The Microsoft AI Insider's Playbook

Your Guide to Cloud Strategy and Digital Transformation

Krishna C. Mukherjee

Apress®

The Microsoft AI Insider's Playbook: Your Guide to Cloud Strategy and Digital Transformation

Krishna C. Mukherjee
New York, NY, USA

ISBN-13 (pbk): 979-8-8688-2729-7 ISBN-13 (electronic): 979-8-8688-2730-3
https://doi.org/10.1007/979-8-8688-2730-3

Managing Director, Apress Media LLC: Welmoed Spahr
Acquisitions Editor: Smriti Srivastava
Development Editor: Laura Berendson
Editorial Assistant: Marina Engler

Cover designed by eStudioCalamar

Distributed to the book trade worldwide by Springer Science+Business Media New York, 1 New York Plaza, New York, NY 10004. Phone 1-800-SPRINGER, fax (201) 348-4505, e-mail orders-ny@springer-sbm.com, or visit www.springeronline.com. Apress Media, LLC is a Delaware LLC and the sole member (owner) is Springer Science + Business Media Finance Inc (SSBM Finance Inc). SSBM Finance Inc is a **Delaware** corporation.

For information on translations, please e-mail booktranslations@springernature.com; for reprint, paperback, or audio rights, please e-mail bookpermissions@springernature.com.

Apress titles may be purchased in bulk for academic, corporate, or promotional use. eBook versions and licenses are also available for most titles. For more information, reference our Print and eBook Bulk Sales web page at http://www.apress.com/bulk-sales.

Any source code or other supplementary material referenced by the author in this book is available to readers on GitHub. For more detailed information, please visit https://www.apress.com/gp/services/source-code.

If disposing of this product, please recycle the paper

In loving memory of my parents, Shri Narayan C. Mukherjee and Shrimati Kshama Mukherjee, to whom I owe more than these pages can express.

Table of Contents

About the Author

Krishna C. Mukherjee is a pioneering Microsoft technologist, software architect, and technology executive whose work in artificial intelligence (AI) and enterprise systems has helped shape widely adopted computing platforms. His career spans mainframes, personal computing, and modern cloud-based AI, with a consistent focus on turning advanced capabilities into practical tools for enterprise use.

He earned his bachelor's degree in electronics and electrical communication engineering from the Indian Institute of Technology (IIT) Kharagpur and his master's degree in computer science and engineering from IIT Kanpur. His early research in AI planning systems and natural language processing at IIT Kanpur laid the foundation for his long-term work in intelligent systems.

Recruited from IIT Kanpur to Microsoft Corporation in 1988, he served on core engineering teams from the late 1980s through the mid-1990s and contributed to foundational technologies that underpin modern software ecosystems. His work included interoperability technologies such as Object Linking and Embedding and the Component Object Model, as well as automation capabilities in Microsoft Word and Microsoft Office. He helped develop WordBASIC, the macro language for Microsoft Word, and later contributed to Visual Basic for Applications. His teams shipped the early, largely rule-based intelligent assistance features in Microsoft Office, including AutoCorrect and AutoFormat. They also developed proofing capabilities, such as spelling and grammar checking, on the personal computer hardware of the time.

At Wolters Kluwer, he shaped technology and business strategy and architected the Intelligent Filing Manager. Its declarative design and service-oriented architecture foreshadowed patterns later common in software as a service (SaaS) platforms. At Bloomberg L.P., he led the creation of the Bloomberg Valuation Service, integrating AI-driven predictive analytics with advanced pricing algorithms to deliver transparent, defensible valuations for millions of financial instruments across asset classes.

He later applied enterprise architecture and Microsoft technologies to modernize operational platforms at Icon Parking Systems (Icon) and Fidelity National Information Services, Inc. (FIS). His recent work centers on cloud strategy and digital transformation, using Azure AI Services to design and deploy interactive voice response systems, intelligent chatbots, and virtual assistants across finance, health care, retail, and legal services.

He has received awards recognizing his contributions to AI and enterprise systems, including distinguished achievement awards from Microsoft and Wolters Kluwer, as well as the Albert Nelson Marquis Lifetime Achievement Award. His work at Bloomberg and FIS earned multiple commendations. In 2014, he received the Microsoft Most Valuable Professional Award in the Microsoft Integration expertise category, recognizing exceptional contributions to technical communities. He is a senior member of the Institute of Electrical and Electronics Engineers (IEEE) and the Association for Computing Machinery (ACM).

About the Technical Reviewer

Mukta Batra is a product leader specializing in the governance of cloud-scale systems, specifically the platforms that manage how AI-powered technologies are safely released through feature management and controlled experimentation.

She builds the control planes that govern configuration and runtime behavior at scale—powering the production environments of global Fortune 500 companies.

Mukta's work focuses on the evaluation and optimization of AI agents, enabling organizations to move beyond the "lab" phase to scale AI innovation with reliability, cost efficiency, and rigorous operational control.

Acknowledgments

This book carries my name on the cover, but it represents the guidance, patience, and encouragement of many people who have shaped my life.

I begin with my parents—my father, the late Shri Narayan C. Mukherjee, and my mother, the late Shrimati Kshama Mukherjee. Their love and values formed the foundation on which every achievement in my life has been built. My father overcame hardship to become a distinguished marine engineer and later a senior director who helped develop India's inland water transport infrastructure. His engineering rigor, integrity, and resilience remain a constant source of inspiration. My mother, a devoted homemaker and an accomplished musician, filled our home with creativity and culture. Together, my parents created an environment that shaped both my character and my career. They showed me that imagination and rigor can coexist and that the technical and the artistic can strengthen one another.

My deepest thanks go to my wife, Jayeeta, and our sons, Shreesham and Shivam. Jayeeta's steady encouragement, patience, and belief in my work carried me through the long stretches when writing demanded evenings, weekends, and quiet persistence. This book would not have been possible without her. Shreesham and Shivam, both deeply engaged with technology in their own right, kept me sharp with their questions, their candor, and their perspectives. They reminded me, again and again, why making complex ideas accessible matters and why the next generation's curiosity deserves clear answers.

I also thank my relatives, both near and far, for the bonds of family and the warmth they have brought to my life over the years. I remain grateful to my schoolteachers and university professors, who recognized my potential even before I did. They gave me both confidence and discipline, and they laid the groundwork for my lifelong relationship with technology and learning.

I am equally grateful for the opportunity to teach. My students have continually energized me with their curiosity and enthusiasm, and their diverse backgrounds and thoughtful questions have influenced many of the insights shared in these pages.

This book benefited greatly from the skill and dedication of the Apress team. I thank Smriti Srivastava, Welmoed Spahr, Sriram N, Laura Berendson, Mukta Batra, Marina Engler, Joseph Quatela, Sowmya Thodur, Abirami D S, and Dulcy Nirmala Chellappa for their guidance and support throughout the publication process. I also thank Aditee Mirashi for her help with the book's marketing and promotion.

Finally, I thank the friends and colleagues who accompanied me throughout my journey—fellow students and alumni across the Indian Institutes of Technology and colleagues at Microsoft, Wolters Kluwer, Bloomberg, Fidelity National Information Services, and other organizations. Their encouragement, collaboration, and high standards shaped my thinking, and their influence can be felt throughout this book.

Introduction

This book draws on my experience building technologies that have helped shape modern computing—from intelligent features in Microsoft's core products to enterprise systems and cloud-based solutions. I wrote it to share what I learned: what these technologies do, how they were designed, and which principles drove success or exposed limitations. The first-person voice reflects that the design trade-offs were not abstract. They were decisions I had to make, ship, and defend in real customer environments.

Computing has transformed how we work, communicate, and understand the world. From early mechanical calculators to today's artificial intelligence (AI) systems, each breakthrough has built on earlier innovations. By tracing the origins of key ideas—from logic and reasoning to modern cloud computing—we can better understand where we have been and where emerging technologies may lead.

We often view cutting-edge computing as the work of a handful of visionaries. However, the history of computing repeatedly challenges that assumption. The roots of AI reach back to ancient philosophy. Thinkers such as Aristotle developed systematic approaches to logical reasoning. These concepts later influenced the formalization of "thinking" as a set of rules and procedures. In the seventeenth century, Gottfried Wilhelm Leibniz advanced a vision of a universal calculus capable of representing human reasoning in mathematical form. That lineage matters in enterprise AI because modern systems still revolve around the same question: how do we represent knowledge in a form that is both powerful and accountable?

AI shifted from philosophy to engineering in the mid-twentieth century. In 1950, Alan Turing's paper "Computing Machinery and Intelligence" reframed "Can machines think?" into a testable proposition through what became known as the Turing Test. That transition, combined with advances in computing, set the stage for the Dartmouth Conference in 1956, which established AI as a distinct scientific field.

Early AI research emphasized symbolic reasoning—representing knowledge explicitly through rules, logic, and structured relationships. This approach powered programs such as the General Problem Solver, which attempted to mimic human reasoning strategies. ELIZA, a natural language processing (NLP) program created by

Joseph Weizenbaum at the Massachusetts Institute of Technology, demonstrated that pattern matching and simple transformations could produce surprisingly human-like responses.

The 1970s and 1980s saw the rise of expert systems—rule-based programs that encoded specialized knowledge to emulate human expertise within well-defined domains. MYCIN, developed at Stanford University, diagnosed bacterial infections and recommended antibiotics. DENDRAL, also from Stanford, inferred molecular structure from mass spectrometry data. Even when these systems were limited, they proved a decisive point: software could capture fragments of expert judgment and make them usable at scale.

Around the same time, AI began reaching mainstream users through productivity software. At Microsoft during the late 1980s and 1990s, I worked on intelligent capabilities in Microsoft Office, including proofing tools, AutoCorrect, AutoFormat, and Office Assistant. These features introduced users to AI-assisted workflows in daily computing and changed expectations: software could actively assist, not merely respond. That experience taught me that "helpfulness" is not a feature. It is a design discipline shaped by timing, defaults, and restraint.

In the late 1990s, I designed the Intelligent Filing Manager (INTELLIFM) to deploy AI in real-world business settings. It combined rule-based intelligence with a modular structure to automate complex document workflows and high-volume forms publishing. Its service-oriented architecture—delivering capabilities as reusable services via secure interfaces—foreshadowed ideas that later became central to cloud computing and software as a service.

The 1990s and 2000s saw the parallel evolution—and eventual convergence—of AI and cloud computing. Statistical machine learning (ML) gained broader adoption as data volumes grew and processing power became more accessible, while early cloud platforms matured into scalable infrastructure for storage and computation. In the 2010s, deep learning—accelerated by graphics processing units (GPUs) and large datasets—pushed AI from a specialized capability into an operational dependency that enterprises could embed into everyday workflows.

Yet the transition has been evolutionary, not revolutionary. Many production systems combine symbolic rules for compliance and transparency with ML models for perception and prediction. Modern NLP tools, including large language models (LLMs), build on the foundations laid by earlier expert systems while leveraging cloud scalability and flexibility. Across industries, new paradigms rarely wipe out the old; they stack, integrate, and gradually converge.

Throughout the book, I return to principles that guided my work: design for constraints, build trust through predictable behavior, apply progressive disclosure, and preserve human judgment. These lessons emerged from building systems under pressure and learning from what broke in production, what confused users, and what earned trust over time.

The book traces this evolution through 14 chapters, drawing on my direct involvement in key developments. The Appendixes provide additional reference material, supporting details, and technical specifications. The Glossary supports both quick lookups and deeper study. Each chapter opens with an accessible introduction, develops the ideas through architecture and implementation detail, and closes with a summary of key takeaways. Readers new to cloud computing and AI may focus on the introductions and summaries, while technical professionals can spend more time in the detailed sections.

I hope this book helps readers at different stages. It is for students and early-career professionals exploring technology, as well as experienced practitioners and decision-makers seeking practical insight into AI and cloud adoption. Understanding the origins of these technologies clarifies where they may go next.

CHAPTER 1

Foundations: Microsoft from BASIC to AI

Technology rarely follows a straight path. When I joined Microsoft in 1988, Bill Gates shared the origin story of how he and Paul Allen built the company. In early 1975, after Allen showed Gates the Altair 8800 on the cover of *Popular Electronics*, the two friends developed Altair Beginner's All-purpose Symbolic Instruction Code (BASIC), Microsoft's first product. They founded the company on April 4, 1975. The name Microsoft, a portmanteau of "microcomputer" and "software," captured their vision of a computer on every desk and in every home. Hearing that story firsthand gave me insight into the company's entrepreneurial DNA and its culture of purposeful innovation.

Since that time, my career has been closely tied to Microsoft's ecosystem. I have worked on foundational software, artificial intelligence (AI), cloud infrastructure, and software as a service (SaaS). These technologies continue to shape the industry. In many ways, Microsoft's story reflects society's evolving relationship with technology, and my own journey parallels that arc: from early work with electronics and microprocessors in India to building AI-powered enterprise systems that serve millions of users.

This chapter traces the foundations that shaped my approach to building software and, eventually, AI systems. It begins with two parallel origin stories: Microsoft's emergence from the Altair era and my own technological awakening in India. It follows these paths through the mainframe era, the rise of personal computing, and Microsoft's early investments in integration and AI. Along the way, it examines the architectural principles that emerged from those years: resource discipline, interoperability, component-based design, and the careful balance between automation and human judgment. It closes with the lessons that Windows taught about evolution, compatibility, and the cost of getting ecosystems wrong—lessons that remain directly relevant to the AI platforms being built today.

K. C. Mukherjee, *The Microsoft AI Insider's Playbook*, https://doi.org/10.1007/979-8-8688-2730-3_1

1.1 Parallel Beginnings

While Microsoft was taking shape in America, my own technological journey began in Kolkata, India, guided by cultural values that would shape how I approached computing. I was fortunate to have parents and teachers who recognized my aptitude and nurtured it.[1] One lesson they repeated often was simple: *waste not, want not.* This lesson became a guiding principle—work hands-on, respect constraints, and use resources carefully.

Growing up in 1970s India meant navigating a technological landscape far removed from Silicon Valley. While the Apple II, the TRS-80, and the Commodore PET were emerging in the West, India's computing resources were concentrated in elite institutions such as the Indian Statistical Institute and the Indian Institutes of Technology (IITs). For most Indians—including me—computers were not merely expensive; they were rarely encountered.

My environment brought its own challenges. Infrastructure that many now take for granted—reliable electricity and running water—often proved unpredictable. Those early constraints shaped my character and became practical lessons in optimization and creative problem-solving, skills that later proved invaluable in software engineering.

Despite the absence of computers at home, my father nurtured my curiosity through unexpected channels. His work with international shipping lines took him around the world, and he returned with carefully chosen artifacts, especially miniature art from Japan and Southeast Asia. The craftsmanship in those pieces, rooted in traditional techniques, demanded close attention to materials, geometry, and proportion. Through them, I learned how remarkable complexity can emerge through miniaturization—a principle that lies at the heart of computing.

That fascination found a perfect outlet when I entered IIT Kharagpur to study engineering after completing my secondary education. To mark the occasion, my father gave me a Casio fx-80 scientific calculator—portable computation that had only recently become available in India. This calculator became my gateway into electronic systems. I could not resist: I carefully disassembled it and discovered the elegant arrangement of integrated circuits and components. Here was proof that transformative technology could fit in one's palm—a lesson that echoed throughout my Microsoft years.

[1] For additional background, see Rod Berger, "Legacies in Technology Forged from Family and Culture," *Forbes*, December 21, 2022, `https://www.forbes.com/sites/rodberger/2022/12/21/legacies-in-technology-forged-from-family-and-culture`.

The cultural foundations of my formative years—humility, resourcefulness, and disciplined attention to detail—proved essential when I joined Microsoft. When colleagues noted that the IITs held prestige comparable to that of the Massachusetts Institute of Technology (MIT) and Harvard University, I felt the responsibility that such recognition entails. The values my parents taught, combined with the rigor of my education, prepared me to contribute to the personal computing revolution that Gates and Allen had set in motion.

Looking back, I see how these parallel narratives—Microsoft's rise in America and my technological awakening in India—converged. The mission to put a computer on every desk and in every home intersected with my journey from a computerless childhood to helping shape software that made that vision a reality. The resource constraints I faced in India shaped how I later designed software at Microsoft, prioritizing efficiency to ensure it worked for users everywhere, not just those with high-end hardware or stable infrastructure. That foundation would prove essential as the personal computing industry entered a transformative phase—beginning with Microsoft's pivotal partnership with International Business Machines (IBM).

Although this book draws heavily on Microsoft's ecosystem—the one I know from the inside—the architectural principles it describes are not proprietary to any single platform. Resource efficiency, interoperability, component-based design, and disciplined automation apply wherever software meets scale, whether the underlying infrastructure runs on Microsoft Azure, Amazon Web Services (AWS), Google Cloud (sometimes informally called GCP[2]), or open source foundations. Readers working in those environments will recognize the same trade-offs under different names.

1.2 The Microsoft and IBM Partnership

In 1980, as IBM prepared to build a new kind of machine—a personal computer (PC) designed for individuals and small businesses—the company approached Microsoft to provide the operating system. To deliver it, Microsoft licensed 86-DOS (also known as QDOS) and adapted it for the IBM PC, and IBM shipped it as PC DOS when the IBM PC debuted on August 12, 1981. Microsoft marketed its own version as Microsoft Disk

[2] GCP is an informal acronym for Google Cloud Platform, a term historically used to refer to Google's core infrastructure and platform services. Google now uses Google Cloud as its primary brand.

Operating System (MS-DOS) and, critically, retained the right to license it to other manufacturers. That nonexclusive structure helped MS-DOS spread rapidly across the growing ecosystem of IBM-compatible machines, turning it into the dominant operating system of the early PC era.

While this decisive shift was unfolding, I was immersed in my engineering studies at IIT Kharagpur. In the institute's hardware laboratory, I encountered a microprocessor for the first time. I remember staring at that tiny chip with genuine wonder. Here was the compact engine behind the PC—small enough to hold on a fingertip, yet powerful enough to execute instructions, coordinate components, and produce behavior that felt almost magical. That moment drew me in. I began studying how microprocessors worked and why their architecture mattered, and that curiosity steadily became a passion.

As the 1980s progressed, PCs gained greater visibility in India. They were still far from common, but they were no longer unfamiliar—especially in universities, research settings, and forward-looking organizations. My work at IIT Kharagpur, combined with my growing understanding of microprocessors, naturally led me to this emerging platform. I began to see these systems not merely as calculation machines, but as tools that could reshape how we create, collaborate, communicate, and even think.

In retrospect, my own path—from being a curious child in Kolkata to becoming an engineering student captivated by microprocessors—mirrors the broader journey of personal computing in India during those years. What began as a distant concept was becoming tangible and increasingly relevant.

Microsoft continued refining MS-DOS through multiple releases and laid the groundwork for one of its most influential contributions: Windows. Before I could contribute to the personal computing wave that followed, my understanding of computing had been shaped by an entirely different world—mainframes, shared systems, and the discipline of scarce resources.

1.3 The Mainframe Heritage

As a graduate student in computer science and engineering at IIT Kanpur, I became absorbed by AI and its promise to change how machines reason, learn, and interact. My undergraduate training in electronics and communication engineering drew me to problems at the intersection of intelligence and hardware. Planning systems and robotics seemed like a natural match. They combined control systems, embedded logic, and signal processing, but they also demanded algorithms that could choose actions, adapt to changing conditions, and recover when reality diverged from the model. Working with faculty collaborators,[3] I studied planning in its most practical form—how to construct sequences of actions that accomplish a goal under real constraints.

Alongside my thesis work, I participated in research on natural language processing (NLP) and machine translation for Indian languages. That work introduced me to Paninian grammar, the ancient analytical tradition underlying Sanskrit, which is remarkable for its rule-based structure and its relevance to modern computational linguistics.[4] We sought more than literal word-for-word translation. We aimed to capture structure, meaning, and nuance—how a sentence hangs together, how intent changes with context, and why two grammatically correct translations can feel markedly different to a native speaker.

The tools we used reflected the nature of the work. Symbolic reasoning and recursion were not side concerns; they were central to the problem. For planning and rule-based inference, we used Programming in Logic (Prolog), a declarative logic programming language built around facts and rules, developed in the early 1970s. For much of our implementation work, we relied on List Processing (Lisp), created by John McCarthy in 1958. Lisp was not only a programming language; it was a way of thinking. Its tree-based representations, automatic memory management, dynamic typing, and the idea of code-as-data made it uniquely suited to building systems that could inspect, transform, and generate logic rather than merely execute it.

The Programmed Data Processor-10 (PDP-10), a family of mainframe systems developed by Digital Equipment Corporation (DEC), was exceptionally well suited to Lisp. These systems became central to AI research during the late 1960s and throughout the 1970s.[5] They played a foundational role at institutions such as MIT, Stanford University,

---

[3] I am grateful to Professors Rajeev Sangal and Harish Karnick, who advised my master's thesis on planning systems.

[4] Paninian grammar is a universal grammar created by an Indian scholar, Pāṇini, who wrote a treatise about the linguistic basis of Sanskrit in the mid-first millennium BCE. This systematic approach to language analysis predates modern computational linguistics by more than two millennia and offers insights that remain relevant to NLP today. I benefited greatly from conversations with Professor Vineet Chaitanya, who shared his ideas on applying Paninian grammar to computational linguistics. See George Cardona, *Pāṇini: His Work and Its Traditions* (Delhi: Motilal Banarsidass, 1997).

[5] The PDP-10's 36-bit word and 18-bit address architecture allowed a Lisp cons cell to be stored in one word, and single instructions could extract the car and cdr parts. See Guy L. Steele Jr. and Richard P. Gabriel, "The Evolution of Lisp," in *History of Programming Languages—II*, ed. Thomas J. Bergin Jr. and Richard G. Gibson Jr. (New York: ACM Press, 1996), 233–330.

and Carnegie Mellon University, where Lisp dialects like Maclisp and Interlisp were developed and widely used. By the 1980s, many research groups were retiring PDP-10 systems and moving to newer platforms: Lisp machines, Virtual Address eXtension (VAX) systems running Interlisp-VAX, and Unix workstations that supported Franz Lisp.

At IIT Kanpur, I did much of my AI development work on a DECsystem-1090—a time-sharing mainframe from DEC in the PDP-10 family. It ran the Time-Sharing Operating System (TOPS-10).[6] The room that housed it had a presence of its own: the hum of cooling systems, the low vibration of spinning drives, and the controlled air that kept the hardware stable. Access was structured—you signed up for time slots in advance, sessions were logged, and you came prepared, because wasted minutes on the machine meant wasted minutes for everyone waiting after you.

What I remember most is how that environment shaped collaboration. With limited time and shared resources, precision mattered. Programs were carefully designed, thoroughly debugged, and documented for whoever came next. Before "real time" became a slogan, the mainframe taught me discipline, patience, and respect for constraints—habits that stayed with me as I built software in strikingly different environments. Years later, when cloud systems made capacity feel infinite, that early discipline kept me wary of waste—and attentive to failure modes.

1.3.1 Evolution and Relevance of Mainframes

My time in mainframe rooms gave me firsthand experience with systems that, although often associated with earlier periods of computing, remain a core platform for many of the world's largest organizations. They support high-volume workloads across government services, banking and financial services, insurance, health care, utilities, and large-scale e-commerce. Nearly everyone has indirectly used a mainframe at some point. For example, when you withdraw cash from an automated teller machine or check an account balance, the back-end transaction may be processed on mainframe systems used by many large banks.

The term *mainframe* originated from the large cabinet that housed the central processing unit (CPU) and main memory of early computers—combining the idea of central importance ("main") with physical structure ("frame"). Mainframes provide centralized, high-performance computing for substantial workloads, complex data

[6] The DECsystem-1090 was installed at IIT Kanpur in 1979 and served as the institute's primary computing resource for approximately a decade. See "History of the Computer Centre," *The Spark* 6 (April 2023), `https://iitk.ac.in/dora/spark/issue-6/`.

processing, and mission-critical applications. They are engineered for resilience and include multiple layers of redundancy—such as secondary cooling, backup power supplies, redundant processors, and specialized cryptographic modules.

Figure 1-1 illustrates a typical mainframe architecture, in which the CPU coordinates peripherals such as disk and tape storage, printers, terminals, and network connections.

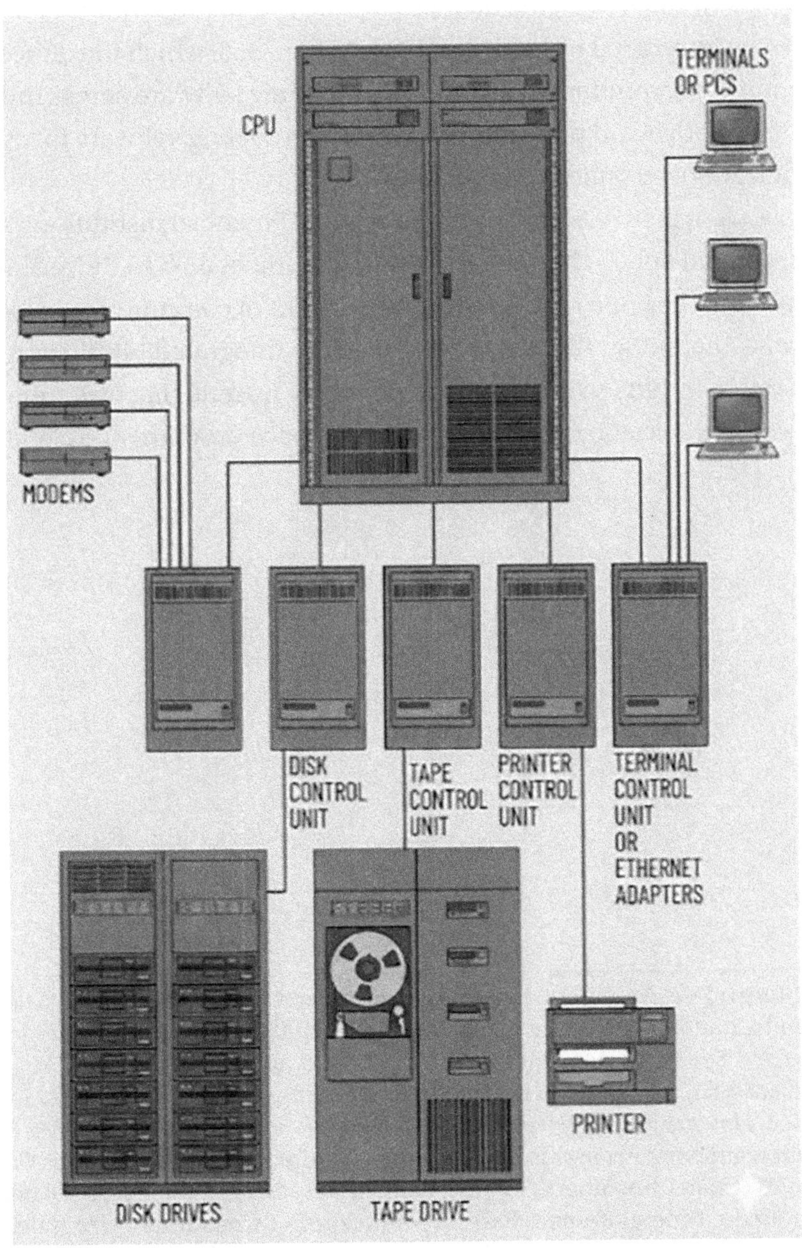

Figure 1-1. *Typical mainframe system architecture. (Image by author)*

Modern mainframes have evolved dramatically. Early milestones in centralized computing include Howard Aiken's Harvard Mark I (1944), a room-sized machine that weighed about five tons and cost roughly $200,000 (approximately $3.7 million in 2026 dollars[7]). Another milestone was the IBM 701 (1952), which helped establish large-scale electronic computing in commercial and scientific settings. IBM broadened adoption with the IBM 1401 in 1960, bringing data processing to a broader range of organizations. A pivotal milestone occurred in 1964 with IBM System/360, which introduced a compatible family of computers that could run the same software across multiple models at different price and performance levels—protecting software investments while allowing organizations to scale incrementally.

Mainframes went on to reshape multiple sectors. Financial institutions automated account management and high-volume transaction processing. In the airline industry, mainframes played a key role in the early development of computerized reservation systems. In India, the Indian Railways introduced the Integrated Multi-train Passenger Reservation System in 1985 to improve ticket booking by reducing wait times and handling immense transaction volumes. In the US space program, the National

[7] IBM's expenditure on the Automatic Sequence Controlled Calculator (Harvard Mark I) project was approximately $200,000, with an additional $100,000 donated to Harvard for operating expenses. See "IBM Dedicates Harvard Mark I, August 7, 1944," EDN, August 7, 2012, `https://www.edn.com/ibm-dedicates-harvard-mark-i-august-7-1944/`. See also I. Bernard Cohen, *Howard Aiken: Portrait of a Computer Pioneer* (Cambridge, MA: MIT Press, 1999). All inflation adjustments in this book use the US Bureau of Labor Statistics Consumer Price Index for All Urban Consumers (CPI-U), with January 2026 as the reference period. CPI data sourced from the Federal Reserve Bank of Minneapolis, "Consumer Price Index, 1913-," `https://www.minneapolisfed.org/about-us/monetary-policy/inflation-calculator/consumer-price-index-1913-`.

Aeronautics and Space Administration (NASA) adopted IBM mainframes in the early 1960s. These systems replaced large teams of "human computers" for trajectory calculations and data analysis during Project Gemini and the Apollo era, including the Apollo 11 moon landing.

These examples highlight why mainframes have remained relevant: they combine scale, reliability, and operational discipline in environments where downtime and errors have serious consequences. Modern mainframes can handle high-volume transactional workloads more efficiently than distributed x86 server farms, often requiring significantly less floor space for equivalent processing.[8]

Figure 1-2 summarizes this evolution—from room-sized systems of the 1950s and 1960s, to progressively more compact designs over subsequent decades, and to the rack-based systems used today in modern data centers.

[8] x86 is a family of instruction set architectures initially developed by Intel based on the Intel 8086 microprocessor and its 8088 variant. The 8086 was introduced in 1978. "2U" refers to the size of the rack required to house the x86-based server, with "U" standing for rack unit (1.75 inches or 44.45 mm). See Intel Corporation, *8086/8088 User's Manual* (Santa Clara: Intel Corporation, 1989).

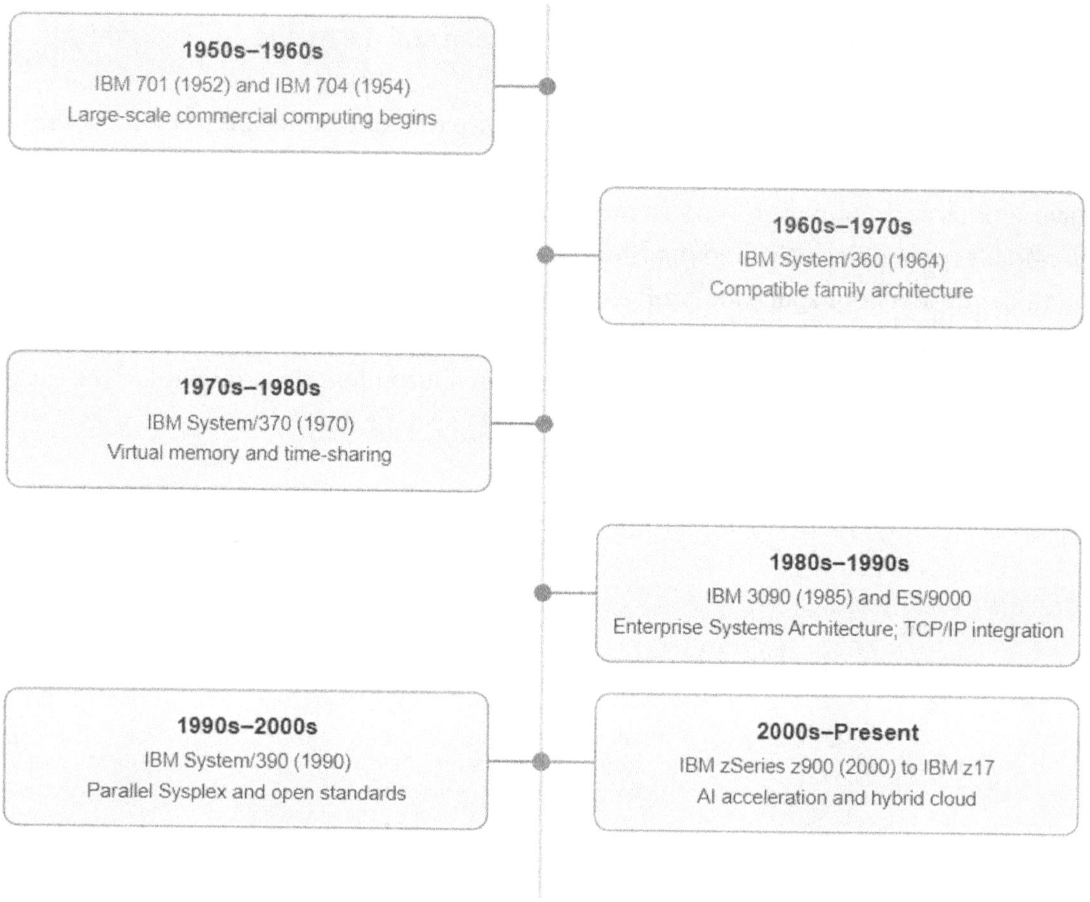

Figure 1-2. *Evolution of mainframe computers. (Image by author)*

1.3.2 From Vacuum Tubes to Semiconductors

The evolution of mainframe technology included sweeping advances in data input, storage, and processing. For much of the early history of computing, punch cards served as a primary medium for both data entry and programming instructions. Each punched hole encoded a character or a unit of data, and the physical workflow was unforgiving—one misplaced, damaged, or out-of-sequence card could derail an entire job. Programmers learned to draw a diagonal line across the top edge of a card deck so that any out-of-sequence card would visibly break the line, making it easier to restore order after an accidental drop. Punch cards were fragile enough that many carried the warning, "Do not fold, spindle, or mutilate." The phrase became so common that it entered popular culture as shorthand for the early computing era.

Figure 1-3 shows a punch card system, with its characteristic rows and columns of holes that encode machine-readable information. Punch cards remained widely used well into the era of commercial computing, before giving way to higher-density, more reliable storage and input methods.

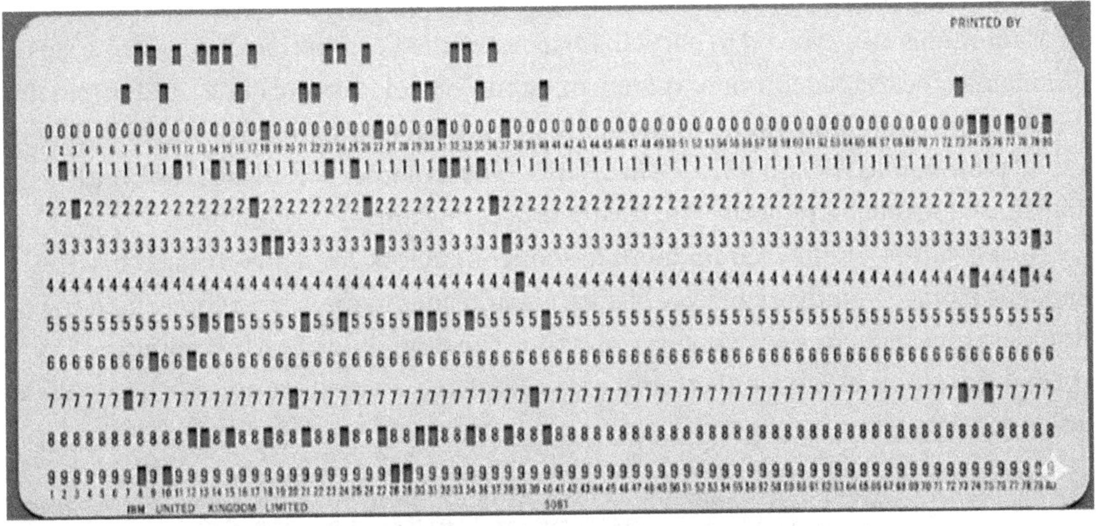

Figure 1-3. *Punch card system for data input and programming. (Pete Birkinshaw, Wikimedia Commons, CC BY 2.0)*

Early mainframes and large computers also relied on vacuum tubes, which powered first-generation systems such as the Electronic Numerical Integrator and Computer (ENIAC) in 1946 and commercial machines that followed in the 1950s. These systems were physically imposing and operationally demanding, often requiring specialized cooling and careful maintenance. The era also produced foundational theoretical progress. Norbert Wiener's work on cybernetics emphasized feedback loops—an idea that later became central to learning, control, and adaptation. Claude Shannon's information theory introduced a rigorous framework for quantifying information, transmission, and error, shaping how engineers approached efficient data handling and reliable communication.[9]

[9] See Norbert Wiener, *Cybernetics: Or Control and Communication in the Animal and the Machine* (Cambridge, MA: MIT Press, 1948); Claude E. Shannon, "A Mathematical Theory of Communication," *Bell System Technical Journal* 27, no. 3 (July 1948): 379–423.

As computing advanced, the practical limits of earlier technologies—data density, reliability, and operating cost—drove a transition to magnetic tape, disk storage, and semiconductor-based memory (see Appendix 1). Silicon-based electronics replaced vacuum tubes, delivering higher performance in smaller, more energy-efficient systems. These advances produced increasingly capable CPUs, later complemented by graphics processing units (GPUs) designed initially for graphics rendering. Over time, GPUs were adapted for the parallel workloads central to machine learning (ML), alongside purpose-built AI accelerators.

Mainframes also evolved to participate in networked computing. By the late 1980s, IBM mainframes had incorporated Transmission Control Protocol (TCP) and Internet Protocol (IP), the protocol suite underpinning the modern internet. These developments helped mainframes remain relevant in sectors such as aerospace, health care, and finance, where reliability, scale, and secure processing are nonnegotiable.

The advances—from vacuum tubes to semiconductors, from punch cards to magnetic storage—were not merely historical curiosities to me. They represented the shoulders on which my own work would stand. The discipline of early computing, where every byte mattered and errors were unforgiving, shaped my approach to software design at Microsoft.

1.3.3 Programming Languages: Bridging Worlds

Programming languages serve as bridges, translating human intent into instructions that a machine can execute. During my formative years working with mainframes in India, I observed firsthand how this translation shaped the design and maintenance of systems. Across decades of change, mainframes have retained an unusual level of flexibility in the languages they support. Traditional languages such as Common Business-Oriented Language (COBOL) and Programming Language One (PL/I) coexist with modern languages such as Java, Python, and R.

This multilingual capability bridges decades of proven business logic with the demands of modern analytics and AI. In finance and health care, for example, long-running COBOL applications can integrate with AI-enabled services, while Python and R connect enterprise data to contemporary model development and analysis. (For details on programming languages used with mainframes, see Appendix 2.)

This flexibility is one reason mainframes remain well suited to applications ranging from traditional transaction processing to AI-driven analytics. High-end systems are designed to support enormous transaction volumes in industries such as banking, airlines, and retail, where consistent throughput and dependable processing are critical.

Mainframes are engineered for high availability, which is essential for workloads that cannot tolerate downtime or data errors. In many environments, organizations use mainframes to consolidate high-volume transactional and batch workloads, streamline operations, and support database-intensive processing, while maintaining strong security controls. Their architecture also enabled early forms of virtualization, allowing multiple virtual machines (VMs) to run on a single physical system. This approach remains valuable for analytics and AI workloads that benefit from parallel processing and shared infrastructure.

The mainframe principles I absorbed—designing for scale, achieving exceptional dependability, and optimizing resource sharing through virtualization—proved invaluable years later when architecting cloud solutions for Microsoft. Those air-conditioned computer rooms taught me batch processing discipline and concurrent workload management. Years later, the same foundations helped me understand how cloud services can deliver mainframe-like resilience at an internet scale.

In this sense, programming languages bridge not only human thought and machine execution but also the past and the future, connecting the hard-won stability of legacy systems to the emerging possibilities of AI.

1.4 Early Microsoft Contributions

My journey in technology gained momentum at IIT Kanpur, where I explored AI and robotics and presented my research at conferences. In 1988, while completing my master's degree in computer science and engineering, I was recruited by Microsoft and relocated to the United States to join the company at its headquarters in Redmond, Washington. At Microsoft, I was responsible for designing software architectures and developing production-grade features. I worked on flagship applications, including Word and Excel, during a formative period when they were still delivered as separate programs, before Microsoft Office was first released as a bundled product in October 1990.

Initially, I helped lead cross-platform development of Office applications on both Microsoft Windows and Apple Macintosh. My teams architected and implemented capabilities that shaped everyday Office workflows. A central focus was improving *What You See Is What You Get* (WYSIWYG) fidelity: reducing the gap between the on-screen composition and the printed output. As on-screen layouts and typography became more accurate, users could format and edit in real time with fewer surprises, and professional-quality documents became practical for a much wider audience.

Typography was pivotal. In the early 1990s, Apple introduced the TrueType font format, developed in collaboration with Microsoft, and both companies built it into their operating systems. Apple shipped TrueType with System 7 in May 1991; Microsoft followed with Windows 3.1 in April 1992. Adobe PostScript Type 1 fonts often depended on separate tools for font management and high-quality on-screen scaling. TrueType integrated scalable outlines and hinting, so the operating system could render text directly. The result was more consistent typography across screens and printers, better legibility at small sizes, and more reliable WYSIWYG behavior. Users could compose with the expectation that the printed page would match what they saw on screen.

These improvements strengthened Windows and reinforced the desktop publishing value of Office. They also reflected disciplined engineering across operating system and application teams, aligning layout, rendering, and printing behavior. In later years, the same design instincts—scale, reliability, and careful coordination across complex subsystems—proved directly relevant when I began architecting cloud solutions.

1.4.1 OLE and COM

Personal computing is more than hardware and software; it expands what people can create and accomplish. From my early school days, I was inclined to view problems from multiple perspectives, and that habit often led me toward simpler solutions to complex challenges. When I joined Microsoft, I found an engineering culture deeply committed to feature richness and backward compatibility—principles needed to support a growing ecosystem of users and legacy systems. But that commitment often came at a cost: products could become complex and, at times, cumbersome.

Windows 2.x ran as an environment on top of MS-DOS, and many tasks still required returning to the DOS command line. Word had to bridge its DOS and Windows versions, preserving shortcut conventions and behavior that complicated the experience. Excel, while groundbreaking, also needed to support Lotus 1-2-3 formats and expectations, adding both user-facing and engineering complexity. Coming from a background grounded in elegant design, I found myself increasingly drawn to simplicity and clarity—qualities that make software more intuitive. My experiences at Microsoft sharpened that sensibility, as I recognized the practical power of restraint in design: making complex tasks feel straightforward.

With that goal in mind, I helped design and develop Object Linking and Embedding (OLE), which shipped in the early 1990s. OLE provided two complementary mechanisms for sharing data across applications: linking and embedding. Linking maintains a live connection, while embedding stores the object within the document. OLE evolved to support in-place editing, so an embedded Excel chart in a Word document could be edited directly within Word. If the chart is linked instead, updates flow back to Word, while editing occurs in Excel.

OLE was also extended to support compound documents and common workflows such as clipboard operations and drag-and-drop. It was widely adopted across Office and by a broad range of third-party applications, marking an essential milestone in desktop interoperability. Developing OLE demanded extensive testing, careful documentation, and sustained collaboration with internal teams and external developers to achieve cross-application compatibility and consistent real-world behavior.

As software systems grew more complex, the need for a more flexible component framework became evident. In 1993, Microsoft developed the Component Object Model (COM), which standardized communication between software components. COM defines a binary standard for interoperability: components expose interfaces that others can use without needing to know internal implementation details or the programming language in which they were written. That approach improved modularity, separation of concerns, and long-term maintainability.

COM became the foundation for a more extensible, component-based implementation of OLE. It also powered ActiveX, which brought components to web browsers. While newer approaches have emerged, the core principles of COM—interface-based programming and language-independent component interaction—remain foundational. Those ideas foreshadow modern interoperability across systems and services, including how cloud platforms integrate across diverse languages, runtimes, and environments.

1.4.2 Introducing AI and Automation

The term *AI* encompasses several distinct generations of computational methodology. Early systems relied on symbolic reasoning and hand-engineered rule sets, executing explicit logic specified by human experts. The emergence of statistical ML introduced models that infer patterns from data rather than following predetermined rules. More recently, foundation models and large language models (LLMs) constitute a further architectural evolution. Trained on massive, heterogeneous corpora, they perform language, code, and analytic tasks with broad functional generality but also exhibit novel forms of stochastic and systemic unpredictability. The continuity across these generations lies in their shared objective of augmenting human cognitive capability, not in any equivalence in computational mechanisms, operational behavior, or risk profiles.

When I joined Microsoft, I recognized an opportunity to bring AI—at the time, primarily rule-based expert systems—into productivity software, beginning with Microsoft Word for Windows (popularly known as WinWord). The first step was to develop proofing tools: a Spell Checker, a Grammar Checker, and a Thesaurus. These had to assist users in real time, which presented a serious engineering challenge. During the late 1980s, most PCs shipped with 1–2 megabytes of random-access memory (RAM) and CPUs operating at 8–20 megahertz, while high-end workstations featured 4–8 megabytes of memory and clock speeds of 33–50 megahertz.[10] Hence, the proofing tools had to perform complex linguistic analysis while remaining sufficiently lightweight so that users could continue editing without interruption.

Working with colleagues, I helped build these proofing tools using rule-based linguistic models and dictionary-driven algorithms, with lexical resources licensed from Houghton Mifflin. To manage memory constraints, we designed them as modular components that applications could load on demand. Word offered the most complete integration of all three tools, whereas Excel and PowerPoint adopted selective subsets based on their primary use cases and performance budgets—a decision driven by the realities of early-1990s hardware.

[10] Personal computer configurations in the late 1980s and early 1990s varied widely. Entry-level systems shipped with 1–4 MB of RAM, while business machines typically included 4–8 MB. Processor speeds ranged from 6 MHz (Intel 80286) to 66 MHz (Intel 80486DX2) by 1992. Winn L. Rosch, *The Winn L. Rosch Hardware Bible*, 3rd ed. (Indianapolis: Brady Publishing, 1994), 67–112.

Customer feedback made the value proposition clear: spelling and grammatical mistakes were among the most common reasons users had to revise documents. Early proofing tools directly addressed this pain point, and their success encouraged further investment in intelligent automation. In response to growing requests for features that reduced mechanical effort, my colleagues and I developed AutoCorrect and AutoFormat.

AutoCorrect, introduced in Word 6.0 in 1993, corrected common typing errors in real time using rule-based pattern matching and a user-editable list of replacements.[11] Although it did not learn in a modern adaptive sense, users could expand the replacement list over time, effectively tailoring the feature to their writing habits. AutoFormat used pattern recognition rules to detect structures, such as numbered and bulleted lists, and automatically applied the corresponding formatting with minimal user intervention. The goal across both features was to reduce friction in the writing process, allowing users to focus on their ideas rather than the mechanics of document preparation.

Earlier, in the late 1980s, I was part of the team that developed WordBASIC—the language that let users write macros to automate tasks in Word. That work laid the foundation for Office automation, transforming standalone applications into a programmable platform. Eventually, WordBASIC gave way to Visual Basic for Applications (VBA), which became the shared automation language across the Office family in the Office 97 era.[12] Around the same time, colleagues on the Visual Studio team developed IntelliSense—an intelligent code assistance feature that used syntactic analysis and symbol tables. The synergy between Office automation frameworks and development environment enhancements created a thriving ecosystem that enabled developers to extend Office with custom workflows and solutions.

Office 97 also introduced the Office Assistant, our most ambitious attempt of that decade to integrate AI into user assistance. Built on Bayesian user modeling developed in the Lumière research project, the system analyzed user actions and document context to predict when help might be needed. The assistant—most famously represented by Clippy, the animated paperclip—used probabilistic models and hand-crafted rules

[11] Word 6.0 introduced AutoCorrect and AutoFormat as new productivity features. See Microsoft Corporation, *Microsoft Word User's Guide*, Version 6.0 (Redmond, WA: Microsoft Corporation, 1993). For a contemporary review, see "MS Word 6.0," Harvard Crimson, December 14, 1993, `https://www.thecrimson.com/article/1993/12/14/ms-word-60-pmicrosoft-word-has/`.

[12] Microsoft Office 97, released in November 1996, unified the macro language across Word, Excel, PowerPoint, and Access under VBA, replacing the application-specific macro languages used in earlier versions. See Microsoft Corporation, *Microsoft Office 97 Resource Kit* (Redmond, WA: Microsoft Press, 1997).

informed by observed usage patterns to offer proactive guidance.[13] User reaction was polarized. Many found the interruptions disruptive, and Microsoft eventually discontinued the feature. Even so, it reinforced an enduring lesson: intelligence must respect attention and timing, or it becomes counterproductive. The Office Assistant pioneered concepts of context-aware assistance that would resurface in more sophisticated forms decades later.

These efforts in the 1990s represented a spectrum of approaches to intelligent software: rule-based systems for writing assistance, automation frameworks for extensibility, and probabilistic reasoning for proactive help. Each taught lessons about what users would accept and where intelligence added genuine value. More broadly, they marked a shift toward systems that adapt to users—not the other way around.

During the late 1990s and 2000s, I created the Intelligent Filing Manager (INTELLIFM) and used it to power SaaS applications for automating document workflows and high-volume forms publishing. Using Microsoft technologies, the system combined AI with a service-oriented design, foreshadowing the cloud model of delivering capabilities as services.

Microsoft subsequently extended this foundation into cloud computing and AI. The company launched its public cloud platform, Windows Azure, in 2010—a name suggestive of the open blue sky—and renamed it Microsoft Azure in 2014. Office 365 launched in 2011, becoming Microsoft's leading SaaS offering and demonstrating its commitment to cloud-based productivity solutions. Beginning that year, Microsoft integrated deep learning technology into its speech recognition products, marking an early step toward the AI-powered services that would follow.[14] In 2017, Microsoft 365 launched as a comprehensive superset of Office 365, designed to meet diverse productivity needs with a broader array of tools and services.

---

[13] Eric Horvitz et al., "The Lumière Project: Bayesian User Modeling for Inferring the Goals and Needs of Software Users," in *Proceedings of the Fourteenth Conference on Uncertainty in Artificial Intelligence* (San Francisco: Morgan Kaufmann, 1998), 256–65.

[14] In 2011, Microsoft Research teams presented breakthrough results applying deep neural networks to large-vocabulary speech recognition at Interspeech 2011 and ICASSP 2011. The first commercial deployment followed in 2012, when the technology was integrated into the Bing Voice Search acoustic model. See Frank Seide, Gang Li, and Dong Yu, "Conversational Speech Transcription Using Context-Dependent Deep Neural Networks," in *Proceedings of Interspeech 2011* (Florence, Italy: International Speech Communication Association, 2011), 437–40; George E. Dahl, Dong Yu, Li Deng, and Alex Acero, "Context-Dependent Pre-trained Deep Neural Networks for Large Vocabulary Speech Recognition," *IEEE Transactions on Audio, Speech, and Language Processing* 20, no. 1 (January 2012): 30–42.

Modern features like Microsoft Editor, which provides nuanced writing suggestions, and Copilot, which generates code and documents, represent the maturation of concepts we pioneered.[15] Earlier systems relied on dictionaries, pattern matching, and hand-tuned heuristics. Today's tools build on transformer architectures and LLMs trained on vast corpora. The architectural lineage remains recognizable, but LLMs introduce a different risk profile—one that breaks traditional enterprise assumptions. Unlike rule-based systems, which are deterministic and auditable by design, LLMs are nondeterministic: the same prompt can yield different outputs across runs. They exhibit emergent behavior that was not explicitly programmed, produce confident but incorrect answers through probabilistic hallucination, and respond inconsistently to variations in prompt phrasing. These characteristics challenge the testability, correctness guarantees, and auditability that enterprise architects have long relied on. They demand new approaches to governance, evaluation, and human oversight. The underlying mission, however, remains unchanged: build technology that understands user intent and helps people achieve more with less. Chapters 11–13 examine how Azure AI Services, the Copilot ecosystem, and Power Platform carry that mission forward at enterprise scale.

1.4.3 OS/2: A Lesson in Ecosystems

In the late 1980s, while Microsoft Word and Excel were gaining traction, IBM and Microsoft partnered to develop Operating System/2 (OS/2) as a successor to MS-DOS. The collaboration was formalized in 1985 and looked promising. OS/2 introduced capabilities that were ambitious for PCs at the time, including preemptive multitasking and a more structured architecture. In 1988, OS/2 introduced Presentation Manager, a graphical user interface (GUI) that delivered a more modern desktop experience.

My team and I worked on adapting Office applications for OS/2 Presentation Manager. OS/2 was ahead of Windows in several respects. It was more stable, was better at multitasking, and had a more robust architecture. We preserved file format compatibility and leveraged OS/2 features where it made practical sense. Early on, the platform appeared well positioned for business computing.

[15] Microsoft Corporation, "Introducing Microsoft 365 Copilot," Official Microsoft Blog, March 16, 2023, `https://blogs.microsoft.com/blog/2023/03/16/introducing-microsoft-365-copilot-your-copilot-for-work/`.

Even with its strengths, OS/2 ultimately failed in the market. This taught me one of the most valuable lessons of my career: technical superiority alone does not guarantee success—ecosystems matter. Windows attracted a larger developer base and a wider range of third-party applications. As a result, hardware manufacturers increasingly bundled Windows on new computers, accelerating adoption. As Windows 3.0 surged in the marketplace, the IBM-Microsoft partnership unraveled, and Microsoft concentrated its efforts on Windows.

That experience shaped my later work. I learned to evaluate not only the software, but also the developer community, hardware support, distribution channels, and complementary products that determine whether a platform can thrive. Those considerations became even more important in AI and cloud computing, where progress depends on broad participation. OS/2 remains a reminder that without a living ecosystem, even a well-designed technology can become an elegant failure.

1.5 Personal Computing: Democratizing Technology

Personal computing is now woven into daily life. It shapes routines, expands what people can do, and changes how they learn and communicate. I witnessed that transformation from two perspectives. In India, I saw PCs move from rare institutional machines to tools within reach of students and professionals. At Microsoft, I helped build software that brought personal computing to a far broader audience.

Personal computing expanded access to knowledge and enabled learning from almost anywhere. It reshaped professional life by supporting collaboration across distance with a naturalness that once seemed improbable. Beyond work and education, it transformed leisure through games, digital media, and increasingly immersive experiences.

Under every PC sits a stack of abstractions that I have come to value not only as a technical structure but also as a model for how complex systems become usable. At the base is digital logic, implemented with transistors, gates, and circuits that make binary decisions. Above that is microarchitecture, the internal design of the CPU that coordinates how instructions are fetched, decoded, and executed. Next is the instruction set architecture, the contract between hardware and software that defines the machine instructions that compilers target and that processors execute.

Above the instruction set sits the operating system. It coordinates memory, processes, storage, and input/output, shielding applications and users from the underlying machinery. As systems grew more complex, additional layers emerged.

Hypervisors support VMs that divide physical hardware into isolated environments. Containers package applications with their dependencies in a lightweight form. Runtime environments and middleware reduce platform-specific details, ensuring that applications behave consistently across different systems. Each layer adds structure, so progress can move forward without requiring every component to change at once.

This way of thinking felt familiar to me. The mainframe discipline I absorbed—where resources were scarce and abstractions had to earn their place—translated directly to personal computing. At Microsoft, I approached features with the same philosophy: hide complexity, surface capability, and keep the experience responsive.

Above these foundations are high-level programming languages that let developers express ideas more closely aligned with human reasoning while still compiling into efficient machine code. At the top sits the user interface, where design, psychology, and engineering meet and where most people actually experience computing.

The microprocessor—the heart of personal computing—sits at the center of this story. It integrates data processing and control into a single chip and serves as the computer's CPU. It executes instructions, performs arithmetic and logical operations, and coordinates data movement across the system. Every program you run is, at its core, the processor carrying out vast numbers of these operations. As the years passed, processing power increased dramatically, and that steady growth helped make possible everything from rich multimedia to the early groundwork for modern AI.

This layered story matters because the same abstraction mindset underlies cloud computing and modern AI platforms. We place complexity behind clean interfaces, making powerful capabilities widely usable, safe, and productive. In a sense, cloud computing extends the PC outward, turning local layers into distributed services. AI adds yet another layer: systems that can interpret, generate, and assist in ways that align more closely with human intent.

1.6 Windows: Lessons in Evolution

Around the same time that Microsoft was developing the text-based MS-DOS, researchers at Xerox Palo Alto Research Center (PARC) pioneered a new approach to human-computer interaction: *the GUI.* In this interface, people manipulate visual representations of files, applications, and commands. As the PC market expanded, Microsoft began developing Windows to bring graphical computing to a broader audience. Since its first release in 1985, Windows has evolved into a family of operating systems, with each major version reflecting changing hardware capabilities, user expectations, and industry requirements. (A fuller timeline of Windows versions appears in Appendix 3.)

The launch of Windows 3.0 in 1990 reshaped the PC software market and signaled a new phase of mass adoption for graphical computing. Windows became not only a product but also a case study in how operating systems evolve to balance capability, compatibility, and usability.

1.6.1 Windows Kernel

The kernel is the core of the operating system. It sits between applications and hardware, coordinating the work that must be done reliably and securely: managing memory, scheduling processes and threads, handling input and output, and coordinating file system operations. It also supports security through mechanisms such as access control and privilege enforcement, provides interprocess communication primitives, and coordinates power management. The kernel works with the graphics subsystem to support the GUI.

While working with Office applications, I interacted with these system services daily—not by modifying them, but by relying on them. Kernel stability and performance shaped whether the features my teams built would behave consistently across millions of machines.

Figure 1-4 illustrates the architecture, divided into User Mode and Kernel Mode. User-mode subsystems—including the Win32 subsystem, the Windows Subsystem for Linux (WSL),[16] the Windows API subsystem, and the graphics subsystem—manage applications through application programming interfaces (APIs). Kernel-mode subsystems—such as the New Technology (NT) Kernel, file system, networking, and memory management—handle core operations and hardware communication, with the Hardware Abstraction Layer (HAL) bridging the kernel and the underlying hardware. The Security subsystem spans both modes. This diagram provides a simplified conceptual overview of the Windows architecture from the Windows NT era. Modern Windows systems incorporate significantly more complex security controls, including authentication, access management, and secure routing layers that are not shown here. (For a detailed explanation, see Appendix 4.)

[16] Linux is an open source operating system kernel created by Linus Torvalds in 1991. It forms the foundation of numerous operating system distributions, including Ubuntu, Red Hat Enterprise Linux, and Debian, and is widely used in servers, cloud infrastructure, embedded systems, and Android devices.

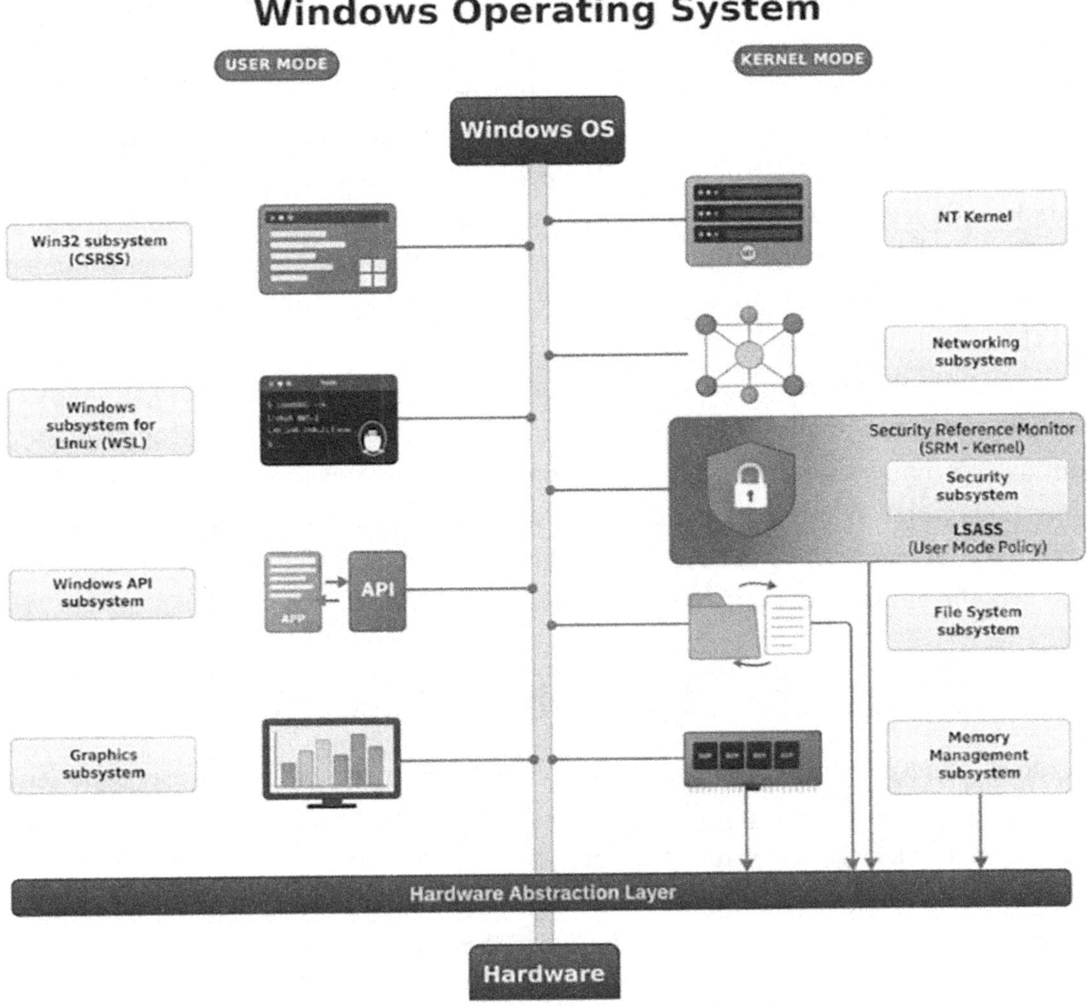

Figure 1-4. *Conceptual architecture of the Windows operating system from the Windows NT era. (Image by author)*

1.6.2 Windows Subsystems

Windows subsystems are components that let the operating system support different application environments. At the core is the Windows NT executive, which comprises the kernel and other foundational services, including memory management, process and thread scheduling, security, and input/output. User-mode subsystems sit above this core and provide specific runtime environments, keeping most application logic in user space while relying on the executive for privileged operations.

Most users interact primarily with the Win32 environment, which supports standard Windows desktop applications. Windows also preserves compatibility across generations. For example, Windows on Windows 64-bit provides a compatibility layer that enables many 32-bit applications to run on 64-bit Windows. More recently, Windows introduced WSL, which lets developers run Linux command-line tools and workflows directly on Windows. WSL 2 expanded on that approach by running a real Linux kernel in a lightweight VM, improving system call compatibility and performance across many workloads.

This architecture enables Windows to run legacy software, modern applications, and cross-platform developer tools within a single operating system. That interoperability has become operationally critical as AI development workflows span heterogeneous runtimes, compilers, and execution backends. When I see developers using WSL to run Linux tools within Windows, I recognize the same interoperability challenge my teams faced decades earlier: how to let different worlds coexist productively. The tools have changed; the problem has not.

1.6.3 Application Compatibility and Security

Windows achieved widespread adoption by combining an approachable user experience with broad application compatibility. That compatibility attracted developers and, over time, produced a large ecosystem of games, creative tools, and productivity software. Microsoft Office became a centerpiece of that ecosystem for many organizations and individuals. I am grateful to have contributed to that work. The Office features I helped build—proofing tools, automation capabilities, and interoperability layers—depended on Windows providing a stable foundation. When Windows worked well across diverse hardware and configurations, our applications could reach users at scale.

Cybersecurity is the practice of protecting systems, networks, and applications from digital threats. Windows includes multiple security capabilities, but no operating system can "solve" security on its own. Protection depends on secure design, safe default settings, timely patching, reliable endpoint tools, and disciplined operational practices. Windows updates address vulnerabilities and enhance defenses incrementally, and built-in components such as a firewall provide an additional layer of protection. Even so, modern threats evolve quickly, and real-world environments remain complex. The intersection of compatibility and security is especially fragile where third-party software operates at deep system levels.

A notable incident in July 2024 underscored both the centrality of Windows in the modern world and the difficulty of protecting large-scale systems. On July 19, 2024, a faulty CrowdStrike update caused widespread Windows failures and disrupted critical services across multiple industries. Microsoft estimated that 8.5 million Windows devices were affected—less than 1% of all Windows machines—yet the operational impact was global because many affected endpoints supported essential enterprise services. Airlines canceled thousands of flights, hospitals postponed procedures, and financial institutions experienced service interruptions.[17]

CrowdStrike endpoint software runs at a highly privileged level on Windows, which is one reason it can be effective but also why faults can be catastrophic. CrowdStrike reported that the outage stemmed from a logic error triggered by a content configuration update, rather than a cyberattack, and that it promptly issued corrective guidance.[18]

The incident also accelerated Microsoft's efforts to enhance resilience. In September 2024, Microsoft described changes aimed at letting security vendors protect endpoints with less reliance on kernel-level access. It also emphasized safer deployment practices such as staged rollouts, broad endpoint testing, and clear rollback plans. Since then, Microsoft has continued to develop resilience initiatives and a vendor platform approach aimed at reducing the blast radius of defective updates while preserving security effectiveness.[19] The episode illustrates a recurring tension in platform design: the same compatibility decisions that welcome third-party innovation into the system also determine where security failures can occur and how far they can spread.

---

[17] John Cable, "Windows Resiliency: Best Practices and the Path Forward," Windows IT Pro Blog, Microsoft, July 25, 2024, `https://techcommunity.microsoft.com/blog/windows-itpro-blog/windows-resiliency-best-practices-and-the-path-forward/4201550`.

[18] CrowdStrike, "Technical Details: Falcon Update for Windows Hosts," CrowdStrike Blog, July 19, 2024, updated July 24, 2024, `https://www.crowdstrike.com/en-us/blog/falcon-update-for-windows-hosts-technical-details/`. See also CrowdStrike, "Preliminary Post Incident Review (PIR): Content Configuration Update Impacting the Falcon Sensor and the Windows Operating System," July 24, 2024, available at the same URL.

[19] David Weston, "Windows Security and Resiliency: Protecting Your Business," Windows Experience Blog, Microsoft, November 19, 2024, `https://blogs.windows.com/windowsexperience/2024/11/19/windows-security-and-resiliency-protecting-your-business/`. Microsoft announced the Windows Resiliency Initiative at Ignite 2024, which included Quick Machine Recovery, safer deployment practices for security vendors, and a new platform enabling security products to operate outside the kernel.

As threats become more sophisticated, AI is becoming a valuable tool in cybersecurity. ML systems can sift large volumes of telemetry to detect anomalies, prioritize alerts, and identify patterns that manual analysis would miss. At the same time, AI introduces its own risks, including adversarial manipulation, reliability concerns, and governance and privacy challenges. The European Union (EU) Agency for Cybersecurity has described AI as a dual-use technology.[20] It has highlighted the need for secure, trustworthy AI and for research into how it can both strengthen and threaten cybersecurity.

1.6.4 Convergence

Early in my career, I watched a colleague demonstrate a Word document that pulled live data from an Excel model linked to a Structured Query Language (SQL) database. It was held together with OLE and COM, and it worked—but every layer of connection was a potential point of failure. That memory stays with me because the same architectural challenge—making heterogeneous systems collaborate reliably—is now the central problem of cloud and AI. Interoperability, the capacity for such collaboration, underpins today's connected computing landscape. It has also been a through-line in my work. From OLE and COM to cloud APIs, I have focused on the mechanisms that let systems collaborate reliably. For me, interoperability is not an abstract ideal; it is the practical foundation on which useful software is built.

Interoperability operates at multiple levels. Technologies such as OLE and COM enable component-based interoperability. They let components written in different languages communicate within a shared platform, supporting modular design and reuse. Application-level interoperability connects systems through APIs, enabling data exchange and coordinated workflows across services. Data-level interoperability relies on shared formats and schemas to ensure that information can be transferred reliably between systems, even when each system stores and organizes data differently. Protocol-level interoperability builds on common standards that make distributed communication predictable. Examples include Hypertext Transfer Protocol (HTTP), Transport Layer Security (TLS), Representational State Transfer (REST), and GraphQL. In practice, modern systems depend on all of these layers working in concert.

[20] European Union Agency for Cybersecurity (ENISA), "ENISA Threat Landscape 2024," 2024, `https://www.enisa.europa.eu/topics/cyber-threats/threat-landscape`.

Modern AI systems exemplify convergence. They depend on multiple forms of interoperability: NLP components integrated with LLMs, retrieval systems that connect models to external knowledge, and data pipelines that unify content from databases, documents, and event streams. Training and deployment further depend on interoperability between frameworks, accelerators, and orchestration layers. Researchers and engineers routinely combine TensorFlow and PyTorch, use scikit-learn for classical ML, and rely on NVIDIA's Compute Unified Device Architecture (CUDA) for GPU-accelerated computing. The point is not the brand names; it is the composability. Progress comes from assembling the best components for each layer and getting them to work together cleanly.

Cloud computing amplifies the same requirement. Applications increasingly span public clouds, private infrastructure, and edge environments. Hence, portability and integration matter as much as raw capability. Containers—portable packages of applications and dependencies—have become a standard building block for this reason. Technologies such as Docker provide standardized container formats, while orchestration platforms such as Kubernetes coordinate containers across clusters, manage placement and scaling, and enable the same workload to run across multiple environments with minimal modification. Interoperability also manifests in developer workflows: WSL allows developers to run Linux-native tools on Windows, reducing friction across toolchains.

Security and governance add another dimension to convergence. As systems connect across organizational and geographic boundaries, identity, authorization, auditing, and key management must interoperate as well. Standards and shared approaches—such as single sign-on, token-based authentication, and policy-driven access control—enhance the trustworthiness of cross-system workflows. Without that layer, integration becomes fragile, and the very connections that create value also expand the attack surface.

Interoperability also determines whether enterprises can adopt AI responsibly. Models must integrate with existing data sources, comply with privacy and regulatory obligations, and support the monitoring of quality, drift, and misuse. Techniques such as retrieval-augmented generation (RAG), model gateways, and evaluation pipelines exist essentially to make AI systems dependable in real-world environments where data, policies, and users vary widely. Interoperability is not only about connecting systems; it is also about ensuring that those connections are reliable, secure, and governable.

Without interoperability, the AI and cloud ecosystem would fragment into isolated silos, slowing innovation and limiting scalability. Interoperability breaks down these barriers and lets developers build intelligent systems that span platforms and environments. It is not merely a helpful feature; it is a prerequisite for the intelligent, scalable future that cloud and AI technologies are shaping.

1.7 Summary

From building programming languages for early PCs to the release of Windows and Office, Microsoft helped reshape how people interact with technology. As a contributor to that journey, I saw each step make computing both more capable and more approachable.

The history of computing extends beyond any one company. Mainframes taught reliability, discipline, and scale—principles that informed the development of cloud architecture. Personal computing brought accessibility and broad participation—ideas that guide today's AI applications. The software bridges we engineered, from OLE and COM to modern containerization, bind these paradigms together.

My path runs from opening a Casio calculator as an engineering student, to researching planning systems and NLP on mainframes in India, and to helping bring these worlds together at Microsoft. Today's AI and cloud combine mainframe-style centralized computation with PC-era usability: immense power delivered through intuitive interfaces. Those foundations now underpin the integration of transformer models and large language systems into everyday products.

As we look ahead, these foundations matter. The ecosystem lessons from OS/2, the interoperability achieved through OLE and COM, and the balance that Windows and Office struck between power and simplicity continue to shape how we design intelligent systems. The convergence is not finished—it is accelerating—promising advances that will make today's milestones feel, like that Casio calculator, a marvel of their moment and a stepping stone to what follows.

The next chapter explores how this synthesis delivers the two core imperatives of modern computing: usability and scalability.

CHAPTER 2

Usability and Scalability: Lessons from Windows

In the late 1980s, Windows was still earning its place. Most PCs lived in a world shaped by MS-DOS: fast to boot, efficient for power users, and highly unforgiving for the broader user base. The GUI was not a given. It was a promise—one that had to be proven every day in code, in design reviews, and, most of all, in the hands of people who did not think of themselves as "computer people."

That tension was immediate as I worked on Word and Excel during a pivotal shift. Applications that once stood alone were becoming parts of something larger, more coherent, and more ambitious—*Microsoft Office*. Integration brought tangible benefits, but it also raised the bar. A change made for one product could ripple through workflows across many. Decisions about menus, keyboard shortcuts, file formats, setup programs, and performance became ecosystem choices rather than local optimizations. That is where usability and scalability intersected, sometimes politely, sometimes in direct conflict.

One memory remains vivid: the Windows 3.0 launch era, when the atmosphere inside Microsoft changed in a way that is hard to convey unless you have lived through it. It felt like we had moved from "this might work" to "this can change how people use computers." The excitement spread fast, with developers, support engineers, and program managers swapping hallway stories about a feature that finally clicked for a user or a demo that ran cleanly after weeks of tuning. The excitement was real, but it was not romantic. It came with a quiet awareness that even a single crash, a confusing dialog box, or a slow operation could turn that momentum into skepticism.

Performance mattered—concretely, measurably, every day. We shipped into a world of low-end hardware: limited memory, modest processors, slow disks, and graphics capabilities that varied widely across machines. Features had to work not only on the best systems on a lab bench, but also on the lowest common denominator in the real world.

K. C. Mukherjee, *The Microsoft AI Insider's Playbook*, https://doi.org/10.1007/979-8-8688-2730-3_2

Those constraints shaped every decision: how we drew text, managed memory, handled errors, and designed user interfaces that stayed responsive under load. "It works on my machine" was never a comfort; it was a warning.

This chapter distills the lessons I carried forward from those years. The core challenge has not changed: to build systems powerful enough for experts yet accessible to everyone. What has changed is the surface area. Today, we are designing AI systems that make decisions, summarize knowledge, generate content, and increasingly mediate how work gets done. The Windows era taught me that usability is not decoration and scalability is not only infrastructure. They are discipline—tested under pressure, refined through feedback, and proven at the edges, where real users live.

2.1 Designing for Constraints

In the early years of Windows and Office, "constraints" were not a theoretical design consideration. Instead, they were the daily reality that shaped every feature discussion and every line of code. An IBM PC 5150 of the early 1980s typically ran at 4.77 megahertz and was often configured with only tens of kilobytes of RAM. Today, a smartphone can have a multicore processor running over two gigahertz with eight gigabytes or more of RAM. If something felt slow, unstable, or inconsistent on the machines people actually owned, it did not matter how elegant the design looked in a meeting room. Constraints were the environment, and the product had to succeed within it.

This remained true even as hardware improved rapidly. In 1965, Gordon Moore observed that the number of transistors on an integrated circuit was doubling approximately every year—a prediction he later revised to every two years. This pattern—Moore's law—held for decades, even though progress has slowed at the leading edge. It drove exponential gains in capability while lowering the cost per transistor. As Moore noted in a 2015 interview, "The message really was: 'Hey, we're going to get lots more components on a chip.' And boy! Did that turn out to be the case."

Figure 2-1 illustrates this trajectory, from the Intel 4004 with approximately 2,300 transistors to modern chips with billions of transistors. But for those of us shipping software, Moore's law was a moving target, not a solution. Each generation raised expectations faster than it removed bottlenecks. Yesterday's luxury became today's baseline. We were not designing for the machines of next year; we were designing for the machines already on desks, in homes, and in offices—machines that were always, in some way, not quite enough.

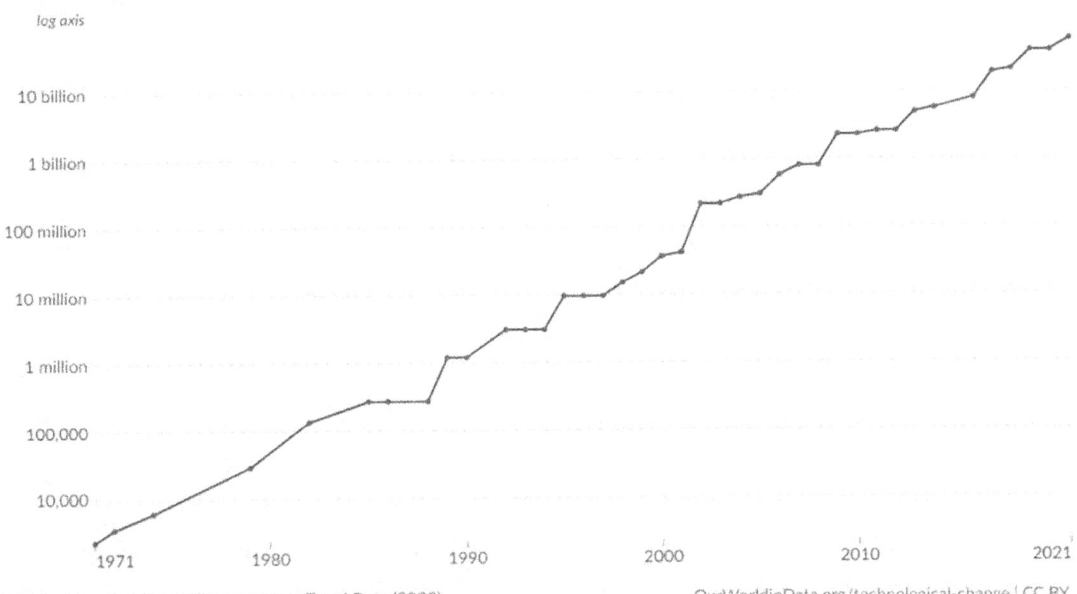

Figure 2-1. *Moore's Law in Action: 1971–2021. This logarithmic graph depicts the evolution of transistor counts per microprocessor across five decades. From approximately 2,300 transistors on the Intel 4004 in 1971 to over 50 billion by 2021, the visualization illustrates a doubling of components roughly every two years. The near-linear progression on this logarithmic scale highlights decades of exponential growth that fueled the digital revolution, even as the industry nears fundamental physical limits of silicon miniaturization. (Data source: Karl Rupp, Microprocessor Trend Data [2022], processed by Our World in Data. CC BY.)*

As transistors approach atomic dimensions at sub-five-nanometer nodes, quantum tunneling and heat dissipation become formidable barriers to further miniaturization. At the same time, the cost of leading-edge fabrication has surged, with new facilities now costing more than $20 billion to build.[1] As these transistor-level gains began to slow, another path emerged for increasing practical performance: parallelism.

GPUs—originally designed to accelerate three-dimensional (3D) rendering by performing many simple operations in parallel—proved well suited to the matrix and vector calculations at the heart of modern ML. Purpose-built AI accelerators further extended this idea. Instead of relying solely on ever-faster general-purpose CPUs, contemporary systems combine CPUs, GPUs, and specialized accelerators to deliver the throughput needed to train and serve large models. The architectural questions remain familiar: how to expose that power in ways that feel responsive, predictable, and trustworthy.

One of the most visible constraints was the performance of screen redraws. Every window repaint had to feel instant, even on slow graphics hardware with limited video memory. Users did not think in terms of graphics pipelines or memory bandwidth; they judged the system by how responsive it felt. A dialog box that appeared late, a scrolling page that smeared, or a window that repainted in chunks undermined trust immediately. Responsiveness was usability. We learned to treat perceived latency as a first-class requirement rather than an afterthought.

Printer driver compatibility was an ecosystem unto itself. We had to support hundreds of printers with varying capabilities, resolutions, and memory limits. The same document had to print correctly across a wide range of devices, even when the printers interpreted commands differently or had tiny buffers. The user expectation was simple: "If it looks right on screen, it should print right." Meeting that expectation meant building for variation, testing relentlessly, and designing output systems that could tolerate imperfect drivers and inconsistent device behavior.

[1] Intel announced an initial investment of more than $20 billion to construct two leading-edge chip factories in Licking County, Ohio. See "Intel Announces Next US Site with Landmark Investment in Ohio," Intel Corporation, January 21, 2022, `https://www.intc.com/news-events/press-releases/detail/1521/intel-announces-next-us-site-with-landmark-investment-in`. TSMC's Arizona fabrication complex, announced in December 2022, carried a projected investment exceeding $40 billion. See "TSMC Announces Updates for TSMC Arizona," TSMC, December 6, 2022, `https://pr.tsmc.com/english/news/2977`.

Display variability posed a similar challenge. Users had monitors ranging from monochrome to 256-color Video Graphics Array (VGA), and the software had to adapt gracefully. Color choices, icons, and layout assumptions that looked fine on one display could become illegible or confusing on another. It imposed discipline on user interface design: favor clarity over ornament, preserve meaning when fidelity drops, and treat accessibility as the default rather than a special case.

Handling large documents was a recurring challenge. Real users created files that exceeded available RAM. That meant we needed virtual memory strategies that did not destroy performance. We could not rely on "just add more memory" as an answer, because many customers could not. The real work was structuring data and algorithms so that everyday tasks—search, pagination, formatting, and editing—stayed smooth while memory management stayed out of the user's way.

Constraints were just as evident in setup and installation. Office had to install and run on machines with minimal free disk space, and every file in the installer was scrutinized. Packaging constraints shaped engineering trade-offs: what shipped by default, what could be compressed, what could be shared, what could be optional, and what always had to be present. Installation was not a footnote; it was the main door. If the door did not open reliably, users could not access the product's best features.

Add internationalization, and the discipline is further tightened. Supporting multiple languages, character sets, and text directions could not come at the cost of multiplying memory requirements. The system had to be flexible without becoming bloated. That pushed us toward generalized solutions—formatting engines, font handling, and resource loading strategies that scaled across locales.

Finally, there was cross-platform parity. Windows and Macintosh versions needed to be consistent in their features despite their different underlying architectures and performance profiles. That required careful thinking about what was truly core, what was platform specific, and how to structure shared logic without sacrificing the native feel users expected.

The lesson was clear: design for the worst machine your users actually have, not the best machine on your test bench. Constraints enforce discipline by revealing what truly matters. They also teach a deeper truth: optimization is not polish applied at the end; it is architecture decided at the beginning. And graceful behavior under pressure is everything. Degrade gracefully, and users stay. Fail suddenly, and they leave.

The same mindset applies directly to modern systems. Edge AI pushes models to phones, tablets, and embedded devices with limited compute resources. Inference latency must feel instant, just as screen redraws once did. The tension between massive cloud models and smaller local models echoes our earlier trade-offs between rich features and constrained hardware. Graceful degradation is now essential. When resources are limited—battery, bandwidth, memory, or processing power—systems must remain usable rather than fail. At a global scale, deployment revives the internationalization challenge in expanded form: diverse devices, networks, languages, and cultural expectations. The surface has changed, but the principle is the same. Great systems respect constraints—and turn them into clarity.

2.2 WYSIWYG and the Trust Equation

The GUI transformed how people interacted with computers, and its modern origins trace back to Xerox PARC.[2] The Xerox Star 8010 Information System, introduced in April 1981, was among the first commercially available systems to bring a GUI into office computing. It helped popularize a visual vocabulary that later became familiar to everyone: icons, folders, windowed documents, and mouse-driven interaction. It also advanced the desktop metaphor—using familiar objects such as files, folders, and a wastebasket to represent computer actions—so digital work felt concrete rather than abstract. At $16,595 per workstation (approximately $59,000 in 2026 dollars)—with complete systems starting at $75,000 (approximately $268,000 in 2026 dollars)—the Star was priced well above most buyers' budgets.[3]

During the early years of modern productivity software, WYSIWYG was not a slogan. It was a promise that shaped whether people felt they could rely on a computer for serious work. The core commitment was simple: what appears on screen should match what prints on paper. I worked on these problems firsthand, and delivering that promise required solving a long list of messy, real-world problems. Getting Word and Excel to render text consistently across screens and printers was a daily challenge—one slight difference in metrics could shift line breaks throughout an entire document. Screens, printers, and operating systems behaved differently, yet users still expected one coherent outcome.

[2] Xerox Palo Alto Research Center (PARC), established in 1970, pioneered many foundational computing technologies, including the GUI, the mouse, Ethernet networking, laser printing, and object-oriented programming.

[3] The introductory workstation price of $16,595 is documented in "Xerox 8010 Star Information System," National Museum of American History, Smithsonian Institution, `https://americanhistory.si.edu/collections/object/nmah_1064205`. The base system price of approximately $75,000 is reported in Jeff Johnson et al., "The Xerox 'Star': A Retrospective," *IEEE Computer* 22, no. 9 (September 1989): 11-26, 28-29.

Before Windows and Office, screen-to-print fidelity was not a given. Early PCs relied on command-line interfaces that demanded memorized commands and arcane syntax. GUIs changed that expectation. Systems such as the Xerox Star, Apple Macintosh, and later Microsoft Windows popularized the desktop metaphor: files and folders on a virtual desk, overlapping windows, and icons that behaved like physical objects.

Technically, this transition also marked the rise of event-driven interaction. Instead of the computer running a single program from beginning to end, the system responded to user actions—mouse clicks, keystrokes, menu selections—and dispatched those events to the appropriate application. That model underlies almost every modern user interface, from productivity software to web applications, and it sets the stage for WYSIWYG editing to feel natural rather than magical.

A major step forward was the integration of scalable fonts that rendered consistently across screens and printers. Technologies such as TrueType, introduced by Microsoft and Apple in the early 1990s, helped narrow the gap by providing consistent underlying font outlines across devices. Before scalable fonts became standard, the same document could look acceptable on one screen and turn into a typographic surprise on another. Printing could feel like stepping into unknown territory. TrueType reduced the "screen says one thing, paper says another" problem and became a foundation for predictable output across devices.

Even with better fonts, however, the technical challenge remained: achieving fidelity across different monitors, printers, and resolutions. Some users had monochrome displays. Others had 256-color VGA displays. Pixel densities varied widely. Printers added an entirely different set of variables—device memory limits, driver behavior, and differences in supported resolutions and printable regions. Each variation could produce subtle shifts: a line break moving by one word, a margin changing slightly, a page breaking one paragraph earlier than expected. Those "small" differences were not minor to a user preparing a report for a client, a contract draft, or a resume.

That is why page layout accuracy became part of the trust equation. Line breaks, margins, and pagination had to match between screen and print. It was not enough to "look close." People built workflows around precise placement—headers aligned, tables fitting cleanly, page counts predictable. If the system could not preserve layout across output contexts, users had to compensate manually, and manual compensation is where frustration grows.

The challenge intensified with cross-platform consistency. Windows and Macintosh versions needed to produce output that was effectively identical from the same document, even though the underlying architectures and graphics systems differed. Users shared files between platforms, and organizations standardized on templates. If the same file printed differently on different machines, the product did not merely feel inconsistent—it felt unreliable.

You could see the impact in the iteration cycle. Users would print, compare, adjust, and reprint. If the document diverged from the screen, they stopped trusting what they saw. Printing became the only authoritative view, which defeated the purpose of WYSIWYG. Every mismatch added friction, and friction turns curiosity into caution. Eventually, even a handful of failures could train users to expect failure, and expectation becomes habit.

One recurring source of mismatch was font substitution. When a font was missing, the system still had to move forward, but without destroying the layout. Substituting a font that changes character widths could trigger reflow: different line breaks, different page breaks, shifted tables. A well-designed system treated font substitution as a controlled fallback: preserving metrics where possible, warning users when output might change, and providing a path to restore fidelity.

The principle endures: users trust systems that behave predictably. "What you see is what you get" is a promise, and breaking it erodes confidence. Consistency across contexts—screen sizes, platforms, and outputs—is important because it protects users from unpleasant surprises. Trust is built incrementally and lost instantly. And fidelity is not a feature added late in development; it is a contract with the user.

That same contract is emerging again in modern AI—though the challenge has shifted. WYSIWYG promised deterministic fidelity: the same document, the same output, every time. AI outputs are probabilistic; the same prompt may yield different results. Nevertheless, the underlying principle holds. Transparency is the new foundation of trust: users need to understand what the system is likely to do and why it produced a particular outcome.

Predictable behavior builds trust; surprising behavior destroys it. In that sense, the WYSIWYG principle has an AI counterpart: "what you prompt is what you get"—not perfectly, but reliably enough that users can form accurate expectations. Explainable AI plays a role similar to screen-to-print fidelity: it reduces the gap between intention and outcome. Consistency matters in AI interfaces as well. When the model, version, and settings are the same, a prompt should yield broadly similar results across sessions and environments, within stated limits. When AI systems behave unpredictably, users lose confidence for the same reason they did when printouts did not match screens: the system broke its own promise.

2.3 Progressive Disclosure

As Office evolved, it became a case study in progressive disclosure: how to expand capabilities without overwhelming users. Early versions of Word were relatively compact. Word 1.0 had dozens of commands that a motivated user could explore within a reasonable period. By the time we reached later releases such as Word 6.0, that modest command set had exploded into the hundreds. The software could do far more, for more people, in more situations. The question was not whether we should add features; it was how to add them without making the product feel intimidating, cluttered, or unpredictable. I participated in these decisions. Seeing users struggle to find features buried in menus shaped my conviction that complexity must be staged, not dumped on the user all at once.

That tension shaped many design decisions. Menu hierarchies became one of the earliest mechanisms for managing interface complexity. Commands were grouped into stable, semantically coherent categories—File, Edit, View, Insert, Format—so the interface matched how users thought about their work. The menu system functioned not just as navigation but as a learning scaffold: if users could infer where a command belonged, they could reliably find it again.

As usage patterns became clearer, toolbars helped solve a different problem: speed. Some actions were used constantly—save, print, undo, copy, paste, bold, italic, and alignment. Toolbars surfaced frequently used actions so that users did not have to navigate menus repeatedly. This reduced friction in the most common workflows, making the software feel lighter, faster, and more approachable.

Productivity software serves novices and experts whose needs differ sharply. That brought us to customization. Power users wanted faster access to specialized tools and were willing to invest in tailoring the user interface. In contrast, many other users never touched customization at all. The goal was not to push everyone to configure, but to let experts expose what they needed while keeping defaults coherent for everyone else. Customization served as an escape valve: it added depth without imposing complexity on the default experience.

Later, the Ribbon emerged as a different solution to the same underlying problem. Instead of organizing commands by type or historical menu categories, it grouped tools by task and user intent. This reduced time spent navigating menus and toolbars by clustering related actions—formatting text, inserting an object, or reviewing a document—rather than requiring users to remember the location of each command in the hierarchy. Whether one prefers menus or the Ribbon, the design challenge was identical: increasing functionality without increasing cognitive load.

Another key technique was the context-sensitive menu. When users right-clicked, the interface presented a focused set of options based on what they were working on. A table surfaced table tools, an image surfaced image tools, and selected text surfaced formatting tools. In other words, context reduced noise. The interface ceased to be a static catalog and became responsive—showing what mattered in the moment and receding when it did not. Beneath these choices was a broader modular design mindset: users should interact primarily with what they need. Advanced features should exist—and be strong—but they should not intrude on someone writing a simple letter. Progressive disclosure is not about removing capability; it is about staging it.

The discipline is straightforward but demanding: hide complexity without removing capability. Surface everyday tasks and make advanced features discoverable without making them intrusive. The user interface should grow with the user's expertise over time. Defaults matter because most users never change them; they must be correct. And discoverability is not the same as visibility—users should be able to find features when needed, but they should not be confronted by everything, all the time.

Modern AI products face the same design challenge in a new form. The user interfaces for prompts must be simple by default, yet powerful when needed. ChatGPT looks straightforward—type a request, get a response—but there is depth beneath the surface: settings, memory limits, connected tools, and structured outputs. In enterprise AI, progressive disclosure often becomes role-based. For example, an executive dashboard should not resemble an analyst's workbench. Copilot-style integration reflects the same principle by embedding assistance within familiar workflows rather than forcing users to use a separate application.

The balance remains delicate: "just works" for most people and "fully configurable" for those who need control. Microsoft 365 reflects this principle across many experiences by personalizing the user interface and suggesting relevant features based on user activity. The best path is progressive complexity—start with natural language, and then expose parameters, controls, and diagnostics for users who are ready to go deeper.

2.4 Cross-Platform Scalability

Cross-platform thinking at Microsoft predates Office on Windows and Macintosh. In the early 1980s, the PC market was highly fragmented across operating systems and processor architectures. To cope with that fragmentation, Microsoft used portability techniques that separated a shared application core from small, platform-specific support layers. One well-known example is Microsoft Multiplan, an early spreadsheet application that used a proprietary portable-code (p-code) compiler to make ports to many systems practical.

The approach relied on a two-part application structure. Most of the application logic could be compiled into compact, machine-independent instructions for a VM. That code was then executed by a relatively small, platform-specific interpreter written for each target environment. Microsoft could move faster by porting the interpreter and a thin platform layer rather than rewriting the entire application for each operating system or processor. The goal was not perfection on day one; it was a disciplined way to preserve functional consistency as software spread across incompatible systems.

This intermediate-code mindset also shows up later in the ecosystem around Word. For example, early versions of Word used a proprietary compiler that emitted p-code, which was executed by an interpreter at runtime. Whether every product used the exact same portability method is less important than the enduring architectural principle: isolate what must behave identically and localize what must vary.

That foundation guided our approach to cross-platform development as Office matured on Windows and macOS. At first glance, the goal sounded straightforward: deliver the same product experience on different operating systems. In practice, that goal drove architectural decisions across the entire product: code organization, testing, release planning, and even what we meant by "the same" behavior. We repeatedly returned to one question: what should be shared across platforms and what must remain platform specific? If we shared too little, we effectively produced two products and incurred twice the engineering, quality assurance (QA), and long-term maintenance costs. If we shared too much, we risked shipping something that felt foreign on both platforms—technically consistent but awkward to use. The best path was deliberate separation: a shared core with platform-specific layers around it.

I experienced these tensions firsthand—first across Windows and Macintosh and later across macOS, Linux, iOS, and Android.[4] Each imposed its own constraints and conventions. macOS emphasized tight integration and careful control over the user experience. Linux required support for diverse distributions, packaging systems, and deployment environments. Mobile platforms introduced their own constraints: battery limitations, touch-based interaction, and app store requirements. Still, the same principle held across all of them: broad adoption depends on combining power with approachability, so users can be productive without becoming experts in system internals.

The cross-platform strategy at Microsoft relied on abstraction layers that enabled code reuse while preserving platform-specific behavior. The shared core held the logic that had to produce identical results, regardless of where it ran. For Office, that meant formatting engines, file parsers, and calculation engines—the machinery that determined document layout, spreadsheet results, and file open/save behavior. Users could tolerate a button being in a different location, but they could not tolerate the same document opening with different pagination or the same formula producing different results. Shared core logic became a single source of truth for correctness.

Around that core, we built platform-specific layers—the parts that needed to feel native to each operating system. User interface rendering, printing subsystems, clipboard integration, and file system access had to respect platform conventions and performance profiles. That was not cosmetic: it affected speed, reliability, and user confidence. The user expectation was simple: "This should behave like a first-class application on my machine." Achieving that required thoughtful adaptation rather than imposing one platform's assumptions on another.

Testing complexity rose rapidly. The same feature had to be verified across multiple operating systems, hardware configurations, and interaction patterns. Edge cases multiplied: device drivers, input methods, font availability, and differences in system services. Even minor changes could have unexpected ripple effects when they crossed the abstraction boundary. Meanwhile, releases had to be synchronized. Coordinating schedules across platform teams required discipline, shared milestones, and a constant focus on potential impediments to parity.

[4] macOS is Apple's desktop operating system, renamed from OS X in 2016. iOS is Apple's mobile operating system, introduced in 2007 for the iPhone. Android is Google's open source mobile operating system, released in 2008.

The cost of divergence was always visible. When platform versions fell out of sync, the support burden multiplied. Documentation became inconsistent, user training became harder, and bug reports became ambiguous: "Does this happen on Windows, macOS, or both?" The deeper cost was trust. Users who share files across platforms expect predictable outcomes. If the product family behaved like separate products, confidence eroded quickly.

This insight is not era-specific. Whether the abstraction was p-code and interpreters in the early years or shared libraries and layered architectures in the Office era, cross-platform portability requires deliberate architectural design from the outset. Abstract the common; optimize the specific. "Write once, run anywhere" is aspirational, but "write once, adapt thoughtfully" is realistic. Users expect a platform-native feel, so abstraction must not erase platform identity. Parity is not sameness: features should behave consistently, even if user interfaces differ appropriately. Underestimating platform differences is a reliable way to deliver poor experiences on all platforms.

Modern systems repeat the same trade-off at larger scale. Cloud-native development increasingly targets multiple providers, including AWS, Azure, and Google Cloud. Teams use containerization tools, such as Docker, and orchestration platforms, such as Kubernetes, as practical abstraction layers that reduce coupling to any single provider. WSL, discussed in Chapter 1, offers a striking example of this convergence—bridging ecosystems that once seemed incompatible by letting developers run Linux tools natively on Windows. Cross-platform deployment in AI introduces an additional dimension: models that run in cloud environments, at the edge, on mobile devices, and in the browser. Standards and frameworks such as TensorFlow, PyTorch, and Open Neural Network Exchange (ONNX) advance portability by providing teams with common formats and runtimes across environments.

The trade-off remains: optimize deeply for one platform, or abstract carefully for many. Early p-code and modern containers are decades apart, but they solve the same problem: build once, and then run well across many machines and operating environments.

Java, introduced in 1995, formalized this approach with its "write once, run anywhere" promise. Java applications compile to platform-independent bytecode that runs on the Java Virtual Machine (JVM), which provides services such as memory management, threading, and just-in-time compilation for each target environment. Microsoft's .NET Common Language Runtime (CLR), introduced in 2002, followed a similar model, using an intermediate language and a managed runtime. I watched this evolution unfold—from the p-code strategies I encountered in my early years at Microsoft to the managed runtimes that later became industry standards. The underlying principle remained constant: abstract the execution environment so application logic stays portable. Both platforms demonstrate the enduring value of the p-code principle. Their ecosystems—Java with Spring and Kafka and .NET with cloud-native libraries—extend this portability into distributed systems and microservices. These were not academic exercises for the teams I worked with. Over the years, we have used these tools to build enterprise systems that run reliably across diverse environments.

2.5 The Ecosystem Imperative

Working with members of my team on OS/2 Presentation Manager applications, I had a front-row seat to one of the most instructive platform failures in the history of personal computing. As discussed in Chapter 1, OS/2 was technically impressive. It offered preemptive multitasking and protected memory—capabilities that many practitioners viewed as ahead of the mainstream Windows experience at the time. On paper, OS/2 appeared to be the stronger foundation. In reality, it lost—and the reasons had little to do with raw technical merit.

The decisive factor was the platform ecosystem. Windows 3.0 gained momentum quickly because it ran on top of MS-DOS and was widely available on new PCs, whereas OS/2 was often sold as a separate add-on. Windows also benefited from broader hardware compatibility and device driver availability, which mattered enormously in a market where "it works with my printer and my graphics card" was a buying criterion, not a detail. As Windows adoption grew, developers followed the users, and applications followed the developers. That feedback loop became self-reinforcing: more applications attracted more users, and more users attracted more developers. OS/2 could not overcome Windows' momentum.

IBM made adjustments over time, but the timing was not in its favor. Once the ecosystem tilted, momentum accelerated. Developers built for Windows because that was where the users were. Users chose Windows because it was where the applications—and compatible hardware—were available. The cycle fed itself, and OS/2 became a cautionary tale.

The lesson is uncomfortable but clear: technical superiority alone does not win. Ecosystems create momentum that features cannot match. Developer adoption is often the leading indicator of platform success—more than benchmarks, architecture diagrams, or executive endorsements. Network effects compound relentlessly. Each new application makes the platform more valuable, attracting more developers, which in turn produces more applications. Timing matters because a head start in developer adoption is extraordinarily difficult to reverse. And perception becomes reality: once a platform is seen as dominant, it attracts investment, talent, and attention that reinforce its position.

This lesson applies directly to modern AI. The major players are competing not only to build the most capable model, but also to own the platforms that developers adopt first. Microsoft's partnership with OpenAI positions Azure OpenAI Service as a tightly integrated entry point for Generative Pretrained Transformer (GPT)-class models, backed by a broad ecosystem of APIs, tooling, and enterprise-grade integrations across Microsoft 365 and Dynamics 365. Google's Vertex AI leverages deep alignment with its cloud, data, and search infrastructure. Amazon's Bedrock aggregates multiple model providers under a unified AWS-native control plane. Each company is building not just a model, but a full-stack platform: APIs, integrations, marketplaces, developer tools, documentation, and governance frameworks that drive large-scale adoption. The competitive race is architectural as much as algorithmic—and, as OS/2 demonstrated, superior technology alone does not guarantee leadership if the surrounding ecosystem lags.

Interface design and developer experience matter enormously. A model that is slightly less capable but far easier to integrate will often see greater adoption than a stronger model that creates friction. Early OpenAI API adoption benefited from straightforward authentication, clear documentation, and a smooth onboarding path—signals that mattered as much as model quality for developers working under tight deadlines. Transparent pricing and responsive support reinforce the message: the platform is worth building on for the long term.

Open source strategies reflect the same ecosystem logic. Meta's Llama releases and models, such as Mistral, represent a deliberate trade: relinquishing some control in exchange for reach. If developers build on an open foundation, the ecosystem can grow even without centralized direction. This is not charity; it is a competitive strategy informed by decades of platform history.

The same ecosystem dynamics play out in domain-specific platforms. Salesforce introduced its Einstein AI layer in 2016 and has since embedded ML, NLP, and generative AI (GenAI) across its customer relationship management (CRM) suite—sales, service, marketing, and commerce. AI capabilities are now built into workflows that millions of users already use. Systems, Applications, and Products in Data Processing

(SAP) has taken a parallel approach with its Joule AI copilot. Joule is now integrated across SAP's flagship Business Suite 4 for High-Performance Analytic Appliance (S/4HANA), SuccessFactors, Concur, and Ariba, embedding intelligence directly into enterprise resource planning (ERP), human resources (HR), and procurement processes. In each case, the platform with the deepest existing integration wins adoption—not by offering the most powerful standalone model, but by reducing the friction between the model and the work.

For enterprise technology leaders evaluating AI investments, the OS/2 lesson remains relevant. Choosing a platform based solely on current benchmarks is risky. The better question is this: Does this platform have a healthy, growing ecosystem—one where developers are building, tooling is maturing, and integrations are multiplying? A platform with a thriving ecosystem today is more likely to remain viable tomorrow—even if a competitor temporarily offers a more impressive demonstration.

Features win attention. Ecosystems win markets.

2.6 Intelligent Assistance: Success and Failure

Some of the most valuable lessons from the Windows and Office years came not from the features that shipped, but from the contrast between what worked and what did not. Nowhere was that contrast sharper than in our efforts to build intelligent assistance into productivity software.

As discussed in Chapter 1, proofing tools have become some of the most widely used and quietly appreciated features in Office. The Spell Checker and Grammar Checker did their work without fanfare. They underlined errors, offered suggestions, and stepped back. Users could accept a correction with a click or ignore it entirely. The tools did not demand attention. They did not disrupt workflow. They waited to be consulted and, when consulted, responded quickly and usefully. That restraint was not a limitation; it was the design.

AutoCorrect and AutoFormat followed a similar philosophy but extended the scope of automation. AutoCorrect fixed common typing errors—replacing "teh" with "the," for example, without asking permission. AutoFormat adjusted formatting as users typed, converting straight quotes to curly quotes and hyphens to dashes. These features acted on the user's behalf, quietly and continuously. Most users appreciated the results without considering the underlying mechanism. The corrections felt natural, almost invisible. When automation is so well calibrated that users forget it exists, it has succeeded.

In usability sessions and hallway demonstrations, I observed that contrast played out in real time. The difference was unmistakable: when proofing features helped, users barely reacted—there was a slight nod, a quick acceptance, and they kept moving. The moment assistance became distracting, the mood changed instantly. Attention shifted from the work to the software, and one could almost feel the trust drain from the interaction.

Then there was the Office Assistant, widely known by its default persona, Clippy. The ambition behind Clippy was genuine. The goal was to offer proactive, context-sensitive help—anticipating what users might need and surfacing guidance before they had to search for it. The underlying technology, rooted in the Lumière Project's Bayesian user modeling, was technically sophisticated. It attempted to infer user intent from user behavior and to provide relevant assistance in real time.

The experience, however, did not match the ambition. Clippy appeared unsolicited, often at moments when users were focused on their own tasks. It asked questions like "It looks like you're writing a letter. Would you like help?" even when users neither wanted help nor were writing letters. The assistant presumed knowledge of user intent that it did not reliably have. Worse, it insisted on being noticed. Dismissing Clippy took effort, and effort breeds resentment. The reaction from users was not mild disappointment—it was intense backlash. Clippy became a symbol of software that tried too hard to be helpful and ended up intruding.

The conclusion is uncomfortable but essential: successful assistance is invisible until needed. Failed assistance barges in, presuming it knows what the user needs. In reality, situational awareness matters more than raw capability. Users accept automation they control; they reject automation that controls them. Timing is everything: help offered at the wrong moment, even when accurate, feels like interference. And confidence calibration is critical—systems that speak with certainty when they should hedge do not feel intelligent; they feel arrogant. The line between helpful and intrusive is thin, and users do not forgive easily.

Modern AI assistants face precisely the same challenge, now at a far greater scale. The design of GitHub Copilot reflects the lessons we learned decades ago. Code suggestions appear inline and in context as the developer types. Accepting a suggestion takes a single keystroke. Ignoring it needs nothing at all—the suggestion simply fades. There is no dialog box, no animated character, no disruption. The assistant proposes; the user disposes. That asymmetry is essential.

Microsoft 365 Copilot follows similar principles. It integrates with familiar workflows—Word, Excel, Outlook, and Teams—without requiring users to learn a separate application. It responds to explicit prompts rather than inferring user intent. When it generates content, it presents drafts for review, not final answers for blind acceptance. The user remains in control.

The Clippy lesson, properly understood, is not that proactive assistance is impossible. Rather, it reveals that proactive assistance must earn trust through restraint, accuracy, and respect for users' attention. Modern AI systems have capabilities that would have seemed remarkable in the Clippy era. LLMs can interpret nuanced requests, generate plausible content, and adapt to context in ways that rule-based systems never could. But power without calibration is dangerous. An AI assistant that intrudes, presumes, or insists will be disabled, ignored, or resented—just as Clippy was.

The risk of repeating Clippy's mistake at larger scale is real. As AI becomes more embedded in daily tools, the temptation to make it more visible, more proactive, and more assertive will only grow. The lesson from Office remains: the best assistance is the kind users forget is there—until the moment they need it.

However, the "forgetting" is no longer just about avoiding a nuisance; it is about managing a new class of systemic risks. Modern AI systems introduce failure modes that earlier tools did not face. LLMs can produce confident but factually wrong outputs—a problem often called hallucination—with no visible signal that something is incorrect. Their behavior can shift unpredictably across prompts, producing different answers to the same question depending on phrasing or context. They can misinterpret intent, degrade silently as data and systems around them change, reflect cultural biases embedded in their training data, and construct reasoning chains that appear sound but rest on flawed premises. Each of these failure modes connects to the lessons of this chapter: confidence calibration, progressive disclosure, respect for user attention, and the principle that automation must remain transparent and reversible. The difference is that in the LLM era, failures are harder to detect and consequences spread faster. Hence, governance is not optional—it is an operational necessity.

2.7 From Desktop to Cloud

One of the defining architectural decisions of the Windows and Office era was a commitment to interoperability. As discussed in Chapter 1, technologies such as OLE, COM, and VBA were not incidental features. They were strategic choices that transformed Office from a collection of applications into a platform—one that developers, enterprises, and power users could extend, customize, and build upon.

OLE made it possible to embed a live spreadsheet in a document or link to external data that updates automatically. A key historical nuance is that OLE 1.0 preceded COM, while OLE 2.0 and later versions were built on COM, which provided the component model and binary contracts that made interoperability reliable. COM standardized how software components communicated, creating stable interfaces that allowed independently developed pieces of software to work together. VBA gave users and developers a programmable layer on top of Office, enabling automation, customization, and integration with other systems. Together, these technologies invited participation. They said, in effect, this is not a closed product; it is a foundation on which you can build.

The benefits were substantial. Third-party developers created add-ins that extended Office into specialized domains such as legal document management, financial modeling, and scientific analysis. Enterprises built internal tools on top of Office rather than starting from scratch. Power users automated repetitive tasks with macros. Each extension increased the platform's value, and visible success attracted more investment from the ecosystem.

Extensibility introduced a clear trade-off: openness entailed risk. A poorly written add-in could destabilize the host application. A macro could introduce security vulnerabilities. Extensibility is valuable, but stability is nonnegotiable. Balancing the two required discipline: clear interfaces, isolation and guardrails where possible, and constant attention to the boundary between the platform and its extensions.

Governance was the invisible requirement: when it worked, no one noticed; when it failed, the consequences were immediate. That lesson applies directly to AI, where the same trade-off between openness and control plays out at a far greater scale. Auditability, policy enforcement, and human accountability must be designed in from the start, not added after deployment.

The takeaway is architectural: interoperability fuels ecosystem growth. When components communicate through stable, well-defined interfaces, developers can build on top of them without needing access to source code or internal knowledge. Extensibility encourages participation. When users can customize, they invest more deeply—and many become advocates. These are not decisions that can be made late in development. Early architectural choices constrain or expand what is possible later.

Interoperability also revealed a deeper architectural principle: the value of maintaining a single source of truth. In the early desktop era, documents were stored as isolated files on individual machines. Users duplicated files, exchanged copies through email, and routinely struggled to determine which version was authoritative. The result was confusion, redundant effort, and errors, as someone inevitably worked from an outdated copy.

Early Microsoft technologies, such as OLE, introduced a partial remedy. By allowing a document to link to an external spreadsheet rather than embed a static copy, OLE enabled multiple files to reference a single, continuously updated source. Although limited in scope and designed primarily for compound documents, this mechanism demonstrated the value of centralizing authoritative data and distributing references to it. That same instinct—centralize truth, distribute access—reappeared in enterprise workflow systems.

The single source of truth principle informed the design of INTELLIFM, which implemented a centralized repository with distributed access—a single authoritative location for documents, available across the organization through controlled workflows. Users no longer maintained personal copies that drifted out of sync. The system enforced a single source of truth, making compliance, version control, and collaborative work tractable rather than chaotic. The architecture anticipated capabilities that cloud computing would later deliver on a global scale. Chapter 4 discusses INTELLIFM in detail.

The broader transition from local files to network shares and ultimately to cloud-based storage can be understood as a progressive consolidation of truth. SharePoint, OneDrive, Google Drive, and Dropbox succeeded not only because they stored files online, but because they solved a daily problem: which copy is the right one. Collaboration features such as Google Docs and Microsoft 365 coauthoring extended that idea by enabling multiple people to work on a single document simultaneously, with a single authoritative version. The usability gains were substantial. Users could trust that what they saw was current, that their contributions would persist, and that colleagues were operating from the same shared foundation. I saw this transition unfold over decades—from the OLE links I helped build, through the centralized architecture of INTELLIFM, and to the cloud collaboration tools that now serve millions of users.

Modern cloud computing is, in many ways, the fulfillment of this architectural vision on a vastly larger scale. The principles are familiar: isolate components, define clear interfaces, and support composition. What OLE and COM did for desktop integration,

APIs do for cloud services. What VBA did for Office automation, serverless functions do for cloud workflows. The vocabulary has changed, but the underlying discipline has remained the same.

The moment this continuity became concrete for me was not during a product launch or an architectural design review. It happened when I watched a colleague edit a shared document from a hotel lobby overseas, the changes appearing in real time on my screen in Redmond. The file was no longer a thing stored on a disk. It had become a service. Everything I had learned about OLE links, COM interfaces, and component boundaries still applied—only now the components were microservices, the interfaces were REST endpoints, and the state lived in a cloud-native substrate rather than on a single machine.

Cloud platforms such as AWS, Azure, and Google Cloud are built around interoperability. Services communicate through APIs, and infrastructure is provisioned on demand. Storage, compute, and networking are disaggregated and reassembled as needed. This architecture enables outcomes that would have been difficult to imagine in the desktop era: large-scale storage accessible from multiple locations, real-time collaboration across geographies, elastic scaling that responds to demand, and deployment models that reduce capital expenditure.

As these platforms matured, two complementary patterns emerged. Cloud computing has effectively made personal and enterprise software location-agnostic. Instead of being limited by the storage and processing power of a single machine, users could access documents, applications, and collaboration tools from almost anywhere with a network connection. At the same time, edge computing pushed selected workloads closer to where data is generated—on devices, sensors, and local gateways—to reduce latency and bandwidth requirements. Together, these patterns extended the lessons on usability and scalability from the desktop era to a world in which computation is distributed across devices, data centers, and networks.

Communication and collaboration platforms—Microsoft Teams, Slack, and Google Meet—share these underlying principles. They integrate with third-party applications through APIs, support extensibility through bots and plugins, and run on cloud infrastructure that scales with usage. The interoperability patterns we learned while building Office apply directly.

AI is now entering this ecosystem as a composable service. Azure OpenAI Service, Amazon Bedrock, and Google Vertex AI expose capabilities through APIs, much as earlier cloud services exposed storage or compute. Developers can integrate language models, image generation, or speech recognition into applications without building those capabilities from scratch. The architectural principle remains consistent: define clear interfaces, support composition, and allow the ecosystem to evolve.

Indeed, composability endows modern AI systems with enormous power, but it also reintroduces familiar challenges in new, sometimes subtler forms. As organizations integrate language models through APIs, they encounter questions that echo long-standing lessons from earlier generations of software design. A RAG pipeline that surfaces outdated, contradictory, or low-quality documents is the single source of truth problem resurfacing in a new form. A chatbot that overwhelms users with unsolicited suggestions repeats the same mistake that made Clippy infamous: the assumption that proactive assistance is always welcome, even when it interrupts the user's focus or misreads their intent. An AI feature whose behavior shifts depending on how a prompt is phrased undermines the consistency that WYSIWYG interfaces taught us to protect. An enterprise deployment that exposes an LLM without role-based access, audit trails, or clear governance boundaries ignores the same lessons that macros, add-ins, and extensibility frameworks forced organizations to learn decades ago. The tools are new; the design discipline is not.

From OLE to APIs, from VBA to serverless functions, from desktop add-ins to cloud-native integrations, the trajectory is coherent. The strongest platforms are not the ones that do everything themselves. They are the ones that make it easy for others to contribute, extend, and build. That was true in the Office era. It remains true in the age of cloud and AI.

2.8 Summary

The lessons from the Windows and Office years are not historical footnotes. They remain directly applicable to the systems we build today—especially the AI systems that are reshaping how work gets done.

Designing for constraints showed us that software must succeed on the machines users actually have, not the machines we wish they had. WYSIWYG fidelity indicates that trust depends on consistency: what users see must match what they receive, or confidence erodes. Progressive disclosure showed us how to stage complexity—surface the common, make the advanced discoverable, and avoid overwhelming users.

Cross-platform scalability reinforced that portability requires a deliberate architectural approach: abstract what must behave identically and adapt what must feel native. The ecosystem imperative reinforced a hard truth: features win attention, but ecosystems win markets; developer adoption is often the leading indicator of platform success.

The contrast between proofing tools and Clippy clarified that successful assistance remains silent until needed, whereas failed assistance intrudes and presumes. Interoperability—from OLE and COM to modern APIs—shows that platforms grow fastest when they make it easy for others to build on them. Finally, the single source of truth principle—seen in OLE linking, INTELLIFM knowledge bases, and modern cloud collaboration—explains why teams move faster when everyone works from a single, authoritative source of data.

Running through all of these lessons is a requirement that is easy to overlook until it fails: governance. Governance is to AI what memory management was to Windows—invisible when done well, catastrophic when ignored. Auditability, lineage, and human sign-off are not compliance add-ons; they are architectural constraints that belong in the design from day one if an AI platform is going to scale safely and credibly.

In fact, these are not separate lessons but facets of one discipline. Usability and scalability are not layers added at the end or infrastructure buried underneath; they are architectural choices made early, tested under pressure, and refined through real-world feedback. They determine whether technology empowers users or frustrates them, whether systems earn trust or erode it, and whether platforms grow or stagnate.

The surface has changed dramatically. We no longer worry about fitting applications into two megabytes of memory or supporting hundreds of printer drivers. But the underlying challenges persist in new forms. Resource constraints now show up in edge deployment and prompt efficiency, not memory limits. Ecosystem challenges have shifted from printer drivers to cloud portability and AI platform adoption. And the human-centered design questions remain: how to assist without overstepping and how to ground AI systems in trustworthy data.

The tools differ, but the discipline remains the same.

These lessons in usability and scalability lead naturally to automation—the subject of the next chapter. Automation, done well, embodies the same principles: it respects constraints, builds trust, manages complexity, and invites extension. When done poorly, it repeats the mistakes we learned to avoid. Next, we explore how automation improves efficiency, reduces human error, and drives innovation—and why getting it right still depends on the lessons we carry forward.

CHAPTER 3

The Need for Automation

The lessons on usability and scalability from the Windows era lead naturally to automation. Done well, automation embodies the same principles: it respects constraints, builds trust, handles complexity, and invites extension. When done poorly, it repeats the mistakes we have learned to avoid.

I saw both outcomes at Microsoft. With early tools like WordBASIC and, later, VBA, the goal was never to take control away from people but to give them the means to automate their own work. A macro that saved someone an hour a week was a success—not because we built it, but because the user did, using the capabilities we provided. VBA respected human judgment. It offered power without presumption: those who wanted automation could script it; and those who preferred manual control could keep it. That balance was intentional, and it became a strategic differentiator for the Office ecosystem.

The same philosophy underpins features such as AutoCorrect and AutoFormat, discussed in Chapter 2. They acted on the user's behalf, fixing common errors and adjusting formatting without interrupting the task at hand. Most users appreciated the results without thinking about the mechanism. When automation is so well calibrated that users forget it exists, it has done its job.

I saw automation succeed, and I also saw it fail in ways that exposed how quickly trust erodes when a system takes too much control. In Word, AutoFormat was meant to be helpful, yet it often worked against the very people who relied on precision. A lawyer drafting a contract, a programmer documenting code, or a writer experimenting with unusual formatting would suddenly find their text transformed: "(c)" became ©, "1/2" turned into ½, and a line beginning with "1." became a numbered list. The feature was intended for convenience, but many users found it an interruption. In response, we chose not to abandon AutoFormat, but to redesign it around user agency. We added an AutoCorrect Options button—a small icon that appeared immediately after an automatic change—so users could undo the change or disable that specific rule. Settings became more granular, allowing users to retain the behaviors they liked and disable the ones they did not.

K. C. Mukherjee, *The Microsoft AI Insider's Playbook*, https://doi.org/10.1007/979-8-8688-2730-3_3

AutoCorrect carried the same risk, but with an added danger: it was often silent. It could silently alter technical terms, product names, or foreign words in unintended ways. A chemical formula or a colleague's unusual name might be "corrected" without permission. The solution followed the same principle: make corrections visible and reversible. Users could review changes, add exceptions to a personal dictionary, and decide which replacements applied.

Windows Update revealed the problem on a larger scale. In some versions, updates enforced restarts to apply patches—sometimes mid-task, sometimes overnight with applications still open. Security came first, but user agency did not, and the backlash was immediate. The response added active hours, restart scheduling, and clearer notifications so people could see what was coming and decide when updates would apply.

The pattern was familiar. Automation that ignored usability became a burden, and automation that ignored scalability became brittle. In each case, the fix was not less automation, but better automation: visible, reversible, and respectful of user intent. The need for automation was real, but the path mattered.

President John F. Kennedy captured the tension in an October 1963 press conference: "So automation does not need to be, we hope, our enemy. ... I think machines can make life easier for men, if men do not let the machines dominate them."[1] Popular culture has long reflected this tension. Charlie Chaplin's *Modern Times* satirized assembly line work, and *I Love Lucy* captured conveyor belt chaos in the candy factory episode "Job Switching," reflecting public anxiety about machines dictating the pace of human life.[2]

That tension—between automation as support and automation as imposition—runs through every system I have worked on. It is not enough for automation to be technically impressive; it must respect human roles, earn user trust, and remain adaptable as circumstances change. The challenge is not whether to automate, but how to do so while preserving human judgment and sustaining trust over time.

Automation technologies can boost operational efficiency, reduce human error, and free resources for strategic, high-value work. By replacing manual workflows with automated systems, organizations can improve accuracy, speed, and consistency. They

---

[1] John F. Kennedy, "News Conference 63, October 31, 1963," John F. Kennedy Presidential Library and Museum, `https://www.jfklibrary.org/archives/other-resources/john-f-kennedy-press-conferences/news-conference-63`.

[2] Library of Congress, National Film Preservation Board, "Modern Times" (film essay), `https://www.loc.gov/static/programs/national-film-preservation-board/documents/modern_times.pdf`; "Job Switching," *I Love Lucy*, season 2, episode 1, directed by William Asher, written by Jess Oppenheimer, Madelyn Davis, and Bob Carroll Jr., aired September 15, 1952 (CBS).

can scale operations, respond more quickly to change, and derive greater insight from their data. These benefits—and the technologies that pursue them—long predate recent advances in AI. A helpful way of envisioning AI applications is to treat them as the next stage in the evolution of automation, inheriting both its promise and its pitfalls.

This chapter examines the factors that determine whether automation succeeds or fails. It begins with the real costs of manual workflows and then explores the principles that distinguish helpful features from those that feel intrusive or presumptive. It examines how intelligent automation can augment human capability rather than replace it and addresses the technical, organizational, and ethical barriers organizations must overcome. Throughout, the lessons from Chapters 1 and 2 remain visible: the same discipline that makes software usable is what makes automation beneficial.

3.1 The Cost of Manual Workflows

At Microsoft, I watched talented people spend hours on tasks that software could have completed in seconds. Engineers reformatted documents by hand. Program managers manually copied data between systems. Support staff sorted incoming messages one by one, scanning each for urgency and context. Software developers waited hours for Office applications to build on their individual workstations, watching progress bars instead of writing code. These were talented people doing work that was structurally necessary but did not require their full ability—not because they lacked skill, but because the right tools did not yet exist. In those earlier years, the gap between human capability and available tools was stark, and it was visible every day in the way brilliant people spent their time.

That observation shaped what we tried to build. Microsoft Office aimed to improve the workflows people actually had: document creation, formatting, repetitive editing, and information retrieval. The goal was never to remove people from the process. It was to redirect effort away from mechanical tasks and toward work that demanded judgment, creativity, and expertise. Even then, we recognized that some tasks benefited from human attention while others could be automated. The discipline was knowing the difference.

The cost of manual workflows is well documented—and persistent. A 2012 McKinsey report found that the average knowledge worker spent an estimated 28% of the workweek managing email and nearly 20% searching for internal information or tracking down colleagues.[3] A decade later, the problem had not diminished. Microsoft's 2023 Work Trend Index, surveying 31,000 workers across 31 markets, found that employees spend 57% of their time communicating—in meetings, email, and chat—and only 43% creating. The survey found that 62% reported spending too much time searching for information and 68% reported lacking sufficient uninterrupted time to focus during the workday.[4] The tools have changed; the pattern has not. Routine communication and information retrieval continue to crowd out the work that requires sustained attention.

Manual tasks are also vulnerable to human error. Data entry, in particular, requires painstaking precision. People enter large volumes of information into databases or spreadsheets, and even small mistakes—such as typographical errors, duplicate entries, or formatting inconsistencies—can compromise data integrity. Industry estimates of manual data entry error rates vary, but even a seemingly low rate—one error per 100 entries—can compound quickly at scale. A single typo in a financial figure can propagate through calculations that depend on it, distorting budgets, forecasts, and downstream decisions.

Complexity and bureaucracy add further friction. Consider a procurement process: an employee submits a request, stakeholders review it, and the approved request then moves through purchasing, finance, and vendors—each with its own documentation and procedural compliance requirements. Every step adds time. In regulated industries, compliance requirements add yet another layer, demanding meticulous recordkeeping to meet legal standards.

The human cost is equally real. Repetitive manual tasks lead to disengagement. Employees who spend their time on routine work may feel undervalued or unchallenged. Gallup research has found that disengaged employees exhibit 37% higher absenteeism, 18% lower productivity, and 15% lower profitability than engaged employees.[5] When people feel overwhelmed by manual workloads or frustrated by a lack of opportunities for growth, they leave—disrupting continuity and incurring the costs of recruiting, onboarding, and training replacements.

---

[3] "The Social Economy: Unlocking Value and Productivity through Social Technologies," McKinsey Global Institute, July 2012, `https://www.mckinsey.com/industries/technology-media-and-telecommunications/our-insights/the-social-economy`.

[4] "Will AI Fix Work?" 2023 Work Trend Index, Microsoft, May 2023, `https://www.microsoft.com/en-us/worklab/work-trend-index/will-ai-fix-work`.

[5] "The Relationship Between Engagement at Work and Organizational Outcomes: 2020 Q12 Meta-Analysis, 10th Edition," Gallup Inc., 2020, `https://www.gallup.com/workplace/321725/gallup-q12-meta-analysis-report.aspx`.

The financial implications are often underestimated. A 2012 International Data Corporation (IDC) report surveyed information workers and information technology (IT) professionals across six countries. It estimated that document-related challenges accounted for about 21.3% of productivity loss—costing nearly $20,000 per information worker each year.[6] At the enterprise scale, the impact is substantial. Beyond lost productivity, manual workflows require physical resources, including paper, filing systems, and storage space. These increase operational costs and have environmental implications.

A core objective for Microsoft Office was to systematically eliminate these inefficiencies. Over time, Microsoft invested in automation, integration, and distributed systems, transforming these workflows. Word gained more advanced formatting automation. Migration tools reduced the need for repetitive transfers. Outlook introduced rules and the Focused Inbox. Office builds moved to a distributed infrastructure.

Seeing the cost of manual workflows is the starting point; turning that insight into effective automation is the real work. Reducing manual effort is valuable only if the automation that replaces it is usable, trustworthy, and adaptable. The following section examines the distinction between automation that helps and automation that hinders.

3.2 What Makes Automation Succeed

Not all automation helps. Some of the systems I encountered at Microsoft created more problems than they solved—not because the technology failed, but because the design ignored how people actually worked. Automation that presumed too much about user intent, removed control, or behaved unpredictably trained users to distrust it. The technology worked; the experience did not.

The automation that succeeded shared common traits. WordBASIC and VBA worked because they respected the user's role. We did not decide what to automate; we gave users the tools to make that decision themselves. A financial analyst could build a macro to format reports. An administrative assistant could automate mail merges. Each person automated what mattered to them, at a pace they controlled.

---

[6] Melissa Webster, "Bridging the Information Worker Productivity Gap: New Challenges and Opportunities for IT," white paper, IDC doc #236480, September 2012, sponsored by Adobe. Originally available at idc.com; archived copy `https://warekennis.nl/wp-content/uploads/2013/11/bridging-the-information-worker-productivity-gap.pdf`.

AutoCorrect and AutoFormat extended that philosophy into continuous, quiet automation. They acted without asking, but they worked on small, predictable things: correcting common misspellings, converting straight quotes to curly quotes, and adjusting formatting as users typed. The changes were minor enough that many users barely noticed and reversible enough that mistakes could be undone with a keystroke. That calibration mattered. If automation changes a user's work without asking, it must be accurate most of the time and effortless to undo when it is not.

The contrast was Clippy. As discussed in Chapter 2, the Office Assistant sought to be proactive—anticipating user needs and providing guidance before users requested it. In practice, it appeared at the wrong moments. It inferred intent from insufficient evidence and demanded attention when users wanted to focus. The technology behind Clippy was sophisticated, but the experience was intrusive. Users rejected it not because it lacked capability, but because it lacked restraint.

Another instructive example was smart tags, introduced in Office XP. The feature automatically recognized entities in a document—such as names, dates, addresses, and stock symbols—and underlined them in purple. When activated, these markers revealed a menu of suggested actions intended to help users complete related tasks without leaving the document.[7] In practice, smart tags often felt intrusive, because the software appeared to insert interactive behavior into text that users had not explicitly designated as actionable. Even when recognition was correct, the feature could still feel socially wrong. It disrupted reading, blurred the line between what the author wrote and what the platform added, and often reduced trust rather than building it. The lesson echoed Clippy: automation that enters a workflow without explicit consent and predictable boundaries tends to create friction, not value.

The principle is consistent: successful automation respects the same lessons we learned about usability. It stays quiet until needed, remains controllable by the user, and behaves gracefully when it fails. Progressive disclosure applies to automation just as it does to user interfaces—start simple, make advanced capabilities discoverable, and avoid overwhelming users.

The same principles apply to enterprise systems, especially document platforms, where automation affects shared content and the cost of manual work remains high and persistent. Modern document organization systems use algorithms and ML to efficiently

[7] "About Smart Tags," Microsoft Office Word 2003 Help, Microsoft Corporation, 2003. The page describes the smart tag indicator as "a purple dotted underline" and states: "The purple dotted lines beneath text in your document indicate the smart tags."

classify and catalog content, replacing manual filing with automated workflows. What distinguishes effective systems is their ability to automate without rigidity—adapting as requirements evolve, integrating with existing repositories like SharePoint, and avoiding wholesale migration.

Figure 3-1 shows how a document platform can unify paper and digital processing through real-time recognition.

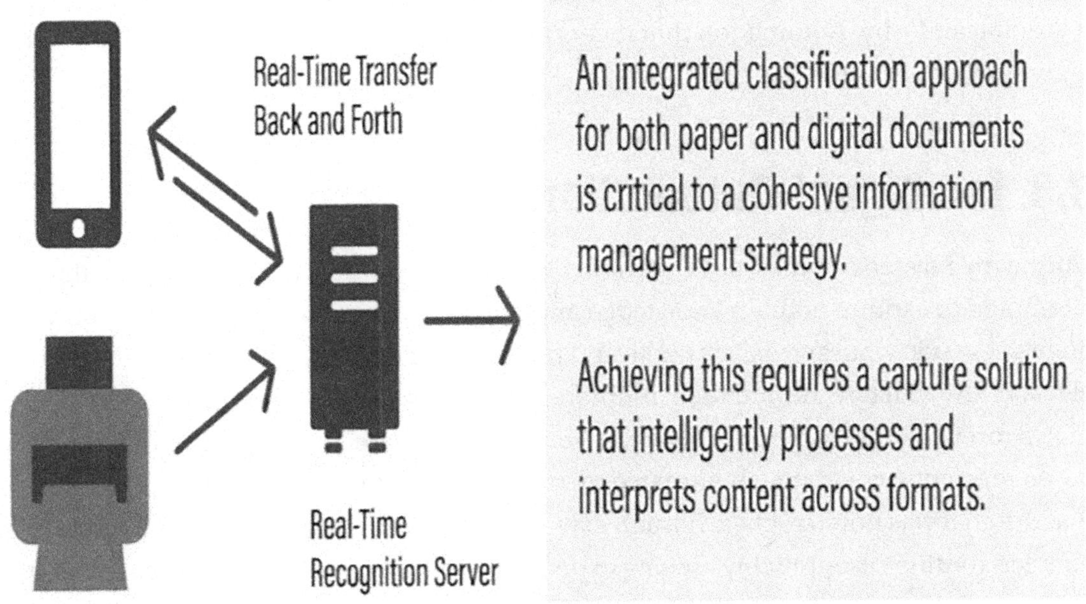

Figure 3-1. *A document management system merging paper and digital document processing through real-time recognition. The central server processes input from mobile devices and scanners, enabling intelligent capture, classification, and workflow automation for improved organizational productivity. (Image by author)*

In a large law firm, a well-designed document system can retrieve the right precedent or filing quickly by indexing matter numbers, parties, and jurisdictions. Without that structure, associates lose time hunting through nested folders and inboxes. Compliance teams in regulated industries use the same approach to pull out the exact version of a policy or submission for a given date and jurisdiction, reducing the risk of acting on outdated information.

Supporting technologies, including optical character recognition (OCR) and robotic process automation (RPA), further extend these capabilities. The former converts scanned documents, images, and Portable Document Format (PDF) files into editable, searchable data, which reduces manual transcription and simplifies integration with applications and databases. Complementing OCR, RPA mimics human actions within digital systems—logging into applications, entering data, and executing calculations—consistently and without interruption. Together, these technologies streamline data entry, minimize errors, and improve workflow efficiency.

However, technical capability alone is only half the equation. The design must preserve user control, handle exceptions gracefully, and remain transparent about what it is doing and why. Automation that meets these standards earns trust. Automation that ignores them earns the fate of Clippy.

3.3 Intelligent Automation

During my master's studies at IIT Kanpur, I worked on expert systems—software that attempted to capture domain knowledge and apply it systematically. The ambition was bold: to encode what specialists know and make that expertise available at scale. Systems like MYCIN, which recommended antibiotics for bacterial infections, and eXpert CONfigurer (XCON), which configured computer hardware, demonstrated that rule-based reasoning could match human experts in specific domains.[8] Early on, I learned that the goal was not to replace human experts but to support them. Effective systems handled routine cases reliably, freeing experts to focus on exceptions, edge cases, and judgment calls. Failing ones tried to do too much, overreaching until users stopped trusting them.

AI has always moved in cycles of ambition, discovery, and recalibration. Expert systems excelled at routine, well-structured cases but became brittle when reality deviated from their rules. By the late 1980s, maintaining massive rule sets for general reasoning had become unsustainable in many domains. Researchers increasingly turned to statistical learning, which allows algorithms to infer patterns from data. This transition powered spam filters, speech recognition, and early recommendation systems. Rule-based approaches continued to thrive when the scope was well defined and the business

[8] For MYCIN, see Bruce G. Buchanan and Edward H. Shortliffe, *Rule-Based Expert Systems: The MYCIN Experiments of the Stanford Heuristic Programming Project* (Reading, MA: Addison-Wesley, 1984). For XCON, see John P. McDermott, "R1: A Rule-Based Configurer of Computer Systems," *Artificial Intelligence* 19, no. 1 (September 1982): 39–88.

logic was explicit. The deep learning revolution of the 2010s further advanced the field. Neural networks trained on unprecedented amounts of data have begun to match or surpass human performance in vision, language, and game-playing.

Despite this technological transformation, the core principle remains: augment human capability rather than replace it. Successful systems—from MYCIN to modern foundation models—follow this pattern. Then and now, failures come from systems that overpromise, hide their limits, or automate decisions that should remain human.

The principles I developed while building expert systems became the architectural foundation for the intelligent features I later designed at Microsoft. The proofing tools in Office—the Spell Checker and Grammar Checker—were early forms of intelligent automation: they analyzed text, identified patterns, and offered suggestions. The user remained the decision-maker, free to accept, reject, or ignore any recommendation. The tools did not presume to know better; they offered options. That restraint was deliberate. We knew language is contextual and that many "errors" are intentional. If the system overrode user judgment, trust would collapse faster than any number of correct suggestions could rebuild it.

The principle holds today, even as the technology has advanced dramatically. Intelligent automation—automation that incorporates reasoning, pattern recognition, and learning—can augment human capability in ways that earlier systems could not. The design challenge remains: use machines for scale, consistency, speed, and pattern recognition while preserving human judgment, context, creativity, and relationships.

Modern examples illustrate the point. In aviation, Rolls-Royce has described using data, analytics, and digital twin techniques to improve maintenance outcomes—for some engines, extending the time between maintenance events by up to 50%.[9] These systems detect patterns across large fleets; humans decide what to do with that signal, when to intervene, and how to balance risk, cost, and operations.

In health care, AI-driven imaging tools increasingly serve as assistants rather than authorities. For example, systems cleared by the US Food and Drug Administration (FDA) that analyze chest X-rays for suspected pneumothorax can support triage and

[9] Peter Sayer, "Rolls-Royce Turns to Digital Twins to Improve Jet Engine Efficiency," CIO, May 19, 2023, https://www.cio.com/article/188765/rolls-royce-turns-to-digital-twins-to-improve-jet-engine-efficiency.html.

notification workflows.[10] The software flags patterns quickly; the clinician remains responsible for interpretation and diagnosis. The value comes from pairing machine consistency with human accountability.

Across operations, AI-powered analytics can combine production data with consumer signals. Organizations can then adjust inventory and schedules while reducing waste. In customer service, chatbots handle routine inquiries, while humans address situations that require empathy and judgment. In scientific research, systems such as DeepMind's AlphaFold solved the protein-folding problem—a challenge that had captivated computational biologists for 50 years. It predicted 3D structures with an accuracy rivaling that of experimental methods. The pattern holds: machines provide scale and pattern recognition; humans provide direction, interpretation, and responsibility. In current AI practice, this approach is known as *human in the loop*—a design principle that keeps human judgment central to automated workflows.

Yet the shift has produced uneven outcomes. In some industries, experienced professionals use AI to enhance strategic work, while traditional entry-level tasks are increasingly automated. In legal services, senior attorneys increasingly use AI for contract analysis, due diligence, and litigation prediction. At the same time, document review—once a common entry point for new associates—is shifting to ML systems. That raises a genuine concern: if routine work disappears, where do newcomers get the repetitions that build judgment? We may end up with a workforce that is more efficient at the top, but with fewer pathways for early-career talent to develop.

India's technology services industry—home to roughly 5.8 million workers in software testing, system maintenance, and business process management—is undergoing a profound shift. According to the National Association of Software and Services Companies (NASSCOM) Strategic Review 2025, the sector generated $283 billion in revenue in fiscal year 2025, accounting for about 7.3% of India's gross domestic product (GDP).[11] As AI tools automate large portions of routine workflows, a critical question emerges: if the entry-level tasks that once trained a generation of engineers

[10] US Food and Drug Administration, "Artificial Intelligence and Machine Learning (AI/ML)-Enabled Medical Devices," `https://www.fda.gov/medical-devices/software-medical-device-samd/artificial-intelligence-and-machine-learning-aiml-enabled-medical-devices`.

[11] National Association of Software and Services Companies (NASSCOM), *Technology Sector in India: Strategic Review 2025* (New Delhi: NASSCOM, 2025). Revenue and employment figures from the NASSCOM press release, available at `https://nasscom.in/knowledge-center/publications/technology-sector-india-strategic-review-2025`. GDP contribution cited by NASSCOM President Rajesh Nambiar at Startup Mahakumbh, April 3, 2025.

disappear, how will the next generation develop equivalent judgment? For a country where technology services are both a major employer and a pathway to upward mobility, this is not an abstract concern but a pressing economic and social policy challenge with global resonance.

A possible response is to use AI to reshape education and workforce development. Adaptive learning approaches can tailor practice and pacing to individual progress. Platforms are experimenting with AI-enabled learning assistants and personalized pathways, and initiatives such as IBM SkillsBuild aim to broaden access to technology training at global scale.[12] Whether these efforts fully offset the opportunities displaced by automation remains an open question. The net employment impact of intelligent automation is still uncertain. The need to invest in human capability alongside machine capability is not.

3.4 Overcoming Barriers

In enterprise deployments, the hardest problems were rarely about cleverness. They were about whether a feature could survive governance, legacy systems, and scale. I saw teams get excited during a demonstration, approve a pilot, and still fail to achieve broad adoption—not because the technology was flawed, but because the design had not anticipated the organization's constraints.

Security was often the first barrier. The same extensibility that made automation powerful—macros, add-ins, scripting, and component-based extensions—also made risk tangible. After major incidents, many organizations aggressively tightened their policies. Macros were disabled, unsigned add-ins were blocked, and anything labeled "automation" was treated as suspicious by default.

ActiveX controls made the trade-off even more explicit. In many enterprise environments, special security settings, approved zones, or administrative policy changes were required. Without that groundwork, an ActiveX control never reached a user's desktop. If that path was not planned up front, adoption stalled—not due to a lack of user interest, but because the enterprise required predictable guardrails rather than a litany of security exceptions.

Even when security teams approved a feature, the corporate desktop environment imposed its own reality. Features that worked perfectly on a developer's machine could fail in a "golden image"—the standardized, locked-down desktop configuration

[12] IBM SkillsBuild, `https://skillsbuild.org/`.

deployed across thousands of machines. Permissions were restricted, and registry access was limited. Component registration might have been disabled, runtimes might have been missing, and group policies might have been strict. In that environment, "it works on my machine" was not a reassurance; it was an early warning. Enterprise adoption requires predictable behavior under least-privilege assumptions. It also needs clear diagnostics when a request is blocked, along with deployment workflows that administrators can automate and support.

Integration was the quieter blocker—connecting identity systems, data sources, and compliance workflows. Enterprises rarely adopt a product as a standalone tool; they adopt it as part of an integration effort. The real work lives in identity and access control, data connectors, file and content models, retention rules, and exception handling. If a feature cannot align with single sign-on requirements, role-based access, auditing, and compliance, it stalls. If it requires users to migrate data to a new repository or modify established workflows overnight, it meets resistance. The fastest pilots are usually the ones that fit into existing systems with minimal disruption.

Finally, scale turns "good enough" into "unusable" quickly. A feature that performs well on small files and clean datasets often breaks down at enterprise scale. Millions of mailboxes, complex documents, and messy shared drives expose every weakness. When performance declines, users rarely file complaints. They quietly revert to old habits. That is why enterprise adoption is as much about operational reliability as it is about feature design: the product must behave predictably, integrate cleanly, and remain supportable when something goes wrong. If it cannot, even a strong idea becomes shelfware—approved, deployed, and quietly unused.

Failure modes matter as much as success paths. Enterprise systems routinely encounter partial outages, messy data, and user errors. Automation that assumes clean inputs and uninterrupted operation collapses quickly. Enterprise reality intrudes every day. The systems that last are designed for recovery. They offer clear error messages, graceful fallbacks, and a way to resume without losing work. Punitive failure—a design flaw where a single error forces a user to start over—effectively trains users to abandon the feature entirely.

These barriers—security, integration, scale, and failure handling—are not unique to Office or Windows. They recur wherever automation meets enterprise reality. AI-driven automation faces the same constraints, and it introduces additional requirements: data provenance, auditability, bias monitoring, and explainability. The potential benefits are immense, but leaders must also address questions spanning ethics, culture, workforce development, and broader societal impact. In enterprise meetings, the first questions are rarely about model accuracy; they center on risk, auditability, and accountability when things go wrong.

That reality leads to a simple conclusion: in an enterprise setting, ethics are a deployment requirement. The moment an AI system touches hiring, lending, pricing, customer support, or health-related decisions, leaders need explicit policies. Those policies must cover data use, fairness, transparency, and human accountability. In practice, this means clear decision boundaries: what the system can recommend, what it must never decide on its own, and the evidence it should present when making a recommendation. The same extensibility concerns I observed with macros and add-ins apply here: powerful capabilities demand governance that anticipates misuse without blocking legitimate work.

Stewardship matters. Every automated behavior needs an owner. Someone has to monitor its impact and adjust it as conditions change. Without ownership, automation drifts: rules become outdated, exceptions accumulate, and no one knows whether the system is still performing as intended. Successful deployments pair a launch strategy with a life-cycle plan: a framework for tuning performance, auditing outcomes, and eventually retiring features that no longer justify their operational cost.

Culture can be just as decisive as technology. AI adoption is more successful when it is framed as augmentation rather than replacement—and when teams have the skills to use it effectively. Training is part of deployment. People need enough literacy to interpret outputs and spot failure modes. They also need enough fluency to ask better questions. A marketing team using AI analytics, for example, still needs domain knowledge and judgment; the tool can surface patterns, but humans decide what those patterns mean and what to do next.

Organizations also need room to experiment safely. Pilots work when they have boundaries: permitted data, permitted use cases, measurable outcomes, and an exit plan if the results do not justify production rollout. This is where leadership matters. If experimentation is punished, teams hide mistakes, and adoption turns brittle. If experimentation is supported, teams quickly learn where AI adds value and where it introduces risk.

Some companies have institutionalized this approach. Google's early "20% time" policy encouraged engineers to spend a portion of their week on experimental projects. That practice contributed to products like Gmail and Google News. The same principle applies to AI adoption. Organizations that train their workforce and provide structured freedom to experiment are more likely to identify where these technologies create genuine value and where they introduce new risks.

Beyond the enterprise, societal impacts feed back into enterprise risk. Large-scale AI increases energy use. It accelerates the spread of misinformation through deepfakes and automated campaigns. It strengthens scams and malware, raising cybersecurity stakes. Privacy concerns also increase because AI systems often rely on large datasets. Poor data practices amplify bias and increase surveillance. These realities prompt enterprises to strengthen internal controls and comply with regulatory frameworks such as the EU General Data Protection Regulation (GDPR). AI-specific regulations are still evolving.

The same discipline that made software usable makes automation adoptable. Trust is earned through predictable, transparent behavior. Users accept automation that they can understand and, when necessary, override. The barriers I encountered at Microsoft—security, integration, scale, governance—reflect a failure to anticipate how organizations operate under real constraints. AI-driven automation will succeed or fail on the same terms.

3.5 Summary

The need for automation is real. Manual workflows consume time, introduce errors, frustrate employees, and drain resources that could otherwise be allocated to higher-value work. The case for reducing that burden is not new. It shaped much of what we built at Microsoft and continues to drive the current wave of AI-driven tools.

Automation is not inherently beneficial. The same principles that governed usability and scalability in the Windows era govern the success of automation today. Design for constraints: automate only what the system can do reliably, and anticipate governance, security, and integration realities in enterprise environments. Build trust: automation should behave predictably and transparently, earning confidence through consistent results rather than demanding it through aggressive defaults. Apply progressive disclosure: start simple, make advanced capabilities discoverable, and avoid overwhelming users with complexity they did not request. Respect user attention: automation should help without intruding—acting quietly when it acts.

Keep human judgment central: augment, and do not replace. The boundary between automation and autonomy is the critical design decision—automation is most effective when it accelerates routine execution while leaving judgment, discretion, and responsibility in human hands. When that boundary blurs, trust erodes, and accountability disappears. Design for failure modes: assume partial outages, messy data, and user mistakes, and make recovery straightforward rather than punitive. Plan for stewardship: every automated behavior should have an owner, a mechanism to monitor its impact, and a process to tune or retire it when conditions change. Lasting systems make people more capable, not unnecessary.

These lessons are practical. They emerged from watching features succeed and fail at scale, across many users and organizations. WordBASIC and VBA succeeded because they respected user control. AutoCorrect succeeded because it was quiet and reversible. Clippy failed because it presumed and interrupted. Smart tags failed because they blurred the boundary between user content and platform behavior. Enterprise pilots stalled when they failed to address security, integration, or scalability. The pattern is consistent: automation that ignores how people actually work becomes a burden rather than a benefit.

The next chapter examines a system that deliberately sought to apply these lessons: INTELLIFM. It automated document workflows and high-volume forms publishing while respecting the constraints, trust requirements, and human judgment described in this chapter. The principles are the same; the application is concrete.

CHAPTER 4

The Intelligent Filing Manager

The usability and scalability lessons from the Windows era—discussed in the preceding chapters—created new challenges even as they solved old ones. Windows 95 and Office 95 democratized access to computing and electronic document creation. The Start button simplified navigation, and the integrated Office suite put word processing, spreadsheets, and presentations within reach of millions. But success introduced a new problem: organizations could now create documents faster than they could organize them.

As electronic workflows spread and the internet accelerated distribution, digital content grew rapidly. Yet file organization and governance remained largely manual. Many companies were soon overwhelmed by inconsistent filing practices, keyword searches that returned too many or too few results, difficulties sustaining consistency across teams, and rising pressure from regulatory and audit requirements. The usability principles that made document creation easy had not yet been applied to document organization at scale.

John McCarthy, who coined the term *artificial intelligence,* envisioned programs that could learn from experience and apply common sense to what they knew.[1] That vision shaped how I approached a growing gap: organizations could create documents faster than they could organize them. I conceived the Intelligent Filing Manager (INTELLIFM) to bring structure and reviewable logic to document-intensive workflows. INTELLIFM

[1] John McCarthy, "Programs with Common Sense," in *Proceedings of the Teddington Conference on the Mechanization of Thought Processes* (London: Her Majesty's Stationery Office, 1959), 75–91, `https://www-formal.stanford.edu/jmc/mcc59.pdf`.

K. C. Mukherjee, *The Microsoft AI Insider's Playbook*, https://doi.org/10.1007/979-8-8688-2730-3_4

blended those ideas with Windows-era usability principles to automate workflows and high-volume forms publishing while preserving human judgment—augmenting domain experts rather than replacing them.[2]

INTELLIFM began as a rule-based expert system. It later expanded into a broader platform for classifying, indexing, and routing large volumes of documents. In regulated industries such as law, finance, and health care, it supports consistent filings and faster retrieval by applying transparent rules and structured metadata that compliance teams can review.

This approach is described in US Patent No. 6,314,415 B1, granted on November 6, 2001. The patent covers methods for automating workflow steps using AI.[3] Beyond improving filing and retrieval, the technology has served as a catalyst for organizational change by streamlining routine tasks and accelerating access to relevant information—an advantage in settings where timely, accurate data often determines outcomes.

Although the INTELLIFM framework has been in use for more than a quarter of a century, it continues to deliver value, both as a standalone solution and as a foundation for modern innovations. Many contemporary systems build on the same core ideas, employing modern technologies such as cloud computing and ML. Many platforms now include AI-assisted organization—classification suggestions, metadata support, and policy-driven retention. Microsoft 365 includes AI-driven document processing services for tasks such as classification, extraction, and content understanding in SharePoint-based workflows—capabilities that echo INTELLIFM's core design. Broad suites such as SharePoint and Google Workspace, along with specialized tools such as DocuWare and Laserfiche, illustrate how these ideas have become mainstream in cloud and mobile environments. Chapter 5 examines in greater detail how these declarative principles evolved into modern Microsoft platforms and document automation workflows. (For a technical discussion of how sophisticated document management systems work in general, see Appendix 5.)

---

[2] Krishna C. Mukherjee, "Automating Forms Publishing with the Intelligent Filing Manager," in *Proceedings of the IEEE International Conference on Systems, Man, and Cybernetics* (IEEE, 1999), I-308–I-313, `https://ieeexplore.ieee.org/document/814108`.

[3] Krishna C. Mukherjee, "Automated Forms Publishing System and Method Using a Rule-Based Expert System to Dynamically Generate a Graphical User Interface," US Patent 6,314,415 B1, filed February 9, 1999, issued November 6, 2001, `https://patents.google.com/patent/US6314415B1`.

This chapter examines why INTELLIFM has endured, focusing on its document-handling capabilities, automated forms publishing, and application integration. It shows how the principles from earlier chapters—design for constraints, build trust, apply progressive disclosure, and preserve human judgment—translate into a working system that has endured for decades.

4.1 Architecture and Design

INTELLIFM's architecture reflected lessons I had learned while building enterprise software. Modularity was not an abstract design goal. It was a practical response to realities I had seen repeatedly: requirements change, components fail, and organizations have different operating models. As systems grow, monolithic designs become difficult to modify and increasingly fragile in day-to-day operations. Tightly coupled designs may appear efficient early on, but they often fail in unexpected ways when a single component changes. In compliance-sensitive domains, such failures are not minor inconveniences; they can lead to operational interruptions, audit findings, or missed deadlines. INTELLIFM had to avoid both traps.

The architecture I envisioned for INTELLIFM required a foundation capable of enforcing clear boundaries between components. Object-oriented languages such as C++ and Java provided the mechanisms to achieve this separation, although they approached it through different design philosophies.

C++ relied on a physical division between header files (.h) and implementation files (.cpp). Header files declared the public interface—effectively serving as a contract that specified what a class or module could do—while the implementation files contained the underlying logic. Encapsulation was reinforced through public, protected, and private access specifiers, which controlled how data and behavior could be accessed.

Java, by contrast, embedded modularity more directly into the language's logical structure. Its package system grouped related classes into cohesive units, and its access modifiers—including the default package-private visibility—allowed developers to hide internal details within those units. This design encouraged clear architectural boundaries and enabled the compiler to enforce them.

These languages gave me the tools. The harder question was where to draw the lines—which responsibilities to isolate, which interfaces to expose, and how to structure knowledge so that regulatory changes would not cascade into system-wide rewrites. That question had no textbook answer. It required understanding both the technology and the domain: the unpredictable cadence of regulatory updates, the jurisdictional variations that multiplied complexity, and the practical reality that compliance officers—not programmers—would need to maintain the rules. The solution was an architecture composed of distinct modules, with components exposed as services.

Each module had a defined responsibility and interacted with other modules through well-defined interfaces. This produced a design that was more flexible and resilient. It could be developed independently, while interface contracts preserved system behavior. Thus, INTELLIFM implemented disciplined change. New capabilities could be introduced without rewriting the platform, and existing capabilities could be upgraded without destabilizing unrelated areas. This mattered because regulated environments are rarely static. A modular architecture made that motion manageable.

Modularity also strengthened reliability. By isolating components and their dependencies, the system could limit the impact of failures in individual modules. If a data extraction component encountered an unexpected document format, the classification module could continue operating rather than fail in a cascading manner. This type of fault containment reduced disruption from software defects, infrastructure issues, and operational surprises. It also simplified troubleshooting. When a system is composed of well-bounded parts, teams can localize root causes more quickly, apply targeted fixes, and return to service without broad rollbacks. In practice, this approach reduced the risk that an improvement in one area would cause unintended regressions in another.

Scalability followed naturally from the same modular approach. The platform supported expansion across users, departments, and integrated systems without sacrificing performance or stability. Organizations could improve document operations incrementally rather than through costly overhauls. The service-oriented architecture provided well-defined APIs for interoperability, positioning INTELLIFM as a central hub that could connect with diverse enterprise systems rather than demanding they conform to it. This point is essential—enterprise document work rarely occurs within a single application. It spans authoring tools, line-of-business systems, compliance databases, archival repositories, and workflow queues. Interoperability is not a luxury; it is the price of admission for operating at scale. A system that cannot connect cleanly becomes a bottleneck, regardless of how capable it may be in isolation.

Ease of use was equally important. Here, the VBA philosophy from Chapter 2 applies directly: we did not decide what users should automate; we gave them tools to make that decision themselves. Domain experts could customize workflow parameters and rules using familiar applications such as Microsoft Excel. A compliance officer could define filing rules, adjust jurisdictional requirements, or update regulatory deadlines without having to learn to program. This reduced deployment time and shortened the gap between policy changes and system updates. It also reinforced accountability. When domain experts can read rules in a transparent format, they can validate, discuss, and revise them with confidence. In regulated work, configuration transparency is a practical advantage. It supports audits, reduces reliance on institutional memory, and makes "Why did the system do that?" a question with a concrete answer. As a result, system behavior remained predictable, even as rules were revised.

The work behind INTELLIFM depended on a close partnership between software engineers and domain specialists—an approach that was less common in enterprise products at the time. I maintained active communication with senior Microsoft colleagues throughout development, hired and trained engineers with deep Microsoft technology expertise, and built INTELLIFM on core Microsoft technologies, including COM—discussed in detail later in this chapter. I presented the architecture and design at international AI conferences, placing the work in the broader context of enterprise AI research at the time. In the late 1990s, the Microsoft–Wolters Kluwer collaboration illustrated a model that became increasingly important in enterprise computing: technology providers working directly with subject matter experts, rather than building in isolation and hoping the result would fit user needs.

Microsoft contributed the Windows platform and a development stack. This included Visual Studio (including Visual C++ and Visual Basic), component-based design through COM, and Microsoft Transaction Server and COM+ for transactional services. Microsoft SQL Server provided the data layer, and Internet Information Services with Active Server Pages handled internet-facing deployment. Data access relied on ActiveX Data Objects and Microsoft Data Access Components, and my teams used tools such as Visual SourceSafe for version control.

Wolters Kluwer contributed decades of accumulated knowledge about legal and regulatory workflows—expertise that most technologists do not gain without years of immersion. Their legal and compliance teams understood the intricate requirements of multijurisdictional filings. These are regulatory submissions that must be filed simultaneously across multiple state or national jurisdictions. Each jurisdiction has its own forms, deadlines, and compliance standards. They also understood the consequences of missed deadlines and the practical constraints of handling hundreds of forms across dozens of jurisdictions.

As the inventor and architect of INTELLIFM, I drew on the combined strengths of Microsoft and Wolters Kluwer—Microsoft's technology stack and Wolters Kluwer's deep regulatory domain knowledge—to build a system whose workflows accurately reflected real-world compliance requirements. Building a system of this complexity and domain specificity would have been far harder without this combination of organizational strengths.

This collaboration shaped the design in concrete ways. The decision to maintain knowledge bases in Microsoft Excel was driven directly by conversations with domain experts who needed to update rules without waiting for software developers or learning programming languages. The modular architecture reflected the reality that different regulatory domains—insurance, corporate compliance, securities, and intellectual property—each carried distinct requirements but could share underlying infrastructure. The question-and-answer (Q&A) session model became one of INTELLIFM's most distinctive features because it reflected the process by which compliance professionals completed complex filings. They worked step by step, with each answer determining the next question, instead of confronting a monolithic form and guessing which sections applied. In other words, the system mirrored the practitioner's reasoning process. That alignment—between how professionals think and how software guides them—often determines whether automation becomes trusted or ignored.

The partnership also anticipated an approach that later became standard practice in enterprise software. Technology providers increasingly recognized that sustainable competitive advantage came not from building generic tools, but from embedding those tools deeply within specific industry workflows. The distinction mattered. Creating solutions with domain partners, rather than merely for them, produced systems that addressed real operational needs. When software engineers and compliance specialists worked side by side—debating requirements, testing prototypes against real regulatory scenarios, and refining interfaces based on observed usage—the resulting system reflected both technical sophistication and practical wisdom. It also improved prioritization. Domain specialists could identify what truly drove risk, cost, and delay, while engineers could translate those priorities into capabilities that were reliable, testable, and maintainable. Over time, that collaborative model influenced how enterprise software partnerships developed, as platform companies sought relationships with organizations that understood particular industries from the inside.

The architecture also enabled parallel development. A document classification module could be built and tested independently of a data extraction component, which allowed multiple teams to work simultaneously without bottlenecks. This reduced the time to market for new capabilities and lowered the risk that one team's work would impede another's progress. It also supported controlled experimentation. Teams could pilot improvements within a single module, measure outcomes, and then adopt changes more broadly. Further, they could achieve these without destabilizing core workflows. In enterprise settings, this ability to adapt carefully is often more valuable than raw speed because it protects operational continuity.

Corporation Trust Company (CT) built the first product on the platform—CTInsurance Advantage—leveraging INTELLIFM's capabilities for insurance regulatory work where errors carry real penalties. It automated multijurisdictional filings at scale for nationwide insurers, covering approximately 700 form types. It covered all 51 US jurisdictions—the 50 states plus the District of Columbia—each with distinct rules and submission requirements.[4] Both client-server and internet-based versions were developed using this technology. By 1999, major insurers were using CTInsuranceAdvantage.

Following CTInsuranceAdvantage's success, my teams built CTAdvantage.com and other applications based on the INTELLIFM architecture. CTAdvantage.com streamlined corporate compliance, entity management, and multijurisdictional filings for legal and corporate professionals.[5] Both applications integrated with the platform's core infrastructure while extending its functionality for targeted vertical markets. The architecture also preserved compatibility across client-server and internet-based environments—accommodating new requirements without disrupting ongoing operations. CTInsuranceAdvantage was later integrated into CT's PINnacle Xchange service.[6]

More broadly, the modular and service-oriented approach provided adaptability, scalability, and interoperability—qualities that have kept INTELLIFM relevant as the technological environment around it has changed. Customers could tailor the system to their needs while preserving the reliability required by enterprise document management. The underlying declarative programming architecture is explored and illustrated in Chapter 5.

---

[4] The District of Columbia is the federal district that contains the US capital, Washington; "Washington, DC" is the common name for the same jurisdiction ("DC" stands for District of Columbia).

[5] "CTAdvantage," CT Corporation, `https://ctadvantage.com`.

[6] "CT Insurance Services Makes XDB Available," Insurance Journal, May 24, 2002, `https://www.insurancejournal.com/news/national/2002/05/24/16931.htm`; "Thrivent Financial for Lutherans Awards CT Insurance Services With Major Outsourcing Contract," PR Newswire, August 8, 2002.

4.2 Responding to an Urgent Need

When I began researching what would become the Intelligent Filing Manager in the 1990s, most organizations still relied on manual, paper-based workflows for repetitive, unforgiving work. Teams produced documents on PCs, printed them, assembled supporting materials, and moved packages from desk to desk for review and signature. Filing calendars were maintained in binders, deadlines were tracked in spreadsheets or on whiteboards, and institutional knowledge resided with a small number of experienced staff. The cost of these manual processes became evident as deadlines approached. As discussed in Chapter 3, this meant overtime, rework, and last-minute scrambles to locate the "right" version of a form or the latest supporting document. Those costs became especially severe for businesses operating across multiple jurisdictions, where legal rules, regulators, formats, and submission procedures varied by location.

Multijurisdictional filing is the recurring preparation and submission of regulated documents across many jurisdictions. The workload is driven by high repetition and high variation: the same core data is repeated, but forms, definitions, attachments, and rules vary by location. That mix is challenging to handle through manual coordination alone.

The insurance industry clearly illustrates the challenge. In the United States, insurance is regulated primarily at the state level, and each state maintains its own regulatory expectations and review processes.[7] Regulatory demands include annual reporting, rate filings, underwriting approvals, and oversight of sales personnel. A large insurer operating nationwide may have to handle hundreds of forms, many of which contain overlapping data fields and require shared supporting information. Even when the information is the same, the presentation often is not. Rules and interpretations also change frequently, which means yesterday's "approved approach" may not satisfy tomorrow's reviewer. Over time, the work begins to resemble a continuous compliance production line, with filings, revisions, resubmissions, and status checks occurring in parallel across states.

[7] "Insurance and Reinsurance Laws and Regulations USA 2025," International Comparative Legal Guides, `https://iclg.com/practice-areas/insurance-and-reinsurance-laws-and-regulations/usa`.

Other heavily regulated sectors face similar pressures. Organizations in food and drug regulation, health care, and social services process large volumes of forms and submissions governed by strict standards.[8] Much of this work is repetitive: names, addresses, policy identifiers, government identifiers such as Social Security numbers, and other core data must be entered repeatedly across different forms and jurisdictions. Repetition increases the chance of inconsistency, and inconsistency invites delays, rejections, and follow-up questions. The operational impact can be substantial, especially when teams are expected to maintain speed without sacrificing accuracy.

Corporate compliance adds another layer of complexity. Lawful and transparent operations require regular interaction with state authorities and careful maintenance of corporate records. The incorporation process includes multiple steps, from filing articles of incorporation to maintaining records and governance materials. Expansion into new states requires a foreign qualification, and ongoing compliance typically includes annual reports and tax-related filings.[9] Each additional jurisdiction adds more deadlines, more forms, and more opportunities for drift between the organization's beliefs and a regulator's expectations.

The pattern was unmistakable: organizations were drowning in paperwork, and the manual processes they relied on could not scale. The same Windows and Office capabilities that made document creation easy—as discussed in earlier chapters—accelerated document volume without providing corresponding tools for organizing, validating, and filing at enterprise scale. I designed INTELLIFM to close that gap by bringing structure, repeatability, and guided decision-making to document-intensive work that had become too large, too variable, and too time-sensitive to remain manual.

4.3 Knowledge Base

Intelligent automation depends on dependable knowledge. Systems that apply AI in regulated, document-intensive work still require a stable foundation of facts, rules, and relationships to guide decisions. A knowledge base provides that foundation by organizing the information an expert system needs to operate consistently and in an

[8] American Hospital Association, *Regulatory Overload: Assessing the Regulatory Burden on Health Systems, Hospitals and Post-acute Care Providers* (Chicago: American Hospital Association, 2017), https://www.aha.org/guidesreports/2017-11-03-regulatory-overload-report.

[9] American Bar Association, "Model Business Corporation Act (2016 Revision)," https://www.americanbar.org/groups/business_law/resources/model-business-corporation-act/.

explainable manner. In regulatory and legal workflows, this knowledge often includes filing deadlines, required documents, jurisdiction-specific rules, and validation constraints. When these elements are captured in a structured format, the system can apply them repeatedly—across teams, offices, and time—without relying on informal memory or ad hoc judgment.

A defining design decision in INTELLIFM was to maintain its knowledge bases in Microsoft Excel. That decision was not merely a technical convenience. It was a usability decision rooted in the same principles discussed in Chapter 2. Domain experts already understood spreadsheets, and spreadsheets offered immediate advantages: information was visible, formulas and logic could be inspected, and changes could be reviewed line by line. Domain experts did not need to learn a specialized interface or a programming language to update rules. They could see decision tables and mappings directly, follow the logic, and make changes with confidence. The principle of progressive disclosure applies here as well: begin with a familiar tool, and then introduce additional structure only when users need it. In practice, this reduced training overhead and shortened the time between a policy change and a system update.

This approach also reflected the lesson from Chapter 3 about automation and user control. Rather than burying logic inside opaque code, the system relied on configurable policies that domain experts could inspect, validate, and revise as regulations evolved. This transparency built trust; users could understand the system's actions and trace decisions back to explicit rules rather than assumptions. It also supported accountability. In regulated industries, achieving the correct outcome is necessary but not sufficient—teams must also explain why it is correct. A knowledge base of configurable policies makes that explanation possible by linking every decision to specific rules and inputs.

Operationally, INTELLIFM managed its knowledge base through configurable policies—rules that domain experts could revise and deploy without touching application code. They could update deadlines, forms, and jurisdiction rules as regulations changed, and those revisions could be deployed to production in a controlled manner. This control was important because frequent updates are routine in regulatory work, and unmanaged change can introduce inconsistencies that are difficult to detect. A practical knowledge base balances flexibility with discipline: updates should be easy to make, and their impact should be clear.

Another innovation was the use of document processing to update the knowledge base at scale. The system applied rule-based NLP—pattern matching, structured parsing, and logical inference—to analyze documents, identify relevant sections, extract key data elements, and propose structured entries. Those proposed entries could then be reviewed by domain experts and incorporated into application-specific knowledge bases, including those used by CTAdvantage.com. This workflow preserved human judgment while reducing repetitive effort, which is often the most expensive and error-prone part of knowledge maintenance. It also improved consistency by allowing the same extraction and structuring logic to be applied repeatedly, rather than being recreated manually for each update.

Maintaining specialized knowledge bases by domain foreshadowed a modern AI lesson: domain specificity improves precision. By dedicating each knowledge base to a particular area of expertise, INTELLIFM reduced ambiguity, improved consistency, and accelerated execution. Newer techniques, such as ML, can add value in some areas, but the underlying discipline remains the same. High-quality outcomes depend on well-structured domain knowledge, transparent rules, and a review process that keeps the system aligned with current requirements.

4.4 Q&A Sessions

INTELLIFM separates business rules from application code so that domain experts can define operational requirements in a structured, human-readable form. In many cases, these rules can be expressed in clear, natural language rather than in a programming syntax. The system interprets the rules and applies them within a consistent decision framework. For example, "If the current date is within 30 days of the incorporation anniversary, then initiate the annual report filing process."

This design keeps operational logic aligned with business processes and regulatory requirements. It also reduces the risk that rules become embedded in technical implementations that only developers can modify. Regular testing and domain review help validate accuracy, and the platform can adapt to changes by updating rules rather than altering core code. That distinction matters in regulated work: policy changes are frequent, but production systems must remain stable and predictable.

To simplify complex workflows for end users, INTELLIFM introduced Q&A sessions—an interface that converts procedural logic into interactive decision trees. Instead of forcing users to interpret dense forms and determine which sections apply, the system guides them through an adaptive sequence of prompts. Each answer determines the next applicable question, and the system can validate inputs, enforce dependencies, and surface exceptions as they occur. This approach streamlines multijurisdictional filings by reducing uncertainty and keeping users focused on a single decision at a time.

I had watched TurboTax[10] guide users through complex tax forms with an interview-style process: one question at a time, while the software handled the underlying complexity. The same idea could be applied to regulatory filings. Rather than presenting a long form and expecting users to know the correct path, INTELLIFM could guide them through a structured conversation that mirrored the reasoning of experienced compliance professionals. Users provided the facts. The system applied the rules, determined the applicable ones, and generated the required steps and outputs. The result was a workflow that was both simpler to complete and easier to review.

This design differed from the generic assistance described in Chapter 2. The Q&A sessions guided users step by step, requested the facts required for each decision, and applied explicit domain rules to determine the next action. That transparency made the guidance easier to trust and easier to review. The result was that users trusted rather than dismissed the assistance, because the guidance was grounded in explicit rules that could be inspected and validated. Chapter 5 presents a case study of Example Automation Inc., illustrating how these sessions help users navigate intricate regulatory tasks with clarity and confidence.

Later releases expanded these dialog capabilities to improve flexibility and responsiveness, including richer prompts and refinements to exception handling. However, the original decision tree structure remained central to guiding users through regulatory requirements. These sessions were refined over time through user feedback and observed usage patterns, improving both efficiency and accuracy. When embedded inside automated workflows, they support faster processing, reduce rework, and help organizations maintain consistent compliance outcomes across teams and jurisdictions.

4.5 Application Integration

Application integration has become central to modern business operations. By connecting systems for data sharing and workflow coordination, organizations can respond more quickly as automation increases. As software ecosystems grow, core work no longer happens inside a single application. It now spans record systems, document repositories, workflow tools, and external service networks—and often requires moving

[10] TurboTax is a consumer tax preparation software product of Intuit, which acquired ChipSoft, the company behind TurboTax, in December 1993. Intuit Inc., Annual Report (Form 10-K), for fiscal year ended July 31, 1996, filed October 24, 1996, `https://investors.intuit.com/sec-filings/all-sec-filings/content/0000891618-96-002383/10-K.txt`.

the same core data reliably across multiple steps. Integration addresses this reality by reducing manual handoffs, minimizing duplicate data entry, and ensuring consistent information across systems.

To support this need, the INTELLIFM framework provides standardized APIs and data conversion capabilities that support interoperability across diverse enterprise applications. Interoperability is more than a convenience; it is how organizations maintain consistency, reduce rework, and sustain throughput as volume grows without shifting deadlines.

The CTAdvantage.com platform demonstrates effective use cases for intelligent automation in business compliance. Developed for CT Corporation—a wholly owned subsidiary of Wolters Kluwer specializing in business incorporation and registered agent services—the platform is built on the INTELLIFM foundation. CTAdvantage.com was designed for legal and corporate professionals who manage complex compliance tasks under time pressure, where accuracy must be repeatable and outcomes must be defensible. The platform provides a full suite of tools as given below:

- Business entity filing manager
- Corporate compliance manager
- Document ordering system
- Forms library
- Uniform Commercial Code (UCC) lien search tools
- UCC filing manager
- Centralized resource center for accessing news and tracking order status

These capabilities are best understood as a workflow, not a menu. Entity data, forms, ordering, searches, filing actions, and status tracking should be integrated into a single, coordinated experience because real compliance work continuously crosses those boundaries.

CTAdvantage.com improves operations in several concrete ways. It delivers immediate results for preliminary due diligence and improves service delivery by automatically routing title search requests to the appropriate regional offices. It handles real-time document retrieval and includes an entity manager that stores search results online for extended periods, enabling users to resume prior work without reconstructing it. These features support a range of scenarios. Mergers and acquisitions, real estate transactions, corporate expansions, and comprehensive due diligence can be consolidated into a single process. When these steps are unified, teams spend less time coordinating and more time completing work—the difference between a system that merely stores information and one that drives execution.

Adaptive Q&A sessions simplify multijurisdictional filings within CTAdvantage.com, streamlining transactions from entity creation and management to secured lending and due diligence. Instead of expecting users to interpret dense forms and determine which fields apply, the platform guides users through adaptive prompts based on their inputs. This method reduces ambiguity, catches inconsistencies earlier, and makes workflows easier to complete correctly on the first pass. Combined with Wolters Kluwer's nationwide service network and the platform's cloud-based interface, CTAdvantage.com supports the formation and qualification of corporations across all 51 US jurisdictions. With this coverage, businesses can address compliance requirements wherever they operate, while maintaining a consistent workflow and data model.

INTELLIFM's integration capabilities were demonstrated by connecting CTAdvantage.com to Secretariat—a software platform from Bridgeway Software that supports corporate governance and compliance. Secretariat assists with the secure management of corporate records, compliance deadlines, and legal entities. The purpose of integrating these systems was straightforward: reduce fragmentation between "where entity information is maintained" and "where filings are executed." Without integration, organizations face duplicate entry, inconsistent entity details, and avoidable errors. These problems often surface at the worst possible time—during an audit or a transaction closing.

The integration was implemented in the early 2000s, with engineering teams at Wolters Kluwer collaborating with Bridgeway Software to develop APIs that supported data synchronization and workflow sharing between the platforms. In 2015, Mitratech acquired Bridgeway Software, expanding its suite of legal technology solutions.[11] Secretariat, the entity management component originally developed at Bridgeway, grew to serve hundreds of corporate legal departments worldwide.[12]

---

[11] "Mitratech Acquires Bridgeway Software," Mitratech, July 7, 2015, https://mitratech.com/resource-hub/pressreleases/mitratech-acquires-bridgeway-software/.

[12] According to Mitratech's product documentation, Secretariat is used in more than 700 corporate legal departments worldwide. "Secretariat User Guide," Mitratech Success Center, https://success.mitratech.com/Suite/Secretariat_User_Guides/Secretariat_User_Guide.

A benefit of integrating Secretariat with CTAdvantage.com is the centralized data management it supports. Data stored in Secretariat can be used directly for multijurisdictional filings in CTAdvantage.com, eliminating redundant data entry and reducing errors. This creates a practical "single source of truth" for entity information, which is especially valuable when multiple teams touch the same records over time. It also strengthens audit readiness. When filings are drawn from a centralized record system, organizations can trace outputs to authoritative inputs rather than reconstructing how a value was entered into a form months earlier. In other words, integration supports not only speed but also defensibility.

This integration provides a consistent user experience. Users can initiate filings in Secretariat and complete them in CTAdvantage.com with entity details prepopulated. For instance, a corporate secretary managing multiple subsidiaries could select an entity in Secretariat, start the filing process, and complete an annual report in CTAdvantage.com with the relevant information already in place. This improves consistency in compliance documentation and supports automated compliance processes across teams and jurisdictions. Real-time updates also matter. When data changes in Secretariat, those changes can be reflected in CTAdvantage.com for the associated filings, keeping compliance-related information current. That reduces the risk of late-stage corrections, rejected filings, and downstream legal or financial exposure. It also lowers operational cost by reducing rework and limiting the "cleanup effort" that typically follows manual processes.

The solution scales as demand and complexity grow because integration reduces repetitive data entry and reconciliation while keeping workflows consistent across jurisdictions. Scaling in this context does not mean merely adding users. It means sustaining performance and correctness as the number of entities, filings, jurisdictions, and concurrent workflows increases. Integration directly contributes to that goal by reducing the number of times information must be re-entered and reconciled and by allowing automated workflows to operate consistently across systems.

While integration offers clear benefits, it also introduces challenges that must be managed deliberately. Transferring data securely requires strong encryption protocols, access controls, and regular audits. Maintaining compatibility when either system is updated requires careful coordination, interface versioning strategies, and thorough regression testing. Adoption also depends on training and interface clarity; if the integrated workflow is confusing, users will revert to manual workarounds, and the integration's value will evaporate. This integration did more than streamline filings. It revealed a broader market need for end-to-end corporate governance and entity management, which directly shaped our decision to build hCue on this foundation.

The success of the CTAdvantage.com and Secretariat integration highlighted demand for complete corporate governance solutions. Recognizing this opportunity, we developed hCue—a new CT Corporation platform within Wolters Kluwer—designed to support entity governance and corporate recordkeeping at scale. It supports corporate secretaries and their teams in maintaining control over entity information, including entity history, management structure, compliance calendars, and ownership records. In practice, these records serve as the backbone of compliance: when recordkeeping is reliable, filings are easier, reviews are faster, and the organization is more resilient during audits and transactions.

The success of this work was recognized by Law Technology News (LTN), which named hCue its Best Records Management Software in its 2006 annual reader awards.[13] That same year, LTN readers nominated CT Corporation for two additional awards: CTAdvantage.com as Top Knowledge Management System and CT Summation Professional Services in the Litigation Support Service/Consultant category. These recognitions reinforced the broader point: INTELLIFM's impact was not confined to automation within a single application; it extended to the practical integration of data, workflows, and compliance execution across systems.

Since then, hCue has matured into a cloud-based entity management solution that helps compliance professionals automate data management and integrate workflows. By integrating with systems such as Workday and Docusign and offering well-documented APIs, hCue provides a secure, customizable platform.[14] As a connected compliance service, hCue integrates directly with other CT Corporation offerings within the Wolters Kluwer portfolio, ensuring consistent corporate record information across related services. This consistency matters because compliance is rarely a one-off. It is an ongoing program, and records must remain coherent as clients grow.

Over time, the integration work reinforced a practical lesson: interoperability is not a one-time engineering effort. It requires ongoing governance—interface contracts, versioning strategies, regression testing, security reviews, and coordination when either system changes. As cloud adoption accelerates and organizations rely on many

[13] "hCue Voted Best Records Management Software," Law Technology News 2006 Technology Awards, CTAdvantage.com, 2006. The LTN vendor awards were an annual reader-voted program administered by the publication; the 2006 program was the fourth annual edition.

[14] "hCue Entity and Subsidiary Management," CT Corporation/Wolters Kluwer, `https://www.wolterskluwer.com/en/solutions/ct-corporation/hcue-entity-management`.

specialized applications, these discipline-driven integration practices become more valuable. Open interfaces and service-based architectures can reduce integration friction, but they do not eliminate the responsibility for maintaining them.

The pattern established with CTAdvantage.com and Secretariat—integrating specialized applications through well-defined interfaces—has since become standard practice across the technology industry. Major acquisitions have often been motivated by workflow integration. Microsoft's 2016 acquisition of LinkedIn and Salesforce's 2020 acquisition of Slack reflect a broader move toward integrating data, collaboration, and execution within unified enterprise ecosystems. Interoperability has become a strategic imperative, not merely a technical convenience. Organizations that master integration adapt faster, serve customers better, and build ecosystems that are difficult for competitors to replicate.

Looking ahead, the importance of application integration will continue to grow. As businesses digitize and specialized software solutions multiply, the ability to connect diverse applications becomes a durable advantage. Cloud computing plays a central role as mobile access becomes ubiquitous and applications require cross-device, cross-platform synchronization. But the central requirement remains the same: systems must work together reliably, securely, and predictably. Organizations that treat integration as an ongoing capability—governed, tested, and maintained—will be best positioned to innovate rapidly, adapt to change, and deliver consistent value to customers.

4.6 Machine Learning Integration

When I created INTELLIFM in the late 1990s, ML was not practical for most enterprise applications. The techniques existed—neural networks, decision trees, and statistical classifiers—but the computing capacity, storage, and training data required to deliver reliable performance were beyond what most organizations could provide at the time. Enterprise customers needed predictable outcomes, traceable logic, and stable behavior under operational constraints. For that reason, my teams built the INTELLIFM applications as rule-based expert systems that delivered consistent results and made the decision logic explicit.

Over the following two decades, ML matured from a research topic into a practical tool for production systems. Large-scale data processing and distributed computing made it feasible to work with far larger datasets, and GPUs accelerated training for deep neural networks. By the late 2010s, widely available pretrained models and transfer learning had often reduced the time and effort required to achieve strong results, enabling practitioners to specialize a general model for a specific enterprise domain. These advances did not eliminate the need for structured domain knowledge, but they expanded the scope of automatability and improved the system's ability to handle complex, variable filing requirements.

4.6.1 Phased Integration Strategy

The question for INTELLIFM was not whether to incorporate ML, but how to do so without compromising reliability. Enterprise document processing and filing systems cannot tolerate silent failures; an incorrect filing category, a missed jurisdiction requirement, or an erroneous submission can create legal exposure, audit issues, or operational delays. Reliability also includes recoverability: when something goes wrong, the system must surface the problem clearly and support correction without disrupting the workflow.

As enterprise data infrastructure matured in the early 2010s, we began incorporating ML into INTELLIFM through a phased, risk-aware strategy. Early integration focused on low-risk assistance, including suggesting filing categories, flagging potential duplicates, and providing predictive assistance during Q&A sessions. In these scenarios, the model's output served as a recommendation rather than a final decision.

INTELLIFM's modular architecture made this possible: new components could be added without rewriting core functionality. We evaluated these features through controlled rollouts, precise performance metrics, and careful exception handling, while preserving deterministic fallbacks for critical steps. As confidence increased, we extended these capabilities to more sensitive tasks, including automated classification, intelligent form prefilling, and pattern detection across large volumes of filing transactions—while remaining mindful of where errors would be costly and where human review remained necessary.

4.6.2 Hybrid Governance Model

The rule-based foundation remained central. ML improved speed, coverage, and adaptability, but final decisions—especially in compliance-critical workflows—remained governed by explicit rules and domain expert oversight. Models could propose; rules decided. Where models were less interpretable, we constrained their role to recommendation and triage, while rule-based checkpoints governed final decisions and compliance-critical outputs. Corrections fed back into later releases through updated rules, curated training examples, and improved models, while preserving transparency for enterprise users. In practice, this meant that the system improved without becoming opaque: users could still trace outcomes to explicit requirements, and domain experts retained the ability to adjust behavior when regulations changed. This hybrid approach—combining adaptability with explainable decision logic—proved more reliable than either approach alone.

ML also strengthened the interactive Q&A experience. Predictive assistance reduced keystrokes, suggested likely next steps, and helped identify required documents for specific filings. The goal was never to displace the expertise encoded in INTELLIFM's rule base but to enhance it—making the system faster, more responsive, and better able to handle the complexity and variability of multijurisdictional filing requirements.

These advances required careful governance. Sectors that process sensitive documents—finance, legal services, and health care—demand strict privacy controls and adherence to emerging standards, including the GDPR and other regional data protection rules. Data quality became decisive. Reliable performance depends on clean, well-documented, representative data, supported by continuous monitoring and periodic updates. These updates address model drift, where performance can degrade as regulations, document formats, and user behavior change. Governance also includes access control, audit trails, and clear rules governing data usage. These rules specify which data may be used for learning, what must remain segregated, and what must be retained or deleted in accordance with policy.

4.6.3 Lessons in Responsible AI

The most important lesson from this evolution was that automation and human judgment are complements, not opposites. The same principle that guided proofing tools at Microsoft applied here: offer suggestions, preserve user control, and build trust through consistent behavior. In enterprise settings, trust is earned through repeatability, transparency, and a clear path for correction.

That is why INTELLIFM's approach treated ML as an enhancement to a disciplined system, not as a substitute for structured domain knowledge and accountable decision-making. These principles resonate strongly in today's agentic AI systems. For an agent to be "responsible," its entire process must be recorded, its logic shared openly, and every decision made fully traceable—placing transparency and consistency at the absolute center of the automation life cycle.

4.7 Summary

INTELLIFM applied lessons in usability, scalability, and automation from the Windows era to document management and regulatory compliance. Developed in the late 1990s for client-server environments, the system later moved to internet-based deployment and adopted cloud delivery and ML. Each migration expanded capability while preserving the disciplined, transparent foundation that enterprise users rely on.

Those principles bear restating. *Design for constraints*: INTELLIFM integrates with existing enterprise environments rather than requiring wholesale replacement of established systems and processes. *Build trust*: transparent rules, predictable behavior, and human-readable knowledge bases give users confidence in outcomes and a clear basis for review. *Apply progressive disclosure*: the Excel-based configuration allows domain experts to begin with familiar structures and introduce complexity only when necessary. *Preserve human judgment*: the system augments compliance professionals rather than replacing them, offering guidance while keeping users responsible for final decisions.

The INTELLIFM platform's longevity, spanning more than a quarter of a century, supports this approach. Technologies changed; discipline endured. The same modular architecture that supported client-server deployment was adapted over time as deployment models and infrastructure matured. The same rule-based foundation that addressed 1990s regulatory requirements was later integrated with ML components without compromising explainability, control, or auditability. CTAdvantage.com, hCue, and their successors built on a foundation designed for evolution rather than obsolescence.

The next chapter explores how declarative programming contributed to INTELLIFM's development and long-term maintainability. This approach—emphasizing desired outcomes over procedural instructions—has become increasingly important in modern AI applications and cloud infrastructure. INTELLIFM aligned with these practices early by separating rules from code and treating domain knowledge as a first-class asset, demonstrating how sound architectural choices can hold up across decades of technological change.

The tools evolve, but the discipline persists.

CHAPTER 5

Declarative Programming

In the late 1990s, as I architected the AI-driven INTELLIFM, I faced a question that would define the entire system: how could compliance officers update filing rules without having to rewrite code? Regulations changed constantly. If every rule change required a programmer to modify application logic, test the changes, and deploy a new release, the system would never keep pace with the jurisdictions it served.

The answer was declarative programming—an approach I first encountered as a graduate student at IIT Kanpur. In Prolog, I learned to express problems in terms of what needed to be true rather than how to make it true. The inference engine handled the procedural details. Years later, while architecting INTELLIFM, I applied the same idea: domain experts would specify business rules in a language they could read and maintain, and the system would execute those rules consistently. The separation was deliberate. Rules lived in knowledge bases and structured artifacts that compliance officers could update; application code lived separately and remained stable when regulations shifted.

This design reflected several principles that recur throughout this book. It respected practical constraints by working within what domain experts could realistically maintain. It built trust through transparency, as users could inspect the rules governing system behavior. It supported progressive disclosure by allowing experts to start with simple rules and gradually add sophistication. And it preserved human judgment by keeping experts in control of the logic shaping filings, rather than burying that logic in opaque software routines.

Declarative programming is not new, but it remains widely used because it changes how problems are framed. SQL lets users specify what data they want without dictating how the database should retrieve it. Configuration-driven systems describe desired states without scripting every step to reach them. Modern user interface frameworks specify the interface's appearance and how it binds to data, while the framework orchestrates the underlying mechanics. What these approaches share

K. C. Mukherjee, *The Microsoft AI Insider's Playbook*, https://doi.org/10.1007/979-8-8688-2730-3_5

is a focus on outcomes over procedures—a subtle reorientation that often yields systems that are easier to understand, easier to maintain, and more adaptable when requirements change.

This chapter explores declarative programming through that lens. We begin by examining how declarative principles shaped INTELLIFM and why separating *what* from *how* made the system resilient to constant regulatory change. We then examine the intersection of declarative rule systems and COM and trace the evolution of declarative user interfaces through data binding and the model-view-viewmodel (MVVM) pattern. From there, we examine practical implementations in Windows Presentation Foundation (WPF) and Extensible Application Markup Language (XAML), as well as JavaScript tools that adopt declarative patterns. Finally, we connect these ideas to prompt engineering, in which specifying intent precisely—what you want an AI system to produce, constrained by context and rules—extends declarative concepts to modern AI-driven development. Throughout, the central lesson remains the same: systems that separate what from how tend to stay more transparent, more maintainable, and better suited to change.

5.1 Characteristics

The declarative approach I adopted for INTELLIFM shared characteristics with other systems built on similar principles. Understanding these characteristics helps explain why the design choices worked and why declarative thinking continues to influence software development decades later.

Declarative programming is often recognized by its declarative syntax: code and notation that read like descriptions of outcomes, constraints, and relationships rather than step-by-step procedures. In practice, this often takes the form of a domain-specific language or structured notation that mirrors how practitioners in that domain already talk and think, improving readability and reducing translation friction.

5.1.1 Separation of Concerns

The most defining characteristic was the precise boundary between business rules and application code. In INTELLIFM, compliance officers defined which filings were required; software engineers built the machinery to execute those requirements.

Neither group needed to understand the other's domain in detail. This division accelerated development and reduced errors because changes to filing rules did not ripple through application code.

The same principle appears wherever declarative approaches succeed. Database administrators write queries without understanding storage engines. User interface designers describe layouts without writing event handlers, and infrastructure engineers declare desired states without scripting deployment steps. The same separation also appears in modern user interface stacks. Designers and product stakeholders can describe the intended states of a screen—layout, visibility, styling, and simple behaviors—while engineers implement the event logic and services that drive them. For example, a product owner might state, "When a user selects an item, highlight the selection and show the related details panel," while engineers implement the event handling and services underlying this functionality.

5.1.2 Domain-Specific Expression

Declarative systems often use languages or notations tailored to a particular field. SQL uses vocabulary familiar to anyone who works with data: SELECT, JOIN, WHERE, and GROUP BY. Prolog uses logical predicates that mirror how experts reason about rules and relationships. In INTELLIFM, we went further: business rules were authored in structured English that compliance officers could read and validate. This alignment between the notation and the domain reduced translation errors and made the knowledge base accessible to those who best understood filing requirements. SQL has endured because it lets developers specify a desired result set, whereas the database decides how to navigate schemas, use indexes, and execute joins.

Prolog takes the same idea into logic—programs declare facts and rules, and the inference engine derives answers through unification and backtracking. It has been used in various contexts, including components of IBM Watson's NLP pipeline,[1] NASA expert systems for spacecraft operations,[2] and bioinformatics applications that analyze

[1] Adam Lally and Paul Fodor, "Natural Language Processing With Prolog in the IBM Watson System," Association for Logic Programming, 2011, `https://logicprogramming.org/2011/03/natural-language-processing-with-prolog-in-the-ibm-watson-system/`.

[2] "Use of a FORTH-based PROLOG for Real-Time Expert Systems: Spacelab Life Sciences Experiment Application," NASA Technical Reports Server, `https://ntrs.nasa.gov/citations/19930073450`.

intricate relationships in biological data.[3] These applications demonstrate why Prolog remains effective for domains where logical reasoning is essential, despite being over 50 years old.

5.1.3 Automatic Optimization

When developers specify outcomes rather than procedures, the execution environment gains the latitude to optimize how those outcomes are achieved. Importantly, this efficiency is engineered rather than learned. The execution environment relies on fixed algorithms and heuristics (often guided by statistics about the current data) to choose an efficient path. That distinction matters because it explains why declarative systems can deliver substantial performance benefits without requiring the system to "learn" from experience.

SQL databases generate query plans based on table statistics, indexes, and available memory—optimizations impractical to hand-code for every query. Prolog's inference engine searches solution spaces using backtracking and unification, strategies that arise from the language's design rather than explicit programmer instructions. INTELLIFM benefited from similar dynamics: the inference engine determined how to traverse rule sets, freeing us to focus on rule accuracy rather than traversal efficiency.

5.1.4 Data and Relationships over Control Flow

Imperative programs list sequences of operations. In contrast, declarative ones describe structures and constraints, leaving the system to determine execution order. This conceptual shift makes code more concise when working with complex data. The pattern is visible in SQL joins, Prolog relations, and the knowledge bases that powered INTELLIFM's filing logic. It makes programs easier to reason about because the reader sees what is true rather than what steps produce that truth.

Several major families of tools reflect these same characteristics in different ways. The functional programming paradigm, for example, emphasizes the evaluation of functions and a reduction in mutable state. While not always purely declarative in

[3] Nicos Angelopoulos and Jan Wielemaker, "Accessing Biological Data as Prolog Facts," in *Proceedings of the 19th International Symposium on Principles and Practice of Declarative Programming (PPDP 2017), Namur, Belgium, October 9-11, 2017*, 29-38, `https://dl.acm.org/doi/10.1145/3131851.3131857`.

practice, its focus on minimizing side effects makes system behavior much easier to reason about and trace. Web markup languages structure content declaratively, defining layout and organization without prescribing how browsers render the result. Style sheets extend this separation by specifying visual presentation independently from content, improving maintainability and flexibility. Configuration formats similarly describe desired settings and states, leaving the system to interpret and apply them consistently.

These characteristics are not exclusive to any single technology. They appear in database languages, logic programming, functional programming, configuration management, and modern user interface frameworks. What unites them is a design philosophy: express intent clearly, and let the system handle execution. That philosophy shaped INTELLIFM from its earliest design, and it continues to shape how I think about building software that must adapt to changing requirements. These characteristics are not confined to application development. They have also transformed how organizations manage the infrastructure on which applications run.

5.1.5 Infrastructure as Code

The move from manual server configuration to infrastructure as code (IaC) is one of the biggest operational changes I have seen in enterprise computing. Early in my career, provisioning a server meant submitting a request, waiting for procurement, and then relying on system administrators to spend hours or even days installing the operating system, configuring networking, and applying patches. Each server ended up slightly different, shaped by the sequence of commands an administrator happened to run. Documentation, when it existed, often became outdated quickly.

IaC changed the model. Instead of building environments by hand, teams define them in configuration files that can be versioned, reviewed, tested, and reproduced. What once lived as unwritten knowledge in the heads of senior administrators can now exist as text in a version control system. When I first encountered this approach in the early 2010s, I immediately saw how it addressed problems I had wrestled with for years: environment drift, inconsistent configuration, and the brittleness created by undocumented changes.

The benefits are practical and measurable. Reproducibility makes development, testing, and production environments match closely, which reduces the "it works on my machine" failures. Auditability means every change is tracked, attributed, and reversible. Speed means work that once took weeks can happen in minutes. In one infrastructure modernization effort I led, provisioning time dropped from three weeks to under two hours. The time savings mattered, but the reduction in configuration errors mattered even more.

Tools such as Terraform, AWS CloudFormation, Azure Resource Manager (ARM), and Ansible have made IaC accessible across organizations. Terraform, in particular, is widely adopted because it can describe resources across multiple cloud providers, supporting hybrid architectures and reducing lock-in. I have seen teams adopt it incrementally—starting with a single application and expanding until the broader cloud footprint is codified. That approach lowers risk and builds capability over time.

IaC also transforms how development and operations teams collaborate. When infrastructure definitions live alongside application code, DevOps becomes a natural extension of the workflow. Infrastructure changes move through pull requests, peer reviews, and automated checks, just like any other code change. Indeed, many core DevOps practices depend on this foundation.

But the discipline should not be underestimated. Poorly structured configurations become as hard to maintain as poorly written software. Teams need modular design, naming conventions, and documentation. State management—reconciling what exists with what the configuration describes—adds complexity that demands careful attention. Teams struggle when they treat IaC as a one-time migration rather than an ongoing practice. Like any codebase, it needs maintenance and periodic refactoring.

Security matters just as much. IaC can encode security defaults—access controls, encryption, logging, and monitoring—so new resources begin with a consistent baseline. At the same time, mistakes can scale fast: a flawed template can create hundreds of vulnerable resources in minutes. Security review and automated scanning should be part of the workflow before changes reach production.

For architects designing cloud-native systems, IaC has become a core expectation. It supports reliability, scalability, and audit readiness across the system life cycle—from first deployment through years of operation and eventual decommissioning.

5.2 The INTELLIFM Approach

The characteristics described above coalesced into a concrete system. INTELLIFM was designed to handle multijurisdictional filings—a problem domain where regulations shifted constantly and compliance officers, not programmers, held the relevant expertise. The architecture had to accommodate that reality. Over time, these ideas were also applied in production deployments, including on platforms such as CTAdvantage.com.

As discussed in Chapter 4, the expert system addressed a persistent challenge in electronic filing: keeping pace with changing compliance requirements. Traditional systems required programmers to rewrite code, test changes, and fix defects each time regulations changed—a process that was expensive, slow, and error-prone. I designed INTELLIFM to break that dependency on code changes. Using declarative programming, the system separated filing rules from application code. When regulations changed, compliance officers could update rules without touching the underlying program.

A distinctive feature was the dynamically generated user interface. It operated according to high-level rules defined by domain experts and adjusted its behavior in response to user input and regulatory context. It activated or disabled controls based on the current state, streamlined queries, and provided guidance tailored to particular filing scenarios. This responsiveness was not hard-coded; it emerged from the declarative rules that governed system behavior.

The platform fostered collaboration between two groups that rarely worked together directly: compliance specialists who understood filing requirements and software engineers who understood system architecture. Domain experts defined high-level rules that shaped application behavior; engineers built the execution machinery without embedding business logic in code. This division of labor embodied the declarative paradigm and yielded products that were both resilient and adaptable.

5.2.1 Architecting with Prolog and C++

To build the core logic of INTELLIFM, I selected Prolog—a language specifically designed for AI applications. Its declarative structure gave me the flexibility to express business rules and logical relationships in near-natural language. This facilitated the translation of complex compliance logic into executable code. Prolog's built-in inference engine and pattern-matching capabilities were well suited to decision trees, rule evaluation, and exception handling. Together, these features supported the rule-heavy reasoning INTELLIFM required.

One of Prolog's most powerful features was backtracking. When a solution path failed, the system automatically revisited earlier decision points and explored alternatives. This was achieved through a choice-point stack—a mechanism that records the state of computation at each decision point, allowing the system to unwind and retry alternative paths when a branch fails. To ensure this did not result in exhaustive, slow searches, Prolog's *first-argument indexing*[4] optimized the process by narrowing the set of candidate clauses before backtracking even began. This capability enabled INTELLIFM to efficiently search large rule sets and resolve ambiguities—an essential requirement for regulatory filings spanning multiple jurisdictions with overlapping and sometimes conflicting requirements.

Prolog also excelled at symbolic computation and list processing, which I used to manipulate the nested data structures common in AI applications. Its support for unification and logical variables allowed the system to reason even when information was incomplete or uncertain. Traditional programming languages handled that kind of reasoning poorly. These capabilities made Prolog the right choice for a knowledge-based platform that had to adapt as business logic was updated.

To support the broader architecture, I designed an object-oriented layer in C++. This layer connected the Prolog inference engine with components that generated user interfaces, supported database interactions, and handled high-volume forms publishing. I chose C++ for its performance characteristics, precise memory management, and ability to model complex relationships across modules.

NLP was another essential component. I wanted business rules to be authored in plain English. To address this, I designed a parser that interpreted high-level, natural language-like statements. This allowed compliance officers and domain experts to contribute directly to rule development without writing code. It also preserved transparency as rules were revised, ensuring the decision-making process remained fully auditable.

INTELLIFM was designed to handle diverse data sources. It extracted information from PDF documents and parsed Excel spreadsheets, capturing business rules expressed in structured English statements. Using rule-based, pattern-driven NLP techniques appropriate to the era—specifically keyword recognition and deterministic transformation to Prolog syntax—the expert system translated these rules into a formal representation and integrated them into its knowledge base. My teams built these knowledge bases on enterprise-grade databases, using Microsoft Access for client-server applications and SQL Server and Oracle for web-based environments. At the time, Oracle was often the preferred choice for large-scale enterprise

[4] First-argument indexing is a Prolog optimization that leverages the type and value of a predicate's first argument to filter out nonmatching clauses. Discarding irrelevant paths before the inference engine even attempts unification prevents the creation of unnecessary choice points and significantly reduces the computational overhead of backtracking.

deployments. We selected these platforms to ensure the scalability and reliability required by stringent regulatory standards. By combining declarative logic, object-oriented design, and high-precision NLP, we created a platform that delivered sound reasoning, cohesive integration, and long-term adaptability. INTELLIFM demonstrates how AI can be architected to solve practical challenges in compliance, document management, and enterprise automation through disciplined, traceable logic.

5.2.2 AI Meets COM Architecture

INTELLIFM was an early example of a knowledge-based system packaged as COM components. This facilitated the integration of the reasoning engine and related services with Windows applications. As discussed in Chapter 1, COM provides a framework for building binary software components that can interact within the Windows environment, independent of the implementation language. In general COM practice, a spell checker implemented as a COM component, for example, could be shared by both a word processor and an email client. A charting component could likewise be reused across spreadsheet and presentation software without reimplementation.

Developers used languages such as Visual C++, Visual Basic, and Delphi to create COM components, ensuring interoperability provided they adhered to the COM specifications. Later extensions, Distributed COM and COM+, expanded these capabilities to support transaction processing and networked component interactions. With the introduction of the .NET Framework, Microsoft added COM Interop, which allowed languages such as C# and Visual Basic.NET to integrate with existing COM components. This backward compatibility helped COM remain part of the Windows ecosystem, particularly in enterprise environments where legacy systems must work alongside modern applications.

INTELLIFM used COM components to achieve a highly modular architecture. Functionalities were encapsulated within components that communicated through well-defined COM interfaces. By separating business rules from procedural code, the system supported complex logic in a form that was easier to implement, test, and adapt over time. My decision to use Excel for rule authoring and COM for component integration drew on familiar tools that enterprises already understood and trusted.

Figure 5-1 illustrates the "AI meets COM" architecture. The system is organized into four modules, each containing one or more components. The diagram highlights one representative component from each module. These are the User Interface Generation (UIG) component from the User Interface module, the SQL component from the Data

Management module, the Encapsulated Prolog Services (EPS) component from the AI and Processing module, and the Persistence and Printing (P&P) component from the Document Management module. The UIG component serves as the central orchestrator, coordinating the other three components in response to user interactions. The SQL component handles operational data retrieval and updates across the reference and reports-and-reminders databases. The EPS component performs inferencing using a knowledge base held in memory. The P&P component handles archival output by writing completed filings to a saved-filings database and generating printed forms. This design preserves a deliberate separation between operational data managed by SQL and archival output managed by P&P.

Figure 5-1. *The "AI meets COM" architecture of INTELLIFM—an AI system developed in the late 1990s and early 2000s using Microsoft COM technology. This architecture is organized into four modules, each implemented by one or more components, with the primary component for each module shown. (For a detailed explanation, see Appendix 6.) (Image by author)*

INTELLIFM's success demonstrated the power of component-based architectures in AI systems, showing how they can support logical reasoning while integrating with enterprise software ecosystems. In the early 2000s, my teams extended this functionality by adapting the platform for web architectures. They developed web service wrappers using Simple Object Access Protocol (SOAP) and Extensible Markup Language (XML)—the dominant standards for web services at the time, for the original COM components. This exposed the components' functionality as APIs and extended the system's reach into the cloud computing era.

INTELLIFM's approach to document workflow automation anticipated capabilities that later became industry standards. SpringCM, a Chicago-based company that had been providing hosted content management since 2005, allowed users to create workflows tailored to particular business processes on a cloud-based infrastructure.[5] Docusign acquired SpringCM in September 2018, and the resulting Docusign Contract Lifecycle Management solution integrated contract life-cycle management with electronic signatures, much as INTELLIFM had integrated document processing with compliance tracking.[6]

The pattern of empowering domain experts through familiar tools also persisted. Templater, developed by the Croatian software company N.G.S. Ltd., allowed nontechnical users to create document templates directly in Microsoft Excel, Word, and PowerPoint.[7] Microsoft Dynamics 365 introduced business document management in late 2019, allowing users to edit and customize Excel and Word templates for automated document generation.[8] Microsoft introduced SharePoint Syntex in 2020. Today, Microsoft 365 document processing and content assembly services, used with Power Automate, can automate document generation from templates and route the resulting

[5] Ron Miller, "SpringCM Scores $18M In Funding; Plans To Expand Sales And Marketing," TechCrunch, April 17, 2014, `https://techcrunch.com/2014/04/17/springcm-scores-18m-in-funding-plans-to-expand-sales-and-marketing/`.

[6] "DocuSign Signs Definitive Agreement to Acquire SpringCM," PR Newswire, July 31, 2018, `https://www.prnewswire.com/news-releases/docusign-signs-definitive-agreement-to-acquire-springcm-300689544.html`.

[7] "About," Templater, `https://templater.info/about`.

[8] "Configurable Business Documents Reporting in Word and Excel," Microsoft Dynamics 365 Release Plan, `https://learn.microsoft.com/en-us/previous-versions/dynamics365-release-plan/2019wave2/finance-operations-crossapp-capabilities/configurable-business-documents-reporting-word-excel`.

documents through workflow steps.[9] These systems echo INTELLIFM's original design principle: document automation achieved without custom coding, with end users controlling their workflows.

Looking back, the broader pattern proved durable: declarative rules, modular components, and domain expert authoring. Modern document automation and workflow platforms share the same idea: reduce custom coding by expressing intent at a higher level and enabling the system to execute reliably. INTELLIFM showed that this approach can scale in real enterprise settings, particularly in domains where requirements change faster than traditional release cycles can accommodate.

5.3 Declarative User Interface: Evolution and Binding

The declarative principles that shaped INTELLIFM later reappeared in technologies I encountered at Microsoft—most notably WPF and XAML.

Both rely on a high-level, human-readable representation of the interface that supports a practical division of labor. Designers can focus on structure, layout, styling, and interaction states, whereas developers can focus on application logic, services, and integration. This collaboration echoes what we built in INTELLIFM: compliance officers defined filing rules; software engineers built the execution machinery. The pattern recurs because it reduces friction and makes change less costly.

The same component-based thinking—modular, reusable elements behind well-defined interfaces—later became a mainstream practice in WPF applications. When Microsoft launched WPF in 2006, it signaled a move toward graphically intensive, interactive applications and formalized workflows that encouraged designer–developer collaboration. To understand why WPF proved effective, two ideas are most important: two-way data binding and MVVM.

[9] Microsoft, "Automate Document Generation with Document Processing and Power Automate," Microsoft Learn, last modified August 4, 2025, `https://learn.microsoft.com/en-us/microsoft-365/documentprocessing/automate-document-generation`.

5.3.1 Two-Way Data Binding

Two-way data binding creates a live connection between the user interface and the underlying data. When a user changes a value in the interface, the data updates automatically. When the data changes—perhaps through a background process—the interface reflects the change without requiring a manual refresh. This synchronization reduces boilerplate code and lowers the risk of the user interface drifting out of sync with application state.

INTELLIFM anticipated this pattern in a different form. The system generated its user interface dynamically at runtime based on rules in its knowledge base, which determined how the interface should look and behave given the current data and regulatory context. If a rule changed—say, a new jurisdiction required an additional field—the interface adapted without code modifications. Presentation and data remained aligned, not because the user interface was hard-coded to the data, but because both were governed by a declarative rule set that served as a shared source of truth.

WPF expresses the same idea through binding expressions in XAML. A binding declaration connects a user interface element to a data property. Setting the binding mode to *TwoWay* activates bidirectional flow: user input updates the bound data, and data changes update the display. The *DataContext* property defines the binding scope (often inherited through the visual tree), making it practical to establish bindings at a container level while allowing nested elements to bind naturally.

WPF also includes built-in conversion and validation options that work directly with bindings. Converters translate between user interface–friendly representations and underlying data types. Validation rules can reject invalid input before it reaches the data layer, providing immediate feedback to the user. The result is a more responsive interface with fewer opportunities for inconsistency or accidental data corruption.

Figure 5-2 illustrates WPF's architecture, which supports advanced graphics, animation, hardware acceleration, data binding, resolution independence, and XML Paper Specification (XPS) printing. It uses XAML for declarative interface definition and customizable styles. The principles visible here—separating presentation from logic, binding data declaratively, and supporting collaboration between designers and developers—reflect ideas we explored in INTELLIFM years earlier.

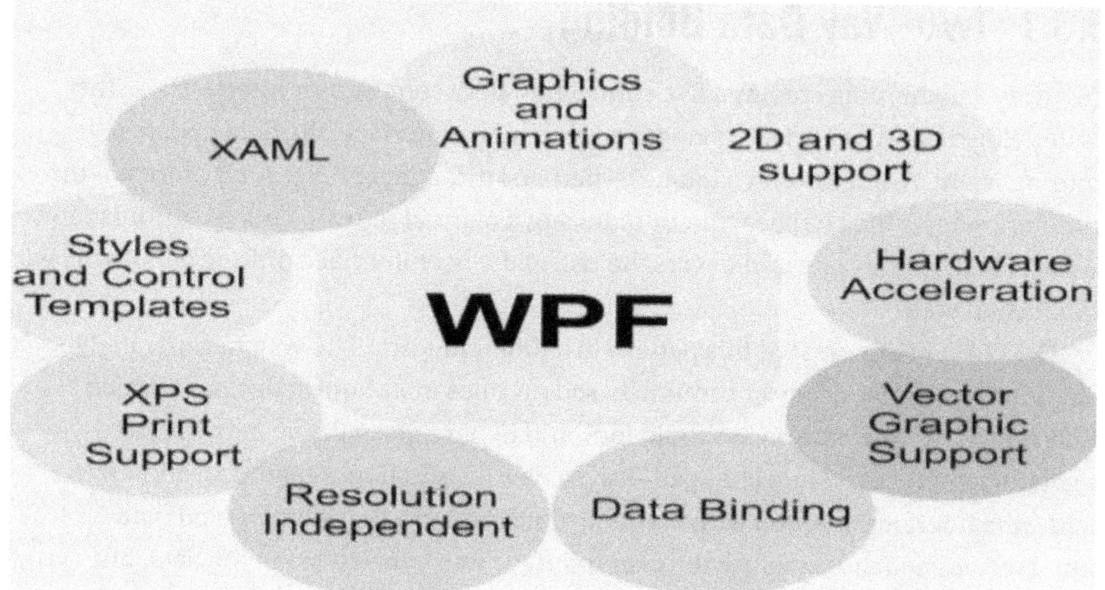

Figure 5-2. *WPF supports 2D/3D graphics, animations, hardware acceleration, data binding, resolution independence, and XPS printing. It uses XAML for declarative user interface definition and styles—echoing INTELLIFM's separation of intent from execution. (Image by author)*

5.3.2 MVVM Architecture Pattern

Two-way data binding made a cleaner architectural pattern possible: MVVM. It addressed limitations in older approaches, in which user interface coordination logic often accumulated in controllers or code-behind, making systems harder to test and modify.

MVVM also introduces a sharper separation: The model represents data and business logic, and the view handles visual presentation. The viewmodel sits between them, exposing model data in a form the view can bind to directly and implementing presentation logic that the user interface needs. Changes in the viewmodel are reflected in the view through binding; user interactions in the view update the viewmodel, which then applies rules, validation, and commands. The view does not manipulate the model directly, and the model remains unaware of the view.

This separation resembles INTELLIFM's architecture. Domain experts defined rules that shaped system behavior; the interface reflected those rules without embedding business logic inside the user interface implementation. The separation enabled parallel work: compliance specialists could refine rules while engineers improved infrastructure, and the two streams integrated cleanly because their connection point was well defined and inspectable.

Figure 5-3 illustrates MVVM in WPF. The solid arrow represents viewmodel calls to access the model; the dashed arrow represents notification callbacks from the model to the viewmodel; the bidirectional arrow represents two-way data binding between the viewmodel and the view. This separation improves modularity, testability, and maintainability—qualities that become decisive as applications grow more complex.

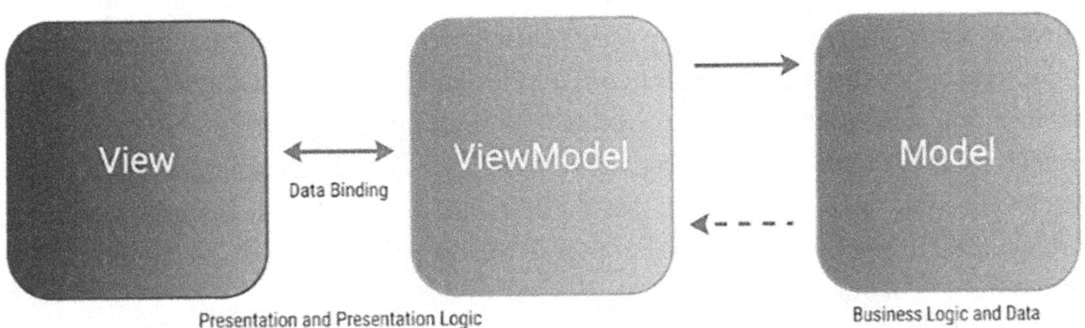

***Figure 5-3.** The MVVM design pattern in WPF, showing three components: the model (business logic and data layer), the viewmodel (intermediary for presentation logic and data binding), and the view (user interface). The arrows represent viewmodel calls to access the model (solid), notification callbacks from the model to the viewmodel (dashed), and two-way data binding between the viewmodel and the view (bidirectional). The separation in MVVM echoes a similar architectural discipline in INTELLIFM: rule definition and execution logic were kept distinct, so each could be updated independently while remaining cleanly integrated. (Image by author)*

Microsoft formalized MVVM guidance in the late 2000s and early 2010s, and the pattern became standard for WPF, Silverlight, and other XAML-based frameworks. Its influence later appeared in other ecosystems as well, including JavaScript frameworks that adopted comparable component-and-state patterns, even when they used different terminology.

5.3.3 WPF and XAML in Practice

WPF and XAML saw practical adoption across Microsoft tooling and enterprise applications. Starting with Visual Studio 2010, Microsoft rebuilt major parts of the integrated development environment (IDE) using WPF, moving beyond the older Windows Forms foundation. The upgrade delivered richer styling, a more flexible layout, and a more extensible user interface surface.

An important part of the WPF landscape was the workflow between Blend and Visual Studio (originally Expression Blend). Blend provided a visual design environment where designers could work directly with XAML to define layouts, styles, animations, and interaction states. On the other hand, developers implemented application logic, services, and view models in Visual Studio. Both tools operated on the same underlying project assets, reducing handoff friction and keeping design and implementation synchronized. In spirit, this echoed INTELLIFM: different specialists contributed through their respective interfaces, but they worked against a shared, declarative representation of intent.

Beyond desktop applications, the same declarative ideas carried over into later Microsoft frameworks. XAML-based development extended to the Universal Windows Platform, and cross-platform approaches such as .NET Multiplatform App User Interface (MAUI) continued to support the goal of describing interfaces and binding state in a structured way. The details changed, but the underlying insight remained durable. When the interface is expressed declaratively and cleanly bound to state, systems become easier to modify, test, and scale as both requirements and teams grow.

5.4 Prompt Engineering

The structured interaction model that was built into INTELLIFM anticipated a concept that has since become central to modern AI: prompt engineering. In INTELLIFM, prompts were not free-form questions. They were designed to guide users through complex filing workflows while capturing exactly the information the system needed. Specificity, sequencing, and structure determined whether users completed filings accurately or abandoned them in frustration.

Modern prompt engineering for LLMs rests on the same core insight: the way a request is framed shapes the response. A vague prompt often produces a vague output. A well-constructed prompt that establishes context, states constraints, and clarifies the expected form of the answer tends to produce better results. The guiding principle behind my original architecture and design of INTELLIFM mirrors that of today's prompt engineering: specify intent clearly and let the system determine the steps to produce the desired result. The critical difference, however, is that declarative systems like INTELLIFM produce deterministic, reproducible outputs: the same inputs yield the same results. LLM prompts, by contrast, produce probabilistic outputs that can vary across invocations. But the distinction goes beyond reproducibility to transparency. INTELLIFM operates as a *white-box* system in which every decision is traceable to its underlying rules. Modern LLMs, by contrast, function as *black-box* models whose internal reasoning is often opaque, making them difficult to audit in regulated environments where explaining the "why" is as important as the "what."

INTELLIFM also had a practical, pre-LLM version of "structured inputs." In the late 1990s, high-volume forms were often created by scanning paper documents and converting them to PDF, with fields tagged using the available tooling. Those identifiers connected the guided Q&A flow to specific form fields, allowing the system to collect data once and apply it consistently across forms and jurisdictions. That workflow reinforced a broader design lesson: when inputs are structured and validated early, downstream automation becomes more reliable.

5.4.1 T Prompts and Q Prompts

In designing INTELLIFM, I categorized prompts into two levels. Transaction-level prompts, prefixed with **T**, captured the user's high-level intent: the type of filing being initiated and the desired outcome. These prompts were form independent and established context before any detailed data entry began.

Form-level prompts, prefixed with **Q**, were specific to the selected transaction type. Based on responses to T prompts, the system determined which Q prompts to present next. Responses to Q prompts populated form fields and triggered the execution of transactions.

This hierarchy served several purposes. It preserved logical sequencing, removed irrelevant questions, and separated intent from implementation: users expressed what they wanted to accomplish, and INTELLIFM handled the procedural work of gathering the correct information in the proper order. The design also supported change. When regulatory requirements changed, we updated prompt definitions rather than rewriting processing logic. This separation of "what to ask" from "how to process answers" was a direct application of declarative principles.

5.4.2 Case Study: Example Automation Inc.

Consider a practical scenario. Example Automation Inc., a fictitious company operating primarily in New York, decides to expand into additional states. In this context, New York is the company's domestic jurisdiction, where it currently operates and complies with state-specific business requirements. Its jurisdiction of incorporation may differ. For example, it might be legally formed in Delaware.

Each state requires a foreign qualification, meaning the company must register formally with that state's authority to conduct business there. Because each state constitutes a separate legal jurisdiction, expanding beyond New York requires the company to file the necessary paperwork and pay the applicable fees with the appropriate state authority (typically the Secretary of State's office). Completing these filings helps the company comply with local requirements, including tax registrations, licensing rules, and other regulatory obligations.

Using CTAdvantage.com, an Example Automation representative begins by responding to T prompts, selecting "Foreign Qualification" as the transaction type on the user interface. The system then presents the applicable Q prompts: entity name, jurisdiction of incorporation, incorporation date, duration, fiscal year-end, and employer identification number. The interface adapts to the selected states because different states require different information.

In practice, the user experience follows a guided sequence. The session typically begins by collecting core entity information, then confirms service details, and finally presents a jurisdiction selection step in which the user selects the states in which the company intends to qualify. As different states are selected, the system dynamically adjusts the questions it asks so that the user sees only those that apply to the selected combination of transaction and jurisdictions. Depending on the states selected, the workflow may also prompt for registered agent representation details required in many jurisdictions.

Internally, that guided flow is driven by the T prompt that establishes intent. The system then assembles and orders the corresponding Q prompt set for the selected transaction and states. Listing 5-1 illustrates the underlying logic.

Listing 5-1. Declarative transaction processing in INTELLIFM (pseudocode).

```
function get_required_prompts(transaction_type):
  if transaction_type == "foreign_qualification":
    return [
      Q_prompt_entity_name,
      Q_prompt_juris_of_incorporation,
      Q_prompt_incorporation_date,
      Q_prompt_duration,
      Q_prompt_fiscal_year_end,
      Q_prompt_employer_id
    ]
  else:
    return []

function process_filing():
  transaction_type = get_user_input("Select transaction type")
  prompts = get_required_prompts(transaction_type)
  answers = []
  for prompt in prompts:
    answers.append(get_user_input(prompt))

  return submit_filing(transaction_type, answers)
```

This pseudocode illustrates how INTELLIFM guided users through regulatory filings using a two-level prompt structure.

First, the system asks the user to select a transaction type, which INTELLIFM treats as a T prompt. In this example, the user selects "foreign_qualification," a filing required when a company wants to do business in a state other than its state of incorporation.

Once the transaction type is selected, the system looks up the corresponding list of questions, known as Q prompts, as shown in Listing 5-1. It then presents each question sequentially, collects the responses, and submits the completed filing.

The insight is that the questions are defined declaratively, as data the system retrieves based on the transaction type, rather than being embedded in procedural code. This separation makes it straightforward to add new transaction types or modify existing ones without rewriting the underlying engine. Domain experts can update the rules, whereas engineers maintain the engine that executes them.

5.4.3 Connection to Modern AI

INTELLIFM operated in a constrained domain: regulatory workflows with defined fields, predictable dependencies, and clear completion criteria. Modern prompt engineering operates in open-ended domains, guiding models to draft text, analyze documents, write code, or answer questions across a broad range of topics. Even in an open-ended setting, effective prompts often follow a familiar structure. They set the context, specify constraints and required fields, and define what an acceptable output looks like.

Research has reinforced the practical value of structured prompting, including approaches that encourage stepwise reasoning on multistep tasks. The lesson is not that every system should expose lengthy reasoning, but that prompting can steer a model toward more careful, staged work when tasks require it.

A notable example is chain-of-thought (CoT) prompting, introduced by Google researchers in 2022.[10] This technique improved the ability of LLMs to solve multistep reasoning tasks by prompting them to generate intermediate steps. In a related discovery, Kojima and colleagues found that simply appending the phrase “Let’s think step by step” to a prompt improved model performance on complex tasks, even without providing examples. They showed that this simple cue can improve performance on multistep reasoning tasks by nudging the model toward a more structured approach—a technique now known as zero-shot CoT prompting.[11]

Prompt engineering is declarative at its core. Users state the goal, constraints, and desired form of the result without dictating the internal procedure for producing it. When the prompt is well constructed, results often improve dramatically—just as well-designed T and Q prompts improved accuracy and completion rates in INTELLIFM. (For a short example of code that illustrates this approach, see Appendix 7.)

5.4.4 Reliability, Ethics, and Limits

Prompt engineering can shape behavior but does not remove responsibility for validation, particularly in high-stakes domains such as compliance, legal work, finance, and security. Thoughtful prompts can reduce risk by requiring citations when

---

[10] Jason Wei et al., “Chain-of-Thought Prompting Elicits Reasoning in Large Language Models,” in *Advances in Neural Information Processing Systems 35 (NeurIPS 2022)*, `https://arxiv.org/abs/2201.11903`.

[11] Takeshi Kojima et al., “Large Language Models are Zero-Shot Reasoners,” in *Advances in Neural Information Processing Systems 35 (NeurIPS 2022)*, `https://arxiv.org/abs/2205.11916`.

appropriate, constraining outputs to approved templates, and requiring fact checks. They can also improve consistency by specifying neutral language, inclusive framing, and explicit decision criteria.

Effective prompt design must anticipate unreliable outputs and adversarial inputs. Consequently, modern architectures supplement optimized prompts with guardrails, including grounded context, output validation, and clear escalation paths for low-confidence results.

Seen in this light, the lesson from INTELLIFM remains practical: invest in prompt design, separate intent from execution, and build systems where the "what" can be developed independently of the "how."

5.5 Summary

As we reflect on the goals and applications of declarative programming, Alan Kay's insight resonates: "Simple things should be simple, complex things should be possible."[12] Kay developed this principle at Xerox PARC while building Smalltalk and GUIs. His goal was to make computing accessible to children, yet powerful enough for sophisticated applications. This philosophy encapsulates the essence of declarative programming and its impact on software development.

This chapter traced declarative programming from a design philosophy to a working architecture. In INTELLIFM, declarative principles solved a practical problem: keeping a complex filing system maintainable as regulations changed constantly, even though the people who understood those regulations were not programmers. The solution was to distinguish what the system should do from how it should do it—capturing intent in rules that domain experts could read and modify, while keeping the execution logic stable beneath the surface.

That distinction shaped every layer of the system. Prolog let us encode compliance logic as facts and rules rather than procedural steps. The COM-based architecture organized functionality into modular components with well-defined interfaces. The dynamically generated user interface adapted to user input and regulatory context

[12] Alan Kay, quoted in Bo Leuf and Ward Cunningham, *The Wiki Way: Quick Collaboration on the Web* (Boston: Addison-Wesley, 2001). For Kay's account of the quote's origin, see `https://www.quora.com/What-is-the-story-behind-Alan-Kay-s-adage-Simple-things-should-be-simple-complex-things-should-be-possible`

without hard-coded behavior. And the T and Q prompt hierarchy guided users through complex workflows by expressing transaction logic declaratively, long before prompt engineering became a term of art.

The same principles appeared later in technologies I encountered at Microsoft—WPF and XAML, two-way data binding, and the MVVM pattern—and have since spread across the industry. JavaScript frameworks such as React, Angular, and Vue adopted related ideas: declarative user interface definitions, reactive updates, and component hierarchies that keep presentation distinct from application logic. The convergence is not coincidental. Developers facing similar problems on different platforms arrived at similar solutions. Declarative thinking scales—not just within a single system, but across an industry.

What made these approaches succeed was not abstraction for its own sake. It was the practical benefit of letting different specialists contribute through different interfaces: compliance officers updating rules, designers shaping interfaces, and engineers building infrastructure. Each group worked in terms they understood, and the system integrated their contributions cleanly because the boundaries were well defined.

The next chapter explores how these principles apply to business process improvement—how organizations can structure workflows, define goals declaratively, and build systems that adapt to emerging requirements.

CHAPTER 6

Business Process Efficiency

In the late 1990s, business process efficiency was not an abstract goal. It was the difference between a system that could keep pace with regulatory change and one that could not. Compliance officers at Wolters Kluwer—the domain experts who owned the filing rules—faced thousands of filings across dozens of jurisdictions, each with different requirements and deadlines. Manual processes resulted in errors, delays, and customer frustration. The challenge was not just technical; it was operational.

I also learned something broader. Efficiency in software systems requires the same discipline that the best-run operations have long applied to complex work—eliminate waste, standardize where possible, and build flexibility into the process so that change does not require rebuilding from scratch. In practice, this is never just a technology problem. It is a balance of people, process, and systems working together under operational constraints.

The principles that guided INTELLIFM run throughout this chapter. Designing for constraints meant working within enterprise realities: legacy databases, domain experts who were not programmers, and regulations that changed faster than release cycles. Building trust required transparent, human-readable rules that users could inspect. Progressive disclosure let experts start with simple rules and expand them over time. Preserving human judgment kept experts responsible for decisions where experience mattered.

This chapter examines business process efficiency through the same lens. It first explains the benefits efficient processes deliver and then outlines practical strategies—lean methods, automation, and technology integration—illustrated through examples from Toyota, Amazon, and McDonald's. It then connects these ideas to collaborative software development and the software development life cycle (SDLC). Finally, it returns to INTELLIFM as a case study in applying these principles to AI-driven automation and to the platforms that followed.

K. C. Mukherjee, *The Microsoft AI Insider's Playbook*, https://doi.org/10.1007/979-8-8688-2730-3_6

6.1 Benefits of Efficiency

The benefits of business process efficiency extend well beyond cost reduction. When my teams built SaaS applications based on INTELLIFM technology, the immediate goal was faster, more accurate filings. But the deeper benefits became clearer over time: a system that could adapt to regulatory change, scale across jurisdictions, and free domain experts to focus on judgment rather than repetitive data entry. Organizations that invest seriously in process discipline see the same pattern. They use resources more effectively, reduce waste, respond more quickly to change, enhance quality, strengthen customer experience, improve financial outcomes, and reduce compliance risk.

The principle I mentioned in Chapter 1—*waste not, want not*—was not merely a childhood lesson. It became a design philosophy. In Kolkata, I watched my mother run our household with a precision that I only later recognized as operational excellence. Food was prepared in measured portions. Clothes were maintained, mended, and passed along. Nothing was discarded that could serve another purpose; nothing was purchased that duplicated what already worked. Resources were allocated with deliberation, and thoughtfulness was treated as a virtue.

That upbringing shaped how I approached system design decades later. When I architected INTELLIFM and other enterprise systems, I instinctively resisted bloated processes, redundant data entry, and workflows that consumed effort without delivering value. A household rule—use what you have fully before acquiring more—translated naturally into software architecture. Reuse components instead of rebuilding them, remove redundant steps, and design systems that deliver more output with less operational overhead.

Efficiency was not merely a performance metric; it was an expression of respect—respect for the users' time, for the organization's resources, and for the craft itself. Compliance officers should not have to enter the same data twice. A system should not demand more infrastructure than the workload justifies. Each unnecessary step is, in a small way, a choice to waste someone's attention. That conviction, absorbed long before I wrote my first line of code, has guided the systems I have built.

> **Effective Use of Resources:** Efficiency begins with deploying human time, expertise, financial investment, and materials to maximize value. In manufacturing, just-in-time approaches reduce excess inventory by coordinating supply with demand. In product organizations, structured time for exploration can be

a deliberate investment in innovation. 3M, for example, is often associated with the "15% rule," which gives employees dedicated time to pursue ideas outside their core responsibilities.[1] In retail, rapid prototyping and smaller production runs can reduce overproduction by aligning output more closely with demand signals. In INTELLIFM, resource efficiency meant that compliance officers could define rules once and apply them across multiple forms and jurisdictions, rather than re-entering the same information for each filing. Strategic resource deployment increases throughput while minimizing avoidable costs.

Waste and Redundancy Elimination: Inefficiency often hides in plain sight. Duplicated work, unnecessary handoffs, and repeated data entry all consume time without improving outcomes. Logistics operations reduce waste by optimizing movement and minimizing unnecessary handling. Large retailers have used cross-docking—moving products directly from receiving to shipping docks—to reduce storage time, handling costs, and inventory carrying expense. The broader point is that reducing unnecessary handling and dwell time often produces outsized efficiency gains.

Enhanced Agility: Well-designed processes make organizations more responsive to change. When workflows are clear, modular, and measurable, teams can adjust quickly to new requirements, fluctuating demand, and changing regulations. Digital businesses use iterative delivery to test, learn, and adjust offerings based on customer behavior. INTELLIFM was designed to be responsive from the start. Because business rules were stored in a knowledge base separate from the application code, regulatory changes could be handled by updating the rules rather than rebuilding the system. That separation made fast response feasible in a domain where requirements shifted frequently.

[1] 3M's "15% rule" has been widely documented in business and innovation literature. See, for example, Kevin Oakes, "Culture Renovation Spotlight: 3M," Institute for Corporate Productivity (i4cp), February 25, 2021, `https://www.i4cp.com/productivity-blog/culture-renovation-spotlight-3m`.

Quality and Consistency: Efficiency and quality reinforce each other. Standardized steps, validation checks, and thoughtful automation reduce variation and prevent avoidable errors. In INTELLIFM, quality meant accurate filings—fields populated correctly, jurisdictional requirements satisfied, and exceptions handled predictably. The system supported this with validation rules that caught common errors early and with transparent, human-readable rules that compliance officers could review and trust. Consistency strengthens credibility and reduces rework.

Customer Satisfaction: Streamlined processes reduce lead times, improve reliability, and increase transparency—qualities customers notice immediately. In consumer services, tracking a task from initiation to completion has become standard to build trust through visibility. For filing services specifically, first-time accuracy is critical. INTELLIFM enhanced the customer experience by reducing turnaround times and minimizing the errors that previously led to rejections, delays, or costly corrections. When the initial submission is correct, customers achieve faster outcomes, and the organization eliminates unnecessary rework cycles.

Financial Performance: Efficiency improves financial performance by reducing operational friction and increasing output per unit of effort. Companies that standardize processes and remove waste often reduce costs and improve margins, freeing resources for new initiatives and growth. Procter & Gamble, for example, describes productivity programs that delivered two $10 billion savings efforts and sets annual cost-of-goods savings objectives of up to $1.5 billion.[2] Southwest Airlines is often cited for turnaround discipline—typically 35 minutes or less, compared with the industry average of around 45 minutes—

[2] "Productivity in All We Do," Procter & Gamble 2023 Annual Report, https://us.pg.com/annualreport2023/productivity-in-all-we-do/; "Fueled by Productivity," Procter & Gamble 2024 Annual Report, https://us.pg.com/annualreport2024/fueled-by-productivity/.

which supports higher aircraft utilization.[3] INTELLIFM delivered practical financial benefits through fewer labor hours spent on repetitive filings, fewer penalties tied to missed deadlines, and lower error correction effort. The larger financial benefit, however, was scalability: growing volumes did not require staffing increases in lockstep.

Risk Mitigation and Compliance: In regulated domains, efficient processes reduce risk by making compliance repeatable and auditable. Standardized controls, consistent validation, and clear accountability reduce the odds of errors that trigger penalties or reputational harm. In medical device manufacturing, the FDA's Voluntary Improvement Program illustrates this principle by using qualified third-party appraisals to assess capability and performance and to promote improvement beyond baseline compliance.[4] Johnson & Johnson MedTech, for example, has described its participation in the program as strengthening alignment with industry standards and best practices while advancing more predictive processes and capabilities that improve device quality and safety.[5] In financial services, large institutions have also reported using ML approaches for transaction monitoring and fraud detection, and senior leaders have publicly linked major AI investments to measurable

[3] "Maximum Velocity," Duke Corporate Education, June 1, 2024, https://www.dukece.com/insights/maximum-velocity/.

[4] US Food and Drug Administration, "Voluntary Improvement Program," updated September 14, 2023, https://www.fda.gov/medical-devices/quality-and-compliance-medical-devices/voluntary-improvement-program; US Food and Drug Administration, *Fostering Medical Device Improvement: FDA Activities and Engagement with the Voluntary Improvement Program: Guidance for Industry and Food and Drug Administration Staff* (September 15, 2023), https://www.fda.gov/media/158180/download/.

[5] MassDevice, "Johnson & Johnson MedTech's participation in the Voluntary Improvement Program, supported by FDA," November 21, 2024, https://www.massdevice.com/johnson-johnson-medtechs-participation-in-the-voluntary-improvement-program-supported-by-fda.

operational benefits.[6] INTELLIFM embedded compliance into the workflow itself: jurisdictional requirements were expressed as rules and validations, audit trails recorded actions and decisions, and the rule base remained readable and updatable by domain experts without requiring programmer involvement. Consequently, compliance officers could verify that system behavior matched policy. In an environment where mistakes carry legal consequences, predictable execution and transparency are central to operational efficiency.

Continuous Improvement: Efficiency is not a one-time project. It is a discipline of measuring outcomes, identifying friction, and refining processes over time. INTELLIFM demonstrated this through iteration: domain experts refined rules as regulations and edge cases evolved, and engineers improved the execution machinery without destabilizing the rule base. Over time, the system became more capable not by adding complexity everywhere, but by strengthening the structure that absorbed change safely.

These benefits reinforce one another. Better resource use reduces costs and frees capacity. Less redundancy improves quality and speed. Agility supports customer satisfaction and resilience. Strong compliance reduces risk; continuous improvement sustains the gains. The examples span many industries, but the underlying principles remain consistent. In fact, the same principles that guided INTELLIFM continue to shape how my teams and I think about system design.

Although these benefits are real, they must be demonstrated to sustain organizational commitment. The next section examines how to quantify efficiency gains in terms that stakeholders recognize and trust.

[6] J.P. Morgan, "AI Boosting Payments Efficiency & Cutting Fraud," November 20, 2023, https://www.jpmorgan.com/insights/payments/security-trust/ai-payments-efficiency-fraud-reduction.

6.2 Quantifying Efficiency Gains

Efficiency improvements must be measured to be sustained. Without quantification, gains remain anecdotal, and the rationale for continued investment weakens over time. I learned this early in my career. When my teams could demonstrate concrete results, support followed. When we relied solely on enthusiasm, budgets tightened. Measurement also imposes a useful discipline: it forces teams to define what "efficiency" means for a specific operation, thereby exposing differing assumptions among stakeholders. To keep the discussion precise, I distinguish between two metrics:

- **Internal Effort (Labor Hours):** Total person-hours staff spend preparing, submitting, and following up
- **End-to-End Cycle Time (Calendar Time):** Elapsed time from kickoff to approvals, including regulator review and external delays

6.2.1 Baseline: Manual Workflow

In the late 1990s, compliance teams struggled with multijurisdictional filings that were almost entirely manual. These filings included insurance producer licensing transactions (such as initial licenses, amendments, and terminations) and entity life-cycle filings (such as incorporations and foreign qualifications). When nationwide coverage was required, a 51-jurisdiction effort meant preparing each jurisdiction's forms individually. Every state and the District of Columbia maintained its own requirements, fee schedules, and procedural rules. Many jurisdictions required wet signatures, notarization, or physical corporate seals. Preparing complete filing packets typically required one to two weeks on the calendar, and physical mailing added two to five days, depending on the service used. Review times varied widely. Some jurisdictions processed filings within three to seven days, others required one to three weeks, and jurisdictions with backlogs could take six weeks or more. Follow-up occurred by phone and fax, and corrections or supplemental materials introduced additional delays.

The manual era was defined by physical bottlenecks that extended beyond data entry. Before digital government portals became common, firms maintained physical libraries of jurisdiction-specific forms or requested them by mail, adding lead time before preparation even began. Because there was no digital validation, a single typographical error could require recreating an entire document from scratch. Many jurisdictions prohibited the use of correction fluid on official filings. Logistics added more overhead: preparing separate envelopes for each jurisdiction, handling postage, and tracking certified mail receipts. Under favorable conditions, a full multijurisdictional filing cycle commonly required three to six weeks from kickoff to approvals. When comments, fee issues, or repeat mailings occurred, delays of six to eight weeks or more were not unusual.

Although preparation often spanned one to two weeks on the calendar, the effort was distributed across that period. What appeared to be "one to two weeks" typically involved several people working in parallel, along with time spent on mailing, tracking, and corrective submissions. In person-hours, preparation, mailing logistics, and follow-up typically totaled 100–165 hours of manual work for a single filing type—such as an insurance producer license, appointment, or corporate qualification—submitted across all 51 US jurisdictions. This estimate is based on my direct experience managing these deployments at Wolters Kluwer.

Those figures align when the staffing assumption is made explicit. A standard workweek is approximately 40 hours per person. If two staff members worked in parallel during the preparation window, one to two weeks corresponds to about 80–160 person-hours (2 people × 40 hours per week × 1–2 weeks). When time for follow-up, corrections, and approval tracking is included, the total typically falls within the 100–165-hour range.

Organizations also maintained a standing state-filings function, often two to four full-time roles, supplemented by paralegals, administrative personnel, or outside counsel for complex jurisdictions. That staffing level reflected the broader workload, not a single filing. Teams typically handled multiple concurrent filings, renewals, regulatory inquiries, recordkeeping, and exception cases across jurisdictions.

6.2.2 Quantified Baseline

The labor burden reflected this complexity. The figures that follow use insurance producer licensing as a representative filing type. While hour ranges vary across filing categories—appointments, corporate qualifications, and entity life-cycle transactions among them—the underlying pattern of effort distribution is broadly consistent across the workflows INTELLIFM was designed to automate. As noted, a single 51-jurisdiction filing required approximately 100–165 hours of manual work, distributed approximately as follows:

- 40–60 hours for form preparation
- 10–15 hours for fee calculations and check processing

- 20–30 hours for copying, assembly, and mailing
- 20–40 hours for follow-ups and corrections
- 10–20 hours for tracking approvals and renewals

These ranges reflect my direct operational experience at Wolters Kluwer. They represent an experience-based estimate rather than an externally validated industry benchmark; actual effort will vary by deployment. At a representative fully loaded cost of $60–$90 per hour, covering base salary, benefits, and corporate overhead for compliance and legal support staff in the late 1990s, direct labor costs ranged from $6,000 to $14,850 per filing. The inefficiency was obvious during filing season. Paper piled up, phones rang nonstop, and fax machines ran all day. Seasoned professionals spent their time on repetitive, error-prone, draining work.

6.2.3 After Automation

Automation changed the workflow by separating rules and data from manual assembly. Using the INTELLIFM technology my teams built for CTAdvantage.com and other applications, the system automatically populated forms, applied jurisdiction-specific rules, calculated fees, and produced consistent filing packages without having to recreate documents from scratch each time requirements changed. Electronic submission and payment replaced much of the mailing-and-tracking overhead. As with the baseline, internal effort and end-to-end cycle time must be kept distinct.

With automation, internal preparation and submission time for a 51-jurisdiction filing commonly fell to three to seven hours of total manual effort (person-hours), distributed roughly as follows:

- One to two hours for automated form population and validation
- Less than one hour each for fee calculation, payment, and submission steps
- One to three hours for limited follow-up and exception handling

This three- to seven-hour figure represents the total human time required, since most of the work is performed by the system. The remaining effort concentrates on review and exceptions.

Using the same fully loaded hourly rate assumption as the baseline ($60–$90 per hour), three to seven hours corresponds to a direct labor cost of approximately $180–$630 per filing. At the low end, 3 hours × $60 = $180; at the high end, 7 hours × $90 = $630. Compared with the manual baseline ($6,000–$14,850 per filing), direct labor savings are approximately $5,820–$14,220 per filing when the low- and high-end assumptions are consistently paired. At the low end, $6,000 – $180 = $5,820; at the high end, $14,850 – $630 = $14,220. Actual savings vary with filing complexity, exception volume, and staffing configuration.

Automation compresses the portion of the process that an organization controls: preparation and submission. It does not eliminate regulator review time, which remains jurisdiction-specific and seasonal. Even so, internal preparation and submission timelines—excluding regulatory review—can shrink from multiple weeks to one to three days because packets no longer wait for printing, mailing, and manual follow-up. Fewer preventable errors can also reduce the number of correction cycles, further shortening end-to-end timelines.

Beyond direct labor savings, the scalability of automated systems represents a profound expansion in organizational capacity. By digitizing workflows, firms can handle much higher volumes of complex filings without increasing headcount. Large firms can realize substantial annual savings. Based on internal project experience and retrospective analysis across client deployments, payback periods were typically measured in months rather than years. The return on investment (ROI) varies by scope and should be modeled per client. In the deployments I oversaw at Wolters Kluwer, staffing requirements fell by an estimated 50–80%. In several client deployments I observed directly, organizations that adopted automation at scale were able to manage comparable filing volumes with a single part-time role rather than a dedicated team.

Filing timelines have compressed significantly as the broader modernization of insurance filing has advanced across related but distinct regulatory workflows. Rate and form filings involve a different submission context from the producer licensing and entity qualification filings quantified above. In this area, insurers can now file electronically through the System for Electronic Rate and Form Filing (SERFF), using standardized transmittal tools and review checklists that reduce administrative friction and shorten the time between preparation and submission.[7]

[7] SERFF, "About the Systems for Electronic Rates & Forms Filing (SERFF)," `https://www.serff.com/`.

Some regulators and coordinated review programs also offer expedited pathways. For example, the Interstate Insurance Product Regulation Commission expedited process states that the initial primary form review will be completed within five business days of the filing being marked Ready for Expedited Primary Review.[8] It states an average turnaround time of 30 review days or fewer, depending on the quality of the filing and the reviewer's responsiveness. Even with electronic submission, end-to-end timelines vary by jurisdiction, workload, and seasonal peaks. Therefore, nationwide initiatives must account for the slowest reviewing authority and objection cycles when they occur.

Further, automation changes capacity planning. The statement that organizations often staffed the state-filings function at two to four full-time roles describes the broader, ongoing workload in the manual era: multiple filings, renewals, regulator communications, recordkeeping, and complex edge cases. With automated workflows, many organizations can handle comparable volumes with fewer dedicated roles because form preparation, fee computation, assembly, and tracking no longer consume most of the week.

Yet effort does not disappear; it shifts upward. Time previously spent on clerical production moves toward review, exception handling, monitoring rule updates, and interpreting regulatory changes. The same professionals who once spent their days copying, collating, and tracking paperwork became strategic contributors, adding genuine value to their employers. This transition—from clerical execution to professional judgment—was one of the most rewarding outcomes of our work. INTELLIFM did not eliminate jobs—it raised the level of the work.

Quantification made these gains visible and supported continued investment. When I could demonstrate that a process requiring weeks of labor and thousands of dollars could be completed in hours at a fraction of the cost, the business case was self-evident. Automated validation also reduced errors before submission, lowering rework and decreasing the likelihood of rejected filings. These automation gains translated directly into faster completion and reduced operational risk. The numbers told a story that no amount of narrative could match.

---

[8] Interstate Insurance Product Regulation Commission, "Instructions for Using Expedited Review Process," revised March 22, 2022, `https://www.insurancecompact.org/sites/default/files/2022-11/insurer_resources_erp_instructions.pdf`.

6.2.4 How to Quantify and Sustain Gains

Effective quantification begins with a baseline. Before any efficiency initiative, teams should document the duration of current processes, the frequency of errors, and the resources they consume. Without a baseline, improvement cannot be demonstrated, only asserted. I have seen projects lose executive support when enthusiasm was not backed by evidence. A project I reviewed reported transformational results but lacked preimplementation metrics. When leadership asked for proof, the team had none. The project was defunded within a year, despite genuine improvements that simply could not be documented.

Metrics should align with business outcomes. Processing time matters when faster processing delivers value, whether by reducing labor costs, improving customer responsiveness, or increasing throughput with a fixed headcount. Faster filing timelines also shorten time to market, enabling organizations to expand operations into new states in days rather than months.

Error rates also matter, but their impact varies. A typographical error in an internal document is not comparable to a compliance error that triggers regulatory scrutiny or a missed filing deadline that carries penalties. Beyond late fees, risk includes preserving good standing, as a missed filing can jeopardize major corporate transactions or credit facilities. Effective measurement distinguishes between what is easy to capture and what reflects meaningful business impact.

Efficiency gains redistribute effort rather than remove it. Automation may reduce data entry time while increasing time spent on review or exception handling. If measurement captures only one side of the change, reported gains will be misleading. Complete measurement accounts for where effort moves, not only where it declines. At Wolters Kluwer, we tracked not only the time saved on form preparation but also the time compliance officers spent reviewing system outputs and handling exceptions. The net savings were substantial but smaller than gross savings on data entry alone. Honest measurement builds credibility; exaggerated claims erode it.

Sustaining efficiency requires ongoing measurement, not only project-phase reporting. Gains can erode as processes drift, systems age, and workarounds accumulate. In AI systems such as INTELLIFM, the core application code may remain stable while external requirements change, including state fee schedules and filing rules. That drift requires periodic updates to the rule logic to keep the automation aligned with current law. When rule logic lags behind changing requirements, exceptions rise, and manual work returns.

Organizations that measure only during implementation miss the gradual degradation that follows. Periodic reassessment, quarterly or annually, depending on the process, identifies when interventions are needed to preserve earlier improvements. I have made it a practice to revisit efficiency metrics long after the initial excitement has faded. The results are often sobering but always valuable.

Finally, quantification strengthens communication. Executives, finance teams, and stakeholders outside the immediate project need evidence expressed in terms they recognize: cost savings, time reductions, capacity increases, and risk mitigation. A well-constructed efficiency case translates operational metrics into business language, making value visible to those who allocate resources. Quantification is not bureaucratic overhead. It is the foundation for sustaining efficiency as an organizational capability, and the discipline I developed while measuring INTELLIFM's impact has informed the initiatives I have led since.

6.3 Strategies for Improving Efficiency

Achieving business process efficiency requires more than good intentions. It demands a clear understanding of how work actually flows, where friction accumulates, and which interventions will produce lasting results rather than temporary fixes. The strategies that mattered most to INTELLIFM were the same as those found in any serious efficiency effort. They included mapping and analyzing processes, selectively applying automation, adopting declarative approaches that separate intent from implementation, standardizing where consistency matters, and building a culture of continuous improvement. These strategies reinforce one another. They succeed only when the workforce is equipped and empowered to carry them forward.

6.3.1 Process Mapping and Analysis

Efficiency begins with understanding. Before improving a process, you must see where work originates, how it moves between people and systems, where delays accumulate, and where errors tend to occur. Process mapping makes workflow patterns visible. It turns undocumented know-how into a shared model that teams can test, challenge, and improve.

Before INTELLIFM, no one in filing operations had a complete understanding of how a multijurisdictional filing actually worked. Requirements varied by state. Forms overlapped but were not identical. Compliance officers carried much of the process knowledge in their heads. Mapping the workflow revealed redundancies—data entered multiple times, handoffs that introduced delays, and validation steps that happened too late to prevent errors. That visibility made improvement possible.

The same principle applies broadly. Logistics companies reduce wasted motion by studying how goods actually move. Manufacturing operations use value stream mapping to identify bottlenecks and excessive handoffs. Financial institutions analyze transaction flows to find steps that consume time without adding value. The tools vary, but the method is consistent: make the invisible visible, and then address what you find.

Amazon's fulfillment operations illustrate process mapping at scale. Workflow analysis highlighted how much time workers spent walking to retrieve items. That insight motivated investments in robotics and warehouse redesign, including the 2012 acquisition of Kiva Systems. The Kiva robots bring inventory shelves directly to workers at packing stations, eliminating the need for employees to walk the warehouse floor hunting for items. The transformation demonstrates how systematic workflow analysis can identify inefficiencies that appear inevitable until they are measured and addressed.[9]

6.3.2 Automation and Technology Integration

Automation and technology integration can be effective catalysts for change, but their application must be tailored to the domain and to customer expectations. Implementing automation is not just about removing manual tasks. When applied appropriately, it introduces new levels of productivity, precision, and consistency. When applied blindly, it can damage experience, trust, and even brand identity.

The goal is not to automate everything—it is to automate the right things. Routine, repetitive tasks with clear rules are good candidates. Tasks requiring judgment, nuance, or human relationships are not. In manufacturing, automation can raise consistency and catch defects earlier. In customer-facing domains, the balance is more delicate: some organizations use kiosks and self-service tools to reduce wait times and improve throughput, while premium services deliberately preserve human touchpoints because the relationship is part of the product. The same tension appears in digital experiences: algorithmic recommendations work well for casual discovery, but live performance and human creativity remain valuable precisely because they are not automated.

[9] Victor Luckerson, "Amazon's New Robots Are Shipping Your Order This Holiday," TIME, December 1, 2014, https://time.com/3605924/amazon-robots/.

INTELLIFM reflected that balance. It automated form population, validation, and document generation—work that was repetitive, rule-governed, and error-prone when performed manually. But it preserved human judgment where it mattered: compliance officers defined the rules, reviewed exceptions, and approved filings. The automation handled volume; the experts handled decisions.

This pattern recurs across industries. Financial institutions use automated systems for routine inquiries while routing complex cases to specialists. Operations teams deploy workflow tools to accelerate standard requests while keeping escalation paths for edge cases and sensitive situations. When deploying ERP systems, workflow automation tools, or CRM platforms, the question is not whether to automate, but what to automate and what must remain in human hands.

6.3.3 Declarative Approaches

As discussed in Chapter 5, declarative programming focuses on outcomes rather than step-by-step procedures. The same principle extends naturally to business process design. A declarative process definition describes what must be achieved and the constraints that must be respected, without hard-coding every procedural pathway. Declarative definitions make processes easier to understand, modify, and align with business goals.

Consider customer onboarding. A procedural design often hardwires today's verification sequence into the workflow. A declarative design can express the intent more clearly: "verify customer identity and create an account." That description remains stable even as verification methods improve and regulations change. The organization can adopt new tools, swap steps, or introduce additional checks without redefining the business objective.

INTELLIFM embodied the same separation. Compliance officers authored filing rules in structured English, specifying what the system should do. Engineers built the inference engine and execution machinery, determining how the system would do it. This separation made the platform adaptable. When regulations changed, the rules changed; the application code remained stable. It also improved collaboration because process definitions were readable to those who understood the domain best.

Adopting declarative approaches is not without challenges. Teams accustomed to procedural methods may resist the adoption. Transitioning existing processes requires training, tooling, and careful change management. But the payoff—flexibility, transparency, and maintainability—often justifies the investment, especially in domains where requirements change faster than software release cycles.

6.3.4 Standardization and Best Practices

Standardization creates consistency, and consistency drives efficiency. Clear protocols make outcomes predictable, training simpler, and errors easier to detect and correct. In regulated industries, standardization is mandatory. But even outside regulation, it reduces variation and frees teams to focus on work that requires judgment rather than reinventing routine procedures.

An important nuance exists: standardization does not have to suppress creativity. When implemented thoughtfully, it supports it. By reducing the burden of repetitive tasks and aligning teams around common expectations, standardized processes create the stability that makes experimentation possible. Organizations that execute well often standardize what must be repeatable while leaving room for creativity where it matters most.

Toyota is widely associated with disciplined standard work paired with continuous improvement. Microsoft standardizes its development pipelines through modern engineering practices to deliver reliably at scale, while also maintaining internal channels where teams can prototype ideas and test new approaches. These are not opposing forces. Discipline and creativity reinforce each other when the boundaries are clear.

Microsoft Garage exemplifies this balance. The program encourages employees to prototype experimental ideas outside their core responsibilities. FindTime, a meeting scheduler that helps users coordinate across organizations, originated with a six-person incubation team exploring ways to make calendaring more efficient. After validation through the Garage's experimental outlet, the tool attracted hundreds of thousands of users and was eventually adopted by the Outlook team as a mainstream product. The path from internal experiment to enterprise feature demonstrates how standardized development practices can coexist with structured experimentation.[10]

In INTELLIFM, standardization showed up in the structure of the knowledge base, the format of filing rules, and the validation protocols applied across jurisdictions. That standardization made the system reliable. At the same time, the system supported refinement. Compliance officers could update rules as regulations changed, and engineers could strengthen the execution machinery without destabilizing the rule base.

[10] "FindTime," Microsoft Garage Wall of Fame, accessed 2025, `https://www.microsoft.com/en-us/garage/wall-of-fame/findtime/`.

6.3.5 Continuous Improvement and Learning

Efficiency is not a destination. It requires ongoing attention—tracking results, uncovering obstacles, and refining how work gets done. Successful organizations build continuous improvement into their culture. They encourage teams to surface problems rather than hide them, to experiment with solutions, and to share what they learn. They treat process improvement as ongoing work, rather than a one-time project.

INTELLIFM incorporated this discipline from the start. Domain experts refined rules as regulations changed and edge cases emerged. Engineers improved performance, expanded validation, and extended the platform's reach. Over time, the system became more capable—not by adding complexity everywhere, but by strengthening the structure that allowed change to be absorbed safely.

6.3.6 People as the Foundation

At the core of any efficiency strategy lies an organization's most valuable asset: its people. Training is not an afterthought; it is an investment in the workforce that discovers inefficiencies, proposes improvements, and sustains new practices. When employees understand the goals, have the skills to contribute, and are trusted with autonomy, improvement becomes a shared discipline rather than a mandate.

In building INTELLIFM, the collaboration between compliance officers and engineers was not incidental—it was essential. Neither group could have built the system alone. The officers understood filing requirements; the engineers understood architecture and execution. The system succeeded because both groups contributed in their own language and because the design made those contributions composable over time.

The same lesson applies broadly. Efficiency strategies that ignore the people who execute them rarely hold. Those that invest in training, foster collaboration, and empower teams to identify and solve problems tend to produce lasting results—precisely because the improvements are owned by the people doing the work.

6.4 Task Agility and Collaboration

Agility and collaboration are closely linked. Agility without collaboration produces isolated speed—teams moving quickly in different directions. Collaboration without agility produces alignment that cannot adapt to changing conditions. Together, they enable organizations to respond to customer needs, adjust to market demands, and absorb disruption without losing coherence. This matters most in customer fulfillment, where expectations can change quickly and slight delays can cascade across the value chain.

Task agility is the ability to dynamically adjust workflows, resources, and processes in response to growing requirements. It goes beyond speed. It involves the capacity to recalibrate operations when circumstances demand it—rerouting work, reallocating resources, or revising priorities—without dismantling the underlying structure.

INTELLIFM was designed for task agility. The separation of business rules from application code—described in Section 6.1—meant the expert system could accommodate regulatory changes without reprogramming. When a jurisdiction updated its filing requirements, compliance officers updated the rules; the execution machinery remained stable.

This separation—supported by a Prolog-based AI inference engine and a component-based architecture—allowed the system to adapt quickly without destabilizing core behavior. Modern intelligent workflow platforms extend the same principle: they can redirect approvals when they detect exceptions or high-priority flags, scale resources in response to volume fluctuations, and adjust routing based on real-time conditions. The underlying insight is consistent—systems that separate intent from implementation can respond to change without rebuilding from scratch.

Collaboration is the disciplined practice of working across roles and boundaries with shared context, clear communication, and joint accountability, going beyond basic coordination. Effective collaboration embeds itself in how work is structured, fostering communication, knowledge sharing, and mutual accountability across boundaries. In practice, it dismantles barriers between people and knowledge domains so that decisions can be made with shared context rather than partial information.

In building INTELLIFM, collaboration between compliance officers and engineers was not a project management technique—it was fundamental to the architecture. The knowledge base served as a shared artifact that both groups could read and refine. Compliance officers contributed domain expertise; engineers contributed technical capability. Neither group dictated to the other. My colleagues developed the INTELLIFM applications using Microsoft technologies precisely because these tools were familiar to enterprise teams and supported the modular, collaborative development the project required. The system succeeded because collaboration was built into the design rather than layered on afterward.

The same principle applies broadly. Cross-functional teams that share context and vocabulary can identify problems earlier, surface better solutions, and execute with less friction. Collaboration platforms reduce communication overhead, but they do not replace the underlying discipline. Tools foster collaboration; culture sustains it.

Together, agility and collaboration drive responsive customer fulfillment. Organizations that can adapt quickly to customer needs—by adjusting offerings, reallocating resources, or speeding up delivery—build loyalty and strengthen their competitive position. Those that combine agility with cross-functional collaboration can move faster without sacrificing coherence.

This combination also improves operational efficiency. When teams share information in real time, errors are detected earlier and corrected more quickly. When workflows can adapt to demand signals, resources align with actual needs rather than forecasts that may no longer apply. Data-driven monitoring and predictive analytics can also surface potential disruptions earlier, giving teams time to reroute work before customers experience delays. The result is leaner operations, shorter lead times, and better use of capacity.

Volkswagen has invested in virtual collaboration technologies across its brands. Engineers, designers, and other professionals use AI-powered virtual twins to simulate, test, and refine vehicle development in collaborative virtual environments before physical production begins. The Volkswagen Digital Reality Hub connects virtual reality applications across Group brands and locations, facilitating cross-site collaboration on production and logistics planning.[11]

The value of agility and collaboration becomes most visible under stress. When conditions change suddenly due to regulatory changes, supply chain disruptions, or demand fluctuations, organizations with agile processes and collaborative cultures can adjust without paralysis. Those with rigid processes and siloed teams often struggle to respond in a timely manner.

[11] "Volkswagen Group Is Backing Virtual Reality Solutions for Interactive Collaboration in Production & Logistics," Volkswagen Group, July 5, 2017, `https://www.volkswagen-group.com/en/press-releases/volkswagen-group-is-backing-virtual-reality-solutions-for-interactive-collaboration-in-production-and-logistics-16361`; "Dassault Systèmes and Volkswagen Group Implement the 3DEXPERIENCE Platform to Optimize Vehicle Development," Dassault Systèmes, February 4, 2025, `https://www.3ds.com/newsroom/press-releases/dassault-systemes-and-volkswagen-group-implement-3dexperience-platform-optimize-vehicle-development`.

The coronavirus disease 2019 (COVID-19) pandemic made the value of agility and collaboration visible. Organizations that could share information quickly across suppliers, logistics, and operations adjusted more rapidly to disruptions, whereas those with rigid processes and siloed teams struggled to respond.

INTELLIFM had to face this test repeatedly. Regulatory requirements changed without warning. New jurisdictions came online with unfamiliar rules. Edge cases emerged that the original design had not anticipated. The system absorbed these changes because it was built for adaptation: rules could be updated, validation could be extended, and the knowledge base could grow without destabilizing the core. The people who operated the system—compliance officers and engineers working together—made those adaptations possible.

Agility and collaboration also encourage experimentation. When teams have latitude to experiment, share ideas across boundaries, and iterate quickly, new approaches emerge. Some organizations formalize this by dedicating time to exploration or by structured programs that invite external input. Others build it into how work is organized—short cycles, rapid feedback, and tolerance for learning through failure.

Google's "20% time" policy—introduced in the early 2000s—allowed employees to dedicate one day per week to projects of their own choosing. As cofounders Larry Page and Sergey Brin wrote in their 2004 initial public offering (IPO) letter, "We encourage our employees, in addition to their regular projects, to spend 20% of their time working on what they think will most benefit Google. This empowers them to be more creative and innovative." Products, including AdSense and Google News, emerged from this program. The policy has matured—by 2012, employees needed managerial approval—but its influence on corporate innovation practices endures.[12]

Procter & Gamble's "Connect + Develop" program, launched in 2001, engages external partners in collaborative innovation. The initiative has produced market-defining products: Swiffer Duster technology was licensed from Unicharm, and the adhesive technology behind Crest Whitestrips was licensed from Corium. By 2010, the program had met its goal of delivering 50% of the company's innovation through external collaboration.[13]

[12] Larry Page and Sergey Brin, "2004 Founders' IPO Letter," Alphabet Investor Relations, 2004, https://abc.xyz/investor/founders-letters/2004/.

[13] Larry Huston and Nabil Sakkab, "Connect and Develop: Inside Procter & Gamble's New Model for Innovation," Harvard Business Review, March 2006, https://hbr.org/2006/03/connect-and-develop-inside-procter-gambles-new-model-for-innovation; "P&G Sets Two New Goals for Open Innovation Partnerships," PR Newswire, October 28, 2010, https://www.prnewswire.com/news-releases/pg-sets-two-new-goals-for-open-innovation-partnerships-105996203.html.

The discipline matters more than the label. Organizations that treat innovation as a separate activity, disconnected from daily operations, often struggle to translate ideas into results. Those that embed experimentation into how work is done—grounded in agile processes and collaborative norms—tend to sustain innovation over time.

Agility and collaboration can also shorten time to market. When cross-functional teams work in short cycles with rapid feedback, they can move from concept to delivery faster than teams organized around sequential handoffs. The reduction in lead time comes not from cutting corners, but from eliminating unnecessary delays, improving information flow, and making decisions closer to the work.

Microsoft's development of Teams illustrates this approach. In response to Slack's growing market presence, Microsoft assembled cross-functional agile teams that worked in short sprints with rapid feedback cycles. The company announced Teams in November 2016 and launched it globally by March 2017—a timeline that would have been impossible under traditional sequential development.

This speed matters in competitive markets where timing affects outcomes. But speed without quality creates its own problems. The goal is not to move fast at any cost—it is to remove friction that slows work without adding value, so that teams can deliver reliably at a pace that matches market needs.

6.4.1 Strategies for Achieving Agility and Collaboration

The concepts discussed above translate into practical strategies. None of these approaches works in isolation; each reinforces the others. Together, they create the conditions for organizations to adapt quickly while maintaining coherence.

1. **Agile Methods:** Implementing agile practices—scrum, kanban, lean, or similar approaches—improves task agility by structuring work into short cycles with frequent feedback. Cross-functional teams can adapt quickly to customer input, market fluctuations, and emerging issues. Chapter 7 examines agile methodologies in depth.

2. **Cross-Functional Collaboration:** Open communication and knowledge sharing across departments improve alignment and outcomes. Collaboration platforms can support real-time coordination, but the underlying discipline depends on

organizational norms: willingness to share information, tolerance for input from outside one's domain, and commitment to shared goals over local priorities.

3. **Customer-Centric Orientation:** Teams that systematically gather and act on customer feedback can align fulfillment processes with actual expectations. This orientation is not the only route to success—some organizations compete primarily on cost or scale—but it helps sustain improvements in outcomes that customers value, not just internal metrics.

4. **Empowered Workforce:** Agility and collaboration depend on people who are equipped to make decisions, test new approaches, and adapt to change. Training, tools, and organizational support prepare the workforce to navigate changing conditions with confidence. When employees understand the goals and have latitude to act, improvement becomes distributed rather than centralized.

These strategies reinforce one another. Agile methods create the structure for rapid adaptation. Cross-functional collaboration keeps adaptation coherent. Customer-centric orientation provides direction. And an empowered workforce sustains the effort over time.

6.5 Real-World Examples

The principles that guided INTELLIFM—designing for constraints, building trust through predictable behavior, enabling progressive sophistication, and preserving human judgment—are not unique to software. They appear wherever organizations pursue sustainable efficiency. The following cases illustrate these principles in action across manufacturing, logistics, and customer service. Each example demonstrates that, properly understood, efficiency is not about cutting corners but about building systems that can adapt and improve over time.

6.5.1 Toyota

The Toyota Production System (TPS) emerged from constraints. After World War II, Toyota lacked the capital, space, and domestic market size enjoyed by American manufacturers. The company could not afford to build inventory and hope for buyers. It needed a different approach—one that delivered precisely what was needed, when it was needed, in the required quantity. From that constraint came the foundation of lean manufacturing.

Two principles anchor the system. *Jidoka*—automation with a human touch—ensures that quality issues are detected and addressed immediately, rather than being passed downstream. When a defect is identified, production stops until the root cause is resolved. This discipline builds trust: every unit that leaves the line meets the standard, and workers know that quality is not sacrificed for throughput. *Just-in-time* production coordinates supply with demand, reducing inventory costs and eliminating waste from overproduction.

Toyota's commitment to *kaizen*—continuous improvement—extends these principles over time. Every team member is encouraged to identify inefficiencies and propose solutions. Frontline workers can halt production when they observe problems. This practice preserves human judgment where it matters most: the people closest to the work have the authority to act on what they observe.

Toyota institutionalized kaizen through its Creative Idea Suggestion System, established in 1951 under the slogan "Good Thinking, Good Products." The program empowers all employees—from frontline operators to engineers—to submit ideas for improving processes, quality, and efficiency. By 1974, cumulative submissions exceeded 1 million; by 1988, 20 million; and by 2011, 40 million. The total now approaches 50 million suggestions over the program's seven-decade history. Most ideas are modest improvements rather than breakthrough innovations, but their cumulative effect is what drives continuous improvement. The system reflects a core Toyota belief: the people closest to the work are best positioned to identify opportunities for improvement.[14]

TPS influenced my thinking about INTELLIFM. Both systems separate intent from implementation—Toyota through standardized work instructions that define what must happen at each station and my platform through a knowledge base that defines filing

[14] "Power to the People—Toyota's Suggestion System," *Toyota UK Magazine*, September 1, 2021, `https://mag.toyota.co.uk/toyota-and-the-power-of-suggestion/`.

rules independent of execution logic. Both systems build trust through transparency—Toyota through visual controls that make workflow status visible and my approach through human-readable rules that compliance officers could inspect and verify. Both systems are designed for adaptation—Toyota through continuous improvement cycles and this architecture through iterative refinement of the knowledge base.

The influence of lean principles extends well beyond automotive manufacturing. Health care providers have applied visual control systems to track patient journeys and identify bottlenecks. Cleveland Clinic, for example, partnered with Palantir Technologies to implement a Virtual Command Center. This cloud-based platform uses AI and ML to forecast patient admissions, discharges, and transfers while monitoring caregiver availability and bed capacity in real time. The system delivers recommendations that help managers adjust staffing levels, reduce wait times, and improve resource utilization. According to the health system, the platform has reduced emergency room wait times by 38 minutes and decreased unused orthopedic operating room time by 40%.[15]

6.5.2 Amazon

Amazon's fulfillment operations demonstrate efficiency at scale. Millions of products are moved from warehouses to customers daily, coordinated by robotics, ML, and data analytics. The system balances automation with human expertise—robots transport goods through facilities, while human workers handle tasks requiring judgment and dexterity.

The underlying principle is selective automation. Amazon automates tasks that are repetitive, rule-governed, and amenable to it—inventory placement, route planning, and demand forecasting. It preserves human involvement where flexibility and judgment matter—quality verification, exception handling, complex picks. This division reflects the same balance that shaped INTELLIFM: automate what machines do well; keep humans in control of tasks that require experience and context.

[15] "Cleveland Clinic and Palantir Technologies Partner to Improve Hospital Performance Through Virtual Command Center," PR Newswire, January 19, 2023, `https://www.prnewswire.com/news-releases/cleveland-clinic-and-palantir-technologies-partner-to-improve-hospital-performance-through-virtual-command-center-301725481.html`; "How AI Assists with Staffing, Scheduling and Once-Tedious Tasks," Cleveland Clinic Consult QD, April 22, 2025, `https://consultqd.clevelandclinic.org/how-ai-assists-with-staffing-scheduling-and-once-tedious-tasks`.

Data-driven decision-making pervades the operation. Analytics converts vast streams of information into insight by recognizing patterns at scale. It helps determine where to stock items, which routes minimize transportation costs, and when to schedule shipments to reduce waste. This transparency—making the state of the system visible and measurable—builds confidence that resources are being deployed effectively.

Amazon's approach involves trade-offs. Investments in fulfillment technology and logistics networks support fast delivery and competitive pricing, but the relentless focus on efficiency has drawn scrutiny regarding labor practices and market power. These tensions illustrate a broader point: operational excellence is not an unqualified good. How efficiency is achieved and who bears its costs matter as much as the outcomes it delivers.

6.5.3 McDonald's

McDonald's drive-through operations illustrate efficiency in customer-facing service. The challenge is consistency at scale: delivering predictable speed and accuracy across thousands of locations with varying demand patterns, staffing levels, and local conditions.

The company addresses this through data and progressive automation. Cloud-based AI systems analyze large volumes of data on customer preferences, peak hours, and popular menu items. This data feeds ML algorithms that predict demand fluctuations across different locations and times, allowing precise adjustments to staffing levels, menu configurations, and food preparation workflows. In some locations, McDonald's has also deployed AI-powered voice recognition technology to take orders more accurately and efficiently.[16]

The layout of the drive-through menu plays a central role in McDonald's efficiency strategy. The company began converting to digital menu boards around 2015, with widespread implementation by 2019. This transformation supported far more dynamic optimization than static boards allowed. McDonald's AI algorithms continuously analyze ordering habits through cloud-based platforms, strategically reorganizing digital displays

[16] McDonald's Corporation, "McDonald's and Google Cloud Announce Strategic Partnership to Update Systems and Deploy AI Solutions to Restaurants Worldwide," December 6, 2023, `https://corporate.mcdonalds.com/corpmcd/our-stories/article/mcd-google-cloud-announce-partnership.html`. For a broader review of AI applications in the food industry, see V. Zatsu et al., "Revolutionizing the Food Industry: The Transformative Power of Artificial Intelligence," *Food Chemistry: X* 24 (2024): 101867, `https://doi.org/10.1016/j.fochx.2024.101867`.

in real time based on time of day, weather conditions, and current promotions. A menu can automatically highlight breakfast items in the morning or promote ice cream on hot days. This responsive design reduces order times by placing likely selections in easily visible positions.

McDonald's implemented AI-powered menu optimization systems by acquiring Dynamic Yield in March 2019 for over $300 million.[17] The company had tested Dynamic Yield's personalization technology in several US restaurants in 2018 and, by late 2019, had deployed it across thousands of US drive-throughs.[18]

These investments reflect the principle of progressive disclosure applied to customer experience. The menu system does not overwhelm customers with every option; it surfaces relevant choices based on context. The underlying complexity—demand forecasting, inventory coordination, preparation timing—remains invisible to the customer, who experiences only the result: faster service with less friction.

The results have been mixed. According to the 2024 Quick-Service Restaurant (QSR) Drive-Thru Study, McDonald's ranked ninth among 10 major quick-service restaurant brands, with an average total order time of 6 minutes and 16 seconds.[19] The industry average for total service time was 5 minutes and 43 seconds, indicating that McDonald's performance was approximately 9% slower than the industry benchmark.[20] This outcome illustrates that technology alone does not guarantee efficiency gains. Execution, integration, and ongoing refinement matter as much as the initial investment.

McDonald's cloud-based platform also links kitchen operations to drive-through demand in real time, helping reduce food waste while maintaining freshness and speed. Other companies have adopted similar strategies. Starbucks uses its Mobile Order & Pay app—supported by ML—to predict store-specific preparation times and adjust pickup

---

[17] "McDonald's to Acquire Dynamic Yield, Will Use Decision Technology to Increase Personalization and Improve Customer Experience," McDonald's Corporate, March 25, 2019, `https://corporate.mcdonalds.com/corpmcd/our-stories/article/dynamic_yield_1164112100.html`.

[18] "McDonald's Acquires AI Company Trying to Automate the Drive-Thru," CNBC, September 10, 2019, `https://www.cnbc.com/2019/09/10/mcdonalds-acquires-ai-company-trying-to-automate-the-drive-thru.html`.

[19] "The 2024 QSR® Drive-Thru Report," *QSR Magazine*, October 2024, `https://www.qsrmagazine.com/story/the-2024-qsr-drive-thru-report/`.

[20] "Annual Drive-Thru Report Released—QSRs Are Getting Faster," NACS, March 1, 2024, `https://www.convenience.org/Media/Daily/2024/March/1/2-Annual-Drive-Thru-Report-QSRS-Faster_Ops`.

notifications accordingly. These examples demonstrate how operational efficiency in customer-facing industries increasingly depends on real-time data and adaptive systems.

6.6 Collaborative Software Development

Modern software requires deep collaboration to maintain alignment with user needs, business objectives, and technical quality from the start. This is not a new insight; in the INTELLIFM blueprint, collaboration between domain experts and engineers is not optional. Such a collaboration is the only way to capture the specialized knowledge that defines the system's value. What has evolved is the formalization of these practices into methodologies and tools that scale across distributed teams and high-consequence projects. Today, this collaboration is most effective when teams are structured from the start to integrate business, technical, and operational expertise into a single, cohesive unit.

Bringing together individuals from different disciplines—domain experts, designers, developers, testers, and project managers—creates an environment in which diverse perspectives inform decisions. That mix of perspectives often produces better solutions for complex constraints than any single discipline can achieve alone. In INTELLIFM, compliance officers understood filing requirements that engineers had never encountered; engineers understood architectural possibilities that compliance officers could not have imagined. Neither group working alone would have produced a system that succeeded in practice. The collaboration was not incidental. It was structural.

Within a collaborative framework, decision-making becomes a collective endeavor. Each stakeholder group contributes a perspective that others lack. Domain experts understand industry challenges and regulatory constraints. Designers translate abstract requirements into concrete interfaces. Developers assess technical feasibility and trade-offs in implementation. Project managers coordinate efforts and manage dependencies. When these perspectives converge, decisions become well rounded—grounded in user needs, business imperatives, and technical feasibility. This inclusive approach improves outcomes and fosters shared ownership among team members.

Collaboration also improves speed and adaptability. When communication flows smoothly across roles and coordination is explicit, teams can identify obstacles earlier, resolve ambiguities faster, and respond to feedback without waiting for handoffs between phases. Software products reach users more quickly and can adapt to emerging requirements. In markets where timing matters, this agility provides a meaningful advantage.

The collaborative model treats quality as a shared responsibility rather than a phase that occurs after development. It is an integrated approach: usability, functionality, performance, and maintainability are shaped together rather than bolted on later. Designers focus on usability. Developers focus on functionality and maintainability. Testers verify that the system behaves as intended. When these roles work together throughout the development cycle—rather than sequentially—the result is a product that reflects all three concerns from the very beginning.

A user-centric orientation reinforces this collaboration. Continuous dialog among designers, developers, and users shapes every feature, interface, and interaction. This approach produces systems that are intuitive and engaging because each element has been examined from the user's perspective. INTELLIFM succeeded in part because compliance officers—the users—were involved throughout the development process. Their feedback shaped the knowledge base, the interface, and the workflow. The system worked for them because it was built with them.

These practices—which I adopted out of necessity in the late 1990s—have since become foundational to both agile methodologies and DevOps. The vocabulary has changed, and the tools have improved, but the core insight remains: effective software emerges from sustained collaboration among people who bring different expertise to a shared problem. (For an overview of the roles involved in collaborative development, see Appendix 8.)

6.7 The SDLC

The SDLC applies the principles of business process efficiency to software itself. It provides a structured approach for managing development from initial planning through deployment and maintenance, helping teams deliver software that meets quality standards, remains within budget, and is delivered on time.

In the late 1980s and early 1990s, products such as Windows and Office operated on multiyear release cycles with sequential phases and late integration. We delivered high-quality software, but the process was rigid, and change requests submitted late in the cycle were costly. By the mid-1990s, Microsoft began experimenting with shorter milestones and earlier integration. This change in strategy reflected a growing recognition that feedback from real users was too valuable to defer until the end. Chapter 7 examines this evolution in more detail.

INTELLIFM's implementation followed a structured development process without calling it an SDLC. The discipline was the same: define objectives clearly, break work into manageable phases, validate continuously, and build in mechanisms for learning and improvement. What has changed since the 1990s is the formalization of these practices into frameworks that organizations can adopt, adapt, and scale.

The SDLC is designed to mitigate risks before launch and to meet customer expectations throughout development and after release. It involves drafting a detailed plan, breaking it into manageable modules, and then systematically executing and assessing each module. This structure helps teams manage changing requirements, keep pace with advancing technologies, and maintain collaboration across disciplines.

Figure 6-1 summarizes the core SDLC phases from planning and analysis through design, implementation, testing, deployment, and maintenance. The value of this structure lies in predictability—stakeholders know what to expect at each stage, and teams can identify problems early rather than after deployment.

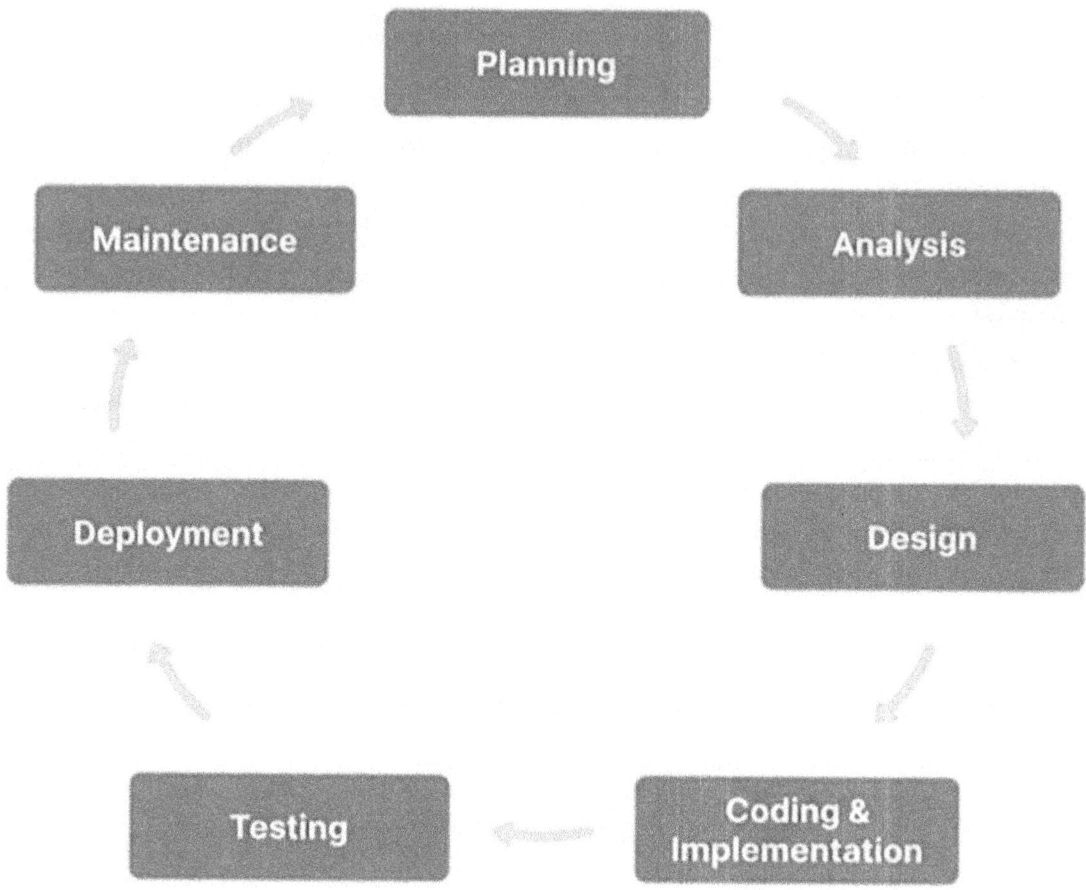

Figure 6-1. *The SDLC stages—planning, analysis, design, coding and implementation, testing, deployment, and maintenance—progress sequentially. (Image by author)*

Planning establishes the foundation: project scope, resources, timelines, cost estimates, risk mitigation strategies, and quality benchmarks. *Analysis* involves domain experts, designers, project managers, and stakeholders working together to understand and define requirements. *Design* transitions from requirements to a detailed technical plan: software architects establish the foundation, while designers create the user interface. *Coding and implementation* brings the design to life through development, unit testing, code reviews, and integration. *Testing* validates that the product meets quality standards through unit, integration, system, performance, and user acceptance testing (UAT). *Deployment* makes the software available in the production environment. This step includes preparing the environment, managing the release, and monitoring the system after the release goes live. *Maintenance* ensures the software remains effective, secure, and relevant through updates, bug fixes, performance optimization, and new features. Some SDLC versions also include a *Disposition* phase that addresses end-of-life activities, such as decommissioning, data migration, and documentation archiving.

Adopting an SDLC framework provides clear advantages. It enhances transparency, improves estimation accuracy, supports structured planning and realistic scheduling, and promotes early risk identification and mitigation. This creates a predictable, controlled development environment in which the final product aligns closely with customer expectations.

The SDLC embodies several principles that also guided INTELLIFM. Separation of concerns is reflected in the distinction between analysis (understanding requirements) and design (determining the implementation). Progressive disclosure is a phased delivery approach in which functionality is revealed incrementally rather than all at once. And preserving human judgment appears in the emphasis on stakeholder involvement throughout—requirements do not emerge from automated processes but from conversations with the people who will use the system.

Modern adaptations of the SDLC compress these phases into shorter cycles and emphasize continuous feedback. But the underlying insight remains: software development benefits from the same discipline that makes any complex process efficient. Define goals clearly, break work into manageable stages, validate continuously, and build in mechanisms for learning and improvement.

For AI systems, the SDLC requires additional considerations. Data quality, model performance, ethical implications, and regulatory compliance introduce challenges that traditional software does not face. The following section examines how INTELLIFM addressed these challenges before modern AI practices emerged and how the SDLC is adapting to meet the demands of AI-driven systems.

6.8 INTELLIFM: Case Study in Business Process Efficiency

The principles discussed throughout this chapter came together in INTELLIFM. When I architected that system, I did not view business process efficiency as a formal discipline. I was solving a practical problem: how to build a filing system that could evolve with regulatory change while remaining accessible to compliance officers who were not programmers.

The solution required bridging two distinct disciplines. On one side were compliance specialists—compliance officers, paralegals, and regulatory affairs professionals—who understood the filing requirements: which forms to use, which fields to complete, and which deadlines applied. Throughout this book, they are referred to as domain experts when serving as subject matter authorities. On the other side were software engineers, who understood system architecture—how to build components that communicated reliably, how to store and retrieve data efficiently, and how to generate user interfaces dynamically. Neither group could build the system alone, and their partnership did more than coordinate tasks: it created bidirectional learning. Engineers developed a deeper understanding of real regulatory workflows, whereas domain experts gained a clearer view of what technology could and could not do.

I structured that collaboration around a shared artifact: the knowledge base. Compliance officers authored rules in structured English, using Excel spreadsheets that they already knew how to use. Engineers built the inference engine, database layer, COM components, and UIG logic. The knowledge base served as the contract between these groups—readable by domain experts, executable by the system, and stable enough to support iterative refinement without constant rework of application code.

This approach anticipated practices that later became standard in agile and DevOps methodologies. Involving domain experts from the outset reduced the risk of costly revisions late in the development cycle. Iterative refinement based on ongoing feedback from those experts fostered continuous improvement. Crucially, the separation between rules and code meant that regulatory changes could be absorbed by updating the knowledge base—rather than touching the underlying code—keeping complexity manageable while still allowing the system to adapt.

INTELLIFM also initiated a broader organizational transformation in how compliance work could be carried out. By breaking down silos between business units and IT teams—at least within the groups responsible for delivering and operating the platform—it strengthened a culture of shared ownership and accountability. Over time, the partnership between engineers and domain experts produced not only better filings, but a reusable base of institutional knowledge that supported future projects and process enhancements—an outcome now widely recognized as central to organizational learning and sustained improvement.

In essence, INTELLIFM was more than a technological innovation. It demonstrated that durable efficiency comes from aligning people, process, and systems—capturing domain expertise in a form that can be updated quickly, while keeping the underlying execution machinery stable and trustworthy.

6.8.1 Adapting the SDLC for AI Development

The SDLC is particularly important for AI development due to the unique challenges AI systems pose. Unlike traditional software, AI incorporates models that learn from data and make decisions with varying degrees of autonomy. This distinction requires specialized considerations throughout the SDLC.

INTELLIFM faced some of these challenges in simpler form. Data quality was critical—the system's outputs were only as good as the rules in its knowledge base. Performance required continuous validation against actual filing requirements. And governance was built in from the start: every rule was traceable, every decision explainable.

Modern AI development faces these challenges at greater scale. Requirements must account for risks such as bias and unintended impacts. Testing must evaluate not only functional correctness but also fairness, explainability, and robustness across representative scenarios. Data collection and preparation have become major early-stage activities in many AI projects, and validation increasingly depends on statistical performance analysis rather than purely deterministic test cases. After deployment, monitoring is essential to detect drift and performance degradation as conditions change.

Regulatory initiatives such as the EU AI Act and emerging industry standards are also raising expectations for documentation and accountability across the life cycle. Cross-functional collaboration—among data scientists, engineers, domain experts, and ethicists—is becoming standard practice. Tools that manage version control not only for code but also for data and models are now essential, and automated safeguards are increasingly integrated into development workflows to identify and mitigate potential harms before release.

The lesson from INTELLIFM remains practical: build systems where domain experts can contribute directly, where rules and decisions are transparent and auditable, and where automation augments human judgment rather than replacing it. These principles do not guarantee success, but they establish a foundation for building AI systems that organizations can trust.

6.9 Summary

This chapter examined business process efficiency as both a discipline and a practice. The examples from Toyota, Amazon, and McDonald's showed that efficiency is not about cutting costs alone—it is about building systems that can adapt, improve, and scale. The same insight applies to software development, where structured approaches such as the SDLC bring the predictability and discipline that complex projects demand.

INTELLIFM illustrated these principles in a specific domain: regulatory compliance and document management. The system succeeded because it was designed for the constraints enterprises actually faced—legacy databases, nontechnical users, and regulations that changed faster than release cycles. It built trust by keeping rules transparent and auditable. It supported progressive sophistication by letting domain experts start with straightforward rules and extend them over time. It also preserved human judgment by keeping compliance officers in control of decisions that required expertise the system could not replicate. Just as necessary, it demonstrated that durable efficiency often depends on structured collaboration: domain experts, designers, and engineers contributing through interfaces and artifacts that match their strengths.

These principles extend beyond any single system. Modern document and information platforms continue to build on the same foundation. They use AI to organize content, surface context, and improve discovery through natural language interaction. They foster collaboration across distributed teams. And they integrate into everyday workflows rather than forcing organizations to rebuild them. Modern document and information platforms reflect this trajectory in different ways, but the pattern remains recognizable: separate *intent* from *execution*. The goal is to allow specialists to contribute through familiar artifacts and to keep system behavior transparent enough for users to trust the results. (For an overview of design and prototyping tools that support collaborative development, see Appendix 9.)

The next chapter examines agile software development, which formalizes many of the collaborative practices pioneered by INTELLIFM before agile methodologies were widespread. Where this chapter emphasized efficiency as a goal, the next focuses on agility as a method—showing how iterative development, cross-functional teams, and continuous feedback help organizations respond to change without sacrificing quality.

CHAPTER 7

Agile Software Development

When I joined Microsoft in 1988, software development followed the industry-standard waterfall model. Teams gathered requirements and produced detailed specifications. Developers implemented them, testing followed, and the product shipped—a cycle that often took months, and sometimes years, to complete. This sequential approach worked well enough for desktop products distributed on physical media, where customers expected periodic, stable releases. Although we delivered high-quality software, the process was inherently rigid. Late change requests were costly, and by the time a product reached customers, their needs had often evolved beyond the original specifications.

By the mid-1990s, the limitations of that model were becoming difficult to ignore. The internet was changing how software was delivered and how quickly users expected improvements. Soon after, the rise of cloud computing further accelerated those expectations. Today, the pressure is even more intense as organizations rush to develop and adopt AI capabilities. In this environment, agility is not a slogan—it is a practical discipline for building software that can adapt to change without sacrificing reliability.

In the late 1990s, INTELLIFM had begun to mirror what would later be codified as agile principles—driven more by pragmatic necessity than by a formal framework. We worked in short cycles, delivered functional components early, and gathered feedback from compliance officers before building the next increment. We maintained a knowledge base that domain experts could read and refine, supporting steady improvement without destabilizing the underlying system. Regular reviews brought engineers and compliance specialists together to examine what was working and what needed adjustment. These were not formal ceremonies, but they reflected the core principles: iterate quickly, involve users continuously, and respond to change rather than resist it.

K. C. Mukherjee, *The Microsoft AI Insider's Playbook*, https://doi.org/10.1007/979-8-8688-2730-3_7

The INTELLIFM effort also deepened the working relationship between Wolters Kluwer and Microsoft. By building an enterprise-grade AI expert system on the Microsoft technology stack, we demonstrated that Microsoft platforms could support mission-critical applications in regulated industries. That early collaboration laid the groundwork for a long-running partnership; over time, Wolters Kluwer expanded its use of Microsoft platforms, including Azure and Microsoft 365.

Those same principles still define effective agile teams today. Time-boxed work cycles force teams to operate within real constraints and deliver value early. Transparency—through frequent reviews and open discussion of obstacles—builds trust and keeps priorities visible. Incremental delivery functions as progressive disclosure, revealing capabilities as they mature instead of waiting for a "complete" system. Human judgment remains central: teams make trade-offs, and product leadership sets priorities. Expertise is respected, not overridden by process or tooling.

This chapter traces the evolution of agile methodologies from their origins as a response to limitations of the waterfall model to their current role as the dominant standard in modern software development. We begin with waterfall—its strengths, its constraints, and why the industry moved beyond it. We then examine the Agile Manifesto and the approaches it inspired, including scrum, extreme programming (XP), and kanban. We explore technical agility and team agility as complementary capabilities, and we address technical debt as both a consequence of rapid iteration and a challenge that disciplined agile teams must manage.

Real-world examples illustrate how organizations have applied agile principles at scale. They reveal what can go wrong when speed outpaces engineering discipline. We also examine the practical challenges of adoption in large enterprises and strategies for overcoming them, drawing on my experience at Microsoft, at Wolters Kluwer, and in broader enterprise architecture roles. The chapter concludes at the intersection of agile and AI: how agile methods support the development of AI systems and how AI tools are beginning to assist in planning, coding, testing, and delivery.

Throughout, the focus remains on principles over checklists. The agile model is not a set of rituals. It is a discipline for building software that stays responsive to change while preserving quality and trust. In fact, that same discipline made INTELLIFM effective in the late 1990s and continues to apply to cloud-first, distributed, and AI-driven development.

7.1 The Waterfall Model

The waterfall model takes its name from the way each phase flows into the next, like water cascading over a series of ledges. Requirements lead to design, design to implementation, implementation to testing, and testing to deployment. Each phase completes before the next begins, and moving backward—revisiting requirements after coding has started, for example—is costly and discouraged.

I experienced this model firsthand during my early years at Microsoft. When I joined in 1988, major products like Windows and Office followed multiyear release cycles with clearly delineated phases. A planning and design period of four to six months determined what features would be built and how. A concentrated coding phase followed, typically six to eight weeks of intense development. After reaching "code complete" status, the project entered a stabilization phase lasting several months, during which no new features were added—only bug fixes and refinements. This cycle would repeat before the final product shipped. The process was thorough, and we delivered software that millions of people relied on. But it was also slow, and by the time a release reached customers, their expectations had often shifted.

The waterfall model's strengths are real. Its structure makes planning straightforward: managers can allocate resources, set deadlines, and track progress against well-defined milestones. Documentation produced at each phase—requirements specifications, design documents, and test plans—provides traceability and supports maintenance long after the original developers have moved on. For projects with stable requirements and predictable outcomes, this discipline reduces risk and supports consistency.

These characteristics made the waterfall model a good fit where requirements change slowly and errors are costly. Examples include heavily customized enterprise accounting systems, legislation-driven government programs, air traffic control, and telecommunications infrastructure governed by strict protocols. Given the high stakes of these environments, the potential cost of failure warrants exhaustive preparation.

The previous chapter described the SDLC in detail. The waterfall model implements those phases—planning, analysis, design, coding, testing, deployment, and maintenance—in strict sequence. While the SDLC provides a general framework, the waterfall model imposes a specific discipline: complete each phase before advancing, document thoroughly at every stage, and minimize iteration. This rigor served the constraints of an era when software shipped on physical media, installation was complex, and updates were infrequent.

But the waterfall model's rigidity became a liability as conditions changed. When requirements are revised during development—as they inevitably are once users encounter working software—the waterfall model offers no graceful way to accommodate those changes. Changes discovered late in the cycle propagate backward through completed phases, requiring rework that delays schedules and inflates budgets. Customers see the product only at the end, after major decisions have been locked in. If assumptions made during requirements gathering prove incorrect, the final product may solve yesterday's problem rather than today's.

I saw these limitations clearly during my early years at Microsoft. As the internet transformed how software was delivered and used, the gap between what we planned and what customers needed grew wider. The software I helped build during that period was developed using a waterfall-like process and was of high quality. But the feedback loops were too slow. By the mid-1990s, Microsoft transitioned to shorter milestones and earlier integration, recognizing that real user feedback was too valuable to defer until the end of a multiyear cycle.

The limitations I observed were not unique. The same friction appears wherever requirements are modified faster than long release cycles can absorb. Projects with well-defined, stable requirements succeeded under the waterfall model. Projects facing fluid requirements, competitive pressure, or rapidly changing technology struggled. The industry's collective experience set the stage for a different approach—one that embraced change instead of resisting it and delivered value in increments, not as a single all-at-once release.

Indian software giants such as Tata Consultancy Services (TCS), Infosys, Wipro, and HCL Technologies have historically used sequential development approaches, particularly for large-scale government initiatives that require strict compliance. Notable examples include TCS's implementation of India's Passport Seva Project, a Mission Mode e-Governance initiative under the National e-Governance Plan, which TCS reports reduced passport issuance turnaround time from about 45 days to about 8 days.[1] TCS

[1] Tata Consultancy Services, "TCS Transforms Passport Services for Indians Across the Globe," TCS Case Study, `https://www.tcs.com/what-we-do/industries/public-services/case-study/e-governance-passport-transform-indian-passport-office`.

also implemented the Andhra Pradesh State Wide Area Network, connecting the state headquarters with 1,088 mandals (administrative units) and 23 district headquarters through a carefully planned, sequential approach.[2]

Still, the core weakness remained: the waterfall model assumes that what you know at the beginning will remain true through delivery. As software transitioned from packaged releases to continuously updated products, customers began expecting frequent improvements and quick responses to feedback. In that environment, long and rigid development cycles became difficult to justify.

Agile approaches emerged to address this evolution. They did not remove discipline. Instead, they kept discipline while shortening feedback loops, reducing late-stage surprises, and delivering value in small increments instead of all at once.

7.2 The Agile Model

The practices used to develop the INTELLIFM technology were not developed from scratch. They drew on ideas that had been circulating for decades—most notably from Toyota's production system, which emphasized continuous improvement, rapid feedback, and respect for the people closest to the work. Chapter 6 examined Toyota in the context of business process efficiency. The same underlying ideas—short cycles, visible progress, rapid problem correction, and empowerment of frontline expertise—would soon reshape how software was built.

By the late 1990s, many software teams had reached similar conclusions. The internet compressed timelines and created a new expectation of "internet time": users preferred frequent updates to annual releases. Traditional, sequential methodologies struggled in that environment. Projects found it challenging to absorb change late in the cycle, and the gap between what plans promised and what delivery realities produced was increasingly hard to ignore.

In February 2001, 17 software practitioners met in Utah to articulate what they had learned. The result was the Agile Manifesto,[3] a short document that distilled their collective experience into four value statements:

---

[2] Tata Consultancy Services, "AP State Government Awards the Largest State Wide Area Network Project in India to TCS," Press Release, September 23, 2009, `https://www.tcs.com/who-we-are/newsroom/press-release/tcs-wins-largest-state-wide-area-network-project`.

[3] "Agile Manifesto," `https://agilemanifesto.org/`.

- Individuals and interactions over processes and tools
- Working software over comprehensive documentation
- Customer collaboration over contract negotiation
- Responding to change over following a plan

The manifesto did not argue that processes, documentation, contracts, or plans are unimportant. It argued that when trade-offs become unavoidable, effective teams prioritize people over bureaucracy, working outcomes over paperwork, partnership over adversarial negotiation, and adaptability over rigid adherence to a predetermined plan.

The manifesto was supported by 12 principles that expanded on these values and provided practical guidance. Taken together, they emphasize early and continuous delivery of working software and frequent, small increments. They also stress the importance of welcoming change, close collaboration between business stakeholders and developers, direct communication, a sustainable pace, technical excellence, and simplicity. Finally, they highlight self-organizing teams and regular reflection to support continuous improvement.

When I first encountered the Agile Manifesto, I recognized that we had already been using some of its practices. INTELLIFM was built through short iterations with frequent delivery. Compliance officers collaborated closely with engineers through shared artifacts and regular reviews. Changing requirements were expected, and not feared, because the architecture separated rules from execution logic, making updates manageable rather than destabilizing. Progress was measured by work capability, not by document volume. The manifesto gave a name—and a shared vocabulary—to an approach that had emerged from necessity.

The connection to the principles that guided INTELLIFM is direct. Agile teams accept constraints by working in time-boxed iterations instead of pretending everything can be known up front. They build trust through transparency: visible backlogs, frequent reviews, and working software that stakeholders can evaluate. They deliver incrementally, letting users respond to real functionality, not speculation. And they preserve human judgment by empowering teams to make decisions, respecting expertise, and keeping people—not process—at the center of the work.

In the years after the manifesto's publication, several frameworks emerged to translate these values into concrete practices. Scrum organized work into sprints with defined roles and recurring reviews. XP emphasized disciplined engineering practices, including pair programming and test-driven development (TDD). Kanban, adapted from lean manufacturing, emphasized visual workflow management and limiting work in progress. Feature-driven development focused delivery around client-valued features. Teams adopted and adapted these approaches in response to contextual constraints and cultural factors.

Agile principles did not remain confined to software development. Teams in marketing, HR, and product development adopted iterative planning and feedback-driven execution, recognizing that uncertainty and change are not unique to engineering. But the agile model is not a universal answer. Its effectiveness depends on organizational culture, the nature of the work, and the willingness to embrace the underlying values. Some teams adopt the ceremonies without the mindset and see little benefit; others blend agile and traditional approaches into hybrid models that fit their realities.

The following sections move from values to practice. We examine how agile methodologies operate in practice, what technical and team capabilities they require, and why disciplined agility—not speed alone—delivers reliable outcomes.

7.3 The Agile Methodologies

The Agile Manifesto established values and principles, but it did not prescribe specific practices. That work fell to the frameworks that emerged in the years that followed. Each offered a different interpretation of agile ideas, and each gained adoption in contexts suited to its strengths.

Scrum is the most widely adopted agile framework. It organizes work into short, time-boxed iterations called sprints, typically lasting two to four weeks. A product owner represents stakeholders and maintains a prioritized backlog. A scrum master facilitates the process, removes impediments, and helps the team improve. The development team—cross-functional and self-organizing—commits to delivering a potentially shippable increment each sprint. Daily stand-ups keep the team aligned. Sprint reviews demonstrate progress to stakeholders. Retrospectives examine what worked and what needs adjustment.

When I view scrum through the lens of INTELLIFM, the parallels are clear. We did not use scrum terminology, but we worked in short cycles, regularly demonstrated progress to compliance officers, and adjusted our approach based on what we learned. The structure was less formal, but the discipline remained the same: constrain the work to what can be accomplished within a defined period, make progress visible, and adapt in response to feedback.

While scrum focuses on process and team coordination, **XP** complements it by emphasizing the technical practices that sustain quality at pace. If scrum provides the framework for how a team organizes, XP provides the engineering toolkit for how they build. These practices—such as pair programming, which places two developers at a single workstation—combine perspectives to catch errors early. TDD further secures this foundation by requiring tests to be written before the code they verify, so every feature begins with verification. To maintain momentum, continuous integration merges code changes frequently, exposing conflicts while they are still small and manageable. Ultimately, these habits enable small, frequent releases to deliver value early and reduce the risk of destabilizing deployments.

Together, continuous integration and continuous delivery (CI/CD) form a disciplined pipeline for moving changes from development into production. In a CI/CD workflow, each change triggers automated builds and tests and then progresses through deployment stages with consistent checks and approvals. When implemented well, CI/CD reduces manual, error-prone release steps and makes deployments routine rather than stressful events.

These practices address a problem I encountered repeatedly: systems that function independently but fail when combined. In INTELLIFM, we did not have the continuous integration tools available today; instead, we built incrementally and tested continuously. The inference engine, the components, and the database layer had to work together reliably. Frequent integration—even without automation—was the only practical way to catch problems before they compounded.

Kanban takes a different approach. Rather than fixed-length iterations, kanban emphasizes continuous flow. Work items move across a visual board from backlog through stages of development to completion. Work-in-progress limits prevent teams from starting more than they can finish, reducing context switching and exposing bottlenecks. The approach originated in lean manufacturing—Toyota, again—and translates naturally to knowledge work, where tasks vary in size and priorities change frequently.

Feature-driven development organizes work around client-valued features. Teams build an overall model of the system and then plan and execute development in short cycles—typically two weeks or less—focused on delivering complete features instead of isolated technical components. This approach keeps development anchored to business value and provides stakeholders with visible progress in terms they can evaluate.

Other methods address specific contexts. Crystal tailors practices to team size and project criticality. The dynamic systems development method fixes time and resources while allowing functionality to vary. Lean software development applies lean principles directly to the software development process. Those principles include eliminating waste, amplifying learning, delivering quickly, and empowering the team.

No single framework fits every situation. Scrum works well for teams that benefit from a regular cadence and clear roles. Kanban suits operations and maintenance work where priorities change continuously. XP appeals to teams that prioritize technical excellence and can sustain the discipline of pairing and test-first development. Many organizations blend elements from multiple frameworks, adapting practices to their culture and constraints.

What matters more than framework selection is alignment with agile values. Teams that adopt scrum ceremonies without embracing transparency gain little. Teams that limit work in progress without addressing the bottlenecks revealed by kanban see no improvement. The frameworks are tools, not solutions. They provide structure for applying agile principles, but the principles themselves—short cycles, visible progress, continuous feedback, and empowered teams—are what produce results.

In my experience, the most effective teams treat frameworks as starting points. They adopt practices that fit their context, discard those that do not, and refine their approach as they learn. The INTELLIFM applications were built before these frameworks became mainstream. However, the discipline was the same: iterate, deliver, collaborate closely with users, and adapt when circumstances change. The frameworks provided the industry with a shared vocabulary and repeatable patterns, but the underlying model predates the labels.

As organizations grow, coordinating multiple agile teams introduces new challenges. Frameworks such as the Scaled Agile Framework (SAFe), Large-Scale Scrum (LeSS), and Disciplined Agile Delivery (DAD) address these needs; Section 7.10 examines scaling in detail.

Traditional waterfall metrics (on-time delivery, task completion rates, milestone progress) measure adherence to the plan. Agile metrics focus more on speed of learning and value delivery. Waterfall projects often rely on Gantt charts that map task completion against a fixed timeline from start to finish. In contrast, agile projects use metrics such as velocity (the amount of work completed in each sprint) and burndown charts (tracking the work remaining). While the waterfall model emphasizes detailed documentation and sequential phase completion, agile emphasizes continuous delivery of working functionality. Metrics in agile environments are therefore oriented toward customer value, responsiveness, and iteration, rather than exhaustive documentation.

The influence of agile extends beyond software development, impacting a wide range of economic sectors by promoting flexibility, collaboration, and continuous improvement. In health care, agile methodologies improve patient care, streamline processes, and support rapid adaptation to regulatory changes. In finance, agile facilitates risk management, expedites product development, and ensures regulatory compliance. In education, agile supports curriculum development and personalized learning through continuous feedback. Retail and e-commerce businesses use agile to optimize inventory management and respond to market trends. In manufacturing, the agile model is applied to prototype new products, adjust supply chains, and bring innovations to market faster. Government and public sector organizations are adopting agile methodologies to enhance transparency, deliver services more efficiently, and implement policies with greater flexibility.

7.4 Technical Agility

Technical agility is an organization's capacity to adapt its technology stack and development practices and to make architectural decisions without disrupting existing functionality. It requires both technical capability—automated testing, modular design, and reliable deployment—and an engineering culture that treats change as the norm rather than the exception.

I have worked on systems where a single configuration change required weeks of planning, multiple approval committees, and a deployment window scheduled months in advance. I have also worked on systems where teams deployed to production multiple times per day with confidence. The difference was not talent or tools alone. It was architecture, discipline, and the accumulation of practices that made change safe.

7.4.1 Foundational Practices

Certain practices appear consistently in technically agile organizations.

1. Continuous integration means merging code changes frequently—ideally multiple times per day—so integration issues are caught when they are still small. I learned this lesson the

hard way on a project where three teams worked in parallel for six weeks before trying to merge. The merge took longer than the original development. After that experience, I pushed for daily integration, even when it seemed like extra work. The extra work was small compared with the alternative.

2. Automated testing creates a safety net that enables change. Unit tests verify that individual components behave correctly. Integration tests confirm that components work together. End-to-end tests validate complete workflows. Without this coverage, every change is a gamble. With it, teams can refactor aggressively and release confidently.

3. Refactoring improves the code structure without changing external behavior. It prevents the gradual decay that often accompanies rapid feature development. I have inherited systems in which developers were reluctant to modify certain modules—not because the code was inherently complex, but because no one understood it well enough to change it safely. That fear is a symptom of deferred refactoring. The longer refactoring is deferred, the more expensive it becomes.

4. Modular architecture supports independent change. When components have clear boundaries and well-defined interfaces, teams can modify one part of the system without needing to understand or affect the rest of the system. This is not just a technical convenience; it is an organizational enabler. Teams can work in parallel, make decisions locally, and deploy on their own schedules. In some environments, this modularity is implemented through a service-based approach, but the goal remains the same: reduce coupling to keep change contained.

5. Version control discipline is another foundation of technical agility. Branching strategies, code reviews, and pull request workflows allow teams to experiment safely, collaborate without stepping on one another's work, and preserve a clear history that supports confident refactoring. In practice, good version control habits are not about bureaucracy; they are what make parallel work safe.

6. Reliable deployment practices institutionalize change. Automation reduces manual steps and makes releases repeatable. Equally important is the ability to roll back quickly when something goes wrong. Continuous integration shows whether the code can be merged; disciplined deployment shows whether it can be released safely.

7. Feature flags separate deployment from release. The code reaches production, but users see the new functionality only when the flag is enabled. This supports gradual rollouts, rapid rollbacks, and controlled experiments without separate deployment cycles. I once watched a team disable a problematic feature within minutes of discovering an issue—no emergency deployment, no late-night firefighting, just a configuration change.

These practices reinforce one another. Automated tests make refactoring safe. Modular architecture makes testing tractable. Continuous integration surfaces problems early. Version control discipline supports parallel development without chaos. Reliable deployment and feature flags reduce the risk of releasing a change. Individually, each practice helps. Together, they create an environment where change is routine.

In enterprise projects for building AI-driven and cloud-based systems, tools such as Jenkins for continuous integration, Selenium for automated testing, and SonarQube for code quality analysis have become staples in technically agile teams. When properly integrated, they create feedback loops that surface problems early, when fixes are least expensive and least disruptive.

7.4.2 Responsiveness and Quality

Technical agility improves responsiveness. When the cost of change is low, teams can incorporate feedback quickly—adjusting features based on user behavior, fixing issues before they spread, and exploring ideas without lengthy planning cycles. It also creates space for controlled experimentation, allowing teams to prototype, validate assumptions, and adopt new approaches without prematurely committing to long-term architectural decisions.

Quality improves as a byproduct. Code reviews catch mistakes before they enter the codebase. Automated tests prevent regressions. Static analysis tools flag potential problems before deployment. Monitoring and observability systems provide rapid feedback on production behavior. When these mechanisms work together, defects are detected early and remedied cost-effectively.

I remember a production incident that took three days to diagnose because the system had no meaningful logging. The fix itself took 20 minutes. After that, we instrumented every significant path. The investment paid for itself within weeks. Observability is not overhead; it is insurance.

Quality also depends on collective ownership. When the team feels responsible for the codebase—not just the person who wrote each module—problems get addressed, not ignored. I have seen teams where developers would walk past obvious issues because "that is not my code." I have seen other teams where anyone who spotted a problem fixed it or flagged it immediately. The second kind of team ships better software.

7.4.3 The Intersection with Team Dynamics

Technical agility and team agility are inseparable. Sophisticated pipelines and automated testing deliver limited value if teams lack the collaboration skills to use them well. Conversely, highly collaborative teams struggle without the technical foundations that make rapid change safe.

Balance matters. Specialists bring deep expertise, but overspecialization creates bottlenecks. If only one person understands a complex system, that person becomes a single point of failure and often burns out from constant demand. Cross-functional teams that share knowledge through pairing, documentation, and rotation are more agile than teams built around individual experts.

I worked on a system in which a single engineer had written the entire data access layer. He was brilliant, and the code was elegant. But when he left for another opportunity, the team struggled for months. We eventually rewrote large portions—not because the original was poor, but because no one else understood it well enough to maintain it confidently. I never made that mistake again. On every subsequent project, I insisted on shared ownership of the significant components.

7.4.4 Managing the Cost of Agility

Technical agility has costs that must be managed consciously. The pursuit of flexibility can lead to overengineering—elaborate abstractions built for changes that never materialize. Every configuration option, every extension point, and every layer of indirection adds complexity that must be understood and maintained.

The connection to technical debt runs in both directions. Taking shortcuts today constrains agility tomorrow. But so does building for hypothetical futures that never arrive. The discipline is knowing which investments will pay off and which will become liabilities.

The most effective teams I have worked with share a common trait: they build just enough structure to support current needs while preserving the ability to adapt. They resist the temptation to solve problems they do not yet have. They refactor when the code tells them to, not on a schedule. They add abstraction when duplication becomes painful, not preemptively.

This pragmatism extends to tool adoption. New frameworks and platforms appear constantly, each promising productivity gains. Technically agile teams evaluate these options skeptically. They ask what problem is being solved, what the migration cost will be, and whether the team has the capacity to absorb the learning curve. Adopting every new technology is not agility—it is churn.

The goal is sustainable delivery. Technical agility is not about moving fast at any cost. It is about maintaining the capacity to respond to change over the long term, without burning out the team or accumulating debt that future developers will inherit.

7.5 Team Agility

Technical practices matter, but they are not sufficient. I have seen teams with excellent tooling—automated tests, continuous integration, and reliable deployment pipelines—that still struggled to deliver. The problem was not their technology—it was how they worked together.

In software development, team agility is the capacity to collaborate effectively, adapt quickly to changing circumstances, and deliver value incrementally without friction consuming their energy. It encompasses communication patterns, decision-making practices, and the trust that allows people to raise concerns, admit mistakes, and propose unconventional solutions without fear of blame. Technical agility makes rapid change possible; team agility determines whether that capability is used consistently and well.

INTELLIFM demonstrated that team agility was as important as any architectural decision. The system required close collaboration between compliance officers and engineers—groups with different vocabularies, different priorities, and different ways of thinking about problems. The technology worked because the team worked. When I have seen similar initiatives fail, the cause was rarely technical. It was people's inability to collaborate across boundaries.

7.5.1 Core Components of Team Agility

Team agility manifests through several interconnected dimensions.

1. **Cross-functional collaboration** breaks down the silos that slow traditional organizations. When a team includes developers, testers, operations perspectives, and someone who understands the business domain, decisions can be made without waiting for handoffs between departments. Questions get answered quickly, within minutes. Problems surface before they become expensive. I once worked with a team that had no dedicated tester. Developers wrote tests, reviewed each other's code, and took turns validating features from the user's perspective. The initial reaction from management was skepticism—surely quality would suffer. Instead, defect rates dropped. Problems were caught earlier because everyone felt responsible for quality, not just the person with "QA" in their title.

2. **Psychological safety** creates an environment where team members feel comfortable taking risks, admitting mistakes, and speaking openly about concerns. This cultural foundation directly affects technical outcomes: teams with high psychological safety are more likely to surface technical debt early and address it proactively, rather than concealing problems that might reflect poorly on individuals. I have been in meetings where engineers remained silent about risks because raising concerns was

perceived as negative. The risks materialized. The projects failed. The connection is direct: teams that cannot discuss problems openly cannot solve them effectively.

3. **Collective ownership** extends beyond code to include architecture decisions, quality standards, and delivery commitments. When teams share responsibility for outcomes, they naturally adopt more sustainable practices and resist the temptation to ship quick fixes that burden future development cycles. In INTELLIFM, collective ownership meant that compliance officers owned the rules and engineers owned the execution machinery, but both groups shared responsibility for the system's success. Neither could blame the other when something went wrong. That shared accountability forced collaboration that would not have happened otherwise.

7.5.2 Enabling Practices and Structures

Team agility does not happen by accident. It requires deliberate practices that reinforce collaborative behavior.

Daily stand-ups, when conducted well, are not status meetings. They are brief coordination sessions in which team members identify blockers, offer help, and adjust plans based on what they learned. The worst stand-ups I have attended were recitations of task lists. The most effective conversations were those that prevented problems from escalating.

Pair programming and mob programming distribute knowledge across the team. Two people at one keyboard catch mistakes earlier and learn from each other continuously. The practice can feel inefficient until you factor in fewer defects, fewer knowledge silos, and faster onboarding of new team members. I was skeptical the first time I tried pairing. Within a week, I was convinced.

Sprint retrospectives provide structured opportunities to examine how the team works. What went well? What did not? What should change? The most agile teams treat these sessions not as perfunctory ceremonies but as vital feedback loops that drive measurable improvements in velocity, quality, and team satisfaction. I have facilitated retrospectives that uncovered process problems previously unarticulated. Once named, those problems became solvable.

The physical and virtual workspace also influences team agility. Colocated teams benefit from spontaneous conversations and rapid problem-solving, in which quick questions are answered before they become impediments. Distributed teams require intentional communication protocols and collaboration tools to maintain cohesion. The transition to remote and hybrid work since 2020 has made this explicit: teams that thrive treat remote collaboration as a skill to be developed, not a constraint to be endured. They invest in explicit asynchronous norms, effective virtual whiteboarding, and deliberate social connection to prevent erosion of trust across distance.

7.5.3 The Relationship Between Team and Technical Agility

Team agility and technical agility are symbiotic. Technical practices such as continuous integration, automated testing, and IaC help teams move quickly with confidence. Conversely, highly collaborative teams are more likely to adopt and sustain technical practices that require coordination and discipline.

A team that cannot agree on coding standards will not sustain a useful test suite. A team that does not trust each other will not embrace pairing. Technical practices depend on team dynamics, and team dynamics, in turn, are reinforced by technical practices.

Architectural decisions benefit from team agility. When teams collaborate effectively, they refine architecture incrementally over time, avoiding disruptive redesign cycles. This evolutionary approach, supported by lightweight decision records and regular reviews, limits architectural drift while maintaining system coherence.

I have watched teams attempt large-scale refactoring efforts that collapsed under their own weight. The technical vision was sound; the team dynamics were not. People worked in isolation, made incompatible assumptions, and discovered conflicts too late. The successful projects were those in which collaboration was strong enough to surface disagreements early and resolve them constructively.

7.5.4 Impact on Technical Debt Management

Team agility profoundly influences how organizations create, manage, and eliminate technical debt. Agile teams treat technical debt as a natural consequence of building software under constraints, fostering honest conversations about trade-offs between delivery speed and long-term maintainability.

When teams are highly agile, they can incorporate debt remediation into regular sprints without requiring special "hardening" sprints or separate technical debt projects. They establish clear criteria for acceptable debt levels and create feedback mechanisms that surface debt before it becomes unmanageable.

Most importantly, agile teams resist the antipattern of individual heroics. I have seen engineers work weekends to fix problems that better collaboration would have prevented. I have seen "heroes" burn out and leave, taking vital knowledge with them. Sustainable pace and collective ownership produce better long-term outcomes than burnout-inducing death marches. The teams that last are the ones that treat sustainability as a requirement, not a luxury.

7.5.5 Scaling Team Agility

Team agility is easier to maintain in small groups. Five people can coordinate informally, develop shared context through daily interaction, and resolve conflicts quickly because relationships are strong.

As organizations grow, these organic processes break down. Communication overhead increases. Shared context fragments. Decisions that once occurred through informal conversations now require meetings, documentation, and formal approvals. Maintaining team agility becomes more difficult, and it requires intentional structures that preserve it while managing complexity.

Framework approaches such as LeSS, DAD, and SAFe provide patterns for scaling. However, success depends less on framework selection than on preserving core agile values: keeping teams small and autonomous, defining clear interfaces between teams, and using lightweight governance that supports team decision-making rather than constraining it. Section 7.10 examines these frameworks in detail.

The insight is that team agility at scale emerges from network effects and strong lateral coordination. When multiple agile teams share common practices, tools, and values, they can coordinate effectively with lightweight artifacts and direct collaboration. This network mode is evident in successful open source communities and modern platform teams. It illustrates that agility can thrive even in large, complex organizations.

The principles that guided INTELLIFM apply here as well. We designed for the constraints of cross-functional collaboration by developing artifacts that both compliance officers and engineers could use. We built trust through transparency—the knowledge base was readable, the rules were auditable, and progress was visible. We preserved human judgment by keeping domain experts in control of decisions that required their expertise. Those same principles help teams maintain agility as they grow.

7.5.6 Adapting Agile to Distributed Teams

The agile practices described in this chapter emerged when most teams shared a physical workspace. Daily stand-ups happened around whiteboards. Sprint reviews took place in conference rooms. Informal desk-side conversations resolved ambiguities that would otherwise require meetings. The transition to distributed and remote work was dramatically accelerated by events in 2020 and has become increasingly permanent for many organizations. It has forced teams to rethink how they apply agile principles without abandoning them.

The underlying values remain unchanged. Individuals and interactions still matter more than processes and tools, but the nature of those interactions changes when team members span time zones and communicate primarily through screens. Working software remains the primary measure of progress, but demonstrating that software requires planning rather than a quick walk to a colleague's desk. Customer collaboration still outweighs contract negotiation, but relationships with stakeholders require more intentional effort as casual encounters diminish.

I have led distributed teams across multiple continents, and the lessons have been consistent.

First, asynchronous communication becomes essential, not optional. Teams that rely on real-time meetings for every decision create bottlenecks when participants span an eight- to ten-hour time difference. Effective distributed teams document decisions, record key discussions, and maintain written artifacts so colleagues in other time zones can catch up and contribute without attending every call. This discipline improves clarity even for colocated teams, but it becomes nonnegotiable for distributed ones.

Second, the informal information flow that occurs naturally in an office must be deliberately replaced. In a shared workspace, team members overhear conversations, notice when someone is struggling, and absorb context without conscious effort. Remote work removes these ambient signals. Teams compensate through structured check-ins, explicit status updates, and communication norms that increase visibility without micromanagement. Some teams designate overlap hours for synchronous collaboration; others rely more heavily on recorded updates and threaded discussions.

Third, tooling matters more than ever, but tools do not create collaboration. They either support it or impede it. I have seen teams adopt sophisticated platforms yet still struggle because the norms governing their use were unclear. Who updates the board? How quickly should messages receive responses? When should a discussion move from chat to a call? These questions have no universal answers; each team must provide explicit responses. The discipline is not choosing the perfect tool. Instead, it is establishing shared expectations about how tools support the work.

Fourth, trust requires deliberate cultivation. In an office, trust often builds through repeated exposure and small interactions over time. Distributed teams must create opportunities for connection that would otherwise happen organically. Some teams begin meetings with brief personal check-ins. Others schedule virtual sessions with no agenda beyond conversation. The specific practice matters less than the recognition that relationships require investment, and that investment does not happen automatically when people work apart.

The COVID-19 pandemic demonstrated that distributed work is viable at scale. It also revealed that simply replicating office practices over video calls is exhausting and unsustainable. The teams that adapted most successfully were those that redesigned their workflows for the constraints and opportunities of distributed collaboration, rather than treating remote work as a temporary inconvenience. As hybrid arrangements become permanent for many organizations, sustaining agile practices across distributed teams has become a core competency, not a contingency plan.

7.6 Technical Debt

Every software system accumulates compromises: a shortcut taken to meet a deadline, a temporary fix that became permanent, or a design decision that made sense at the time but now constrains what the system can do. Technical debt is the accumulated cost of these expedient choices—the future work required to address what was deferred or done imperfectly in the past.

The metaphor is helpful because, like financial debt, technical debt is not inherently bad. Borrowing to ship a feature faster can be rational if the benefit outweighs the cost of repayment. But unmanaged debt compounds. “Interest” is characterized by slower development, more defects, and increasing brittleness. Eventually, even small changes require disproportionate effort.

Agile practices can unintentionally exacerbate this problem when short cycles are treated as a license to cut corners, even though they are intended to promote technical excellence. Iteration makes trade-offs visible; it does not remove them. Without deliberate attention to quality, teams may deliver quickly in the short term while quietly increasing the cost of every future change.

I have inherited systems in which debt accumulated over the years. Simple feature requests took weeks because every change required navigating layers of workarounds. Engineers spent more time understanding the existing code than writing new code. The original developers were no longer available, and their shortcuts had become permanent constraints. These experiences taught me that managing technical debt is not optional—it is a core discipline of sustainable software development.

7.6.1 The Nature and Sources of Technical Debt

Technical debt takes many forms.

Code-level debt includes duplicated logic, unclear naming, tangled dependencies, and missing tests. Developers encounter this debt daily as they read and modify code. It slows comprehension, increases the likelihood of defects, and makes onboarding more difficult.

Architectural debt includes poor component boundaries, inappropriate technology choices, and missing or misplaced abstraction layers. This debt is less visible but often more damaging. A system with clean code and flawed architecture remains difficult to change because its boundaries are misconfigured. I once worked on a system where nearly every feature request required changes across six services because the domain had been sliced incorrectly. The code in each service was fine; the architecture was the constraint.

Infrastructure debt accumulates through deferred upgrades, manual processes that should be automated, and inadequate monitoring. This debt increases operational risk. Systems running on outdated platforms become harder to secure and maintain. Manual deployment processes introduce errors and slow delivery.

Security debt includes outdated dependencies with known vulnerabilities, insufficient access controls, and gaps in security testing. This debt can create immediate risk and often demands attention regardless of other priorities. I have seen organizations discover that a critical vulnerability had been flagged months earlier but never addressed. The debt had been accumulating silently.

Debt accumulates for many reasons. Time pressure is the most common—teams take shortcuts to meet deadlines. Requirements emerge and invalidate earlier designs. Team turnover leaves code that no one fully understands. Technology advances, turning yesterday's best practice into today's legacy. Even strong teams accumulate debt simply because software must adapt to change, and adaptation is never perfect.

7.6.2 Impact on Technical and Team Agility

Technical debt directly erodes technical agility. As debt accumulates, the practices that make change safe—automated testing, continuous integration, and confident refactoring—become harder to sustain. Systems grow fragile. Builds slow down. Deployments become risky. Modular boundaries degrade into tangled dependencies.

The impact extends to team dynamics. Developers become frustrated as simple changes require them to navigate workarounds. Velocity declines while defect rates rise, creating pressure for even more shortcuts. Psychological safety deteriorates as teams spend more time firefighting than building. Over time, knowledge silos form because only a few people understand the safest path through the codebase. Onboarding becomes an exercise in learning exceptions, even though teams need shared principles.

In INTELLIFM, we faced the same pressures as any other project: deadlines, changing requirements, and regulatory variation. The system I architected replaced a legacy approach that embodied the very technical debt we sought to eliminate—a tangle of manual, jurisdiction-specific workflows accumulated over years. These processes were impossible to scale and required constant human intervention to handle exceptions. That legacy represented the organizational equivalent of technical debt: processes so deeply embedded that replacing them required not just new software, but a fundamentally new architecture. The solution was not incremental; it was a complete reimagination of how multijurisdictional filings could be automated. We deliberately designed the system to absorb change without accumulating crippling debt. By decoupling the rules from the execution logic, regulatory updates could be managed within the knowledge base rather than by repeatedly modifying application code. This single design choice reduced the cost of change for years to come.

7.6.3 Lessons from Industry

Debt becomes most visible when organizations attempt to "fix everything" at once or ignore compounding constraints until they become existential.

Netscape's late-1990s rewrite effort is often cited as a cautionary example. Attempting to eliminate debt through a complete replacement can freeze delivery long enough for competitors to outpace you. The lesson is not that rewrites are always wrong—it is that incremental debt reduction is often less risky than big-bang replacement.

Early scaling challenges at high-growth technology companies provide a second lesson: architectural debt that is tolerable at a small scale can become a hard constraint as growth accelerates. Systems that were "good enough" for an initial audience can become bottlenecks when usage explodes, and unwinding those constraints later can take years.

Not all debt stories end badly. I worked with an organization that took a deliberate approach, allocating time for planned refactoring during quieter business periods and treating debt reduction as everyday work rather than a crisis response. Over time, bug-fix cycle time dropped, and developer satisfaction rose. The investment paid for itself in regained velocity and reduced operational stress.

7.6.4 Strategic Management Approaches

The most effective approach is usually incremental: integrate refactoring and debt repayment into regular development cycles rather than attempting to eliminate all debt at once. Teams allocate time within each sprint to address targeted issues, preserving feature delivery while steadily improving the codebase.

Prioritization matters because not all debt is equally costly. Effective evaluation considers the debt's impact on current delivery speed, the risk it creates for stability and security, its effect on team morale, and its relevance to upcoming business initiatives. High-impact debt that impedes daily work or increases production risk should be prioritized over cosmetic issues that are merely unpleasant.

A simple question helps keep this practical: "What will this cost us if we ignore it for another six months?" Some debt compounds rapidly. For example, gaps in test coverage become more dangerous as a system grows. Other debt remains stable. For example, an ugly but rarely changed module may not justify immediate refactoring. The key is to tell the difference and schedule the work accordingly.

7.6.5 Prioritization and Team Collaboration

Debt management works best when it is visible, shared, and discussed without blame. Teams benefit from regular "technical debt grooming" sessions—similar to backlog grooming—in which developers collectively identify, size, and prioritize technical debt items.

Transparency with nontechnical stakeholders matters. Business leaders often support debt reduction once they see the connection to delivery speed and reliability. The conversation turns from "engineering wants to rewrite code" to "this investment reduces risk and accelerates future delivery."

Team practices influence debt accumulation as much as tools do. Code reviews and pair programming prevent avoidable technical debt from entering the codebase. Collective ownership reduces bottlenecks in the most problematic areas. Most importantly, teams must treat debt repayment as part of delivering value, not as a side project reserved for a "cleanup crew."

7.6.6 Automation, Measurement, and Judgment

Automation facilitates the systematic identification and management of technical debt. Static analysis can flag code smells and complexity trends. Continuous integration pipelines can enforce quality gates to prevent new debt from entering unnoticed. Dependency scanning can surface outdated libraries and security risks early.

But tools cannot decide what matters. They must be paired with engineering judgment. A tool may flag hundreds of issues; experienced teams learn which items represent meaningful risk and which are noise. Documentation also matters: when teams document the reasoning behind shortcuts and trade-offs, they avoid "fixing" code that was intentionally structured that way for valid reasons.

Teams can track debt trends using metrics such as test coverage, defect rates, bug-fix cycle time, and the balance between new features and refactoring. Operational delivery measures—deployment frequency, lead time, change failure rate, and time to recovery—can also reveal when debt is making delivery brittle. Metrics do not replace judgment, but they can show when debt is compounding faster than it is being repaid.

7.6.7 Building Sustainable Practices

Managing technical debt requires balancing competing pressures: shipping new features, maintaining stability, and improving quality. The most successful teams treat debt management as part of normal development rather than a separate activity. They refactor as they learn, invest in tests and observability as the system grows, and make trade-offs explicit.

The goal is not to eliminate technical debt. Some debt is rational and deliberate, taken to achieve a business objective. The goal is to keep debt at sustainable levels so systems can adapt without sacrificing reliability or exhausting the people who support them.

This pragmatic discipline aligns with the principles that guided INTELLIFM: design for constraints, build trust through transparency, and preserve human judgment. Shortcuts were sometimes necessary, but we made them visible and planned for remediation. We built with the expectation that change was inevitable. I have seen these same principles validated across decades of enterprise AI work, from early expert systems in manufacturing and logistics to the ML platforms I work with today. The discipline helps teams navigate the trade-offs inherent in building software under real-world constraints.

7.7 Real-World Examples

The principles of technical agility, team agility, and technical debt management come to life through real-world implementations. The examples in this section demonstrate how organizations across different industries have successfully applied—or failed to apply—agile concepts. From technology companies pioneering new practices to traditional banks reinventing themselves, these cases illustrate both the rewards of agility and the consequences of technical rigidity.

I have discussed my experiences at Microsoft and Wolters Kluwer. But the principles are not unique to those organizations. The examples that follow—Netflix, Amazon, ING Bank, and cautionary tales from Netscape and Twitter—offer a broader perspective on how these ideas play out across industries and contexts.

7.7.1 Netflix: Technical Resilience Through Chaos Engineering

Netflix exemplifies technical agility through its approach to system resilience and architectural evolution. The streaming service serves hundreds of millions of users globally, and its engineering culture reflects the demands of operating at that scale.

At the heart of Netflix's technical agility is its pioneering Chaos Engineering practice, embodied in the Chaos Monkey tool—part of a broader suite called the Simian Army. Chaos Monkey randomly terminates instances in Netflix's production environment.[4] Rather than passively waiting for system failures, Netflix proactively simulates failure scenarios, keeping its systems in a constant state of readiness.

This approach drives continuous improvement among engineering teams. Every service must be designed from the ground up to withstand these tests, making resilience a fundamental aspect of the architecture rather than an afterthought. The practice exemplifies the technical agility principles described in Section 7.4—building systems that anticipate change and adapt without disruption.

Netflix's architecture offers a concrete example of technical agility in practice. The company moved from a monolithic system to a microservices architecture, making it possible to develop, deploy, and scale components independently. This modular approach allows Netflix to update services rapidly while maintaining system stability. Individual services can be scaled according to demand, enabling the platform to handle massive traffic spikes during the release of popular shows.

The company's approach to technical debt provides valuable lessons. Rather than allowing debt to accumulate to crisis levels, Netflix continuously refactors and improves its systems. The microservices architecture itself emerged from a deliberate effort to address the technical debt inherent in their original monolithic design. By investing in architectural improvements while maintaining service delivery, Netflix avoided the fate of competitors who failed to adapt their technical infrastructure to changing market conditions.

[4] Netflix Technology Blog, "The Netflix Simian Army," Netflix TechBlog, July 19, 2011, `https://netflixtechblog.com/the-netflix-simian-army-16e57fbab116`.

7.7.2 Amazon: Scaling Innovation Through Service Orientation

Amazon demonstrates how technical and team agility can drive business growth. The company's transformation from online bookstore to cloud computing giant illustrates the power of agile principles applied at scale.

Jeff Bezos's 2002 mandate required all teams to expose functionality through service interfaces.[5] This decision laid the foundation for both AWS and the company's ability to scale rapidly. The service-oriented architecture exemplifies technical agility. Each service can be updated independently, teams can experiment without affecting the entire system, and new capabilities can be added incrementally. This architectural decision, initially met with internal resistance, ultimately helped AWS grow from an internal efficiency initiative to a business generating tens of billions of dollars annually.[6]

Amazon's two-pizza team structure embodies the team agility principles outlined in Section 7.5.[7] These small, autonomous teams—sized so that two pizzas can feed the entire group—maintain ownership of specific services end to end. This structure facilitates rapid decision-making, reduces coordination overhead, and fosters innovation. Each team operates like a small startup within the larger organization, with the freedom to experiment and the responsibility for outcomes.

The company's leadership principles reinforce this agility. "Invent and simplify" encourages innovation while maintaining focus on elegant solutions. "Learn and be curious" promotes continuous improvement and adaptation. The principle that "frugality drives innovation" recognizes that constraints force creative problem-solving—teams must work within limitations rather than simply adding resources.

These principles manifest in concrete practices. Amazon's deployment pipeline supports thousands of deployments each day across hundreds of services, illustrating

[5] Steve Yegge, "Stevey's Google Platforms Rant," October 2011, preserved at `https://gist.github.com/chitchcock/1281611`; see also Kristopher Sandoval, "The Bezos API Mandate: Amazon's Manifesto for Externalization," Nordic APIs, September 5, 2023, `https://nordicapis.com/the-bezos-api-mandate-amazons-manifesto-for-externalization/`.

[6] Amazon, Inc., Annual Report (Form 10-K), 2023; see also "AWS Posts $24.2bn in Revenue for Q4, 2023," Data Center Dynamics, February 2, 2024, `https://www.datacenterdynamics.com/en/news/aws-posts-242bn-in-revenue-for-q4-2023-yoy-increase-of-13/`.

[7] Amazon Web Services, "Amazon's Two Pizza Teams," AWS Executive Insights, `https://aws.amazon.com/executive-insights/content/amazon-two-pizza-team/`.

the CI/CD practices central to technical agility. The company pioneered the "working backward" approach, starting with customer needs and writing press releases before coding begins. This ensures that technical decisions align with business value—an important aspect of managing technical debt effectively.

7.7.3 Google: Scientific Excellence in AI Innovation

Google exemplifies technical agility through a research-driven engineering culture and a commitment to open innovation. Operating at a scale that spans billions of users and petabytes of data, the company has developed ways of working that balance rapid experimentation with system reliability.

At the core of Google's approach is the idea that research and production are complementary, not separate. Engineers publish findings in peer-reviewed venues, thereby contributing to the broader technical community while advancing their own capabilities. This publication model accelerates learning: teams build on one another's work rather than solving the same problems independently. As discussed earlier, Google also promoted a structured form of autonomy, encouraging engineers to pursue exploratory projects. This novel approach helped produce innovations such as Gmail and Google News, illustrating how disciplined freedom can yield breakthrough results.

Google's engineering practices reinforce this model. The company maintains a monolithic code repository that supports code sharing and visibility across teams. Rigorous code review is mandatory, with every change reviewed by at least one other engineer before submission. Site reliability engineering (SRE) applies software engineering principles to infrastructure and operations, treating reliability as a feature to be designed and measured. Automated testing at scale helps prevent regressions across interdependent systems.

Google's 2018 AI Principles formalized a commitment to scientific excellence in AI development. The commitment holds that AI work should remain grounded in the scientific method, emphasizing open inquiry, intellectual rigor, integrity, and collaboration.[8] This approach has supported notable advancements. In 2015, Google released TensorFlow as an open source framework, which has become a widely used

[8] Google, "AI at Google: Our Principles," Google Blog, June 7, 2018, `https://blog.google/technology/ai/ai-principles/`.

platform for building and training ML models.[9] In 2018, Google researchers introduced Bidirectional Encoder Representations from Transformers. This language model achieved state-of-the-art results on multiple NLP tasks and helped reshape how machines process language.[10]

The lesson from Google's example is that technical agility includes learning velocity and knowledge sharing, not only deployment speed. By making research accessible—through publications, open source releases, and internal knowledge sharing—Google amplifies the impact of individual innovations across the organization and the industry.

7.7.4 ING Bank: Team Agility in Traditional Industries

Published case studies of ING suggest that agile transformation can succeed even in highly regulated, traditional industries. The Dutch banking group launched a full-scale agile transformation in the summer of 2015, restructuring its operating model to compete with digital-native challengers.[11]

Drawing inspiration from companies such as Google, Netflix, and Spotify, ING reorganized around approximately 350 squads of 9 people each, grouped into 13 tribes. Spotify's squad-based model is often cited as an influential example of how organizational structure can support technical agility, although results vary when the model is applied outside Spotify's specific context.[12] Autonomous squads own specific features end to end, encouraging rapid experimentation while maintaining system coherence and consistency. At ING, each squad functions as a fully cross-functional team, bringing together marketing professionals, product experts, user experience designers, data analysts, and IT engineers. This structure exemplifies the team agility principles of cross-functional collaboration and collective ownership described in Section 7.5.

[9] Google Open Source Projects, "TensorFlow," `https://opensource.google/projects/tensorflow`.

[10] Jacob Devlin et al., "BERT: Pre-training of Deep Bidirectional Transformers for Language Understanding," Google Research, October 2018, `https://research.google/pubs/bert-pre-training-of-deep-bidirectional-transformers-for-language-understanding/`.

[11] Bart Schlatmann and Peter Jacobs, "ING's Agile Transformation," McKinsey Quarterly, January 2017, `https://www.mckinsey.com/industries/financial-services/our-insights/ings-agile-transformation`.

[12] Henrik Kniberg and Anders Ivarsson, "Scaling Agile @ Spotify with Tribes, Squads, Chapters & Guilds," Crisp, October 2012, `https://blog.crisp.se/wp-content/uploads/2012/11/SpotifyScaling.pdf`.

The transformation required addressing technical debt accumulated over decades of traditional banking operations. Legacy systems built for batch processing had to be reimagined for real-time digital services. Rather than attempting a complete system replacement—the approach that doomed Netscape—ING adopted an incremental strategy, progressively modernizing its infrastructure while maintaining operations.

The results validated this approach. ING reduced its release cadence from five to six major releases annually to deployments every two to three weeks—a dramatic improvement in technical agility.[13] This acceleration enabled innovations such as instant lending, in which existing customers can apply for and receive loans within two minutes through fully automated processes. The bank's mobile app became one of the highest-rated banking apps in European markets.

These technical achievements translated into measurable business outcomes. Published case studies report that the Net Promoter Score for the ING Business Platform improved from -30 to +30 within one year.[14] Employee engagement scores reached 88%, according to the bank's Winning Performance Culture survey. INSEAD case studies document the transformation and discuss the reported outcomes.[15]

ING's transformation suggests that team agility and technical excellence mutually reinforce one another. The squad structure accelerated iteration and experimentation, while investments in technical capabilities gave teams the tools to deliver value quickly.

7.7.5 Lessons from Failure: Cautionary Tales

Not all attempts at technical transformation succeed. Understanding failures provides valuable insights into the importance of balance in pursuing agility.

Netscape's decline in the late 1990s illustrates the dangers of attempting to eliminate all technical debt at once. Instead of incremental refactoring, Netscape pursued a complete rewrite—a choice that consumed time and reduced its ability to respond

[13] Schlatmann and Jacobs, "ING's Agile Transformation."

[14] Adam Walendziewski, "Case Study: ING Bank's Digital Platform Tribe Goes Agile," Agile Business Consortium, `https://www.agilebusiness.org/resource-report/case-study-ings-digital-platform-tribe-goes-agile.html`.

[15] Lucia Del Carpio, Yves L. Doz, Maria Guadalupe, and Nancy J. Brandwein, "Embracing Digital: ING's Pioneering Journey to Agile," INSEAD Publishing; Maria Guadalupe, "Three Ways to Make Your Organisation Agile," INSEAD Knowledge, April 23, 2018, `https://knowledge.insead.edu/leadership-organisations/three-ways-make-your-organisation-agile`.

quickly to competitive pressure.[16] This multiyear effort left the company unable to respond to Internet Explorer's rapid improvements, ultimately resulting in the loss of their market-leading position. Three lessons emerge from this failure. First, technical debt must be managed continuously rather than addressed in dramatic, all-or-nothing efforts. Second, a working system—however imperfect—retains an "option value" that a rewrite cannot preserve during the transition. Third, the opportunity cost of a complete rewrite is rarely visible until it is too late to recover.

Twitter's early scalability challenges, widely reported at the time, illustrate how early architectural decisions can constrain growth in ways that are difficult and costly to reverse. The company's monolithic Ruby on Rails architecture was adequate for a startup but became a severe bottleneck as usage exploded. The infamous "Fail Whale" error page became synonymous with the impact of technical debt on user experience.[17] Twitter eventually invested heavily in decomposing its monolith into services, but the multiyear effort and reputational damage could have been reduced with earlier attention to architectural agility. The lesson is not that monolithic architectures are always wrong—it is that architectural decisions made under startup constraints must be revisited deliberately as scale increases, before constraints become crises.

Knight Capital Group's trading failure in August 2012 illustrates the catastrophic consequences of inadequate deployment controls. A flawed software deployment activated dormant legacy code in Knight's automated trading system, triggering 45 minutes of erroneous trades that generated a loss of approximately $440 million, forcing the firm into an emergency sale within days.[18] The failure resulted from a manual deployment process that lacked automated validation and consistent environment management. Crucially, one of the eight servers was not updated with the new software version, leaving legacy code active on a live system. Three lessons emerge from this failure. First, continuous delivery requires rigorous deployment controls, and speed without discipline becomes catastrophic. Second, even a single inconsistent server in a cluster is a latent existential threat. Third, the absence of automated, tested rollback mechanisms transforms recoverable errors into terminal ones.

[16] Joel Spolsky, "Things You Should Never Do, Part I," Joel on Software, April 6, 2000, `https://www.joelonsoftware.com/2000/04/06/things-you-should-never-do-part-i/`.

[17] Neil McAllister, "Twitter Survives Election After Ruby-to-Java Move," *The Register*, November 8, 2012, `https://www.theregister.com/2012/11/08/twitter_epic_traffic_saved_by_java/`.

[18] US Securities and Exchange Commission, "SEC Charges Knight Capital With Violations of Market Access Rule," Release No. 34-70694, October 16, 2013, `https://www.sec.gov/litigation/admin/2013/34-70694.pdf`.

These failures underscore a fundamental insight: sustainable velocity matters more than raw speed. Teams that sacrifice long-term adaptability for short-term gains eventually lose both. The success stories in the preceding sections—Netflix, Amazon, Google, and ING—share a common discipline: they managed change incrementally, maintained working systems throughout, and treated architectural health as an ongoing investment rather than a one-time project.

7.7.6 Common Patterns and Success Factors

Across these examples, several patterns emerge that distinguish successful agile transformations.

Incremental evolution consistently outperforms revolution. Amazon and Netflix gradually refined their architectures, maintaining service while improving them. Netscape's attempt to change everything at once froze its competitive response. ING modernized progressively rather than replacing legacy systems wholesale. The pattern holds across industries: sustainable transformation occurs in stages, not in leaps.

Cultural and technical change must proceed together. ING's success required both organizational restructuring and technical modernization; neither alone would have sufficed. Netflix's Chaos Engineering works because the culture expects and rewards resilience. Amazon's service orientation succeeded because the two-pizza team structure aligned organizational boundaries with technical boundaries.

Proactive debt management separates thriving teams from struggling ones. Companies that address technical debt continuously as part of normal operations avoid the crises that force dramatic interventions. Netflix refactors constantly. Amazon's service architecture prevents debt from accumulating across boundaries. ING's incremental modernization addressed debt without halting delivery.

Investment in foundations lays the groundwork for future agility. Amazon's service interfaces, Netflix's Chaos Engineering, and ING's automated deployment pipeline are foundational investments that have paid dividends over the years. These foundations create the conditions for agility rather than agility itself.

Empowered teams with clear accountability consistently outperform traditional hierarchical structures in rapidly changing environments. Amazon's two-pizza teams, Netflix's engineering culture, and ING's squads all share this characteristic: small groups with end-to-end ownership, the autonomy to make decisions, and the responsibility for outcomes.

However, achieving and maintaining agility presents ongoing challenges. Organizations encounter resistance to change, constant demands for learning and upskilling, and the challenge of balancing innovation with operational stability. Overcoming these hurdles requires leadership commitment, a culture that embraces continuous improvement, and strategic investments in both technology and human capital.

These examples demonstrate that technical agility, team agility, and effective management of technical debt are essential to organizational success. The companies that master these capabilities—integrating them into their culture, processes, and technical architecture—position themselves to thrive in a constantly changing environment. The principles that guided INTELLIFM decades ago still hold: design for constraints, build trust through transparency, and preserve human judgment. These patterns recur because they address fundamental challenges of building systems that must adapt over time.

7.8 Challenges in Agile Adoption

Transitioning to agile methodologies presents substantial challenges for organizations accustomed to traditional development approaches. The benefits of agile are compelling, but successful implementation requires navigating cultural, structural, and operational obstacles that can derail even well-intentioned transformations.

I have participated in numerous agile adoptions—some resulting in clear breakthroughs, others falling short of their intended impact. The most instructive experiences were rarely the nominal successes; instead, they were the difficult transitions where committed teams encountered obstacles that no framework or methodology could resolve in isolation. In almost every instance, the primary challenges were not technical. They were human: a collision of entrenched habits, professional fears, and misaligned incentives deeply embedded in the organizational fabric. Organizations that approach agile adoption as a mere process change, rather than a fundamental cultural transformation, consistently underestimate the institutional inertia they are destined to face.

7.8.1 Cultural Resistance and Mindset Shifts

The most fundamental challenge lies in cultural transformation. Agile emphasizes flexibility, collaboration, and adaptability—values that often conflict with predictable, hierarchical structures. Team members comfortable with detailed upfront planning and clearly defined phases may resist the ambiguity and constant change inherent in iterative delivery.

This resistance shows up in familiar patterns. Senior stakeholders accustomed to detailed plans and fixed deliverables question the value of incremental progress. Middle management can feel threatened by self-organizing teams that reduce the need for traditional oversight. Engineers who take pride in extensive documentation may struggle with agile's preference for working software over exhaustive specifications.

I once worked with a project manager who had built a career on detailed Gantt charts and milestone tracking. When the organization adopted scrum, he tried to map every sprint to a traditional project plan, producing elaborate documentation that no one used. He was not resisting out of malice; he was trying to demonstrate value using the only methods available to him. The transition improved only after leadership helped him focus on roadmap planning and dependency management. In that role, his strengths mattered, and sprint execution did not become performative.

The culture required for agile adoption also connects to building trust through transparency. Agile makes work visible—backlogs, burndown charts, and daily coordination expose progress and problems in ways that traditional methods can obscure. In organizations where information is power and visibility is treated as a risk, transparency can be perceived as threatening. Teams must learn that surfacing problems early is safer than delaying their resolution until they become crises.

7.8.2 Redefining Roles and Responsibilities

Agile restructures team dynamics by promoting cross-functional collaboration and shared ownership. Traditional organizations often operate with clearly delineated responsibilities: developers code, testers test, and analysts analyze. Agile reduces these silos, expecting team members to contribute beyond their primary specialization and to share accountability for outcomes.

This change can create confusion and anxiety. A database specialist may be drawn into discussions of user interfaces. A business analyst may need to understand technical constraints in greater depth. The product owner role—central in many agile frameworks—often lacks a clear precedent in traditional organizations. These ambiguities can trigger territorial disputes, accountability gaps, and reduced throughput during the transition.

In INTELLIFM, we faced a version of this challenge. Compliance officers and engineers had distinct expertise and initially resisted crossing boundaries. The breakthrough came when we created shared artifacts—the knowledge base that both groups could read and refine. Compliance officers did not need to write code, and engineers did not need to master regulatory law. But both required enough shared understanding to discuss rules constructively. The shared artifact became the bridge.

The lesson applies broadly: role ambiguity resolves more quickly when teams have concrete objects to collaborate on. Abstract debates about responsibility often generate conflict; working together on tangible deliverables builds mutual understanding.

7.8.3 Adapting to Iterative Development

Teams accustomed to the waterfall model's linear progression often struggle with the iterative nature of agile. The concept of delivering potentially shippable increments every few weeks challenges ingrained beliefs about what constitutes "complete" software. Engineers trained to perfect their work before release may view frequent delivery as rushed or unprofessional.

I have heard engineers describe early iterations as "embarrassing"—they wanted more time to polish before showing progress. That instinct is understandable, but it undermines the purpose of iteration. The value lies in getting feedback before perfection, when course corrections are still cheap. Discomfort is part of the learning loop.

Stakeholder feedback also becomes continuous rather than episodic. Instead of gathering requirements once and building to specification, agile teams must remain responsive to changing priorities throughout development. This can feel chaotic to those who prefer the stability of fixed requirements.

Progressive disclosure helps teams navigate this transition. Rather than promising a complete system and delivering everything at once, agile teams reveal capabilities incrementally. Users see working software early and often, and their feedback shapes what comes next. This approach reduces the risk of building the wrong thing, but it requires accepting that early iterations will be incomplete by design.

7.8.4 Communication and Collaboration Barriers

Agile depends on frequent, effective communication, and this requirement exposes weaknesses in organizational communication habits. Daily coordination, sprint reviews, and retrospectives demand transparency that many organizations have not practiced. Team members must discuss blockers openly, admit mistakes, and offer constructive feedback—behaviors that may conflict with existing norms.

I have facilitated retrospectives in which no one spoke candidly because the room included people who controlled promotions. I have also observed that daily stand-ups have devolved into status reports for managers rather than peer coordination. The ceremonies are easy to adopt; the honesty they require is harder.

Geographic distribution can amplify these challenges. Colocated teams benefit from spontaneous conversations and rapid problem-solving, whereas distributed teams must intentionally create communication channels and maintain engagement across time zones. Distributed agile is possible, but it demands more discipline than colocated work.

Trust is the prerequisite. Teams that lack psychological safety will not communicate honestly, regardless of the methodology. Organizations seeking to adopt agile must invest in trust-building before expecting the communication patterns required by the agile model.

7.8.5 Technical Infrastructure Gaps

Many organizations undergoing an agile transformation lack the technical foundation needed for rapid iteration. Legacy systems without automated testing make frequent releases risky. Monolithic architectures resist modular change. Manual deployment processes create bottlenecks that prevent teams from delivering value quickly.

These limitations often become visible only after adoption begins, forcing teams to retain waterfall-like practices despite mandates for agility. The resulting hybrid—usually referred to as "water-scrum-fall"—satisfies neither approach and frustrates teams seeking improvement. Teams go through the motions of sprints and stand-ups, but delivery remains constrained by the same bottlenecks as before.

I have seen this pattern repeatedly: an organization announces an agile transformation, trains everyone in scrum, and then wonders why throughput does not improve. The answer is often technical debt and infrastructure gaps that no amount of process change can overcome. Section 7.6 examined technical debt in detail. The point here is simpler: without the technical investments that remove bottlenecks, agile rituals alone rarely improve delivery.

The constraint principle applies. Teams must design their adoption around the constraints they actually face, not the constraints they wish they had. If the deployment pipeline supports only monthly releases, the sprint cadence will not translate into weekly delivery. If the test suite takes hours to run, continuous integration becomes difficult to practice consistently. Effective adoption sequences technical improvements alongside process changes, building the infrastructure that makes agility practical.

7.8.6 Strategies for Successful Adoption

Despite these challenges, organizations can navigate agile transitions successfully by acknowledging obstacles openly and addressing them systematically.

Start with willing teams. Pilot programs with motivated groups build momentum and generate visible wins that persuade skeptics. Forcing agile on resistant teams before demonstrating value tends to create opposition instead of learning.

Invest in coaching. Experienced coaches bring pattern recognition and objectivity that internal champions may lack. They can identify dysfunction that insiders have normalized and suggest adjustments that fit the organizational context.

Align incentives. If performance reviews reward individual heroics, agile's emphasis on collaboration will conflict with career advancement. If managers are measured primarily on predictability instead of value delivered, they will resist the uncertainty that iteration introduces. Incentive structures must reinforce the behaviors required by the agile model.

Sequence the technical and cultural change. Technical improvements without cultural change produce sophisticated tools that teams do not use well. Cultural change without technical investment produces motivated teams that are constrained by infrastructure limitations. Sustainable adoption treats both as necessary.

Accept that transformation takes time. Organizations that have operated under the waterfall model for decades will not become agile in a quarter. The ING transformation discussed in Section 7.7 took years and required rethinking how work was organized. Patience and persistence matter more than speed.

The same principles that guided INTELLIFM transfer well to agile adoption: design for real constraints, build trust through transparency, deliver in increments that users can validate, and keep experts responsible for judgment-heavy decisions.

7.9 Resolution Strategies

Successfully addressing agile implementation challenges requires strategies that address both human and technical dimensions. The obstacles described in Section 7.8—cultural resistance, role confusion, communication barriers, and infrastructure gaps—do not resolve on their own. Organizations that tackle these obstacles deliberately can transform resistance into engagement and confusion into clarity.

The following strategies draw on my experience at Microsoft and in other enterprise roles. Each addresses a specific dimension of agile adoption: building culture through practice, strengthening distributed collaboration, integrating DevOps disciplines, learning from failure without blame, establishing improvement rhythms, and leading transformation with architectural intent.

7.9.1 Building Culture Through Practice

Cultural transformation cannot be mandated; it must be cultivated through consistent practice and visible results. Successful organizations avoid forcing wholesale change. They start with pilot teams that demonstrate agile value through delivery. These early adopters become advocates, sharing what worked, what did not, and how they adjusted.

I have seen this pattern work repeatedly. On one occasion, three teams were willing to experiment with scrum while the rest of the company continued with traditional methods. Within six months, those teams increased their delivery frequency and reduced defects. Other teams noticed. Requests for coaching moved from mandated training to genuine interest. Culture followed demonstrated value rather than preceding it.

Daily practices reinforce cultural change. Stand-ups promote transparency by surfacing progress and blockers. Retrospectives create space for continuous improvement. Pair programming reduces knowledge silos while building trust. These ceremonies may feel awkward at first, but with repetition and refinement, they gradually reshape how teams work together.

Trust grows through transparency. Agile practices make work visible. Teams learn that openness is rewarded, not punished. That learning comes through experience, not instruction.

7.9.2 Supporting Distributed Collaboration

Sections 7.4 and 7.5 addressed the practices and dynamics that make teams effective. This section focuses on the tools and working agreements that support those practices when teams are not colocated—a reality for many organizations since the transition to remote and hybrid work.

Through my work at Microsoft, I have seen collaboration tools advance from email and shared drives to integrated platforms that support real-time coordination across continents. That evolution accelerated with Microsoft Teams, which serves as the hub for many agile teams by combining chat, video, file sharing, and application connectors. For organizations already standardized on Microsoft 365, integration with SharePoint, OneDrive, and Outlook can reduce routine coordination overhead for distributed teams.

Azure DevOps complements this by supporting backlog management, source control, and pipeline automation. Teams use boards to manage backlogs, plan sprints, and track progress. Integration between collaboration tools and development workflows can reduce context switching. Commits, pull requests, and build notifications can surface in the same place where teams coordinate every day.

Other tools address specific needs. Slack offers flexible messaging and automation. Zoom supports reliable video meetings and breakout discussions. Visual collaboration platforms such as Miro and Mural provide digital canvases for story mapping, retrospectives, and design workshops—replicating the spontaneity of physical whiteboards while adding features such as voting, timers, and reusable templates.

AI features are increasingly embedded in these platforms. Meeting summaries, action item extraction, and coding assistants are still maturing, but they already show how AI can augment collaboration without removing human ownership. Section 7.12 explores the intersection of agile and AI in greater depth.

However, tools alone do not create effective collaboration. I have seen teams with excellent tooling fail because they lacked working agreements. Successful distributed teams establish explicit norms: response time expectations, core collaboration hours across time zones, and protocols for asynchronous communication. They define which decisions require synchronous discussion and which can proceed asynchronously. They also create space for informal connection—virtual coffee sessions, celebrations, and social channels—to maintain the social fabric that colocated teams build naturally.

The tools support the practices, but the practices must be intentional. A team with excellent video conferencing but no agreement on response times or core hours will struggle. Distributed agile often requires more explicit discipline than colocated work because fewer norms form automatically.

7.9.3 Learning from DevOps Integration

My experience leading a payment platform consolidation illustrates how DevOps practices can accelerate agile maturity. We were tasked with unifying multiple payment systems into a single cloud-based solution, a complex undertaking that required coordination across development, operations, and security.

Initially, our sprints were hampered by deployment bottlenecks. Development teams delivered features on schedule, but operations required weeks to provision environments and deploy changes. Security reviews were delayed and frequently triggered by rework. We were following agile ceremonies but not achieving agile outcomes.

The breakthrough came when we embedded DevOps engineers directly into the agile teams. They participated in stand-ups, planning, and retrospectives. They were not external service providers; they were full team members with shared accountability for delivery. This integration surfaced downstream constraints early—issues that previously emerged just before release were now identified and addressed during development.

One incident stands out. During sprint planning, a DevOps engineer pointed out that our proposed architecture would require manual configuration changes across multiple regions for each deployment. What seemed like a minor technical decision to developers represented hours of error-prone work for operations. By identifying the issue early, we redesigned the solution to use IaC, thereby eliminating what would have become a recurring bottleneck.

This reinforced the principle of designing for constraints. The constraint was not technical skill. The constraint was organizational: siloed teams lacked early visibility into downstream consequences. Embedding DevOps capabilities within the teams directly addressed that constraint.

7.9.4 Implementing Blameless Learning

Blameless postmortems are essential for maintaining psychological safety and agility. When incidents occur—and they will—the default impulse is to assign fault. That behavior drives problems underground, as people hide mistakes even though they could be shared as learning opportunities.

Blameless postmortems reverse this dynamic. After a major incident, the team constructs a timeline of events and focuses on system behavior and decision context rather than individual failings. We ask, "What information did we have at the time?" instead of "Who made the wrong choice?"

These sessions follow a structured format. We begin by confirming the incident is resolved and recognizing the team's response. We then collaboratively build a timeline, with participants contributing observations without judgment. Analysis focuses on systemic factors: missing alerts, unclear documentation, brittle architecture, or process gaps. We conclude with specific, assignable actions to reduce the chance of recurrence.

The principle of preserving human judgment applies directly. People make decisions based on the information available at the time. Hindsight makes every mistake obvious; foresight operates under uncertainty. By focusing on systemic improvement rather than blame, teams create an environment where judgment can be exercised without fear.

In INTELLIFM, we applied similar thinking to rule failures. When the system produced an incorrect filing recommendation, we did not blame the compliance officer who authored the rule or the engineer who implemented the logic. After examining the edge case, assumptions, and rule logic, we updated the knowledge base and supporting checks. That approach kept both groups engaged in improvement rather than defensive about their contributions.

7.9.5 Establishing Continuous Improvement Rhythms

Sustainable transformation requires embedding improvement into regular work. Retrospectives provide scheduled reflection, but teams also need protected time for debt reduction, automation, and experimentation.

We implemented "Improvement Fridays," dedicating Friday afternoons to addressing technical debt, automating manual work, or experimenting with new practices. This regular investment prevents impediments from compounding and creates space for new ideas without threatening sprint commitments.

The practice requires leadership support. Teams must trust that improvement time will not be canceled whenever deadlines approach. If improvement disappears under pressure, teams learn that it is optional, and it stops happening. Protecting improvement time signals that sustainable pace and continuous improvement are organizational priorities.

AI tools are beginning to assist in identifying improvements by surfacing debt patterns, recurring incident themes, and opportunities for automation. These capabilities complement human judgment rather than replacing it. The team still decides what to prioritize; the tools help reveal patterns that might otherwise be missed.

Other rhythms complement retrospectives and Improvement Fridays. Monthly architecture reviews surface debt before it becomes a showstopper. Quarterly planning aligns priorities with strategy. Annual technology assessments evaluate whether platforms and tools still fit emerging needs. Each rhythm operates at a different timescale, creating a layered system of reflection and adjustment.

7.9.6 Leadership's Role in Transformation

Leaders must model the behaviors they expect from teams. This means admitting uncertainty, supporting learning from failure, and prioritizing agile principles even when under pressure. When executives demand fixed deadlines and detailed plans while advocating agility, teams receive mixed signals that undermine change.

I have worked for leaders who understood this and leaders who did not. The difference showed up quickly. When a leader responded to a missed sprint goal by asking what the team learned rather than who was responsible, the team became more honest about risks in subsequent planning. When a leader praised an experiment that failed but produced valuable insights, other teams became more willing to try new approaches.

Effective leaders focus on removing impediments and clearing the path for teams, leaving task decisions with the people doing the work. They ask, "What is blocking you?" instead of "What is your status?" They protect teams from organizational resistance—processes and policies that conflict with agile practices. They also treat improvement work as real work, not discretionary work.

The principle of building trust through transparency requires leaders to go first. Teams will not be transparent with leaders they do not trust. Leaders earn trust by sharing strategic context, acknowledging mistakes, and explaining the reasoning behind decisions. That reciprocal transparency provides the foundation for the honest communication required by the agile model.

The strategies in this section address the challenges outlined in Section 7.8. They include building culture through practice, supporting distributed collaboration, integrating DevOps, learning without blame, establishing improvement rhythms, and leading by example. None is sufficient alone. Successful adoption requires attention to all of these dimensions, appropriately sequenced for the organizational context and sustained over time. Teams that succeed treat transformation as ongoing work, not a project with an end date.

7.10 Scaling Agile

As organizations succeed with individual agile teams, they encounter a new challenge: scaling these practices across dozens or hundreds of teams while preserving the core benefits of agility. Scaling agile requires deliberate orchestration: preserving team autonomy while coordinating roadmaps, dependencies, and enterprise priorities.

Earlier sections described the evolution from waterfall to agile at the team level. As organizations grow, short cycles, continuous feedback, and cross-functional collaboration remain effective, but they are harder to sustain without explicit alignment mechanisms. Scaling frameworks aim to preserve the benefits of agility while addressing dependencies between teams, shared roadmaps, and enterprise-wide priorities.

I have worked in organizations at various stages of this journey. Some scaled too quickly, imposing frameworks before teams had internalized the principles of agile. Others scaled too slowly, leaving successful teams isolated while the rest of the organization continued with traditional methods. The organizations that succeeded treated scaling as an evolution—building on what worked rather than replacing it wholesale.

7.10.1 Frameworks for Scaling

Several frameworks have emerged to address scaling challenges, each with distinct philosophies and practices. The right choice depends on organizational context, existing culture, and the nature of the work.

LeSS maintains scrum's simplicity while scaling to multiple teams. It resists adding layers of coordination, instead emphasizing direct communication between teams and shared ownership of the product backlog. Organizations willing to restructure around products rather than projects often find LeSS appealing. I have seen it work well when teams share a single product and can coordinate directly, but it struggles when organizational boundaries prevent the structural changes it requires.

DAD adopts a pragmatic approach, recognizing that different situations require different practices. It provides a toolkit of strategies that organizations can adapt to their context, from initial project visioning through delivery and operations. Its flexibility appeals to organizations with diverse work types that resist one-size-fits-all approaches. The trade-off is complexity: DAD's breadth can overwhelm teams looking for a clear starting point.

SAFe has gained widespread adoption, particularly in large enterprises. According to the 16th State of Agile Report, 53% of organizations practicing agile at scale use it.[19] Its systematic approach guides portfolio, program, and team levels. Agile Release Trains coordinate multiple teams working toward shared objectives, and Program Increment planning establishes a delivery cadence that many executives prefer. Critics argue that SAFe's prescriptive structure can become bureaucratic, but organizations that adapt it thoughtfully often find value in its coordination mechanisms.

No framework guarantees success. I have seen organizations adopt SAFe and achieve meaningful improvement. I have also seen organizations adopt SAFe and produce elaborate ceremonies that increased overhead without improving delivery. The difference was not the framework; it was whether teams internalized the underlying principles or merely followed prescribed practices.

7.10.2 Coordination Without Control

Successful scaling preserves team autonomy while achieving coordination. This balance requires both technical and organizational practices that foster alignment without centralized control.

Technical foundations support independent team operation. Service-based architecture allows teams to deploy independently while maintaining system integration. Clear API contracts define boundaries between components, reducing coordination overhead. Feature flags support continuous integration while controlling when capabilities become visible to users. Thorough automated testing provides confidence that changes will not break existing functionality. These are not optional refinements; at scale, they determine whether autonomy is feasible.

[19] Digital.ai, "16th State of Agile Report," Digital.ai Software, Inc., 2022, `https://digital.ai/resource-center/analyst-reports/16th-state-of-agile-report/`.

I learned the value of these practices through their absence. I once attempted to scale agile across eight teams sharing a monolithic codebase. Every deployment required coordination across all teams. Merge conflicts were frequent, and a defect introduced by one team blocked releases for all teams. We spent more time coordinating than building. The eventual migration to service-based architecture took 18 months, but it made independent delivery feasible for the first time.

Organizational practices create shared context without adding bureaucracy. Communities of practice connect specialists across teams, spreading knowledge and establishing consistent standards. Architecture guilds help guide decisions that affect multiple teams, balancing standardization with local flexibility. Regular system demos create transparency about progress and dependencies, replacing status meetings with working software.

The principle of building trust through transparency operates at scale just as it does within teams. When teams can see what other teams are building, dependencies become visible earlier. When architectural decisions are discussed openly, teams understand the rationale rather than experiencing constraints as arbitrary mandates. Transparency at scale requires more deliberate effort than transparency within a single team, but the benefits compound as coordination complexity increases.

7.10.3 Challenges at Scale

Scaling introduces complexities that do not exist at the team level. Dependencies multiply as the number of teams increases. A feature requiring changes from three teams creates coordination points, and each point adds delay, communication overhead, and risk of rework. I have watched features that would take a single team two weeks stretch to three months when dependencies required sequential handoffs across multiple teams.

Technical debt also becomes systemic at scale. Individual teams might maintain clean code, but the interfaces between systems can accumulate complexity. Inconsistent patterns across teams create cognitive overhead for anyone working across boundaries. Legacy systems that cannot support rapid deployment become bottlenecks that affect multiple teams, even when individual teams are performing well.

Cultural drift emerges as well. Teams that began with a shared understanding of agile principles can diverge over time as practices adapt to local contexts. Some adaptations are healthy; others represent a gradual erosion of core values. Without mechanisms for alignment, organizations end up with teams that claim to practice agile but operate in incompatible ways.

The constraint principle applies directly. Organizations must design their scaling approach around the constraints they actually face. If legacy systems cannot support independent deployment, scaling approaches that assume service-based architecture will produce frustration rather than improvement. If the organizational structure prevents cross-functional teams, frameworks that require them will fail. Honest assessment of constraints—technical, organizational, and cultural—must precede framework selection.

7.10.4 Sustainable Scaling Strategies

Organizations that successfully scale agile adopt strategies that systematically address these challenges.

Technical excellence must precede scaling. Before expanding to more teams, organizations should establish sound engineering practices. Continuous integration, automated testing, and deployment automation become exponentially more valuable—and their absence more painful—at scale. I have seen organizations attempt to scale without these foundations, and the result was predictable: agile ceremonies layered atop the same bottlenecks that existed before.

Platform capabilities accelerate team productivity. Rather than having each team independently solve common problems, platform teams provide shared services, including deployment pipelines, monitoring systems, data platforms, and authentication. These investments pay dividends across every team that uses them. The challenge is to ensure that platform teams remain responsive to the teams they serve rather than becoming gatekeepers.

Lightweight governance replaces approval gates with automated quality checks. Instead of architecture review boards that meet monthly, fitness functions can continuously verify architectural constraints. Instead of change advisory boards that manually review deployments, automated checks verify that releases meet defined criteria. This approach scales governance without scaling bureaucracy.

Communities foster alignment without hierarchy. Communities of practice, guilds, and chapters create organic knowledge sharing across teams. Engineers solving similar problems in different areas connect, share solutions, and establish patterns others can adopt. These communities work because participation is voluntary and the value is immediate—people join because they benefit, not because they are assigned.

Team stability enables performance. Stable teams develop trust, shared context, and working rhythms that support sustained delivery. Constantly reorganizing teams in response to changing priorities undermines that foundation. I have seen organizations churn team composition quarterly and then wonder why performance did not improve. The teams never had time to develop the cohesion that makes agility possible.

The four principles that guided INTELLIFM also apply at scale. Design for constraints by assessing the organization's capacity before selecting frameworks. Build trust through transparency by making work visible across teams and discussing architectural decisions openly. Deliver incrementally by scaling gradually rather than attempting to transform everything at once. Preserve human judgment by keeping decisions with the people closest to the work rather than centralizing control in scaling bureaucracies. These principles do not change as organizations grow; they become more nonnegotiable.

7.11 Benefits of Agile

After examining the challenges and strategies of agile implementation, it is worth revisiting why organizations undertake this transformation. The difficulties described in Sections 7.8–7.10 are real, but so are the rewards. Organizations that navigate the transition successfully gain capabilities that extend beyond faster delivery.

I have witnessed these benefits across my career. The patterns are consistent. Teams that embrace agile principles deliver more value, respond more quickly to change, and sustain higher morale than teams operating under traditional methods. Evidence in industry reports and large-scale studies confirms what practitioners have observed for decades, including the annual State of Agile Report[20] and the State of DevOps Report.[21]

[20] Digital.ai, "16th State of Agile Report."

[21] Nicole Forsgren, Jez Humble, and Gene Kim, *2023 State of DevOps Report* (Google Cloud and DevOps Research and Assessment (DORA), 2023), `https://cloud.google.com/devops/state-of-devops`.

7.11.1 Accelerated Value Delivery

Agile's iterative approach delivers working software in weeks rather than months or years. The Standish Group's CHAOS Report found that agile projects are three times more likely to succeed than waterfall projects.[22] This acceleration is not just about speed—it is about validating assumptions and delivering value before investing in complete solutions.

Early delivery produces compounding benefits. Revenue can begin to flow sooner, yielding an ROI that can fund continued development. Equally important, honest user feedback guides improvement, directing effort toward features that matter.

In INTELLIFM, we experienced this directly. Early releases to compliance officers revealed which filing rules worked and which needed refinement. We adjusted before investing months in the wrong direction. That pattern—deliver early, learn, and adapt—became foundational to my approach to every project.

7.11.2 Enhanced Quality

Contrary to traditional beliefs, faster delivery through agile can improve quality. The State of DevOps Report found that, under its definitions, elite performers deploy 973 times more frequently than low performers while maintaining higher quality, with a change failure rate of 0–15%.[23]

As described in Section 7.4, the technical practices that drive this outcome include continuous integration, automated testing, and refactoring. These practices catch defects early, prevent regression, and maintain code health as systems grow. Quality is built in rather than tested out at the end.

[22] The Standish Group International, Inc., *CHAOS Report 2020: Beyond Infinity* (Boston: The Standish Group International, Inc., 2020), `https://www.standishgroup.com`.

[23] Forsgren, Humble, and Kim, *2023 State of DevOps Report.*

7.11.3 Stakeholder Engagement

Agile transforms stakeholder relationships from transactional handoffs to collaborative partnerships. Product owners work closely with development teams to build a shared understanding that extends beyond documented requirements. Regular demonstrations keep stakeholders engaged and informed, reducing the surprise and disappointment that often accompany big-bang deliveries.

Agile transparency builds trust by making progress, priorities, and impediments visible, replacing status meetings with collaborative problem-solving. The principle of building trust through transparency operates directly here. When stakeholders regularly see working software, they develop confidence in the team's ability to deliver. When problems surface early, they become shared challenges rather than blame assignments.

7.11.4 Adaptive Capability

Agile organizations develop institutional capability for change. Teams comfortable with iteration adapt quickly to new technologies, market fluctuations, or regulatory requirements. Innovation also flourishes because short iterations encourage experimentation—teams can try new approaches knowing that failure costs weeks, not years. This adaptability proved valuable during the widespread adoption of remote and hybrid work. Organizations with mature agile practices transitioned more smoothly, having already established the collaboration patterns required by distributed teams.

Given the pace of technological advancements, traditional long-term planning is often challenged. Agile teams excel in this fast-moving environment, focusing on rapid execution and adaptability. They pursue short- to medium-term goals while maintaining awareness of the broader long-term vision. This approach, often described as "see long, act short," underscores the importance of flexibility. It empowers teams to adapt swiftly to change without being hindered by rigid plans.

7.11.5 Team Morale and Retention

The 16th State of Agile Report indicates that organizations cite improved team morale as a benefit of agile adoption. Developers prefer working in environments where they can see their impact and receive rapid feedback. The autonomy of self-organizing teams supports mastery and purpose that traditional command structures often suppress.

Section 7.5 described the collaborative practices—pair programming, cross-functional teams, and retrospectives—that help create these environments. The regular rhythm of ceremonies provides structure without rigidity. Teams that feel ownership over their work deliver better results and stay longer.

7.11.6 Financial Performance

McKinsey's 2021 global survey found that organizations with highly successful agile transformations were nearly three times as likely to be top-quartile performers among their peers.[24] The same study found that organizations in the top quartile of agility achieve shareholder returns 2.7 times higher than those in the bottom quartile.

These effects reinforce one another over time. Faster delivery supports more experiments, accelerating learning. Higher quality reduces maintenance burden, freeing capacity for innovation. Engaged employees contribute discretionary effort and creative solutions.

7.11.7 Risk Mitigation

Agile's iterative approach alters the risk profile by continuously testing assumptions rather than deferring validation until final delivery. Technical risks emerge early through architectural spikes and proofs of concept. Market risks are validated through regular releases and user feedback. Integration risks are addressed through continuous integration rather than big-bang integration phases. The principle of progressive disclosure applies: capabilities are revealed incrementally, and course corrections occur while they remain affordable.

7.11.8 Learning Organizations

One of agile's most important benefits is the creation of organizations that continuously learn and improve. Failure is treated as a learning opportunity rather than a trigger for blame. Teams develop hypothesis-driven approaches, treating features as experiments rather than fixed requirements.

[24] McKinsey & Company, "The Impact of Agility: How to Shape Your Organization to Compete," McKinsey Global Institute, 2021, `https://www.mckinsey.com/capabilities/people-and-organizational-performance/our-insights/the-impact-of-agility-how-to-shape-your-organization-to-compete`.

INTELLIFM embodied this approach before the terminology existed. We treated every release as an opportunity to learn. Compliance officers told us what worked; we adjusted what did not. The knowledge base improved continuously in response to real-world feedback. That cycle of delivery, feedback, and improvement is what the agile model formalizes and scales.

Organizations that adopt agile's learning culture respond more quickly to opportunities, recover more quickly from setbacks, and innovate more consistently. The four principles that guided INTELLIFM—design for constraints, build trust through transparency, deliver incrementally, and preserve human judgment—align directly with these benefits. Agile methodologies succeed not because of their ceremonies or frameworks, but because they operationalize principles that have always distinguished effective teams from struggling ones.

7.12 Agile and AI

The integration of agile methodologies with AI development represents a natural convergence. INTELLIFM combined rule-based intelligence with iterative refinement—an approach that anticipated today's agile-AI fusion. What has changed is scale. Modern ML requires rapid experimentation and continuous feedback, and AI tools now strengthen agile practices.

ML development differs from conventional software engineering in ways that change how agile practices apply. Requirements are often probabilistic rather than deterministic: for example, a model achieving 95% accuracy may be acceptable, whereas one achieving 92% may not—depending on the context and metric. "Done" must include evaluation against baselines and real-world performance, not just passing tests. Data pipelines are part of the product, not merely inputs, and their quality directly affects outcomes. Monitoring and drift detection are first-class concerns from day one, not operational afterthoughts. These differences do not invalidate agile principles, but they require thoughtful adaptation.

The core principles of adaptability, continuous feedback, and iterative development align well with the dynamic and often unpredictable nature of AI projects. Traditional methodologies such as scrum and kanban are being adapted to meet AI's unique demands. Scrum sprints in AI projects often incorporate extended experimentation phases to accommodate the iterative nature of model training and refinement. Kanban boards for AI projects may include additional columns for data preparation, model training, and ethical review processes.

The iterative sprints of agile provide a structured framework for rapid prototyping and experimentation, supporting swift hypothesis testing and frequent refinement. But applying agile to AI projects presents distinctive challenges. Uncertainty in model performance and the need for extensive data preparation can strain traditional sprint timeframes.

Teams often address this by incorporating flexible sprint lengths or introducing "research spikes"—time-boxed periods, typically lasting one to three days, dedicated to exploratory work. For example, a developer might spend half a day evaluating cloud services, APIs, or open source tools to address a video processing challenge or run experiments with a new algorithm to assess feasibility before implementation. These spikes have clear deliverables such as written reports, proof-of-concept code, or brief presentations to the team, so the knowledge gained informs future sprint planning with more accurate estimates and technical direction.

The emphasis on collaboration and cross-functional teams in agile development is particularly beneficial for AI projects, which require integrating diverse skills and perspectives. Section 7.12.1 examines the specific collaboration challenges that arise when data scientists, engineers, and product managers must align around ML-specific concerns.

Agile methodologies also promote transparency and visibility, which are valuable in AI projects given the "black-box" problem, in which the internal workings of complex models are not easily interpretable. Regular sprint reviews can showcase the capabilities and limitations of AI models to stakeholders, building trust and accountability. This transparency reflects the same principle I applied in INTELLIFM: making the system's reasoning visible to users so they could understand and trust its recommendations.

By maintaining an iterative development and testing cycle, agile practices help AI projects adapt quickly to new insights and challenges. Teams can integrate ethical review processes into sprint cycles through "ethics checkpoints" that evaluate AI decisions for unintended biases or consequences.

Health care illustrates how teams apply agile practices in heavily regulated environments. Companies such as PMX, NeuralMed, and Digital Diagnostics have developed AI diagnostic tools that iteratively refine ML models and adapt to new medical research, potentially accelerating the path to regulatory approval.

PMX's ChestOMX analyzes computed tomography scan reports for lung infections, NeuralMed's Harpy extracts information from radiology reports, and Digital Diagnostics improves diabetic retinopathy detection using AI algorithms. These examples show how agile methodologies can adapt to stringent compliance requirements while maintaining the flexibility AI development demands.

7.12.1 Adapting Agile for ML-Enabled Systems and AI Agents

While agile methodologies provide valuable frameworks for iterative development, applying them to ML systems requires thoughtful adaptation. The term *ML-enabled systems* encompasses a broad spectrum—from classical ML models and cognitive services to LLMs and, increasingly, AI agents that autonomously execute multistep tasks. Researchers have observed that traditional life-cycle models—waterfall, spiral, and agile—often clash with the experimental nature of ML.[25] Unlike conventional software, where logic is deterministic and requirements translate into predictable code, ML development is inherently stochastic. It proceeds through hypothesis testing and data experimentation, producing probabilistic outcomes that resist the rigid constraints of standard sprint planning and estimation. These difficulties are most visible when moving from a stable prototype to a production environment, where data dependencies and model drift can turn a successful deployment into a moving target.

The collaboration challenges are particularly acute. ML-enabled systems require expertise spanning data science, software engineering, infrastructure operations, and domain knowledge. Each discipline brings different assumptions about quality, documentation, and success criteria. ML scientists may focus primarily on model accuracy and devote less attention to coding standards and operational robustness, while software engineers emphasize maintainability, reliability, and system performance. Product managers may hold overly optimistic expectations about what ML can deliver, particularly when they lack technical depth in the field. Without explicit mechanisms to connect these perspectives, teams often discover integration problems late in the development cycle—frequently during production deployment, when the cost and risk of remediation are highest.

[25] J. J. Wu, "An Exploratory Study of V-Model in Building ML-Enabled Software: A Systems Engineering Perspective," in *Proceedings of the Conference on AI Engineering Software Engineering for AI (CAIN 2024), Lisbon, Portugal* (ACM, 2024), `https://doi.org/10.1145/3644815.3644951`.

Effective adoption of agile for ML-enabled systems requires several adaptations. First, teams should draw clear boundaries between system-level concerns and component-level work. This involves defining explicit interfaces and responsibilities for ML components, data pipelines, and infrastructure services. Each element requires its own requirements, acceptance criteria, and validation processes to ensure work can proceed in parallel without creating hidden dependencies. Second, verification and validation should occur continuously at multiple levels—not only through unit tests and code reviews, but also through data quality checks, model performance monitoring, and system integration testing. The research spikes discussed earlier in this chapter are essential for managing uncertainty; they provide structured time for exploration without turning every sprint into open-ended experimentation. Third, documentation practices need to support cross-functional communication rather than serve solely as a technical recordkeeping function. Table 7-1 summarizes how agile practices adapt to each stage of ML development.

Table 7-1. *Adapting agile practices for machine learning development stages.*

ML Stage	Agile Adaptation	Typical Artifact
Data readiness	Treat as a backlog item with acceptance criteria	Data quality checklist
Model iteration	Use research spikes + experiment tracking	Experiment log
Evaluation	Define "done" as metrics + guardrails	Evaluation report
Deployment	Include monitoring from day one	Monitoring dashboard, alerts
Governance	Embed review gates in the sprint cycle	Model card, risk review note

When an ML scientist documents a model, the documentation should be understandable to the software engineers who will deploy it and the product managers who will explain its behavior and limitations to stakeholders. Agile teams working on ML-enabled systems benefit from explicit completion criteria that address ML-specific concerns:

- Training and evaluation are reproducible.
- Baseline comparison is documented.
- Bias and safety checks have been performed.
- Monitoring hooks are in place.

- A rollback plan is documented.
- Cross-functional review is complete (data science, engineering, product).

Some organizations have found value in examining alternative life-cycle models to identify practices that complement agile. The V-Model in Systems Engineering, for example, emphasizes system decomposition, explicit boundaries of responsibility, and rigorous verification at each integration level. While the V-Model's rigidity makes it a poor fit as the sole governing process for fast-moving ML experimentation, its focus on clear interfaces and multilevel validation addresses gaps that agile often leaves open. A practical synthesis might retain agile's iterative sprints and customer focus while incorporating V-Model-inspired practices for system boundary definition, traceability, and testing at system, subsystem, and component levels. This hybrid approach acknowledges that ML-enabled systems are genuinely more complex than many traditional software applications and require proportionally greater attention to integration and validation.

The organizational implications extend beyond process. Teams building ML-enabled systems benefit from colocation or, where that is not possible, from regular synchronous collaboration between ML scientists, software engineers, and other stakeholders. Code review practices should flow in both directions—engineers reviewing scientists' code for maintainability and operational quality and scientists reviewing engineers' integration code for correct use of models, features, and data. Retrospectives should explicitly address cross-functional friction points and recurring integration issues, rather than focusing only on velocity or estimates. Sprint planning should account for resource dependencies introduced by ML workloads, including access to suitable datasets, data labeling capacity, and compute infrastructure for training and evaluation.

The emergence of AI agents introduces a new layer of systemic complexity. Unlike static ML models, agents possess stochastic agency—executing multistep workflows, invoking external tools, and making autonomous decisions. Agile teams must move beyond traditional acceptance criteria, which struggle to account for the nondeterministic paths agents may take toward a goal. Furthermore, the reliance on external APIs introduces cascading failures that are difficult to predict during standard testing. Architectural agility in this context requires embedding safety and governance into the very first sprint. Consequently, sprint planning must evolve to include explicit guardrails testing, human-in-the-loop checkpoints, and compensating transactions. These measures are designed to roll back or neutralize unintended autonomous actions before they affect the enterprise.

When these adaptations are made thoughtfully, agile practices provide a solid foundation for ML development and agent-based systems. When they are neglected, teams frequently end up with impressive prototype models that never become reliable, maintainable production systems.

7.12.2 AI-Assisted Agile Development

The previous section examined how agile practices must adapt when building AI systems. But AI is also transforming the tools available to agile teams, regardless of what they are building. The emergence of AI-assisted development tools has introduced a new dimension to software engineering workflows. Tools like GitHub Copilot, Amazon CodeWhisperer, and similar offerings use LLMs trained on vast code repositories to suggest completions, generate boilerplate, and even produce entire functions from natural language descriptions. When I first experimented with these tools, I was struck by how fundamentally they changed the rhythm of coding by transforming the blank editor into an active collaborator that anticipates intent and offers possibilities.

The impact of these tools extends beyond the code editor to the broader agile life cycle. AI-driven project management tools now apply ML to improve planning and resource allocation by analyzing historical project data to flag patterns that may affect scope, dependencies, or delivery risk. Predictive sprint planning features in platforms such as Jira and Azure DevOps provide timeline forecasting that can inform team discussions. However, these systems should inform, not replace, team judgment. Models trained on historical data may not always reflect current team composition or novel technical challenges.

The productivity gains can be substantial. Repetitive tasks that once consumed considerable time—writing unit tests, implementing standard patterns, converting data between formats—can now be accomplished in seconds with AI assistance. Developers report spending less time on mechanical work and more time on design decisions and problem-solving. In organizations I have advised, AI coding assistants have reduced the time required for specific task categories—such as unit test generation and boilerplate refactoring—by 30–50%. These gains are most pronounced among experienced developers, whose ability to critically evaluate and refine AI-generated logic prevents technical debt from creeping into the codebase.

These modern engineering assistants increasingly support core development activities, including code review, vulnerability detection, and automated test generation. The next evolution—already emerging—is toward AI agents that go beyond suggestion and assistance to autonomously execute development tasks such as writing and running tests, submitting pull requests, and resolving issues end to end. By automating large portions of the SDLC, these tools deliver efficiencies that mirror the lasting impact of early architectural breakthroughs like INTELLIFM. Just as earlier systems transitioned professionals from clerical execution to high-value judgment, AI lets current engineers shift from mechanical production toward evaluation and design.

However, AI-assisted development introduces risks that teams must manage deliberately. The code these tools generate is probabilistic, not verified. It may contain subtle bugs, security vulnerabilities, or violations of organizational coding standards. I have reviewed AI-generated code that looked correct at first glance but failed under edge cases the model had not anticipated. The tools are confident even when they are wrong, which can mislead developers who trust their suggestions without careful review. Every AI-generated line must be treated as a starting point for human judgment and not a finished product.

Security concerns are particularly acute. AI models trained on public repositories may suggest code patterns that contain known vulnerabilities or inadvertently reproduce proprietary code from their training data. Organizations handling sensitive information must assess whether AI coding tools comply with their data handling policies. Notably, some tools transmit code to external servers for processing, which may conflict with confidentiality requirements. I recommend that security and legal teams review AI tool adoption before developers begin using them on production codebases.

Beyond technical and security risks, teams must consider the sociological limitations of these models. AI systems can inadvertently perpetuate biases present in their historical training data, leading to skewed technical decisions or project forecasts. Overreliance on AI-driven insights without a critical human lens can diminish the intuition and creativity essential for complex problem-solving. Balancing these automated capabilities with human judgment is a fundamental principle that guided my teams' work on INTELLIFM and other mission-critical applications. They remain equally vital today.

The impact on learning and skill development is a subject of ongoing debate. Junior developers who rely heavily on AI assistance may miss opportunities to develop a deep understanding of the languages and frameworks they use. The struggle to solve a problem independently involves consulting documentation, experimenting with alternatives, and understanding error messages. It builds knowledge that persists. AI assistance that short-circuits this process may produce developers who are productive with tools but fragile without them. I encourage teams to be intentional about when AI assistance is appropriate and when independent problem-solving serves long-term skill development.

Integration with existing workflows requires thought. AI suggestions work best when developers provide clear context. Well-named variables, descriptive comments, and coherent file organization help the model understand intent. Codebases with inconsistent conventions or sparse documentation yield poorer suggestions. In this sense, AI-assisted development rewards the same practices that benefit human collaboration—clarity, consistency, and communication. Teams that invest in code quality find that AI tools amplify their investment.

Finally, AI-powered agents are streamlining delivery and operations by automating incident summarization, release notes generation, and meeting capture. Microsoft's SRE agent exemplifies this shift toward autonomous operations. It monitors system health in real time, triages multiservice incidents, and proposes specific remediation steps, substantially reducing the time engineers spend on reactive, "toil-heavy" work. This evolution continues the iterative AI philosophy seen in industry leaders like Amazon, which has refined its operational algorithms over decades of real-time feedback loops. While these agents substantially reduce coordination overhead, human-in-the-loop verification remains essential. This is especially true for incident response and customer-facing communications, where nuanced context and empathy must not be sacrificed for speed.

The tools are advancing rapidly. Capabilities that seemed impressive months ago are quickly superseded by new models with broader context windows, better reasoning, and tighter integration with development environments. Architects and engineering leaders should expect continuous change and plan for periodic reassessment of tool choices. What matters most is not which specific tool a team adopts, but whether it establishes practices for critically evaluating AI suggestions, maintaining code quality standards, and preserving the human judgment that remains essential to building reliable systems.

AI-assisted development does not replace skilled engineers. It changes the nature of their work, redirecting effort from mechanical production to evaluation, integration, and design. Teams that embrace this change—treating AI as a capable but fallible collaborator—will realize benefits while avoiding the pitfalls of uncritical adoption.

Those who expect AI to replace engineering judgment will often, and painfully, discover the limits of current technology. The most effective approach lies between these extremes: informed optimism tempered by professional skepticism. (For a full overview of AI-powered development tools, see Appendix 10.)

7.12.3 The Future of Agile–AI Integration

Looking ahead, integrating agile methodologies with AI is poised to drive advances in personalized medicine, autonomous systems, and smart cities. The current landscape of AI-powered development tools provides a foundation for understanding how these capabilities will develop. As these tools mature from assistive technologies to collaborative partners, they will reshape how agile teams approach software development.

I expect new agile frameworks to emerge that are explicitly tailored for AI development, incorporating extended experimentation phases and embedded ethical review processes. These frameworks may include specific stages for data quality assessment, model interpretability checks, and continuous ethical evaluations throughout the development cycle.

Ethical considerations in AI development present a unique challenge that agile methodologies are well positioned to address. By incorporating ethical reviews into each sprint and making transparency a core principle, agile teams can develop AI systems with fairness, accountability, and social responsibility in mind. Future agile frameworks may include tools such as fairness audits and bias detection algorithms integrated into the development pipeline.

The emergence of explainable AI is also likely to influence future agile practices. As demand for transparency in AI decision-making grows, agile methodologies may expand to include steps to demonstrate model interpretability. This could lead to new roles within agile teams, such as "AI ethicist" or "model interpretation specialist."

Federated learning—a technique for training AI models on distributed datasets without requiring centralized data collection—exemplifies how privacy-preserving approaches are reshaping AI development.[26] This approach increases data privacy by

---

[26] Brendan McMahan, Eider Moore, Daniel Ramage, Seth Hampson, and Blaise Agüera y Arcas, "Communication-Efficient Learning of Deep Networks from Decentralized Data," in *Proceedings of the 20th International Conference on Artificial Intelligence and Statistics* (PMLR, 2017), 1273–1282, `https://proceedings.mlr.press/v54/mcmahan17a.html`.

keeping sensitive information on local devices, reduces bandwidth usage by transmitting only model updates, and provides access to training data from multiple sources. But federated learning also introduces challenges, including managing computational heterogeneity across devices, handling non-IID data (data that is not independent and identically distributed across devices), and protecting against model poisoning through advanced encryption protocols.

Google's Gboard uses federated learning to improve predictive text suggestions without accessing users' private messages.[27] NVIDIA has applied the technique in its autonomous vehicle platform, enabling collaborative training across global partners without sharing raw data. Voice assistants such as Siri and Google Assistant use federated learning to refine speech recognition models on devices. Similarly, mobile facial recognition systems, health care diagnostic tools for detecting tumors, and Industry 4.0 predictive maintenance platforms all use federated learning to train models across decentralized environments. Industry 4.0, also known as the Fourth Industrial Revolution, refers to the ongoing transformation of manufacturing through digital technologies, including advanced connectivity, data analytics, human–machine interaction, and robotics.[28]

As these applications mature, agile AI development frameworks must adapt. This adaptation requires flexible sprint structures that accommodate the asynchronous, distributed nature of federated model updates. In highly regulated sectors, we are witnessing the rise of "compliance-driven agile" methodologies that embed regulatory checkpoints and documentation processes directly into the agile workflow. Industries such as finance, health care, and pharmaceuticals are adopting these methodologies to meet complex regulatory requirements with agility, flexibility, and speed.

The integration of agile methodologies with AI represents a productive fusion of flexibility and creative capacity. However, the principles that made early systems such as INTELLIFM effective remain central. Design for constraints by accepting that ML outcomes are probabilistic and by building processes that accommodate uncertainty. Build trust through transparency by making model behavior visible and explainable.

---

[27] Brendan McMahan and Daniel Ramage, "Federated Learning: Collaborative Machine Learning without Centralized Training Data," Google Research Blog, April 6, 2017, `https://research.google/blog/federated-learning-collaborative-machine-learning-without-centralized-training-data/`.

[28] See McKinsey & Company, "What Are Industry 4.0, the Fourth Industrial Revolution, and 4IR?" August 17, 2022, `https://www.mckinsey.com/featured-insights/mckinsey-explainers/what-are-industry-4-0-the-fourth-industrial-revolution-and-4ir`.

Apply progressive disclosure by delivering ML capabilities incrementally as confidence increases. Preserve human judgment by keeping domain experts informed for pivotal decisions. Organizations that ground agile and AI practices in these principles will be well positioned to deliver systems that are technologically sound, aligned with user needs, and rooted in responsible development practices.

7.13 Summary

The evolution of software development from waterfall to agile methodologies represents a profound change in how teams deliver value. The waterfall model served its purpose when requirements could be fully specified in advance, but the pace of internet time revealed its limitations. The Agile Manifesto offered a different path—one that prioritized working software over comprehensive documentation, customer collaboration over contract negotiation, and responding to change over following a plan.

This chapter traced that evolution through specific practices. Scrum and kanban provide complementary frameworks: scrum offers structured sprints and defined roles, while kanban emphasizes flow and continuous delivery. Technical agility—supported by continuous integration, automated testing, and IaC—helps teams deploy confidently and frequently. Technical debt, when managed deliberately, becomes a strategic tool and not an uncontrolled liability. Team agility depends on cross-functional collaboration, psychological safety, and empowered decision-making. Scaling agile across large organizations requires balancing coordination with autonomy, as frameworks such as SAFe and LeSS aim to do.

The benefits of agile are well documented: faster delivery, improved quality, stronger stakeholder engagement, and higher team morale. More recently, agile methodologies have become essential for AI development projects, supporting iterative experimentation, rapid prototyping, and continuous feedback. At the same time, AI tools are strengthening agile practices themselves by improving planning, automating routine tasks, and providing real-time insights.

Throughout this chapter, I have shown how agile practices embody the same principles that guided the development of the INTELLIFM technology decades ago. Design for constraints appears in time-boxed sprints and limited work in progress. Trust through predictable behavior emerges from transparency—daily stand-ups, sprint demos, and retrospectives that make progress visible. Progressive disclosure is achieved through incremental delivery, revealing functionality as it becomes available. And preserving human judgment remains central: agile empowers teams to make decisions, keeps product owners in control of priorities, and resists the temptation to automate away expertise. These principles are not artifacts of a particular era; they address fundamental challenges inherent in building complex systems and will remain essential as technology continues to advance.

As we will see in the following two chapters, agile principles also serve as a cornerstone of cloud computing and subscription-based software delivery, supporting rapid iteration, reliable deployments, and fast responses to changing user requirements. Together, these technologies extend agility beyond development into delivery and scaling.

CHAPTER 8

Cloud Computing Essentials: Understanding Azure

When I joined Microsoft, the PC revolution was dismantling an older model of computing. In the time-sharing era of the 1960s and 1970s, organizations rented time on centralized mainframes, accessed them via terminals, and paid for computing time by the hour. The PC changed that calculus. Suddenly, computing power sat on individual desks, owned outright, ready whenever needed, with predictable costs and full independence from a central system. The migration from shared to personal, from leased to owned, seemed like permanent progress.

Nearly four decades later, we have come full circle, but not as a simple return. It is more accurate to think of the journey as a spiral: the same core idea reappears, but at a vastly greater scale and with far higher levels of abstraction. Cloud computing revives the fundamental premise of time-sharing—shared resources accessed over networks—while transforming it beyond recognition. Where time-sharing often meant a single mainframe serving a building or campus, cloud computing spans millions of servers across continents. Where time-sharing supported batch workloads and interactive terminal sessions, cloud computing delivers everything from VMs and containers to managed databases and AI APIs. The economics have changed as well. Time-sharing costs typically limited access to large organizations, whereas cloud economies of scale have made capabilities once reserved for the few accessible to many.

I have witnessed this transformation. I have seen Microsoft grow from a packaged software vendor—the enterprise that helped make personal computing ubiquitous—into a cloud-first company. The same company that built its fortune on software installed on owned machines recognized that the future lay in services delivered over the internet.

K. C. Mukherjee, *The Microsoft AI Insider's Playbook*, https://doi.org/10.1007/979-8-8688-2730-3_8

Microsoft introduced Windows Azure in 2008 and brought it to general availability in 2010,[1] marking a clear commitment to that future—one that has since reshaped the technology industry. Microsoft partner companies grew alongside Microsoft's transition. Many moved from one-time license revenue and project-based systems integration to recurring, service-based models built on subscriptions, managed services, and cloud marketplaces. Partners that once differentiated themselves through on-premises deployments and customization expanded into cloud migration, security, data, and application modernization, often packaging their expertise as repeatable offerings. In the process, their business models advanced from selling implementations to delivering ongoing outcomes—operational reliability, continuous improvement, and measurable business value over time.

This chapter introduces the foundations of cloud computing with particular attention to Microsoft Azure, the platform I know most intimately. We will trace the architectural evolution from the rigid constraints of mainframes—systems like the DECsystem-1090, known to the IIT Kanpur community as the DEC-10[2]—to the elastic, distributed infrastructure of today. This is not merely a history lesson; it is the story of how we built the necessary engine for the AI revolution.

We will examine the core characteristics that distinguish cloud computing—scalability, cost structure, and reliability—and contrast them with those of the mainframe and client-server systems that preceded it. Crucially, I will show how the principles behind INTELLIFM anticipated the modern cloud era: centralized intelligence coupled with distributed access and a clean separation between infrastructure and application logic.

For the enterprise leader, the cloud is the infrastructure layer that makes large-scale AI viable. Without the high-performance GPU clusters, managed vector databases, and global distribution that Azure provides, the AI strategies explored in this book would remain theoretical. Understanding the cloud is not a detour from the AI playbook—it is the mastery of the factory where AI is built.

---

[1] Doug Hauger, "Windows Azure General Availability," Official Microsoft Blog, February 1, 2010, `https://blogs.microsoft.com/blog/2010/02/01/windows-azure-general-availability/`.

[2] "CSE Evolution at IIT Kanpur: A Tribute," *The Spark* (IIT Kanpur DORA Office), no. 3 (April 2022): 89. The section "Anecdotes around the arrival of the DEC-10" uses "DEC-10" and "DEC-1090" interchangeably in describing the 1979 commissioning.

- Explain the infrastructure as a service (IaaS), platform as a service (PaaS), and SaaS service models and identify when each is appropriate.
- Describe Azure's organizational hierarchy—management groups, subscriptions, and resource groups—and understand how governance decisions cascade through it.
- Choose an Azure region based on latency, compliance, and service availability considerations.
- Articulate the shared responsibility model and identify which security obligations remain with the customer.
- Recognize how identity and access management (IAM) serves as the primary security boundary in cloud environments.
- Apply cost management and governance tools to encode organizational intent into infrastructure.

8.1 Core Concepts

Cloud computing delivers computing resources as services over the internet. Those resources include servers, storage, databases, networking, software, and analytics. Instead of purchasing and maintaining physical infrastructure, organizations draw from shared pools of configurable resources that can be provisioned rapidly and released when no longer needed. The National Institute of Standards and Technology (NIST) defines cloud computing by five characteristics: on-demand self-service, broad network access, resource pooling, rapid elasticity, and measured service. These collectively distinguish cloud platforms from traditional data center operations.[3]

These characteristics extend beyond technical specifications. They signal a fundamental change in how organizations relate to computing infrastructure. On-demand self-service means a developer can provision a VM, a database, or an entire application environment without waiting for procurement cycles or data center

[3] Peter Mell and Timothy Grance, "The NIST Definition of Cloud Computing," National Institute of Standards and Technology Special Publication 800-145, September 2011, `https://csrc.nist.gov/publications/detail/sp/800-145/final`.

staffing. Broad network access means resources are reachable from any device with an internet connection. Resource pooling means that the provider's infrastructure serves multiple customers simultaneously, thereby achieving economies of scale that no single organization could easily replicate. Rapid elasticity refers to the capacity to expand or contract in response to demand, sometimes automatically. Measured service means usage is tracked and billed precisely, converting computing from a fixed cost to a variable one.

The cloud computing model is commonly described through three primary service categories, each reflecting a different level of abstraction from the underlying infrastructure.

IaaS provides the most basic building blocks: VMs, storage, and networking. The customer controls operating systems, middleware, and applications, whereas the provider handles the physical hardware, the virtualization layer, and much of the networking. Amazon Elastic Compute Cloud (Amazon EC2), launched in 2006, pioneered this model.[4] Microsoft Azure VMs and Google Compute Engine offer comparable services. IaaS offers maximum flexibility but also carries substantial responsibility, as customers remain accountable for everything above the hypervisor.

PaaS raises the level of abstraction by providing managed environments for application development, testing, and deployment. The provider manages operating systems, middleware, runtime environments, and often databases, freeing developers to focus on application code. Azure App Service, Google App Engine, and Heroku exemplify this approach. PaaS accelerates development but also constrains architectural choices because applications must align with the platform's supported languages, frameworks, and patterns.

SaaS abstracts away infrastructure by delivering complete applications over the internet. Customers access software through web browsers or thin clients, with no installation, maintenance, or infrastructure administration required. Microsoft 365, Salesforce, and the document management solutions I helped develop at Wolters Kluwer follow this model. SaaS reduces operational burden but offers less customization because customers adopt the application as delivered by the provider.

These categories are not rigid boundaries; they are points on a spectrum. Serverless computing—exemplified by Azure Functions and AWS Lambda—moves further along that spectrum by removing even the concept of servers. Developers deploy individual

[4] Amazon Web Services, "Announcing Amazon Elastic Compute Cloud (Amazon EC2) - beta," AWS News Blog, August 24, 2006, `https://aws.amazon.com/blogs/aws/amazon_ec2_beta/`.

functions that run in response to events, whereas the platform handles resource allocation behind the scenes. Container services such as Azure Kubernetes Service (AKS) occupy a strategic middle ground between IaaS and PaaS. They offer more control than fully managed platforms while transferring substantial infrastructure toil to the provider. In AKS, Microsoft manages the Kubernetes control plane, cluster upgrades, node pool life cycles, and underlying VM patching—leaving teams to focus on their application workloads and container configurations. For AI-enabled systems, this abstraction is critical; it allows architects to scale GPU-enabled node pools dynamically to meet demand bursts driven by LLMs or autonomous agents, without the operational burden of maintaining the orchestration layer itself.

Cloud deployment models add another dimension of choice. *Public clouds*—Azure, AWS, and Google Cloud—deliver services over public networks, with physical hardware and data center facilities shared among multiple customers. *Private clouds* dedicate infrastructure to a single tenant, hosted on premises or by a third party, in exchange for higher cost and greater control. *Hybrid clouds* combine public and private resources, placing workloads where they fit best. *Multicloud strategies* use services from multiple providers, reducing vendor lock-in and giving organizations access to specialized capabilities.

Over time, cloud computing has broadened access to technologies that once required major capital investment. AI, ML, and big data analytics—capabilities that previously demanded major infrastructure commitments—are now available as managed services. A startup with a credit card can tap the same class of computing power used by Fortune 500 companies. This change has accelerated innovation across industries, lowering barriers to entry and supporting business models that would have been difficult to sustain in an era defined by capital-intensive infrastructure.

8.2 Evolution of the Cloud

The path from mainframes to cloud computing spans roughly seven decades of technological and economic changes and emerging business needs. Each phase built on what came before, while introducing capabilities that earlier generations would have considered improbable. Understanding this progression clarifies why cloud computing emerged when it did and why it reshaped enterprise computing so fundamentally.

8.2.1 The Mainframe Era

The origins of shared computing lie in the mainframe systems of the 1950s and 1960s. These large, centralized machines performed data processing, scientific calculations, and business applications while serving multiple users through structured scheduling and controlled access. IBM System/360, introduced in 1964, established an architectural foundation that shaped enterprise computing for decades.[5] Mainframes delivered extraordinary capability, but at high cost. A single mainframe in the early 1960s could cost between $1 million and $5 million—roughly $10–$50 million in 2026 dollars.[6]

That expense drove innovation in resource sharing. Time-sharing systems emerged to maximize utilization: multiple users connected through terminals, each receiving a slice of processing time. Companies such as General Electric, Tymshare, and CompuServe built commercial time-sharing services that allowed businesses to rent computing capacity rather than own it outright. The model foreshadowed the cloud's core economic proposition, even though the technology and scale were fundamentally different.

8.2.2 The Client-Server Transition

The 1980s brought a major architectural transformation. PCs placed processing power on individual desks, while local area networks connected those machines to shared resources. The client-server model distributed computing tasks across the network. Clients handled user interaction and local processing, while servers managed shared data and centralized functions.

This transition broadened access to computing inside enterprises, but it also created new burdens. Each server required procurement, installation, configuration, patching, and ongoing maintenance. Scaling often meant purchasing additional hardware, waiting for delivery, and planning deployments. The total cost of ownership (TCO) extended well beyond acquisition, including facilities overhead—power, cooling, and space—and specialized personnel.

[5] IBM, "The IBM System/360," IBM History, `https://www.ibm.com/history/system-360`.

[6] IBM, "The IBM 1401," IBM History, `https://www.ibm.com/history/1401`, notes that "large mainframes cost more than USD 1 million to purchase outright." Higher-end systems such as the IBM System/360 Model 195 could cost $7–$12.5 million. See Ken Shirriff, "Iconic Consoles of the IBM System/360 Mainframes," Right to Repair Blog, April 2019, `http://www.righto.com/2019/04/iconic-consoles-of-ibm-system360.html`.

During this period, I architected INTELLIFM, which centralized document management and provided secure remote access for distributed users. The system reflected principles that would later become hallmarks of cloud services: centralized administration, network-based access, and intelligent automation that reduced manual intervention. The expert system ran on a client-server infrastructure, but the architectural direction was already clear to me: centralized control with distributed reach, supported by automation that made complex workflows practical at scale.

8.2.3 Virtualization and the Internet

Two developments in the 1990s laid the technical groundwork for cloud computing. First, the public internet expanded beyond academic and government networks into commercial infrastructure, bringing broad connectivity to organizations large and small. Second, virtualization matured, making it practical to run multiple VMs on a single physical server.

Virtualization decoupled software from underlying hardware. A single physical server could host multiple isolated environments, each behaving like an independent machine with its own operating system and applications. This improved infrastructure utilization and supported rapid provisioning. Creating a new server increasingly became a software-driven operation, with resources allocated on demand through automation. VMware, founded in 1998, commercialized x86 virtualization and brought these capabilities into mainstream enterprise environments.[7]

The combination of ubiquitous connectivity and efficient virtualization created the necessary conditions for cloud computing. Critically, virtualization enabled multitenancy at scale—multiple customers sharing the same physical hardware in logically isolated environments—which serves as the economic foundation of the cloud model. A provider's ability to pool resources across thousands of customers drives the economies of scale that make elastic, pay-as-you-go computing viable. Resources can be provisioned, scaled, and reconfigured remotely through software, bypassing the need for physical intervention. In the AI era, this model is what democratizes access to the massive, specialized compute power required for model training and inference—capabilities that were once the exclusive domain of the world's largest research labs.

[7] Kristin Morris, "Turtles, Blocks, and Memories," Computer History Museum, December 13, 2023, `https://computerhistory.org/blog/turtles-blocks-and-memories/`.

8.2.4 The Cloud Emerges

The early 2000s saw the emergence of the first large-scale cloud platforms. Salesforce, founded in 1999, helped pioneer the SaaS model by delivering CRM through a web browser.[8] Users needed no installed software, no local servers, and no staff dedicated to maintaining the application—they subscribed and logged in.

In late 2002, CTAdvantage.com was launched to deliver web-based multijurisdictional filing—an early capability in its category.[9] Built on the INTELLIFM foundation of centralized management and intelligent automation, CTAdvantage.com showed that sophisticated corporate compliance workflows could be delivered over networks years before "cloud-first" became a standard industry phrase. From my perspective, it was a familiar pattern reappearing: intelligent, centralized information management—now delivered with far broader reach and far more elastic infrastructure.

Amazon EC2 was launched in 2006. It established infrastructure as a commercial service. For the first time, organizations could rent virtual servers by the hour, scaling capacity up or down without capital investment. What once required procurement cycles and data center planning became available on demand via a web interface.

Microsoft entered the market with Windows Azure in 2008, reaching general availability in 2010. The platform combined infrastructure services with higher-level platform offerings that simplified application development and deployment. Office 365, launched in 2011,[10] extended the cloud strategy into productivity software and proved that even flagship products could move from installed software to subscription-based services. In the early 2010s, Google expanded its enterprise cloud offerings, making the same class of infrastructure that powered its consumer services available to organizations.

---

[8] Marc Benioff and Carlye Adler, *Behind the Cloud: The Untold Story of How Salesforce.com Went from Idea to Billion-Dollar Company—and Revolutionized an Industry* (San Francisco: Jossey-Bass, 2009).

[9] The Intelligent Filing Manager was also marketed as the "Internet Filing Manager."

[10] "Microsoft Launches Office 365 Globally," Microsoft News, June 28, 2011, `https://news.microsoft.com/source/2011/06/28/microsoft-launches-office-365-globally/`.

8.2.5 The Partner Ecosystem Transformation

As cloud platforms matured, the industry's economics transformed alongside the technology. Microsoft partners—systems integrators, independent software vendors, and managed service providers—faced a change not only in what they delivered, but also in how they sustained their businesses.

In the era before cloud computing, partners generated revenue primarily through one-time license sales and project-based implementations. A typical engagement involved selling licenses, customizing the solution for a client environment, deploying it on premises, and then providing support when something broke. Revenue was front-loaded, and relationships often became transactional after deployment.

Cloud computing changed those incentives. Subscription pricing spread revenue over time and aligned it with ongoing delivery and customer retention. Ongoing services replaced episodic support, creating long-running operational relationships instead of isolated projects. Cloud marketplaces became essential distribution channels, letting partners package their expertise into repeatable offerings that scale across customers and deployments.

I watched this transition play out in real time. Partners that once differentiated themselves through deployment skills expanded into cloud migration, security and compliance, data and analytics, and application modernization. The best partners I encountered redirected their focus from "finishing the implementation" to sustaining outcomes—reliability, predictable operations, continuous improvement, and measurable business results over time. In that sense, the partner network mirrored the broader cloud transition itself: from ownership to service, from installation to ongoing delivery.

8.2.6 Edge Computing and the Internet of Things

The cloud continues to expand through edge computing, which complements centralized services by processing data closer to its source. Rather than transmitting all data to distant data centers, edge computing performs time-sensitive processing at or near the devices that generate it, reducing latency and bandwidth requirements.

This approach matters for workloads that cannot tolerate delays. Autonomous systems process sensor data locally because milliseconds affect safety. Industrial systems monitor equipment in real time, detecting anomalies before they become failures. Smart home devices respond to voice commands without waiting on round trips to remote servers.

Edge computing does not replace the cloud; it extends it. Edge systems handle immediate processing, while cloud services provide long-term storage, advanced analytics, and centralized governance. Services such as Azure Internet of Things (IoT) Edge, AWS IoT Greengrass, and similar offerings blur the boundary between edge and cloud by supporting consistent workloads across both environments. These platforms exemplify the growing convergence of cloud infrastructure and IoT, enabling organizations to manage connected devices at scale while processing data at the edge.

8.2.7 Global Adoption Patterns

Cloud adoption has not followed a single path worldwide. In regions with mature IT footprints, adoption often meant migrating existing systems and integrating cloud services with long-standing on-premises investments. Organizations weighed transition risk, governance constraints, and operational readiness against the gains in scalability and flexibility. In my experience, the deciding factors were rarely technical alone; connectivity, compliance requirements, and risk tolerance often determined the pace.

In other regions, many organizations leapfrogged traditional infrastructure. Without extensive on-premises data centers already in place, they adopted cloud-based solutions directly—similar to how mobile services in parts of Africa reshaped financial access, as Kenya did through mobile money services such as M-Pesa. Cloud computing offered capabilities that would have been prohibitively expensive to build independently, and it reduced the need for large upfront capital investment.

Challenges remain. Limited connectivity still constrains adoption in many areas. Data sovereignty requirements complicate cross-border deployments. The digital divide between connected and unconnected populations persists. Yet the overall trajectory is clear: cloud computing has expanded access to enterprise-grade capabilities for organizations that could never have justified equivalent infrastructure on their own.

8.3 Cloud versus Mainframe

Having worked with both mainframe and cloud computing systems, I bring a unique perspective to the comparison of these paradigms. My hands-on experience with the strengths and limitations of each has given me a clear view of how computing has progressed. It has also shown me why certain design principles endure, even as the underlying technology changes.

As discussed in Chapter 1, mainframe computing is characterized by large, centralized systems serving numerous users simultaneously. Emerging in the 1950s, mainframes became the backbone of large-scale computing for government agencies, financial institutions, and corporations. Their ability to process vast amounts of data made them indispensable for census tabulation, financial transactions, and complex scientific calculations. IBM System/360, introduced in 1964, set the standard for enterprise mainframe computing.

The advent of PCs in the 1980s and the rise of the internet in the 1990s challenged mainframe dominance. As networking matured, distributed computing gained traction, and cloud platforms emerged in the early 2000s. The result was not merely a new hosting option, but a change in operating assumptions. Resources—from servers and storage to applications and analytics—could be provisioned on demand and reached from almost anywhere. That architectural transformation affects scalability, flexibility, cost structure, reliability, and security, and it is one reason cloud adoption has reshaped how organizations build and run software.

8.3.1 Scalability and Elasticity

Scalability is where the practical differences between the paradigms become apparent quickly—especially for organizations with uneven demand. Mainframe environments were often designed around peak loads. Scaling up typically meant adding physical resources—processing power, memory, and storage—while incurring high costs and requiring time for planning, procurement, and installation. Scaling down was rarely symmetrical; excess capacity remained on the books with little return.

Cloud platforms take a different approach. Capacity can expand or contract in response to demand, with far less dependence on hardware lead times. For many workloads, this elasticity aligns costs more closely with usage. Autoscaling policies can automatically adjust capacity, reducing the operational friction that used to accompany every growth cycle.

In my experience, this difference is most pronounced when demand fluctuates widely. A tax preparation service faces a different world in April than in August. Retail infrastructure often spikes during holiday seasons. Under the mainframe model, those organizations were provisioned for peak demand and maintained surplus capacity for the remainder of the year. Cloud computing ties capacity—and therefore spending—

more directly to actual usage. That change affects budgets, but it also changes business expectations: teams start designing around variability rather than treating it as a problem to absorb.

When I designed INTELLIFM in the late 1990s, scaling meant something fundamentally different. Capacity planning happened months in advance, based on projections of document volumes, concurrent users, and workflow complexity. If we underestimated, the system slowed or queued requests until we could procure and install additional hardware. If we overestimated, expensive resources sat idle. The infrastructure could not expand on demand; it expanded on schedule, after budget approvals and procurement cycles.

INTELLIFM addressed these constraints through careful architecture rather than elastic infrastructure. The system used modular components that could be distributed across available hardware, efficient indexing structures that minimized storage and retrieval overhead, and workflow designs that batched operations to reduce peak load. We built headroom into capacity plans and monitored utilization closely to anticipate growth before it became a crisis. These were sound engineering practices, but they were also workarounds for a fundamental limitation: the infrastructure was fixed, and the application had to adapt to it.

Cloud elasticity inverts that relationship. The infrastructure adapts to the application. What we designed around—hardware constraints, procurement delays, the mismatch between peak demand and average utilization—becomes a configuration decision rather than an architectural constraint.

Cloud elasticity fundamentally reshapes architectural design patterns and failure domains. Mainframe architectures were traditionally stateful by necessity—sessions and application state were tightly coupled to specific hardware, meaning a single hardware fault could be catastrophic. Cloud-native design inverts this with stateless architectures, where any instance can handle any request because state is decoupled from compute. This architectural pivot enables horizontal scaling—adding more instances rather than larger ones—which fundamentally shrinks the failure domain. In this model, if an instance fails, traffic is automatically routed to surviving nodes; the failure is localized and contained rather than system-wide. In the AI playbook, this stateless discipline enables dynamic scaling of inference endpoints and training pipelines across GPU node pools. While capacity planning still matters, its role has shifted: it is no longer a matter of system survival, but a strategic tool for cost optimization.

8.3.2 Flexibility

Flexibility is where cloud computing changed day-to-day engineering behavior. Cloud platforms offer multiple service models—IaaS, PaaS, and SaaS—so organizations can choose how much control they want versus how much operational work they want to avoid. This spectrum supports iterative approaches to building and refining systems because teams can prototype quickly, revise architectures, and terminate experiments without committing to hardware.

Mainframes, while exceptionally robust, often present friction when integrating with newer technologies and diverse partner ecosystems. Proprietary interfaces and legacy architectures can create silos of data and functionality, making interoperability more difficult than teams would like. At the same time, this constraint reflects a set of virtues: stability, security, and backward compatibility. Organizations running risk-sensitive operations—banking, insurance, and government—often accept reduced flexibility as a reasonable trade-off for predictable behavior and long-term continuity.

Cloud platforms generally lean toward openness. They provide APIs, integration tooling, and patterns for connecting cloud-native and on-premises systems. This makes it practical to compose larger systems from interoperating components: a cloud-based CRM system can integrate with analytics, marketing automation, and data pipelines without bespoke integration at every layer.

I have observed that this flexibility changes what smaller organizations can undertake. Airbnb migrated to AWS within a year of its 2008 launch, scaling from a small startup into a global marketplace operating in more than 190 countries without building its own data centers. Airbnb leaders have described AWS as appealing because teams could manage and customize their stack and scale quickly without lengthy procurement cycles or minimum-usage commitments.[11] Netflix began migrating to the cloud in 2008 after a database corruption incident caused a multiday outage, and it completed the migration in 2016 as streaming demand grew dramatically.[12]

Azure has powered similar transformations. Walgreens Boots Alliance migrated its 100-terabyte SAP landscape to Azure, the largest such migration at the time. The

[11] Amazon Web Services, "Airbnb Case Study," AWS Customer Success Stories, `https://aws.amazon.com/solutions/case-studies/airbnb-case-study/`.

[12] Yury Izrailevsky and Ariel Tseitlin, "Completing the Netflix Cloud Migration," Netflix Technology Blog, February 11, 2016, `https://about.netflix.com/en/news/completing-the-netflix-cloud-migration`.

migration supported pharmacy systems, e-commerce, and supply chain management across thousands of locations in more than 25 countries.[13] Perplexity AI, a startup building conversational AI products, used Azure AI Studio and Azure OpenAI Service to bring its product to market in six months with a lean team and limited budget.[14]

These examples—whether on AWS or Azure—demonstrate a common pattern. Cloud platforms remove infrastructure constraints that once limited how fast organizations could grow and adapt.

Hybrid and multicloud strategies further extend this flexibility. Many organizations combine cloud services with existing on-premises infrastructure, including mainframes, placing workloads where they fit best. In practice, this supports gradual modernization. Teams can integrate stable, proven systems with new, scalable capabilities and modernize in stages, with each step delivering value on its own.

8.3.3 Cost Structure

Cost is where many cloud discussions start, but it is also where simplistic comparisons fail. Mainframe environments can entail high upfront costs—hardware, licensing, and maintenance contracts—and often require specialized personnel and facilities overhead. For organizations with limited financial resources, that entry barrier can be decisive.

Cloud adoption alters the spending profile. Planning and migration can be expensive—architecture work, implementation effort, data transfer, and retraining often add up. But cloud adoption can convert large upfront capital investments into usage-based operating expenses. Organizations pay for what they consume and can reduce idle capacity costs by designing and operating with discipline.

Cloud platforms also provide detailed cost visibility: usage tracking, budget alerts, and optimization recommendations. In my work with enterprise clients, the organizations that achieved the best cloud economics treated cost control as an ongoing discipline, not a one-time migration task.

---

[13] "Walgreens Boots Alliance moves a mountain of SAP assets to Azure in a key modernization move," Microsoft Customer Stories, June 10, 2020, `https://www.microsoft.com/en/customers/story/792300-walgreens-boots-alliance-azure-sap-migration-technical-retailer`.

[14] "Trailblazing AI answer engine Perplexity.AI doubles throughput, cuts cost with Azure AI Studio," Microsoft Customer Stories, November 15, 2023, `https://www.microsoft.com/en/customers/story/1701944358715641785-perplexity-ai-azure-partner-professional-services-usa`.

TCO still requires careful analysis. It includes transition costs, productivity changes, staffing, and long-term strategic value from increased agility. Mainframe cost models must account for the shrinking pool of specialized expertise in some markets, which can raise labor costs over time. Cloud cost models must account for architectural choices that can inflate spending if left unchecked—overprovisioned services, data egress surprises, and poorly governed sprawl.

Vendor dependency exists in both paradigms. Mainframes can create deep dependence on a single vendor's hardware, software, and support environment. Cloud platforms offer more competition, but lock-in can still emerge when applications become tightly coupled to provider-specific services. Many organizations respond by adopting portable patterns where appropriate, such as containers and orchestration. They also separate application logic from platform services, preserving leverage while still using managed capabilities.

8.3.4 Reliability and Resilience

Reliability is central to both paradigms and warrants a balanced comparison. Mainframes have earned their reputation for stability, especially in high-volume transaction environments. They can be engineered with impressive redundancy, and many organizations have decades of operational maturity.

At the same time, resilience is not only about how well a system behaves under normal conditions; it is about how it responds to failures, outages, and regional disruptions. Many mainframe deployments concentrate risk into fewer physical locations than typical cloud designs, and full disaster recovery can be complex and expensive when it requires duplicate environments and specialized configurations.

Cloud platforms approach resilience through geographic distribution and layered redundancy. Providers operate multiple data centers and regions, with replicated storage and failover options that can be integrated into application architectures. Disaster recovery patterns—backup and restore, warm standby, and active-active—are available in scalable forms. So organizations can start with what they need and expand coverage as requirements grow. Recovery time and recovery point targets can often be materially improved if the application is designed to take advantage of those capabilities.

Even so, technology alone does not produce resilience. The shared responsibility model creates three distinct layers of accountability. First, infrastructure availability—encompassing data center uptime, physical hardware, and the network backbone—remains the provider's responsibility. The provider delivers the underlying infrastructure, but not the way a specific system uses it. Second, application resilience—how software handles failures, scales under load, and recovers from faults—is the customer's responsibility. In the AI era, this also includes ensuring the stability of model inference endpoints and gracefully handling API timeouts. Finally, operational maturity—the human and procedural elements, including runbooks, tested recovery procedures, monitoring, and incident response—also falls to the customer. In practice, organizations that achieve the highest reliability combine cloud capabilities with a disciplined internal culture that treats clear ownership and operational rigor as design requirements rather than afterthoughts. From this perspective, continuity is not an inherent feature of the cloud; it is the result of how a system is architected and operated.

INTELLIFM was designed with the same priorities, though the available mechanisms were different. Reliability meant redundant hardware components—duplicate disk controllers, mirrored storage, and backup power systems—but these operated within a single facility. Geographic redundancy required maintaining a separate installation with its own hardware, software licenses, and operational staff, which few organizations could justify for a document management system, regardless of how pivotal the workflows it supported.

Recovery planning required anticipating failure modes and building manual procedures to restore service. We documented step-by-step recovery processes: which tapes to retrieve, which systems to restore first, and how to verify data integrity before resuming operations. We tested these procedures periodically, but each test required scheduling downtime and coordinating across teams. The recovery time objective was measured in hours or days rather than minutes because the restoration process was manual and sequential.

Cloud platforms have automated much of what we used to do manually. Cross-region replication runs continuously, keeping data synchronized in near real time. Failover can run automatically, rerouting traffic without waiting for an operator to intervene. Recovery point objectives measured in seconds are achievable for workloads designed to use them. The underlying discipline—treating continuity as a design requirement—remains the same. What has changed is the infrastructure's ability to support that discipline without heroic operational effort.

8.3.5 Security, Governance, and Regulatory Reality

Security is frequently framed as though one approach is "secure" and the other is "risky," a binary that ignores the reality of shared responsibility and defense-in-depth—the practice of layering multiple security controls so that no single failure becomes catastrophic. My experience suggests a more accurate view: they present different security problems and different operational disciplines.

Mainframes have long been regarded as highly secure for good reasons: centralized control, mature access models, and a long history of operating in tightly regulated environments. Many deployments also benefited from relative isolation compared with today's internet-connected systems. But isolation is only one layer. Modern threats pressure every layer: identity, data governance, monitoring, and incident response. Those pressures apply whether systems run on a mainframe, in a private data center, or in the public cloud.

Cloud security has improved substantially, in part because major providers invest heavily in security engineering, audits, and operational controls. Encryption in transit and at rest, multifactor authentication (MFA), key management, continuous monitoring, and broad compliance attestations are now baseline expectations. The change is operational. In the cloud, access is easier, but it must be governed continuously. IAM becomes the primary security boundary, and misconfiguration is one of the most common ways in which otherwise strong security measures are undermined. Chapter 9 illustrates this division in detail (see Figure 9-1), but the core principle applies here: providers secure the infrastructure, while customers remain accountable for identity, data, configuration, and application-level decisions.

That is why governance matters as much as technology. Organizations need precise data classification, retention policies, access controls, and audit trails that span services and regions. They also need practical guardrails—configuration baselines, policy enforcement, and monitoring that detects drift before it becomes exposure. The cloud can support this rigor, but only if teams treat governance as part of the architecture rather than an afterthought.

INTELLIFM enforced governance through its workflow engine, embedding compliance requirements into system behavior rather than relying on user discipline. Users could not bypass approval steps because the system would not advance a document to the next stage without the required signatures. Access controls were tied to roles defined in the system's security model: a clerk could initiate a filing, but only a supervisor could approve it, and only an administrator could modify the workflow definitions themselves. Audit trails captured every action—who accessed which document, when, and what they did with it—creating an unbroken chain of accountability.

These controls were application-level constructs. The underlying operating system and database had their own security models, but the compliance logic lived in INTELLIFM's rule set and configuration. This meant governance was tied to the workflows we had designed, and extending it to entirely new scenarios—ones outside the system's original rule set—required additional configuration or development effort.

By design, the INTELLIFM blueprint prioritized deterministic integrity over open-ended flexibility at the infrastructure level. In an era before cloud-native policy engines, expressing compliance requirements as explicit, engine-enforced rules was the most reliable way to ensure an unbroken chain of accountability. This approach created operational silos—requiring deliberate engineering effort to bridge seams during integration—but it provided a level of regulatory certainty that manual procedures could never achieve. This historical model highlights precisely why the transition to platform-level governance in the cloud is so impactful: it allows organizations to maintain that same rigor while removing the seams that once slowed down integration.

Azure Policy and governance guardrails operate at the infrastructure layer, applying controls across all resources regardless of which applications use them. A policy requiring encryption applies to every storage account in scope, not just those that are explicitly encrypted. The principle—embedding compliance into system behavior—is the same principle INTELLIFM implemented at the application level. The difference is scope: infrastructure-level governance applies universally, whereas application-level governance applies only where developers implement it.

Regulatory complexity has intensified as systems have become more distributed and globally reachable. Organizations must now navigate a dense web of privacy and security frameworks—most notably the GDPR in Europe and the California Consumer Privacy Act (CCPA) in the United States—alongside sector-specific requirements governing the storage, processing, and transfer of data. While global reach is a core cloud advantage, it requires rigorous attention to data residency and sovereignty: the specific geography where data resides, the jurisdictions that apply to it, and the legality of cross-border transfer mechanisms. In regulated environments, these are not merely theoretical concerns; they shape architectural decisions, provider selection, and the design and deployment of AI agents that may inadvertently process sensitive data across borders.

A legal-access dimension also applies that architects cannot ignore. Under the Clarifying Lawful Overseas Use of Data (CLOUD) Act of 2018, US-based providers may be compelled through lawful process to produce data stored outside the United States, though the Act also includes mechanisms for providers to challenge orders that would conflict with qualifying foreign laws. Targeted cross-border mechanisms, such as the US–UK Data Access Agreement, provide defined channels for qualifying law enforcement requests between participating countries.,[15][16][17] These frameworks continue to evolve and should be reviewed with qualified counsel. Organizations selecting cloud providers must weigh these legal frameworks alongside technical capabilities when assessing where and how their data will be stored.

8.3.6 Performance and Latency

Scalability is not the same as performance, and the difference matters. Mainframes remain renowned for high-volume transaction processing with highly consistent latency. They excel in workloads such as core banking transactions, airline reservation systems, and other environments where predictability and throughput are nonnegotiable. That stability is the result of specialized hardware architectures, optimized operating systems, and decades of operational refinement.

Cloud performance has a different character. The distributed nature of public cloud infrastructure can introduce variability, particularly in multitenant environments. Yet cloud providers have narrowed these gaps through region selection, dedicated capacity options, optimized networking, and architectures that place compute and data closer to users. Content delivery networks, edge computing, and geographic distribution can reduce latency for global applications in ways that centralized environments struggled to match.

In practice, the choice depends on the workload. For applications that require strictly consistent, low-latency transaction processing at enormous scale, mainframes can remain the correct answer. For applications with variable demand, global users, or

[15] Clarifying Lawful Overseas Use of Data Act, Pub. L. No. 115–141, Division V, 132 Stat. 348 (2018), codified at 18 U.S.C. § 2713.

[16] Congressional Research Service, "Cross-Border Data Sharing Under the CLOUD Act," R45173, updated April 23, 2018, `https://www.congress.gov/crs-product/R45173`.

[17] US Department of Justice, "CLOUD Act Resources," Criminal Division, `https://www.justice.gov/criminal/cloud-act-resources`.

rapid change cycles, cloud architectures often provide a better overall fit. The advantage is not that any single instance is "faster," but that the system can be distributed, scaled, and placed closer to users. These performance decisions increasingly intersect with another consideration that has gained prominence in recent years: the environmental impact of computing infrastructure.

8.3.7 Sustainability in Enterprise Architecture

Environmental sustainability has become an architectural concern that enterprise teams can no longer afford to ignore. In the early stages of my career, the energy consumption of computing infrastructure was rarely discussed outside facilities management. Data centers were evaluated on uptime, capacity, and cost per square foot—not on carbon footprint or energy efficiency. That perspective has changed dramatically. Today, sustainability influences vendor selection, architecture decisions, and corporate reporting requirements. For architects, this change introduces both constraints and opportunities.

The scale of the challenge is large. Data centers consume roughly 1–2% of global electricity (recent estimates are around 1.5%),[18] and demand continues to rise as cloud adoption expands and AI workloads proliferate. Training large models can also consume substantial energy, with some training runs comparable to the annual electricity use of many households, depending on model size and assumptions.[19] These numbers are not abstractions. They translate into real environmental impact and, increasingly, real costs as energy prices rise and carbon pricing mechanisms expand.

Cloud providers have responded with major investments in renewable energy and efficiency improvements. Further, they publish sustainability metrics that customers can use to estimate the footprint of their workloads. Choosing a cloud region with a cleaner energy mix can reduce an application's carbon footprint without changing a single line of code. I advise teams to consider regional energy sources as part of the deployment strategy, alongside latency and compliance requirements.

---

[18] International Energy Agency (IEA), "Data Centres and Data Transmission Networks," IEA, updated 2023, `https://www.iea.org/energy-system/buildings/data-centres-and-data-transmission-networks`.

[19] David Patterson et al., "Carbon Emissions and Large Neural Network Training," arXiv, April 21, 2021, `https://doi.org/10.48550/arXiv.2104.10350`. For a high-level summary of environmental impacts, see Stanford Institute for Human-Centered AI, *AI Index Report 2024*.

Architecture decisions also influence sustainability outcomes. Right-sizing compute resources requires matching instance types and quantities to actual workload demand. This exercise reduces both cost and energy consumption. Serverless architectures, which provision resources only when code executes, can be more efficient than continuously running VMs for intermittent workloads. Efficient algorithms consume less computing time and therefore less energy. Optimization that once seemed premature now offers environmental and performance benefits.

Data storage presents similar opportunities. Tiered storage strategies that move infrequently accessed data to lower-power storage classes reduce energy consumption while also reducing costs. Data retention policies that eliminate unnecessary copies and expired records shrink storage footprints. I worked with an organization that identified seven redundant copies of certain datasets across different systems. Consolidating them reduced storage consumption by more than 60% and the associated energy use by a proportional amount.

AI workloads deserve particular attention. Training large models is computationally intensive. However, inference, which requires running trained models to generate predictions, often dominates total energy consumption because it occurs continuously at scale. Techniques such as model distillation, quantization, and efficient inference frameworks can reduce the compute required for deployed models without materially degrading accuracy. Architects should evaluate these techniques as part of AI system design, balancing capability against resource consumption.

Measurement is essential. Organizations cannot improve what they do not measure. Cloud providers now offer carbon footprint dashboards that estimate emissions associated with cloud resource usage. These tools are imperfect because they rely on estimates and averages, but they establish a starting point for tracking progress. Some organizations have begun including sustainability metrics in architectural review processes, treating energy efficiency as a quality attribute alongside performance, security, and reliability.

Sustainability is not merely a compliance obligation or a public relations concern. It reflects a broader responsibility that technology professionals carry as stewards of systems that consume substantial resources. The decisions we make about architecture, infrastructure, and operations have environmental consequences that extend beyond our organizations. Designing systems that accomplish their objectives efficiently—using only the resources they need, when they need them—is good engineering practice that also happens to be good environmental practice. This alignment gives me confidence that sustainability will remain a durable consideration in enterprise architecture rather than a passing trend.

8.4 Understanding Azure

Having traced the evolution of cloud computing and compared it with mainframe paradigms, we turn now to Microsoft Azure itself. This section introduces the platform organizational model, global infrastructure, core services, and management capabilities. The goal is not exhaustive documentation—Microsoft documentation serves that purpose.[20] It aims to provide a conceptual foundation for deeper exploration of Azure AI Services in Chapter 11.

8.4.1 Organizational Structure

Azure organizes resources through a hierarchy that governs access, policy enforcement, and billing. Understanding this structure matters before provisioning anything, because decisions made at the organizational level ripple through everything built beneath them.

At the apex of the Azure hierarchy are management groups, which provide the structural framework for organizing multiple subscriptions under a unified governance model. Large organizations use management groups to establish a distinct governance posture—such as segregating business units or enforcing specific regulatory boundaries—across a broad portfolio. Subscriptions, meanwhile, serve as the primary operational boundaries, providing the necessary isolation for distinct environments such as production, staging, and development. Policies applied at the management group level cascade downward through the hierarchy, promoting consistent compliance and security controls without requiring repetitive configuration.

Subscriptions form the primary boundary for billing and access control. Each subscription is a container for resources and a unit of Azure billing. Organizations commonly maintain separate subscriptions for different environments—development, testing, staging, and production—or for different departments and cost centers. In my experience advising enterprise clients, subscription design can look administrative

[20] For current documentation on Azure services and capabilities, see "Microsoft Azure Documentation," `https://learn.microsoft.com/en-us/azure/`.

at first, but becomes architectural over time. A poorly chosen subscription model can complicate cost allocation, access management, and compliance reporting for years to come.

Within subscriptions, resource groups provide logical containers for related resources. A resource group can contain all components of a single application—VMs, databases, storage accounts, and networking—so they can be managed, monitored, and deleted as a unit. Resource groups also serve as a scope for access control. Permissions granted at the resource group level apply to all resources within the resource group.

This hierarchy—management groups, subscriptions, resource groups, and individual resources—reflects a principle I encounter consistently: good architecture cleanly separates concerns. Just as the INTELLIFM blueprint distinguishes administrative control from user-facing access, Azure's organizational hierarchy separates governance posture from operational execution. In Azure, governance is defined at the higher scopes—management groups and subscriptions—where policies, compliance rules, and access controls cascade downward. Operational activity, by contrast, occurs at the lower scopes—resource groups and individual resources—where teams deploy, configure, and manage workloads. This structural separation allows governance decisions made by platform teams to be applied consistently across all operational activities, eliminating the need to repeat compliance configurations for every resource deployed. Role-based access control (RBAC) and policies can be applied at each level, and higher-scoped rules cascade downward—one more reason early structural choices tend to persist.

8.4.2 Global Infrastructure

Azure operates through a global network of data centers organized into regions. Each region is a geographic area containing one or more data centers, deployed within a latency-defined perimeter and connected by a dedicated, low-latency network. As of early 2026, Azure spans more than 70 regions globally and is supported by more than 400 data centers.[21] This extensive footprint is not merely a matter of scale; it is the physical foundation that enables business-critical AI workloads and rigorous data sovereignty compliance in the modern enterprise. Geographic distribution improves performance by placing resources closer to users. However, it also introduces variability in latency, capacity, and failure domains.

[21] Microsoft Azure, "Global Infrastructure," Microsoft, 2026, `https://azure.microsoft.com/en-us/explore/global-infrastructure`.

In many regions, Azure offers availability zones: physically separate data centers within a region, each with independent power, cooling, and networking. Deploying resources across availability zones protects against facility-level failures. If one zone experiences an outage, resources in other zones can continue operating. For applications requiring high availability, this architecture provides resilience without requiring geographically distant deployments.

Region pairs extend resilience further. Azure pairs many regions within the same geography, typically separated by a substantial distance. Some services can replicate data across paired regions, and platform updates are often sequenced so that paired areas are not updated simultaneously. This design supports disaster recovery scenarios where an entire region becomes unavailable.

I have found that organizations new to Azure often underestimate the importance of selecting the appropriate region and zone. The decision affects latency, compliance posture, service availability, and cost. Not all services are available in every region, and pricing varies. In regulated industries, region selection is often constrained by data residency requirements before any technical factors come into play. The flexibility is genuine, but so is the responsibility to choose thoughtfully.

8.4.3 Core Infrastructure Services

Azure infrastructure services provide the fundamental building blocks for cloud deployments. These correspond to the IaaS layer discussed in Section 8.1, offering maximum control alongside meaningful operational responsibility.

Azure VMs provide on-demand compute capacity running Windows or Linux. VMs come in a wide variety of sizes and configurations—general purpose, compute optimized, memory optimized, storage optimized, and GPU enabled—allowing organizations to match resources to workload requirements. Unlike physical servers, VMs can be provisioned in minutes and resized as needs change.

Azure Storage offers multiple storage types for different use cases. Blob storage handles unstructured data such as documents, images, and media files. File storage provides managed file shares using standard file system protocols, supporting legacy applications that rely on traditional interfaces. Queue storage supports messaging between application components. Table storage offers key-value storage for structured datasets that do not require relational semantics. Each storage type supports multiple redundancy options, from locally redundant storage within a single data center to geo-redundant storage replicated across regions.

Azure Virtual Network provides private network environments within Azure. Organizations define address spaces, create subnets, configure routing, and control traffic flow through network security groups. Virtual networks can connect to on-premises infrastructure via secure gateways or Azure ExpressRoute, supporting hybrid architectures in which cloud and on-premises resources operate as a unified network.

Azure Load Balancer and Azure Application Gateway distribute traffic across multiple instances, improving availability and supporting horizontal scaling. Load Balancer operates at the transport layer, distributing traffic based on the IP address and port. Application Gateway operates at the application layer, supporting address-based routing, encrypted connection termination, and web application firewall capabilities.

These services echo patterns I worked with decades ago, now scaled globally. When I designed INTELLIFM, centralized storage with controlled access was a major engineering challenge. Today, Azure Storage provides that capability as a managed service, with built-in replication, encryption, and access controls. The problems remain recognizable; the solutions operate at a different order of magnitude.

8.4.4 Identity and Access Management

Identity is the control plane of cloud security. In environments where resources are reachable over public networks, verifying who is requesting access—and what they are permitted to do—becomes the primary security boundary.

Microsoft Entra ID (formerly Azure Active Directory) serves as the primary IAM plane for Azure and thousands of integrated third-party applications. Beyond simple authentication and group management, Entra ID enforces advanced security controls through MFA and Conditional Access policies—rules that evaluate real-time signals such as location and device health before granting access. For enterprises maintaining legacy infrastructure, Entra ID synchronizes with on-premises Active Directory, creating a unified identity fabric across hybrid environments. In the modern enterprise playbook, this identity layer has become the new security perimeter. It forms the foundation for securing not only human users, but also the autonomous AI agents and service principals that power the next generation of software.

RBAC serves as the authorization plane, governing the specific actions that authenticated users, service principals, and AI agents can perform. RBAC functions by assigning roles—predefined or custom collections of permissions—to security principals at granular scopes. For example, an engineer might hold Contributor access at the development resource group level to facilitate rapid iteration, while being restricted to Reader access in the production environment to prevent unauthorized modifications. While Azure provides an extensive library of built-in roles for common scenarios, organizations can create custom roles when the precision of the "Principle of Least Privilege" requires finer-grained access.

Managed identities address a persistent challenge in distributed systems. The challenge is to authenticate applications to other services without embedding credentials in code or configuration. A managed identity assigns an Azure resource (such as a VM, a function app, or a container) an identity in Entra ID. The resource can then authenticate to services that support Entra ID authentication, and Azure handles credential management automatically. This eliminates a category of credential exposure risk that I have observed to cause serious incidents in organizations that rely on embedded secrets.

The shared responsibility principle discussed in Section 8.3.4 applies to identity with particular force. Microsoft secures the identity platform itself, but organizations remain responsible for how they configure access: who holds which roles, how authentication policies are enforced, and whether access reviews occur regularly. In my experience, organizations with the strongest cloud security posture treat identity governance as a continuous discipline rather than a one-time setup task.

INTELLIFM addressed the same fundamental challenge in its era. It distinguished who could administer the system from who could use it and ensured that access decisions were auditable and consistent. The expert system maintained its own user directory, separate from the operating system accounts used to log in to workstations. When a user accessed INTELLIFM, they authenticated against this directory, and their role assignments determined which documents they could view, which workflows they could initiate, and which administrative functions they could perform.

This design reflected a practical reality: enterprise identity infrastructure in the late 1990s was fragmented. Enterprises might have multiple authentication systems—mainframe security, Novell NetWare, and Windows NT domains—none of which communicated with one another. INTELLIFM could not rely on a unified identity platform because none existed. Instead, the system implemented its own identity model and managed the complexity of mapping users across environments.

Microsoft Entra ID represents what we built toward but could not achieve: a unified identity platform that spans applications, devices, and organizational boundaries. The architectural insight—that identity determines what is possible and everything else follows from that boundary—was present in INTELLIFM's design. What was missing was the infrastructure to implement that insight consistently across an enterprise, rather than application by application. Cloud identity platforms close that gap, making the principle achievable at a scale that application-level solutions could never reach.

8.4.5 Management and Automation

Azure offers multiple interfaces for managing resources, supporting different workflows and automation strategies.

The Azure Portal is a web-based interface for provisioning, configuring, and monitoring resources. It offers a graphical experience that makes exploration intuitive, particularly for those learning the platform or performing infrequent administrative tasks. Dashboards can be customized to display metrics, alerts, and resource status relevant to designated roles or applications.

Azure Command-Line Interface and Azure PowerShell provide command-line interfaces for scripting and automation. Both tools can perform any operation available through the portal and integrate with shell-based workflows. Azure PowerShell follows the standard PowerShell Verb-Noun cmdlet convention (for example, Get-AzVM), whereas Azure Command-Line Interface organizes commands as az <group> <command> (for example, az vm create). Both tools support repeatable, version-controlled operations that reduce manual errors.

IaC represents a more systematic approach to automation. ARM templates define resources declaratively in JavaScript Object Notation (JSON), specifying the desired state of the environment and letting the platform handle the creation details. Azure compares the template to the current state and applies the required changes. Bicep, a domain-specific language developed by Microsoft, provides a more concise syntax that compiles to ARM templates. Third-party tools such as Terraform provide cross-platform infrastructure definitions that are useful for organizations operating across multiple cloud providers.

I have long believed that automation separates sustainable operations from fragile ones. Automation is central to the INTELLIFM blueprint, which relies on intelligent workflows to reduce manual intervention and enforce consistency. The same principle applies to cloud infrastructure. Organizations that manage Azure through automated, version-controlled definitions gain compounding advantages over those that rely on manual portal operations. First, they can reliably reproduce environments, eliminating the configuration drift that accumulates when teams make undocumented manual changes. Second, tools such as Terraform, through their plan-and-apply workflow, reveal the exact delta between the desired and current states before any change is executed, reducing the risk of unmanaged divergence. Third, IaC supports scaling with consistency: environments can be replicated across regions to enable global GPU-enabled inference without introducing manual errors. Finally, when combined with Azure Policy, IaC enforces compliance automatically. Every deployed resource is validated against governance rules at the moment of creation, closing the gap between strategic intent and operational reality.

8.4.6 Platform Services

Beyond raw infrastructure, Azure offers platform services that offer higher levels of abstraction, allowing teams to focus on application logic rather than underlying systems.

Azure App Service provides a managed environment for hosting web applications, REST APIs, and mobile backends. Developers deploy code or containers; Azure handles operating system patching, load balancing, and scaling. App Service supports multiple languages and frameworks—.NET, Java, Node.js, Python, and Hypertext Preprocessor (PHP)—and integrates with deployment pipelines for continuous delivery.

Azure SQL Database delivers Microsoft SQL Server as a managed service. Azure handles patching, backups, high availability, and many performance management tasks, while customers focus on schema design, queries, and application integration. Service tiers range from basic workloads to business-critical deployments with zone-redundant high availability. For organizations with existing SQL Server expertise, Azure SQL Database offers a familiar programming model with reduced operational overhead.

Azure Cosmos DB provides a globally distributed, multimodel database service. It supports multiple APIs and targets single-digit millisecond read and write latencies at the 99th percentile, depending on configuration and workload.[22] Cosmos DB supports automatic replication across regions, with configurable consistency levels that allow developers to balance consistency guarantees against latency and availability.

[22] Microsoft, "Azure Cosmos DB Documentation," https://learn.microsoft.com/en-us/azure/cosmos-db/.

Azure Functions exemplifies serverless computing. Developers write individual functions triggered by events—HTTP requests, queue messages, timer schedules, database changes—and Azure executes them on demand without server provisioning. Billing is based on execution count and duration, making Functions economical for sporadic or event-driven workloads.

These services illustrate the spectrum described in Section 8.1. The primary benefit is a marked reduction in operational burden: App Service and Functions relieve teams of the infrastructure management required by VMs, allowing them to focus on application logic. Similarly, Cosmos DB and Azure SQL Database shift the complexities of database administration to the platform while preserving application-level control over schemas and queries. The trade-off is consistent across managed services: reduced operational toil in exchange for some architectural flexibility. For most enterprise teams, this is a favorable trade-off, as the productivity gains achieved by offloading infrastructure management far outweigh the constraints on low-level architectural choices.

8.4.7 Cost Management and Governance

Cloud economics reward attention. Without deliberate governance, cloud spending can outpace the value it delivers—a pattern I have observed in organizations that treated cloud adoption as a one-time migration rather than an ongoing operating discipline.

Azure Cost Management provides visibility into spending across subscriptions and resource groups. It tracks costs by service, region, and resource, and it supports budgets and alerts that notify stakeholders when spending approaches defined thresholds. Cost analysis tools help identify spending trends, anomalies, and optimization opportunities.

Azure Advisor provides recommendations across cost, security, reliability, operational excellence, and performance. For cost specifically, Advisor identifies underutilized VMs, idle resources, and opportunities to purchase reserved capacity at discounted rates. These recommendations surface optimizations that might otherwise go unnoticed.

Azure Policy enforces organizational standards across the environment. Policies can require specific configurations—such as encryption enabled, certain regions permitted, and specific tags applied—and can audit or prevent noncompliant deployments. Policy initiatives group related policies to support consistent application. In regulated industries, Azure Policy provides evidence of control enforcement that supports audit and compliance requirements.

Azure Blueprints packages policies, role assignments, and resource templates into repeatable definitions for environment setup.[23] A blueprint might define a compliant landing zone for a new application, helping teams start with appropriate governance controls already in place.

The underlying principle is one I have maintained throughout my career: systems behave as they are designed to, and governance is integral to that design. INTELLIFM embedded compliance logic into its workflows to prevent users from inadvertently bypassing required approvals. Azure governance tools serve a similar purpose at the infrastructure scale: they encode organizational intent, making compliance structural rather than dependent on individual vigilance.

8.4.8 Principles in Practice

The connections between INTELLIFM's design principles and Azure's architectural patterns are not coincidental. Both address the same fundamental challenges—governing distributed resources, automating complex workflows, and embedding compliance into system behavior:

- **Centralized Governance with Distributed Access:** Management groups and Azure Policy cascade rules downward; users access resources without direct administrative control.
- **Separation of Concerns:** Subscriptions separate billing from deployment; resource groups separate applications from one another; RBAC scopes separate permissions by role and context.
- **Automation-First Operations:** ARM templates, Bicep, and Terraform encode infrastructure as version-controlled definitions; pipelines enforce repeatable deployments.
- **Centralized Storage with Controlled Access:** Azure Storage provides managed replication, encryption, and access controls—capabilities that once required substantial engineering effort.

[23] Microsoft has announced plans to deprecate Blueprints, so many organizations standardize governance primarily through Azure Policy and landing zone patterns.

- **Compliance Embedded in Workflow:** Azure Policy and governance guardrails encode organizational intent at the structural level, preventing noncompliant configurations before they occur.
- **Identity as the Control Plane:** Microsoft Entra ID and managed identities make authentication the primary security boundary, replacing network perimeter models.

8.4.9 Cloud Architecture Checklist

Before deploying workloads to Azure, ensure you have addressed

- **Region and Zone Selection:** Chosen based on latency requirements, data residency constraints, and service availability
- **Organizational Structure:** Management groups, subscriptions, and resource groups designed to support governance, billing, and access control
- **Identity and Access:** Microsoft Entra ID configured; RBAC roles assigned at appropriate scopes; managed identities used where possible
- **Network Boundaries:** Virtual networks, subnets, and security groups defined; hybrid connectivity planned if required
- **Security Validation:** Threat modeling completed; least-privilege access confirmed; external exposure and attack surface reviewed; IAM and network controls validated against security baseline
- **Data Classification:** Sensitivity levels established; encryption, retention, and access policies aligned with classification
- **Cost Controls:** Budgets set; alerts configured; tagging strategy enforced
- **Logging and Monitoring:** Diagnostic settings enabled; alerts defined for critical metrics and security events
- **Backup and Disaster Recovery:** Recovery time and recovery point objectives defined; replication and failover tested

8.5 Summary

This chapter traced the arc of computing from centralized mainframes through personal computing and client-server architectures to the distributed, service-oriented model of cloud computing. The journey is not a simple linear progression but a spiral in the sense that shared, network-accessible resources return in new forms—reshaped by scale, abstraction, and economics.

Cloud computing delivers infrastructure, platforms, and software as services over the internet. The five NIST characteristics introduced in Section 8.1—on-demand self-service, broad network access, resource pooling, rapid elasticity, and measured service—allow organizations to provision resources in minutes rather than months, scale capacity with demand, and convert capital expenditures into operating expenses.

The evolution unfolded in stages. Mainframes established centralized computing and time-sharing economics. Client-server architectures distributed processing while creating new operational burdens. Virtualization decoupled software from hardware. The public internet provided ubiquitous connectivity. Cloud platforms—Salesforce, AWS, Azure, and Google Cloud—combined these foundations into commercial services that reshaped enterprise technology. Along the way, the partner network also transformed. It moved from one-time license revenue and project-based implementations to recurring subscriptions and outcome-oriented managed services.

Comparing cloud computing with mainframe systems reveals trade-offs rather than simple superiority. Cloud platforms offer elasticity, flexibility, and cost models aligned with variable demand. Mainframes offer stability, predictable performance, and decades of operational maturity in high-volume transaction environments. Reliability, security, and governance depend less on the chosen platform and more on execution. What matters is how rigorously teams apply disciplined practices within their selected environment. Regulatory and legal considerations—data residency, privacy frameworks, and laws governing access to data—shape architectural decisions regardless of where systems run.

Microsoft Azure provides a full-featured cloud computing platform. Its organizational model—management groups, subscriptions, and resource groups—separates governance from operations and billing from deployment. Its global infrastructure spans more than 70 regions and availability zones (as of early 2026), supporting performance optimization and regulatory compliance. Core infrastructure services deliver VMs, storage, networking, and load balancing. Microsoft Entra ID and RBAC establish identity as the primary security boundary. Management interfaces and IaC tools support automation that separates sustainable operations from fragile ones. Platform services raise the level of abstraction, reducing operational burden in exchange for architectural constraints. Cost management and governance tools encode organizational intent, thereby making compliance structural.

Throughout this chapter, I have drawn connections to principles that guided my earlier work. INTELLIFM embodied centralized administration with distributed access, intelligent automation, and clean separation of concerns—concepts that cloud computing has since brought into the mainstream at a global scale. The problems I worked on decades ago remain recognizable; the solutions now operate at a different order of magnitude.

This foundational architecture prepares the ground for the strategic developments that follow. The cloud infrastructure explored in this chapter is not merely an operational concern; it is the engine that makes enterprise AI viable at scale. GPU-enabled compute, elastic scaling, managed identity, and governance automation are essential prerequisites for the AI strategies advanced in this book. In the modern playbook, the cloud serves as the high-velocity data plane and large-scale parallel processing environment required to transform static code into dynamic, reasoning systems.

Chapter 9 builds on these concepts by exploring SaaS and cloud-native applications. It examines how the platform capabilities introduced here translate into the software experiences that organizations and users encounter daily and how AI is beginning to transform those experiences from within. We will also examine how the transition from cloud-native to AI-native design is redefining the application layer, moving traditional software from a passive tool to an intelligent partner capable of autonomous action and predictive insight.

CHAPTER 9

The Evolution of SaaS: From Cloud Modernization to AI-Native Design

Software once came in boxes. Customers purchased a license, installed the product on their machines, and hoped it would run reliably until the next upgrade cycle. Distribution was physical, updates were infrequent, and the relationship between vendor and customer often ended at the point of sale.

That model served its era, but it strained under its own weight. Support calls flooded in from users running different hardware configurations. Bug fixes took months to reach customers. Organizations that needed the latest capabilities had to plan costly upgrade projects, often deferring improvements indefinitely because the cost and effort were more than they could justify. I saw this pattern repeat at Microsoft and other technology companies—talented teams building excellent software, only to watch adoption stall because the delivery mechanism could not keep pace with innovation.

The transition to SaaS changed everything. Providers no longer shipped disks and waited for adoption. Instead, they delivered applications over the internet, continuously updated them, and maintained a living relationship with users. When my teams launched CTAdvantage.com[1]—a flagship enterprise deployment of the INTELLIFM platform—in the early 2000s, I saw firsthand how this model transformed not only distribution but also the fundamental nature of software development. We could respond to customer feedback within days, whereas packaged releases often meant waiting months for the next update. We could observe how users actually worked with

[1] Debra Levy, "Finding Forms," *Legal Assistant Today*, November/December 2001, `https://www.legalassistanttoday.com/feature_nd01-2/`.

K. C. Mukherjee, *The Microsoft AI Insider's Playbook*, https://doi.org/10.1007/979-8-8688-2730-3_9

the system and refine it accordingly. The software became a service in the truest sense: a continuous value stream that we delivered, maintained, and improved for the people who depended on it.

This chapter examines the rise of SaaS and its relationship to cloud computing. Cloud infrastructure provides the foundation—scalable resources, global reach, and operational resilience. SaaS builds on that foundation to reshape how software is distributed, consumed, and experienced. Together, they represent a fundamental change in the economics and practice of enterprise technology—one I have witnessed and shaped over the years.

The sections that follow trace this transition from multiple angles. First, I examine why organizations migrate from legacy systems, what patterns succeed, and how workforce and governance must adapt. Next, I define SaaS, compare it with other cloud service types, and discuss where the industry is heading. I then turn to my own journey and describe how the constraints of PC-era software shaped my thinking and how cloud architecture changed what I believed software could become. The chapter concludes by examining how SaaS and cloud reinforce one another, how AI is reshaping the model, and what the market trajectory implies for practitioners and leaders.

A word on sequencing is warranted. The chapter title promises an evolution that culminates in AI-native design, but the journey begins with cloud migration and modernization. This is deliberate. SaaS did not emerge in a vacuum. It was made possible by the infrastructure transformation that preceded it, and AI-native design is only intelligible against the backdrop of what SaaS replaced and what it has since become. Why organizations migrate, how SaaS reshaped the software delivery model, and where AI is now taking that model are not three separate topics; they are three phases of the same story. The sections that follow are structured to tell that story in sequence, so that by the time we arrive at AI-native design, its significance is grounded in the full arc of the transformation rather than presented as an abstraction.

9.1 From Mainframe to Cloud

The transition from mainframes to cloud computing is one of the most far-reaching changes I have observed in enterprise technology. It is not simply a change in infrastructure—it is a transformation in how organizations think about computing, how they structure IT departments, and how they deliver value to customers. It also changes how executives measure progress: from "projects completed" to "capabilities delivered," from fixed capacity planning to elastic consumption, and from periodic upgrades to continuous improvement.

I have seen this transition from multiple vantage points. I understood mainframe architectures as an engineer, designed cloud migrations as an enterprise architect, and led the organizational change that accompanies these moves as a technology executive. The technical challenges are real, but the human challenges are often greater. Migrating code is difficult; migrating culture is harder. The deeper work is not moving applications. It is a redesign of decision-making: who approves changes, how risk is assessed, how teams collaborate across domains, and how accountability shifts when infrastructure is defined by software.

Many organizations today still run core systems on mainframes. These machines are not relics—they are reliable, secure, and optimized for high-volume transaction processing. Banks, airlines, and government agencies continue to depend on them because they work. In many cases, the mainframe remains the system of record—the place where the final transaction settles, where the authoritative customer balance lives, and where audit trails are strongest. But maintaining mainframe expertise is increasingly difficult, and the economics of cloud computing offer compelling alternatives. In parallel, user expectations have changed. Customers now expect mobile-first experiences, real-time notifications, and features that improve steadily rather than arriving in multiyear leaps. For most enterprises, the question is not whether to migrate, but how and at what pace.

That question cannot be answered with a single playbook. Some systems are candidates for a straightforward move, whereas others require modernization that reshapes application boundaries and data models. Many organizations find that cloud adoption is a portfolio decision. In practice, it means keeping specific workloads on the mainframe, offloading selected functions, wrapping legacy cores with modern APIs, and building new digital experiences on cloud platforms. A thoughtful migration distinguishes between what must be preserved—correctness, security, resilience, and compliance—and what can be reimagined: user journeys, operational workflows, analytics, and delivery cadence.

A final reality often surprises executives: cloud migration is not only a technology initiative. It is a new operating model. Procurement changes. Finance changes. Security changes. Engineering changes. The enterprise moves from owning assets to consuming services, from static budgets to consumption discipline, and from long release trains to smaller, more frequent deployments. Each of those changes creates friction if leadership treats the cloud as a data center replacement rather than an organizational transformation.

9.1.1 Workforce and Operating Model

When I led cloud migration projects, the scarcity of professionals who understood both mainframe systems and cloud architectures was immediately apparent. Mainframe developers had spent decades mastering COBOL, job control language, and the intricacies of batch processing. Cloud engineers thought in terms of containers, microservices, event-driven integration, and continuous deployment. Bridging these two worlds required deliberate effort—not only in skills training, but in building mutual respect. Mainframe professionals often carried deep domain knowledge and a disciplined approach to stability; cloud professionals brought tooling, automation, and a mindset optimized for speed and iteration. Successful programs created mixed teams that could translate between paradigms rather than forcing one side to "convert" overnight.

The migration process itself demands a deep understanding of legacy systems that often exists only in the minds of experienced professionals. Business logic written decades ago may be poorly documented or entirely undocumented. I encountered systems in which business rules were embedded in code comments or existed only as institutional knowledge held by a handful of people nearing retirement. That knowledge becomes a strategic asset. Retaining and valuing these experts throughout the migration matters—not as obstacles to progress, but as guides to what the new system must preserve. In practice, this requires disciplined knowledge capture efforts: domain workshops, decision logs, reverse engineering of business rules, and targeted refactoring that encapsulates logic into modular, testable components.

Modernization introduces roles that many mainframe enterprises have not previously needed. Platform engineers build internal tooling and standardized templates. Reliability specialists design for high availability and rapid recovery. Security engineers shift from perimeter defenses to identity-centered controls. Cost-aware architects connect technical decisions to usage patterns, since cloud spending behaves differently from traditional data center budgets. These roles are not optional; they determine whether a migration results in a stable platform or an expensive tangle of ad hoc services.

Beyond technical skills, migration requires a cultural adjustment. Mainframe environments operate under a different operating model: change is deliberate, deployments are scheduled, and stability is paramount. Cloud environments embrace continuous delivery, rapid iteration, and architectures designed to recover quickly from component failures. Professionals accustomed to the measured pace of mainframe operations may find the velocity of cloud development disorienting. This adjustment requires not just training but a change in mindset, along with clear communication about career paths to maintain morale and retain talent. Leaders also have to rewrite incentives. If teams are rewarded only for avoiding incidents, they will resist change. If they are rewarded only for speed, resilience will suffer. Balanced measures create alignment. Those measures include reliability, security, delivery cadence, and customer outcomes.

The impact extends beyond IT. As cloud technologies introduce new capabilities and more agile workflows, business units must adapt their processes accordingly. Finance teams accustomed to capital expenditure models must learn to govern operating expenses and usage-driven cost behavior. Procurement processes designed for hardware purchases must accommodate subscription-based services and new vendor relationships. Risk and compliance teams must adapt to shared responsibility models, where the provider secures the underlying platform and the enterprise secures its configuration and use. Legal teams may need new approaches to data residency, retention, and audit access. HR also plays a role, as recruiting, reskilling, and retaining talent become central constraints.

A well-run migration, therefore, treats workforce impact as a first-class workstream, not an afterthought. Technology moves only as fast as the enterprises can absorb new ways of building, operating, and governing systems. When that reality is recognized early, the mainframe-to-cloud journey becomes less of a jarring leap and more of a disciplined evolution. It respects what the legacy environment got right while capturing the flexibility and velocity the business now demands.

9.1.2 Enterprise Migration Examples

The transition from legacy systems to cloud takes many forms. I have observed organizations pursue complete replacement, hybrid architectures, and phased migrations—each approach reflecting business constraints, risk tolerance, regulatory obligations, and technical realities. The experiences of Icon Parking (Icon), Danske

Bank, the Cleveland Clinic, Walmart, and Microsoft illustrate this range. Icon is a case I led directly; the Microsoft transition is one I witnessed from the inside; the others represent patterns I have studied and advised on. Each addressed industry-specific pressures by harnessing the flexibility, scalability, and operational advantages of cloud platforms.

Icon: Phased Migration with Parallel Run

Icon, the leading parking operator in Manhattan, is a case I know intimately. With nearly 200 locations across New York City, Icon needed to modernize its operations for a digital-first world. As a technology executive and Microsoft enterprise architect, I led the migration of Icon operations from a legacy VAX platform to a cloud-based infrastructure. Once a staple in many enterprises, this environment had become a limiting constraint: it could not support the speed of change, integration needs, and scale that modern urban services demand.

The migration required careful planning around data conversion, interface integration, and operational continuity. We adopted a phased approach, moving capabilities in logical increments while keeping indispensable business data accessible throughout. I insisted on parallel operation during the transition—the legacy environment and the new platform running side by side—so we could validate results, reconcile transactions, and catch issues before they affected customers. That discipline also gave business stakeholders confidence: they could see the new system earning trust, day after day, before we retired the old one.

The results were visible quickly. The migration helped position Icon as an industry leader in cashless parking payments. Through IconParkingSystems.com and the mobile application, Icon GO, customers can reserve spaces and pay digitally. The AutoPay system, which I architected and my team developed, supports several payment options: credit and debit cards, commuter benefit cards, and direct bank transfers from checking or savings accounts. Customers appreciated the reduced friction—payment in a few taps—and easy access to a complete parking history and digital receipts, which reduced payment disputes and simplified recordkeeping. What struck me most was how rapidly behavior changed once friction disappeared; customers who had always paid cash adopted digital payments within weeks.

On the operational side, AutoPay delivered measurable improvements. Manual cash handling declined, which lowered processing errors and reduced administrative overhead. Ticket validation became faster, and transaction tracking became more reliable. Those operational gains, combined with customer convenience, strengthened trust and supported a more effective parking operations platform. Just as important, the new environment made data usable: arrival patterns, duration distributions, location utilization, and payment preferences could be analyzed to improve pricing decisions and capacity planning in ways the legacy system could not.

Security posture also strengthened following the migration. Moving away from cash reduced exposure to physical theft and counterfeit currency, enhancing safety for both customers and operators. The transition necessitated rigorous cybersecurity controls to protect customer information; the resulting platform supports encrypted digital transactions and granular access controls. A key takeaway from this project is that security improvements are often undervalued during the planning phase—only to be deeply appreciated once the system is live.

Danske Bank: Regulated Migration with Strong Controls

In the financial sector, Danske Bank presents a compelling model for cloud migration—one that reflects the caution appropriate to highly regulated industries. As Denmark's largest bank, serving millions of customers across Northern Europe, it faced long-term pressure from legacy complexity, rising maintenance demands, and the need to deliver new digital capabilities faster. Rather than attempt a single cutover, Danske pursued a staged, risk-managed program that moved selected workloads and data to cloud platforms while preserving the reliability and control required for core banking operations.

This pattern is typical in financial services: the highest-trust systems remain tightly governed, while innovation accelerates in customer-facing channels, analytics, and integration layers. Regulatory obligations—including EU privacy mandates and data sovereignty requirements—shape the architecture from the beginning. They determine service boundaries, data flows, and the governance controls that must be in place before any workload or AI model moves to the cloud. In practice, that means controls such as approved data residency, encryption standards, continuous monitoring, periodic audits, and disciplined IAM. In these environments, compliance is not a postdeployment audit; it is a primary design constraint that dictates the very perimeter of the technical solution.

Cleveland Clinic: Modernization to Support Care and Research

In health care, the Cleveland Clinic's cloud journey sought to improve both care delivery and research capability. Central to this effort was the deployment of Epic's electronic health record (EHR) platform on Azure, including MyChart, the patient-facing SaaS portal. MyChart gives patients direct access to health records, appointment scheduling, test results, and communications with care teams. By moving these core systems and analytics to the cloud, the organization improved collaboration among clinicians, streamlined patient data operations, and expanded its capacity for medical research. This architectural shift reduced operational bottlenecks and opened new opportunities for personalized medicine and data-driven clinical decision-making.

Health care migrations carry unique weight because the data is intensely personal and the consequences of failure are immediate. I have worked on similar initiatives, and the pattern is consistent: success depends on earning clinicians' trust, not merely the approval of IT leadership. If physicians and nurses do not believe that the new workflows will help them care for patients, adoption will stall regardless of technical elegance. That is why governance, usability, training, and reliability belong in the critical path, not in a postlaunch checklist.

Walmart: Scale, Peak Demand, and Internal Capability Building

In retail, Walmart's cloud modernization stands out for its scale. By migrating large portfolios of internal applications to cloud-native architectures, Walmart improved elasticity—particularly during demand spikes such as Black Friday—and strengthened integration between digital commerce and physical stores, thereby supporting a more unified omnichannel experience.

What makes Walmart's approach instructive is its emphasis on building internal capabilities. At that scale, operating discipline matters as much as technology choice: standard patterns, platform engineering, cost controls, and reliability practices can determine whether a migration delivers lasting advantage or merely relocates complexity to a different environment. Walmart's willingness to invest in internal platforms reflects both its scale and its need to govern cost, performance, and operational behavior over the long term.

Microsoft: From Packaged Software to SaaS at Global Scale

The most consequential SaaS transition in enterprise computing history may well be Microsoft's own. For decades, Microsoft Office stood as the defining example of packaged software: licensed, installed on individual machines, and upgraded on multiyear cycles. Beginning in 2011 with the launch of Office 365, Microsoft started moving its flagship productivity suite to a subscription-based, cloud-delivered model. This transformation was not merely a change in distribution. It required rearchitecting applications for continuous delivery, rebuilding the update and telemetry infrastructure, and shifting the commercial model from one-time license revenue to recurring subscriptions.

I witnessed this transformation from the inside, and what struck me most was the organizational discipline it demanded. Every team had to learn to ship continuously rather than through discrete releases, and every customer-facing decision had to reflect the reality that all users would be on the current version. Today, Microsoft 365 serves hundreds of millions of users worldwide and has become a benchmark for enterprise SaaS transitions. The lesson for leaders is that even the most successful product line can be reinvented and that this SaaS foundation now supports the rapid, global infusion of generative AI into the daily workflows of millions.

9.1.3 When Legacy Persists

Some organizations—particularly those handling extremely sensitive data, hard real-time constraints, or sustained high transaction volumes—continue to rely on mainframes and other tightly controlled legacy environments, and for good reason. Government agencies and airlines, for example, often prioritize predictable throughput, operational stability, and long-established controls.

The industry saw a version of this trade-off during the CrowdStrike outage in July 2024.[2] Organizations whose systems were not running the affected agent configuration reported less disruption than those running it. Analysts discussed whether a smaller "blast radius," a slower cadence of change, or legacy dependencies contributed to reduced impact in some instances. The broader point is not that old systems are inherently safer, but that exposure to systemic failures is shaped by architecture,

[2] For a detailed account of the CrowdStrike incident and its impact on Windows systems, see Chapter 1.

operational discipline, and the software actually deployed. Sometimes, the most resilient environment is the one whose constraints prevent a problematic update from reaching critical paths.

Cloud migration is not a one-size-fits-all approach. Each organization must assess its unique needs, operational constraints, regulatory obligations, and business objectives. The right approach varies: a focused migration with parallel operations (as in Icon), a risk-managed staged program (as many banks adopt), or a broad, large-scale modernization (as in Walmart). The common thread across all these migrations is not the cloud provider or the toolset. Modernization succeeds or fails based on discipline: careful planning, respect for legacy knowledge, and investment in fundamentals. Without that discipline, modernization yields brittle systems; with it, it yields durable platforms.

In my experience, the decision framework becomes clearer when framed as three questions. First, when should legacy persist? The answer is typically when hard real-time constraints exist, when regulatory sensitivity demands proven controls, when throughput requirements are already met with high reliability, or when the change cadence is stable and modernization offers limited upside. Second, when should modernization surround legacy rather than replace it? This applies when channel innovation is needed—mobile apps, partner APIs, analytics layers—but the core transaction engine remains sound. APIs can decouple the legacy core from new experiences without rewriting existing functionality. Third, when should migration replace the legacy system entirely? This path makes sense when skills scarcity threatens supportability, when economics favor cloud operating models, or when new experience requirements cannot be met by layering on top of the existing architecture. These are not mutually exclusive; many organizations pursue all three strategies across different parts of their portfolio.

9.2 SaaS Explained

SaaS has been one of cloud computing's most impactful innovations—both for the industry and for my career. When I first encountered the model, it solved a problem I had struggled with for years: keeping software current for users who could not or would not upgrade. In the boxed-software era, even a well-designed product could stagnate in the field because the distribution channel, the installation burden, and the upgrade economics discouraged change. SaaS replaced that stagnation with a delivery model built for continuous improvement. It narrows the gap between engineering progress and the experience customers actually have.

SaaS delivers applications over the internet from provider-managed infrastructure and centrally operated environments. End users typically access the software via a web browser or client application. In contrast, organizations integrate it with other systems via APIs rather than installing and maintaining local binaries across fleets of machines. This approach reduces the traditional cycle of purchase, installation, patching, and upgrading that has long defined enterprise software. It also changes the operational posture. Instead of each customer maintaining its own instance and patch cadence, the provider maintains a controlled production environment with standardized deployment, monitoring, and incident response. Popular examples include CTAdvantage.com, built on INTELLIFM technology; Salesforce, which popularized the CRM model; and Microsoft 365, which introduced subscription-based delivery of productivity software at scale.

The impact has been broad across industries and organizational sizes. In health care, SaaS has accelerated the adoption of EHR systems and related clinical platforms, improving care coordination, documentation workflows, and operational throughput when implemented well. In education, SaaS-based learning management systems have expanded online and distance learning far beyond what was practical with installed software, while supporting faster iteration in course delivery and assessment tooling. In finance, SaaS has provided small businesses with access to accounting, payroll, invoicing, and financial management capabilities that were previously available only to large enterprises with specialized staff. The pattern is consistent: SaaS lowers barriers, accelerates adoption, and moves software economics from capital expenditure to operating expense. It also raises expectations. Customers increasingly assume frequent enhancements, rapid support responsiveness, and integration with the broader set of tools they already use.

Not all enterprise SaaS platforms emerged through migration. A distinct and increasingly influential category consists of organizations born in the cloud—built from inception on cloud infrastructure rather than evolved from a legacy predecessor. Snowflake, founded in 2012, exemplifies this pattern. Its cloud-native data platform was designed from the ground up to separate compute from storage, allowing organizations to scale each independently and pay only for the resources they use. Rather than simply replacing an on-premises data warehouse, Snowflake introduced a fully managed, continuously updated environment that made advanced data infrastructure available to businesses of many sizes. Today, it serves thousands of enterprises across industries, with deep integration across AWS, Azure, and Google Cloud.

The broader significance of cloud-native SaaS lies in how it expands access to enterprise-grade capability: a founding team can build and scale a product on cloud infrastructure to serve Fortune 500 clients without the massive capital investment traditional software development once required. This is one of the most profound shifts cloud computing has produced—not only in how software is delivered, but also in who can build and compete in the enterprise market.

9.2.1 Key Features and Benefits

A defining characteristic of SaaS is broad accessibility. Users need an internet connection and a browser or client application, and they can begin using the service without procuring hardware or deploying complex local installers across hundreds or thousands of endpoints. Configuration still exists in SaaS. But it is typically managed centrally within the service rather than through per-machine installation and ad hoc compatibility work. I remember the contrast vividly from my years at Microsoft: we would spend months preparing a release, ship it on physical media, and then wait—sometimes years—for customers to deploy it across diverse environments. With SaaS, the gap between development and delivery collapses. Users run the current production version, and providers can observe usage patterns and respond to feedback in days rather than release cycles. That immediacy changes product strategy: teams can prioritize improvements based on what users actually do rather than what they report, and they can assess whether a new feature delivers real value rather than merely shipping on schedule.

The subscription model changes the economics for both sides and alters how organizations plan technology roadmaps. Customers avoid hefty upfront license fees and pay on a per-period basis, with costs scaling with usage, capacity, or functionality tiers. This approach benefits small and midsize businesses that lack the capital or appetite for traditional enterprise software purchases. It also gives larger enterprises an option to align costs with adoption rather than overbuying licenses "just in case." Providers benefit as well, gaining predictable, recurring revenue and durable relationships with users that make long-term improvement financially rational. Free trials, which are impractical with shrink-wrapped software, become standard practice—customers can evaluate before committing, reducing risk for everyone and raising the competitive bar for product quality.

SaaS transfers the operational burden from the customer to the provider, thus reshaping the role of IT. The provider operates the infrastructure, applies security patches, manages upgrades, and rolls out new capabilities. Users no longer need to schedule costly upgrade projects or maintain compatibility across multiple versions deployed across the enterprise. For organizations without deep IT staff, this transfer of responsibility can materially change how IT budgets are structured. I have worked with organizations that moved from allocating a large share of their IT budgets to maintenance to redirecting that capacity toward business initiatives. That does not eliminate governance; it changes it. Instead of controlling every server and every patch window, customers focus on vendor management, identity controls, data governance, and integration quality. On the other hand, providers focus on reliability engineering, operational automation, and platform resilience.

Scalability is inherent in the model because the provider controls the environment and can allocate resources dynamically. Customers can scale usage up or down without purchasing hardware or negotiating new licenses and expand into new geographies without building local infrastructure. This elasticity is not limited to peak traffic; it also encompasses organizational growth, seasonal variation, and business experimentation. Shopify, for example, has helped thousands of small businesses launch and scale online stores with minimal upfront investment. A generation ago, achieving the same outcome would have required substantial capital and specialized technical expertise. The same principle applies within enterprises: teams can quickly pilot a capability, measure adoption, and scale it broadly when it demonstrates value.

Many SaaS platforms use multitenancy. A shared software environment serves multiple customers, with data isolation and access separation enforced through industrial-grade architecture, controls, and operational discipline, rather than by maintaining separate physical infrastructure for each customer. This approach drives efficiency for the provider, which can translate to lower costs for customers and faster rollout of improvements. It also concentrates security investment. A well-run multitenant platform can apply hardened configurations, continuous monitoring, and rapid patch deployment at a level that many individual organizations struggle to sustain. The trade-off is that multitenancy demands rigorous engineering and governance, because failures in isolation or access control can have outsized consequences. That demand is why mature SaaS providers invest heavily in testing, segmentation, auditing, and incident response.

The model also encourages integration. SaaS applications expose APIs and event hooks. Hence, they can connect to other systems—CRM to marketing automation, collaboration tools to project management, analytics to operational dashboards, and identity providers to access controls. Slack, for instance, integrates with hundreds of other services, giving teams a way to run workflows that span departmental and organizational boundaries. Integration changes organizational behavior: once data can flow across tools, teams begin to expect visibility and automation rather than manual handoffs and spreadsheet-driven reconciliation. I saw this pattern take hold at enterprises where departmental silos had resisted integration for years; SaaS made connection the default rather than the exception, especially when combined with integration platforms and standardized identity.

Security in SaaS is a shared responsibility, and that point becomes more important—not less—as organizations adopt more services. Providers invest heavily in encryption, access controls, compliance certifications, vulnerability management, and continuous monitoring. Large providers such as Microsoft, Amazon, and Google undergo independent audits against standards such as International Organization for Standardization (ISO) 27001 and System and Organization Controls (SOC) 2 and publish extensive documentation and assurance reports for enterprise customers. However, customers remain responsible for configuring access, managing credentials, governing data classification, and enforcing policies such as least privilege and retention. The best outcomes occur when both sides clearly understand their roles and when the customer treats identity, logging, and policy enforcement as first-class components of the architecture rather than administrative afterthoughts. In practice, many of the most serious failures arise not from provider infrastructure but from misconfiguration, excessive permissions, weak authentication, or uncontrolled third-party integrations.

Finally, SaaS supports continuous innovation in a way that traditional delivery models cannot. Providers can release features incrementally, test variations, and respond to market changes without waiting for customers to upgrade. Microsoft 365 delivers new capabilities regularly; users benefit without scheduling downtime or managing installers. Providers also learn from usage. When Slack introduced Dark Mode in 2019 or Zoom added waiting rooms in 2020, these changes reflected patterns observed in how customers used the products and what they needed to remain productive and safe. That feedback loop—expensive and slow with shrink-wrapped software—is one of the SaaS model's most powerful advantages. It also introduces responsibility. Providers must communicate changes clearly, manage backward compatibility, and provide administrative controls so that enterprises can adopt new capabilities in a governed manner rather than being surprised by them.

9.2.2 SaaS, IaaS, and PaaS

SaaS is one of the three core cloud service models, alongside IaaS and PaaS. Thinking of them as a spectrum makes the trade-offs clear: the further you move from IaaS toward SaaS, the more responsibility the provider takes on. As the provider assumes more of that responsibility, organizations gain greater speed, simplicity, and focus on business outcomes, while reducing the need to manage underlying technology. Many organizations use all three models to balance agility with control.

IaaS provides virtualized computing resources over the internet: servers, storage, and networking. Users retain control over operating systems, middleware, and applications, much as they would in a traditional data center, but without owning physical hardware. Amazon EC2, Azure VMs, and Google Compute Engine are well-known examples. IaaS suits organizations that require fine-grained control, have compliance requirements that demand direct oversight, or want to migrate existing workloads without rearchitecting them. It is often the first step in a migration strategy because it reduces dependence on the data center while preserving familiar operational patterns. The trade-off is operational responsibility: the customer manages everything above the virtualization layer, including patching, hardening, scaling strategy, and many aspects of availability.

PaaS abstracts further by providing a platform for building, deploying, and running applications without requiring management of the underlying infrastructure. Developers work with runtime environments, databases, message queues, and middleware that the provider maintains. Google App Engine, Azure App Service, and Heroku are representative examples. PaaS accelerates development by removing infrastructure concerns and standardizing common operational patterns, thereby improving consistency across teams. It also encourages architectural discipline, because applications must conform to platform constraints around scaling, state management, and deployment. The trade-off is reduced flexibility: certain platform decisions become difficult to reverse, and teams must accept a degree of provider-defined convention in exchange for speed and operational simplicity.

SaaS abstracts the most as the provider manages the infrastructure, platform, and applications. Users consume finished software with limited visibility into the underlying stack. This model suits organizations seeking capability without operational complexity:

email, collaboration, CRM, accounting, procurement, analytics, and many other functions delivered as services rather than as long-running deployment projects. In practice, SaaS can also become a strategic choice for functions that do not differentiate—areas where excellence is essential but building and operating a custom solution does not create a unique advantage.

Figure 9-1 illustrates this spectrum, showing how responsibility shifts from the customer to the provider as you move across service models.

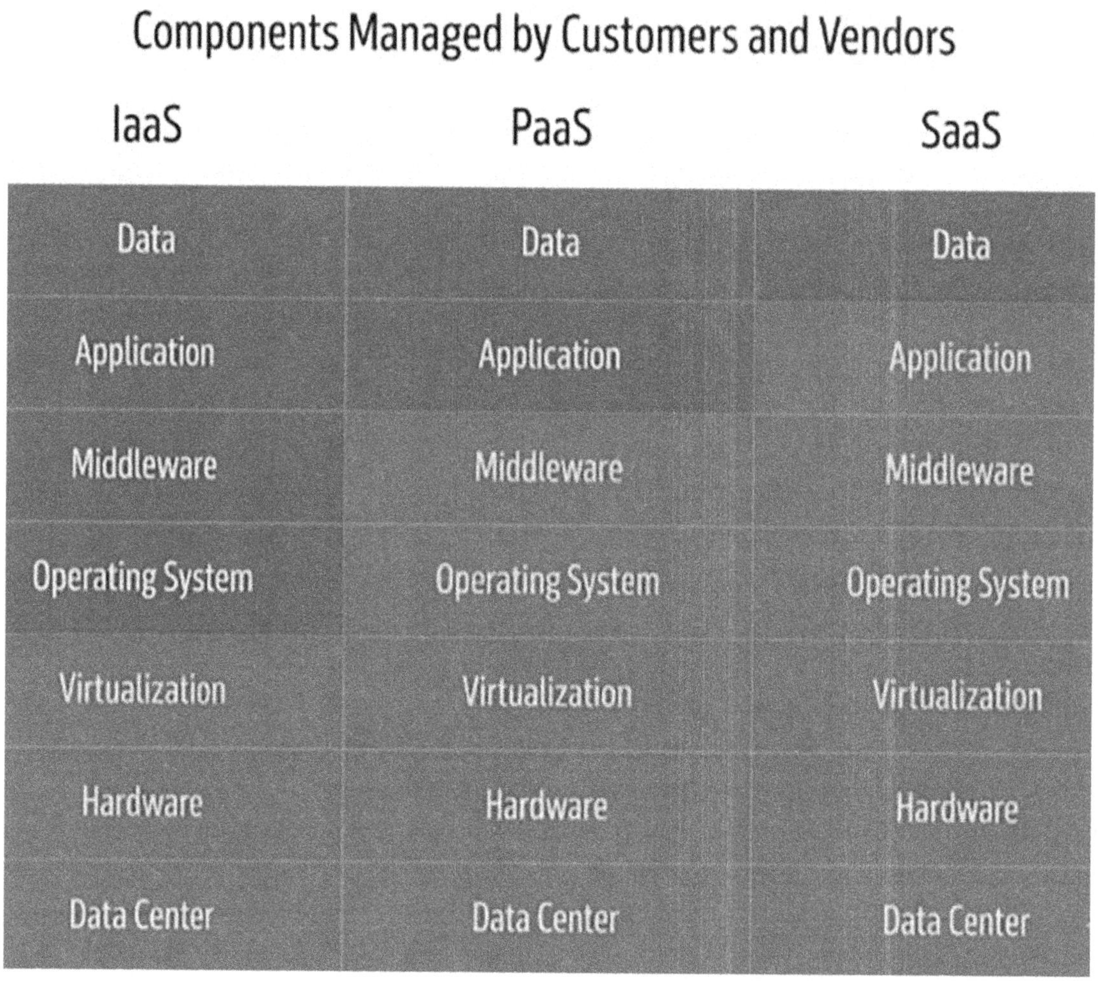

Figure 9-1. *Cloud service models (IaaS, PaaS, and SaaS) showing customer-managed components in teal and vendor-managed components in orange. The progression across models demonstrates increasing vendor management of the cloud computing stack. (Image by author)*

These models are not mutually exclusive. I have worked with enterprises that use IaaS for legacy workloads requiring specialized configurations, PaaS for new application development and standardized delivery, and SaaS for business functions where building in-house would drain attention from higher-value work. The question is not which model is best in the abstract, but which model fits each workload's requirements for control, speed, compliance, resilience, integration, and operational capacity. Mature organizations manage these choices as a portfolio, with governance that evaluates risk, cost, and long-term sustainability rather than defaulting to a single preferred pattern.

In practice, the selection follows a straightforward logic. IaaS is well suited to workloads where control or migration constraints predominate—when compliance requires direct oversight, when specialized configurations cannot be abstracted, or when an existing application must be migrated without rearchitecture. PaaS suits workloads where standardization and development speed dominate—when teams benefit from managed runtimes and want to avoid infrastructure decisions. SaaS suits capabilities that are essential but not differentiating—where operational burden should be transferred to a provider and internal teams should focus elsewhere.

Newer patterns blur the boundaries between IaaS and PaaS. Serverless computing, often described as Function as a Service (FaaS), extends the PaaS model by abstracting away server and container management. Developers write individual functions that execute in response to events, while the platform automatically handles provisioning, scaling, and runtime management. Because developers still write and own the application logic, FaaS aligns more closely with PaaS than with SaaS, where the provider manages the application entirely. The pay-per-invocation pricing model changes the economics of intermittent workloads and encourages architectures built around event-driven message flows. Crucially, this model shifts the financial risk of idle capacity from the customer to the cloud provider. Because serverless environments can scale to zero, organizations avoid the cost of overprovisioned infrastructure sitting idle during periods of low activity. This transition from fixed infrastructure commitment to granular, execution-based operating expense keeps costs closely aligned with actual business value. These developments reflect a consistent trend: as cloud platforms mature, they assume greater operational responsibility and provide higher-level building blocks. As a result, customers can focus on business outcomes and product value rather than infrastructure maintenance.

9.2.3 Where SaaS Is Heading

Several forces are shaping how SaaS will develop, and many reinforce the same underlying trajectory: greater intelligence, greater specialization, stronger governance, and tighter integration across the enterprise landscape.

AI is becoming embedded rather than optional. Providers are integrating ML into core functionality, including predictive analytics, intelligent search, automated classification, anomaly detection, and conversational interfaces. When building CTAdvantage.com, my teams incorporated rule-based intelligence to guide filing decisions, reduce errors, and preserve explainability. Today's SaaS platforms go further, learning from usage patterns across broad customer populations and incorporating LLMs through APIs. This trend will accelerate as model tooling improves, as enterprises demand auditable controls, and as customers expect software to assist with decisions rather than merely record them. At the same time, it will raise new questions about trust, transparency, governance, and the boundaries between automation and accountability.

Vertical specialization is increasing. Early SaaS platforms were horizontal—CRM, email, and collaboration—serving broad markets with general-purpose tooling. Increasingly, providers are building for specific industries. Veeva Systems serves the life sciences industry with cloud-based clinical trial management and regulatory submissions; Procore is widely used for construction project management; and Toast provides point-of-sale, payroll, and inventory management tailored to restaurant operations. In health care, MEDITECH and Epic offer EHR platforms designed around clinical workflows and regulatory requirements.[3] These vertical SaaS solutions embed domain knowledge, regulatory awareness, and workflow patterns that horizontal platforms often cannot match. As markets mature, differentiation shifts from "Can it do the basics?" to "Does it understand my process, my constraints, and my compliance obligations?"

The compliance dimension deserves particular attention. Vertical SaaS platforms operating in regulated industries carry obligations that horizontal platforms can often leave to customers. Data residency, audit trails, access controls, and retention policies must be built into the product architecture from the start, not bolted on later. Enterprises

[3] For overview information on the vertical SaaS platforms cited, see Veeva Systems, "Life Sciences Cloud Solutions," `https://www.veeva.com`; Procore, "Construction Management Software," `https://www.procore.com`; Toast, "Point of Sale Software," `https://pos.toasttab.com`; MEDITECH, "EHR Solutions," `https://ehr.meditech.com`; and Epic Systems, "Company Overview," `https://www.epic.com`.

evaluating vertical SaaS should scrutinize compliance certifications, data handling practices, and the provider's track record in their specific regulatory environment. I expect this trend to continue as providers compete on domain depth, regulatory fluency, and operational fit rather than on generic feature lists.

A related development is the rise of "point solutions"—sometimes called micro-SaaS in developer communities—highly focused products that solve narrow problems, frequently as extensions to larger platforms. Loom, which began as a standalone asynchronous video messaging tool before its full integration into the Atlassian suite, proved how effortlessly a specialized tool can integrate with Slack, Notion, and GitHub. Calendly simplified appointment scheduling without requiring changes to the underlying calendar platform, while Typeform redefined data collection through a conversational interface that connects with hundreds of third-party services.[4] These tools address specific friction points and thrive within broader ecosystems rather than competing directly with large horizontal platforms. For developers, this model represents an accessible path into the market; for enterprises, it offers a way to fill functional gaps without commissioning custom development or waiting for platform vendors to address niche requirements.

Edge computing is extending the reach of the cloud service model, bringing the same management, security, and intelligence once reserved for the data center directly to the network edge where data originates. SaaS has traditionally assumed reliable connectivity to centralized infrastructure. Edge architectures push processing closer to users and devices, reducing latency and supporting operations in environments with intermittent connectivity. Retail point-of-sale systems, manufacturing sensors, and field service applications increasingly combine cloud-based management with edge-based execution. This hybrid pattern also addresses data locality and resilience: pressing functions can continue to run even when connectivity is degraded, while centralized services synchronize state when connectivity returns. The rollout of fifth-generation (5G) networks will further amplify this pattern by enabling richer, more responsive applications on mobile and embedded devices.

Multicloud and hybrid strategies are also gaining importance as organizations seek resilience, prudent cost management, and freedom from provider lock-in. Rather than committing entirely to a single cloud provider, enterprises increasingly distribute

[4] For overview information on the point solution products cited, see Atlassian, "Loom | Async Video Messaging for Work," `https://www.atlassian.com/software/loom`; Calendly, "Free Online Appointment Scheduling Software," `https://calendly.com`; and Typeform, "Typeform: People-Friendly Forms and Surveys," `https://www.typeform.com`.

workloads across providers—using each for its strengths and maintaining the ability to switch if pricing, reliability, or capabilities change. This approach adds architectural and operational complexity, but for organizations with the maturity to manage it, the flexibility can be substantial. Hybrid strategies, which blend on-premises infrastructure with cloud services, remain relevant for workloads with data residency constraints, latency requirements, or legacy dependencies that cannot yet be fully migrated.

Compliance and data sovereignty are becoming architectural constraints rather than documentation exercises. Regulations across multiple jurisdictions require providers and customers to control where data resides, how it is moved, how it is retained, and who can access it. Providers are responding with regional deployments, granular residency controls, customer-managed encryption options, and certifications that demonstrate adherence to specific frameworks. For organizations in regulated sectors, these capabilities are not "nice to have." They are prerequisites that determine whether adoption is possible at all, and they influence vendor selection as much as price or functionality.

Sustainability is increasingly influencing procurement decisions. Large data centers consume substantial energy, and enterprises increasingly ask about environmental footprint alongside reliability, security, and cost. Providers are investing in renewable energy sourcing, efficient cooling, workload optimization, and improvements in hardware life-cycle management. Over time, environmental performance may become a differentiator comparable to security posture, especially as organizations incorporate sustainability metrics into corporate governance and supplier evaluation.

Quantum computing remains in early stages, but cloud providers are already offering access to quantum processors and simulators through managed services. For most enterprises, practical applications are still years away. Yet the trajectory is worth watching: problems in optimization, cryptography, and simulation that are intractable for classical computers may eventually yield to quantum approaches. Organizations that begin exploring the technology now—even experimentally—may be better positioned when it matures. The more immediate implication for SaaS providers is the need to prepare for a post-quantum cryptographic landscape, where current encryption methods may need to be replaced.

Blockchain technology has moved past its initial hype cycle into more targeted applications. In supply chain management, it offers auditable provenance tracking. In finance, it supports settlement mechanisms that reduce dependence on intermediaries. For SaaS providers, blockchain may influence how certain transactions are recorded, verified, or shared across organizational boundaries—particularly where trust between parties is limited and transparency is valued. The technology is not a universal solution, but in specific contexts where immutability and distributed verification are critical, it is finding practical traction.

User experience remains a battleground. As functionality converges across categories, design quality, workflow elegance, and time-to-value become primary differentiators. Personalized dashboards and richer mobile experiences are expanding users' expectations. Emerging interaction models—including voice interfaces and augmented reality—are beginning to influence SaaS design, particularly in field service, training, and remote assistance applications. These remain niche today, but they signal a broader trend. As devices diversify, SaaS providers must design for experiences beyond the traditional screen and keyboard.

The most successful SaaS products reduce cognitive load. Hence, they make the right action obvious, guide users through complex processes, and surface insights when needed rather than burying them in reports. Providers who fail to keep pace with rising expectations risk losing customers to competitors whose products appear more modern and more intuitive.

Finally, integration has become a baseline requirement. Enterprises use dozens of SaaS applications, and the value of each depends on how well it connects to the others. Reliable APIs, prebuilt connectors, identity federation, event-driven integration, and integration platforms are no longer premium features; they are baseline requirements. The SaaS economy rewards platforms that work well with others and penalizes those that create data silos or force customers into brittle point-to-point integrations. In enterprise environments, software is evaluated not only by features but also by how well it fits within the surrounding IT landscape. Providers that pair strong core capabilities with integration, security, and operational excellence will lead the next phase.

9.3 PC to Cloud, Software to SaaS

The preceding sections examined the enterprise reality of cloud migration: organizational patterns, governance changes, and the economics of SaaS adoption. This section turns inward, to the personal journey. It describes how I experienced the transition from PC-era software to cloud architecture, the constraints that shaped my early thinking, and how those constraints dissolved as the delivery model evolved.

When I joined Microsoft, my mission was clear—to make computing valuable and accessible to businesses and individuals who had never had that power at their fingertips. Our shared ambition was captured in a phrase that defined a generation of software development: "a computer on every desk and in every home."

The software I helped build ran on individual machines. We developed spell checkers, grammar checkers, and features that made word processors and spreadsheets more intelligent and capable. Each application had to fit within the constraints of a PC, namely, limited memory, modest processing power, and restricted storage. Those limits demanded discipline. Every byte mattered. Every algorithm had to run efficiently on hardware that would seem primitive by today's standards.

But the challenges went beyond raw performance. Ensuring that software behaves reliably across different hardware configurations introduced an additional layer of complexity. A feature that ran flawlessly on one machine might fail on another because of differences in graphics cards, memory layouts, or peripheral devices. My teams spent countless hours chasing defects that appeared only on specific setups. Sometimes, we could not reproduce those problems in our own development environments. Distribution compounded these difficulties. Updates meant shipping physical disks and, later, downloading releases over slow dial-up connections. Many customers stayed on older versions for months or years because upgrading was inconvenient, disruptive, or risky.

Those constraints shaped how I thought about software. They taught me to design for resource efficiency, anticipate variability, and build systems that degraded gracefully when conditions were less than ideal. The lessons were invaluable, but they also revealed the limits of the PC model. Even the best software could not escape the fact that it ran on isolated machines with finite resources and no dependable way to stay current.

When the internet emerged in the 1990s, I recognized that something fundamental had changed. The network was not merely a new distribution channel; it was an architectural turning point. Computing resources no longer had to reside on the user's desk. Applications could run on remote servers with far greater capacity than any PC. Data could be stored centrally and accessed from anywhere. Updates could be applied once, with all users benefiting immediately.

I began to focus on what would become cloud computing because it addressed the constraints I had struggled against for years. Cloud computing replaced the limitations of local execution with centralized, elastic infrastructure, bringing dynamic scaling, global accessibility, and advancement decoupled from the limits of end-user hardware. It did not merely improve how we built and managed software; it fundamentally transformed both the economics of software and the scope of what software could achieve.

9.3.1 Designing for the Cloud

The advent of cloud computing forced me to reconsider architectural assumptions I had carried for years. In the PC era, software lived in a world of ownership and boundaries. An application ran on a known machine, depended on predictable hardware, managed memory within a single process, and stored data in proximity. The cloud replaced that certainty with a different premise: computing as a shared, elastic fabric—available on demand, distributed across many machines, and constantly in motion. It felt liberating, and it also took time to trust it.

To work in that new environment, I had to stop thinking in terms of "bigger servers" and start thinking in terms of "more copies." I began designing systems that scaled horizontally by adding instances rather than upgrading individual machines. I learned to view failure as the norm, not the exception. Any component could fail without warning, and the system must continue operating. Redundancy was no longer a comfort; it became part of the baseline. Stateless design, which initially felt unnatural, gradually became familiar: applications that did not retain state between requests, relying instead on shared storage and caching services. Over time, I came to appreciate what those patterns made possible—elasticity that could expand under pressure and contract when demand subsided.

As my understanding deepened, serverless computing became one of the moments that reshaped my intuition. Services such as AWS Lambda and Azure Functions let me focus on logic and behavior rather than the mechanics of provisioning and maintaining infrastructure. The first time I deployed a function and watched it execute purely in response to an event (an API call, a file upload, a message arriving in a queue), it felt like a small revelation. I paid for the compute time I used, and nothing more. There were no servers to size, no capacity to reserve "just in case," and no patch cycles to schedule. For workloads that spiked unpredictably, the model was not merely convenient; it was a better fit for reality.

The movement toward microservices also felt familiar, even if the vocabulary was new. INTELLIFM was designed as a collection of modular components that interacted through well-defined interfaces. The inference engine, the forms publisher, and the knowledge base manager could be developed, tested, and updated independently. We did not describe that structure as "microservices" at the time. Still, many of the principles were the same: decompose complex systems into smaller components, define clear contracts, and establish boundaries that allow teams to move quickly without stepping on one another's work.

Cloud platforms gave those instincts operational force. Services could be deployed independently, scaled based on demand, and updated without requiring an all-or-nothing release. A surge in document processing did not require scaling the entire system—only the services that carried that workload. Failures could be contained so that a single weak link did not bring everything down. What had once been an architectural preference became an operational discipline because the cloud rewarded systems prepared for change.

Designing for distributed environments also introduced a set of concerns that had barely surfaced in the PC world. Services needed ways to discover one another without hard-coded addresses. Communication required choices: synchronous calls when immediacy mattered, asynchronous messaging when resilience mattered, event-driven patterns when decoupling mattered most. Data no longer resided in a single place, which raised new questions in daily engineering conversations—consistency, partitions, replication, and eventual convergence. These were not abstract ideas; they were practical trade-offs that shaped reliability and user experience.

The transition reshaped not only architecture but also the rhythm of work. DevOps practices—tight collaboration between development and operations teams, automated provisioning, and CI/CD pipelines—became central rather than optional. Deployments moved from quarterly events to routine moments. Infrastructure became code: version-controlled, testable, and repeatable. The feedback loop between committing a change and seeing its impact in production compressed dramatically, reshaping how teams learned. We could now observe, adjust, and improve in days—or even hours—rather than waiting for a months-long release cycle to validate our assumptions.

Perhaps most importantly, the cloud made possible a class of capabilities that had previously been out of reach on standalone machines. At scale, storage and analytics were no longer scarce resources. We could observe usage patterns across millions of interactions and use those signals to refine systems over time. ML models that once required specialized hardware could now be trained or served on demand. Personalization moved from aspiration to implementation because data and compute could be brought together at a scale that the PC era simply could not support. The cloud did not merely provide me with new tools. It changed what I believed software could be.

Table 9-1 summarizes the key differences between PC-based and cloud-based development.

Table 9-1. *Comparative analysis of PC-based and cloud-based development.*

Aspect	PC-Based Development	Cloud-Based Development
Scalability	Limited by local hardware	Virtually unlimited; scales on demand
Deployment	Complex, often manual	Automated and continuous
Updates	Challenging to distribute; users often ran outdated versions	Seamless and immediate; applied centrally
Resource utilization	Often inefficient; capacity fixed	Dynamic and optimized; pay for what you use
Global reach	Limited; requires physical distribution	Inherent; accessible from anywhere
Failure handling	Application-level recovery	Built-in redundancy and failover
Data insights	Isolated to individual machines	Aggregates across users; supports analytics

Adopting cloud architecture did more than change where my code ran. It changed how I approached problems. The cloud became more than a platform—it became a canvas for innovation, powering solutions that could reach users globally in ways that were unimaginable during the PC era. The constraints that had defined my early career—limited memory, isolated machines, cumbersome updates—gave way to possibilities I am still exploring decades later.

9.3.2 Challenges and Solutions

The architectural patterns described in the previous section shaped my approach to design. The lessons that follow shaped how I approached deployment, governance, and the organizational changes that accompany any major platform transition.

The promise of cloud computing came with its own set of hard lessons. Scalability, resilience, security, and data management demanded fresh thinking and, for me, a willingness to set aside instincts that had served me well in the PC era. I had spent years learning how to tune performance on known machines with known limits. The cloud asked me to trust a world in which machines were interchangeable, failure was routine, and capacity could expand or vanish without warning. The first time I watched a healthy instance disappear and a new one take its place, I remember thinking, "This is both brilliant and unsettling." It felt as if the ground under the application was moving—because it was.

Scalability, in particular, forced me to rethink what "growth" meant. In the PC world, scaling often meant purchasing more powerful hardware and planning upgrades months in advance. In the cloud, scaling meant multiplying—adding instances at the right moments and then removing them just as quickly. Early on, I did what many engineers do: I designed for maximum capacity. It felt safe. It also created waste. That lesson became real during an early production rollout when we overprovisioned "just in case" and then watched the usage curve flatten out. The system performed beautifully, but the cost dashboard told the uncomfortable truth. After that, I began treating cost as an architectural signal, not merely a financial concern. Over time, I learned that the real goal was to achieve right-sized capacity, sufficient to meet demand without paying for idle resources. In practice, this meant building autoscaling architectures that respond to load, using elastic resources across platforms such as AWS, Azure, and Google Cloud. The satisfaction came not from seeing the largest system run, but from seeing a system expand calmly under pressure and then return to normal when the surge passed.

Resilience demanded an even more fundamental rethinking. In the PC world, reliability often meant preventing failures. In the cloud, reliability begins with accepting that failure is normal. Hardware fails. Networks partition. Services become temporarily unavailable. The question is not whether something will go wrong, but how the system will respond when it does. I remember a project that raised the stakes sharply: my teams were responsible for mission-critical financial applications with a 99.99% uptime target. That number looks abstract until you translate it into what it means operationally—how little room it leaves for error, how quickly minor incidents become big ones. I still recall the tone of our readiness reviews: not fear, but seriousness. We approached every dependency and every recovery path with the question, *What happens at 2 AM when no one is watching?*

We achieved the target by deploying redundancy across multiple geographic regions, implementing automatic failover, and supporting real-time data replication. I can still recall a full-load failover test in which we intentionally forced a component to drop out. For a moment, the monitoring screens spiked, and alarms fired—precisely as they should. Then the traffic shifted, the system stabilized, and user-facing performance barely moved. That was the moment resilience ceased to be a theory for me. It became a discipline: assume components will fail and make those failures survivable.

Security brought a different kind of pressure. When data resided on isolated PCs behind corporate firewalls, risk was perceived as bounded. In cloud environments—where applications and data are hosted remotely—protecting sensitive information and meeting regulatory requirements became nonnegotiable. I saw this most clearly in regulated industries. In health care projects, my teams implemented MFA and encryption protocols to comply with the Health Insurance Portability and Accountability Act (HIPAA). In financial services, we developed secure payment processing systems compliant with the Payment Card Industry Data Security Standard (PCI DSS) requirements. The hardest part was rarely choosing the proper control. The hardest part was making security usable. I recall a pilot in which a control sequence was technically correct but, in practice, painful. Users began finding "creative" ways around it within days. That experience taught me to treat usability as a security requirement. Overly restrictive controls frustrate users and invite workarounds that create new vulnerabilities. The systems that succeed are the ones that make the secure path the easy path.

Sustaining that balance demanded ongoing attention. Threats multiply, regulations change, and yesterday's configuration may not satisfy tomorrow's requirements. I learned how easily systems drift out of alignment: a new service gets introduced, a permission is broadened to unblock a deployment, and an exception becomes permanent. Over time, those small decisions accumulate. That is why my teams build monitoring and adaptation into the foundation of every cloud solution. We track access patterns, audit configurations, and stay current with regulatory changes so that we respond methodically rather than scramble at the last minute. Some of the most valuable work happens quietly—before an incident ever reaches a user.

Not every challenge was technical. Cloud computing depends on connectivity, and connectivity is not universal. Early in my cloud work, I became more aware of the digital divide—the gap between those with reliable internet access and those without. It is easy to assume the network is always there when your own world has constant access. But reality looks different in many communities, and that gap shapes who benefits from technology. That awareness prompted my teams to adopt an offline-first design: systems that preserve core functionality in low-connectivity environments and synchronize with cloud services when connectivity is restored. One project that stayed with me was an agricultural information system used by farmers in remote regions. In early field feedback, the recurring theme was simple: *"The signal comes and goes."* So we built around that reality. Farmers could record crop data, receive planting guidance, and access market prices on mobile devices without a constant connection. When connectivity was restored, the data synchronized automatically. Watching that system succeed reminded me that architecture is not only about elegance and performance. It can also be about inclusion.

The broader ethical dimensions of cloud computing also shaped my thinking. Data privacy remains a persistent concern. When information resides on remote servers, questions of ownership, access, and jurisdiction become complex—especially when systems span countries and legal regimes. My teams learned to navigate international data protection frameworks—GDPR, CCPA, and a growing patchwork of regional regulations—so that the systems we built respected user rights and met legal obligations. More than once, I found that the most crucial design conversations were not about databases or services, but about trust: what users expect, what they consent to, and what we owe them when they share their data.

Environmental impact is another consideration I take seriously. Large data centers consume substantial energy, and the carbon footprint of cloud infrastructure is not trivial. Many providers have made meaningful commitments to renewable energy and efficient operations, but responsibility does not end with the provider. I began to see that efficiency is not only a cost issue but also an ethical one. In my own work, I focus on optimizing resource utilization—choosing right-sized infrastructure, avoiding wasteful always-on capacity, and writing efficient code where it matters. Those choices add up. The cloud offers extraordinary capabilities, but using them responsibly means acknowledging both the costs and the benefits while being deliberate about the trade-offs we make.

9.3.3 Software Transformation Examples

The transition from PC-based software to cloud computing and SaaS reshaped the technology industry in ways that were difficult to foresee. It democratized computing resources, allowing startups to compete with established players without the burden of building their own data centers. It gave rise to new business models—SaaS, PaaS, and IaaS—that transformed how software is sold, delivered, and maintained. It elevated IT departments from maintenance hubs to strategic drivers of capability. Most importantly, it redefined user expectations: ubiquitous access, continuous updates, and the ability to work from any device. Along the way, it also raised persistent concerns about data privacy and security that remain at the forefront of modern architectural debate. The following examples illustrate how this transformation unfolded across the industry.

In the late 1990s, much of the software industry still relied on physical distribution. Microsoft products, such as Windows and Office, were shipped on CD-ROMs. As a result, installation, upgrades, and fixes depended on customer-installed media and local environments. During the same period, CTInsuranceAdvantage and CTAdvantage were distributed on CD-ROMs as client-server products. Customers installed the client software on PCs and deployed the server components within their own environments. They applied updates themselves and operated within the constraints of local infrastructure, including storage, processing capacity, and network configuration.

I experienced this era firsthand. We carefully prepared releases, shipped them, and then waited days or weeks for feedback. Often, the first response was an urgent call when installations failed or when customer environments behaved differently than expected.

In March 1999, Salesforce was founded as a cloud-delivered, subscription-based CRM platform, an early example of the SaaS model. Recognizing the far-reaching potential of the internet, we transitioned to cloud-based platforms in the early 2000s, launching CTInsuranceAdvantage.com and CTAdvantage.com. These were among the earliest industry-specific SaaS solutions in the document management space.

As distribution moved online, the constraints of physical distribution disappeared. Users no longer needed to install software or wait for disc-based updates. They could access the platform from any internet-connected device, and we could deploy improvements continuously rather than bundling them into infrequent releases. I recall the first time we implemented a meaningful improvement and observed users benefit without requiring any local installation. It was a quiet moment, but it clarified the industry's direction: the delivery mechanism was becoming part of the product. That experience gave me an early view of what SaaS would eventually become. It reinforced principles I still apply today: design for accessibility, deliver value continuously, and treat the relationship with the user as ongoing rather than transactional.

The following industry examples illustrate three distinct delivery patterns that emerged as software moved to the cloud. Each pattern reflects different trade-offs between accessibility, performance, and user experience. Each has found its place depending on the workload and audience.

Pure SaaS: Browser-First Delivery

Intuit's QuickBooks illustrates this browser-first pattern in vertical software. Initially distributed on discs as PC-based accounting software, QuickBooks Online was launched by Intuit in 2001, giving users browser-based access to their financial data.[5] Thus, users were freed from single-machine constraints and could collaborate across locations.

These early adoptions in vertical markets anticipated a broader trend. Microsoft's transition to Office is an important milestone. For decades, Microsoft Office was distributed on floppy disks and later compact discs, requiring installation on individual computers. In 2011, Microsoft introduced Office 365, moving from the traditional PC-based model to a SaaS approach. Users could access Word, Excel, PowerPoint, and other applications directly through web browsers, with documents stored in the cloud. Real-time collaboration became possible, and access from multiple devices enhanced workplace efficiency. For Microsoft, the subscription model provided more predictable revenue and enabled continuous improvement. By 2017, Microsoft expanded these offerings with Microsoft 365, a broader suite of productivity tools and services. The full consumer rebrand from Office 365 to Microsoft 365 followed in April 2020.

Hybrid: Desktop SaaS

Adobe's transition to Creative Cloud in 2013 represents a different pattern: a hybrid model rather than a purely browser-based delivery system. Previously, Adobe Creative Suite—Photoshop, Illustrator, and InDesign—was sold in physical boxes with installation discs. With Creative Cloud, the software is downloaded and installed locally, but delivery, licensing, updates, and cloud-integrated features are all managed through a centralized service. This transition transformed a static, one-time purchase into an evergreen relationship, giving users immediate access to the latest versions and AI-driven capabilities without waiting for a physical release cycle.

This combination of local execution and cloud-based delivery persists because creative tasks, such as graphic design and video editing, demand intensive local processing and low-latency performance that browser-based environments cannot yet match. The result is what might be called "desktop SaaS": software that runs locally but

[5] Intuit Inc., "QuickBooks Online," Intuit Corporate History; see also "History of Intuit Inc.," FundingUniverse, `https://www.fundinguniverse.com/company-histories/intuit-inc-history`.

connects to the cloud for licensing, storage, synchronization, and continuous feature updates. This model has become the standard for professional, resource-intensive applications where full-browser delivery would compromise the user experience.

Streaming and Edge-Constrained Delivery

Cloud migration reached even the gaming industry, where physical discs and powerful local hardware had long been essential. In 2014, Sony launched PlayStation Now, a cloud gaming service that streams games directly to users' devices. Microsoft followed with Xbox Cloud Gaming, part of Xbox Game Pass, and NVIDIA introduced GeForce NOW, which streams games from users' existing libraries. These services demonstrated that even the most resource-intensive applications could transition to cloud delivery.

Yet this pattern reveals the outer boundary of what cloud delivery can currently achieve. Gaming demands real-time responsiveness measured in milliseconds; any perceptible delay between a player's input and the screen's response breaks the experience. Unlike productivity software, where a half-second delay is tolerable, interactive entertainment requires latency low enough that users cannot distinguish cloud rendering from local processing. That constraint pushes compute infrastructure closer to users, specifically into edge data centers positioned for proximity rather than scale.

The same dynamics apply to other latency-sensitive workloads: remote video editing, 3D rendering, and real-time simulation. In each case, the cloud provides elastic capacity and eliminates the need for expensive local hardware, but only if the network path is sufficiently short and consistent to preserve responsiveness. Google's Stadia service, which launched in 2019 and shut down in 2023, illustrated the difficulty of meeting these constraints at scale; despite substantial investment, the experience varied too much across network conditions to sustain a broad user base.[6]

Streaming delivery remains a frontier rather than a settled pattern. As edge infrastructure expands and network performance improves, more workloads will cross the threshold into viable cloud delivery. However, for now, this model operates

[6] Google Stadia launched November 19, 2019, and shut down January 18, 2023, after failing to gain sufficient user traction despite substantial investment in cloud gaming infrastructure. Phil Harrison, "A Message about Stadia and Our Long Term Streaming Strategy," Google Blog, September 29, 2022, `https://blog.google/products-and-platforms/products/stadia/message-on-stadia-streaming-strategy`.

under tighter constraints than browser-first or hybrid approaches, underscoring that the physics of distance and the realities of network variability still shape what software architecture can achieve.

Business Model and Relationship Implications

The evolution from PC-based software to cloud computing and SaaS transformed both software development and deployment, as well as how companies generate revenue. One-time purchases gave way to subscription models, providing software providers with more predictable income and sustaining continuous product improvement. This change placed greater emphasis on customer retention and long-term value creation. IT spending adjusted correspondingly—from periodic capital expenditures, such as hardware purchases, to ongoing operational expenditures, in which organizations pay for services as they are consumed.

Perhaps the most lasting change is in the relationship between software companies and their customers. Traditional software sales were transactional: a customer purchased a license, received a disc, and the relationship ended, typically until the next major version. SaaS changed that. Subscription models require companies to maintain ongoing connections with customers—monitoring usage, addressing issues, and continually adding value. Customer success teams now work proactively to help users get the most from the software, rather than merely resolving problems after they arise. I noticed that this also changed the internal conversation: release day ceased to be the finish line and became one checkpoint in a continuous cycle of improvement and accountability. The relationship has become continuous, and that continuity has reshaped expectations on both sides. (For a broader survey of popular SaaS products, see Appendix 11.)

9.4 SaaS–Cloud Synergy

Over the years, I have watched cloud computing and SaaS mature from promising ideas into cornerstones of modern IT. They have reshaped how organizations operate, how services are delivered, and how technology investments are planned. But their impact extends well beyond the enterprise. The experiences that define daily life for billions of people—streaming video, social media, instant messaging, photo sharing, and video calling across continents—are all delivered through the cloud. Instagram,

WhatsApp, and TikTok exist at their current scale only because cloud infrastructure made it economically viable to serve vast numbers of users simultaneously. The smartphone accelerated this transformation: the device in every pocket became a portal to experiences that would have been inconceivable in the era of installed software. As a Microsoft veteran, I have had a front-row seat to this evolution, from the age of packaged software to the rise of cloud platforms and subscription-based services that now shape nearly every aspect of work and daily life. Throughout that journey, I have helped organizations navigate change by designing architectures, guiding migrations, and solving the complex problems that arise when systems must scale, adapt, and remain available. Looking back, what stands out is the depth of the interdependence between cloud and SaaS. Each strengthens the other, and together they create possibilities that neither could achieve alone.

The relationship is best understood as a flywheel: a set of reinforcing loops in which progress in one area accelerates progress in others. Three loops, in particular, explain why cloud and SaaS have grown together and why that growth is likely to continue.

The first loop connects adoption, scale, and economics. As more organizations adopt SaaS, cloud providers achieve greater scale. That scale lowers the unit costs of compute, storage, and networking, making SaaS offerings more economically viable and, in turn, driving further adoption. Applications such as Salesforce for CRM and Dropbox for file storage rely on scalable compute, resilient networking, durable storage, and strong security controls to deliver the experience users expect. In my own work—spanning Microsoft environments and enterprise deployments beyond Microsoft—I have helped design and implement these underlying layers so that SaaS providers can serve customers reliably. Without that infrastructure, SaaS would be a promise without a delivery mechanism. When the infrastructure functions well, users do not think about it. That invisibility is the goal.

The second loop connects platform capabilities and user expectations. As cloud providers introduce richer primitives—managed databases, identity services, AI APIs, and serverless compute—SaaS providers can iterate more quickly and deliver more sophisticated features. Those features raise user expectations, which in turn prompt cloud providers to further expand their platforms. Microsoft, for example, has built a global network of data centers to support cloud services and deliver low-latency access and high availability for products such as Microsoft 365, Dynamics 365, and a growing portfolio of Azure-based services. The scale of that investment reflects the scale of the opportunity: SaaS adoption creates demand, and cloud providers respond with more capacity, richer platform services, and broader geographic reach.

The third loop connects security investment and enterprise trust. Cloud providers invest heavily in compliance certifications, encryption, identity management, and audit capabilities. That investment builds trust among regulated industries—finance, health care, and government—that had previously resisted cloud adoption. As those industries move workloads to SaaS, their requirements drive further security and compliance investment, which expands the addressable market for both cloud and SaaS.

I have seen this flywheel in action through my work with SaaS providers, cloud teams, and Microsoft partners. One example is Kliger-Weiss Infosystems Inc. (KWI), a company founded in 1985 that became a pioneer in cloud-based retail technology. KWI offers a unified omnichannel platform that integrates mobile point of sale, merchandising, inventory management, e-commerce, order management, and CRM—all on a single database. Long before the term “SaaS” was common, when similar offerings were often described as “service bureau” models, KWI delivered centrally hosted solutions to retailers. That early vision anticipated what would later become standard: software delivered as a service, maintained by the provider, and accessible from anywhere. KWI’s trajectory illustrates all three loops: adoption driving scale, platform evolution driving richer features, and compliance investment opening new market segments.

The practical benefits of this flywheel are concrete. Scalability allows systems to absorb rapid surges in demand—Black Friday traffic spikes, major product launches, unexpected viral moments—without advance provisioning or manual intervention. Reliability derives from multiregional redundancy and automated failover, so a problem in one location does not affect users. Cost efficiency follows from shared infrastructure and economies of scale; customers pay for what they use rather than maintaining idle capacity. Secure accessibility supports work from any location, which has become not a convenience but an expectation.

The COVID-19 pandemic in early 2020 made these benefits visible in ways that no marketing campaign could. As remote work became the norm, the cloud pay-as-you-go model and the accessibility of SaaS helped businesses maintain continuity. Teams that had never worked from home began collaborating via cloud-based tools within days. Organizations that had resisted cloud migration accelerated their plans out of necessity. What might have taken years happened in weeks. The pandemic did not create the SaaS-cloud synergy, but it demonstrated its value under pressure. Moreover, it changed the conversation for organizations that had been hesitant. For many, the debate went from “Should we move to the cloud?” to “How quickly can we get there?”

9.5 SaaS Meets AI

AI is reshaping the next wave of SaaS innovation by changing not only what software can do, but also how quickly it improves. Since the early 2000s, when I helped launch CTAdvantage.com, AI and ML have steadily advanced from experimental features to core capabilities that shape product design and customer value. The most important shift lies in the pace of improvement. Traditional software improved according to its release cycle: new features arrived when engineering teams completed them. AI-powered SaaS, by contrast, improves through a continuous feedback loop of data, model updates, retrieval, evaluation, and operational tuning. Recommendations become more precise, anomaly thresholds adjust, and system behavior improves as usage patterns accumulate. I remember how quickly expectations changed once users realized that software could learn from their behavior rather than wait for the next version. Today, that data-driven adaptation is visible in products that many users take for granted. Zoom uses AI for noise suppression and virtual backgrounds; Spotify refines recommendations with every listen; and Gmail suggests replies and completes text as users write. What these features share is not just intelligence, but continuous, usage-driven improvement that no traditional release cycle could replicate.

The capabilities AI brings to SaaS can be understood in three tiers, each representing a different level of autonomy and impact. The first tier is assistance: AI that summarizes, routes, and suggests. Recommendation systems exemplify this capability. Netflix analyzes viewing histories to suggest content; Spotify creates personalized playlists based on listening habits. In business platforms, Salesforce Einstein predicts which leads are more likely to convert and suggests next steps. Recommendation and assistance features reduce friction and make software feel more responsive, while leaving human decision-making in control.

The second tier is automation: AI that executes workflows and reduces repetitive operational effort. AI-based chatbots and virtual assistants handle routine customer inquiries, route complex issues to human agents, and provide round-the-clock support. By reducing repetitive Tier 1 workload, cutting response times, and enforcing consistent resolution patterns across channels, these tools deliver measurable operational gains. Zendesk AI agents, for example, suggest relevant solutions and can resolve certain inquiries autonomously, illustrating how such systems can reduce ticket volume and improve first-contact resolution. When I speak with support leaders, I hear the same message repeatedly: fewer repetitive conversations for agents, faster responses for customers, and greater reliability across service channels.

The third tier is autonomous decision-making: AI that assesses risk, detects fraud, or personalizes at scale without waiting for human approval at each step. This tier differs from the first tier, where AI suggests and humans decide, and from the second tier, where AI executes predefined workflows. In the third tier, the AI has already decided and acted; the human reviews the outcome afterward rather than authorizing it in advance.

A bank's fraud detection system that autonomously blocks a credit card transaction from an unfamiliar location illustrates the point well: the decision is made in milliseconds, the customer is notified, and a human reviewer later examines flagged cases in a queue. Similarly, automated pricing engines adjust rates in real time based on demand signals, and content recommendation systems personalize feeds without human intervention at the point of delivery. The benefits are considerable—speed, scale, and consistency beyond what any human workflow could match—but so are the responsibilities. When AI makes high-stakes decisions autonomously, governance requirements such as transparency, explainability, and appeal mechanisms become indispensable.

These tiers carry cumulative obligations that extend beyond SaaS itself. Privacy concerns, algorithmic bias, audit requirements, and accountability frameworks apply to any AI system making consequential decisions—whether delivered as SaaS, built on PaaS, or integrated into custom applications. A bank's loan approval model carries the same governance responsibilities as a SaaS-based fraud detection service. The reason to address these issues here is practical: SaaS is the primary channel through which most enterprises now encounter and consume AI capabilities. When leaders evaluate AI-enhanced SaaS products, they are also making governance choices—about which models to trust, what oversight mechanisms to require, and what accountability they can demonstrate to regulators and customers. Governance includes who reviews model outputs, how bias is detected and corrected, what audit trails exist, and how users can override or appeal automated decisions. Providers must offer transparent practices and clear explanations so that customers can place confidence in the outcomes. AI is not a feature to be added at the margins; it belongs at the center of how enterprise software, in any delivery model, is designed and evaluated.

I saw the potential of this approach firsthand at Fidelity National Information Services (FIS)—a global leader in financial services technology—where I led engineering efforts to reposition the provider as a forward-looking software innovator. Using the INTELLIFM architecture and modern Microsoft technologies—including Nuance's conversational AI and speech recognition platform—my teams developed conversational AI systems that integrated interactive voice response (IVR), chatbots, and virtual assistants. This work proved that even the most complex, regulated financial environments could be transformed through the strategic application of intelligent, cloud-delivered interfaces.

We used NLP and ML to deliver efficient self-service experiences without turning customers into menu navigators. I recall reviewing call flows in which a slight change in phrasing or intent detection produced a measurable difference in outcomes. By integrating these front-end systems with the automatic call distributor, we reshaped the customer service model. The result was higher customer and agent satisfaction, lower operating costs, more streamlined sales operations, and stronger security protocols. That project reinforced my conviction that AI must be an architectural priority, not an afterthought.

The impact of AI-driven SaaS varies across industries, but the pattern is consistent: AI provides capabilities that were previously impractical. In health care, AI-supported SaaS platforms are optimizing clinical workflows and assisting with diagnostic imaging analysis. In finance, they strengthen fraud detection and support data-driven trading and risk analysis. In retail, they improve inventory decisions and drive personalized marketing at scale.

AI is also reshaping internal operations among SaaS providers. Automation handles routine work, such as data entry, workflow routing, and system monitoring, freeing staff to focus on higher-value initiatives. AI-assisted integration tools reduce manual effort in mapping, conversion, and synchronization across systems. AI-based analytics helps providers refine pricing, improve customer relationships, and identify operational bottlenecks in real time. Compared with earlier generations of SaaS, these solutions go beyond hosting and delivery; they also provide prediction, guidance, and partial decision automation.

Predictive analytics deserves particular attention. By tapping into historical data, AI helps SaaS providers anticipate trends and make evidence-based decisions rather than relying on intuition. Sales forecasts gain precision, market opportunities emerge from patterns that might otherwise remain hidden, and resource allocation improves when planning is informed by data rather than heuristic guesswork. Implementing these capabilities requires selecting the right architectural approach for the data at hand. For structured data—tabular records such as sales figures, usage metrics, and customer records—traditional ML models such as gradient boosting and regression techniques often deliver the most accurate, interpretable results. Deep learning and neural networks often become the preferred approach when the data is unstructured: text, images, audio, or behavioral sequences where pattern complexity may exceed what traditional models can capture. NLP techniques, which sit at this boundary, are increasingly central to SaaS analytics as providers mine support tickets, user feedback, and communication logs for strategic insight.

For me, the most important lesson is that AI and SaaS are now developed together. Early platforms such as CTAdvantage.com and other solutions built on the INTELLIFM framework offered an early view of what AI could contribute to cloud-delivered software: more personalized experiences, operational efficiency, and continuous improvement. As technology advances, potential grows, but so do responsibilities. Providers must address privacy, algorithmic fairness, and transparent design choices in ways that preserve user trust. AI is becoming integral to what SaaS offers, and that integration calls for discipline as much as ambition.

The operational risks that accompany AI integration differ from those of traditional software and deserve explicit attention. Hallucination—the tendency of LLMs to generate plausible but factually incorrect outputs—requires grounding strategies such as RAG, in which responses are anchored to verified data sources rather than produced from the model alone. Prompt injection and tool injection attacks, in which malicious inputs manipulate AI agents into taking unintended actions, create a new attack surface that security teams must proactively address. In multitenant SaaS environments, preventing data leakage and enforcing tenant boundaries are baseline expectations. The system must be designed so that one customer's data cannot surface in another customer's context, whether through shared embeddings, cached completions, or improperly scoped retrieval pipelines. These risks are not merely theoretical; early AI-enhanced SaaS deployments have already shown how readily such failures can emerge in practice. The lesson from earlier eras of software development applies here as well: security and reliability must be designed in, not bolted on. Organizations that treat AI operational risks as something to address after deployment will find them far harder to manage than those that build mitigations into the architecture from the start.

The assistance, automation, and autonomous decision-making tiers described above represent AI in its current role: a capable layer added onto SaaS platforms originally designed for a different era. The emerging frontier is more fundamental. AI-native design refers to software conceived from the ground up with AI as a central architectural principle—not as a feature added after the fact, but as the foundation shaping data flows, decision logic, and user interaction.

Illustrations of this evolution can already be seen in products such as Harvey for legal services, Sierra for customer experience, Cursor for software engineering, and Attio for CRM.[7] In each case, AI sits much closer to the center of the workflow than in earlier SaaS designs. In an AI-native system, the application does not merely use AI; it reasons, adapts, and improves as a core part of its operating model. This shift reflects a change in the underlying assumptions of software design: from passive tools that respond to user commands to active systems that anticipate needs, learn from outcomes, and operate with increasing autonomy. This is the direction SaaS is moving in. Enterprise leaders who invest now in data architecture, governance frameworks, and AI literacy will be best positioned as AI-native platforms increasingly shape the competitive baseline in their sectors.

9.6 Cloud and SaaS Markets

The scale of the cloud and SaaS markets underscores how deeply these technologies have reshaped enterprise computing. What began as an alternative delivery model has become the center of gravity for IT investment worldwide.

According to IDC's Worldwide Semiannual Public Cloud Services Tracker, worldwide public cloud services revenues totaled $669.2 billion in 2023, representing a 19.9% increase from $558.3 billion in 2022.[8] This growth reflects the continuing expansion of the cloud industry across regions and industries.

SaaS applications remained the largest segment, generating $298.5 billion in 2023 and accounting for 44.6% of the total market. While revenues rose 17.4% from $254.4 billion in 2022, the segment's market share declined slightly from 45.6% as other categories grew more quickly.[9]

The tracker breaks that market down further by category. IaaS was the second-largest category, generating $133.4 billion in 2023 and accounting for 19.9% of the market. The segment expanded 15.6% from $115.5 billion in 2022, though its share declined from 20.7%,

[7] For overview information on the AI-native platforms cited as of early 2026, see Harvey, `https://www.harvey.ai`; Sierra, `https://sierra.ai`; Cursor, `https://cursor.com`; and Attio, `https://attio.com`.

[8] International Data Corporation, "Worldwide Public Cloud Services Revenues Grew 19.9% Year Over Year in 2023, According to IDC Tracker," press release, June 10, 2024, `https://www.businesswire.com/news/home/20240610550557/en/`.

[9] IDC, "Worldwide Public Cloud Services Revenues Grew 19.9%."

making it the slowest-growing category. PaaS recorded the fastest growth, surging 29.3% to $123.3 billion in 2023. Its share increased from 17.1% to 18.4%, reflecting rising enterprise adoption of development platforms and middleware for application modernization and deployment. SaaS-System Infrastructure Software completed the picture, with $114.0 billion in 2023 revenues and 17.0% of the market. This segment grew 22.5% from $93.1 billion in 2022, when it held 16.7% of the market, signaling greater enterprise investment in cloud-based system management and infrastructure software. IDC projects that worldwide public cloud services revenues will exceed $800 billion in 2024 and reach $1.6 trillion by 2028, with a compound annual growth rate of 19.5% over the 2023–2028 period.[10]

Cloud computing now represents a substantial and rapidly expanding segment of global technology spending. It can offer cost advantages and operational flexibility in many scenarios and provides a scalable platform for hosting enterprise applications and fostering innovation in data, AI, and edge computing. Gartner's February 2026 forecast projected worldwide IT spending to reach $6.15 trillion in 2026, a 10.8% increase over 2025.[11] This acceleration is driven largely by demand for AI infrastructure: server spending is projected to grow 36.9% year over year, and total data center spending is expected to surpass $650 billion in 2026.[12]

The cloud's growing influence is evident in the steady migration of enterprise IT budgets to public cloud services. An earlier Gartner forecast published in 2022 had projected that the share of enterprise IT spending on public cloud services—across application software, infrastructure software, business process services, and system infrastructure—would rise from 41% in 2022 to 51% by 2025, a directional shift that the subsequent spending trajectory has broadly borne out.

Within the public cloud market, the cloud infrastructure services segment—which industry trackers such as Synergy Research define as IaaS, PaaS, and hosted private cloud services, excluding SaaS applications—is dominated by a small group of technology companies offering large-scale platforms, commonly referred to as *hyperscalers*. AWS, Azure, and Google Cloud lead this segment. These platforms are recognized for their ability to dynamically scale computing resources to meet global demand.

---

[10] IDC, "Worldwide Public Cloud Services Revenues Grew 19.9%."

[11] Gartner, Inc., "Gartner Forecasts Worldwide IT Spending to Grow 10.8% in 2026, Totaling $6.15 Trillion," press release, February 3, 2026, `https://www.gartner.com/en/newsroom/press-releases/2026-02-03-gartner-forecasts-worldwide-it-spending-to-grow-10-point-8-percent-in-2026-totaling-6-point-15-trillion-dollars`.

[12] Gartner, "Worldwide IT Spending to Grow 10.8% in 2026."

As of the fourth quarter of 2025, AWS accounted for 28% of the global cloud infrastructure services market, followed by Microsoft Azure at 21% and Google Cloud at 14%. The three companies collectively accounted for 68% of the public cloud infrastructure services market, up gradually over prior years as the "Big Three" continue to take share from smaller providers. Worldwide cloud infrastructure services revenues reached $119.1 billion in the quarter, bringing full-year 2025 revenues to $419 billion—growth of 30% year over year and the highest growth rate the market has seen in more than three years, driven substantially by generative AI.[13]

Although AWS has maintained its lead for nearly two decades, its share has eroded modestly as Microsoft and Google continue to post higher growth rates. AWS held 31% in the first quarter of 2024 and 30% in the fourth quarter of 2024 before settling at 28% by the end of 2025. Azure and Google Cloud have each gained ground over the same period, with Google Cloud, in particular, reaching its highest-ever share of 14%. Among Tier 2 providers, CoreWeave has emerged as a top-10 cloud provider, generating more than $1.5 billion in quarterly revenue through its AI and GPU-focused services—a vivid illustration of how rapidly the AI boom is reshaping the competitive landscape. These figures reflect the market through the end of 2025; the underlying patterns—hyperscaler dominance, AI-driven growth, and a gradual redistribution of share toward Microsoft and Google—are more durable than the specific numbers.

Each of the three platforms brings distinct strengths. AWS offers breadth and maturity across virtually every service category. Azure integrates deeply with the Microsoft technology stack that many enterprises already depend on. Google Cloud is widely recognized for its strengths in data analytics and ML, anchored by services such as BigQuery and Vertex AI. For organizations I advise, the choice often depends less on raw capability than on existing investments, workforce skills, and specific workload requirements. Multicloud strategies are now common in enterprise architectures, typically adopted to balance risk, manage cost, and reduce vendor lock-in.

---

[13] Synergy Research Group, "GenAI Helps Drive Quarterly Cloud Revenues to $119 Billion as Growth Rate Jumped Yet Again in Q4," February 5, 2026, `https://www.srgresearch.com/articles/genai-helps-drive-quarterly-cloud-revenues-to-119-billion-as-growth-rate-jumped-yet-again-in-q4`.

These leading platforms continue to expand their dominance through sustained investment in AI, next-generation data centers, and a widening portfolio of integrated services. While hyperscale platforms power much of the enterprise cloud market, a range of smaller providers compete by focusing on specific industries, regional regulatory needs, or specialized workloads.

Hyperscalers employ multifaceted strategies to maintain their market positions. They are expanding their global reach by establishing new data centers in different regions, thereby improving service performance for an increasingly diverse international customer base. At the same time, hyperscalers continually enhance their platforms with advanced features and functions, integrating technologies such as AI, ML, analytics, and security solutions.

By diversifying their offerings, hyperscalers cater to a broader range of sectors, including finance, health care, manufacturing, and entertainment. In health care, cloud services provide secure management of patient data and analysis of medical images. In manufacturing, cloud-based IoT platforms optimize production-line efficiency and support predictive maintenance. These industry-specific capabilities have become important competitive advantages.

The expansion of the cloud market reflects a growing reliance on cloud-based services to drive performance, efficiency, and connectivity in an increasingly digital world. Regional variations in adoption are notable. Industry trackers consistently report that North America leads in absolute cloud spending, while Asia-Pacific generally posts the fastest growth rate, driven by rapid digital transformation in countries such as China and India. Europe's adoption tends to be more measured, shaped by stringent data protection regulations such as the GDPR that influence how providers operate and how enterprises architect their solutions.

According to Precedence Research, the global SaaS market reached $314.54 billion in 2023 and expanded to $358.33 billion in 2024. The market is expected to continue its upward trajectory, reaching $1.38 trillion by 2035, with a compound annual growth rate of 12.95% between 2025 and 2035.[14] Forecasts from different research firms vary in their methodologies and endpoint assumptions; most project sustained double-digit growth through the decade. The growth reflects a structural change in how organizations allocate IT budgets. SaaS is increasingly the default consumption model, replacing on-premises deployments across ERP, CRM, supply chain management, data management, security, and compliance.

[14] Precedence Research, "Software As A Service (SaaS) Market" (Ottawa, ON: Precedence Research, 2025), 1.

Multiple converging factors drive this expansion. Global digitization, expanded cloud infrastructure, and the widespread adoption of hybrid and distributed work models are accelerating SaaS adoption across Europe, the Middle East, Africa, Asia-Pacific, and Latin America. Technology catalysts—generative AI copilots, low-code and no-code platforms that democratize development, and vertical-specific SaaS solutions tailored for niche markets such as legaltech, edtech, and medtech—are creating new growth vectors.

Despite having reached maturity in developed regions, the market's continued annual growth rate above 10% indicates strong expansionary momentum. Growth in the SaaS installed base typically comes from several commercial levers. These include add-on modules and new integrations, higher usage on consumption-based pricing tiers, seat expansion as customer organizations grow, cross-selling into adjacent product categories, and lower churn through improved retention.[15]

Figure 9-2 illustrates the projected growth trajectory from 2023 to 2035.

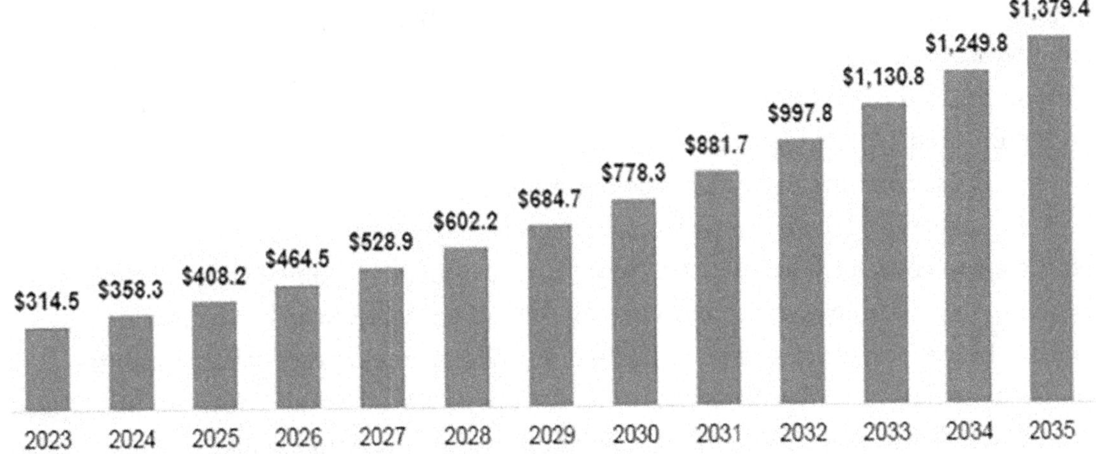

***Figure 9-2.** Illustrative long-range projection of global SaaS market growth from 2023 to 2035, based on the 2025 edition of published estimates from Precedence Research. The figure is included to illustrate the market's directional trajectory rather than to imply certainty about year-by-year outcomes. (Source: Precedence Research, "Software As A Service (SaaS) Market," ©2025 Precedence Research. Used with permission.)*

[15] Precedence Research, "Software As A Service (SaaS) Market," 1–3.

Growth projections for cloud computing and SaaS underscore their expanding influence across sectors and geographies. For enterprises navigating this landscape, the imperative is clear: stay informed about market developments, evaluate platforms against specific business requirements, and adapt strategies to draw on the capabilities these technologies offer. The market will continue to develop, and the organizations that benefit most will be those that treat cloud and SaaS not as static choices but as ongoing strategic decisions.

9.7 Summary

The arc from boxed software to cloud-delivered services is not something I have only observed—it is something I have lived through and helped shape. In the era of packaged software, applications were products that users purchased, installed, and maintained on their own hardware. I remember how much effort went into planning releases, shipping upgrades, and supporting customers who could not always upgrade on schedule. Today, software is a service accessed through a browser—updated continuously, scaled on demand, and woven into workflows that span organizations and geographies. This fundamental shift has reshaped not only how software is built and delivered, but also how businesses operate, how teams collaborate, and how value reaches customers.

Looking back, what stands out to me is how deeply cloud computing and SaaS reinforce each other. Cloud infrastructure provides elastic building blocks, including compute, storage, networking, and security, at a global scale. SaaS builds on those building blocks to deliver applications that improve in small, practical increments—shaped by real usage rather than assumptions. I have seen firsthand how this pairing can lower barriers that once kept sophisticated tools out of reach for smaller organizations, while also helping large enterprises move faster than legacy delivery models ever allowed.

The integration of AI is driving this evolution. Features that were once considered futuristic—intelligent recommendations, conversational interfaces, and predictive analytics—are rapidly becoming standard expectations. I saw early signs of this direction when my teams built CTAdvantage.com using the INTELLIFM architecture. Those systems taught me a lesson I still rely on: the most valuable automation is the kind that quietly removes friction, respects the user's intent, and fits into a larger workflow without calling attention to itself.

That lesson points toward what comes next. The trajectory from packaged software to cloud-delivered SaaS to AI-enhanced platforms now leads to a more fundamental shift: AI-native design, where AI is not a layer added to existing architecture but the foundational principle around which software is built. This transition will redefine what enterprise software looks like, how it is evaluated, and what it means to deliver value to users. Today, the tools are more powerful, the data more abundant, and the opportunities more expansive. But the principle has not changed: technology succeeds when it serves people, reduces friction, and earns trust through reliability and transparency.

Challenges persist, and I have encountered many of them in practice. Security demands constant vigilance. Integration across systems and vendors requires discipline and clear ownership. Organizations must develop new skills and rethink processes designed for a different era. AI introduces its own set of hurdles—managing hallucinations, keeping model outputs grounded in reliable sources, conducting systematic evaluations to validate accuracy and fairness, and maintaining visibility into where AI is making decisions and on what basis. These realities are not arguments against adoption; they are operating conditions that must be addressed deliberately. The organizations that thrive will be those that treat cloud computing and SaaS not as one-time migrations but as ongoing capabilities to steward, refine, and extend.

The next chapter examines how these forces converge in cloud-based AI architectures—the technical foundations and the organizational choices that determine whether AI delivers lasting value or becomes another layer of complexity. The groundwork laid in this chapter sets the stage for that discussion.

CHAPTER 10

Strategic Cloud–AI Architecture

The scale of cloud and AI adoption is now large enough to affect competitive outcomes, and small execution errors can have enterprise-level consequences. Organizations across industries are adopting cloud and AI technologies at an unprecedented pace, yet many struggle to translate that adoption into measurable results. For executives, the benefits are clear—faster decisions, improved customer experiences, and new revenue streams. But the downside is equally real. When these initiatives fail, the damage is not theoretical. Production incidents, audit findings, uncontrolled spend, and reputational loss can arrive in the same quarter.

I have observed this transformation unfold throughout my career and contributed to it by building systems that integrate intelligence directly into business workflows. In the packaged software era, progress occurred through discrete releases, and customers bore much of the operational burden, such as installation, upgrades, patches, and compatibility issues. Cloud computing changed the delivery model, and SaaS altered the business model. Now, AI is changing the product itself. I saw this transition happen when my teams developed CTAdvantage.com. The breakthrough was not a technological novelty. Rather, it was embedding intelligence into workflows in a way that remained dependable, auditable, and maintainable.

What has caught many organizations off guard is not experimentation. It is the operationalization of integrating AI into real workflows without compromising control over risk, cost, and accountability. Many companies are using AI in at least one business function, but only a small fraction have achieved sustained profitability gains.[1] The model is rarely the deciding factor. Sustained results come from the surrounding system:

[1] McKinsey & Company, "The State of AI in 2025: Agents, Innovation, and Transformation," November 5, 2025, `https://www.mckinsey.com/capabilities/quantumblack/our-insights/the-state-of-ai`.

K. C. Mukherjee, *The Microsoft AI Insider's Playbook*, https://doi.org/10.1007/979-8-8688-2730-3_10

disciplined data pipelines, clean integration points, redesigned workflows, security and access controls, governance, production-grade operations, and the ability to scale responsibly.

I have seen these outcomes repeatedly in real deployments. From Microsoft to the partner ecosystem—including Wolters Kluwer, Icon, and FIS—the pattern has been consistent. Architecture and operating discipline determine whether AI becomes a durable capability or a short-lived experiment. The core architectural principles that made systems like INTELLIFM resilient remain highly applicable in today's cloud and AI (cloud–AI) landscape. Those principles include modularity, separation of concerns, declarative design, and progressive disclosure. While the scale and speed have changed, these foundations keep platforms comprehensible and extensible.

Architecture determines whether these outcomes are repeatable or whether the system collapses under growth, complexity, and risk. Over decades of enterprise work, I have learned that early architectural choices are hard to undo. How components connect, where intelligence lives, how change is absorbed, and how risk is contained often determine whether a platform thrives or becomes a burden. The most successful architectures are rarely the most elaborate. Instead, they remain comprehensible, maintainable, and extensible as requirements evolve and technologies advance. Those same principles—not novelty—are what keep cloud–AI systems dependable at scale. What has changed is the scale, the speed, and the stakes.

This chapter argues that cloud–AI outcomes are driven more by architecture than by algorithms. It explains how platform choices create path dependence, why hybrid deterministic–probabilistic designs win in regulated work, and what "enterprise-grade" requires in practice. It closes with a decision framework and checklist that executives and architects can apply immediately.

10.1 Microsoft's Cloud Journey

In the mid-1990s, Microsoft was already a technology giant, and the momentum inside the company was unmistakable. I still remember the intensity of that period—how every release felt like a make-or-break milestone and how the company's execution muscle was built around shipping packaged software at scale. Windows and Office were not just successful products; they anchored a fast-growing community of developers, partners, and customers. Windows 95 reinforced the sense that Microsoft's trajectory in personal computing was nearly unstoppable. Launched in August 1995, it became a commercial phenomenon within weeks, reinforcing Microsoft's belief that the packaged software playbook would continue to win.

That success also shaped how Microsoft saw the world. The business model had been refined around software licenses and periodic desktop upgrades, and the strategy remained anchored to Windows and client applications even as the internet began to gain traction. But the internet introduced a different center of gravity. Strategic value gravitated toward connected networks, browser-based experiences, and services that improved through continuous iteration rather than discrete versions. In the early and mid-1990s, it was easy to underestimate how quickly this new model would reshape distribution, competition, and customer expectations. In retrospect, the challenge was not capability or talent. It was recognizing that the rules of the market were changing and that winning would require a different operating rhythm.

The competitive pressure became undeniable. Netscape moved fast, and Microsoft had to accelerate. I remember the internal realization that we were no longer setting the pace—we were reacting to it. Publicly and internally, the company's stance changed as the stakes became clear. In May 1995, Bill Gates issued the "Internet Tidal Wave" memo, pushing Microsoft to treat the internet as a top priority. Microsoft introduced the Internet Explorer browser and integrated it more directly into Windows. But the deeper challenge was cultural: instincts built for the desktop era had to be rebuilt for an "always connected" world.

Legal and strategic turbulence arrived at the wrong time. In 1998, the US Department of Justice and a coalition of state attorneys general filed the antitrust case that came to define the era. Prolonged litigation creates drag. It pulls senior attention toward legal strategy, heightens internal caution, and narrows the range of moves a company feels comfortable making while the spotlight is on. The case culminated in a settlement in 2001 that reshaped Microsoft's approach to competition and product bundling.

Another tension was interoperability. Microsoft built powerful frameworks such as OLE and COM, designed for high-performance integration across complex software components. I used these frameworks in INTELLIFM because they provided precisely the guarantees an enterprise expert system required: strong interface contracts, predictable execution, and efficient communication within a process and across processes. But the web developed around a different set of priorities. Open standards and cross-platform compatibility became the norm, favoring looser coupling and broader reach over tightly integrated binaries.

Microsoft's instinct to extend its existing platform strengths was understandable. Platform companies protect platforms. However, that instinct also created friction with a developer community that prioritized openness over control. This friction illustrates a lesson that applies equally to cloud–AI architectures today. During major platform transitions, failures rarely reflect technical limitations. They reflect the operating model—misaligned incentives, slow feedback loops, and a company built for a prior era.

By the time the next phase arrived, the industry had changed. Internet-native companies had taken dominant positions in search, e-commerce, and online services. Then the cloud era began in earnest: AWS launched in 2006, and Microsoft launched Azure in 2010. The general availability of Windows Azure marked more than a product release. It signaled a commitment to a future Microsoft had long debated. I remember watching it unfold with a mixture of relief and professional curiosity. The platform I had built my career around was adapting, but the deeper question was whether the culture could change at the same pace as the technology.

Azure's early years were uneven. It began as a PaaS offering that excited developers but felt unfamiliar to enterprise IT teams accustomed to owning the full stack. AWS had a head start and had trained customers to think in infrastructure primitives. Microsoft corrected its course by expanding its infrastructure capabilities, closing a credibility gap that affected enterprise decisions.

Around the same time, Office 365 became the clearest evidence that Microsoft was willing to reinvent its business model. Office became a cloud subscription rather than a perpetual license. Once the product was "always on," conversations moved away from a single ship date and toward reliability, update cadence, and customer experience in the course of daily work. The incentives changed—Microsoft won only if customers continued to find value month after month. The Office suite has since grown into one of the most widely adopted productivity platforms in enterprise computing.[2]

A deeper inflection point followed in 2014, when Microsoft's leadership committed to a "cloud-first" future. The company's actions began to match its rhetoric. The Office suite appeared on competing mobile platforms, and Azure treated Linux as a first-class citizen. Microsoft's new strategy resonated with me. During my engineering studies at IIT Kanpur, I worked with Unix systems and came to admire their elegance. Subsequently, I watched large organizations run mission-critical workloads on Unix and Linux, often

[2] By mid-2025, Microsoft 365 had more than 430 million users. Microsoft Corporation, "FY25 Q3 and Q4 Earnings, 2025"; Statista/Enlyft, "Number of companies using Office 365 worldwide," February 2025.

built in Java for portability and robustness. Embracing Linux on Azure acknowledged a reality that enterprise systems had long embodied. Microsoft also opened .NET and invested more deeply in open source communities. These were not token gestures. They signaled that Microsoft would compete on the quality of its services rather than rely on lock-in as the default strategy.

Then came the OpenAI partnership, which I regard as one of Microsoft's most strategic moves in recent history. The initial investment in 2019 positioned Azure as a primary channel for accessing OpenAI models at enterprise scale. When generative AI captured public attention in late 2022, Microsoft was prepared to operationalize demand across products and platforms. Microsoft 365 Copilot saw rapid enterprise adoption following its 2023 launch.

I have seen a pattern repeat in every durable technology transition. Winners invest ahead of certainty, and they build the operational muscle to turn that investment into repeatable value. The cloud story follows a lesson: timing and architecture compound. When a platform arrives later, it can still succeed, but it must overcome an accumulated advantage in operational maturity, developer adoption, and ecosystem pull. These are not features a team ships in a single quarter. Instead, they are capabilities built through years of iteration, reliability work, and hard-earned customer trust.

For those of us building enterprise systems during this period, Microsoft's transformation offered both inspiration and practical opportunity. As Azure embraced openness, it became more hospitable to diverse workloads, and the enterprise AI market grew significantly stronger. This evolution underscores a central theme of this chapter. Cloud-AI outcomes depend on building the operational foundation around the model, not on the model alone. That foundation comprises governance, integration, reliability, and change management.

Microsoft's journey—from platform protectionism to cloud-first openness and ultimately to AI integration—illustrates at an enterprise scale why architectural decisions compound over time and why platform choice is never purely technical. Every organization now making cloud-AI decisions is navigating the same terrain Microsoft navigated—only faster and with far more at stake.

10.2 Platform Choice as Path Dependence

Platform choice in cloud-AI is not merely a procurement decision; it is an architectural commitment with consequences that persist for years. The major providers—AWS, Azure, and Google Cloud—have each developed distinct strengths, and understanding these differences matters for any organization building systems intended to last.

AWS established early leadership in cloud computing by training a generation of developers to think in infrastructure primitives. It approaches AI through breadth and modularity, consistent with its heritage of providing building blocks. For example, Amazon Bedrock focuses on managed access to multiple foundation model families, whereas Amazon SageMaker supports organizations that require granular control over training and deployment. This "Lego-block" approach allows enterprises to assemble custom AI stacks, though it places a greater burden on architects to ensure that the pieces fit together securely.

Azure gained momentum through enterprise integration—identity, productivity, and collaboration tools that many enterprises already use. By integrating OpenAI's models directly into the Azure environment, it has positioned itself as the bridge between frontier research and enterprise-grade reliability.

Google Cloud has positioned itself strongly for analytics and AI research workloads, with deep credibility in the ML community. Its impact on core primitives remains substantial: Kubernetes, developed at Google, has become the standard for container orchestration across all clouds. Understanding these cultural leanings helps architects predict how a provider's roadmap will likely develop. Each provider continues to invest heavily in AI infrastructure, and competitive positions will realign.

The current scale of this competition is staggering. In Q2 2025, AWS accounted for approximately 30% of the global cloud infrastructure services market, with Azure at 20% and Google Cloud at 13%.[3] Together, these providers account for two-thirds of a market approaching $99 billion in quarterly revenue. Growth rates further highlight the momentum. In the same period, Azure grew 39% year over year, whereas Google Cloud

[3] Synergy Research Group, "Q2 Cloud Market Nears $100 Billion Milestone - and it's Still Growing by 25% Year over Year," August 2025, `https://www.srgresearch.com/articles/q2-cloud-market-nears-100-billion-milestone-and-its-still-growing-by-25-year-over-year`.

grew 32% and AWS grew 17.5%.[4] These data suggest that AI capabilities and go-to-market execution are reshaping competitive positions in ways that historical scale alone cannot determine.

What matters for architects is not which provider leads in a given quarter, but which platform aligns with an organization's long-term needs. Five factors shape that alignment:

1. **Integration Surface:** Cloud–AI does not operate in isolation. It connects to identity systems, collaboration tools, data warehouses, and line-of-business applications. The depth of native integration between a cloud platform and an organization's existing technology stack affects implementation cost, security posture, and operational complexity. For organizations already invested in Microsoft technologies, Azure's integration with Entra ID, Microsoft 365, and Dynamics reduces friction. Identity is particularly important. It serves as the control plane for access, security, and governance across cloud services.[5] For organizations built on AWS primitives, the breadth of AWS services creates similar advantages. Architects should evaluate integration surface not as a feature checklist but as a measure of how naturally AI workloads will fit into existing operations.

2. **Model Strategy:** The AI landscape now includes foundation models from multiple providers, open source alternatives, and models optimized for enterprise domains. Platform choice affects which models are available, how easily they can be deployed, and the degree of practical customization. Azure's partnership

[4] Microsoft Corporation, "Fiscal Year 2025 Fourth Quarter Earnings Conference Call," July 30, 2025, https://www.microsoft.com/en-us/investor/events/fy-2025/earnings-fy-2025-q4; Alphabet Inc., "Q2 2025 Earnings Release," July 2025, https://www.sec.gov/Archives/edgar/data/1652044/000165204425000056/googexhibit991q22025.htm; Amazon.com, Inc., "Amazon.com Announces Second Quarter Results," July 31, 2025, https://ir.aboutamazon.com/news-release/news-release-details/2025/Amazon-com-Announces-Second-Quarter-Results/.

[5] Microsoft research indicates that 99.9% of compromised accounts lack multifactor authentication, reinforcing identity as a foundational architectural concern. Microsoft Learn, "Security at your organization - Multifactor authentication (MFA) statistics," https://learn.microsoft.com/en-us/partner-center/security/security-at-your-organization.

with OpenAI provides streamlined access to GPT models and offers broader model selection through Microsoft Foundry. AWS offers Bedrock for managed access to multiple model families and SageMaker for organizations that require greater control over training and deployment. Google Cloud provides Vertex AI with access to Gemini and other models. The strategic question is whether an organization wants a primary model relationship, a multimodel portfolio, or the capability to train and fine-tune its own models. Platform choice should reflect that strategy.

3. **Data Gravity:** Data is the heaviest object in enterprise architecture in the practical sense that it is the hardest to move at scale. As datasets grow, they anchor the systems around them—compute, applications, analytics, and AI workloads naturally migrate toward where the data resides. Moving a trained model is relatively straightforward; moving petabytes of structured and unstructured data is not. Organizations should make platform choices based on existing data realities rather than assuming data will follow platforms. The cost and complexity of data egress reinforce this effect. Cloud providers price data transfer asymmetrically, making it inexpensive to move data in and expensive to move it out.

4. **Operational Maturity:** Cloud–AI systems require monitoring, incident response, cost management, and governance capabilities that extend beyond the AI workload itself. Organizations should evaluate whether a platform's operational tooling aligns with their existing practices and whether their teams have the skills to operate effectively on it. A platform with superior AI capabilities but unfamiliar operational patterns may underperform compared with a platform on which the organization already has operational expertise. Operational maturity also includes compliance capabilities such as audit logging, access controls, data residency options, and industry-specific certifications.

5. **Economic Levers:** AI workloads introduce cost structures that differ from traditional cloud computing. Training runs consume GPU hours in bursts; inference costs accumulate continuously at scale; storage costs grow with data volume and retrieval

frequency. Each provider offers distinct pricing models, reserved-capacity options, and optimization tools. Architects should model costs across the full AI life cycle rather than optimizing for a single phase. That life cycle includes experimentation, training, fine-tuning, inference, and storage. The economic sustainability of an AI initiative often depends on these calculations.

These five factors interact. An organization with strong data gravity in AWS but a strategic preference for OpenAI models faces a trade-off between data proximity and access to models. An organization with deep Microsoft integration but limited Azure operational experience must weigh the benefits of integration against the learning curve. There are no universal answers; only trade-offs must be evaluated in context.

My own experience spans multiple providers, though my deepest work has been with Microsoft technologies. I have observed that success rarely depends on the provider an organization selects. It depends on how thoughtfully the organization designs its architecture to preserve optionality while exploiting the strengths of its chosen platform. Providers will adapt, partnerships will realign, and new capabilities will emerge. Architectures that anticipate this reality will outlast those that assume today's competitive landscape is permanent. Anticipation means building abstraction layers, portable workloads, and disciplined integration patterns.

The practical implication is that platform selection should be deliberate rather than default. Organizations that select a platform because it is familiar or because a vendor offers favorable terms often discover the constraints only when requirements change. Organizations that evaluate platforms against these five factors make decisions that they can sustain. Those factors are integration surface, model strategy, data gravity, operational maturity, and economic levers.

10.3 From Deterministic Rules to Probabilistic Intelligence

Expert systems relied on explicit, deterministic logic. Modern AI relies on probabilistic behavior learned from data. This transition has profound implications for how systems are designed, governed, and trusted. Having built systems on both sides of this divide, I have come to see it not as a replacement but as an expansion. New capabilities are layered over enduring principles.

INTELLIFM operated through codified rules. If a document matched defined criteria, it was filed accordingly. The system captured domain expertise as decision trees that executed with predictable precision. I spent months interviewing compliance specialists, studying jurisdictional requirements, and translating that knowledge into formal logic. The result was a system that could explain its routing decisions. When a filing was sent to a particular jurisdiction, the system could trace the path through the decision tree and show which rules applied. This transparency was not a convenience. On the contrary, it was a requirement in regulated work, where accountability cannot be delegated to an opaque mechanism.

Thus, in INTELLIFM, intelligence was explicit and authored. Experts encoded their knowledge into rules that the system executed faithfully. My architecture allowed domain specialists to create and maintain those rules in a structured, high-level form without requiring programming skills. When requirements changed, they updated the rules. When edge cases emerged, they extended the decision tree. INTELLIFM followed instructions that the experts themselves could refine. This approach was chosen deliberately to ensure sustainability, allowing domain owners to make updates without needing developer involvement for every change. Within the boundaries of the rules covered, the system was precise and reliable. Outside them, it failed visibly, surfacing exceptions for human review rather than relying on guesswork.

INTELLIFM also reduced user effort through "remember and resume." A customer answered a single set of questions, and the system populated the corresponding underlying forms. If a project was paused, the customer resumed it without restarting because the system retained the state and context. Today's agentic systems pursue similar continuity through session state, conversation history, and vector-based retrieval of past interactions rather than explicit workflow checkpoints.

LLMs operate differently. Instead of coding rules, we train LLMs on large corpora so they learn statistical structure in language. Capability emerges from learned representations, not from an explicitly authored decision tree. An LLM can draft a contract clause, summarize a regulation, or answer a compliance question not because someone encoded that specific answer, but because the model has absorbed enough related language to generate a plausible continuation. In many cases, work that once required days of rule engineering can now be approached with careful prompting and supporting context.

However, this capability comes with a different risk profile. Deterministic systems return consistent outputs for identical inputs. Probabilistic systems can vary with model parameters and generation settings, such as temperature, even when the prompt remains unchanged. Outputs can be made more stable, but they are not guaranteed to be as stable as rule execution. More concerning, an LLM can produce fluent, confident responses that are factually wrong. In compliance-sensitive domains, an AI that guesses where a regulated filing belongs introduces unacceptable risk. The consequences of error can include regulatory penalties, legal liability, and loss of client trust.

The architectural implications are far-reaching. Deterministic systems can be validated more systematically by testing branches and verifying outputs. Probabilistic systems resist that approach because behavior emerges from large parameter spaces that cannot be enumerated. Validation turns toward statistical evaluation, including accuracy, calibration, and measured failure modes across representative samples. That approach is valuable, but it is still incomplete. An LLM can perform well on evaluation data and still fail on inputs that differ subtly from what it has seen.

For that reason, many of the most effective enterprise architectures are hybrid by design. ML enables pattern recognition at scale, including document classification, entity extraction, draft generation, and the identification of relevant passages from large corpora. Expert rules serve as a safety layer that constrains probabilistic outputs to acceptable bounds. An LLM might draft a response, while a rule engine verifies formatting, checks required fields, blocks prohibited terms, and enforces jurisdictional constraints. The probabilistic layer proposes, and the deterministic layer decides whether the output is acceptable, requires revision, or must be escalated.

This pattern extends an older enterprise principle: automate the routine and route uncertainty to people who can take responsibility. In modern systems, confidence scores and explicit policy checks determine which actions can proceed automatically and which require human review. The underlying principle remains the same, even as the technology changes.

Viewed through this lens, the rule-based principles embodied in INTELLIFM can serve as governance mechanisms for systems whose internal reasoning is not fully inspectable. The rules do not replace AI capability; they preserve accountability. They make the system's behavior auditable, its constraints explicit, and its escalation paths traceable. That combination—probabilistic intelligence bounded by deterministic governance—is what enterprise-grade AI requires.

This transformation fundamentally redefines how systems improve. In the era of INTELLIFM, progress was achieved through logical refinement. We analyzed failures, identified gaps in the decision trees, and updated the rules in a deliberate, traceable manner. Today, cloud-AI systems improve through statistical adaptation, incorporating new data, refining prompts and retrieval pipelines, tuning models or policies where appropriate, and re-evaluating performance across large samples. The improvement loop is faster and broader, but it is also less transparent and harder to audit than rule refinement.

Further, the feedback loops differ in kind: one is explicit and driven by human expertise, while the other is probabilistic and driven by data patterns. Both approaches have distinct merits. Strong architectures combine both approaches—LLMs to capture nuanced data patterns and deterministic rules to enforce nonnegotiable constraints.

What stands out when looking across both eras is how persistent the foundational questions remain. How do we make the system do what we intend? How do we detect failure early? How do we preserve accountability when decisions are automated? How do we update the system as requirements change? The implementation details differ, but the design questions remain.

The practical guidance is straightforward. Apply LLMs where language understanding, pattern recognition, and scale provide real leverage. Apply deterministic rules where consistency, auditability, and compliance with explicit requirements are nonnegotiable. Define clear, auditable interfaces between the layers. Instrument both for observability. Reserve human judgment for decisions where the consequences of error are unacceptable.

That synthesis is where my career has led me to: not a choice between old and new, but an architecture that integrates both. The expert systems I built taught me the value of explicit reasoning and traceable decisions. The LLMs I work with today demonstrate capabilities that rule-based approaches could not achieve. The systems that endure will combine probabilistic power with deterministic discipline, with capability bounded by governance and decisions anchored in accountability.

10.3.1 Wolters Kluwer's AI Evolution

The groundwork laid by INTELLIFM has continued to shape Wolters Kluwer's trajectory. By 2023, Expert Solutions—Wolters Kluwer's segment encompassing software products and information services—accounted for 58% of total company revenue.[6] That same year, the company increased its focus on LLMs, recognizing their potential for scalability

[6] Wolters Kluwer, "Wolters Kluwer 2023 Full-Year Report," press release, February 21, 2024, `https://www.wolterskluwer.com/en/news/wolters-kluwer-2023-full-year-report`. The Expert Solutions figure appears under "Progress against 2022–2024 strategy."

in knowledge-intensive domains. That groundwork included testing with select clients and beta deployments in health care, legal services, and regulatory compliance, much of it in collaboration with Microsoft and other technology partners.

Throughout 2024, Wolters Kluwer expanded generative AI capabilities across multiple products, including enhanced search, summarization, question answering, and assistant-style interfaces.[7] These capabilities were built on the same foundational principles—modularity, human-in-the-loop review, and governance by design—that had guided INTELLIFM decades earlier. As Wolters Kluwer moved through 2025, the company's investments in cloud-based platforms reflected a commitment to the same goals pursued by INTELLIFM: helping professionals navigate complex work with greater speed and accuracy.

10.4 Principles of Strategic Cloud–AI Architecture

The architectural principles that guide durable cloud-AI systems are not new. They are the same principles I learned while building enterprise software over decades, now applied to a different technological substrate. What has changed is the vocabulary and the scale, not the underlying logic. Systems that endure share common structural choices, and recognizing these patterns across eras is one advantage of having worked through multiple technology transitions.

The recurring patterns are straightforward: modularity, abstraction, respect for data gravity, progressive disclosure of complexity, preservation of human judgment, governance as architecture, and observability at every layer.

10.4.1 Modularity with Clear Interfaces

When I designed INTELLIFM, I separated the document analysis engine from the workflow orchestration layer and the user interface. Each component could be updated independently, and failures in one area did not cascade into others. The same logic applies to modern cloud-AI architectures.

[7] Wolters Kluwer, "Wolters Kluwer AI," `https://www.wolterskluwer.com/en/about-us/artificial-intelligence`.

The data layer, model layer, inference layer, and application layer should be distinct, connected through well-defined APIs rather than tightly coupled implementations. Organizations that embed AI logic directly into application code will find themselves rewriting systems whenever the underlying models improve. In the current environment, that can become a recurring cycle. A model that performs well today may be surpassed quickly. If the application cannot swap models without a structural change, every improvement turns into a reconstruction project.

Modularity also supports the separation of compute and storage that modern AI workloads demand. Most enterprises do not train foundation models from scratch; that remains the domain of organizations such as OpenAI, Anthropic, Google, Meta, and Microsoft with its Phi models and Copilot-related adaptations. More commonly, enterprises fine-tune pretrained models on domain-specific data or access foundation models such as GPT, Claude, or Gemini through managed APIs.

Even so, the separation of compute and storage remains important: fine-tuning requires GPU-intensive computation in bursts, inference requires sustained availability with variable throughput, and storage scales independently. Data lakes store raw corpora at petabyte scale, while vector stores optimized for similarity search support RAG, in which relevant passages are retrieved and supplied as context for generation. When these tiers are decoupled, each can be optimized for its own access patterns and cost profile. When they are tightly coupled, optimization in one area often creates constraints in others.

10.4.2 Abstraction for Portability

In the packaged software era, we built abstraction layers to insulate business logic from operating system dependencies. The goal was to support multiple platforms without rewriting core functionality. Today, the same reasoning applies to cloud providers and model families.

Organizations benefit from designing systems that can switch between foundation models or cloud platforms without wholesale reconstruction. This portability does not mean ignoring the distinctive capabilities of a chosen provider. It means exploiting those capabilities through abstraction layers that preserve optionality. The model gateway pattern exemplifies this approach. A routing layer manages calls to multiple models, internal and external, allowing the application to treat model selection as a configuration rather than an architectural decision. IaC serves a similar function by defining environments declaratively, enabling deployments to be reproduced across providers with far less rework.

Abstraction also supports edge and cloud hybridity. Time-sensitive tasks such as voice recognition, anomaly detection on sensor streams, and near-real-time translation can run closer to data sources, while the cloud handles computationally intensive work such as model updates and longer-horizon learning. Without abstraction, workloads become locked to specific deployment targets. With it, architects can place computation where latency, bandwidth, and cost considerations dictate.

10.4.3 Respect for Data Gravity

In practical terms, data resists relocation more than any other architectural element. As datasets grow, they anchor the systems around them—compute, applications, analytics, and AI workloads naturally gravitate toward where the data resides.

I learned this at Wolters Kluwer, where decades of compliance records and filing histories anchored our architectural decisions. The lesson for cloud–AI is to think carefully about where data lands before committing to a platform. Moving a trained model is often feasible; moving petabytes of structured and unstructured data is far harder.

For example, I have seen a global bank with years of transaction history, customer records, call center transcripts, and compliance archives face pressure to "standardize" on an AI platform that would require relocating everything to a single vendor's cloud. On paper, the platform looked compelling. In practice, migrating petabytes of regulated data would have taken months, triggered data residency and security reviews, and introduced ongoing egress costs as other systems continued to operate outside that environment. The bank succeeded by starting from the data it already had, where it already lived. It retained sensitive datasets, added a governed metadata and access layer, and deployed an AI architecture that operated near the data through well-defined interfaces. Over time, it migrated selectively, on its own timeline, rather than attempting an abrupt lift-and-shift. Successful organizations treat data architecture as foundational. They make AI platform choices based on existing data realities, rather than assuming the data will automatically align with the platform.

Cloud providers reinforce this gravity through pricing. Data ingress is typically inexpensive or free, whereas data egress incurs a high cost. Once data accumulates in one environment, the economic friction of moving it compounds the technical friction. Architects who understand data gravity make deliberate choices about where data is initially placed, knowing that those choices constrain subsequent options.

Data structures—and the systems that manage them—have become more complex. In the relational database era, teams relied on strict schemas and on atomicity, consistency, isolation, and durability (ACID) guarantees: all-or-nothing operations, rules and constraints preserved, concurrent operations that do not interfere with one another, and committed data that persists even after system failures. If a record did not conform to the schema, the database rejected it. This discipline strengthened auditability and referential integrity in regulated industries, but it required architects to anticipate data structures in advance.

Many modern AI architectures take a different approach: schema-on-read. In this model, diverse datasets, such as images, documents, transaction logs, and sensor streams, are ingested with minimal upfront structure and interpreted at query time. This flexibility helps when assembling large, heterogeneous corpora for model training. However, the hybrid reality persists. Critical metadata still benefits from relational discipline. Pointers that link a model prediction to its training lineage, audit records that trace a decision to its inputs, and compliance artifacts that regulators demand require strong referential integrity. Effective architectures layer structured metadata over unstructured content, preserving governance while accommodating the scale and variety required by modern AI.

10.4.4 Progressive Disclosure of Complexity

This principle was central to how I designed INTELLIFM, and I still see it as fundamental for AI systems intended for broad use. Users should encounter simple interfaces first and discover advanced capabilities only as their needs grow. For example, a user forming a new corporation began with a single question: "In which state will you incorporate?" Based on that answer, CTAdvantage.com presented only the questions relevant to that jurisdiction. A Delaware incorporation required different information than a California one, but users never saw the full decision tree. They answered what was in front of them, and the system revealed the next step. Only when a filing involved exceptions, such as foreign qualifications or multistate coordination, did the interface surface additional options. Users who filed routine documents never encountered the complexity that power users navigated daily.

In cloud–AI terms, this means offering sensible defaults, prebuilt prompts, and turnkey integrations for everyday use cases while preserving access to fine-tuning, custom model deployment, and advanced orchestration for teams that require them. Systems that expose full complexity at the first interaction overwhelm users. Systems that hide complexity entirely frustrate experts. The balance requires deliberate design.

The same principle applies to operational interfaces. A well-designed dashboard surfaces the metrics that matter most, such as accuracy, latency, cost, and error rates, without burying operators in data they cannot act on. Drill-down capability should be available for investigation, but the default view should support rapid orientation. Progressive disclosure is not simplification; it is organization. The complexity remains available, but it is revealed in layers that match how people actually work.

10.4.5 Preservation of Human Judgment

Automation should augment expertise, not replace it. This principle has grown more pressing as AI capabilities have expanded. Generative models can draft contracts, summarize regulations, and propose investment strategies, but the stakes of error in compliance-sensitive domains call for human review.

The architectural pattern is consistent across domains. AI handles volume and consistency; humans provide judgment and accountability. Virtual assistants address routine inquiries, process standard transactions, and guide users through common workflows. When a situation requires interpretation, such as a disputed charge, an exception to policy, or a request that falls outside established patterns, the system escalates to a human agent with the relevant context. The threshold for escalation should be explicit and adjustable, tuned to the domain's risk tolerance.

Architectures that treat AI as an autonomous agent rather than an augmentation tool invite risk that responsible enterprises cannot accept. The emphasis on explainability, audit trails, and human-in-the-loop workflows reflects this reality. In regulated industries, the question is not whether AI can perform a task, but whether the organization can demonstrate accountability for the outcome. Human oversight is not a constraint on capability. In fact, it is required for deployment in demanding contexts.

10.4.6 Governance as Architecture

In regulated industries, compliance requirements shape what systems can do, where data can reside, and how decisions must be documented. I saw this repeatedly in financial services and legal technology. Modern cloud-AI architectures require governance by design. Model versioning, access controls, bias monitoring, data lineage, and auditability work best as built-in features rather than bolt-on additions.

Organizations that treat governance as something to minimize often discover they must rebuild when auditors or regulators arrive. Those that treat governance as a design requirement build systems that scale with far less rework.

Modern governance extends across the full model life cycle. Machine Learning Operations (MLOps) applies CI/CD discipline to AI systems by standardizing how models are built, tested, deployed, and monitored in production. Automated pipelines monitor production data for drift—a phenomenon that occurs when observed input distributions diverge from the model's original training conditions. When drift appears, the system can alert teams and trigger evaluation and retraining workflows before accuracy degrades. Version control tracks not only code, but also model weights, training data snapshots, and hyperparameter configurations, thereby helping teams reproduce prior states and roll back when new deployments underperform.

Governance also includes cost. AI workloads consume substantial resources, and unmanaged infrastructure spend accumulates quickly. Effective architectures treat cost as an operational signal, not a surprise. Teams schedule training jobs with pricing awareness, right-size inference endpoints to match demand, and decommission resources promptly when workloads complete. Organizations that treat efficiency as an afterthought often discover that AI initiatives cost far more than projected. Those who design for efficiency from the earliest stages build systems that remain economically viable as they scale.

10.4.7 Observability at Every Layer

You cannot manage what you cannot measure, and AI systems introduce uncertainty that traditional software did not. Model performance can degrade as data distributions drift. Inference latency varies with load. Costs accumulate in ways that are difficult to predict. Effective cloud-AI architectures instrument every component. Data pipelines, training jobs, inference endpoints, and application integrations should emit metrics, logs, and traces that feed unified monitoring systems.

Observability in AI systems includes metrics that traditional software rarely requires. Uptime and latency remain important, but model quality metrics become equally central. Accuracy is one of the dimensions. Calibration matters too, meaning whether confidence scores reflect the real likelihood of correctness. Factual grounding also matters, meaning whether outputs are grounded in retrieved or authoritative context rather than improvised. A model that returns answers quickly but confidently wrong is more dangerous than one that declines to answer. Effective pipelines include automated evaluation gates that compare candidate models against held-out test sets and block degraded versions from reaching production.

The philosophy I learned at Microsoft applies here: users experience latency, not architecture. A beautifully designed system that makes users wait is a failed system. The metrics that matter most are the ones users feel, such as time to first response, time to task completion, and responsiveness under load. Internal metrics such as CPU utilization and memory consumption matter primarily insofar as they shape the user experience.

Observability is not merely an operational hygiene. In reality, it is the foundation for continuous improvement and cost control. Without instrumentation, teams cannot distinguish between a model failure and a pipeline failure. Without metrics, they cannot identify which component to optimize. Without traces, they cannot diagnose why a particular request took longer than expected. Investment in observability pays dividends throughout the system life cycle, enabling evidence-based evolution that separates durable platforms from brittle experiments.

10.4.8 Enduring Principles

The seven principles described in this section are not independent. They reinforce one another, and architects who apply them together build systems that are more resilient than the sum of their parts.

Modularity enables abstraction. Clean interfaces between components create natural points for portability layers. Abstraction respects data gravity by allowing compute to move toward data rather than forcing data to move toward compute. Progressive disclosure depends on modularity. Complexity can only be revealed in layers if the underlying system is structured in layers. Human judgment is preserved when governance is built in, because audit trails and escalation thresholds make it possible to know when and why a human intervened. Observability supports all the other principles by making their effects visible. Without measurement, architects cannot know whether modularity prevents failures, whether abstraction preserves optionality, or whether governance controls function as intended.

These relationships reflect a deeper truth about systems that endure: durability comes from coherence, not from isolated excellence. A system with superb observability but poor modularity will generate metrics that are difficult to act on because failures will cascade unpredictably. A system with strong governance but weak abstraction will enforce controls that become obsolete when platforms change. The principles work because they work together.

Architects fail by chasing novelty without grounding it in principle. They adopt the latest framework, the newest model, or the most fashionable architecture and build systems that must be rebuilt when the next wave arrives. Architects also fail by clinging to the familiar, refusing to adopt new capabilities because the old ways were comfortable. Both failure modes stem from the same mistake: confusing the principle with its implementation.

I believe the architects who succeed hold principles firmly and implementations loosely. They recognize that a model gateway today serves the same purpose as an abstraction layer did decades ago: it insulates the application from dependencies that will inevitably change. They understand that MLOps is CI/CD applied to a new domain, not a new invention. For architects designing cloud-AI systems today, the practical implication is to invest in understanding the principles themselves, not just in mastering current tools. Tools will change. The systems that survive will be those whose architects applied these principles with discipline from the start.

10.5 Applying the Principles

The principles outlined in Section 10.4 emerged from building systems that had to operate in production under real constraints for demanding users. At Wolters Kluwer, where my teams developed SaaS applications using the INTELLIFM framework, these principles were repeatedly tested in production deployments. This section translates those principles into practice, drawing on lessons from enterprise deployments and industry-specific considerations.

10.5.1 Lessons from Enterprise Deployments

Across years of enterprise deployments, I have seen patterns that outlast any particular platform, language, or architecture style. Some lessons came from successes. Others came from watching carefully designed systems fail in ways their architects did not anticipate. Both shape how I approach cloud-AI architecture today.

As discussed in Section 10.3, earlier expert systems embodied deterministic, rule-based decision-making, whereas today's LLMs learn statistical patterns from large corpora and therefore produce probabilistic outputs. The architectural discipline must remain. Probabilistic intelligence still needs deterministic guardrails, such as validation rules, policy constraints, audit trails, and human review, to ensure automation remains accountable in enterprise and regulated workflows.

In recent years, many established enterprise software companies, including Wolters Kluwer, have introduced generative AI capabilities, such as enhanced search, summarization, IVR systems, chatbots, and virtual assistants. What matters architecturally is that these additions still depend on the same foundations: modular services, human-in-the-loop review for critical decisions, and governance woven into the workflow by design, consistent with the discipline that guided INTELLIFM.

Workflow and Deployment

The most common deployment failures often stem from decisions made before the first line of code was written. The following practices consistently separate successful rollouts from troubled ones:

Start with the Workflow, Not the Technology: A common mistake is selecting a platform or model first and then searching for problems it might solve. Durable systems begin with a clear understanding of the work people actually do: the decisions they make, the exceptions they handle, and the constraints they operate under.

At Wolters Kluwer, we mapped the decision trees that domain experts navigated daily before the developers wrote a line of code. We documented which forms applied to which jurisdictions, the required supporting documents, and the exceptions that triggered manual review. The Q&A sessions described in Chapter 4 emerged directly from this mapping. Each question led to the next relevant question, and exception paths were explicit rather than improvised. That investment paid dividends because the system addressed real operational pain rather than hypothetical use cases.

The same discipline applies to AI deployments. An LLM can generate fluent responses, but fluency is not the same as usefulness. Understanding the workflow means knowing what users actually ask, what constraints govern acceptable answers, and where confidence thresholds should trigger human review. It also means defining the boundaries of automation up front. Decide what the system may assist, what must remain human, and what requires escalation under specified conditions.

Pilot Narrowly, and Then Expand Deliberately: Large-scale rollouts without focused pilots tend to surface problems at the worst possible time. At Icon, we piloted the AutoPay system with a small number of parking facilities before expanding to the full portfolio. This mirrors the disciplined approach I learned at Microsoft, where new products undergo controlled beta testing with a carefully selected group of customers long before general availability. These early adopters reveal real-world behaviors, integration challenges, and usability issues that internal QA environments cannot replicate. Our pilot surfaced edge cases that would have been far more expensive to fix after a broad launch, including transaction timing anomalies, network reliability under load, and user confusion at kiosks.

When we later migrated billing functions from legacy infrastructure to a cloud-based system, we followed the same structured, phased methodology. A small group of facilities migrated first, while the rest remained on the legacy platform. Just as Microsoft's beta cohorts isolate risk and provide a controlled environment for rapid iteration, our pilot group absorbed the early turbulence. Issues affected only a limited set of sites, giving us time to diagnose, correct, and validate before additional locations went live. By the time the final facilities migrated, the process had become routine and predictable.

This principle is equally central to UAT, which has become an integral stage of the modern SDLC. UAT is, in many ways, a formalized version of the same idea: expose the system to a small, representative group of real users before full deployment. Their workflows, expectations, and edge cases become the ultimate validation that the system behaves as intended in real operational conditions. UAT provides a structured checkpoint where business stakeholders confirm that the solution meets functional requirements, performance expectations, and usability standards. It is the last safeguard before scale, ensuring that what works in development and testing also works in the hands of actual users.

A practical rule of thumb applies across enterprise rollouts, beta programs, and UAT alike. Expand only when the pilot has reached a stable operating baseline. That baseline must be defined by measurable indicators such as error rates, latency percentiles, user experience metrics, and clear support procedures. Whether you are rolling out a cloud billing system, conducting UAT for a new enterprise workflow, or preparing a global software release, disciplined piloting and selective early testing are the mechanisms that transform innovation into reliability.

Resilience and Operations

At Microsoft, we learned that unhandled exceptions could crash millions of machines. That discipline—*designing for failure, not just success*—applies with equal force to cloud–AI.

Design for Containment and Limit the Blast Radius: Production systems fail, and cloud–AI adds new ways to fail. The question is not whether a component will degrade or misbehave, but whether that failure stays local. Architect for containment through isolation, rate limits, circuit breakers, and clear trust boundaries between data, models, and execution.

If an AI component produces an unsafe or incorrect output, the system should degrade gracefully: fall back to a simpler path, request clarification, or escalate to a human rather than letting failure propagate into customer impact. A useful test: ask what happens when the model returns nonsense, when latency spikes tenfold, or when the service becomes unavailable entirely. If the answer is "the application crashes" or "users see raw errors," the containment design needs work.

The same principles apply directly to IVR systems and chatbots, which often sit at the front line of customer interaction. In practice, IVR systems typically begin with a call flow diagram that maps every path a caller might take, including invalid input, silence, and repeated errors. The diagram also defines escalation points and the context passed to a human agent. Chatbots do not always require a traditional call flow diagram. However, any chatbot that performs transactions, touches regulated data, or drives material outcomes should have an explicit conversation model. That model can be an intent-and-state flow that defines allowed paths, validation checks, fallback behavior, and handoff conditions.

A well-designed IVR should detect when speech recognition confidence drops and automatically switch to keypad input rather than trapping callers in an endless loop. Likewise, a chatbot should detect uncertainty, policy violations, or incoherent responses and route the user to scripted flows, a retrieval-backed answer, or a live agent with the relevant context. In both cases, AI should be treated as an enhancement, not a single point of failure, so that when the intelligent layer falters, the customer still experiences a stable, predictable, and recoverable path forward.

Invest in Exception Handling Early: Optimistic architectures assume the happy path. Production systems allocate much of their complexity to adverse paths: network failures, malformed inputs, unexpected user behavior, and upstream systems that do not respond as documented.

I have seen AI deployments fail not because models were inadequate, but because surrounding infrastructure handled exceptions poorly. Timeouts, retries, fallback responses, and graceful degradation deserve as much design attention as core functionality. When failures occur, the system should capture diagnostic context, including timestamps, request identifiers, input parameters, and relevant state at the time of the error. A log entry that says "error at line 247" confirms something broke. A log entry with full context explains why it broke and how to reproduce it.

This philosophy echoes practices that became part of Microsoft's engineering DNA over time. On the Windows and Office teams, we learned that an unhandled exception could crash millions of machines worldwide. Such exceptions included out-of-memory conditions, null pointer dereferences, and corrupted file handles. As a result, defensive coding, structured exception handling, and graceful fallback paths became nonnegotiable. Developers were trained to assume that any API call could fail and that every failure must be handled predictably, without exposing raw system errors to the user. The goal was always the same: the application must survive, even if a component does not.

That mindset carries directly into modern cloud and AI systems. Just as early Microsoft products had to recover from low-memory conditions or unexpected runtime states, today's distributed services must recover from model failures, transient network partitions, and unpredictable latency spikes. The principle has not changed—only the failure modes have.

Prepare for Incident Response, Not Just Incident Prevention: Even well-contained failures require a response plan. Define escalation paths, on-call responsibilities, and communication templates before the first incident occurs. When production issues arise, teams should know who to contact, what information to gather, and how to communicate status to stakeholders. A runbook written during a crisis is always worse than one written in calm.

I have established tiered support structures—from front-line triage through specialist diagnosis to engineering-level remediation—with explicit escalation criteria at each level. Before any product release, I require that these criteria be documented: the conditions that trigger escalation, the information required for the handoff, and the response time targets. These preparations are reviewed during release readiness assessments and treated as prerequisites for go-live, not optional refinements to be added later.

Plan for Disaster Recovery, Not Just High Availability: High availability keeps systems running through localized failures. Disaster recovery addresses scenarios where an entire region, data center, or critical dependency becomes unavailable. AI systems introduce recovery challenges that traditional applications do not face, and those challenges require planning before a disaster strikes.

Traditional applications recover by restoring code, configuration, and data from backups. AI systems depend on additional artifacts, such as model weights, embedding indices, vector databases, prompt templates, and evaluation datasets. If any of these are lost or corrupted, the system may not function correctly even if the application code is restored. Recovery plans must account for where these artifacts live, how they are versioned, how often they are backed up, and how long restoration will take.

Model-serving infrastructure adds another layer of complexity. A system that depends on a specific GPU configuration may not recover quickly if equivalent hardware is unavailable in the failover region. Vector indices that took hours to build cannot be reconstructed instantly. RAG systems that rely on indexed corpora require those corpora to be replicated and kept in sync. Unless these dependencies are explicitly addressed, the recovery time objective for an AI system is often longer than for a traditional application.

I learned to take disaster recovery seriously after watching a team lose about three weeks of fine-tuning work when a storage failure corrupted model checkpoints that had not been replicated. The original training data still existed, but the computational cost and time required to reproduce the model were substantial. After that incident, I instituted a policy: every artifact that affects model behavior must be versioned, replicated to a secondary location, and tested for restorability. The policy added overhead, but it turned a potential catastrophe into a manageable inconvenience when a similar failure occurred later.

Practical disaster recovery for AI systems requires answering several questions in advance. Where are model weights stored, and how quickly can they be restored? Are vector indices replicated, or must they be rebuilt from source documents? What is the dependency on specialized hardware configurations, and are equivalent resources available in failover regions? How long will recovery take, and is that duration acceptable for the business? If the answers are unclear, the recovery plan is incomplete.

The goal is not to eliminate risk but to make recovery predictable. When a disaster occurs, teams should execute a documented plan rather than improvise under pressure. That plan should be tested periodically—not merely reviewed, but executed in a controlled environment—so gaps are discovered before they matter.

Security and Governance

AI systems expose unique vulnerabilities that traditional perimeter-based security models do not fully address. Among the most pervasive is prompt injection, which exploits the way cloud-AI models treat developer instructions and untrusted user data as part of a single combined context. This blending of control and data allows attackers to bypass safety guardrails through direct "jailbreaks" or indirect injections, such as malicious payloads hidden in retrieved documents or emails that subvert the model's objectives during a RAG cycle. Furthermore, the rise of autonomous agents introduces the risk of excessive agency. A hijacked model may be induced to misuse tools—for example, by exfiltrating data through an authorized "ping" tool or executing destructive commands under the guise of routine maintenance. Other critical risks include model inversion, which can expose sensitive training data through systematic probing, and context poisoning, in which shared embeddings inadvertently leak information across tenant boundaries.

Architectures that treat these models as trusted components create systemic risk. To mitigate these threats, disciplined organizations should implement layered controls such as semantic firewalls, scoped tool access, and deterministic validators. Where appropriate, a dual-LLM pattern adds a smaller, hardened "judge" model that validates the primary model's inputs and outputs before any external action is executed. Addressing these risks requires architectural discipline across several dimensions.

Secure the seams. The vulnerabilities described above share a common architectural response: treat every integration point as a potential attack surface. AI systems introduce attack surfaces that traditional applications do not have. Prompt injection can manipulate model behavior through malicious input. RAG can be poisoned if the source corpus is compromised. Tool-using agents can be tricked into unauthorized actions. Data exfiltration can occur if models are prompted to reveal training data or context that they should not disclose.

Security incidents are inevitable in a long career, but one episode stands out—not because it involved AI directly, but because of what it taught me about the discipline AI security now demands. During a large-scale data integration rollout, I noticed an anomaly in the access logs: a pattern subtle enough that most systems would have ignored it. It turned out to be an automated credential-stuffing attempt targeting a legacy API. We shut it down quickly, but the real value came from what followed. I led the redesign of the authentication layer, introduced zero-trust principles, and implemented continuous monitoring. That moment reinforced something I have always believed. Security is not a feature; it is a discipline. In AI systems, security must be designed at every integration point. Validate and sanitize inputs before they reach the model. Constrain outputs before they reach users or downstream systems. Limit what tools an agent can invoke. Audit what data flows through the pipeline. Treat the model as an untrusted component whose inputs, outputs, permissions, and tool access are tightly constrained, not as a trusted component with implicit permissions.

Version everything that affects system behavior. In traditional software, version control tracks code. In AI systems, behavior depends on more than code: model weights, prompt templates, retrieval configurations, policy rules, and evaluation datasets all influence outputs. If any of these change without tracking, reproducibility and reliable root cause analysis become far more difficult.

I learned this the hard way. In one project, a missing versioning strategy for a shared data contract caused a cascade of failures across dependent services. A single schema change, harmless in isolation, broke analytics pipelines, reporting dashboards, and a customer-facing workflow. It was a painful day. But that experience led me to formalize a versioning framework that became standard practice across the organization: semantic versioning, backward compatibility rules, and automated contract testing.

The chaos of that incident produced a culture of predictability and traceability. In AI systems, the same discipline applies with greater urgency. Version control should extend to models, prompts, system instructions, retrieval indices, and configuration parameters. When a user reports that the system behaved differently last week, the team must be able to reconstruct exactly what was running. The goal is not bureaucracy but the ability to reproduce, compare, and roll back.

Make accountability an artifact. In mission-critical workflows, accountability cannot be a slogan. Create a decision log for AI-assisted outcomes that captures the model version, the prompt or policy template, retrieved sources, key inputs, confidence signals, and the human approver, when applicable. This turns accountability from an assurance into something that can be inspected, audited, and improved. When regulators or auditors ask how a decision was made, the answer should be a record, not a reconstruction.

Address bias and fairness as architectural requirements. AI systems can perpetuate or amplify biases present in training data, and those biases can cause real harm to individuals and organizations. In regulated industries, such as financial services, health care, employment, and housing, biased outcomes may also violate laws or regulations. Responsible AI is not a separate initiative. Indeed, it is an architectural discipline that must be embedded by design.

Bias in AI systems takes multiple forms. Training data may underrepresent certain populations, leading to models that perform poorly for those groups. Historical data may encode past discrimination, causing models to replicate patterns that society has since rejected. Proxy variables may correlate with protected characteristics, producing disparate impact even when sensitive attributes are excluded from the input data. These risks do not disappear because intentions are good; they require systematic detection and mitigation.

The architectural response begins with data governance. Teams must understand what data trains their models, where it comes from, and what populations it represents. Gaps in representation should be identified and addressed before training, not discovered after deployment. Documentation should capture data provenance, known limitations, and populations for which performance may be degraded.

Evaluation must extend beyond aggregate accuracy. A model that performs well on average may perform poorly for specific demographic groups, and that disparity may not be captured by standard metrics. Disaggregated evaluation reveals performance disparities across relevant subgroups and helps determine whether the system may be producing inequitable outcomes. This should occur before deployment and continue throughout the system's operational life, because data distributions and model behavior can drift over time.

Mitigation strategies vary by context. Some teams improve representation by adjusting the training data. Others use algorithmic methods that steer models toward more equitable outcomes. Still others apply rules after the model produces an output to flag results for review or adjust them when bias indicators appear. The best approach depends on the domain, the nature of the bias, and the regulatory environment. What matters is that the work is deliberate, documented, and revisited regularly.

Governance structures should include diverse perspectives. Teams composed entirely of people with similar backgrounds may not recognize biases that affect populations unlike themselves. Including diverse voices in design reviews, evaluation criteria, and deployment decisions improves the likelihood that harmful biases will be identified before deployment. External audits—whether conducted by internal compliance teams, third-party assessors, or regulators—can strengthen accountability.

I have seen organizations treat responsible AI as a compliance checkbox, addressed once and then forgotten. That approach fails. Bias mitigation is not a one-time activity but an ongoing commitment that must be resourced, measured, and continuously improved. The systems that earn trust are those that demonstrate sustained attention to fairness, not those that merely claim it.

Economics and Measurement

AI initiatives often stumble not on technical limitations, but on economics. Systems that perform impressively in pilots can become unsustainable at production scale if cost structures are not understood from inception.

Establish cost guardrails before scaling. AI workloads can become expensive quickly, and cost drivers differ from those in traditional computing. Token-based pricing means that verbose prompts and long outputs accumulate charges with every request. Embedding generation and vector search add costs that scale with corpus size. Fine-tuning and training consume GPU hours that can dwarf inference costs.

I learned this lesson during a cloud-native AI modernization project as part of my enterprise transformation work. We had architected a system that was elegant and scalable: elastic compute, distributed inference, and real-time analytics. Within weeks of deployment, the cloud bill ballooned far beyond projections. The culprit was not incompetence; it was success. Usage spiked faster than anticipated, and our autoscaling rules were too generous. I had to redesign the workload patterns and introduce cost-aware orchestration. That experience shaped my view: AI must be capable, but it must also be economically sustainable. Build cost awareness into the architecture from the start. Set budgets and alerts, monitor cost per transaction, optimize prompts for efficiency, cache repeated queries where appropriate, and model the economics before scaling. A pilot that costs hundreds of dollars per month may cost hundreds of thousands at production volume.

Treat evaluation as a product requirement, not a research exercise. In enterprise AI, the model is rarely the primary bottleneck. Data readiness, workflow fit, access controls, exception handling, and measurement determine success more often than model brand or benchmark scores. Evaluation is where discipline becomes visible.

Define what "good" means in advance using representative test sets, acceptance thresholds, and regression gates. Without an evaluation harness, teams argue by anecdote, and quality becomes a matter of opinion rather than evidence.

That constraint is also where the concept of a minimum viable product (MVP) becomes essential. An MVP forces teams to identify the smallest set of capabilities that must work reliably before anything is exposed to real users. It prevents overengineering and ties evaluation criteria to concrete, testable behaviors rather than aspirational feature lists.

A practical approach is straightforward: Before deployment, establish test cases that cover normal operation, known edge cases, and adversarial inputs. Run them automatically before any model or prompt change reaches production. An MVP that passes these gates becomes the baseline for safe iteration, so progress stays measured, controlled, and grounded in evidence rather than enthusiasm.

Measure what matters, not what is easy. Dashboards overflowing with metrics can create a comforting illusion of observability. The real question is whether the metrics reflect outcomes that matter: accuracy, latency, user satisfaction, cost per transaction, and error rates by category. A dashboard showing 99.9% availability is of little value if the remaining 0.1% of failures consistently occur during peak hours. Likewise, an average response time of 200 milliseconds can mask the reality that the 95th percentile extends to several seconds—a reality that leaves many users experiencing unacceptable delays.

That distinction is why effective measurement emphasizes percentiles over averages, user-facing latency over internal proxies, and outcomes over raw activity counts. In my project management meetings, I have consistently advocated for treating latency measurement—especially for web service calls—as a systematic requirement during the testing phase. Rather than assuming performance will hold under load, I push teams to instrument interservice boundaries, define percentile-based performance targets, and incorporate latency checks into automated test suites. This discipline ensures that regressions are caught early and that the system behaves reliably under realistic conditions.

The rule of thumb remains simple and universal: measure what users actually feel and what auditors ultimately ask for.

Build feedback loops into production. The best AI systems improve with use. Design mechanisms that capture signals from production. Track which outputs users accept, edit, or reject; whether confidence scores align with correctness; and when fallback paths trigger. These signals feed evaluation datasets, inform prompt refinement, and guide decisions about where human review adds most value.

Some of my most meaningful improvements have come directly from users. I remember a knowledge management platform I built that was technically sound but initially underutilized. Instead of defending the design, I spent weeks listening to the people using it. Their feedback revealed friction points that no amount of architectural planning could have predicted. We redesigned the interface, simplified workflows, and added features that aligned with how people actually worked rather than how we assumed they worked. Adoption increased markedly.

This approach reflects a tradition I saw early at Microsoft. The company regularly held user meetings to gather candid feedback on product features. Those sessions often surfaced insights that internal teams would never have uncovered on their own, and they shaped the culture of building software with users rather than merely for them. That philosophy has stayed with me throughout my career.

The experience reinforced a truth I carry into every project: technology succeeds only when it resonates with the people it serves. The feedback loop should be deliberate, not accidental. Without it, the system remains static as user needs grow and change.

Organization and Sustainability

INTELLIFM has endured for more than a quarter-century not only because of its architecture, but because we invested in staff onboarding, documentation, and change management from the start. In my experience, organizational factors are more likely than technical ones to cause technology deployments to fail.

Plan for the people, not just the system. Users resist systems that disrupt familiar workflows without a clear benefit. Managers lose patience with projects that exceed timelines. Executives withdraw support when early results fail to meet inflated expectations. I have seen technically sound architectures abandoned because sponsors did not invest in change management, training, and setting of expectations. Cloud-AI systems are particularly susceptible because attention can outpace realistic delivery timelines.

To be effective, readiness must be organization-wide. It cannot be siloed within engineering or product teams. Instead, it must encompass every department that interacts with or supports the system—including product support, client services, operations, compliance, and any other groups affected by the change. When these cross-functional groups understand the new workflows, escalation paths, and user expectations, the organization operates as a cohesive unit rather than a collection of disconnected fragments.

A full-scale rollout also requires strong self-service resources. A well-maintained Frequently Asked Questions (FAQ) site should be created to answer common questions, clarify expected behaviors, and provide quick guidance for routine issues. Alongside this, teams must supply detailed explanations of application logs so that support staff can interpret errors, trace workflows, and diagnose problems without guesswork. These artifacts reduce friction, shorten resolution times, and facilitate teams across the enterprise to operate confidently.

A practical safeguard: treat rollout, staff enablement, documentation, and support as part of the architecture itself, not as project management footnotes.

Respect the legacy. In enterprise environments, greenfield deployments are relatively uncommon. Most enterprise AI work involves integrating with existing systems, some well documented and others understood mainly by the people who built them years ago. The temptation is to treat legacy systems as obstacles. The wiser approach is to understand why they persist. They often encode institutional knowledge, edge case handling, and regulatory accommodations that are not obvious from their interfaces. My teams have succeeded when we respected what existing systems did well and targeted genuine gaps rather than forcing wholesale replacement.

Design for the long term, even when timelines are short. Pressure to deliver quickly can lead to shortcuts that accumulate as technical debt. The cost compounds: systems become harder to modify, debug, and hand off. Cloud–AI architectures face added pressure because the field moves quickly and stakeholders expect rapid results. This makes it even more important to dedicate sufficient time to the architecture and design phase before major implementation work begins.

The core discipline is to protect replaceability: keep models, prompts, and policies swappable without requiring application rewrites. The model you deploy today is unlikely to be the same model you run two years from now.

These lessons from enterprise deployments are not unique to AI or cloud computing. They reflect patterns I observed building client-server systems in the 1990s, web applications in the 2000s, and cloud-native architectures in the 2010s. The technologies change; the organizational and operational patterns persist.

Figure 10-1 illustrates the cloud–AI architecture, including the AI gateway, AI agents, and Model Context Protocol (MCP) tools that connect the orchestration layer to back-end systems. (For a detailed explanation, see Appendix 12.)

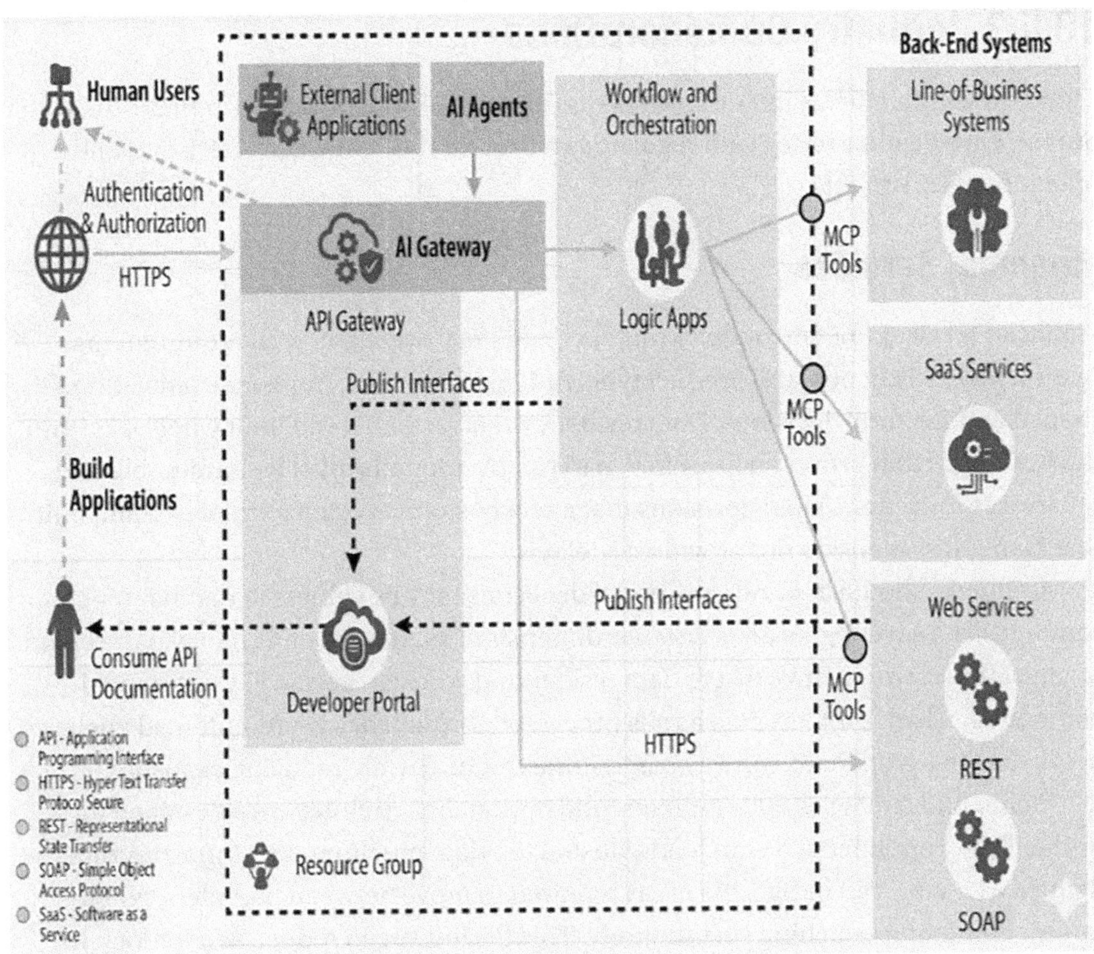

***Figure 10-1.** A high-level conceptual diagram of a cloud–AI architecture, showing the flow from external client applications and AI agents through an AI gateway and API management layer (gateway and developer portal) to a workflow and orchestration layer. The orchestration layer coordinates both human-initiated requests and agent-driven workflows, using MCP tools to invoke back-end systems including organization-specific services, SaaS platforms, and web services exposed via REST or SOAP. The diagram illustrates how humans and AI agents share a unified, governed API surface, with the AI gateway enforcing authentication, authorization, rate limiting, and policy controls for both. A dashed boundary denotes a single, governed resource group. (Image by author)*

10.5.2 Industry Considerations

Cloud-AI architecture is not uniform across industries. The principles remain consistent, but their application varies with regulatory requirements, data characteristics, and operational constraints.

Financial Services

Financial services operate under stringent regulatory oversight, with requirements that vary by jurisdiction and product type. At FIS, I saw how compliance obligations shaped architectural decisions. Data residency requirements can limit where data and the workloads that process it are allowed to run. Audit trails must be immutable and retrievable for years. Model decisions that affect customers often require explainability that many AI systems do not provide by default.

Architects should assume that model decisions may be subject to audit or regulatory scrutiny. Data sovereignty adds another dimension: as AI workloads move to the cloud, organizations must control where data resides and who can access it. Confidential computing, which protects data as it is processed through hardware-enforced enclaves, helps sensitive workloads run on shared infrastructure while reducing exposure.

Multicloud strategies add resilience and optionality. Architectures designed for portability—containerized workloads, abstracted data pipelines, and infrastructure defined as code—can reduce the effort required to move between providers, albeit rarely eliminating switching costs entirely. This flexibility can reduce vendor lock-in and provide leverage in commercial negotiations, but it requires deliberate investment in abstraction layers and operational tooling. Organizations that design for a single provider often discover the switching costs only when circumstances force a transition. Planning for portability as a foundational requirement preserves strategic options that competitors have foreclosed.

Latency requirements also differ by use case. Fraud detection must operate in milliseconds, whereas portfolio analytics can tolerate batch processing. Effective architectures separate these workloads rather than forcing them through a single pipeline. In this sector, a practical rule is conservative by default: if the system cannot justify an output with policy and evidence, it should escalate rather than improvise.

Legal Technology

Legal work combines high stakes with high variability. Contracts, filings, and litigation documents follow patterns, but exceptions are frequent. At Wolters Kluwer, we learned that legal professionals trust systems that make reasoning visible. Black-box recommendations face resistance in a profession built on argumentation and evidence.

Cloud-AI in legal technology should emphasize transparency. When a system recommends a filing deadline or flags a contract clause, users need to understand why. This expectation influences both model selection and interface design. Interpretable approaches often outperform more powerful but opaque alternatives in user adoption, and interfaces should expose confidence levels, alternative readings, and supporting evidence. Scale is another constraint: large litigation matters can involve millions of documents, and e-discovery workflows must process them under tight deadlines. A practical guideline is to treat provenance as a feature—every output should link back to the sources and reasoning cues that justify it.

Health Care

Health care introduces unique challenges around data sensitivity and interoperability. Patient records are subject to strict privacy regulations, including HIPAA in the United States and GDPR in Europe. Cloud-AI systems that process protected health information must satisfy compliance requirements that constrain infrastructure, data handling, and training approaches.

Interoperability remains difficult. Health care data is fragmented across EHRs, imaging systems, laboratory information systems, and administrative platforms. Standards such as Health Level Seven and Fast Healthcare Interoperability Resources improve data exchange, but integration remains labor-intensive. The stakes of error are also higher than in most industries. Just as a misclassified document in corporate compliance causes inconvenience, a misclassified diagnostic image can affect patient outcomes. This reality reinforces the need for conservative confidence thresholds and human review for consequential decisions. A reusable rule here is "first, do no harm" in system form: default to escalation when uncertainty intersects patient impact.

Cross-Industry Patterns

Despite differences, certain patterns recur. Regulated sectors require governance by design, auditability, and explainability. Document-intensive industries benefit from modularity and abstraction regardless of domain. High-stakes decisions in any sector require human oversight and clear accountability.

AI systems also introduce distinctive failure modes that cut across industries. Hallucination occurs when the model generates plausible but false information. Prompt injection occurs when malicious input manipulates model behavior. Inadvertent disclosure occurs when sensitive data leaks through model outputs. Tool misuse occurs when agents connected to external systems take unauthorized actions. Durable architectures assume these risks and build controls that detect them early.

Architects who succeed across industries separate universal requirements from domain-specific ones. Universal requirements can be addressed with common patterns and reusable components. Domain-specific requirements demand specialized knowledge and close collaboration with practitioners who understand operational realities. The most effective teams combine both deliberately.

10.6 Architecture Decision Framework

The Introduction promised a framework that executives can use to evaluate strategy and that architects can use to design systems. The following checklist distills the chapter's guidance into questions worth asking before committing to a cloud–AI initiative.

10.6.1 Checklist

Before committing resources to a cloud–AI initiative, product development teams should work through these questions systematically. The checklist covers strategy and platform, architecture and design, governance and operations, and human factors. A "no" or uncertain answer to any question signals an area that warrants further attention before proceeding.

Strategy and Platform

1. Have we defined the business problem before selecting the technology? A clear workflow analysis should precede any platform or model decision.
2. Have we evaluated platform choice against the five factors: integration surface, model strategy, data gravity, operational maturity, and economic levers?
3. Have we modeled the full cost of the AI life cycle, including experimentation, training, inference, storage, and egress, rather than optimizing for a single phase?
4. Have we assessed our organization's operational readiness to run AI workloads on the chosen platform?
5. Have we designed for portability so that changing models or providers does not require rebuilding the application?

Architecture and Design

1. Is the architecture modular, with clear interfaces between data, model, inference, and application layers?
2. Have we established where data will reside and accepted the gravitational consequences of that decision?
3. Have we designed for containment so failures in one component do not cascade into others?
4. Have we invested in exception handling, including timeouts, retries, fallbacks, and graceful degradation?
5. Have we secured the seams by treating the model as untrusted code and validating inputs and outputs at every integration point?
6. Have we assessed the quality, provenance, and representativeness of the data used for training or retrieval integration and documented any known gaps or limitations?

Governance and Operations

1. Is governance built into the architecture, with model versioning, access controls, audit trails, and bias monitoring treated as first-class features?
2. Have we versioned everything that affects behavior, including models, prompts, retrieval configurations, and policy rules?
3. Have we defined what "good" means in advance, with representative test sets, acceptance thresholds, and regression gates?
4. Have we identified and documented the AI-specific failure modes relevant to our system—including hallucination, prompt injection, adversarial inputs, data leakage, and tool misuse—and defined detection, escalation, and remediation procedures for each?
5. Have we instrumented every layer for observability, capturing not only uptime and latency but also accuracy, calibration, and factual grounding?
6. Have we established the cost guardrails, including budgets, alerts, and cost-per-transaction monitoring?

Human Factors

1. Have we preserved human judgment for critical decisions, with explicit escalation thresholds and clear accountability?
2. Have we planned for the people, treating rollout, training, and support as part of the architecture rather than afterthoughts?
3. Have we built feedback loops to capture signals from production and improve the system over time?
4. Have we made accountability an artifact, with decision logs that can be inspected and audited?
5. Have we respected the legacy, integrating with existing systems rather than forcing wholesale replacement?

10.6.2 Antipatterns to Avoid

The following patterns recur in failed or troubled AI initiatives. Recognizing them early can prevent costly rework:

1. **Selecting the Model Before Understanding the Workflow:** Teams that begin with a model and search for problems often build impressive demonstrations that fail in production. The workflow defines what success looks like. The model is one component in achieving it.

2. **Treating Governance as a Constraint to Minimize:** Organizations that defer compliance considerations discover them at the worst time: during an audit, a regulatory inquiry, or a production incident. Governance, which is designed into the architecture, scales. Governance bolted on afterward creates rework.

3. **Assuming Data Will Follow the Platform:** Data is heavy. Once it accumulates in one environment, it resists movement. Organizations that select platforms without considering existing data realities often find themselves paying for data movement they did not anticipate or maintaining integrations they did not plan.

4. **Optimizing for Average Performance:** Averages hide problems. A system with a 200-millisecond average latency may have a 95th-percentile latency of several seconds, meaning many users experience unacceptable delays. Effective measurement focuses on percentiles and on the metrics users actually feel.

5. **Deploying Without an Evaluation Harness:** Without defined test sets and acceptance thresholds, quality becomes a matter of opinion. Teams argue by anecdote rather than evidence. Regression gates become impossible to enforce. The system drifts until users complain.

6. **Scaling a Pilot Without Validating Unit Economics:** A pilot that costs hundreds of dollars per month may cost hundreds of thousands at production volume. Token-based pricing, embedding costs, and GPU hours accumulate in ways that surprise teams who did not model the full life cycle.

7. **Deploying Agentic AI Without Appropriate Guardrails:** Agentic systems that plan, use tools, and execute multistep workflows can deliver measurable value. But autonomy requires boundaries. In regulated industries, accountability cannot be delegated to software. Systems that take high-impact actions—such as submitting filings, executing transactions, or communicating with customers—need explicit constraints. Those constraints should define which actions are permitted, under what conditions, and at what level of human oversight. The question is not whether to use agentic architectures, but how to appropriately scope their autonomy. Architectures that treat all agentic use cases identically, or remove human oversight for high-stakes actions, create risks that responsible organizations cannot accept.

8. **Ignoring AI-Specific Failure Modes:** Hallucination, prompt injection, inadvertent disclosure, and tool misuse are not edge cases. They are predictable risks that require deliberate controls. Architects who assume models are reliable may be surprised when they prove not to be.

9. **Chasing Novelty Without Grounding in Principle:** The latest framework or model is not inherently better than its predecessor. Teams that adopt new technologies without understanding the underlying principles often rebuild systems when the next wave arrives.

10. **Clinging to the Familiar Without Adapting:** The opposite failure is equally damaging. Teams that refuse to adopt new capabilities because old approaches were comfortable miss genuine opportunities. The discipline is to distinguish between principles, which endure, and implementations, which are updated as conditions change.

10.7 Summary

The journey from packaged software to cloud–AI architecture spans the arc of my career, and this chapter has sought to distill the lessons it has taught me. What strikes me most, looking back, is how much has changed and how much has remained constant.

The scale of transformation is undeniable. Organizations across industries are investing in AI and cloud infrastructure at levels that would have seemed improbable a decade ago. These investments signal a fundamental reordering of how organizations create and capture value. I have watched this transformation unfold from the inside: from the early days of building proofing and automation capabilities for Word and Excel, through CTAdvantage.com, to the cloud migrations and AI integrations of recent years. Each transition felt momentous at the time. In retrospect, each was preparation for what came next.

The architectural principles that guided my earliest work hold true today. These include modularity with clear interfaces, abstraction for portability, respect for data gravity, progressive disclosure of complexity, preservation of human judgment, governance as an architectural principle rather than an afterthought, and observability at every layer. These are not abstract preferences. In fact, they are the distillation of lessons learned building systems that had to work in production, under real constraints, and for demanding users. The vocabulary changes. We now speak of MLOps, vector databases, and confidential computing rather than OLE, COM, and client-server architectures. But the underlying logic persists.

What has changed is the nature of intelligence itself. INTELLIFM embodied deterministic logic. Domain experts encoded jurisdictional knowledge into decision trees that executed with predictable precision and could explain every routing choice. Today's LLMs learn statistical patterns from text at a scale no human could replicate, producing capabilities that emerge from data rather than explicit programming. Yet the hybrid reality endures. Probabilistic outputs require deterministic guardrails, and the high-level business rules of the earlier era now serve as safety layers over ML predictions. The most effective modern architectures blend both approaches. They use AI for pattern recognition at scale while preserving the auditability and governance that regulated industries demand.

I have been fortunate to work alongside brilliant colleagues throughout this journey at Microsoft and its partner companies. Their insights sharpened my thinking, and their challenges pushed me to find better answers. Isaac Newton's observation remains apt: "If I have seen further, it is by standing on the shoulders of giants." The collaborative spirit of this industry, the willingness to share knowledge, debate approaches, and build on one another's work, has shaped whatever I have contributed.

The competitive landscape continues to take shape. AWS, Azure, and Google Cloud each bring distinct strengths, and investment activity shows no sign of slowing. Organizations that select platforms thoughtfully, design for portability, and treat governance as foundational will navigate this landscape successfully. Those who chase features without architectural discipline will find themselves rebuilding systems when the next transition arrives. In this industry, the next transition is always around the corner.

Looking ahead, the integration of AI, cloud computing, and SaaS promises to unlock capabilities we are only beginning to imagine. The principles explored in this chapter will remain important even as the technologies continue to advance. My hope, as it has been throughout my career, is to help democratize these capabilities. It is to make AI's power accessible to organizations of all sizes, capable of solving complex problems, and aligned with human values and judgment.

Having established the strategic foundations of cloud–AI architecture, we now turn to the Microsoft technologies that operationalize this vision. Azure AI Services, together with Microsoft Foundry and the broader Azure platform, illustrates how these principles translate into practical cognitive capabilities at enterprise scale. These include integrated identity and access controls, governed data pipelines, model evaluation and life-cycle management, and production-grade observability. In the next chapter, I examine how these services fit together architecturally and how to apply them in regulated enterprise environments.

CHAPTER 11

Azure AI Services: A Deep Dive

The architectural principles that underpin today's Azure AI Services will feel familiar to anyone who has designed layered enterprise AI systems. Similar design principles guided systems I worked on decades earlier when "artificial intelligence" still meant expert systems and hand-tuned rules. The INTELLIFM technology, which my teams created in the late 1990s, reflected foundational patterns—such as modularity, explicit contracts, and composable services—that remain highly relevant in modern cloud-AI platforms. While the implementation paradigm has since shifted from rule-based logic to ML and transformer architectures, the core architectural ambitions remain consistent. This chapter traces that journey: from the constraints that shaped my early thinking, through the breakthroughs that transformed what machines can do with language, to the enterprise-grade platform that realizes those original architectural ambitions with capabilities I could only have imagined.

In the early 1990s at Microsoft, I found myself deep in the trenches, debugging a grammar-checking engine that struggled to tell a dangling modifier from a split infinitive. The work was meticulous—finite-state machines and hand-coded rules, thousands of them, tuned line by line by computational linguists. Each time the system caught an error that a careful human editor would notice, we celebrated as though we had bent language itself to our will. Yet true semantic understanding remained a distant horizon, something we dreamed about over coffee but could not engineer into shipping software.

More than three decades later, I observe developers provision Azure AI Services that accomplish, in a fraction of the time, work that once required years of effort. The transformation is not incremental. It represents a rupture, a fundamental break in what machines can do with human language, images, and speech. Having lived this arc from

K. C. Mukherjee, *The Microsoft AI Insider's Playbook*, https://doi.org/10.1007/979-8-8688-2730-3_11

the inside—from rule-based grammar engines to transformer models with billions of parameters—I can explain not only what Azure AI Services offers, but why it matters and how it came to be.

This chapter examines Azure AI Services as both a technical platform and an architectural milestone. It begins with the historical context that shaped the platform's design and then traces the multilayered architecture that connects infrastructure to intelligence. The core service categories—Azure OpenAI Service, Azure Speech, Azure Language, and Azure AI Vision and Document Intelligence—are examined in turn, followed by architectural patterns for conversational AI, including service integration, orchestration, security, and data flow. The chapter then addresses advanced chatbot and virtual assistant development patterns before concluding with implementation best practices and performance optimization strategies for production-grade deployments.

AI has moved from academic curiosity to foundational enterprise technology. I have witnessed other inflection points—the shift from mainframes to client-server, the rise of the web, the migration to cloud computing—but this one feels qualitatively different. The capabilities emerging from LLMs and multimodal systems are not incremental improvements. Instead, they are qualitative leaps in what software can accomplish.

Azure AI Services is Microsoft's strategic response to this shift. It delivers a production-grade portfolio of cognitive services, engineered for integration into mission-critical workflows while maintaining security and compliance. What once demanded bespoke architecture and months of integration now begins with configuration rather than custom code. Data residency and compliance, once the bane of enterprise architects, are now addressed through Azure's global footprint. With a broad global footprint and a mature compliance portfolio, the platform can support many regulated workloads, subject to service availability, region, and tenant configuration. Validating the specific certifications and controls relevant to the intended use cases is an essential step.

Having worked on high-impact projects for organizations subject to strict regulations, I know how consequential this is: what once required elaborate architecture is now achieved through deliberate configuration. The result is freedom. Engineers can redirect their energy away from foundational model training and infrastructure upkeep—tasks Azure now shoulders—and toward the distinctive business challenges that define their markets. This is the promise I glimpsed in service-oriented architecture decades ago, now realized at a scale we could scarcely imagine. Azure AI Services has moved well beyond experimentation and now sits within Microsoft's broader enterprise AI platform strategy. Its managed deployment model, ecosystem integration, and expanding platform capabilities have made it a practical foundation for many production-oriented AI initiatives. Microsoft's investment underscores the strategy—purpose-built data centers for AI training and inference reflect the central role of AI in Azure's growth.

I have seen this pattern before. Cloud computing followed a similar trajectory: skepticism giving way to pilots, pilots expanding into production, production becoming indispensable infrastructure. AI services are on the same path, but accelerated. The question for most organizations is no longer whether to adopt AI, but how quickly they can scale it.

A brief note on naming. At Microsoft Ignite on November 18, 2025, Microsoft rebranded Azure AI Foundry as Microsoft Foundry and renamed the underlying service family from Azure AI Services to Foundry Tools. As of early 2026, Microsoft documentation uses Microsoft Foundry as the unified platform name and Foundry Tools for the underlying service family. However, the capabilities, architecture, and integration patterns described in this chapter are unchanged by the rebrand. For clarity and continuity, this chapter retains "Azure AI Services" as a familiar umbrella term in general discussion, while using newer terminology—Microsoft Foundry for the unified platform and specific product names such as Foundry Tools, Foundry Agent Service, and Foundry IQ—where those current names are more precise.

11.1 Historical Context

The limitations I encountered building those early grammar engines shaped my subsequent thinking about AI system design. When I developed INTELLIFM, I deliberately chose a different architectural approach. Rather than embedding intelligence monolithically inside desktop applications, the expert system emphasized modular design, declarative business rules, and direct incorporation of domain expertise. The system evolved from desktop COM components to client-server applications and, eventually, to web services, anticipating the principles that would later be recognized as the SaaS model. This progression moved beyond error detection to parsing business intent from natural language input—anticipating the eventual transition of Office to Office 365 and Microsoft 365.

The true inflection point arrived with ML and, later, deep learning. The convergence of cloud computing, large-scale training datasets, and transformer architectures has enabled semantic generalization at a scale that rule-based architectures were never designed to address. Azure AI Services packages these advances in a service-oriented architecture that will be familiar to anyone who has worked with INTELLIFM: modularity, clear contracts, and composable capabilities remain central, now powered by transformer-based models rather than declarative rules.

Patterns established in those earlier systems now operate on a global scale. Where components once coordinated on a single machine via COM interfaces, Azure orchestrates intelligent services across a global infrastructure via REST APIs. Client-server protocols matured into stateless, resource-based designs that scale massively. The principles—*modularity*, *interoperability*, and *clear interfaces*—remain constant, and their impact is now enterprise-wide. Deployments that once took months of custom integration can often be completed in days through standardized endpoints and managed services.

Nevertheless, the hard-won lessons from earlier implementations remain relevant. Production systems need to degrade gracefully, handle errors comprehensively, and anticipate conditions no test environment can fully simulate. These lessons, learned from debugging Microsoft's earliest grammar engines and refined through enterprise deployments across financial services, health care, and government, inform everything that follows in this chapter.

11.2 The Architectural Foundation

The principles I learned building INTELLIFM—modularity, clear contracts, and composable capabilities—remain highly relevant in modern AI platforms. Azure has evolved from an infrastructure that runs applications to one that embeds intelligence into them. Large-scale models provide the reasoning engine for interpreting text and images; Foundry Tools expose these advanced capabilities through stable APIs; and orchestration frameworks connect organizational knowledge to these models, producing grounded, context-aware responses. What I once built for an expert system now appears, in more advanced form, across enterprise AI platforms operating at a global scale.

This transition reflects an industry insight that took years to crystallize: AI is no longer a feature layered on top of cloud services. It has become one of the primary reasons organizations choose a cloud platform. Compute, storage, and networking remain foundational, but differentiation increasingly lies in the depth, reliability, and integration of the intelligence stack, as well as in how well that stack aligns with an organization's data, identity, and compliance posture.

What stands out to me, after decades on both sides of the enterprise software boundary, is how Azure's AI platform embodies lessons learned through earlier generations of system design. Pretrained models are continuously optimized and exposed through standardized APIs, making state-of-the-art capabilities available without requiring every organization to build foundational models from scratch. This approach removes a layer of complexity that once consumed entire teams.

The result is a production-ready AI platform spanning core domains such as vision, speech, language, document intelligence, and knowledge retrieval. These capabilities are delivered through Foundry Tools as discrete, composable units with well-defined contracts and enterprise-oriented operational characteristics. Their latency and throughput profiles vary by service, model, deployment type, and workload, but they can be managed through sound architectural and deployment choices.

The broader Microsoft Foundry stack includes Foundry Models for access to foundation and partner models, Foundry Agent Service for orchestrating and hosting agents, and Foundry IQ as a managed knowledge layer that grounds agents in enterprise data. Together, these components support perception, language understanding, retrieval, grounding, generation, and agentic execution. Final decisions in enterprise systems, however, usually emerge from application and orchestration layers that combine AI outputs with business logic, policies, governance controls, and human oversight where required. Organizations can therefore begin with focused use cases and expand as their maturity grows—mirroring the incremental adoption pattern I originally designed INTELLIFM to support, now realized at enterprise scale.

This modular architecture extends across the broader Azure platform. Foundry Tools integrate natively with existing infrastructure and inherit enterprise-grade security controls with minimal configuration. They can also support compliance requirements for standards and regulatory frameworks, such as SOC 2 Type 2, ISO 27001, and HIPAA, depending on the specific service, region, and deployment configuration. Furthermore, geographically distributed deployment options support resilient, low-latency architectures that can scale globally while adhering to local data residency requirements. Microsoft Foundry, which evolved from Azure AI Studio to Azure AI Foundry and now to its current form, serves as the unified platform for building and operating enterprise AI applications—bringing together models, agents, tools, and knowledge under a unified governance framework.

These principles come together in a carefully structured five-layer architecture, which I examine in the next section.

11.3 The Multilayered Architecture

The five-layer framework that follows represents a conceptual model for understanding the structure of Azure AI Services, informed by decades of enterprise deployments. While not drawn from official Microsoft architectural documentation, this model reflects the patterns consistent with how these services behave in practice.

This architectural approach will feel familiar to anyone who has designed layered enterprise systems. It follows the same principle I applied in INTELLIFM and other enterprise applications: each layer abstracts complexity from the layer above, exposing only the interfaces required for that layer to function. What has changed is the scale—and the sophistication of what each layer now delivers. For executives, this structure provides a predictable, low-risk path to AI adoption. For engineers, it offers a clear, composable foundation that avoids the pitfalls of monolithic design.

The infrastructure layer comprises globally distributed clusters of high-performance GPUs and specialized field-programmable gate arrays (FPGAs), interconnected via low-latency fabrics such as InfiniBand and networking enabled with remote direct memory access. These clusters are optimized for parallelized AI inference and training, with schedulers that balance heterogeneous workloads—batch, streaming, and real-time—while maintaining tenant isolation. Hyperscale storage systems manage petabytes of model artifacts and training data, with topology-aware caching to reduce cold-start latency. Edge devices extend this layer into constrained or intermittently connected environments, delivering consistent performance across retail sites, manufacturing floors, and clinical settings. For business leaders, this means global reach, predictable performance, and the ability to scale from pilot to production without rearchitecting systems or building specialized AI operations teams.

The model layer hosts a diverse portfolio of continuously updated pretrained models, ranging from compact, quantized variants for edge deployment to large foundation models. This ecosystem includes specialized models for language, speech, and vision, further strengthened by Microsoft's 2022 acquisition of Nuance Communications, which brought deep expertise in health care and clinical language understanding to the platform. To support reliability, each model deployment moves through a rigorous life cycle across staging, canary, and production rings. This process is backed by automated regression detection, telemetry-informed retraining, and rollback mechanisms. This managed approach gives engineers access to advanced capabilities without the burden of managing the underlying infrastructure. Ultimately, executives benefit from a model ecosystem that can improve over time, reducing the likelihood of disruptive replatforming and limiting the need for costly custom development.

The service layer operationalizes these models and serves as the platform's hub for security, governance, and reliability. At this layer, the architecture draws on broader Azure platform services—including Azure API Management (APIM), secure authentication through Microsoft Entra ID and Open Authorization (OAuth) 2.0, and rate limiting—to deliver predictable performance during peak demand. Engineers gain deep observability: distributed tracing across model and service boundaries, real-time metrics for throughput and saturation, and structured diagnostics for failure analysis. Request and response logging can be configured in Azure Monitor and APIM, with redaction policies applied per the organization's logging and privacy requirements. Governance tools such as Azure Policy can enforce configuration baselines when the relevant policies are applied. Model versioning and deployment instrumentation can make inference activity traceable to the model version and configuration in effect at the time of the request, depending on how telemetry and data lineage are implemented. For executives, this layer reduces regulatory exposure, strengthens audit readiness, and keeps AI initiatives scaling safely and responsibly.

The software development kit (SDK) layer offers language-specific libraries and unified abstractions for Python, C#, Java, JavaScript, and Go. Modern SDKs eliminate the integration friction I remember from early COM-based systems—no more marshaling data across process boundaries or debugging interface mismatches. Engineers benefit from built-in retry logic and telemetry hooks that integrate directly with Azure Monitor. Circuit breakers are typically implemented at the gateway or application layer (for example, APIM policies or resiliency libraries). Organizations can extend or override default behaviors, plug in custom vector stores, or integrate private embeddings without breaking the abstraction. For executives, this translates into faster delivery cycles, reduced dependency on scarce AI specialists, and a more productive engineering workforce.

The applications and solutions layer is where organizations realize tangible business outcomes: intelligent customer service, automated documentation, personalized experiences, and domain-specific copilots. Microsoft Foundry provides a unified workspace for prompt design, RAG, safety configuration, evaluation, and deployment. The portal experience and product naming evolve over time, but the underlying life cycle remains consistent. Engineers can test latency budgets, validate prompt injection defenses, and integrate private data sources with fine-grained access control. Executives see accelerated time to market, reduced operational overhead, and the ability to turn internal knowledge into a strategic asset. GitHub Copilot, running on Azure infrastructure, exemplifies the productivity transformation this layer delivers—code generation accelerates, features ship faster, feedback arrives sooner, and the gains compound across the delivery pipeline.

Figure 11-1 illustrates this stack. Each layer provides clear functional contracts while abstracting away implementation complexity, making it easier for organizations to adopt the stack incrementally as their expertise grows.

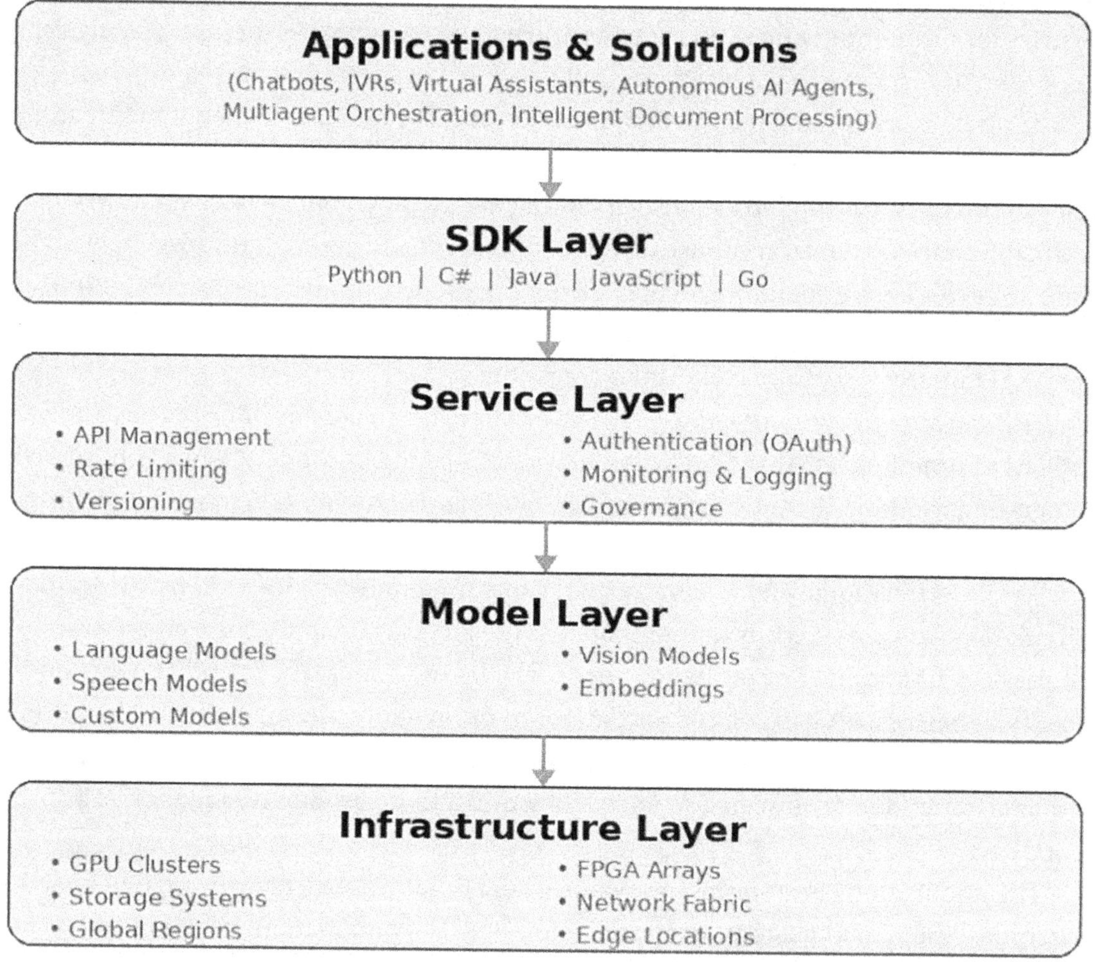

Figure 11-1. *The diagram illustrates a five-layer technology stack. The layers are as follows: (1) applications and solutions; (2) SDK layer supporting multiple programming languages; (3) service layer with API management, authentication, and governance; (4) model layer featuring language, speech, vision, and custom AI models; and (5) infrastructure layer including GPU clusters, storage systems, FPGA arrays, and edge devices. (Image by author)*

This incremental path is critical for executives managing risk: AI adoption becomes a series of controlled, measurable steps rather than a disruptive overhaul. For engineers, the layered architecture lets each component evolve independently without destabilizing the system.

What distinguishes Azure AI Services from academic or experimental offerings is its commitment to industrial-grade engineering: end-to-end encryption, thorough audit logging, real-time diagnostics, automatic failover, and geographic redundancy. The platform is designed with explicit failure modes in mind—GPU node loss, regional outages, model unavailability—and provides engineered resiliency mechanisms and documented degradation paths for common scenarios.

These capabilities protect against operational disruption and reputational risk, which often matter more than raw model accuracy in enterprise settings. Having operated systems where downtime was measured in millions of dollars per hour, I can attest that these operational characteristics determine whether AI becomes a strategic asset or a liability. Azure's architecture is built for organizations that cannot afford uncertainty. Table 11-1 summarizes each service's primary functions, key capabilities, common enterprise use cases, and pricing model.

Table 11-1. *Azure AI Services portfolio showing primary functions, key capabilities, common enterprise use cases, and pricing models. Each service offers REST APIs and SDKs for seamless integration and operates within Azure's security controls. Compliance coverage varies by service and region. Verifying requirements against Azure's compliance documentation prevents assumptions about coverage.*

Service	Primary Function	Key Capabilities	Common Use Cases	Pricing Model
Azure OpenAI Service	Generative AI and language models	Text generation; multimodal models; embeddings; function calling; fine-tuning (where available)	Content generation; code assistance; summarization; RAG; conversational AI	Usage-based (per 1,000 tokens); provisioned throughput where supported
Azure AI Speech	Speech recognition, synthesis, and translation	Speech-to-text (STT); text-to-speech (TTS); neural voices; custom speech models; real-time and batch processing	Contact centers; IVR modernization; accessibility; meeting transcription; voice assistants	STT: per audio hour; TTS: per million characters; custom models billed separately
Azure AI Language	Natural language understanding (NLU)	Sentiment analysis; entity recognition; personally identifiable information (PII) detection; key phrase extraction; conversational language understanding (CLU)	Document analysis; customer feedback insights; chatbot intent classification; compliance workflows	Per 1,000 text records or transactions (varies by feature)
Azure AI Vision	Image and video analysis	OCR; object detection; image classification; spatial analysis; face detection (availability varies)	Visual inspection; content moderation; accessibility; retail analytics	Per 1,000 transactions; video features billed per minute

(continued)

Table 11-1. (*continued*)

Service	Primary Function	Key Capabilities	Common Use Cases	Pricing Model
Azure AI Document Intelligence	Structured document processing	Form recognition; layout extraction; table parsing; prebuilt models for invoices, receipts, IDs, contracts	Invoice automation; claims processing; contract review; onboarding workflows	Per page processed; custom model training billed separately
Azure AI Search	Cognitive search and retrieval	Semantic search; vector search; hybrid retrieval; indexers; RAG integration	Knowledge mining; enterprise search; document discovery; domain-specific copilots	Provisioned search units (per hour) plus storage
Azure AI Translator	Multilingual translation	Text translation; document translation; transliteration; 100+ languages	Localization; multilingual chat; global content distribution; cross-border documentation	Per million characters
Azure AI Content Safety	Content moderation and safety	Detection of harmful text and images; configurable severity thresholds; safety signals for LLM apps	Platform safety; moderation of user-generated content; enterprise risk controls; LLM guardrails	Per 1,000 transactions

11.4 Azure OpenAI Service

In early proofing tools, success meant catching a misplaced modifier or rescuing a sentence from syntactic confusion. I remember poring over rule sets late into the night, adjusting one clause only to break another. At the time, the idea that a machine could generate coherent analyses across multiple paragraphs, retain context across long conversations, or reason through complex problems felt like something out of speculative fiction. Yet today, Azure OpenAI Service does exactly that. In my view, it is the most strategically transformative component within Azure AI Services.

Azure OpenAI Service provides enterprise access to OpenAI's models hosted within Azure—including GPT, DALL-E, Whisper, and embedding models—for text, multimodal, and semantic search applications. Organizations requiring access to other LLMs, such as Meta's Llama or Anthropic's Claude, can do so through the Microsoft Foundry model catalog. Model offerings vary by region, service tier, and tenant configuration, and they evolve over time. As a result, teams often rely on current Azure documentation to confirm which models and features are available in a given deployment region. For executives, this means access to frontier AI capabilities within Azure's security and compliance boundary, subject to the certifications and controls available for the selected region and service. For engineers, it offers production-grade APIs backed by meaningful service-level agreements (SLAs), where available for the selected service tier and region.

The defining distinction from the public OpenAI API is Azure's trust boundary. Customer prompts, input data, and model outputs are processed in Azure and governed by Azure security controls and the organization's configuration (for example, private endpoints, logging, and data residency options). Most importantly, customer data is not used to train or improve OpenAI models. Organizations that require custom models can opt into fine-tuning scenarios where training occurs entirely within their secure Azure environment. Having spent years navigating data governance challenges in regulated industries, I know how consequential this assurance is. It turns generative AI from a compliance liability into a deployable enterprise capability.

Context window size determines how much a selected model can process in a single interaction. Some models support very large context windows and multimodal inputs, while others emphasize lower cost and faster response times. Model selection is typically guided by workload requirements and regional availability.

Performance characteristics can support real-time enterprise workloads, but latency varies with model choice, token volume, region, concurrency, and application design. Benchmarking under representative load and monitoring both first-token latency and end-to-end response time in production are common practices for setting expectations and detecting regressions. For workloads requiring predictable capacity, provisioned throughput units (where supported), reserve dedicated capacity to reduce variability during peak demand. Usage-based pricing applies, and batch processing can lower costs for workloads that tolerate higher latency.

For conversational AI, the linguistic sophistication of these models is transformative. They grasp nuance, maintain long-range context across dozens of turns, and generate responses that feel genuinely human. The contrast with the rule-based systems I once built could not be sharper. Where we once labored over individual grammar rules, these models generalize across the full complexity of human language.

Success, however, depends on effective prompt engineering. Few-shot prompting establishes desired formats through examples. Step-by-step prompting can improve accuracy on complex analytical tasks by encouraging the structured decomposition of problems. In enterprise settings, auditability comes from verifiable artifacts such as logged tool calls, structured outputs, retrieval citations, deterministic calculations performed by external services, and end-to-end telemetry that traces inputs to actions and outcomes.

Prompting can influence reasoning and formatting, but it cannot eliminate hallucinations, block prompt injection, or compensate for weak grounding. These risks require architectural controls that extend beyond the prompt itself, providing a defense-in-depth approach to protect the application from a range of vulnerabilities. Such controls may include an AI gateway for input and output filtering, helping detect malicious prompt injection or unintended disclosure of sensitive data before information reaches the model or the end user. They also include RAG and circuit breakers, which help keep the application accurate and resilient during periods of heavy demand or service instability.

Function calling extends these models into agentic applications by allowing the model to act as a reasoning engine that interacts with external systems. Rather than simply generating text, the model determines when to invoke tools—such as APIs for data retrieval, computation, or business process execution—and formats those requests in machine-readable form. Combined with Foundry Agent Service for stateful agent execution and structured outputs for reliable JSON generation, Azure OpenAI Service supports sophisticated workflows. This architecture connects language understanding with concrete action, giving developers the foundation to build systems that not only answer questions but also carry out complex business processes.

Azure OpenAI Service includes content filtering that evaluates prompts and responses for harmful content—hate speech, violence, sexual material, and self-harm—across configurable severity levels. When additional moderation workflows are required, organizations can integrate Azure AI Content Safety as a separate service. They can configure thresholds to balance safety with legitimate business needs. Fine-tuning, where available for the selected model and approved for the subscription, supports specialized tasks such as legal summarization, medical terminology, and domain-specific classification. Training data and artifacts remain governed by the organization's Azure controls and configuration.

11.5 Azure Speech

The early systems processed text—words on a screen, parsed and analyzed in silence. Voice belonged to a different universe, handled by systems with their own constraints, latencies, and failure modes. Integrating the two meant bridging not only technologies but disciplines: acoustic engineering, signal processing, and telephony infrastructure. I remember how fragile those bridges were. Today, Azure Speech bridges the divide, converting spoken language into structured data and text back into natural-sounding speech within a unified platform. For organizations building conversational AI, it provides the foundational layer that connects human voice to digital intelligence.

The service encompasses three core capabilities. STT converts spoken words into written text, giving applications a way to understand and process human speech. TTS operates in reverse, generating natural-sounding synthetic speech for voice responses. Speech translation combines recognition and synthesis to translate speech in real time, making communication across languages possible. For executives, these capabilities unlock voice-enabled customer experiences without the burden of specialized infrastructure. For engineers, they offer production-grade APIs that abstract the complexity of acoustic modeling and neural synthesis.

Each capability exhibits distinct performance characteristics that vary with configuration and use case. STT accuracy can improve with customization and domain terminology. TTS quality is often assessed in terms of naturalness and intelligibility, and custom neural voices can reinforce brand identity. Speech translation performance varies across language pairs, audio quality, and deployment conditions. Hence, representative audio and real deployment environments are commonly used for testing.

The service supports extensive language coverage that continues to expand, with availability varying by feature and region. STT supports dozens of languages and regional variants, with availability varying by region and service tier. Neural TTS offers a similarly broad range, using deep neural networks to generate speech with natural rhythm and emotional context. Verifying the availability of current language versions for the specific regions and requirements confirms production readiness.

Customization involves two complementary processes. Language model customization incorporates domain-specific text data, unique terminology, and anticipated phrases to sharpen the recognition of specialized vocabulary—medical terminology, product codes, and financial jargon. The acoustic model is trained on audio from real deployment environments, helping the service adapt to noisy call centers, varied microphone types, diverse acoustic conditions, and regional accents. Technically, this provides fine-grained control over recognition behavior. From a business perspective, it translates into measurably higher accuracy in domain-specific deployments without building custom speech systems from scratch.

Real-time applications require sophisticated audio processing. Acoustic echo cancellation eliminates speaker feedback in two-way communication. Voice activity detection distinguishes speech from silence, optimizing processing resources. Endpointing algorithms determine precisely when a user has finished speaking, helping keep interactions responsive. These were once the kinds of signal processing challenges that demanded dedicated hardware and specialized teams. Azure now delivers them as managed services with configurable parameters.

TTS supports the Speech Synthesis Markup Language (SSML), an XML-based standard that provides developers with precise control over voice output. SSML facilitates adjustments to prosody—rhythm, pitch, and intonation—to create more engaging interactions. Developers can control speaking rates, add pauses, emphasize specific words, and shape emotional delivery to match application requirements. Having worked on early text processing systems in which output formatting was a constant challenge, I appreciate the expressive range SSML provides within a standardized framework.

Custom neural voice is a strategic capability for enterprises that require branded voice experiences. The technology typically requires several hours of professional-quality training audio to create production-ready voices, though rapid prototyping options are available with smaller datasets. The process adheres to Microsoft's responsible AI guidelines, which require documented consent from the voice talent and a thorough review of the intended use cases. Organizations can create unique voices aligned with brand identity while maintaining the naturalness and clarity of neural synthesis.

Integration with other Azure services extends the platform's reach. Azure Speech works directly with Azure Language for intent recognition, Azure AI Translator for multilingual scenarios, and Azure OpenAI Service for generative responses. It also connects with Azure Communication Services for telephony and with current agent and application frameworks for conversational AI. This composability reflects the same modular philosophy I applied in INTELLIFM—discrete capabilities with clear interfaces, assembled into solutions that exceed what any single component could deliver.

Pricing follows a consumption-based model. STT charges are based on the hours of audio processed. TTS pricing is based on the number of characters synthesized. Custom models and neural voices incur additional training and hosting costs. Real-time and batch processing options provide flexibility for different workload patterns and budget constraints.

Azure Speech transforms modern IVR systems in ways I could only have imagined when building early natural language interfaces. Callers can express complex requests conversationally—providing an account number, transfer amount, and date in a single natural utterance rather than navigating menu trees. This is the kind of intent parsing I designed INTELLIFM to support, now operating in real time over telephone networks at enterprise scale. In well-designed deployments, this can reduce menu friction, improve containment for routine requests, and shorten handling time for selected call types, although outcomes depend heavily on recognition quality, journey design, and back-end integration. For executives, this delivers measurable ROI from voice automation. For engineers, it demonstrates how speech, language understanding, and business logic integrate into coherent conversational experiences.

11.6 Azure Language

Of all the services in the Azure AI portfolio, this one feels the most personal. Azure Language accomplishes what I spent years trying to achieve with rule-based systems: interpreting user intent, extracting structured data from unstructured text, and navigating the ambiguities of human expression. The rule-based expert systems excelled at error detection. INTELLIFM extended this foundation to parse business intent through declarative rules and domain expertise—an approach that delivered precision and explainability within its intended scope. Azure Language now applies neural architectures to process unconstrained natural language across dozens of languages and domains, trading the explainability of rule-based systems for broader generalization. What once demanded years of custom development now executes in milliseconds.

Azure Language remains important in many production systems, especially for text analytics and existing conversational workloads. However, some of its conversational features now sit within a transition period. Microsoft has announced that CLU and custom question answering will retire on March 31, 2029, and recommends directing new projects toward Microsoft Foundry models while migrating existing workloads over time.[1]

The service delivers multiple core capabilities for text analysis. Entity recognition identifies and categorizes information within text, supporting prebuilt categories such as Person, Location, Organization, DateTime, and Currency. Organizations can create custom entity models to capture domain-specific terms—"Medicare Plan G," "Series A Preferred Stock," "EBITDA adjustments"—with each recognized entity including confidence scores and positional metadata. At the implementation level, this provides precise extraction with tunable thresholds. The business outcome is structured data that emerges automatically from unstructured documents.

PII detection provides specialized recognition and redaction. The service automatically identifies sensitive data—financial accounts, social security records, passport identifiers, and telephone numbers. Organizations configure detection sensitivity and choose between redaction, masking, or flagging. Having worked in regulated industries where a single exposed Social Security number could trigger compliance failures, I appreciate how this capability transforms a manual, error-prone process into automated policy enforcement.

Sentiment analysis operates at multiple levels of granularity. Document-level analysis provides overall sentiment scores. Sentence-level analysis tracks emotional progression through text. Aspect-based sentiment identifies targeted opinions within complex documents—detecting positive sentiment toward "camera quality" while flagging negative sentiment toward "battery life" in the same review. Each analysis includes confidence scores and detailed breakdowns to support a nuanced understanding. Strategically, this turns customer feedback into actionable intelligence. Technically, it provides structured sentiment data ready for dashboards and alerts.

Custom question answering, a feature of Azure Language, has supported rapid deployment of knowledge-based conversational systems and remains relevant for existing workloads during the current support window, although Microsoft now

[1] Microsoft, "Conversational Language Understanding," Foundry Tools, Microsoft Learn, https://learn.microsoft.com/en-us/azure/ai-services/language-service/conversational-language-understanding/overview.

recommends Foundry models for new projects. The service ingests unstructured documents, FAQ pages, and technical manuals to build knowledge bases. It can automatically generate interfaces that understand natural language questions and return relevant answers. It also handles question variations, contextual follow-ups, and ambiguous queries while maintaining coherence across a conversation.

This is close to what I envisioned when developing INTELLIFM's knowledge-driven interfaces. That vision is now realized through a managed service that does not require a custom inference engine. The quality of the answers, however, depends directly on the quality of the underlying knowledge base. Source accuracy, document freshness, chunking strategy, and ongoing evaluation all shape whether retrieval produces useful results or merely plausible but unhelpful responses.

These systems are also limited by the content they ingest. They cannot reliably generate new knowledge or reason well beyond the available context. When the knowledge base is sparse or contains conflicting information, the risk of hallucination increases because the model may fill gaps with plausible but incorrect statements. In addition, maintaining the knowledge base across its full life cycle is an operational challenge. Without strong governance to remove outdated documentation and verify new material, system reliability will gradually decline, undermining user trust.

Intent classification and entity extraction power conversational AI implementations. When users interact with chatbots or voice assistants, the service determines their goals—"transfer money," "check balance," "report fraud." Entity extraction identifies required parameters from natural language: "pay my bill next Friday" yields both the payment intent and a specific date for "next Friday" that back-end systems can process. I designed INTELLIFM to do precisely this—parse business intent from natural language input. The differences now lie in scale, speed, and the transition from declarative rules to learned representations.

Azure Language supports extensive language coverage across its text analytics and understanding capabilities, with availability varying by feature and region. For translation scenarios, Azure Language integrates with Azure AI Translator, which provides broad language coverage for text and document translation. Custom models can be trained for specific languages and regional variants to improve local accuracy.

Integration with other Azure services facilitates the development of end-to-end solutions. Azure Language connects with Azure OpenAI Service for generative capabilities, Azure AI Search for intelligent document retrieval, Copilot Studio or custom channel applications for conversational experiences, and Power Platform for low-code development. This composability reflects the modular philosophy I have advocated throughout my career—discrete capabilities with clear contracts, assembled into solutions that exceed what any single component can deliver.

Deployment options accommodate diverse requirements. Fully managed cloud endpoints provide automatic scaling and high availability. Container deployment is well suited to edge processing and air-gapped environments. Batch processing efficiently handles large document collections. Real-time APIs support interactive applications with low-latency response times. This flexibility aligns the service with architectural constraints while accommodating deployment of language understanding wherever the business requires it.

Pricing follows Azure's consumption-based model. The standard tier charges per 1,000 text records, with volume discounts available. Custom models incur training and hosting fees. Free tier options support development and testing. Commitment tiers provide discounted pricing for predictable workloads.

Azure Language transforms how organizations process unstructured text at scale. Customer service systems categorize and route tickets by intent and sentiment. Compliance teams use PII detection to verify the safety of documents. Research departments extract insights from thousands of documents simultaneously. Health care organizations process clinical notes to identify conditions, medications, and outcomes. Financial institutions analyze earnings calls and regulatory filings. The service converts the ambiguity of human language into structured, actionable data—the goal I pursued for decades, now realized as enterprise infrastructure.

11.7 Azure AI Vision and Document Intelligence

The early systems I built for Microsoft processed text that arrived already digitized—characters on a screen, ready for parsing. But most enterprise information does not begin that way. It arrives in the form of scanned contracts, photographed receipts, faxed forms, and handwritten notes. Before any semantic analysis can occur, the visual information needs to be structured as data. Azure AI Vision and Azure AI Document Intelligence solve this problem by transforming images and documents into structured input that downstream services—including Azure Language and Azure OpenAI Service—can process. For organizations drowning in paper and PDFs, these services represent the first step toward intelligent automation.

Azure AI Document Intelligence extracts structured data from unstructured and semistructured documents at enterprise scale. The service goes beyond traditional OCR to understand document context, relationships, and hierarchies—identifying key-value pairs, tables, selection marks, and signatures while preserving logical structure. For engineers, this means APIs that return parsed, validated data rather than raw text. For executives, this means invoices, receipts, contracts, and forms are processed automatically without manual data entry.

Prebuilt models handle common document types without training. Invoice processing extracts vendor information, line items, totals, and payment terms. Receipt analysis identifies merchant details, transaction dates, and itemized purchases. Identity document processing extracts data from passports, driver's licenses, and ID cards. W-2 and other tax form models are used to handle complex financial documents. Each prebuilt model delivers production-ready accuracy out of the box—the kind of capability that once required months of custom development and ongoing maintenance.

Custom document models address organization-specific requirements through supervised ML. Organizations train models using as few as five sample documents for simple layouts. However, more complex documents benefit from larger training sets. The training process identifies fields, tables, and selection marks specific to proprietary forms. Models learn to handle variations in formatting, handwriting styles, and document quality, achieving high accuracy even with poor-quality scans. Having overseen digitization initiatives where document variability was the primary obstacle, I appreciate how dramatically this reduces implementation risk.

Azure AI Vision provides advanced image analysis for visual understanding tasks. Object detection identifies and localizes multiple objects using bounding boxes and associated confidence scores. Image classification categorizes images into thousands of predefined categories. OCR extracts printed and handwritten text in dozens of languages. Spatial analysis examines the physical layout and relationships among elements. For engineers, these capabilities compose into sophisticated visual pipelines. For executives, automation unlocks capabilities in domains such as quality inspection, content moderation, and visual search that previously required human review.

Advanced vision capabilities support specialized scenarios. Face detection can identify human faces and return locations and selected landmarks, with outputs shaped by the scenario and policy settings. Identity-related recognition and other sensitive biometric scenarios are typically handled under separate controls and may be subject to restriction. Responsible AI guidance, along with current documentation, is often used to confirm feature availability, requirements, and appropriate use. Brand detection identifies logos and trademarks. Adult content detection flags inappropriate material for moderation. Custom vision models can be trained to recognize organization-specific objects, defects, or conditions. This makes it possible to tailor quality inspection workflows to specific manufacturing contexts.

Integration with other Foundry Tools creates complete visual-intelligence solutions. Document Intelligence and Vision connect directly with Azure OpenAI Service for multimodal understanding, Azure AI Search for visual search across repositories, and Power Automate for low-code workflow automation. Azure Storage integration provides the processing pipelines. This composability follows the same pattern I have emphasized throughout my career—discrete services with clear interfaces, assembled into solutions that address specific business problems.

Performance characteristics meet enterprise requirements. Document Intelligence processes pages rapidly, with performance varying by document complexity, page count, and selected features. Benchmarking with representative documents establishes baseline expectations grounded in actual performance. Vision analysis returns results in milliseconds for most operations. Both services scale automatically to handle thousands of concurrent requests, with batch processing supporting the digitization of millions of documents. These metrics inform architectural decisions. Further, they translate into predictable throughput and the ability to address document backlogs that have accumulated over time.

Deployment options support diverse architectural patterns. Cloud endpoints provide fully managed services with automatic scaling. Container deployment facilitates on-premises processing to meet regulatory compliance requirements. Edge deployment via Azure IoT brings vision capabilities to remote locations, including manufacturing floors, retail stores, and field service operations. Both services maintain data residency within specified regions.

Security and compliance features support enterprise-grade protection. Data is typically protected in transit and at rest using industry-standard encryption, although the specific protocols and algorithms can vary by service and region. Published Microsoft security documentation is commonly used to confirm the applicable configurations for a given deployment. Azure participates in compliance programs such as SOC and ISO, and many services are eligible for regulated workloads. HIPAA support is typically addressed through service eligibility and a business associate agreement. Applicability varies by service, region, and configuration. Customer data is not used for model training without explicit consent, and audit logs track all API access.

Pricing follows Azure's consumption-based model. Document Intelligence charges per page, with different rates for prebuilt versus custom models. Vision pricing is transaction-based and varies by operation type. Free tiers support development, while volume commitments offer discounts for large-scale deployments.

These services drive transformative business processes across industries. Insurance companies automate claims processing by extracting data from accident photos and medical forms. Health care organizations digitize patient records and extract clinical information. Manufacturing deploys Vision for quality inspection and defect detection. Retail applications span visual search, inventory management, and receipt processing. Financial institutions accelerate loan processing through automated document extraction. The pattern is consistent: unstructured visual information becomes structured data, ready for the kind of semantic processing that drives modern business applications.

11.8 Architectural Patterns for Conversational AI

The move to conversational IVR marks a genuine paradigm shift—one I have watched unfold over many years. At FIS, I led engineering efforts to integrate IVR systems, chatbots, and virtual assistants using the INTELLIFM architecture and modern Microsoft technologies, including Nuance. The challenge was bridging silos: telephony from one vendor, speech processing from another, and business logic buried in legacy systems that predated both. We succeeded, but only through custom integration at every layer. Today, Azure offers a unified platform where these components connect through standardized APIs and managed services. Transitioning from linear phone trees to systems that understand natural speech still requires a multilayered architecture, but those layers now compose reliably at enterprise scale.

The foundational element is the telephony integration layer, which manages voice connectivity via Session Initiation Protocol trunking, either through Azure Communication Services or via certified providers. These providers are third-party vendors approved for compatibility and regulatory compliance. The integration layer delivers high-quality audio transmission and includes essential features, such as WebRTC support for browser-based calling. It also supports call recording with built-in privacy controls suitable for compliance-sensitive environments.

The sophisticated speech processing pipeline follows immediately, capitalizing on Azure AI Speech's low-latency capabilities to achieve impeccable audio quality and accurate recognition. It employs acoustic echo cancellation to eliminate feedback and high-precision voice activity detection to filter out the background noise. The system uses highly tuned endpointing to accurately determine when a user has completed their utterance. Taken together, these features provide barge-in functionality, so users can interrupt system prompts naturally.

The cognitive layer centers on the NLU component, using Azure Language for advanced parsing. This includes recognizing multiple user intents to handle compound requests simultaneously. For example, it can process "I need to check my balance and also change my personal identification number (PIN)" as two distinct actions. The system resolves ambiguous time and date expressions into standard formats and maintains conversation context across multiple exchanges.

The NLU layer acts as a translator, passing highly structured requests to the business logic integration layer. This layer connects the conversational interface to core enterprise systems through sophisticated API orchestration. It manages sequential actions such as checking the account balance before processing transfers. Robust transaction management preserves data integrity during updates. A workflow engine coordinates complex multistep processes. This layer is frequently augmented by a high-speed in-memory cache, often implemented with Azure Cache for Redis. The cache stores frequently accessed customer data markers and policy information. This reduces latency and lowers the transactional load on core legacy database systems. Table 11-2 provides a framework for selecting among these patterns, comparing architectural complexity, performance characteristics, cost profiles, and optimal use cases.

Table 11-2. *Comparison of AI implementation patterns, showing architectural complexity, performance characteristics, cost profiles, and optimal use cases. Selection depends on specific requirements for latency, scale, and budget constraints.*

Pattern	Architecture Complexity	Latency	Cost Profile	Best For	Typical Response Time
Direct API	Low—single service calls	Network + service overhead (model dependent)	Low—pay per use	Simple queries, prototypes	Subsecond intervals to seconds
Cached response	Medium—Redis/memory layer	Very low (cache lookup)	Medium—cache infrastructure	Repeated queries, FAQs	Near real time for cached answers
Orchestrated	High—multiple services	Network + orchestration + model computation	High—multiple API calls	Complex workflows	Seconds (workflows that span multiple services)
Hybrid local/ cloud	High—edge + cloud	Low for edge inference; cloud path adds latency	High—infrastructure costs	Latency-sensitive apps	Milliseconds (local) to seconds (cloud)
Batch processing	Medium—queue-based	N/A—async	Low—bulk pricing	Large-scale analysis	Minutes to hours
Streaming	High—event-driven	First update in subsecond range and then continuous	Medium—continuous processing	Real-time monitoring	Continuous (incremental output)

11.8.1 Service Integration and Orchestration

While each Azure AI Service offers powerful capabilities individually, their true potential emerges when they work together. Think of them as instruments in an orchestra—each has its unique sound, but the symphony comes from their coordination. The following sections explore how these services connect and collaborate to create comprehensive conversational AI solutions.

11.8.2 How the Services Connect

Foundry Tools (formerly Azure AI Services) share a common foundation. They all operate within the same Azure environment, use common security controls, and communicate through standardized formats. This shared foundation simplifies integration compared with cross-platform composition, although meaningful engineering effort is still required.

Consider a typical customer service call. A customer speaks a request, and Azure Speech captures the audio and converts it to text. Azure Language analyzes the text to understand the customer's intent. Azure OpenAI Service then generates an intelligent response based on that understanding, which Azure Speech converts back into natural-sounding audio. The entire flow typically completes within a few seconds under normal conditions, though actual latency varies considerably depending on model selection, token count, region, concurrency, cold-start behavior, and response length. Each service passes data to the next in sequence.

The services communicate using standard JSON formats, which reduces format conversion overhead. Even so, composition requires deliberate engineering. Payloads often need to be shaped to match each service's expected input structure, and retry logic must address transient failures at each integration point. Latency accumulates across service boundaries, and each service imposes its own rate limits, token quotas, and timeout thresholds. Teams that treat service composition as a simple configuration task rather than an engineering problem often encounter these constraints in production.

11.8.3 Orchestration Patterns

Three primary patterns govern how services work together in conversational AI implementations.

Sequential processing is the most common pattern, in which services execute in order, with each completing before the next begins. When a customer states, "I need to check my balance and transfer $50 to checking," Azure Speech first transcribes this utterance. Azure Language then identifies two intents: balance inquiry and transfer request. Azure OpenAI Service processes each intent sequentially, maintaining a logical flow. This pattern makes debugging straightforward and maintains clear transaction boundaries.

Parallel processing accelerates complex tasks by running multiple services simultaneously. While Azure Speech transcribes a customer's question, Azure AI Vision can simultaneously analyze their uploaded insurance claim form. Both results merge to provide a comprehensive response. This pattern substantially reduces the total processing time for multimodal interactions, thereby improving the user experience by delivering faster responses.

Event-driven processing creates reactive intelligence, with each service responding to events from other services. When a customer uploads a document, Azure AI Document Intelligence is triggered to perform extraction. The extracted data is automatically sent to Azure Language for validation. If anomalies are detected, Azure OpenAI Service generates clarifying questions. This creates a dynamic, responsive system that adapts to user input in real time.

11.8.4 The Orchestration Layer

Several Azure services can be used alongside Foundry Tools to orchestrate conversational AI workflows. Azure Logic Apps offers a visual designer for connecting services. Developers can place Azure Speech onto the canvas, connect it to Azure Language, and then link both to Azure OpenAI Service. The resulting flow becomes the running application, making the conversational logic easier to understand and modify.

For more complex scenarios, Azure Functions provides programmatic control. A single function can manage the entire conversation flow. It receives audio input, calls Azure Speech for transcription, processes the text through Azure Language, generates responses via Azure OpenAI Service, and returns synthesized speech. The function maintains context, handles errors, and facilitates smooth interaction throughout the conversation.

Semantic Kernel remains a flexible SDK for application-level orchestration and AI integration. It allows developers to expose enterprise functions as callable tools and coordinate workflows that combine model calls with deterministic business logic. For newer applications that require richer agent patterns, long-running workflows, or more advanced multiagent orchestration, Microsoft now positions Microsoft Agent Framework as the direct successor to Semantic Kernel and AutoGen, an earlier open source multiagent framework from Microsoft Research. Foundry Agent Service complements this stack by providing a managed Azure runtime for deploying and operating agents at enterprise scale.

State management ties the architecture together. Azure Cache for Redis stores conversation context markers, including previous intents, pending actions, and collected information. This shared memory allows services to work cohesively rather than operate in isolation. When Azure OpenAI Service generates a response, it can reference the entire conversation history represented by these context markers, not just the current utterance.

These patterns are sound in principle, but orchestration introduces operational challenges that require deliberate engineering. Transient failures at any service boundary require retry logic with appropriate backoff strategies. Operations that may be retried, such as initiating a payment or sending a notification, must also be designed for idempotency so that duplicate calls do not create unintended side effects.

Partial failures, in which one service succeeds while another fails, require compensation logic to reverse, isolate, or otherwise handle incomplete work rather than leaving the system in an inconsistent state. Teams that do not address these concerns during design usually encounter them later under production load.

11.8.5 Security and Data Flow

The security of AI applications is a shared responsibility. Although the platform provides strong infrastructure controls, system integrity depends on how those controls are configured to protect data as it moves through the architecture.

Shared Responsibility and Infrastructure Controls

Securing AI applications built on Foundry Tools follows a shared responsibility model. The platform provides core infrastructure controls, including encrypted transport, managed identity support, Azure Key Vault integration, RBAC, and audit logging. However, the implementer is responsible for making sure these controls are enabled and properly configured.

Identity and Secrets Management

To eliminate the risk of embedded credentials, managed identities should be used for all service-to-service authentication. When keys are strictly required, they should be stored in Key Vault and rotated automatically. RBAC policies should also be limited to the minimum permissions required. Granting broad access for convenience creates unnecessary exposure across the data flow.

Data Classification and Protection

Data classification should guide how information moves between services. Each component should receive only the data required for its function. Sensitive data, such as PII, should be masked or encrypted before being passed between services. This adds protection even if transport-layer safeguards are compromised.

Egress, Governance, and Auditability

Egress to external systems should be treated as a deliberate architectural decision. Policy-controlled endpoints and network segmentation reduce the risk of unintended data exposure. Audit logs provide visibility, but they must also be actively configured and monitored in line with organizational governance requirements. Teams that treat these controls as defaults rather than design decisions often discover the gaps only during audits or security incidents.

11.8.6 Practical Integration Example

A health care virtual assistant demonstrates this integration in day-to-day use. A patient calls to schedule an appointment, and their voice enters through Azure Communication Services. Azure Speech transcribes their request: "I need to see a cardiologist next week."

Azure Language extracts the key information, including the specialty requirement (cardiology) and timeframe (next week). It also identifies missing information, such as specific date or time preferences.

Azure OpenAI Service accesses the appointment system through secure APIs, finds available slots, and generates a natural response: "I can schedule you with Dr. Smith on Wednesday at 2 PM or Friday at 10 AM. Which works better?"

Azure Speech synthesizes this response in a warm, professional voice configured for health care settings. The entire interaction feels natural and instantaneous, though four services collaborated behind the scenes to deliver the result.

If the patient mentions they have referral documents, Azure AI Document Intelligence automatically extracts the referral details while the conversation continues. The services work harmoniously, creating an experience that feels like speaking with a knowledgeable human assistant who can handle multiple tasks simultaneously.

11.8.7 Cost and Performance Optimization

Integration requires thoughtful optimization to manage both cost and performance effectively. Each service call incurs cost and adds latency to the overall response time. Intelligent caching prevents redundant calls—if Azure Language has already analyzed a phrase, the result is cached for reuse. Batch processing groups multiple operations when real-time response is not critical, reducing per-transaction costs.

Service proximity materially impacts performance. Deploying all services in the same Azure region minimizes network latency between components. Using Azure's backbone network helps maintain consistent performance regardless of external internet conditions. Premium tiers provide dedicated capacity for predictable performance under load, which is essential for high-volume contact centers.

Systematic monitoring spans all services via Azure Application Insights, providing end-to-end visibility from speech input to output. Every service interaction is tracked, and bottlenecks become immediately visible through detailed metrics. Performance data guides optimization efforts, helping identify which services need scaling or caching improvements.

This integrated approach assembles individual AI services into complete conversational solutions. The orchestration complexity is managed by Azure's platform. Users experience intelligent interaction that feels natural and responsive. That is the power of proper service integration and orchestration—complex technology working together to create simple, compelling user experiences.

11.9 Advanced Chatbot Development Patterns

Modern conversational AI systems require sophisticated architectural patterns that combine multiple approaches to achieve enterprise-grade performance and reliability. These patterns have evolved over decades of NLP experience, progressing from simple rule-based systems to today's hybrid architectures that harness the full power of Azure AI Services.

11.9.1 The Hybrid Architecture Pattern

The hybrid architecture pattern combines deterministic rule-based logic with AI flexibility to create resilient conversational systems. This approach addresses a fundamental challenge in enterprise chatbots: maintaining absolute accuracy for critical operations while providing natural, flexible interactions for general queries. This hybrid approach reflects a lesson I learned building INTELLIFM: some decisions must be deterministic. An expert system that occasionally produced hallucinations in financial calculations would have been unusable. The same principle applies today—AI enhances the conversation, but rules govern the transaction.

Rule-based components handle sensitive, high-stakes decisions where deterministic outcomes are essential. Financial transactions require exact precision—funds must be transferred exactly as specified, without interpretation. Compliance checks demand consistent application of regulations without variation. Medical dosage calculations need absolute accuracy without the possibility of hallucination. These scenarios use traditional procedural code to produce predictable results.

AI components handle NLU and general informational queries, thereby enhancing the user experience. Azure Language interprets user intent from natural speech patterns and handles variations in how people express the same request. Azure OpenAI Service generates contextually appropriate responses to open-ended questions, providing detailed explanations and recommendations. Azure Speech powers natural voice interactions that adapt to speaking styles and accents.

The integration between these components requires careful orchestration. Azure Logic Apps or Azure Functions coordinates the flow, determining when to invoke AI models versus when to apply business rules. A request such as "transfer $500 to my savings" flows through AI-based intent recognition, rule-based transaction validation, and AI-generated confirmation. Thus, it combines natural interaction with deterministic safety checks.

11.9.2 The Multimodel Ensemble Pattern

The multimodel ensemble pattern uses multiple AI models in parallel, selecting the optimal response based on confidence scores and contextual information. This approach substantially enhances accuracy and coverage compared with single-model systems.

The pattern typically combines three or more specialized components. A domain-specific intent model or classifier can handle high-precision transactional requests. A retrieval layer grounded in enterprise content can answer FAQ and policy queries. Azure OpenAI Service or other Foundry-hosted models can address complex, open-ended requests that require reasoning and synthesis. In environments that already use CLU or custom question answering, those components can remain part of the ensemble during the migration window, but they should no longer be treated as the default architecture for new projects. Specialized models can handle domain-specific tasks, such as medical terminology or legal language.

An intelligent arbiter coordinates these models, which are implemented using Azure Functions, Azure Machine Learning, or another orchestration layer. The arbiter sends each user query to the relevant models or retrieval components, collects responses and confidence signals, and evaluates them against business rules and threshold criteria. For a routine transactional request, a domain-specific classifier or structured workflow may return a high-confidence result, triggering its response. For a more complex troubleshooting query, the OpenAI model's broader reasoning and synthesis may make it the better choice, even when confidence is expressed less explicitly.

Azure OpenAI Service's function-calling capability provides an elegant implementation of the arbiter. The service can be configured with function definitions for each specialized model, allowing it to intelligently route queries. For example, when configured with functions for "check_balance", "dispute_transaction", and "general_inquiry", Azure OpenAI automatically determines which function to invoke based on the user's request, effectively serving as a semantic router while maintaining conversation context.

The arbiter also handles edge cases where multiple models return high confidence. It may combine responses, request clarification, or escalate to human agents. Azure Application Insights tracks model performance over time, identifying patterns where specific models excel or struggle. This data drives continuous improvement through retraining and threshold adjustments.

11.9.3 Context-Aware Conversation Management

Effective conversational AI requires sophisticated memory management—a challenge I confronted in INTELLIFM, where each user response had to be stored in a database so the system could resume a Q&A session without losing context. That approach worked reliably and provided the precision required in legal, financial, and health care applications. The trade-off, however, was meaningful engineering effort: every branch, dependency, and exception required explicit encoding, and context was preserved structurally rather than interpreted semantically.

Modern architectures within Microsoft Foundry shift much of this burden to the orchestration layer. That layer manages context explicitly by passing conversation history, retrieved state, and relevant prior interactions into each model request. The model itself remains stateless, processing only what the application provides in the current invocation. The improvement lies not in any inherent memory within the model, but in the platform's ability to store, retrieve, and organize context more efficiently than the handcrafted approaches required by earlier systems.

Short-term memory functions as a rolling buffer that retains recent conversational turns. Implemented using a low-latency cache (such as Azure Cache for Redis), it provides fast access to context within the current session. This memory primarily resolves anaphoric references—when users say "it," "that," or "the same one"—by maintaining entity chains. If a customer inquires about mortgage options and then asks, "What documents do I need for it?" short-term memory links "it" back to the mortgage discussion. The buffer is scoped to the session and cleared at its end, supporting privacy by default.

Long-term memory persists across conversations, storing customer history, preferences, and interaction patterns. Azure Cosmos DB provides globally distributed storage with configurable consistency levels, selected to balance correctness, latency, and availability. Each customer profile includes interaction history, stated preferences, successful query patterns, and personalization data. When customers return after weeks, the system remembers their previous inquiries, account details, and communication preferences. Privacy controls allow customers to view and delete their stored information.

Episodic memory tracks the specific state of ongoing tasks within a conversation. Stored in Azure Table Storage or Cosmos DB, it maintains transaction details, progress of multistep processes, and pending actions. During a wire transfer, episodic memory stores the source account, destination, amount, and the completed verification steps. If the conversation is interrupted, the system can resume exactly where it left off. This memory expires when the task completes or a timeout occurs.

Semantic memory contains persistent domain knowledge, business rules, and organizational policies. Azure AI Search indexes this information for rapid retrieval. It includes product specifications, pricing rules, compliance requirements, and procedural workflows. Unlike other memory types, semantic memory remains consistent across all conversations and customers. Updates to policies or procedures propagate immediately to all active conversations.

Privacy compliance requires careful consideration across all memory layers. Under GDPR and similar regulations, any memory that contains personal data must be tied to a defined purpose and processed on a valid, lawful basis. It must also be limited in scope and retention, protected through appropriate technical and organizational safeguards, and erased or anonymized when it is no longer needed or when deletion rights apply. Azure's built-in compliance features, including encryption at rest, audit logs, and data residency controls, support regulatory compliance while maintaining data confidentiality.

11.9.4 Implementation Architecture

These patterns integrate through a layered architecture built on Azure and Microsoft agent technologies. The presentation layer uses Copilot Studio, the Microsoft 365 Agents SDK, or custom channel applications to manage user interactions across channels. The orchestration layer, implemented through Azure Functions, Logic Apps, Microsoft Agent Framework, or Foundry Agent Service, coordinates pattern execution and service calls. The AI layer combines Azure Language, Azure OpenAI Service, and other Foundry-hosted models. The memory layer uses Redis, Cosmos DB, and Azure AI Search to support different storage and retrieval needs. The monitoring layer uses Application Insights and Azure Monitor to track performance, errors, and user outcomes.

Azure AI Content Safety integrates across all pattern implementations to safeguard the responsible deployment of AI. It automatically filters harmful content in both user inputs and system responses, checking for violence, self-harm, sexual content, and hate speech. This filtering occurs transparently within the conversation flow, with configurable thresholds that balance safety and legitimate business communications.

11.9.5 Practical Implementation Example

Consider a banking chatbot handling a complex customer interaction. The customer says, "I noticed an unusual charge on my statement yesterday."

Short-term memory is activated to track the "unusual charge" as the topic of conversation. Azure Language identifies the intent as "dispute transaction" with high confidence. The hybrid architecture employs AI to handle NLU and rules governing the dispute process. The multimodel ensemble activates multiple services: a domain-specific intent model identifies the specific transaction dispute intent, the knowledge base retrieves dispute procedures, and Azure OpenAI Service generates empathetic responses.

The customer continues: "It was for $847 at a store I've never heard of."

Episodic memory stores the amount and merchant details. The system asks clarifying questions while semantic memory retrieves dispute policies. Long-term memory checks if this customer has a history of previous disputes. The conversation continues as the system gathers the required information while maintaining context.

If the customer later says, "Actually, can we handle that tomorrow? I need to check my mortgage payment first," episodic memory preserves the dispute state while the customer switches contexts. The system seamlessly transitions to mortgage inquiries and can return to the dispute upon request.

11.9.6 Performance and Optimization Considerations

These advanced patterns require careful optimization to maintain responsiveness. Parallel model execution in the ensemble pattern adds latency that varies with model selection and infrastructure. This overhead can be mitigated through aggressive caching and model warm-up strategies. Memory operations benefit from careful optimization. Redis provides access to active context in under a millisecond, and Cosmos DB provides distributed, long-term storage.

Cost management involves balancing model calls with cached responses. The ensemble pattern increases API costs. Therefore, adjusting confidence thresholds helps prevent unnecessary model invocations. Memory storage costs scale with the user base, necessitating retention policies and data life-cycle management.

These patterns transform simple chatbots into sophisticated conversational agents capable of handling complex, multiturn interactions while maintaining context and accuracy. The combination of hybrid architectures, ensemble models, and advanced memory systems creates AI assistants that feel truly intelligent and helpful.

11.10 Virtual Assistant Architecture

Virtual assistants represent the pinnacle of conversational AI—combining speech, language understanding, orchestration, and integration into a unified experience. My teams built unified conversational AI systems at FIS that anticipated many of these patterns. Today, Microsoft's current stack—Copilot Studio, the Microsoft 365 Agents SDK, Microsoft Agent Framework, and Foundry Agent Service—supports these capabilities within a more standardized enterprise architecture, with much of the custom plumbing required by earlier implementations substantially reduced.

11.10.1 Core Architectural Components

The tooling for building virtual assistants has evolved substantially. The Bot Framework SDK and Bot Framework Emulator, which underpinned earlier generations of Azure bot development, have been archived and are no longer maintained. Microsoft's current stack more clearly separates low-code and pro-code paths. Copilot Studio provides a graphical environment for designing agents and flows. The Microsoft 365 Agents SDK serves as the modern pro-code path for enterprise agent development and migration from legacy Bot Framework solutions. Foundry Agent Service provides a managed Azure platform for building, deploying, and scaling agents. Microsoft Agent Framework adds a modern orchestration layer for single-agent and multiagent execution patterns. Together, these tools support a current architecture centered on tools, models, grounding, state, and policy-driven orchestration rather than on legacy dialog trees and skill registries.

The resulting architecture still follows a layered design optimized for flexibility and scalability. The *channel layer* connects to communication platforms such as Teams, web chat, short message service (SMS), email, and telephony via appropriate clients and services, including Azure Communication Services for voice. The *orchestration layer* manages tool invocation, state, and workflow execution. The *intelligence layer* combines models, retrieval, and cognitive services. The *integration layer* securely connects the assistant to enterprise systems via APIs, event buses, and governed data sources.

11.10.2 The Orchestration Engine

The orchestration layer governs the assistant's interaction flow, deciding how tools and capabilities are used in response to the current context and the user's intent.

In modern agentic architectures, this coordination is often model-driven rather than controlled by a separate skill router or intent classifier. For example, when a user says, "I need help with my mortgage and want to check my savings balance," the model can evaluate the available tools—such as a mortgage assistance function and an account inquiry API—and decide which ones to call, in what order, and with what parameters.

Enabled by function-calling and tool use mechanisms in models such as those available through Azure OpenAI Service, this approach replaces the static skill registries and confidence-based routing of earlier frameworks with reasoning that adapts to context without requiring explicit routing rules. In Foundry Agent Service, the orchestration layer supports this model-driven pattern through stateful agent execution, tool registration, and multiturn conversation management. This allows teams to focus on defining tools and interfaces rather than building the routing logic that connects them.

The *context manager* maintains conversation state across sessions, channels, and devices. Built on Azure Cosmos DB for global distribution and Redis Cache for performance, it tracks user identity, conversation history, preferences, and in-progress transactions. When a customer starts a conversation on web chat and then continues via voice on their phone, the context manager maintains continuity. It preserves partial inputs, maintains authentication state, and remembers user preferences across all touchpoints.

In current architectures, structured workflows still exist, but they are typically implemented via tool schemas, workflow engines, policy checks, and application state rather than hard-coded dialog trees. The orchestration layer determines when a request can be handled through direct tool invocation, when it requires retrieval from enterprise knowledge, and when it should fall back to a more guided workflow for data collection or confirmation.

Corrections, interruptions, and topic shifts are handled through state tracking and model-driven replanning. When a user changes direction midstream, the orchestration layer preserves the relevant task state, updates the active context, and either resumes the interrupted workflow later or discards it, depending on business policy. This produces the same user-facing effect that earlier dialog frameworks tried to achieve, but through a more flexible combination of state, tools, and runtime policy.

11.10.3 Intelligence Services Integration

The orchestration layer communicates with Foundry Tools through unified APIs and SDKs, using them to perform actions and retrieve information required for a given interaction.

Azure OpenAI Service provides the reasoning, language generation, and decision support capabilities of the assistant. The orchestration layer uses function calling to invoke specific tools while maintaining conversation context through structured prompts. For open-ended questions or situations that require reasoning, the assistant relies on GPT models to generate responses. This integration also involves token management to control cost, prompt design to improve consistency, and content filtering to support safety.

In enterprise virtual assistant deployments, a knowledge retrieval layer is equally important. Rather than relying only on the model's built-in knowledge, most production systems ground responses in verified organizational content through RAG.

Foundry IQ provides a managed knowledge layer for this purpose, while Azure AI Search supplies the underlying indexing and retrieval infrastructure. Together, they can index documents, FAQs, product catalogs, and policy content, supporting vector and hybrid search across structured and unstructured sources. When a user asks a question, the retrieval pipeline identifies the most relevant content and passes it to the model as grounding context, reducing hallucinations and helping responses reflect current, organization-specific information.

A health care IVR system, for example, can draw on a curated knowledge base of clinical FAQs and policy documents rather than generate answers from the model alone. In this architecture, the retrieval layer sits between the orchestration layer and the model. Its quality—especially the accuracy of indexed content, the freshness of the knowledge base, and the relevance of retrieved chunks—directly affects the reliability of the assistant's responses.

Azure Language continues to provide text analytics and existing conversational capabilities in many systems. It can support entity extraction, sentiment analysis, and certain legacy conversational patterns, although Microsoft now recommends Foundry models for new CLU and custom question answering projects. In practice, Azure Language remains useful where organizations already depend on it, while newer agent architectures increasingly consolidate orchestration and reasoning around Foundry models and retrieval layers.

Azure Speech powers natural voice interactions with real-time transcription and synthesis. The orchestrator manages speech sessions, handles interruptions via barge-in detection, and coordinates turn-taking in conversations. Custom neural voices preserve brand consistency, while speech translation provides multilingual support.

Azure AI Document Intelligence and Vision process uploaded documents and images within conversations. When users share insurance claims, invoices, or identification documents, the orchestrator coordinates the extraction, validation, and integration of visual data with conversational context. This handles scenarios such as "I uploaded my receipt. Can you process the return?" in which visual and conversational modalities merge.

11.10.4 Channel Management and Deployment

Virtual assistants need to operate consistently across channels while adapting to the constraints of each one. In current Microsoft architectures, channel integration is handled through Copilot Studio, the Microsoft 365 Agents SDK, custom web and mobile clients, and services such as Azure Communication Services for voice and telephony scenarios. The design challenge is no longer simply exposing a bot on multiple endpoints; it is maintaining consistent grounding, identity, policy enforcement, and user experience across those endpoints.

Authentication flows still need to adapt to channel capabilities through Microsoft Entra External ID and related identity patterns. Single sign-on can work smoothly in Teams and enterprise applications, while web and voice channels require different token, session, or verification models. Proactive messaging remains important for time-sensitive scenarios, but it must respect channel rules, user preferences, and regulatory limits on outbound communication.

11.10.5 State Management Architecture

Effective state management preserves context across complex, long-running interactions in virtual assistants.

The conversation state tracks the immediate dialog context, including the current turn, active dialogs, and collected values. Stored in Azure Cache for Redis with automatic expiration, it provides millisecond access for real-time interactions. The state includes partial inputs, validation results, and navigation history within the current session.

User state persists across conversations, maintaining preferences, history, and personalization data. As mentioned earlier, Azure Cosmos DB provides globally distributed storage with configurable consistency levels, selected to balance correctness, latency, and availability. Each user profile includes interaction patterns, communication preferences, completed transactions, and learned behaviors that improve over time.

Configuration state stores agent definitions, tool registrations, policy settings, runtime parameters, and deployment metadata. Depending on the implementation, this state may live in a version-controlled configuration, managed service metadata, blob storage, or platform-level agent definitions. The important architectural point is that runtime behavior should be governed through explicit configuration and policy rather than hidden application logic.

The private conversation state provides a secure way to handle sensitive information. Encrypted with keys managed in Azure Key Vault, it stores payment details, PII, and health data in a restricted data store (for example, Azure SQL Database or Azure Cosmos DB) with tightly scoped access controls. The orchestrator treats this data as highly sensitive. It is excluded from application logs, not cached in shared stores, and transmitted only through approved, encrypted channels and private connectivity, as required.

11.10.6 Practical Implementation Example

Consider a health care virtual assistant deployed across multiple channels, demonstrating the complete architecture in action.

A patient initiates contact through the hospital's web portal, saying, "I need to schedule a follow-up for my surgery and update my insurance information." The orchestration layer receives the request, recognizes that it contains two tasks, and evaluates the available tools: appointment scheduling, insurance verification, document extraction, and knowledge retrieval. Azure Language or a Foundry-hosted model extracts the key entities, while the runtime preserves both tasks in state.

The agent first retrieves the patient's surgical history through secure APIs and proposes available follow-up appointments. When the patient says, "Actually, wait. I need to check if my new insurance covers Dr. Johnson first," the orchestration layer updates the active context, pauses the scheduling workflow, and invokes the insurance verification tools instead. If the patient uploads an insurance card, Azure AI Document Intelligence extracts the relevant information, which is then validated against eligibility systems.

Once coverage is confirmed, the orchestration layer returns to the earlier scheduling task, presents the appointment options again, and completes the booking. From the patient's perspective, the conversation feels continuous. Architecturally, the experience depends on state preservation, tool invocation, retrieval grounding, and policy-driven orchestration rather than on a fixed dialog tree.

11.10.7 Performance Optimization Strategies

Virtual assistants require careful optimization to maintain responsiveness across high-volume deployments.

Skill parallelization reduces latency when multiple operations can execute simultaneously. While one skill checks appointment availability, another retrieves patient history. Results merge for complete responses. Azure Durable Functions orchestrates these parallel executions with automatic retry and timeout handling.

Response streaming improves perceived performance for long-running operations. The assistant provides incremental updates—"Checking your coverage ... Verifying network status ... Confirmed, Dr. Johnson is in-network,"—maintaining engagement during processing. Azure SignalR Service delivers real-time streaming across all channels.

Caching strategies balance freshness with performance. Frequently accessed data, like provider directories, is cached in Redis with a sliding expiration. User preferences are cached locally and synchronized periodically. Dynamic content, such as appointment slots, cannot be cached but benefits from connection pooling and query optimization.

11.10.8 Monitoring and Analytics

With strong observability in place, virtual assistants can sustain high quality and keep improving over time.

Azure Application Insights provides end-to-end conversation tracking. Every interaction generates correlated telemetry showing channel entry, skill invocation, service calls, and response generation. Performance metrics identify bottlenecks while conversation analytics reveal user behavior patterns.

Conversation analytics can be derived from Application Insights telemetry and custom events, including metrics such as completion rates, abandonment points, skill usage, and error frequency. Custom events capture business metrics, such as scheduled appointments or processed claims. These insights drive continuous improvement by identifying points of confusion and optimization opportunities.

Azure Monitor alerts on operational issues, including service failures, performance degradation, or unusual patterns. Automated responses can scale resources, restart services, or route requests to human agents as needed.

11.10.9 Security and Compliance Considerations

Virtual assistants need to maintain security across all architectural layers while ensuring compliance with relevant regulations.

Channel security requires the use of current TLS standards for all communications, with certificate pinning for sensitive channels. OAuth 2.0 and OpenID Connect provide secure authentication, including token refresh and revocation. Channel-specific security features, such as Teams' compliance boundaries, are fully supported.

Data protection keeps sensitive information secure throughout processing. Redacting conversation logs to remove PII protects both the user and the organization. Where recordings are required, encrypt them with customer-managed keys. Retention and purge policies, defined explicitly and enforced through storage life-cycle controls, complete the data protection picture. Azure Purview can be used to classify and govern the data sources and storage locations associated with an assistant, including logs and conversation transcripts where they are retained. Coverage depends on the data ingested, where it is stored, and the governance policies applied.

Compliance features support regulations across health care, financial services, and privacy, including HIPAA, PCI DSS, and GDPR. Audit logs capture all actions for regulatory review. Data residency controls ensure geographic compliance, and consent management tracks user permissions for data use.

This architecture elevates virtual assistants from simple conversational interfaces into sophisticated business automation platforms. The combination of intelligent orchestration, reliable service integration, and rigorous state management creates assistants that handle complex, multistep processes while maintaining natural, context-aware conversations across all channels. The architecture is designed to scale from small deployments to high-concurrency workloads, subject to capacity planning and appropriate service tier selection, while supporting the security, performance, and reliability expectations of production systems.

11.11 Implementation Best Practices

Successful deployment of Azure AI Services requires rigorous adherence to proven practices that build security, reliability, and maintainability. Architecture and algorithms receive attention, but implementation details determine whether systems survive deployment to production.

I learned this through incidents that taught more than any design document: credential leaks from hard-coded secrets, cascading failures from missing circuit breakers, and compliance findings from inadequate audit trails. The practices outlined here reflect what matters most when systems need to operate under regulatory scrutiny—lessons learned over decades of enterprise deployments. These practices, drawn from enterprise implementation patterns, form the foundation for production-ready conversational AI systems. While architectural patterns define how services connect, implementation practices determine whether those connections remain secure, stable, and sustainable over time.

11.11.1 Security and Compliance Framework

Conversational AI systems require a rigorous security framework because these interactions often involve sensitive personal, financial, and proprietary information. Deployments follow zero-trust principles. No user, device, or service is trusted by default, even within the network perimeter.

Data protection standards are typically aligned with organizational policy and applicable compliance requirements. Azure services support encryption at rest and in transit using industry-standard cryptography, while configuration choices determine how those controls apply in a given deployment. Logging and monitoring pipelines often incorporate data masking and PII redaction before storage to reduce the risk of inadvertent exposure of sensitive information.

Access control through Microsoft Entra ID and RBAC enforces the principle of least privilege. Service principals with managed identities eliminate the need for embedded credentials in code. These identities automatically authenticate Azure resources with other services, removing the need for developers to manage connection strings or secrets. This approach reduces the risk of credential leakage and simplifies key rotation.

Network security can be strengthened by using private endpoints, which route traffic to AI services via private IP addresses within the organization's virtual network rather than over the public internet—a configuration often required in regulated industries. Network security groups and Azure Firewall provide additional defense by controlling traffic flow between services. Security and operational logs can be ingested into Microsoft Sentinel for centralized security information and event management (SIEM), where they can be correlated and used for response across the environment.

11.11.2 Error Handling and Resilience Patterns

Production conversational AI systems that gracefully handle the inevitable failures in distributed systems prove far more resilient. Robust error handling prevents single-point failures from cascading into system-wide outages.

Retry logic with exponential backoff handles transient failures in AI service calls. When Azure OpenAI Service experiences temporary throttling, the system progressively delays retries to avoid overwhelming the service. Azure SDK retry policies are configured automatically, whereas custom implementations require careful tuning. Maximum retry attempts, base delay intervals, and maximum delay caps should be carefully balanced to offer a positive user experience and protect the service.

Circuit breaker patterns prevent repeated calls to failing services. After detecting multiple failures, the circuit breaker opens, causing subsequent calls to fail immediately without attempting the remote service. This protects both the failing service and the calling application. APIM implements circuit breakers at the gateway level, while the Polly library provides an application-level implementation for.NET applications.

Fallback strategies help conversations continue during service disruptions. When Azure OpenAI Service is unavailable, systems may shift to Azure Language for basic intent handling. When speech services fail, interaction can continue through text. These graceful degradations preserve user engagement while services recover. Fallback responses work best when they acknowledge limitations plainly, such as "I am having trouble with advanced features right now, but I can still help with basic requests."

Timeout management prevents hanging requests from blocking the flow of conversation. In well-designed systems, each service call has explicit timeouts matched to the operation it performs. Speech transcription often allows up to 30 seconds for long utterances, whereas simple entity extraction typically times out after about 2 seconds. Timeout values are tuned using observed performance metrics rather than assumptions.

11.11.3 Development Workflow and DevOps Integration

Efficient development workflows accelerate delivery while maintaining quality. IaC principles provide reproducible deployments across environments.

Azure Resource Manager templates or Terraform defines all infrastructure components declaratively. Every AI service configuration, network setting, and security policy exists in version-controlled templates. This approach produces consistent deployments, simplifies disaster recovery, and provides audit trails for compliance.

Template parameterization allows environment-specific values while maintaining configuration consistency.

Continuous integration pipelines validate changes before deployment. Azure DevOps or GitHub Actions run automated tests on every commit. Pipeline stages include syntax validation, security scanning, and configuration verification. AI-specific validations include prompt injection testing, response quality checks, and performance benchmarking. Failed validations block deployment, preventing degraded experiences from reaching production.

Environment progression follows strict promotion paths. Development environments allow rapid experimentation with relaxed security. Staging environments mirror production configurations for realistic testing. Production deployments require approval gates and automated rollback capabilities. Blue-green deployments allow instant rollback if issues emerge after deployment.

Feature flags allow the rollout of capabilities without requiring code changes. Azure App Configuration centrally manages flags, facilitating the gradual rollout of new AI features. A newly integrated model may initially serve only 5% of users, with that share increasing as confidence grows. Feature flags also provide instant kill switches if issues arise, disabling problematic features without requiring a full redeployment.

11.11.4 Monitoring and Observability Patterns

End-to-end observability helps teams understand system behavior and user experience. Effective monitoring spans both technical metrics and business outcomes.

Structured logging captures every notable event with consistent formatting. Each log entry includes correlation IDs that trace requests across services. When a user query flows through speech recognition, language understanding, and response generation, correlation IDs link all related logs. Azure Application Insights automatically correlates distributed traces, while custom instrumentation adds business-specific context.

Custom metrics track AI-specific performance indicators. Response relevance scores, conversation completion rates, and escalation frequency provide insight beyond standard latency metrics. Token consumption per conversation type drives cost optimization. Model confidence distributions reveal when retraining might improve performance. These metrics feed dashboards that provide real-time visibility into system health and user satisfaction.

Alerting strategies strike a balance between responsiveness and noise reduction. Critical alerts for service failures require immediate response. Warning alerts for degraded performance trigger investigation during business hours. Informational alerts track trends without requiring action. Alert fatigue destroys team effectiveness. The most effective alerting strategies keep alerts actionable and necessary.

Cost tracking at granular levels prevents budget surprises. Tags on every resource support cost allocation by department, application, or feature. Azure Cost Management tracks spending trends and forecasts monthly costs. Budgets with alerts prevent runaway consumption. Regular cost reviews identify optimization opportunities, such as moving to reserved capacity or adjusting model selection.

11.11.5 Prompt Engineering and Content Management

Prompt management is crucial for maintaining consistent, high-quality AI responses while the team can iterate rapidly.

Prompt templates separate static structure from dynamic content. Base prompts define personality, constraints, and response format. Variable injection adds user context, conversation history, and retrieved knowledge. This separation allows prompt updates without code changes. Azure App Configuration or dedicated prompt management systems support versioning and the independent deployment of prompts.

Prompt testing frameworks validate changes before deploying to production. Well-designed test suites include edge cases, adversarial inputs, and regression tests so that new iterations do not degrade existing performance. Within Microsoft Foundry, automated evaluation can use built-in and custom evaluators designed for conversational AI. Groundedness measures whether responses are supported by retrieved or provided source content, while rubric-based evaluation assesses quality against defined criteria such as accuracy, tone, and completeness. Teams can also track task success rates to determine whether the assistant achieved the user's objective and use safety evaluations to verify compliance with content and policy requirements.

Beyond predeployment testing, A/B testing in production compares prompt variants using real user interactions. Statistical testing helps determine whether measured improvements are repeatable rather than the result of random variation. Teams that incorporate these practices into their delivery pipeline can release changes with greater confidence and reduce the risk of unintended behavior in complex, customer-facing scenarios.

Content moderation applies at multiple layers. Azure AI Content Safety filters both inputs and outputs for harmful content. Custom business rules enforce organization-specific policies. Human review queues capture edge cases for policy refinement. Moderation involves striking a balance between safety and user experience because overly aggressive filtering can frustrate legitimate users.

Response caching reduces costs and improves performance for common queries. Semantic similarity matching identifies when cached responses can be used to serve new queries. Cache invalidation strategies keep responses current. Privacy considerations determine what can be cached—personal responses require careful handling or exclusion from caches.

11.11.6 Documentation and Knowledge Management

Thorough documentation contributes to system maintainability as teams evolve while serving multiple audiences with varying technical expertise.

Architectural decision records document the rationale for selecting specific approaches. Each record documents the context, decision, and consequences of key choices. Why was Azure OpenAI Service selected over competitors? Why does the system use synchronous rather than asynchronous processing? These records prevent future teams from repeating past investigations or unknowingly reversing important decisions.

Runbooks provide step-by-step procedures for operational tasks. Deployment procedures, rollback processes, and incident response flows benefit from thorough documentation and testing. Runbooks are often written with minimal context in mind, since operators responding to incidents may not have the bandwidth to recall complex procedures. Azure Monitor Workbooks can support this goal by automating common diagnostic and remediation tasks.

API documentation built on OpenAPI specifications often provides clear integration guidance. Teams typically describe each endpoint, parameter, and response format consistently. Example requests and responses tend to speed developer onboarding. Postman collections or similar tools often support interactive API exploration. When specifications are generated from code, the documentation tends to remain aligned with the implementation over time.

Knowledge base maintenance processes help keep conversational content up to date. Regular reviews identify outdated information, policy changes, and emerging topics. When subject matter experts propose updates, those changes are routed through appropriate approval chains. Version control tracks all changes with attribution and rollback capabilities. Automated testing validates that updates do not break existing functionality.

These implementation best practices transform theoretical architectures into reliable production systems. Security protections safeguard sensitive data, resilience patterns handle inevitable failures, and operational excellence delivers sustainable growth. When combined with robust monitoring and documentation, these practices help conversational AI systems to deliver consistent value while adapting to evolving requirements.

11.12 Performance Optimization Strategies

Performance optimization for Azure AI Services requires balancing response latency, throughput, and cost while maintaining quality. Early in my career, optimization meant squeezing functionality into kilobytes of memory and shaving milliseconds from operations that ran on hardware a fraction as powerful as today's smartphones. The constraints have changed—memory is abundant, and compute is elastic—but the discipline remains essential.

Users expect responsive interactions regardless of the underlying complexity. The strategies that follow reflect this discipline applied to modern AI workloads, where the cost of careless implementation can compound with every API call. Meeting latency and throughput targets within cost constraints often depends on coordinated optimization across infrastructure configuration, application design, and model selection. Refined through real-world deployments, these strategies support large-scale systems operating under heavy load.

11.12.1 Caching Strategies for AI Services

Intelligent caching represents the most impactful optimization for conversational AI systems. Multiple caching layers work together to minimize latency and reduce redundant processing.

Response caching stores answers to FAQs, thereby eliminating the need for repeated calls to AI services. Azure Cache for Redis maintains a semantic cache that returns precomputed responses for similar queries. The system uses embedding vectors to measure semantic similarity rather than relying on exact string matching. A query about "password reset" retrieves the same cached response as "forgot my password" or "can't log in." Cache entries can include confidence scores that teams can use to determine when a cached response is appropriate. Time-based expiration and event-driven invalidation help keep responses up to date as knowledge bases are updated.

Model caching keeps inference endpoints warm, thereby eliminating cold-start penalties. Azure Container Instances and Azure Kubernetes Service maintain preloaded model instances ready for immediate use. LLMs that take time to initialize remain memory-resident, reducing cold-start delays. End-to-end response time varies with model choice and output length, ranging from subsecond intervals to several seconds. Predictive scaling anticipates demand patterns and warms up additional instances before traffic spikes. This approach trades memory costs for dramatically improved response times during critical business hours.

Session state caching preserves conversation context, eliminating the need for repeated database queries. Redis stores active conversation state with sliding expiration windows. Each user interaction refreshes the cache timeout, keeping active conversations memory-resident. Archive completed conversations to persistent storage, freeing up cache capacity. This pattern supports thousands of concurrent conversations with state access in under a millisecond.

Embedding caches accelerate similarity searches and RAG. Precomputed embeddings for documents, FAQs, and knowledge base articles are stored in vector databases. Azure AI Search maintains these vectors with efficient indexing structures. New queries compute embeddings once and then perform similarity searches against cached vectors, rather than computing embeddings again for entire document collections.

11.12.2 Model Selection and Configuration Optimization

Choosing the appropriate model for each workload has a direct effect on performance. Many queries do not require the most powerful model available.

Model routing based on query complexity optimizes both speed and cost. Simple factual questions route to smaller, faster models that prioritize low latency. Complex reasoning tasks are delegated to more capable models in exchange for higher latency. Classification tasks use lightweight custom models deployed in Azure Machine Learning. This tiered approach reduces average response time while maintaining quality for complex queries. APIM implements routing rules based on intent classification, transparently directing requests to the most appropriate models.

Parameter tuning affects both response quality and generation speed. Lower temperature settings produce more deterministic responses and facilitate effective cache behavior. Reducing *max_tokens* limits the length of the generated text. *Top_p* adjustments balance creativity with consistency. These parameters are dynamically tuned by query type: creative tasks allow higher temperatures, whereas transactional queries use near-zero temperatures for consistency.

Prompt optimization reduces token consumption and processing time. Concise system prompts minimize overhead for every request. Few-shot examples use minimal tokens while maintaining quality. Dynamic prompt assembly includes only relevant context, rather than the entire conversation history. Token counting before submission prevents exceeding limits that force truncation or errors.

Fine-tuned models for specific domains outperform general models on specialized tasks. A customer service model trained on organization-specific data handles routine queries faster than general-purpose models. The smaller, focused model loads quickly and infers efficiently. Azure Machine Learning manages these custom models with automated scaling and version management.

11.12.3 Infrastructure and Network Optimization

Strategic deployment of infrastructure helps minimize network latency and maximize throughput.

Regional deployment positions services close to users. Azure AI Services can be deployed across multiple regions, with Azure Traffic Manager or Azure Front Door routing requests based on performance, geography, or other criteria. Geographic distribution reduces network latency for users worldwide, with the magnitude of improvement depending on user locations and network paths. Data residency requirements guide regional selection, while performance metrics validate placement decisions.

Connection pooling and reuse reduce TCP and TLS handshake overhead. Persistent connections (HTTP/2 or HTTP/3) keep channels open to AI services, avoiding the cost of repeatedly establishing new connections. Connection pools can scale dynamically based on traffic patterns, and health checks remove failed connections while keeping healthy ones active.

Content delivery networks (CDNs) accelerate the delivery of static resources. Azure CDN or similar services cache JavaScript libraries, images, and static responses at edge locations, allowing web chat interfaces to load from nearby servers rather than distant origins. Dynamic content can also benefit from CDN features such as compression and optimized routing.

Load balancing distributes traffic across service instances. Azure Application Gateway or Azure Front Door can route requests based on health probes, latency, and routing rules, directing traffic away from degraded instances. Weighted routing supports the gradual rollout of configuration changes. Conversation continuity can be maintained through session affinity or, more commonly in modern architectures, through externalized session state in a shared store.

11.12.4 Asynchronous Processing Patterns

Not all operations require synchronous responses. Asynchronous patterns can improve perceived performance and system throughput.

Queue-based processing efficiently handles operations that are not time-critical. Azure Service Bus can queue tasks such as document processing, report generation, and bulk operations. Users receive immediate acknowledgment while processing continues in the background, with completion notifications delivered via webhooks, email, or in-app messages. This pattern prevents long-running operations from blocking conversational flows.

Streaming responses improve perceived responsiveness for extended generations. Rather than waiting for a complete response, applications can stream partial model outputs as they arrive. Azure SignalR Service or similar technologies can deliver these incremental updates to clients in real time. Users see progress immediately, which can reduce abandonment, and early cancellation avoids unnecessary processing costs.

Batch aggregation consolidates multiple operations into fewer requests. Rather than processing multiple individual extractions separately, the system can batch them, reducing per-request overhead and improving throughput. For large-scale offline workloads such as bulk document processing, services like Azure Batch can distribute work across compute resources. The scheduling can be timed to take advantage of lower-priority or off-peak capacity when cost optimization is a goal.

Background prefetching can anticipate user needs. While users read responses, the system may prefetch likely follow-up information based on conversation patterns. Prefetched results are cached speculatively and served immediately if users follow expected paths. Cache misses have minimal impact since prefetching occurs asynchronously and does not block the primary interaction.

11.12.5 Monitoring and Performance Analysis

Systematic monitoring identifies optimization opportunities and validates improvements.

Distributed tracing tracks requests across all services. Azure Application Insights correlates traces from speech recognition through response generation. Each service span shows precise timing, allowing bottlenecks to be identified immediately. Slow database queries, network delays, and processing bottlenecks become visible. Performance regression detection alerts when optimizations degrade.

Custom performance metrics capture AI-specific indicators. First-token latency measures the time it takes for users to see the initial response. Token generation rate tracks streaming performance. Cache hit ratios validate caching effectiveness. Model inference times guide scaling decisions. These metrics feed real-time dashboards accessible to operations teams.

Load testing validates performance under stress. Azure Load Testing can simulate traffic at scale through configurable virtual user patterns, with the specific concurrency profile determined by the test design and allocated capacity. Tests include a range of query types, conversation lengths, and user behaviors. Performance baselines establish expected behavior. Regular testing prevents performance degradation as systems evolve. Chaos engineering tests resilience by introducing failures during load tests.

Cost performance analytics balance optimization efforts. Azure Cost Management correlates spending with performance metrics. High-cost queries identify optimization targets. Performance improvements quantify the ROI in optimization. Reserved capacity recommendations reduce costs for predictable workloads.

11.12.6 Query and Retrieval Optimization

Efficient information retrieval accelerates knowledge-based responses.

Search query optimization improves retrieval precision and speed. Query expansion automatically adds synonyms and related terms. Query reduction removes stop words and redundant terms. Semantic search using vector similarity outperforms keyword matching. Azure AI Search implements these optimizations transparently, improving both relevance and speed.

Index optimization structures data for rapid retrieval. Selective field indexing reduces index size and search time. Compound indexes accelerate multifield queries. Partitioned indexes distribute load across shards. Regular index maintenance prevents fragmentation that degrades performance.

Retrieval result filtering reduces processing overhead. Relevance thresholds exclude low-quality matches before processing. Document freshness filters prioritize current information. Security trimming removes unauthorized results early. These filters reduce the volume of data flowing through subsequent processing stages. Retrieved documents are cached with their embeddings for the immediate retrieval of similar queries.

11.12.7 Real-Time Optimization Techniques

Real-time adjustments maintain performance as conditions change.

Dynamic timeout adjustment prevents cascade failures. Initial timeouts are set conservatively and then adjusted based on observed latencies. Services experiencing slowdowns temporarily receive extended timeouts. Consistently fast services use aggressive timeouts. This adaptation prevents unnecessary failures while maintaining responsiveness.

Adaptive batch sizing optimizes throughput dynamically. Small batches during low traffic minimize latency. Large batches during peak traffic maximize throughput. Queue depth triggers automatic adjustments to batch size. This elasticity maintains performance across varying loads.

Circuit breaker patterns (as discussed in Section 11.11.2) prevent the propagation of overload. Performance-based circuit breakers open when latency exceeds thresholds, not just in response to errors. Gradual recovery tests performance before fully closing circuits.

Priority queuing prioritizes critical requests. Health-related queries surpass general inquiries. Authenticated users receive priority over anonymous traffic. Time-sensitive operations, such as payment processing, take priority over browsing. Azure Service Bus priority queues implement these patterns declaratively.

These optimization strategies work synergistically to deliver responsive, cost-effective conversational AI systems. The combination of intelligent caching, appropriate model selection, infrastructure optimization, and continuous monitoring positions systems to meet demanding performance requirements while controlling costs. Regular analysis and adjustment keep optimizations effective as usage patterns evolve.

11.13 Testing, Quality Assurance, and Feedback

Testing conversational AI systems presents unique challenges beyond traditional software validation. With rule-based systems, I could trace every decision path and deterministically verify every outcome. Language models offer no such certainty—the same input may yield different outputs, and correctness itself becomes probabilistic. This shift demands a different testing philosophy: one that validates boundaries and distributions rather than exact matches, that measures quality through human judgment as well as automated metrics, and that accepts uncertainty while still maintaining standards. The methodologies described here have evolved through that transition.

11.13.1 Test Strategy and Planning

Test strategies for agents built with Foundry Tools must address multiple dimensions of quality. Two distinct testing approaches are required to reflect the hybrid nature of modern agent systems.

Deterministic testing applies to the system's structural behavior: components that must produce consistent, verifiable outcomes regardless of model variation. API contracts, tool invocations, state transitions, authentication flows, and integration responses all fall into this category. These behaviors can be validated with conventional unit and integration tests that assert specific, repeatable results. Microsoft's current Foundry tooling also treats function calling and tool execution as explicit application behaviors, with the application responsible for executing functions and returning outputs.

Probabilistic evaluation applies to model-generated outputs. Unlike deterministic systems, where the same input produces the same output, language model responses can vary across invocations. Evaluation, therefore, measures quality against acceptable ranges rather than exact matches, using methods such as groundedness scoring, rubric-based review, task success rates, and safety checks. These evaluation patterns align with Microsoft Foundry's support for both built-in and custom evaluators for generative AI applications.

Teams that conflate these two modes—by applying probabilistic tolerances to system behavior or by expecting exact matches from model outputs—often create testing gaps that later surface as production incidents.

Test coverage planning begins with identifying critical conversation paths and failure modes. High-risk scenarios, such as financial transactions or medical advice, require thorough testing with clearly defined acceptance criteria. Low-risk informational queries allow more flexible validation. Risk matrices guide resource allocation and promote thorough testing of critical functions while maintaining development velocity.

Test environment management presents unique challenges for AI services. Production models often differ from development versions in both performance and behavior. In many Azure deployments, test environments mirror production configurations, including model versions, scaling parameters, and integration points, to reduce surprises during release. Achieving that level of parity often involves close attention to service quotas, regional deployments, and data residency constraints. Foundry Local supports local development and testing by running selected models on-device, allowing teams to iterate on prompts, tool configurations, and agent behavior before deploying to the cloud.

Test data management strikes a balance between realism and privacy protection. Production conversation logs provide realistic test scenarios but require careful anonymization. Synthetic data generation addresses gaps when real data is insufficient or sensitive. Test data libraries maintain approved datasets for regression testing, performance benchmarking, and model comparison. Azure Data Factory orchestrates test data pipelines to refresh datasets on a schedule while maintaining privacy compliance.

Success criteria often span both technical metrics and business outcomes. Response accuracy, measured through precision and recall, can provide quantitative baselines. Conversation completion rates often reflect task success. User satisfaction scores can capture subjective quality. Together, these measures can form quality scorecards that track improvement over time and help prioritize optimization efforts.

11.13.2 Unit Testing for AI Components

Unit testing validates individual AI service components in isolation before integration. These tests focus on measurable behaviors rather than attempting to validate all possible responses.

Intent classification testing verifies that user utterances are mapped to the correct intents with acceptable confidence scores. Test suites include canonical examples, boundary cases, and adversarial inputs. Each intent requires both positive examples that match and negative examples that do not. Confidence thresholds steer the system toward requesting clarification when inputs are ambiguous rather than making incorrect guesses.

Entity extraction testing focuses on the accurate identification and categorization of information within text. Tests typically cover both entity detection and value extraction. Date entities are evaluated against varied formats, such as “next Wednesday,” “March 15th,” or “3/15.” Currency amounts are checked to confirm they parse correctly across common notations. Custom entities are exercised with domain-specific variations and representative phrasing. Edge cases, including overlapping entities and ambiguous references, often receive targeted test coverage.

Response generation testing for systems using Azure OpenAI Service focuses on consistency and appropriateness rather than exact matching. Tests validate that responses remain within defined boundaries, maintain an appropriate tone, and include all required information. Automated checks detect hallucinations by verifying factual claims against knowledge bases. Safety validations verify that responses do not contain harmful content, even when exposed to adversarial prompts.

Model performance benchmarks establish baselines for latency, token usage, and resource consumption. Automated tests track these metrics across model updates, flagging regressions before they impact production. Performance budgets define acceptable ranges for each metric. Builds that exceed these limits are reported as failures.

11.13.3 Integration Testing for Conversational Flows

Integration testing verifies that AI services function correctly in conjunction with other systems. These tests examine complete conversation paths, including service orchestration, state management, and external integrations.

End-to-end conversation testing simulates complete user journeys from initial greeting through task completion. Conversation test harnesses, transcript-based regression suites, channel simulators, and scripted integration flows validate multiturn interactions across the application stack. Tests verify that context is carried correctly across turns, pronouns are resolved accurately, and the conversation state is maintained appropriately. Interruption scenarios validate that users can change topics mid-conversation without breaking the system.

Service orchestration testing verifies correct coordination between Azure AI Services. When users upload documents, tests verify that Document Intelligence extracts content, Language Service processes text, and OpenAI Service generates appropriate responses. Timing scenarios validate that synchronous and asynchronous operations coordinate correctly. Fallback paths confirm that service failures trigger appropriate alternatives.

Back-end integration testing validates connections to enterprise systems. Mock services simulate interactions with CRM, ERP, and databases during testing. Contract testing verifies API compatibility as systems evolve. Transaction testing verifies data consistency across distributed operations. Security testing confirms that credentials and sensitive data are handled appropriately throughout integrations.

Channel-specific testing accounts for platform variations. Microsoft Teams, web chat, and voice channels each have distinct capabilities and constraints. Tests often verify that rich cards render correctly, that voice responses include appropriate SSML, and that platform-specific features, such as suggested actions, work as intended. Adaptive Cards are typically designed to degrade gracefully on constrained platforms while utilizing the full functional depth of the host environment where available.

11.13.4 Conversation Quality Testing

Conversation quality testing evaluates subjective aspects of user interaction that traditional testing cannot capture. These assessments verify that responses are natural, helpful, and contextually appropriate.

Dialog coherence testing validates that conversations maintain logical flow across multiple turns. Tests assess whether responses acknowledge prior context, maintain a consistent personality, and progress toward resolution. Conversation transcripts are analyzed automatically for coherence metrics, including topic drift, response relevance, and completion efficiency. ML models trained on human-rated conversations provide a scalable approach to quality assessment.

Context preservation testing assesses whether systems correctly maintain and reference conversation history. Tests often verify that pronouns such as "it" and "that" refer to their intended antecedents. Temporal references, such as "what I mentioned earlier," are evaluated to determine whether they refer to the correct prior information. Requests with multiple intents are exercised to see whether all components are handled without losing context. Longer conversations help reveal memory limits and how performance degrades as context increases.

Ambiguity handling tests evaluate whether responses remain appropriate when user input is ambiguous. Effective systems recognize ambiguity and prompt for clarification rather than relying on assumptions. Test cases often include homonyms, incomplete sentences, and contradictory requests. Clarification dialogs are validated for natural phrasing and for their efficiency in gathering the required information. Edge cases, such as typos and speech recognition errors, typically receive targeted attention.

Personality consistency testing checks that responses maintain appropriate tone and style throughout interactions. Professional contexts require formal language while consumer applications allow casual conversation. Tests verify that personality remains consistent even when handling errors or unusual requests. Emotional intelligence tests validate appropriate responses to user frustration or satisfaction.

11.13.5 Synthetic Data Generation and Testing

Synthetic data generation exponentially expands test coverage beyond manually created scenarios. Generative models create diverse, realistic test conversations that expose edge cases human testers might miss.

Azure OpenAI Service generates synthetic test conversations by simulating both user inputs and expected system responses. Prompt engineering creates user personas with different communication styles, technical expertise, and goals. Generated conversations include common patterns and unusual scenarios that stress system boundaries. Parameters control the complexity, length, and distribution of conversation topics.

Adversarial testing uses synthetic data to probe system weaknesses. Generated inputs attempt to inject prompts, manipulate roles, and perform information extraction attacks. Fuzzing techniques create malformed inputs that test error handling. Stress patterns include rapid topic changes, contradictory requests, and recursive loops. These tests identify vulnerabilities before malicious users discover them.

Corner case generation focuses on unusual but valid scenarios. Synthetic data includes rare entity combinations, extreme parameter values, and unlikely conversation paths. Cultural variations test system behavior across different communication norms. Multilingual scenarios validate the use of language switching and translation accuracy. Accessibility scenarios verify compatibility with screen readers and voice-only interaction.

Data quality validation verifies that synthetic data remains realistic and relevant. Statistical analysis compares synthetic conversations to production patterns. Human reviewers sample synthetic data for quality assessment. Diversity metrics provide adequate coverage across user segments and scenario types. Feedback loops refine generation parameters based on discovered gaps.

11.13.6 A/B Testing and Experimentation

A/B testing provides a safe way to validate changes through controlled experiments on production traffic. These tests measure the actual impact on users rather than simulated scenarios.

Experiment design for conversational AI requires careful consideration of continuity in the user experience. Users participating in extended conversations must not switch between variants during the same dialog. Azure App Configuration manages feature flags that assign users to consistent experimental groups. Sample size calculations account for the variability of the conversation and the desired statistical power.

Model comparison experiments evaluate different AI services or configurations. For specific query types, tests might compare smaller, faster models against more capable alternatives. Response quality metrics, latency measurements, and cost analysis inform model selection. Gradual rollout strategies minimize risk while gathering sufficient data for decisions.

Prompt variation testing optimizes response generation without modifying the model. Different prompt templates, few-shot examples, and parameter settings are systematically compared. Automated evaluation metrics provide rapid feedback, while human assessment validates qualitative improvements. Winning variations are deployed automatically once statistical significance is achieved.

Feature testing validates new capabilities with limited exposure. New skills or conversational flows are initially deployed to small user segments. Monitoring tracks success metrics, error rates, and user feedback. Automatic circuit breakers disable features that degrade performance. Successful features are gradually rolled out to all users, whereas failed experiments are rolled back without disruption.

11.13.7 Automated Testing Frameworks

Automation drives continuous validation throughout development and deployment cycles. These frameworks integrate multiple testing approaches into a single pipeline.

Automated testing frameworks combine conventional unit and integration test tooling with evaluation pipelines for model behavior. Standard unit test frameworks such as Jest, Mocha, NUnit, xUnit, and pytest validate tool execution, workflow state, API contracts, and policy enforcement. For conversational behavior, teams typically utilize transcript-based regression suites, channel simulators, synthetic conversations, and custom evaluation harnesses tied to the application's orchestration layer. For example, they deploy harnesses built on top of Foundry Agent Service traces or the Microsoft 365 Agents SDK's built-in telemetry instead of relying on legacy Bot Framework testing libraries. In environments that still maintain Bot Framework solutions, existing test assets remain useful for support and migration work, but new development should align with current agent architectures and evaluation pipelines.

Azure DevOps pipelines orchestrate automated testing across environments. Pipeline stages progress from unit tests through integration testing to deployment validation. Quality gates prevent promotion of builds that fail critical tests. Parallel execution reduces testing time while maintaining coverage. Test results feed dashboards that track quality trends over time.

Load testing frameworks validate performance under realistic usage patterns. Azure Load Testing can simulate traffic at scale through configurable virtual user patterns, with the specific concurrency profile determined by the test design, workload characteristics, and allocated capacity. Tests measure response times, throughput, and resource utilization. Stress tests identify breaking points and degradation patterns. Soak tests validate stability over extended periods. Performance baselines allow regression detection across deployments.

Continuous testing in production monitors live system quality. Synthetic monitors conduct periodic test conversations to validate availability and response quality. Real user monitoring tracks actual conversation metrics. Anomaly detection identifies quality degradation before users complain. Automated alerts trigger an investigation and, if thresholds are breached, a potential rollback.

11.13.8 Feedback Collection and Analysis

User feedback provides essential insights that automated testing cannot capture. Structured collection and analysis processes transform feedback into actionable improvements.

Explicit feedback collection gathers direct user ratings and comments. Surveys sent after the interaction capture satisfaction scores and specific feedback, while feedback options during the interaction allow an immediate response to problems. Feedback prompts balance data collection needs with user experience impact. Response rates improve through thoughtful timing and minimal friction.

Implicit feedback derives from user behavior patterns. Conversation abandonment indicates potential problems. Repeat questions suggest unsuccessful initial responses. Task completion rates measure actual success in relation to perceived satisfaction. Session duration and turn counts reveal the efficiency of conversation. These behavioral signals often provide a more honest assessment than explicit ratings.

Sentiment analysis of conversation transcripts identifies emotional patterns. Azure Language analyzes user messages for signs of frustration, satisfaction, or confusion. Shifts in sentiment trends indicate emerging issues. Sentiment correlation with specific intents or responses guides optimization priorities. Automated alerts flag conversations with extremely negative sentiment for review.

Feedback prioritization frameworks aid in the efficient allocation of resources. Issue severity, frequency, and user impact combine into priority scores. Root cause analysis identifies systemic problems versus isolated incidents. Feedback trends guide roadmap decisions and investment priorities. Regular reviews channel feedback into continuous improvement rather than leaving issues unaddressed.

11.13.9 Human-in-the-Loop Validation

Human review remains essential for validating subjective quality and handling edge cases that automated testing cannot assess.

Review queue management routes conversations for human validation based on confidence scores, risk levels, and random sampling. Low-confidence responses require expert review before being used in the future. High-risk scenarios, such as medical or financial advice, mandate human oversight. Random samples promote statistical representation across all conversation types.

Annotation workflows streamline efficient human review at scale. Reviewers assess response quality, identify errors, and suggest improvements. Standardized rubrics provide a consistent basis for evaluation across reviewers. Batch interfaces allow rapid assessment of multiple conversations. Quality scores feed back into model training and testing pipelines.

Expert validation draws on domain specialists for specialized content. Medical professionals review health-related responses. Legal experts validate compliance scenarios. Domain specialists safeguard the technical integrity of the content. This expertise layer provides QA that general reviewers cannot offer.

Continuous learning processes incorporate human feedback into system improvements. Corrected responses become training data for model updates. Identified gaps guide test scenario creation. Common errors trigger systematic fixes rather than individual corrections. This feedback loop facilitates system evolution based on live deployment metrics instead of purely simulated benchmarks.

These QA and feedback frameworks align conversational AI systems with both technical specifications and end user needs. The combination of automated validation, human oversight, and continuous feedback creates high-quality processes that scale with system growth while maintaining high standards.

11.14 Enterprise Use Cases

Azure AI Services deployments across industries demonstrate measurable business transformation through intelligent automation and enhanced customer engagement. Having led technology initiatives in financial services—including the conversational AI systems my teams built at FIS—I have seen firsthand how thoughtfully implemented conversational AI reshapes operations. Our work at FIS demonstrated that financial institutions could move beyond rigid IVR menus to natural conversation. The use cases that follow illustrate how Azure AI Services now makes this transformation accessible without the extensive custom engineering we once required.

11.14.1 Telecommunications: Automated Network Troubleshooting

Telecommunications providers handle millions of technical support requests each month across phone, chat, and digital channels. Network-related troubleshooting accounts for a substantial share of these interactions and materially escalates operational costs. Industry analyses report that technical support calls involving connectivity issues typically require extended handling times of 10–15 minutes and are often escalated to specialized technicians.[2]

A network support assistant built on Azure AI Services addresses this challenge through intelligent diagnostics and automated resolution. The process begins with Azure Speech, which converts customer descriptions of connectivity problems into structured data. NLP identifies technical indicators embedded in colloquial phrasing. A statement such as "My internet keeps dropping" maps to intermittent connectivity patterns associated with specific diagnostic workflows.

The assistant interfaces with network management and service assurance systems via secure APIs to retrieve real-time telemetry, including signal strength, packet loss rates, device health, and outage logs. Azure OpenAI Service analyzes these data streams and correlates customer-reported symptoms with network conditions. Automated diagnostic tests connect to multiple vantage points and determine whether issues originate from customer equipment, local access infrastructure, or broader regional disruptions.

When customer action is required, the assistant generates personalized troubleshooting steps tailored to the user's equipment model, service tier, and network configuration. Visual guides are delivered through web and mobile channels, while voice instructions are adapted for phone-based support. The system tracks completion of each step and dynamically adjusts subsequent instructions based on observed results. Industry case studies indicate that automated network troubleshooting systems can resolve a substantial share of technical issues without human intervention and meaningfully reduce average handle times for cases that still require escalation.[3]

---

[2] TM Forum, "Customer Experience and Technical Support Benchmarking Report," 2022–2024; Analysys Mason, "Telecoms Customer-Care Trends," 2023.

[3] McKinsey & Company, "AI in Telecommunications: Improving Customer Experience and Reducing Costs," 2021; Deloitte, *AI-Driven Service Operations in Telecom* (2022); Accenture, *Automation and AI in Network Operations* (2023).

11.14.2 Retail: Intelligent Product Discovery

Retail organizations process millions of product-related inquiries across digital and voice channels each year. Industry research consistently shows that friction in product discovery reduces conversion rates and customer satisfaction, although the National Retail Federation (NRF) does not publish a specific correlation metric. Recent NRF and IBM research makes clear that consumers increasingly expect intuitive, AI-powered discovery experiences that interpret natural language and reduce cognitive load during shopping.[4]

An intelligent shopping assistant built on Azure AI Services enhances product discovery by letting customers describe their needs in their own words—"I need something waterproof for hiking in Scotland"—rather than navigating rigid category hierarchies or filter trees. Azure Language extracts intents, entities, and contextual qualifiers from these natural descriptions, identifying product attributes, use cases, constraints, and preferences.[5]

The system maintains a product knowledge graph indexed in Azure AI Search. Each product entry combines structured attributes, unstructured descriptions, and sentiment-analyzed customer reviews enriched through Azure Language. Vector embeddings power semantic similarity matching, allowing the assistant to identify relevant products even when customer terminology differs from the catalog's vocabulary. A request such as "something to keep my coffee hot during my commute" correctly surfaces insulated travel mugs through semantic understanding rather than keyword overlap.[6]

Personalization layers refine recommendations using purchase history, browsing patterns, and stated preferences. The assistant explains its reasoning through natural dialog, highlighting why specific products align with the customer's needs. As customers provide additional context—"I prefer sustainable materials"—the system dynamically adjusts recommendations while maintaining conversational coherence. Industry studies on conversational commerce report notable increases in average order value and

[4] IBM and National Retail Federation, *Consumers Want It All: Hybrid Shopping, Sustainability, and the New Consumer Mindset* (Armonk, NY: IBM Institute for Business Value, 2022).

[5] Microsoft, "Azure Language Documentation," Microsoft Learn, `https://learn.microsoft.com/azure/ai-services/language-service`.

[6] Microsoft, "Azure AI Search: Vector Search Overview," Microsoft Learn, `https://learn.microsoft.com/azure/search/vector-search-overview`.

reductions in product return rates due to improved initial product matching, though these findings come from broader market research rather than NRF-specific studies.[7]

11.14.3 Manufacturing: Predictive Maintenance Intelligence

Manufacturing operations generate vast volumes of sensor and machine state data that require real-time analysis to prevent equipment failures and production interruptions. Industry studies estimate that unplanned downtime can cost manufacturers tens of thousands of dollars per hour, with some analyses placing the figure near $50,000 per hour and others—particularly in asset-intensive sectors—reporting substantially higher costs.[8]

An intelligent maintenance system built on Azure AI Services integrates IoT telemetry with advanced analytics to predict and prevent equipment failures. Azure Language processes maintenance logs and technicians' notes, extracting patterns from natural language descriptions of symptoms, observations, and repair histories. Terms such as "grinding noise from bearing housing" map to known failure modes within established reliability taxonomies, helping the system convert unstructured text into structured diagnostic signals.

The system continuously analyzes streaming sensor data, including vibration signatures, temperature profiles, pressure readings, and acoustic patterns. Azure AI Vision augments these signals by processing thermal images and visual inspection data to identify wear patterns, alignment deviations, and early-stage component degradation. ML models trained on historical failure events estimate the remaining useful life of critical components and detect anomalies that exceed learned thresholds. When such conditions arise, the system generates natural language alerts that explain the issue, its likely cause, and recommended corrective actions.

Maintenance technicians interact with the system through conversational interfaces to query equipment status, retrieve repair procedures, and access parts inventories and

---

[7] McKinsey & Company, "The Future of Conversational Commerce," 2023; Salesforce, *State of the Connected Customer*, 5th ed. (2023).

[8] Deloitte, *The Smart Factory: Responsive, Adaptive, Connected Manufacturing* (2017); Aberdeen Group, *The Cost of Downtime* (2016); Siemens, *The True Cost of Downtime 2024* (2024), `https://assets.new.siemens.com/siemens/assets/api/uuid:1b43afb5-2d07-47f7-9eb7-893fe7d0bc59/TCOD-2024_original.pdf`.

maintenance schedules. Azure Speech supports hands-free operation in high-noise industrial environments through custom acoustic models and noise-robust speech recognition. Industry research indicates that AI-driven predictive maintenance can materially reduce equipment downtime and extend asset life, consistent with findings from multiple large-scale studies.[9]

11.14.4 Government: Citizen Service Automation

Government agencies handle millions of citizen inquiries each year, spanning permit applications, benefit eligibility, licensing, and public service requests. The Partnership for Public Service estimates that federal agencies collectively manage well over one billion customer service interactions annually, with some years approaching two billion when accounting for calls, web inquiries, in-person visits, and correspondence.[10] State and local governments process similarly large volumes across 311 systems, unemployment services, and social service programs.

Intelligent citizen assistants built on Azure AI Services streamline service delivery while supporting accessibility, multilingual communication, and regulatory compliance. Multichannel deployment delivers voice, text, and web interactions across devices and languages. Azure Speech with neural voice synthesis provides clear, natural communication for citizens with varying literacy levels, while real-time translation supports non-English speakers without requiring separate systems.

The assistant guides citizens through complex processes such as permit applications or benefit enrollment. Azure AI Document Intelligence extracts structured data from uploaded documents—including identification, proof of residence, and income verification—while detecting missing fields and prompting for corrections. Integration with government case management systems and eligibility databases offers real-time status checks and automated verification. Secure authentication using multifactor verification protects sensitive information while maintaining accessibility for diverse populations.

NLU accommodates the many ways citizens express their needs. A question such as "I just lost my job. What help is available?" triggers an eligibility assessment across

---

[9] McKinsey & Company, "Predictive Maintenance and the Smart Factory," 2018; PwC, *Digital Factories 2020: Shaping the Future of Manufacturing* (2017).

[10] Partnership for Public Service, *Government for the People: Profiles on Federal Customer Experience*, multiple editions (Washington, DC: Partnership for Public Service, 2018–2024).

relevant programs. The assistant explains qualification criteria, required documentation, and application steps in clear, concise language. When human assistance is needed, the system provides warm transfers with full context, eliminating the need for repetitive explanations. Case studies reported by *Government Technology* show that AI-enabled citizen service systems can effectively reduce call volumes and improve satisfaction scores by providing 24-hour availability and consistent service delivery.[11]

11.14.5 Financial Services: Fraud Detection and Prevention

Financial institutions process billions of transactions each day across card networks, Automated Clearing House (ACH) rails, wire systems, and digital banking channels. Industry research places global payment fraud losses well above $30 billion annually, though this figure reflects worldwide estimates from commercial analysts rather than Federal Trade Commission reporting, which focuses on US consumer fraud losses.[12] Real-time fraud detection requires analyzing complex behavioral and transactional patterns across multiple data streams while minimizing false positives that disrupt legitimate customers.

This trajectory mirrors what I observed at FIS, where early conversational AI deployments focused on customer service automation but rapidly expanded into fraud prevention, risk scoring, and compliance workflows. The same natural language capabilities that improve customer interactions also enhance threat detection—a convergence that financial institutions are only beginning to exploit at scale.

Intelligent fraud detection systems built on Azure AI Services identify suspicious activity through behavioral analytics and NLP. Azure Language analyzes transaction descriptions, merchant identifiers, and communication patterns to detect anomalies. Unusual linguistic structures in transaction metadata, atypical merchant categorizations, and irregular communication sequences trigger enhanced scrutiny.

The system evaluates customer interactions across channels to identify social engineering attempts and account takeover indicators. Speaker recognition capabilities

---

[11] *Government Technology*, various case studies on AI-enabled 311 systems, unemployment assistance platforms, and digital service centers, 2021–2024.

[12] Federal Trade Commission, *Consumer Sentinel Network Data Book*, annual editions (Washington, DC: Federal Trade Commission, 2022–2024); Nilson Report, *Global Payment Card Fraud*, various editions.

in Azure Speech, which are specialized and subject to access controls and scenario restrictions, can support impersonation detection in approved use cases, while conversation analysis models identify scripted, coached, or coerced responses. NLU recognizes urgency patterns commonly associated with scams (for example, phrases such as "urgent wire transfers" or "cryptocurrency investments") and triggers real-time fraud education and risk-aware guidance.

When potential fraud is detected, the assistant engages customers through adaptive dialog rather than rigid authentication scripts. Dynamic questioning, informed by account history and behavioral baselines, helps distinguish legitimate customers from fraudsters. The assistant clearly explains security concerns, reinforcing trust and guiding customers through protective measures. Connecting to case management systems streamlines handoffs to human agents and provides a direct escalation path for complex scenarios. Industry analyses indicate that AI-enhanced fraud detection programs curtail fraud losses and lower false-positive rates, consistent with findings from multiple large-scale financial services studies.[13]

11.14.6 Education: Personalized Learning Support

Educational institutions serve diverse student populations with varying learning needs, schedules, and levels of prior preparation. International organizations such as the United Nations Educational, Scientific, and Cultural Organization (UNESCO) emphasize the importance of personalized and inclusive learning approaches, particularly for remote, adult, and marginalized learners, but do not report specific, quantifiable improvements in outcomes attributable to personalization.[14]

Intelligent tutoring systems built on Azure AI Services provide 24/7 personalized learning support across subjects and skill levels. Students engage through natural conversation, asking questions in their own words rather than navigating rigid content hierarchies. Azure Language interprets educational queries, mapping informal phrasing to learning objectives, curriculum standards, and prerequisite concepts.

---

[13] McKinsey & Company, "Fighting Fraud with Advanced Analytics," 2020; Deloitte, *AI in Financial Crime Prevention* (2021); IBM, *AI-Driven Fraud Detection in Financial Services* (2022).

[14] UNESCO, *Guidance for Generative AI in Education and Research* (Paris: UNESCO, 2023); UNESCO, *Reimagining Our Futures Together: A New Social Contract for Education* (Paris: UNESCO, 2021).

The system adapts explanations based on student comprehension and learning preferences. When students struggle with a concept, the assistant offers alternative explanations, visualizations, and targeted practice problems. Azure OpenAI Service generates unique practice questions and worked examples, reducing answer-copying while maintaining alignment with instructional goals. Real-time conversational assessment identifies misconceptions and adjusts instructional strategies accordingly.

Integration with learning management systems gives organizations visibility into progress across courses and assignments. The assistant reminds students of deadlines, suggests study strategies based on performance patterns, and connects related concepts across disciplines. Voice interaction empowers learners with reading difficulties or visual impairments, while multilingual capabilities guarantee accessibility for nonnative speakers. Research in the educational technology literature indicates that AI-driven tutoring systems can improve learning outcomes and reduce dropout rates in online courses, though these ranges reflect findings from multiple studies rather than a single journal source.[15]

11.14.7 Transportation and Logistics: Supply Chain Intelligence

Global supply chains process millions of shipments each day across ocean, air, rail, and parcel networks. Industry analyses estimate that logistics costs account for roughly 8–12% of global GDP, though this figure reflects the total cost of logistics rather than inefficiencies alone.[16] Visibility gaps, coordination challenges, and process delays exacerbate these costs and remain persistent impediments to multinational supply chain operations.

Intelligent logistics assistants built on Azure AI Services provide real-time visibility and proactive issue resolution across complex supply chain ecosystems. Natural language interfaces allow stakeholders to query shipment status, inventory levels, and delivery schedules conversationally. A question such as "When will our Shanghai orders

[15] See, for example, Kurt VanLehn, "The Relative Effectiveness of Human Tutoring, Intelligent Tutoring Systems, and Other Tutoring Systems," *Educational Psychologist* 46, no. 4 (2011): 197–221; and multiple meta-analyses summarized in the *International Journal of Artificial Intelligence in Education* and *Computers & Education*, 2018–2024.

[16] Council of Supply Chain Management Professionals, *State of Logistics Report*, annual editions (Lombard, IL: CSCMP, 2018-2024); World Bank, *Connecting to Compete: Trade Logistics in the Global Economy*, various editions.

arrive?" triggers federated queries across transportation management systems, carrier APIs, customs databases, and warehouse management platforms, aggregating data into a unified response.

Azure AI Document Intelligence processes unstructured shipping documents—including bills of lading, customs declarations, commercial invoices, and delivery receipts—extracting structured data and supporting multilingual documentation without manual translation. Automated validation detects discrepancies among ordered, shipped, and received quantities to identify potential issues early, before they disrupt downstream operations.

Predictive analytics models anticipate delays by analyzing weather patterns, port congestion, geopolitical disruptions, and carriers' historical performance. The assistant proactively notifies stakeholders of emerging risks and recommends alternative routing, mode shifts, or expedited options. Natural language generation provides clear explanations of complex logistics scenarios, giving nontechnical stakeholders a clearer understanding of operational impacts and decision pathways. When disruptions occur, the system coordinates resolution through conversational workflows that maintain context across interactions among shippers, carriers, and receivers. Industry research indicates that AI-enabled supply chain management can reduce logistics costs and improve on-time delivery performance, consistent with findings from multiple large-scale studies.[17]

11.14.8 Energy and Utilities: Intelligent Grid Management

Energy providers manage increasingly complex grids that incorporate distributed energy resources, variable renewable generation, and dynamic demand patterns. International organizations such as the International Energy Agency emphasize that digitalization and intelligent grid management are essential for improving efficiency, reducing losses, and enhancing reliability, though they do not provide a specific, quantified estimate of the global reduction in energy waste attributable to these technologies.[18]

[17] McKinsey & Company, "Digital Logistics: The Next Frontier," 2021; Boston Consulting Group, *AI in the Supply Chain: Creating End-to-End Resilience* (2022); Gartner, *Supply Chain Technology User Survey* (2023).

[18] International Energy Agency, *Digitalization and Energy* (Paris: IEA, 2017); International Energy Agency, *Electricity Grids and Secure Energy Transitions* (Paris: IEA, 2023).

Conversational grid management systems built on Azure AI Services offer operators a natural language interface for monitoring and controlling complex energy systems. Operators can query system status, investigate anomalies, and execute control actions conversationally rather than navigating intricate control interfaces. Azure Language interprets technical terminology and industry-specific jargon, understanding requests such as "Show me transformer loading in the downtown district during yesterday's heat event."

The system analyzes high-volume sensor data from smart meters, weather stations, and grid equipment. Natural language generation produces concise summaries of complex grid conditions, highlighting issues requiring operator attention. When anomalies occur, the assistant provides probable cause analysis based on historical patterns and current telemetry. Integration with predictive models promotes proactive management by anticipating equipment failures, overload conditions, and demand spikes.

Field technicians interact with the system through voice interfaces during maintenance and emergency response. The assistant provides step-by-step guidance for complex procedures, accessing technical manuals and safety protocols as needed. Real-time translation supports a multilingual workforce while maintaining technical accuracy. Augmented reality integration with Azure AI Vision supports remote expert assistance, allowing senior engineers to guide field repairs via visual annotations and voice instructions. Industry research indicates that AI-enabled grid management systems can reduce outage duration and improve operational efficiency, with gains observed across multiple utility case studies rather than a single standardized benchmark.[19]

These diverse use cases demonstrate the reach of Azure AI Services across industries. Each implementation addresses distinct operational challenges while adhering to established architectural patterns and best practices. Success requires careful attention to industry-specific requirements, regulatory compliance, and organizational change management. Organizations that thoughtfully deploy these capabilities realize substantial operational gains while optimizing both customer and employee experiences.

[19] McKinsey & Company, "AI and Advanced Analytics in Power and Utilities," 2021; Deloitte, *Digital Transformation in Power and Utilities* (2022); Electric Power Research Institute, *AI Applications in Grid Operations*, various technical briefs (2020–2024).

11.15 Future Directions and Regulatory Outlook

The evolution of Azure AI Services reflects broader shifts in AI, cloud computing, and regulation. I have navigated previous technology transitions—mainframes to client-server, client-server to web, web to cloud—and each followed a familiar pattern: technology advanced, adoption accelerated, and regulation eventually caught up. AI is different. Regulatory frameworks are being developed alongside the technology rather than years later, and organizations face the challenge of navigating both simultaneously. The trajectories outlined here carry genuine uncertainty, but understanding them is essential for investments intended to retain value across multiple planning horizons. Organizations that keep pace with rapid advances while addressing emerging governance requirements and competitive pressure are best positioned for long-term success. Understanding these trajectories supports strategic planning for AI investments that retain value despite uncertainty about specific technological and regulatory outcomes. For architects and enterprise designers, these shifts matter not as background context but as active constraints—shaping which services to bet on, which abstractions to trust, and where to preserve optionality in the stack.

In 2026, the pace of AI advancement has far eclipsed the steady two-year heartbeat commonly associated with Moore's Law, driven by a shift from shrinking individual chips to building warehouse-scale clusters of specialized GPUs. These clusters can now reach on the order of 100,000 GPUs, with the scale of training systems defined as much by networking, power delivery, and cooling as by transistor density.[20] While traditional hardware progress is often framed as doubling every two years, the training compute used for frontier models has been rising roughly fourfold to fivefold per year—equivalent to about a doubling every five to six months.[21] This growth has been fueled by major capital investment and sustained architectural innovation.

Simultaneously, the capability doubling rate has been trending upward. This rate is measured by the "time horizon" of tasks an AI system can complete autonomously—a metric developed by the research organization Model Evaluation and Threat Research (METR). The doubling time was roughly seven months from 2019 to 2025, with evidence

---

[20] NVIDIA, "NVIDIA Ethernet Networking Accelerates World's Largest AI Supercomputer, Built by xAI," NVIDIA Newsroom, October 28, 2024, `https://nvidianews.nvidia.com/news/spectrum-x-ethernet-networking-xai-colossus`.

[21] Jaime Sevilla and Edu Roldán, "Training Compute of Frontier AI Models Grows by 4–5x per Year," Epoch AI, May 28, 2024, `https://epoch.ai/blog/training-compute-of-frontier-ai-models-grows-by-4-5x-per-year`.

that the pace may have accelerated to about four months in 2024. In practical terms, earlier language models could reliably handle only very short, seconds-long tasks, whereas frontier systems can now sometimes complete software and research tasks that take human experts hours, even though reliability still drops on longer and messier work. If these trends persist, extrapolations suggest that day-scale task horizons could arrive relatively soon, though such forecasts remain uncertain.[22]

This acceleration is sustained not only by raw computational scale but also by algorithmic efficiency. OpenAI has documented that between 2012 and 2019, researchers reduced the compute needed to match AlexNet-level image recognition performance by a factor of 44.[23] In addition, the Stanford AI Index has highlighted that by 2024, a model with 3.8 billion parameters could reach the same Massive Multitask Language Understanding benchmark threshold that required a 540-billion-parameter model in 2022.[24] In effect, intelligence is being densified through smarter designs—such as mixture-of-experts routing, improved scaling methods, and distillation—even as physical scaling faces tighter constraints.

This rate of progress carries profound regulatory implications. Traditional technology regulation operates on legislative timescales of years or decades; Moore's Law, with its relatively predictable cadence, gave policymakers a comfortable window in which to observe, deliberate, and act. AI capabilities are now advancing on cycles measured in months, meaning that a regulatory framework drafted today may be addressing a technological landscape that has doubled or tripled in capability by the time it takes effect. The gap between the pace of AI advancement and the pace of governance is itself widening rapidly, creating a compounding deficit of oversight precisely when the stakes—autonomous decision-making in finance, health care, criminal justice, and national security—are at their highest. If regulation cannot keep pace with even a fraction of this tempo, society risks ceding foundational decisions about safety, accountability, and fairness to the momentum of deployment rather than to the deliberation of democratic institutions.

---

[22] METR, "Measuring AI Ability to Complete Long Tasks," March 19, 2025, `https://metr.org/blog/2025-03-19-measuring-ai-ability-to-complete-long-tasks`.

[23] OpenAI, "AI and Efficiency," May 5, 2020, `https://openai.com/index/ai-and-efficiency`.

[24] Stanford Institute for Human-Centered Artificial Intelligence, "AI Index 2025: State of AI in 10 Charts," April 7, 2025, `https://hai.stanford.edu/news/ai-index-2025-state-of-ai-in-10-charts`.

11.15.1 Technical Evolution and Emerging Capabilities

Azure AI Services is evolving toward more sophisticated, autonomous, and context-aware systems, building on current capabilities while addressing current limitations.

Multimodal AI represents a fundamental architectural shift from single-modality processing to the concurrent interpretation of text, speech, vision, and structured data. Current preview features demonstrate systems that link visual elements to spoken descriptions during structured database queries. A medical consultation system may simultaneously analyze patient speech patterns, review uploaded test images, and query EHRs. This convergence calls for orchestration beyond sequential service calls—specifically, parallel pipelines that maintain temporal synchronization across modalities.

Advanced reasoning moves beyond pattern matching toward genuine problem-solving. CoT, now achieved largely through prompt engineering, is poised to become a native capability of the model. Temporal reasoning for scheduling and sequencing is shifting from rule-based implementations to learned behaviors, and causal reasoning focuses on cause-and-effect relationships rather than correlations. These capabilities remain largely experimental. Production deployment still requires stronger guarantees for consistency, accuracy, and explainability.

Edge AI addresses latency, privacy, and connectivity constraints through local processing. Specialized models optimized for edge devices handle targeted tasks—such as voice command recognition, entity extraction, and simple intent classification—on constrained hardware without relying on cloud dependencies. The architectural challenge is maintaining consistency between edge and cloud models while managing the distribution of updates and version synchronization. Current implementations keep edge workloads narrow and well defined rather than general-purpose conversations.

Autonomous agent development is progressing toward proactive systems that initiate actions in response to triggers rather than waiting for user queries. These agents monitor business events, execute multistep workflows, and adapt behavior based on outcomes. Today, they require extensive guardrails and human oversight, and genuine autonomy is constrained by goal specification, safety limits, and accountability mechanisms. Production deployments, therefore, focus on narrow, well-scoped tasks with clear success criteria rather than broad autonomy.

11.15.2 Emerging Architectural Patterns

Future architectures aim to address current limitations while unlocking new capabilities built on production experience and research advances.

Federated learning improves models without centralizing sensitive data by training locally and sharing updates rather than raw information. Health care organizations can collectively refine diagnostic models without sharing patient data, and financial institutions can strengthen fraud detection without exposing transaction details. Challenges include achieving model convergence, preventing adversarial updates, and maintaining fairness across participants.

Hybrid quantum-classical approaches use quantum computing for specific optimization problems within broader AI systems. Quantum processors may optimize routing, portfolio allocation, or molecular simulations, while classical systems handle tasks such as NLP and user interaction. These hybrids require orchestration patterns that account for quantum constraints, such as coherence times and error rates, with near-term applications focused on narrow optimization rather than general-purpose quantum AI.

Self-improving architectures detect performance drift and initiate retraining or fine-tuning, monitoring accuracy, distribution shifts, and changing patterns. Current designs typically require human approval for updates and rigorous testing before deployment. Fully autonomous improvement remains constrained by safety concerns and the difficulty of defining appropriate optimization objectives. Production systems typically adjust parameters rather than alter core architectures.

Compositional architectures dynamically assemble specialized models for specific tasks, rather than relying on monoliths to handle everything. For example, a customer service interaction may invoke sentiment analysis, product knowledge, and transaction processing models as needed. This approach reduces compute requirements and can improve explainability, but it depends on sophisticated orchestration and consistent interfaces between components.

11.15.3 Global Regulatory Landscape

Regulatory frameworks continue to emerge worldwide, with marked differences in approach and requirements, forcing organizations to navigate complex and sometimes conflicting obligations.

The European Union's AI Act uses risk-based categories and imposes stringent requirements on high-risk applications in employment, education, law enforcement, and critical infrastructure, including conformity assessments, technical documentation, and human oversight. Prohibited uses include social scoring and real-time biometric identification in public spaces with limited exceptions. Its extraterritorial scope extends to any organization serving residents of the European Union, prompting global companies to adopt the Act's requirements across all their operations rather than maintaining separate compliance regimes.

In the United States, progress occurs through multiple channels, often without the need for comprehensive federal legislation. The National Institute of Standards and Technology AI Risk Management Framework provides voluntary guidance increasingly referenced in procurement. Federal agencies enforce sector-specific regulations—for example, health care applications that make diagnostic recommendations may fall under FDA medical device regulations—and financial services are subject to scrutiny under fair lending laws for credit decisions. States such as California and New York add bias audit and transparency requirements.

China emphasizes algorithmic governance and transparency in recommendation systems, requiring algorithm registration, regular assessments, and user controls for personalized recommendations. Deep-synthesis rules impose labeling for deepfakes and generated content, and cross-border data transfer restrictions complicate international deployments. Operating in China typically requires algorithm explanations and user preference controls.

The United Kingdom follows a principles-based path through existing regulators rather than a single statute. The Information Commissioner's Office addresses AI through data protection law. The Financial Conduct Authority examines AI in financial services, and the Competition and Markets Authority investigates algorithmic collusion and market manipulation. This distributed approach offers flexibility but requires organizations to interpret how existing rules apply to AI.

International standards, as outlined in ISO/IEC JTC 1/SC 42—a joint technical committee of ISO and the International Electrotechnical Commission (IEC)—are shaping common frameworks for governance, risk management, and testing. These standards are increasingly influencing national regulations and procurement, positioning organizations for cross-jurisdictional compliance, although adoption remains voluntary in most regions.

11.15.4 Compliance and Governance Implementation

Translating regulation into operations requires governance across technical, organizational, and procedural dimensions.

Bias detection and mitigation often span the full life cycle. Predeployment testing can reveal demographic disparities, production monitoring can surface emerging bias patterns, and mitigation can include data augmentation, reweighting, or algorithmic adjustments. Because fairness can be defined in multiple, sometimes conflicting, ways—such as equal opportunity, demographic parity, and individual fairness—teams often document the criteria they adopt and retain evidence of ongoing monitoring over time.

Explainability requirements vary by risk level and jurisdiction. High-risk decisions may call for detailed explanations of individual outcomes, while lower-risk applications may rely on broader model descriptions. Common techniques include feature importance analysis, counterfactuals, and example-based reasoning. Model selection is often shaped by the trade-off between transparency and accuracy, as simpler, more interpretable approaches may sacrifice some performance relative to complex neural networks. The balance depends on the use case and the applicable obligations.

Audit trails and documentation often extend beyond traditional logs to include model versions, training data characteristics, and decision rationales. Immutable logs are typically designed to capture enough detail to reconstruct predictions when needed. Documentation includes model cards detailing the intended use, performance, and limitations, as well as the architecture and training procedures and validation results. The workload suggests the need for automated generation and standardized templates at scale.

Human oversight remains central to accountability in high-risk applications. A common pitfall is a "rubber-stamp" review, in which reviewers accept recommendations without critical evaluation. Effective oversight tends to depend on clear user interfaces, adequate review time, and training that equips reviewers to exercise judgment. In mature governance programs, oversight is evidenced by operational safeguards with measurable effects, rather than by processes that primarily serve as theatrical compliance.

Data governance for AI extends privacy practices to include training data quality, lineage tracking to identify and remediate problematic data, and consent mechanisms that reflect AI-specific uses, such as model training and improvement. Data minimization principles can conflict with big data approaches, so teams often balance the data required for effective AI with privacy obligations and protection requirements.

11.15.5 Market Dynamics and Competitive Forces

Competition in AI platforms is intense, with rapidly evolving capabilities and shifting differentiation.

AWS draws on the scale of its infrastructure and its enterprise reach. AWS Bedrock offers access to multiple foundation models—including Anthropic's Claude and Amazon's Titan—and SageMaker provides comprehensive development and deployment tooling. AWS's edge lies in infrastructure flexibility and the breadth of model choices, although tighter integration with productivity tools used by business users remains a challenge.

Google Cloud brings strengths in search, knowledge graphs, and the TensorFlow ecosystem. Vertex AI unifies services with robust ML operations, while Google's research leadership in transformers and LLMs informs core platform features. Integration with Google Workspace enhances productivity through collaboration and workflow tools, though enterprise adoption lags Microsoft 365.

Open source options, such as Hugging Face, LangChain, and a range of foundation models, offer flexibility and prevent vendor lock-in, giving organizations the freedom to deploy models on any infrastructure, customize them freely, and maintain complete control. The trade-off is taking on governance, security, and performance optimization, which demands technical depth and operational maturity. Many teams adopt hybrid models that combine open source components with cloud services.

Specialized providers target particular capabilities or industries. Anthropic focuses on AI safety and constitutional techniques, Cohere on enterprise search and retrieval, and Scale AI on data labeling and evaluation. These firms often partner with major cloud providers while maintaining independent offerings, thus paving the way for organizations to combine specialist services with platform capabilities.

Microsoft's position rests on ecosystem integration rather than any single technical edge. Azure infrastructure, Microsoft 365, and long-standing enterprise relationships reinforce one another. Customers already using Microsoft 365 can quickly deploy Copilot. Microsoft Entra ID supplies unified identity, and Power Platform supports citizen development of AI applications. This ecosystem raises switching costs and accelerates deployment for existing Microsoft customers.

11.15.6 Organizational Readiness and Change Management

Successful adoption requires organizational change beyond technology.

Skills gaps are a primary constraint. Teams need AI architects who understand business context and technical options, ML engineers who implement and optimize models, prompt engineers who design effective interactions with LLMs, and data scientists who select and validate models. Scarcity drives compensation pressure and talent competition, so companies balance external hiring with internal upskilling through training and partnerships with educational institutions.

Governance structures are adapting to AI-specific issues that traditional IT frameworks do not fully address, such as bias, explainability, and continuous learning systems. New roles are emerging, including AI ethics officers, model risk managers, and algorithmic auditors. In response, cross-functional committees often coordinate legal, compliance, technical, and business stakeholders. Decision rights for deployment, update approvals, and incident response are clarified through defined responsibilities and escalation paths.

Change management often differs because employees may worry about job displacement and loss of autonomy. Transparent communication that frames AI as augmentation rather than replacement, together with training that helps employees work effectively with AI assistants, can improve acceptance. Success metrics often prioritize the quality of human–AI collaboration over automation rates alone.

Process re-engineering opportunities arise when AI opens the way for a deeper redesign. Customer service can shift from ticket resolution to proactive issue prevention; financial analysis can shift from periodic reporting to continuous monitoring with exception-based alerts; and health care delivery can shift from reactive treatment to prevention and early intervention. Realizing these gains requires reimagining workflows rather than merely inserting AI into existing steps.

Cultural shifts toward data-driven decision-making and experimentation also matter. Teams need to be comfortable with probabilistic systems, tolerate controlled failure in experiments, and be transparent about limitations to avoid overreliance. Trust grows through pilot projects that demonstrate value before being rolled out more broadly.

11.15.7 Risk Management and Mitigation Strategies

AI introduces risks that necessitate targeted identification, assessment, and mitigation beyond traditional IT practices.

Model degradation over time is expected as data distributions shift. Monitoring typically tracks accuracy, prediction distributions, and changes in feature importance, with thresholds that can trigger retraining or replacement. Because it can be difficult to distinguish natural variation from meaningful drift, many teams maintain model inventories with refresh schedules and sunset plans.

Adversarial threats include crafted inputs that cause misclassification, prompt injection to override instructions, data poisoning during training, and model extraction via repeated queries. Defenses such as input validation, anomaly detection, and rate limiting are helpful, but a perfect defense is unrealistic and does not align with incident response playbooks.

Vendor dependencies introduce exposure to service discontinuation, price fluctuations, and capacity constraints. Mitigation includes abstraction layers between applications and AI services, contingency plans for alternative solutions, and negotiated SLAs. Multicloud strategies increase flexibility but add complexity.

Liability and insurance gaps can persist. Errors-and-omissions policies may exclude algorithmic decisions, while cyber coverage may not address AI-specific attacks. These raise questions about board oversight of AI among directors and officers. Risk programs often respond by reviewing coverage terms, negotiating AI-specific provisions where feasible, and retaining reserves for exposures that remain uninsured.

Reputation risk can exceed direct financial loss. Biased outcomes affecting protected groups invite scrutiny, hallucinated information damages credibility, and privacy violations trigger backlash. Managing reputation risk requires proactive communication, rapid incident response, and transparent accountability.

11.15.8 Strategic Planning Considerations

Strategic approaches often read like a balancing act. Leaders look for ways to capture opportunity without taking on disproportionate risk, and they keep enough flexibility in the plan to adapt as conditions change and the future reveals itself.

Platform strategies often aim to reduce premature lock-in by introducing abstraction layers between applications and AI services. They combine multiple providers where prudent and invest in platform-agnostic skills and tools. Enterprise agreements can support pricing predictability while preserving flexibility to adopt emerging capabilities.

Capability roadmaps are frequently sequenced by business value, feasibility, and risk tolerance. Many programs begin with internal productivity to build familiarity, demonstrate progress through high-value, low-risk use cases, and defer complex, high-risk applications until governance and operations are mature. Roadmaps also tend to remain flexible enough to incorporate new capabilities without constant rework.

Investment frameworks need to account for rapid evolution and uncertain returns. Option value thinking better captures flexibility, portfolio approaches balance safer incremental gains with bolder initiatives, and staged pilots and proofs of concept sustain learning while limiting commitment.

Partnership strategies can accelerate progress while maintaining strategic control. Cloud providers and AI specialists offer cutting-edge capabilities; implementation partners contribute proven methods and experienced resources; academic partners advance research and talent pipelines; and strategic customers codevelop solutions and provide real-world validation. These collaborations work best with clear governance, aligned incentives, and well-drafted intellectual property terms.

The convergence of technological advances, regulatory maturation, and organizational readiness creates both opportunities and challenges for the adoption of Azure AI Services. Organizations that navigate these dimensions carefully, while keeping options open, position themselves for a durable advantage. Success depends not only on technical implementation but also on comprehensive transformation across all aspects of skills, processes, governance, and culture. Benefits will accrue to organizations that combine human judgment with AI capabilities while managing the attendant risks and regulatory obligations.

Underpinning the Azure AI Services portfolio is Microsoft Foundry, Microsoft's unified platform for building, evaluating, and deploying AI applications and agents. While Azure AI Services provides discrete cognitive capabilities as consumable APIs, Foundry provides the development environment in which those capabilities can be assembled into complete solutions. Its model catalog offers access to models from OpenAI, Meta, Mistral, and other providers alongside Microsoft's own models, giving architects flexibility beyond the OpenAI-only model scope of Azure OpenAI Service. Prompt flow supports the structured development and evaluation of LLM-based pipelines, while Microsoft Foundry Agent Service supports the design and deployment of autonomous agents that orchestrate tools, state, and reasoning across multistep workflows. For organizations building enterprise AI applications, Foundry has become the primary workspace where model selection, prompt engineering, evaluation, safety configuration, and deployment converge into a governed, repeatable process.

11.16 Summary

Azure AI Services has evolved from experimental technology into the production-grade foundation for enterprise conversational AI systems. Reflecting on the arc from those early grammar engines to today's platform, I am struck by how much has changed—and how much remains constant. The technology is unrecognizably more powerful, but the principles that made systems work then still apply now: modularity, clear contracts, graceful degradation, and respect for the complexity of human language. What has changed is that these principles can now be applied at a planetary scale, with capabilities that would have seemed miraculous to my younger self, debugging finite-state machines late into the night. Deployments in enterprise contact centers have reported improvements in first-call resolution, self-service rates, and average handling time, improving both customer experience and operational efficiency.

The architectural foundation of Azure AI Services rests on a five-layer stack that systematically abstracts complexity while delivering industrial-strength capabilities. From GPU clusters and FPGAs at the infrastructure layer, through pretrained models, service orchestration, and SDKs, to complete applications, each layer exposes clear contracts while hiding implementation complexity. With this modularity, organizations can adopt AI incrementally while maintaining enterprise-grade security and compliance.

The progression from scripted call routing to context-aware conversational interfaces represents a fundamental shift in human–computer interaction. Through integrated services—Azure Language for understanding, Azure Speech for voice interaction, Azure AI Vision and Document Intelligence for visual processing, and Azure OpenAI Service for generation and reasoning—the platform provides a complete toolkit for intelligent applications. Success comes from the thoughtful orchestration of these services through proven architectural patterns, including hybrid systems that combine rule-based logic with AI models, multimodel ensembles, and sophisticated memory management spanning conversational, user, episodic, and semantic contexts.

Implementation excellence distinguishes successful deployments from failed experiments. Zero-trust security with managed identities, error handling with circuit breakers, and IaC practices establish solid foundations. Performance optimization through intelligent caching, appropriate model selection, and asynchronous processing can materially reduce latency and improve responsiveness at scale. A multifaceted testing strategy incorporating automated validation, synthetic data generation, and human-in-the-loop review secures the reliability and quality of the final solution. These practices, refined through deployments across telecommunications, health care, financial services, and other industries, demonstrate the versatility and transformative potential of conversational AI.

The regulatory landscape and competitive dynamics continue to evolve rapidly. Many organizations navigate complex compliance obligations, including the European Union's AI Act and sector-specific regulations, while managing risks that range from model degradation to adversarial attacks. Microsoft's ecosystem integration can be an advantage for organizations already invested in Microsoft 365, while AWS, Google Cloud, and open source alternatives offer compelling capabilities. Successful adoption often combines technical implementation with organizational change, including closing skills gaps, updating governance practices, and supporting cultural shifts.

Looking forward, Azure AI Services continues to advance toward multimodal integration, edge deployment, and autonomous agents, while organizations develop strategic approaches that balance opportunity capture with risk management. The convergence of technological advancement, regulatory maturation, and organizational readiness creates unprecedented opportunities for those who thoughtfully combine human judgment with AI capabilities.

The capabilities described in this chapter—cognitive APIs, orchestration patterns, RAG pipelines, and evaluation frameworks—form the building blocks of the agentic era now emerging across enterprise AI. Where earlier implementations relied on human-triggered workflows, modern agent architectures built on Foundry Agent Service and the Microsoft 365 Agents SDK can plan and execute multistep tasks, invoke tools, and maintain state across interactions. Rather than simply responding to prompts, these systems can function as reasoning engines that decompose high-level business objectives into sequences of logical operations. They can select and invoke appropriate tools—whether querying a real-time data stream, updating a legacy ERP system, or orchestrating a multiparty approval process—while tracking progress against the stated goal. When designed with evaluation, feedback, and recovery mechanisms, such agents can transform software from a passive utility into an active participant in the business process. The architectural patterns examined here provide the foundation on which these systems are constructed.

Azure AI Services represents just one component of Microsoft's broader AI strategy. While these services provide foundational AI capabilities, they achieve their full potential when integrated into daily workflows. This brings us to the next evolution: the Copilot ecosystem. Where Azure AI Services provides the underlying intelligence infrastructure, Copilot embeds that intelligence directly into familiar applications. As we will explore in the next chapter, Copilot transforms AI from a capability into a collaborator—making intelligence not just available but ambient throughout the modern workplace.

CHAPTER 12

The Copilot Ecosystem

The Copilot ecosystem represents a foundational shift in enterprise computing. AI-powered assistants can work alongside people to augment decision-making, accelerate productivity, and support new workflows across business functions. These systems extend beyond traditional automation by generating drafts, summaries, and recommendations that users review and refine in the context of their work. This chapter focuses on Microsoft Copilot offerings across Microsoft 365, GitHub, and related Microsoft platforms. These AI assistants are becoming increasingly integral to how many organizations execute knowledge work.

Microsoft has reported expanding enterprise interest and growing deployments of Copilot offerings, including adoption by large enterprises. The broader pattern suggests that many organizations are moving beyond pilots and integrating Copilot into operational workflows, while governance, security, and change management increasingly determine outcomes.

Built on the Azure AI Services infrastructure detailed in the previous chapter, Copilot embeds this intelligence directly into familiar workplace applications. The underlying Azure OpenAI Service, Azure Language, and other services provide the foundational capabilities, while Copilot delivers these through natural interfaces within the tools people use daily. This architectural approach transforms AI from a separate capability requiring specialized knowledge into an ambient intelligence woven throughout the digital workplace.

The path to modern AI assistants took a more practical form in the 1980s and 1990s, as foundational productivity tools began to incrementally improve specific aspects of knowledge work. Although the broader field of AI has much deeper historical roots, these decades marked an important transition as software moved from passive data entry toward more active, intelligent assistance.

Early innovations included spell checkers, grammar tools, and formatting assistants that enhanced document correctness. Through my long association with Microsoft, I contributed to capabilities such as the grammar engine and spell-checking

K. C. Mukherjee, *The Microsoft AI Insider's Playbook*, https://doi.org/10.1007/979-8-8688-2730-3_12

infrastructure that helped make Word more intelligent and improved writing assistance at scale. Development environments gained code completion features that accelerated programming by predicting common patterns. These tools improved efficiency within narrow domains but did not fundamentally alter how people approached their work.

Each generation of tools expanded capability while revealing limitations. Grammar checkers could identify errors, but could not improve writing style. Code completion could suggest syntax, but could not understand the programmer's intent. These tools remained reactive—responding to specific triggers rather than understanding the broader context. They improved the mechanics of work without addressing its substance.

Copilot represents a fundamental advance from these incremental improvements. Rather than correcting errors or completing patterns, it understands objectives and generates appropriate responses. This shift from mechanical assistance to intelligent partnership marks a transformation in human-computer interaction.

The journey to today's generative Copilots spans decades of AI development. Early rule-based systems of the 1980s and 1990s operated on if-then logic. They required programming for every possible scenario. While useful for structured tasks, these systems lacked flexibility and could not adapt to novel situations. The late 1990s and 2000s saw the rise of statistical learning and early NLP. My work on the INTELLIFM technology during this period demonstrated both the promise and the limitations of this era. We could parse business rules from domain experts using declarative programming, but the system still required structured input rather than true NLU. Assistants like Clippy could offer contextual suggestions, though still limited by predefined responses.

The breakthrough came with deep learning in the 2010s. The transformer architecture introduced in 2017 laid the groundwork for LLMs. Today's generative Copilots represent a major advance in capability: they can interpret prompts, incorporate available context, and generate drafts and options for users to evaluate. Unlike earlier rule-based systems that followed explicit scripts, modern Copilots can support more flexible workflows. Improvements typically arise from periodic updates to models, tooling, and services rather than from per-user training during everyday interactions.

This chapter explores Microsoft's Copilot ecosystem and how it embeds AI assistance directly into familiar workplace applications. It examines the technical architecture that powers Copilot across Microsoft 365, GitHub, and other platforms. It covers practical applications in sales, marketing, development, and operations. It also analyzes how Copilot integrates with existing enterprise systems and the standards behind this connectivity.

The discussion includes user experience design principles and how people interact with these AI assistants. It addresses enterprise deployment challenges, security requirements, and governance frameworks that organizations must consider. The chapter also examines the developer community and partner network, which are expanding Copilot's capabilities.

Finally, the chapter addresses limitations—from accuracy issues to adoption barriers—and looks ahead to how this technology is expected to evolve. Through this examination, readers will gain a deeper understanding not only of what Copilot does but also of how it fundamentally reshapes the relationship between humans and AI in the modern workplace.

12.1 Architectural Foundations

The power of Microsoft's Copilot and agent ecosystem stems from a multilayered architecture that combines frontier AI models with enterprise-grade infrastructure. These foundations explain how Copilot can evolve from a standalone assistant into an integrated intelligence layer across Microsoft's productivity environment.

Like many Azure and Foundry services, Copilot-related architectures can be understood through a control plane and data plane model. The control plane governs configuration, policy enforcement, identity, and routing—managing how services are provisioned, which models and tools are available, and what governance rules apply. The data plane handles execution: model inference, retrieval and grounding through the relevant context layer, tool invocation, and response generation. In Microsoft 365 Copilot, that context commonly comes through Microsoft Graph and the Semantic Index; in Foundry-based agent architectures, it can come through Foundry IQ.

Foundry documentation explicitly distinguishes control plane actions, such as creating deployments and projects, from data plane actions, such as building agents, running evaluations, and uploading files. This separation allows teams to apply governance controls independently to retrieval, tool execution, and model inference, and it gives Azure-experienced architects a familiar mental model for reasoning about security boundaries, policy enforcement, and operational management.

12.1.1 Core Components: The Technical Stack

At the heart of Copilot lie three essential components that work in concert: LLMs provide the generative capability, orchestration layers manage the interactions and tool use, and user interfaces deliver the experience. This layered architecture echoes principles my teams helped establish decades earlier with OLE and COM at Microsoft—the idea that complex capabilities are best exposed through well-defined interfaces, allowing components to evolve independently while maintaining seamless integration.

The hardware foundation supporting Copilot spans both cloud infrastructure and, in some scenarios, device-level acceleration. Modern devices with neural processing units (NPUs) can perform selected, latency-sensitive tasks locally, which can reduce round-trip times for certain interactions and limit the amount of data that must be transmitted for processing. In most enterprise Copilot experiences, however, higher-order reasoning and cross-application synthesis remain cloud-mediated and are governed by tenant identity, permissions, and policy controls.

Work is allocated between device and cloud based on the task, the user's context, tenant configuration, and the capabilities of the endpoint. Device-local processing is typically limited to narrowly scoped functions that benefit from immediacy, while cloud processing handles tasks that require richer context, synthesis across multiple documents, or access to organizational data. This hybrid model can improve responsiveness for supported local operations, but end-to-end performance and feature availability vary by product, workload, and deployment settings.

The model foundation primarily relies on LLMs hosted on Azure's secure infrastructure. Different Copilot experiences can draw on different model families, including general-purpose models for language tasks and code-focused models for software engineering workflows. Model selection and availability vary by product, plan, and configuration. Rather than treating model capacity as a fixed constant, Copilot manages context through orchestration techniques such as retrieval, summarization, and selective inclusion of relevant artifacts, so that the interaction remains grounded in permitted enterprise data while staying within model limits.

The orchestration layer coordinates the end-to-end flow of each interaction across three distinct subsystems. *Prompt orchestration* handles context assembly, token management, and prompt construction. It selects and structures artifacts to stay within the model's context limits while preserving the information most relevant to the current task. *Retrieval orchestration* manages the RAG pipeline, determining what content to retrieve through the relevant grounding layer, how to rank it, and how to pass it to the model as grounding context. Depending on the product surface, that grounding layer may rely on Microsoft Graph and the Semantic Index or on Foundry IQ and related retrieval infrastructure. *Tool orchestration* governs the invocation of external systems, APIs, and workflows through the appropriate tool layer. Depending on the product surface, that layer may include Foundry Tools, product-specific connectors, or plugin frameworks. It also manages sequencing, error handling, and result integration.

Each subsystem can be governed independently, allowing teams to apply different access controls, logging policies, and compliance rules to retrieval, tool execution, and model inference. The orchestration layer also applies safety and quality checks before responses are returned to the user, subject to tenant policy and product configuration. This framing aligns with Microsoft's architecture guidance, which distinguishes control plane management from data plane execution.

User interfaces represent sophisticated interaction layers that understand user intent before it reaches the LLM. In Word, the interface recognizes whether users are drafting, editing, or formatting and adjusts Copilot's responses accordingly. In Excel, it distinguishes between data analysis and visualization tasks and automatically selects appropriate statistical methods or chart types. These contextual cues shape prompt construction. In Word, a request to "make this better" may trigger stylistic improvements, whereas the same request in Excel may prompt changes to formulas or data organization.

This context-aware behavior represents a natural evolution of the programmability model my teams helped create with WordBASIC and VBA. Where macros required users to explicitly script their intentions, Copilot infers intent from context—a shift from imperative to declarative interaction that we could only dream of in the early 1990s. Table 12-1 provides a reference architecture for Copilot-style systems. It uses representative components and technologies to illustrate how the layers fit together. Specific Microsoft products may implement these layers differently.

Table 12-1. *Reference architecture layers for Copilot-style systems showing representative components, primary functions, and key technologies. Actual implementations vary by product, tenant configuration, and enterprise governance requirements.*

Layer	Components	Primary Function	Key Technologies
AI models	Frontier and code-focused language models; domain models where applicable	Core reasoning and generation	Azure OpenAI Service; model catalog varies by product
Orchestration	Agent/orchestration frameworks and policies; prompt templates; tool invocation	Request routing, chaining, and tool use	Orchestration frameworks (for example, Semantic Kernel); API management; service mesh
Grounding	RAG; Microsoft Graph; enterprise search	Context grounding and personalization	Azure AI Search; Microsoft Graph API; Semantic Index (for Microsoft 365 Copilot)
Data layer	OneDrive; SharePoint; Dataverse (as applicable)	Organizational knowledge	Storage services; databases
Integration	Plugins; connectors; APIs	Application connectivity	REST APIs; OAuth; webhooks
Interface	Chat interfaces; sidebars; embedded panels	User interaction	Web frameworks; Adaptive Cards
Security	Microsoft Entra ID; data loss prevention (DLP); encryption	Access control and compliance	Identity platform; secrets and key management (for example, Key Vault)

12.1.2 Integration Architecture: The Microsoft Ecosystem

Microsoft 365 Copilot's integration with Microsoft 365, Azure, and Power Platform reflects deep platform embedding rather than a superficial overlay. By grounding responses in Microsoft Graph data and the Semantic Index, Microsoft keeps the assistant operating within the enterprise's existing security, permissions, and compliance boundaries. This architecture allows the system to draw on real-time organizational context while respecting user-level access controls and tenant boundaries.

Within Microsoft 365, Copilot commonly integrates via Microsoft Graph, which provides unified access to user and organizational data across services, subject to tenant licensing, configuration, and access permissions. This integration supports contextual assistance without bypassing governance controls. For example, when a user asks Copilot to "summarize yesterday's meeting about Project Phoenix," Copilot can draw on available and permitted meeting artifacts, including the transcript or recording, associated chat, shared files, and related calendar context. From these sources, it synthesizes a summary that highlights decisions, action items, and follow-up tasks. The fidelity of the result depends on what was captured, what is retained, and what the user is authorized to access.

Azure integration extends beyond hosting infrastructure. Copilot uses Foundry Tools—the rebranded Azure AI Services portfolio—to perform specialized tasks such as real-time translation and clinical documentation. Azure Speech supports meeting transcription with speaker diarization, which identifies who spoke at what times. Azure AI Search retrieves enterprise knowledge from large document collections. Azure Language performs sentiment analysis and extracts named entities. Azure OpenAI Service hosts models and provides dedicated capacity. This modular approach supports independent scaling of specific capabilities—for example, transcription capacity can be increased during meeting-heavy periods while maintaining consistent chat performance.

Security architecture maintains strict tenant isolation through multiple layers. Microsoft Entra ID enforces authentication and authorization at service boundaries. Data is protected in transit and at rest through Microsoft 365 and Azure security controls, as well as industry-standard cryptography. However, the specific algorithms, protocol versions, and enforcement mechanisms vary by service, region, and tenant configuration. Tenant data remains logically separated through compute and storage partitioning with strict access controls. Zero-trust principles reinforce authentication and authorization at each boundary, limiting lateral movement if a control is compromised and supporting tighter containment during incident response.

Integration with Power Platform transforms Copilot from a productivity assistant into a business process automation engine. Power Automate flows are triggered by Copilot interactions—when Copilot identifies action items in meeting summaries, it can automatically create tasks in project management systems. Conversely, Copilot can initiate workflows from natural language requests. For example, "Schedule follow-up meetings with everyone from today's review" triggers a complex workflow that includes calendar checks, meeting room bookings, and invitation sends.

Power BI aims to make business intelligence (BI) more accessible by translating business questions into technical queries and visualization suggestions. Copilot's integration with Power BI allows natural language data exploration, where users can ask, "What were our top-selling products last quarter?" and receive both visualizations and narrative insights.

Microsoft's infrastructure investments support Copilot's scale and reliability requirements. Geographic distribution across many Azure regions can reduce latency for users. Nevertheless, end-to-end response times still depend on task complexity, model selection, orchestration overhead, and tenant configuration. Infrastructure scale can improve resilience, but outcomes remain workload-dependent and warrant validation with measurement in the target environment.

12.1.3 Semantic Intelligence: Grounding and RAG

The sophistication of Copilot's responses comes from three interconnected capabilities: semantic indexing, grounding, and RAG. Together, they can improve relevance by selecting permitted organizational content and using it as context for generation. Results still depend on indexing coverage, retrieval quality, and governance controls.

Semantic indexing supports meaning-based retrieval across organizational content by combining embeddings with metadata signals. Unlike keyword-only indexing, it can surface related concepts even when terminology differs. Indexing latency and coverage vary with workload, connectors, retention settings, and tenant configuration. As a result, the time from content creation to discoverability should be treated as variable rather than guaranteed. In enterprise deployments, the retrieval layer introduces meaningful operational complexity: content must be chunked into appropriate segments, embedded or otherwise indexed, and enriched with metadata to support hybrid filtering and ranking.

In addition, incremental ingestion and refresh workflows must be maintained so that the index stays current as source content changes. Teams that underestimate the overhead of this retrieval layer often encounter stale-grounding problems, where the assistant produces answers based on outdated versions of organizational documents.

Grounding seeks to anchor responses in permitted organizational sources by retrieving relevant items and using them as context for generation. Outcomes vary with retrieval quality, indexing coverage, and permissions. Some experiences can surface source references or links when that capability is available. High-impact facts are often checked against the underlying documents and systems of record, especially when data changes frequently or when governance constraints limit retrieval.

RAG combines retrieval and generation to produce answers that reflect relevant organizational context. For a query such as "What are the dependencies for launching our European expansion?" the system can retrieve relevant artifacts (for example, strategic plans, regulatory guidance, market analysis, and project timelines), rank them by relevance, and assemble an evidence set within the defined context. End-to-end latency varies with retrieval scope, network conditions, and the amount of context assembled. The model synthesizes retrieved information into a structured response. Dependencies and high-impact details are often checked against authoritative sources such as project plans and systems of record. This architectural foundation allows Copilot to deliver responses that are not only linguistically fluent but also factually accurate, organizationally relevant, and appropriately contextualized.

12.2 Functional Domains

The Copilot ecosystem encompasses a wide range of business functions, with each implementation tailored to specific workflows and user needs. From writing documents to analyzing security threats, these specialized Copilots demonstrate how AI assistance adapts to different professional contexts while maintaining a consistent underlying architecture. Table 12-2 summarizes the primary Copilot products, their target users, integration points, and licensing models.

Table 12-2. *Comparison of Microsoft Copilot products showing primary functions, target users, integration points, and licensing models across the ecosystem. Each product addresses specific domain needs while sharing standard architectural foundations.*

Product	Primary Function	Key Users	Integration Points	Licensing Model
Microsoft 365 Copilot	Productivity assistance across the Office apps	Knowledge workers, executives	Word, Excel, PowerPoint, Teams, Outlook	Per user/month
GitHub Copilot	Code generation and completion	Software developers	VS Code, Visual Studio, JetBrains IDEs	Individual/business
Security Copilot	Threat detection and incident response	Security analysts, SOC teams	Sentinel, Defender, Intune	SCU (Security Compute Units)-based capacity; exact entitlements vary by offer
Dynamics 365 Copilot	CRM and ERP assistance	Sales, service, finance teams	Dynamics apps, Power Platform	Per user/month
Copilot in Windows	Operating system–level assistance and automation	All Windows users	Windows 11, Edge browser	Included with Windows for baseline experiences; advanced capabilities may require additional licensing
Power Platform Copilot	Low-code development assistance	Citizen developers	Power Apps, Power Automate, Power BI	Per user/month
Copilot Studio	Custom agent and assistant development; autonomous workflow automation	IT developers, citizen developers, business analysts	Microsoft 365, Teams, Power Platform, Azure AI, third-party APIs	Per user/month; consumption-based for messages and agent execution

12.2.1 Productivity Copilots: Transforming Knowledge Work

Microsoft 365 Copilot is a suite-level offering that brings AI assistance across the Microsoft 365 application portfolio. Rather than functioning as a single monolithic tool, it delivers app-specific Copilot experiences within Word, Excel, PowerPoint, Outlook, Teams, and related Microsoft 365 services. Each experience is tailored to the context, data structures, and user workflows of its host application.

While the underlying intelligence is powered by frontier models, the system's orchestration and app-specific integration adapt the assistant's behavior to the task at hand. For example, Copilot in Teams emphasizes meeting recap, synthesis, and action item follow-up, while Copilot in Word is optimized for drafting, rewriting, and document refinement. This suite-level approach gives organizations a consistent security, permissions, and compliance model across Microsoft 365 while still delivering specialized capabilities for different professional workflows.

Word Copilot excels at document creation and refinement through NLU. It drafts initial content from brief prompts, expands outlines into full documents, and rewrites sections for different audiences. The system uses style-aware models or context-sensitive mechanisms to match linguistic patterns—formal register for legal documents, conversational tone for marketing copy, and technical precision for documentation. When generating content, it analyzes existing document context to align vocabulary complexity, sentence length, and paragraph structure where appropriate. Word Copilot can transform a technical specification into an executive summary by identifying key points and abstracting implementation details while preserving essential business impact.

Excel Copilot aims to make data analysis more conversational by applying semantic understanding to business data. Users describe analytical goals in natural language, and Copilot generates appropriate formulas, pivot tables, and visualizations. The system can surface statistical summaries and pattern detection results, potentially drawing on time-series analysis, correlation metrics, and variance estimates to help identify trends and anomalies. For example, when analyzing sales data, it may surface recurring patterns—such as periodic revenue dips related to billing cycles—that manual review could miss. Excel Copilot can explain findings in plain language and translate common statistical concepts into business-relevant phrasing. Analytical assumptions and interpretations are often validated by users before conclusions are shared.

PowerPoint Copilot accelerates presentation creation through intelligent design assistance and content transformation. It converts Word documents into structured presentations by identifying key themes, extracting supporting points, and organizing information hierarchically. The system applies design principles, including visual balance, color theory, and typography rules, to suggest appropriate layouts. When generating speaker notes, it creates complementary narratives that expand on slide content rather than repeating it. PowerPoint Copilot maintains brand consistency by analyzing established templates and applying organizational design standards across new presentations.

Teams Copilot synthesizes information across permitted communication channels, subject to tenant settings and access permissions. During meetings, it generates real-time summaries, tracks action items, and identifies unresolved questions. The system understands conversational dynamics—distinguishing between brainstorming, decision-making, and information sharing. After meetings, Teams Copilot creates structured recaps that include participant contributions, decisions reached, and follow-up assignments. It can answer questions about past discussions within the scope of available and permitted data by searching authorized chat history, shared files, and meeting recordings, subject to tenant licensing and admin controls.

Outlook Copilot manages communication complexity through contextual awareness and configured user preferences. It drafts responses by analyzing the user's previous emails to match their tone, level of formality, and typical response length. The system summarizes long email threads by identifying key decisions, extracting action items, and highlighting unresolved issues. When scheduling meetings, it considers factors such as time zone differences, meeting room availability, and calendar patterns visible through Microsoft Graph. Outlook Copilot may refine suggestions based on configured preferences and usage patterns, subject to tenant settings and privacy controls.

Copilot in Windows provides AI assistance for system tasks such as finding settings, troubleshooting common issues, and completing repetitive actions, subject to available operating system controls and user permissions. The system can interpret natural language requests—such as asking to improve battery life—and, where supported, suggest or apply settings changes such as enabling energy saver, reducing background activity, or opening relevant system controls. Microsoft has also introduced a Copilot-powered agent in Windows Settings that can help users find and change settings through natural language. On Copilot+ PCs, some AI-powered experiences and models run locally on the NPU, which can improve latency and support on-device privacy for those specific features. In practice, this can also make technical tasks more accessible to nontechnical users by reducing the need to manually navigate deeply nested settings.

12.2.2 Developer Copilots: Accelerating Software Creation

GitHub Copilot has accelerated software development by bringing AI assistance directly into the coding environment. It suggests entire functions from natural language comments, completes complex algorithms from partial implementations, and generates test suites. The system uses contextual signals to infer code semantics beyond syntax. It can suggest design patterns, error handling approaches, and refactorings (structural improvements to code that preserve its behavior) to promote architectural consistency.

GitHub Copilot is trained on a large body of code from existing code repositories, and the default inline-suggestions model is documented as being trained on high-quality public GitHub repositories. GitHub also applies product policies and safeguards to improve relevance and reduce the likelihood of suggestions that closely match publicly available code. GitHub provides controls for suggestions that match public code, including the ability to block such suggestions or to show code references to similar public sources. GitHub's disclosures in this area continue to evolve as product features, training practices, and legal frameworks develop. This managed approach allows teams to adopt AI-assisted development within enterprise policy and compliance boundaries while accounting for intellectual property concerns.

The system's effectiveness stems from its ability to understand developer intent through multiple signals. Comment analysis extracts functional requirements, variable names indicate data types and purposes, and surrounding code provides architectural context. When a developer types a comment like "// Calculate compound interest with monthly contributions," GitHub Copilot generates not just the formula but also parameter validation, edge case handling, and appropriate documentation. It adapts to project conventions by analyzing existing code patterns, matching indentation styles, naming conventions, and comment formats.

Visual Studio integration extends capabilities through deeper IDE hooks. Copilot can provide inline documentation, explain unfamiliar code in the project context, and suggest potential performance optimizations using available profiling or telemetry data, where permitted. The system can use debugging context to suggest variable watches and describe execution flow when such context is available in the IDE. During refactoring, Copilot may flag potential code smells—such as duplicated logic or high complexity—and suggest alternative implementations that aim to preserve functionality and improve maintainability. Integration with static analysis tools allows Copilot to predict potential runtime errors and suggest preventive fixes before code execution.

12.2.3 Business Intelligence: Data-Driven Decisions

Power BI Copilot translates business questions into technical queries and visualization suggestions. Users ask questions in natural language, and Copilot can generate Data Analysis Expressions (DAX) measures, propose visualizations, and summarize insights for further validation. The system can use business context and configured glossaries to interpret terms such as "customer churn," including relevant calculations, time windows, and segmentation criteria when context is available. When analyzing financial data, it may apply configured accounting conventions, such as fiscal year boundaries and currency conversion rules, if those settings or contextual signals are available. Power BI Copilot can provide statistical summaries and signal potentially noteworthy trends. It may apply techniques such as regression or hypothesis testing while recommending that analysts verify the methodology and assumptions.

Dynamics 365 Copilot embeds intelligence across business operations with role-specific implementations. In sales, it analyzes customer interaction history to estimate deal probability, identifies cross-selling opportunities based on purchase patterns, and drafts personalized proposals using shared templates and historical examples. The system can incorporate engagement metrics—such as email open rates, meeting attendance, and document interactions—into opportunity health signals when those telemetry sources are enabled and permitted.

In customer service, Dynamics 365 Copilot can suggest ticket routing based on inferred issue complexity and agent skills, propose solutions from knowledge base articles, and maintain conversation context across permitted channels. Resolution rates vary by deployment, and any specific claims are typically supported by product telemetry.

In finance, Dynamics 365 Copilot can assist with the month-end close by automating reconciliation workflows. It can flag transactions that exceed configured deviation thresholds and draft variance explanations that reference available business events for human review.

Viva Copilot enhances employee experience by personalizing workplace interactions within policy boundaries. It can analyze collaboration patterns to suggest focus time, identify meeting overload, and recommend relevant learning resources. It can surface workload and collaboration signals (for example, meeting load, focus-time availability, and after-hours collaboration patterns) and recommend practices such as protected focus blocks or learning plans, subject to tenant policies and privacy controls. Viva Copilot can generate daily briefings that summarize upcoming commitments and priority items, supporting productivity while recognizing organizational governance requirements.

12.2.4 Security and Compliance: Protecting Digital Assets

Microsoft Security Copilot augments security teams by helping prioritize and investigate threats using AI-assisted analysis and automation. It can correlate signals from Microsoft Defender, Sentinel, and integrated third-party tools and map adversary behavior to frameworks such as MITRE ATT&CK when integrations and permissions are enabled. Scale and outcomes vary by deployment: data sources, telemetry volume, retention windows, and detection coverage differ across tenants. When investigating incidents, Security Copilot can help construct timelines, identify affected assets, and summarize findings to accelerate analyst investigation. Nevertheless, validating outputs against existing tools and procedures remains essential.

The system accelerates incident response by automating initial triage and investigation. Upon alerting, Security Copilot can initiate configured playbooks that collect recent logs, query threat intelligence sources, and search for related incidents within permitted telemetry windows defined by tenant configuration. Customers have reported a reduction in mean time to respond in some deployments, thanks to automation and playbook-driven triage. Specific improvement percentages vary by environment and are best cited from deployment telemetry. The system adapts its response based on threat severity—commodity malware receives automated remediation while targeted attacks trigger enhanced monitoring and manual review. Security Copilot generates executive-ready incident reports that translate technical details into business impact assessments, including potential data exposure, regulatory implications, and remediation costs.

Compliance-related capabilities can support control mapping, evidence gathering, and posture assessment when connectors and policies are configured. Mapping cadence, scoring frequency, and drift detection depend on the tenant's governance design rather than a universal real-time default. Automation can help teams assemble audit-ready documentation and highlight areas that require attention. Compliance conclusions are typically confirmed through the organization's established risk, legal, and audit processes.

12.2.5 Custom Copilots: Extending the Ecosystem

Solution teams use Copilot Studio to build specialized assistants tailored to unique business needs without extensive programming expertise. Using a visual workflow designer, businesses create Copilots that understand industry-specific terminology, follow proprietary processes, and integrate with existing systems. Typical implementations include HR onboarding assistants that guide new employees through paperwork and training, procurement advisors who navigate approval workflows and vendor selection, and technical support agents who troubleshoot product issues using internal knowledge bases.

The platform offers numerous prebuilt connectors for standard enterprise systems, covering major vendors such as SAP, Oracle, Workday, and ServiceNow. Exact counts and supported versions depend on the product edition and updates. Custom APIs allow integration with proprietary applications through REST or GraphQL interfaces. NLU adapts to organizational vocabulary through glossary management and entity extraction training. For example, a pharmaceutical company can teach Copilot to recognize drug names, understand clinical trial phases, and follow regulatory submission processes. Testing capabilities include conversation simulation, performance monitoring, and A/B testing to optimize responses.

Microsoft Foundry and related Azure AI platform capabilities support evaluation, prompt workflows, and model customization under supported options. In the broader Azure ecosystem, privacy-preserving training approaches and hybrid patterns may be used. The availability varies by service, model, and deployment architecture and is best treated as scenario-dependent. Custom grounding implementations can draw on curated knowledge sources such as technical manuals, regulatory databases, and internal repositories. Fine-tuning can improve domain performance in some cases. The results depend on dataset quality, task definition, and evaluation methodology and are typically validated for each deployment.

Modern Microsoft agent implementations depend on capabilities that extend beyond simple connectors and grounding. Memory and session management govern how context is retained and recalled across turns and, in some architectures, across sessions, subject to tenant policy and product design. Tool execution frameworks define how agents interact with external systems through structured tool or action calls, including sequencing, error handling, and result integration. State management tracks task progress and pending actions across multistep workflows, allowing agents to resume interrupted processes and maintain coherent behavior. Together, these capabilities distinguish modern agentic implementations from earlier connector-centric approaches. They are central to building reliable, enterprise-grade solutions across Copilot Studio, Microsoft Agent Framework, and Foundry Agent Service, although each product exposes them through a different runtime and authoring model.

Enterprise planning benefits from early attention to compute and latency requirements. Resource requirements (for example, GPU counts) vary widely by model size, latency targets, and concurrency and must be benchmarked for each workload. Data requirements vary by use case. Some conversational assistants benefit from tens of thousands of historical interactions, while highly specialized advisors may require substantially larger, high-quality corpora. Exact needs depend on the desired performance and scope.

Licensing commonly includes per-user subscriptions, consumption-based pricing options, and enterprise agreements. Exact pricing tiers, entry points, and features vary by product, region, and contract. Implementation timelines can range from a few weeks for lightweight Copilot Studio deployments to several months for complex Microsoft Foundry customizations that require model adaptation and deep integrations. Timelines depend on scope, compliance needs, and integration complexity.

12.3 Ecosystem Interoperability

Copilot's value emerges from its ability to operate across Microsoft's technology stack. This interoperability creates a unified intelligence layer that follows users across devices, applications, and workflows, subject to configuration and permissions.

12.3.1 Cross-Platform Integration

Copilot's cross-platform architecture provides AI assistance across environments through Microsoft Graph grounding and shared service infrastructure. When permissions and technical capabilities allow, the integration can carry forward relevant work context across Microsoft 365 experiences.

Cross-application awareness depends primarily on the signals and artifacts available via Microsoft Graph at the time of the request. It is always subject to tenant configuration, permissions, and product behavior. In addition, Microsoft 365 Copilot can retain certain personalization and memory data—such as saved memories, details inferred from chat history, and custom instructions—when those features are enabled. This behavior is governed by tenant and user settings and should not be treated as a universal, global memory layer across all Copilot experiences.

Windows integration embeds Copilot directly into the operating system. Copilot in Windows offers system-level assistance for adjusting settings, troubleshooting, and performing cross-application tasks. When configured appropriately, it can maintain limited awareness between Microsoft applications. For example, when working on a budget in Excel and switching to Outlook, Copilot may suggest relevant attachments from recent work. However, this requires explicit Graph API permissions and only functions within the Microsoft 365 ecosystem. Context preservation depends on application support, user permissions, and tenant configuration.

Edge browser integration extends Copilot to web experiences via a sidebar. It can summarize articles, compare products on supported shopping sites, and assist with form completion where technically feasible. The browser integration operates within security sandboxes—Copilot can analyze visible page content subject to the page context permissions and security boundaries described below.

Before sending page context to the model, Copilot in Edge uses content from the active tab when the user or administrator has allowed page context access. Microsoft documents this in terms of page content or page context, rather than as direct access to arbitrary browser data. This behavior is governed by Copilot in Edge privacy settings and administrative policies. Copilot can use content from the current web page or PDF in the active tab when that permission is enabled, but the exact scope of what is passed is subject to product behavior, tenant controls, and applicable security policies. In some enterprise scenarios, Copilot in Edge can also reference encrypted content from the active tab, depending on DLP controls and the underlying protection rights.

Teams provides Copilot's most integrated collaborative implementation within the Microsoft ecosystem. During meetings with appropriate licenses, it transcribes conversations using Azure Speech, identifies potential action items through NLP, and tracks stated decisions. The system can generate role-appropriate summaries when meeting recordings and transcriptions are enabled. Context from after the meeting persists in Teams channels and associated SharePoint sites, but it requires manual invocation in other applications. Data retention and availability depend on tenant policies and workload-specific retention settings.

Mobile integration adapts Copilot interfaces to device constraints while maintaining session continuity through Microsoft Graph. Mobile applications often prioritize concise responses and voice interaction due to screen limitations. Document synchronization is handled through OneDrive and SharePoint, supporting continuity of work across devices. However, mobile context preservation can be limited—complex formatting, macros, and certain features may not transfer. Session lifetimes and reauthentication intervals are governed by tenant-wide configurations and Conditional Access policies. Most Copilot features require network connectivity because inference and retrieval are typically cloud-mediated. Offline support is limited and depends on the host application and the specific feature.

Microsoft Graph powers cross-device synchronization by maintaining user activity feeds, recently accessed documents, and search queries. This synchronization respects data residency requirements and privacy settings. Graph maintains an activity window whose duration is governed by retention policies and tenant configuration. Not all application state transfers—such as local drafts, unsaved work, and application-specific settings—remain device-bound.

Session lifetime, reauthentication, and data retention are governed by tenant identity and compliance policies. In Microsoft 365, retention is typically governed by mechanisms such as retention labels, retention policies, and e-discovery/legal hold requirements, and it can vary by workload (for example, Teams, Exchange, SharePoint, and OneDrive). Enterprise designs often treat session persistence and retention as policy-driven controls rather than assuming fixed default durations. These settings are typically confirmed for the target tenant and workload.

12.3.2 API and Plugin Architecture

The plugin architecture allows organizations to extend Copilot with specialized capabilities while maintaining security boundaries. Plugins operate under strict sandboxing with defined data access patterns and rate limits.

In modern Copilot and agent architectures, plugins, connectors, and tools provide capabilities that the orchestration layer invokes through structured tool or action calls. As a result, Copilot performs actions such as retrieving data, executing workflows, or interacting with external systems in a controlled and auditable way.

Plugin specifications adhere to OpenAPI 3.0 standards, supplemented with Microsoft-specific extensions for authentication and data handling. Plugins must declare required permissions in their manifest, support OAuth 2.0 or Microsoft Entra authentication, and gracefully handle rate limiting. Data access remains restricted to explicitly granted scopes, and plugins cannot directly modify user data without consent.

Teams message extensions integrate Copilot with line-of-business applications through Adaptive Cards and task modules. These extensions can surface information within conversation flows when users explicitly invoke them. For example, a project management extension may display task status when a task is mentioned, but only for users with appropriate project access. They cannot access conversation history beyond the current message context and must respect Teams information barriers when configured.

Graph connectors ingest external data into Microsoft 365's Semantic Index for search and discovery. Connected content becomes searchable across Microsoft 365 while respecting source system permissions via access control lists. Connectors require Microsoft Entra application registration and appropriate Graph API permissions and typically consume Azure resources that are billed separately.

The certification process for production plugins includes security review, performance testing, and compliance validation. Microsoft reserves the right to throttle or disable plugins that violate performance thresholds or security policies.

Some Microsoft Copilot and agent platforms also support MCP—an open standard originally developed by Anthropic for connecting AI systems to external tools and contextual data through a common interface. In Microsoft's ecosystem, Copilot Studio, Microsoft 365 Copilot declarative agents, and Microsoft Agent Framework all provide MCP-related integration paths, although the implementation differs by product. MCP servers expose tools and resources that agents can discover and invoke at runtime, reducing integration effort and improving interoperability across platforms and vendors.

Plugins, connectors, and MCP-based integrations are subject to quotas, payload limits, timeouts, and concurrency controls that vary by product, licensing tier, and deployment configuration. High-availability designs often incorporate fallback behaviors such as progressive responses, asynchronous execution for long-running tasks, retries with backoff, and graceful degradation as service limits are approached. This helps teams maintain reliability during peak workloads or partial system failures.

12.3.3 Data Governance and Identity

Enterprise adoption of Copilot requires a governance foundation, which Copilot implements through Microsoft Entra identity management, Conditional Access policies, and information protection controls.

Microsoft Entra provides the identity foundation for Copilot interactions. Authentication occurs at session initiation and may be revalidated during extended use. Reauthentication frequency is governed by Conditional Access and risk-based policies, and it varies by tenant configuration and user context. Authorization checks occur on a per-request basis, evaluating user permissions against the requested resources. Copilot respects existing Microsoft 365 permissions—if users cannot access a document directly, Copilot cannot surface its contents. This permission model extends to granular controls where supported. Users may have permission to read financial data, but lack permission to share it externally.

Conditional Access policies facilitate context-aware security controls. Organizations can restrict Copilot based on location (IP ranges, geographic regions), device compliance (managed devices, encryption status), risk scores from Identity Protection, application sensitivity levels, and session duration requirements. These policies apply uniformly across access methods but may impact user experience. Stringent policies may require reauthentication frequently or block specific features entirely on noncompliant devices.

Microsoft Purview provides information protection and governance capabilities. Sensitivity labels automatically classify content based on patterns, keywords, and metadata. Copilot respects these classifications and will not include content marked "Confidential" in responses to users without appropriate clearance. DLP policies can block Copilot from processing specific data types (credit card numbers, health records) in unauthorized contexts. Retention is primarily governed by the underlying workloads (for example, Exchange, SharePoint, OneDrive, and Teams) and by audit and log retention settings. Copilot interactions and related audit events are subject to Microsoft Purview Audit configuration and licensing. Defining retention by policy—confirming behavior for each workload—closes the gap between assumption and reality.

Audit logging tracks Copilot interactions for security and compliance purposes. Logged events typically include the user involved, timestamps, the host application or session context, and references to resources that Copilot or the agent accessed while generating a response. Depending on the product and logging surface, records can also include plugin or tool details, message metadata, model details, and, in tracing scenarios, telemetry about tool invocations and agent execution flow.

Full prompt and response content is not handled uniformly across Microsoft's Copilot and agent stack. In Copilot Studio, audit records in Purview generally store metadata and transcript thread identifiers rather than full conversation text, while transcripts may be available separately through Microsoft's data security posture management (DSPM) for AI and governed by retention policies. In Foundry tracing, sensitive content such as user inputs, model outputs, and tool arguments can be captured when content recording is enabled, and Microsoft recommends disabling that in production environments.

Audit and tracing data support evaluation, debugging, and compliance review. They capture relevant access, policy, authentication, and execution signals where supported, rather than providing a complete record of every permission check and authorization decision.

Audit logs integrate with the Microsoft 365 compliance center and support exporting data to SIEM systems via APIs. Audit retention is determined by the Microsoft Purview Audit capability level (for example, Standard versus Premium) and can also be affected by licensing, tenant configuration, and policy settings. Retention periods have changed over time. Consequently, the correct duration is typically checked against current Microsoft Purview Audit documentation for the tenant's licensing and configuration. Expanded audit logging is often enabled explicitly, since it can affect performance and generate substantial data volumes.

A unified access control model often leads to more consistent enforcement of security policies across tools and data sources. At the same time, the introduction of finer-grained controls tends to increase configuration complexity, and teams often see the trade-off immediately. Tighter restrictions can improve security posture, but they can also limit what Copilot can retrieve and reduce the usefulness of its responses. Over time, many organizations treat this as an ongoing calibration exercise, using periodic access reviews and audit signals to refine policies and keep security and productivity in reasonable alignment.

12.4 Developer and Partner Ecosystem

The Copilot ecosystem expands through contributions from developers and partners who extend, customize, and enhance core capabilities. This collaborative approach creates opportunities for innovation, specialization, and value creation across the industry.

12.4.1 Copilot Studio: Democratizing AI Development

Copilot Studio provides Microsoft's low-code environment for building custom Copilots. Organizations with the appropriate licensing can create specialized AI assistants using visual tools and prebuilt components, although complex scenarios may require additional technical expertise.

Copilot Studio's scope expanded considerably in 2024–2025. Beyond conversational assistants, the platform now supports two distinct agent types. Declarative agents follow natural language instructions and knowledge sources to respond in Microsoft 365 Copilot and other channels. Autonomous agents monitor triggers, initiate multistep workflows, and take actions without a human prompt. The latter reached general availability in 2025 and represent the platform's primary growth vector for enterprise automation. Organizations building at this level of autonomy benefit from narrowly scoped agent permissions, clearly defined escalation paths, and established governance policies before deployment. While the authoring environment is accessible, production-grade agent operation requires the same rigor as any business-critical workflow and often uses MCP to provide secure, standardized access to enterprise data and external applications.

The development environment offers a visual interface for creating conversational experiences. Developers define conversation flows using visual designers that map prompts, actions, and responses. In practice, these flows typically use a hybrid approach that combines structured logic with LLM-based reasoning. This combination allows agents to interpret user intent dynamically while keeping complex operations within the boundaries of controlled workflows.

Copilot Studio manages orchestration within configured parameters. NLU relies on available models, context management operates within memory limits, and response generation follows defined templates and rules. While basic flows require minimal coding, advanced scenarios often require custom development for API integration, error handling, and performance optimization.

Testing capabilities help validate functionality before deployment. The studio includes conversation simulators for testing common user paths and basic edge cases. Developers can validate responses against expected outputs and measure response times under simulated loads. The built-in testing experience is best suited for functional validation—verifying typical user paths, edge cases, and regression checks. Modern AI deployments also require evaluation frameworks that measure qualitative characteristics such as response quality, groundedness, and safety. Within Copilot Studio and Microsoft Foundry, built-in evaluation tools and custom evaluators can be used to assess whether responses are accurate, grounded in permitted organizational content, and free from harmful or policy-violating outputs. These evaluations are typically performed during predeployment reviews and repeated whenever prompts, tools, knowledge sources, or underlying models are updated. For production-scale performance validation, teams benefit from dedicated performance testing approaches (for example, testing through supported channels and APIs) and measure latency, error rates, and throughput under representative load.

Publishing workflows manage deployment to target audiences. Custom Copilots can deploy to specific security groups or entire tenants, subject to administrative approval. Copilot Studio records the version history of agent flows in Dataverse, giving developers the ability to review prior saved and published states during development. Prompt and configuration versioning is an equally important operational practice: prompts, system instructions, tool definitions, and grounding configurations should be treated as versioned artifacts.

These artifacts should be stored in source control alongside application code and promoted through environments as part of a managed release process. This practice allows teams to audit the exact production state at any point in time, reproduce issues, and roll back safely when a change causes unexpected behavior. In the Foundry Agent Service ecosystem, this “Prompts as Code” approach helps keep nondeterministic AI behavior subject to deterministic governance.

In production, organizations typically treat agents as assets that move through a managed life cycle, with changes promoted across environments and tracked in source control or managed pipelines. If an issue occurs, teams can roll back by restoring a previous packaged state and republishing it. Deployment targets include development, staging, and production environments, though each requires separate licensing. Geographic deployment depends on data residency requirements and regional availability.

Integration occurs through prebuilt and custom connectors. Copilot Studio includes prebuilt connectors for standard Microsoft services and select third-party applications (exact count varies by license tier and region). Custom connectors require REST API endpoints that support OAuth 2.0 authentication and must gracefully handle rate limiting. Enterprise systems, such as SAP, ServiceNow, or Salesforce, require appropriate API licenses and may incur additional transaction costs. Specific rate limits, timeouts, and connector quotas vary by product version and licensing tier and warrant confirmation in the current documentation.

The platform offers different tools and entitlements across Copilot types and licensing tiers. Capacity, including usage, connector availability, and advanced features, varies by plan, region, release wave, and adjacent service dependencies. Some scenarios also depend on related services, such as Power BI or Power Automate, with their own licensing and capacity requirements. For that reason, architecture decisions that depend on numeric limits or entitlement assumptions should be validated against the current Microsoft licensing documentation at the time of deployment.

Note Published licensing terms, quotas, and service limits change frequently. Therefore, it is advisable to treat numeric limits as time-bound rather than permanent and verify them in the current Microsoft documentation before finalizing architecture, pricing, or rollout commitments.

12.4.2 Software Vendor and Integrator Opportunities

Independent software vendors and systems integrators can build businesses around Copilot, although success requires a large investment in technical capabilities and a partnership with Microsoft. Independent software vendors are companies that develop, market, and sell software products that run on one or more platforms but are not owned or controlled by the platform provider. Systems integrators are firms that specialize in bringing together diverse technology components—hardware, software, networking, and services—into cohesive, functioning solutions tailored to an organization's specific needs. Together, these partners extend the Copilot ecosystem by providing industry-specific solutions, implementation expertise, and ongoing support that complement

Microsoft's platform capabilities. In practice, implementation work typically spans several core disciplines: integration engineering, prompt design, retrieval system configuration, evaluation framework setup, and governance implementation.

These activities require cross-disciplinary expertise and hands-on experience with Microsoft Foundry and Copilot Studio. Teams that rely on partners for these capabilities often benefit from established best practices and a shorter time to value when navigating the complexities of production-ready AI.

Commercial terms for Copilot-related solutions, including pricing, revenue share, support obligations, intellectual property rights, and change notification practices, often vary by program and contract. Partner economics and legal obligations are typically driven by the specific agreement terms rather than by universal platform rules. In many engagements, intellectual property ownership, service levels, support models, and change management responsibilities are defined in the governing contracts, statements of work, and related service agreements rather than in partner program terms alone. Depending on the architecture and tooling used, partners may also contribute domain-specific knowledge bases, curated datasets, and retrieval configurations to help ground Copilot responses in specialized content.

The quality and currency of these knowledge assets directly affect response accuracy. Thus, ownership, maintenance responsibilities, and update cadences should be defined explicitly in the engagement agreement. This helps keep the life cycle of the grounding data—from ingestion to retirement—transparent and manageable for all teams involved.

12.4.3 Community and Open Source

The developer community contributes to Copilot's evolution through knowledge sharing, open source projects, and collaborative development, although participants should be aware of intellectual property implications.

GitHub hosts many Copilot-related repositories under a range of open source licenses. Developers share prompt templates, integration libraries, and sample applications. Licensing considerations can be nuanced, since some Copilot APIs have restrictive terms and some prompt engineering approaches may reflect proprietary methods. When open source components are adopted, license terms and support limitations are often reviewed as part of due diligence.

Community forums provide peer support and knowledge exchange. The Microsoft Tech Community includes specialized areas where developers can troubleshoot issues and share practical experience. While Microsoft employees do participate selectively, most solutions are community-generated rather than part of an official support channel. Participation requires sign-in and adherence to community guidelines.

Teams should treat community-generated solutions as peer guidance rather than vendor-backed commitments. In addition, open source contributions often include evaluation datasets, benchmarking tools, and orchestration frameworks. Teams can adapt and build on these assets, provided they comply with the applicable open source licenses.

Educational initiatives support the development of Copilot skills across multiple channels. Microsoft Learn offers free online training, although certifications require paid exams. Microsoft role-based certification exams are priced by country or region and may change over time. Current pricing is available on the Microsoft certification website. Universities participating in Microsoft's academic programs can access Copilot resources for curriculum development. Community colleges and technical schools offer programs ranging from two-day workshops to six-month certificates.

While various initiatives are expanding the talent pool, demand continues to exceed the supply of experienced AI architects and developers. Building production-ready Copilot systems requires a synthesis of AI engineering, data architecture, software integration, and user experience design. Few individuals possess deep proficiency across all these domains. Understandably, successful implementations depend on teams—cross-functional groups of professionals—rather than isolated contributors. This collaborative approach helps balance the nondeterministic nature of AI with the deterministic rigor of enterprise software engineering and data governance.

12.5 User Experience and Interaction Models

The effectiveness of Copilot depends on creating interactions that feel natural and intuitive while respecting technical limitations and privacy requirements. Microsoft has developed AI assistants that can interpret context within defined parameters, adapt to work patterns when permitted, and integrate into existing workflows where technically feasible.

12.5.1 Natural Language and Multimodal Input

Copilot interprets intent primarily through probabilistic language modeling informed by contextual prompts—a marked departure from the deterministic intent classification used in traditional conversational AI systems.

The natural language interface can often handle varied phrasing when sufficient context is available, but its behavior is implementation-dependent and may vary across applications and configurations. "Make this more professional," "Rewrite formally," and "Adjust tone for executives" are common phrases that prompt similar refinements in document editing. This flexibility has limits—incomplete requests such as "schedule it for next week" succeed only when recent context within the same application session clearly identifies the meeting. Otherwise, Copilot may request clarification. Context is generally application-scoped. Cross-application continuity may be possible when tenant configuration and integrated connectors permit it, but it is not automatic.

When ambiguity exceeds system capabilities, Copilot may request clarification or misinterpret intent. This behavior varies depending on the host application and specific tenant configurations. The effectiveness of natural language interaction depends on prompt specificity and the availability of relevant contextual signals through the grounding layer. Ambiguous requests often produce inconsistent results because the model must infer intent from insufficient or conflicting signals. Teams that ignore these constraints often encounter prompt drift, where users become frustrated by response variability. Consequently, establishing clear patterns for contextual grounding is a prerequisite for moving from experimental pilots to reliable, production-grade implementations.

In supported Microsoft Copilot experiences, voice-related functionality depends on the host application, available hardware, user permissions, and licensing. In Microsoft Teams meetings and calls, Copilot generally relies on transcription or STT processing to interpret what was said. Copilot's reasoning then operates primarily on the resulting text rather than on raw audio alone. In these scenarios, the interaction is grounded in a meeting transcript or STT context and remains subject to the product's standard security, compliance, and policy controls. When licensing, transcription settings, and product support are in place, users can ask Copilot to identify action items or summarize recent discussions, although availability depends on the specific Teams feature, policy configuration, and rollout status.

Voice commands require clear audio input and can be less accurate in the presence of heavy accents, background noise, or specialized technical terminology. Response accuracy varies based on audio quality and speech patterns.

Visual input processing operates within specific Microsoft applications when the feature is enabled and available on that host and under that license. In PowerPoint, dragging images into slides can trigger layout suggestions when the feature is available and enabled for the tenant or user. In Excel, selecting data may trigger visualization recommendations when Copilot features are active, and the environment is configured appropriately. These visual cues require explicit user action and are available only for supported content types. Integration between visual and text inputs remains constrained by the capabilities of the specific application and retrieval pipeline. In many enterprise implementations, visual inputs are preprocessed into searchable or structured representations—such as extracted text, document objects, table structures, captions, metadata, or embeddings—before they are used for retrieval or grounding.

In practice, multimodal reasoning may operate either on these derived representations or, in some newer pipelines, on multimodal embeddings that directly incorporate image and text content. Within Microsoft Foundry and Azure AI Search, the key design goal is to bring visual and textual artifacts into a governable retrieval pipeline rather than treat images as an entirely separate channel. Accordingly, teams need to optimize the preprocessing and indexing layer for their document types so that important visual information is not lost before retrieval and grounding occur.

Touch gesture support is available primarily on Surface devices and on Windows tablets running compatible applications, with gesture behavior determined by the operating system and the application. Users can employ standard touch interactions, such as pinch-to-zoom or selection gestures, although specialized Copilot gestures remain implementation-dependent. Most gesture recognition is handled at the operating systems level rather than by Copilot itself, although Copilot-enabled apps may expose gesture-driven flows. Cross-device gesture continuity depends on application synchronization mechanisms such as OneDrive and on tenant and application support and may not persist across sessions.

Context switching between input methods can be implemented within a single application session, but it is subject to implementation-dependent limitations that vary by host and configuration. Users can type a request and, in some hosts, refine it by voice within the same conversation thread. Still, context generally remains application-scoped unless cross-application features are explicitly enabled. Session continuity varies depending on the tenant configuration, application behavior, and activity patterns. Stating it as a universal time-bound default would be misleading. Input method changes may introduce processing delays or interpretation errors, depending on the system state and available resources.

12.5.2 Contextual Memory and Adaptive User Experience

Copilot's memory capabilities operate within privacy constraints, product boundaries, and tenant controls. In many enterprise scenarios, the assistant relies primarily on session-scoped context, meaning that much of its working context is limited to the current interaction rather than treated as a universal long-term record of all past interactions.

When available and enabled, some Copilot experiences can also use personalization and memory features, such as saved memories, details inferred from chat history, and custom instructions, subject to tenant policy and user settings. Cross-application awareness depends primarily on the contextual signals available through Microsoft Graph or other product-specific grounding layers at the time of the request. For this reason, readers should not assume that Copilot maintains an omniscient running memory across all products, sessions, and applications.

Short-term memory may preserve the context of a conversation during active sessions. Duration and behavior vary depending on the application, tenant settings, and product updates. Copilot can reference earlier requests in the same conversation thread, understand pronouns referring to recent content, and build on previous responses within the same document or chat. This memory is typically application-specific. Context from Word does not automatically transfer to Excel unless specific cross-application integrations are enabled.

Session memory behavior depends on timeout settings, application state, and tenant policies. Conversation context is also constrained by model context limits and orchestration policies that determine which prior interactions remain relevant to the current request. As conversations grow longer, earlier exchanges may fall outside the active context window and become unavailable to the model, even within the same session.

Orchestration layers address this by summarizing, pruning, or selectively retaining prior turns based on relevance and configured policy. In current Microsoft agent architectures, this kind of compaction and session management is handled by the orchestration framework or runtime, rather than by Foundry IQ, which instead serves as the managed knowledge layer for grounding enterprise data. This strategic management helps teams maintain coherent interactions while operating within the token limits of the underlying models.

Personalization in enterprise Copilot systems is typically derived from activity signals available through Microsoft Graph—such as frequently accessed documents, collaboration patterns, and organizational context—rather than from the model learning directly from user conversations. When enabled and permitted by administrative settings and retention policies, Microsoft 365 Copilot can use contextual intelligence layers such as the Semantic Index and Work IQ to surface recurring preferences, such as frequently used templates, common recipients, or regular meeting participants.

This synthesis remains subject to tenant configuration and compliance controls, so personalization does not bypass established security boundaries. Teams responsible for deployment should recognize that this form of personalization is dynamic and grounded in current organizational signals, rather than being a static profile stored inside the LLM itself.

This personalization operates through aggregated patterns rather than storing specific interactions. Users can typically disable personalization through privacy settings, and organizations can restrict data collection through compliance policies. Tenant configuration, admin policies, and applicable compliance requirements determine the pattern data retention period. Stating retention periods without a supporting citation risks inaccuracy. Interface adaptation may adjust basic preferences when supported, but substantive interface changes usually require manual configuration or admin action. Feature availability usually depends on subscription level and administrator enablement—behavioral signals alone do not guarantee access to advanced features.

When properly configured and enabled in admin settings, organizational context awareness uses data from Microsoft Graph and Microsoft Entra ID. Copilot may access reporting structures, team membership, and role information that are subject to administrative settings. This awareness could affect suggestions—email tone might vary based on the recipient's seniority as defined in the directory. However, Copilot cannot infer relationships beyond the documented organizational structure and does not account for informal dynamics or project-specific roles not reflected in official systems.

Privacy controls allow users and administrators to limit memory and personalization features to meet organizational requirements and compliance policies. Organizations can disable cross-session learning, restrict data retention periods, or prevent specific pattern recognition methods through administrative policies. Users may clear interaction history or opt out of personalization, subject to compliance requirements. These controls may impact Copilot's effectiveness, but they support compliance with privacy regulations.

12.5.3 Organizational Culture and Work Rhythms

Organizations implementing Copilot report varied impacts on work patterns and behaviors, though comprehensive longitudinal studies remain limited. Early adoption data suggest emerging patterns whose outcomes vary by organization size, industry, and implementation approach.

Task initiation patterns may show changes in some organizations. Microsoft's Work Trend Index reports that, in some contexts, employees using Copilot attempt complex tasks more readily. This effect depends on training, support, and organizational culture. AI assistance can reduce psychological barriers to starting projects when organizations provide clear use cases and adequate training. When guidance and review processes are lacking, AI-generated outputs often require substantial revision.

Meeting and collaboration dynamics may evolve in organizations with widespread Copilot adoption, though patterns vary. Some teams transition from extended planning discussions to iterative refinement of AI-generated drafts when clear processes for AI integration and quality review are established. Organizations that lack defined workflows typically see more variable results from AI adoption.

Time allocation shifts can be difficult to quantify consistently across organizations. Users often report time savings on routine tasks, but the magnitude varies by role, usage patterns, and implementation maturity. Some employees reinvest the time they save into higher-value work, while others face higher output expectations. For this reason, productivity expectations are often set in context, and workload changes are monitored over time.

Adoption typically follows standard technology diffusion curves rather than delivering immediate transformation. An initial phase of enthusiasm is often followed by a plateau as users encounter limitations or develop proficiency in prompting. Organizations that report positive outcomes typically invest in sustained change management activities, with timelines varying by size and complexity.

12.5.4 Copilot Personas and Task Orchestration

Copilot adjusts response style based on task type and user preference. These styles are prompt-driven variations, not separate AI entities. Users can request different styles, but consistency and availability depend on application context and configuration.

The instructional approach provides step-by-step guidance for defined tasks when the feature is available. In Excel, requesting "explain how to create a pivot table" could trigger detailed instructions with examples when the feature is available. This mode typically works best for defined tasks with clear procedures. Instructional responses often draw on Microsoft documentation and may not reflect organization-specific customizations.

The creative approach generates multiple options for variety or innovation within supported scenarios and template constraints. In PowerPoint, requesting "creative slide designs" may yield alternatives constrained by templates and licensing. In Word, requesting "different ways to start this proposal" could generate varied introductions when properly configured. Creative outputs benefit from human review to verify appropriateness and accuracy.

The analytical approach may emphasize data validation and pattern identification when working with quantitative information in supported applications. Excel Copilot can check formula consistency and flag potential errors when the feature is available and properly configured. Power BI Copilot may suggest correlations based on statistical analysis when available. Analytical conclusions warrant human verification because interpretation accuracy varies.

Multistep task orchestration typically runs within a single application unless cross-application automation is configured. When asked to prepare meeting materials, Copilot can generate content within the active application. However, coordinating across applications usually requires Power Automate flows or custom integration. Cross-application workflows typically require manual triggering in each application or a dedicated integration setup, such as Power Automate or custom connectors.

Response consistency across sessions and users varies with model updates, differences in prompts, context availability, and system conditions. The same request can generate different outputs depending on numerous variables. Organizations seeking consistent outputs benefit from standard prompts and review procedures rather than relying on default behavior.

12.6 Enterprise Deployment and Governance

Deploying Copilot across an enterprise requires careful planning, strong governance structures, and clear operational frameworks. The central tension lies in balancing innovation and control, ensuring that AI capabilities enhance productivity while upholding standards for security, compliance, and responsible use. Having led technology organizations, I have seen firsthand that the success or failure of technology initiatives hinges on governance and change management, rather than technical capability alone.

12.6.1 Licensing and Deployment Models

Microsoft offers multiple licensing tiers and deployment options, each designed for different organizational needs and maturity levels. Understanding these options, along with their associated costs and prerequisites, helps organizations choose the most suitable implementation.

Microsoft 365 Copilot is generally offered as a per-user add-on for Microsoft 365 enterprise subscriptions. License prerequisites and bundle details can change over time. They are often reviewed against current Microsoft product terms during procurement and rollout planning. This model often appeals to organizations seeking productivity gains without major infrastructure changes. Baseline prerequisites still matter, including Microsoft Entra ID configuration, adequate network bandwidth, and Exchange Online deployment. The licensing includes access to Copilot features across Microsoft 365 applications, subject to regional availability and feature rollout schedules. Organizations commonly begin with pilot groups, though the size and composition vary by organizational structure and change management approach.

Microsoft Fabric uses consumption-based pricing for data and analytics. Organizations purchase capacity that scales with workload, and total spend is driven by configuration, usage, and autoscaling policies. The model supports variable demand: when autoscaling is configured, capacity—and therefore costs—typically scales up and down in response to load. Actual spend patterns depend on autoscale thresholds, usage limits, and the granularity of the service's billing model. Some Fabric AI features, including Copilot, consume the same capacity units, which means AI activity is often folded into the analytics budget. The specific Copilot capabilities that draw on capacity can vary and are commonly checked against current product pricing terms. In all cases, realized costs reflect usage patterns, query complexity, and the volume of data processed.

Azure-hosted implementations (including Azure OpenAI Service) allow custom Copilot integrations and typically bill for usage-based resources. Specific pricing models and technical requirements vary by service and deployment. This model is suited for specialized applications or organizations that embed Copilot capabilities into custom solutions. Implementation costs include not only consumption charges but also development resources, testing infrastructure, and ongoing maintenance.

Hybrid deployments can combine Microsoft 365 Copilot with Azure-based custom solutions. This approach tends to introduce operational and governance complexity, particularly when multiple licensing and integration surfaces are involved. Teams often face multiple licensing agreements, limitations on interaction between different Copilot implementations, and increased administrative overhead.

Deployment typically follows a staged approach tailored to an organization's readiness. Typical phases include a readiness assessment (evaluating data quality, security posture, and training needs), a pilot deployment with representative user groups, measurement of success against predefined metrics, and a phased expansion based on pilot results. The specific timeline and scale depend on organizational size, technical maturity, and change management capabilities.

Success requires preparing people, processes, and data governance—not just technical infrastructure. Licensing decisions and architectural design choices must be evaluated together because the cost profile of Copilot and agent solutions varies with model invocation frequency, retrieval and grounding architecture, and the number of workflow steps requiring model inference.

Organizations that treat licensing as a purely procurement decision, separate from architecture, often encounter cost surprises during production scale-up. Teams that incorporate financial modeling into the early architectural phase are better positioned to optimize for both performance and predictability.

Table 12-3 summarizes the key adoption considerations for Copilot.

Table 12-3. *Key considerations for enterprise Copilot deployment, including technical requirements, common implementation challenges, and recommended best practices. Addressing these factors systematically improves the likelihood of successful adoption.*

Aspect	Requirements	Common Challenges	Best Practices
Licensing	Microsoft 365 E3/E5 base, Copilot add-on	Cost justification, user allocation	Start with pilot groups, measure ROI
Data readiness	Clean SharePoint, proper permissions	Legacy data, inconsistent metadata	Data cleanup sprint, governance review
Security	Zero-trust, Conditional Access	Oversharing risks, data exposure	Sensitivity labels, DLP policies
Network	Sufficient bandwidth, low latency	Remote office connectivity	Edge caching, traffic optimization
Training	Prompt engineering, AI literacy	User resistance, skills gaps	Champions program, use case library
Governance	Usage policies, ethical guidelines	Shadow IT, uncontrolled adoption	Center of Excellence (CoE), clear policies
Change management	Communication plan, success metrics	Cultural resistance, job concerns	Transparent communication, reskilling
Compliance	Data residency, audit trails	Regulatory requirements	Regional deployment, audit logging

12.6.2 Administrative Controls and Analytics

Enterprise Copilot deployment requires administrative oversight capabilities. Microsoft provides controls that allow IT departments to manage, monitor, and optimize Copilot usage, though effective governance requires proper configuration and ongoing management.

The Microsoft 365 admin center serves as a primary control point when properly configured. Administrators can enable or disable Copilot features for specific users or groups through RBAC. Feature availability can be managed at a granular level—

organizations may activate certain Copilot functions while restricting others based on business or compliance requirements. Data source access requires explicit configuration, allowing administrators to control which repositories Copilot can query.

With telemetry enabled and configured, administrators can capture logs and metrics on Copilot activity. The specific data collected and its retention period depend on audit policies, licensing tier, compliance settings, and storage configuration. Properly analyzed, this telemetry supports multiple organizational goals: security teams can identify anomalous behavior, IT can diagnose performance bottlenecks, and business analysts can track adoption and usage trends.

For Microsoft 365 Copilot, reporting and oversight typically come from the Microsoft 365 admin center, the Microsoft Copilot Dashboard, Copilot Analytics in Viva Insights, and Microsoft Purview audit logs. These reporting surfaces help organizations track adoption, usage patterns, and compliance signals across the tenant. For Foundry and custom agent workloads, observability is typically surfaced through Foundry monitoring dashboards, tracing, and Azure Monitor Application Insights, which can expose signals such as latency, token consumption, tool invocations, error rates, and evaluation outcomes. Taken together, these reporting and observability surfaces support performance monitoring, cost analysis, and governance. This evidentiary trail is important for organizations seeking to assess AI ROI and demonstrate adherence to internal safety and compliance standards.

Usage analytics capabilities often vary by license level and configuration. Where they are available, dashboards can show adoption patterns, feature utilization, and user engagement signals. These metrics tend to require interpretation in an organizational context, and they frequently influence training programs and feature rollout decisions. Baseline measurements are commonly captured before deployment so that later changes can be compared against a consistent starting point.

Microsoft Purview and the Microsoft 365 compliance center can be used to govern Copilot interactions. The available controls and their effectiveness depend on configuration and licensing. Retention policies for Copilot interactions must be explicitly configured to meet regulatory requirements. These policies require regular review and updates as regulations and organizational needs evolve.

Privacy controls balance operational visibility with employee privacy concerns. Organizations configure data visibility levels, although the available options vary by licensing and regional regulations. Common approaches include aggregating department-level data, restricting individual metrics to HR and IT administrators, and using time-delayed reporting. Clear communication about monitoring practices fosters trust while maintaining necessary oversight. Feature flight and preview controls are important operational mechanisms in Copilot deployment.

Administrators can use the Microsoft 365 admin center, Copilot-specific settings, and Targeted release options to expose new Copilot capabilities to selected users before broader rollout. This tiered approach allows organizations to validate new features, gather feedback, and manage change at a controlled pace, reducing the operational friction of simultaneous tenant-wide updates.

12.6.3 Security, Compliance, and Responsible AI

Enterprise Copilot deployment addresses security requirements, regulatory compliance, and ethical use of AI through appropriate configuration and ongoing management.

Security implementation often depends on coordinated configuration across multiple controls. Tenant isolation keeps organizational data segregated when Microsoft Entra ID settings and data residency controls are configured correctly. Geographic residency must satisfy applicable regulatory obligations, while region and licensing constraints vary by service. Residency settings and any processing outside primary regions are commonly reviewed for legal compliance, recorded accurately, and approved through established governance processes.

Threat protection depends on the selection and configuration of the Microsoft Defender product. Scanning and detection capabilities for Copilot scenarios vary with licensing and settings. Organizations typically configure scanning rules, define response procedures, and periodically assess the effectiveness of their threat detection systems. Integration between Copilot and security tools generally involves explicit configuration and testing.

Compliance alignment necessitates substantial configuration effort beyond selecting settings. Organizations subject to regulations like GDPR, HIPAA, or financial services requirements must configure multiple systems, including data classification, retention policies, access controls, and audit logging. Compliance is not achieved through simple activation. Instead, it requires comprehensive configuration, regular auditing, and thorough documentation. Many organizations engage compliance experts to verify proper implementation and to maintain evidence of ongoing compliance efforts. External support can also come from established providers such as Wolters Kluwer, particularly for regulatory content, control frameworks, and audit-ready documentation.

Responsible AI implementation is often treated as both a technical and a governance problem. Content filtering can reduce the risk of inappropriate outputs when it is configured and monitored, for example, by blocking hate or harassment, explicit sexual content, or self-harm instructions in user-facing assistants. Over time, many teams find that filter settings require tuning as usage patterns evolve and new edge cases arise. A customer support bot, for instance, may initially flag legitimate troubleshooting language as incorrect, whereas a health-related workflow may trigger false positives with clinical terms.

False positives (over-filtering) and false negatives (missed violations) should be monitored to refine filtering configurations, escalation paths, and review processes. Responsible AI programs also include periodic evaluations of model behavior across representative prompts and datasets to test for bias, safety failures, groundedness issues, and unintended outputs. These systemic evaluations complement runtime guardrails and governance oversight. They are typically repeated whenever prompts, tools, grounding configurations, or underlying models are updated. This iterative process helps teams maintain a high safety bar as the system evolves.

Human oversight structures often take the form of governance committees with defined charters, regular review cycles, and clear authority to adjust policies. In many organizations, these groups set acceptable use policies that reflect local culture and risk posture, such as whether employees may paste customer data into assistants, which teams may deploy external-facing chatbots, and which approval steps apply to automated actions. They also tend to review incident reports and usage patterns, for example, recurring prompts that trigger policy violations, spikes in blocked requests, or repeated failure modes in a high-impact workflow. Controls are then updated in response, such as by tightening access to premium connectors, strengthening DLP rules, expanding human review for sensitive scenarios, or revising training materials. Documentation of these decisions and their rationale commonly supports consistent enforcement and provides evidence for audits and regulatory inquiries.

12.6.4 Copilot as Organizational Learning Infrastructure

Copilot deployment can impact organizational knowledge management and learning patterns, although outcomes vary widely depending on the implementation approach and organizational culture.

Knowledge accessibility can improve when Copilot is integrated well with organizational knowledge bases, but the gains tend to depend on the underlying information discipline. When content is high quality, indexed properly, and paired with effective search configuration, new employees may find answers faster, such as locating the most recent onboarding checklist, the correct policy for an exception, or the latest approved troubleshooting steps. Results are typically stronger when sources are organized, metadata is explicit, and content is maintained, for example, by retiring outdated versions, standardizing titles, and tagging documents by product, region, and audience. In contrast, loosely named files, duplicate folders, and stale pages often remain hard to navigate even with an assistant. This implies Copilot does not automatically turn disorder into clarity.

This pattern echoes my experience building the INTELLIFM technology and enterprise applications: the intelligence layer is only as strong as the data foundation beneath it. At Wolters Kluwer, taxonomy and metadata governance often required as much sustained effort as the filing logic itself, because those structures determined whether knowledge could be found, trusted, and reused.

Iterative interactions between users and Copilot can create feedback loops that potentially improve both user proficiency and system effectiveness within defined parameters. Users may learn to formulate more effective queries, while usage patterns may inform improvements to prompt engineering. However, these improvements require active management, regular analysis of interaction patterns, and systematic incorporation of learnings into training and configuration updates.

Some organizations report changes in experimentation patterns following Copilot deployment, though results vary widely. Factors influencing outcomes include organizational culture, leadership support for innovation, clear use case definition, and psychological safety for experimentation. The ability to rapidly generate and test ideas may lower barriers to exploration in some contexts, but this requires appropriate governance to maintain quality and manage risks. Based on my observations of enterprise application deployment, establishing clear criteria for evaluating AI-generated outputs and processes for human review and validation provides the framework for continuous improvement.

Organizational transformation through AI deployment often depends on factors beyond the technology itself. Many rollouts succeed when change management is treated as ongoing work, with clear communication about what the system can and cannot do, training tailored to job roles, and accessible support for day-to-day questions.

Early experience also tends to shape adoption: if users encounter inconsistent answers, unclear boundaries, or a lack of guidance on appropriate use, enthusiasm can fade quickly. By contrast, programs that provide practical examples, such as how to draft a first-pass report, summarize meeting notes, or find policy guidance, often see more durable behavior change.

Expectations about timing matter as well. Productivity gains may appear first in routine tasks, while broader process changes often emerge later as governance, workflows, and skills mature. In that sense, Copilot is commonly treated as a tool that can support new ways of working when it is implemented thoughtfully, rather than as a deployment that automatically produces transformation on its own.

12.7 Challenges and Limitations

Despite its capabilities, the Copilot ecosystem is often shaped by technical, operational, and governance constraints that vary across products, licensing tiers, tenant configurations, and geographic regions. Many organizations discover these differences during pilots, for example, when a feature is available in one environment but not another, when throughput changes under shared versus Premium capacity, or when a compliance setting alters what content can be retrieved and cited. These constraints tend to influence deployment strategy, set expectations for stakeholders, and drive priorities for governance, monitoring, and change management.

For that reason, statements about feature availability or behavior are usually framed in a product-specific way. Discussions typically identify the target Copilot product and the relevant configuration, including tenant settings, licensing tier, and region, rather than treating capabilities as uniform across the entire ecosystem.

12.7.1 Hallucination Risks and Mitigation

Generating plausible but incorrect information—commonly referred to as hallucination—poses a serious challenge for LLM-driven assistants, including Copilot products. Hallucination arises from the probabilistic generation of next tokens, incomplete or noisy context, retrieval failures, and ambiguous or underspecified prompts. It reflects both the characteristics of current model architectures and imperfections in retrieval and context modeling. Addressing hallucination requires a layered mitigation strategy that combines preventive controls, detective mechanisms, and corrective processes.

Manifestations vary by application and context. In Excel, Copilot can produce incorrect calculations or misinterpret data relationships when working with complex, poorly structured, or ambiguous datasets. In Word, factual inaccuracies can appear when content is generated without grounding in authoritative sources. In meeting summaries, details can be omitted, speakers conflated, decisions misstated, or action items misinterpreted out of context. Automated or high-risk actions, such as large-scale bulk edits, formula generation, or policy-driven changes, increase the potential for harm and are typically routed through restricted modes or require additional verification.

Mitigations are usefully organized into preventive, detective, and corrective layers. Preventive measures include input validation, constrained prompts or task-specific templates, narrow or specialized models, and prompt design that reduces ambiguity. Detective mechanisms encompass provenance and explicit citation of retrieved sources, calibrated confidence scores and uncertainty indicators, truthfulness classifiers, and automated cross-checking against authoritative data. Corrective processes include human-in-the-loop review gates for high-risk outputs, automated requerying of authoritative sources, correction and rollback workflows, and explicit refusal or "I don't know" modes for out-of-scope requests.

Grounding responses with RAG and explicit citations to organizational sources can materially improve accuracy when retrieval is configured correctly and relevant, authoritative material exists. However, retrieval errors, poor relevance ranking, or misinterpretation of retrieved content can still produce incorrect outputs.

The availability and design of uncertainty indicators, provenance metadata, and visual verification prompts vary by Copilot product, tenant settings, licensing tier, and region and are not universal. Verification workflows are most effective when classified by risk tier, with automation applied to routine checks and clear human-in-the-loop gates for high-risk categories. User training that emphasizes recognizing hallucinations, verifying citations and provenance, understanding role-based approval workflows, and treating AI outputs as draft artifacts supports appropriate validation behavior.

12.7.2 Scalability, Latency, and Cost Trade-Offs

Enterprise Copilot deployments require deliberate architectural and operational planning to balance performance, scale, cost, SLAs, and compliance constraints. Scalability planning commonly addresses infrastructure capacity, autoscaling policies, quotas, API rate limits, token limits, geographic distribution, and licensing tier constraints.

Demand management techniques, such as prioritized queues and throttling, are often used to maintain responsiveness during peak loads. Deployment controls frequently include capacity forecasting, model version pinning, staged rollouts, and automated validation and smoke tests. These controls reduce the risk of service disruption and limit unexpected behavior following base model updates or custom fine-tuning.

Latency characteristics depend on the workload: simple text generation under optimal conditions is typically fast, whereas complex analytical tasks that aggregate multiple data sources or require large context windows are slower. Real-time features such as meeting transcription or interactive guidance impose different architectural and provisioning requirements than batch summarization or offline analytics. Latency measurements under representative regional network and load conditions provide a realistic basis for production readiness assessments and SLA definition.

Cost structures vary depending on the licensing model, token consumption, custom training and fine-tuning fees, and infrastructure choices. TCO generally encompasses licensing, compute, storage, observability and monitoring, support, and change management costs across the system life cycle. Financial models that include these elements produce more accurate comparisons between deployment alternatives and help clarify where operational savings or hidden costs may arise.

Optimization strategies include caching responses with clear freshness windows and invalidation rules, refining prompts and templates to minimize token consumption, precomputing common outputs on a defined refresh schedule, batching nonurgent requests, and introducing tiered service levels to balance cost, latency, and quality. Each optimization introduces trade-offs, including the risk of staleness, additional storage and maintenance overhead, and added engineering complexity. Engineering controls for cache governance and provenance checks help prevent stale or misleading outputs when cached responses are used in authoritative workflows.

Operational monitoring typically tracks latency, error rates, and hallucination incidence, token consumption, cost per transaction, and user impact metrics to inform capacity planning, charge-back models, and SLA definitions. Resource management and deployment controls—such as usage quotas, prioritized queues, autoscaling, model version pinning, and staged rollouts—are used to align the user experience with budget and risk tolerance. Reported benefits from Copilot deployments often vary by role and use case. Hence, organizations frequently develop a detailed business case for each major use case, including metrics for accuracy, error remediation cost, compliance effort, and human review time.

12.7.3 Governance, Observability, and Model Life Cycle

Effective Copilot deployment incorporates governance and observability controls that extend beyond technical mitigations. Logging and audit trails for queries, retrieved sources, and generated outputs support post hoc review and legal defensibility. RBAC, least-privilege data access, dataset lineage, and model change management, including versioning, predeployment validation, and rollback procedures, address compliance and operational risk. Observability metrics, which include accuracy, hallucination incidence, confidence calibration, fairness and bias indicators, usage patterns, and key performance indicator trends, help detect regressions and guide remediation.

12.7.4 Ethical Considerations and Trust

Copilot adoption raises questions about AI's role in decision-making, privacy, data residency compliance, accountability, and preservation of human skills and agency. Bias in AI outputs remains a persistent and active area of research. Models can reproduce or amplify patterns present in training data, producing disparate outcomes in contexts such as resume screening, performance feedback, or targeted marketing content. Mitigation approaches include dataset auditing, contextual fairness testing, deployment-time monitoring for disparate impacts, and targeted human review for high-risk decisions. The effectiveness of these techniques varies by scenario and requires ongoing evaluation.

Privacy and compliance considerations extend beyond technical security controls. Copilot functionality often depends on accessing organizational information. Data flows are typically mapped to capture where data is stored, how it is processed, and which jurisdictions apply. Data residency commitments, retention policies, least-privilege access controls, and contractual protections with vendors are central to compliance. Transparent data use disclosures and role-based controls help address employee concerns about AI-mediated analysis of work products.

Attribution and accountability questions arise when AI contributes to content creation or informs decisions. Practical governance encompasses policies that define when AI involvement should be disclosed, rules that assign responsibility for outputs and downstream decisions, intellectual property and recordkeeping practices for AI-assisted work products, and legal and compliance frameworks for evaluating potential liability. Audit logs and provenance metadata that record inputs, retrieved sources, model versions, and decision paths support post hoc review and legal defensibility.

Skill maintenance and human agency warrant proactive attention as AI handles routine tasks and reduces practice in core skills such as writing, analysis, and problem-solving. Approaches to preserve capability include periodic skill assessments, role design that retains critical human responsibilities, and deliberate practice programs that maintain expertise for oversight and escalation.

Longitudinal effects are still under study, and monitoring for unintended skill erosion is advisable. Transparency about system capabilities, limitations, provenance practices, and governance builds appropriate trust. Documentation that describes model versions, known failure modes, mitigation controls, provenance practices, and incident response procedures supports informed use. Communicating with stakeholders about when AI is used and how humans participate in review and decision-making helps set realistic expectations and supports responsible adoption.

12.8 Future Trajectory

The Copilot ecosystem continues to evolve, with current capabilities providing a foundation for potential expansions in functionality and scope. Understanding likely directions of development helps organizations prepare for changes in workflows, decision-making processes, and value creation. At the same time, specific timelines and features remain subject to technical progress, regulatory developments, and market feedback. Vendor roadmap statements are point-in-time and may be subject to revision. Verification through official vendor channels and incorporation of roadmap volatility into planning assumptions improve decision accuracy.

12.8.1 From Assistants to Agents

The transition from reactive assistants to autonomous agents is already underway. Copilot Studio's agent capabilities, the Microsoft 365 Agents SDK, Microsoft Agent Framework, and Foundry Agent Service represent Microsoft's current production tooling for building agents that plan, invoke tools, and execute multistep workflows—not a future roadmap item but an available architectural pattern as of 2026. Future workflows may monitor conditions and suggest or initiate actions within defined parameters. For example, a sales-focused implementation might identify patterns in deal progression and recommend or trigger interventions. Security implementations could flag anomalies for investigation based on configured thresholds. Such capabilities would operate within strict authorization boundaries and require logging, provenance metadata, auditable decision trails, and explicit operational policies that define when and how actions are permitted.

More sophisticated orchestration could foster management of structured, multistep processes under clearly defined escalation and audit rules. In scenarios such as financial closing, systems might coordinate data gathering, perform defined reconciliations, and generate standardized reports while escalating exceptions for human review. These uses depend on careful scoping, exhaustive testing, and clear accountability frameworks. Operational safeguards include monitoring, rollback capability, staged canaries, and incident response playbooks to mitigate risk and support recovery.

Microsoft's published roadmaps suggest graduated capability releases, though these are subject to revision based on technical progress and market feedback. Initial implementations may focus on well-defined tasks within a single application, with later phases involving cross-application coordination, depending on technical feasibility, security considerations, and customer demand. Verification through official vendor channels and incorporation of roadmap volatility into planning assumptions provide a firmer basis for organizational decisions.

The technical requirements for more autonomous operations differ from current implementations. Such systems require enhanced state management, temporal awareness, goal decomposition, error handling, and traceable reasoning with citations. Operationally, they also necessitate observability, provenance capture, rollback mechanisms, and model version management. These requirements pose engineering and organizational challenges, particularly in defining roles, assigning responsibilities, and establishing accountability structures.

12.8.2 Ambient Intelligence and Workplace Transformation

Integration with ambient computing environments could reduce the visibility of AI assistance while increasing its availability. However, adoption will depend on hardware readiness, privacy regulations, and organizational usage patterns. Context-aware assistance may operate without explicit invocation in certain scenarios. For instance, entering a meeting room could trigger a relevant briefing on authorized devices, document creation could present related materials based on content analysis, and calendar conflicts could be proactively detected and surfaced. Such features require sophisticated context detection, explicit consent models, local data minimization, and configurable privacy controls.

Physical workspace integration may extend beyond traditional computing devices. With appropriate hardware, meeting rooms could provide real-time transcription and analysis. Digital whiteboards might capture and structure brainstorming content, and, where available and permitted, augmented reality devices could overlay contextual information. The value of these integrations depends on hardware costs, sensor and device coverage, model performance at the edge, and organizational readiness to change interaction patterns. Context-aware features that act proactively must include transparent disclosure of data use and mechanisms for user review and opt-out.

Conversational interfaces and natural language orchestration could let users describe their objectives rather than navigate application flows, potentially broadening access to technology. This linguistic approach requires careful design to handle ambiguity, surface provenance, preserve security and authorization, and require explicit confirmation for consequential actions. Organizational structures and work practices may adapt as AI assistance becomes more widespread. Some organizations may flatten decision layers as information becomes more accessible, while others may retain structures and redefine roles. Human judgment, escalation, and social coordination will remain essential to many organizational functions.

12.8.3 Strategic Implications for Technology Leaders

As AI capabilities expand, technology leaders face infrastructure, data, security, and organizational challenges, with priorities shaped by context, constraints, and strategic considerations. Data architecture and data quality investments materially affect AI effectiveness. Organizations with well-structured, accessible data typically realize benefits more quickly than those with fragmented systems. Investment in governance and integration strongly influences implementation success, requiring sound technical infrastructure and effective change management.

Security and compliance models often need to be adjusted when agents operate across system boundaries. Many organizations find that familiar controls become more important, not less, because cross-system actions expand the potential blast radius of a mistake or compromise. Zero-trust principles, granular access controls, strong auditability, and incident response readiness typically receive renewed emphasis, especially when an agent can read from one system, write to another, and trigger downstream actions. For example, an agent that can pull customer data from a service system and then initiate a refund in a finance system may require tighter approval gates, clearer separation of duties, and more detailed audit trails than a single-application workflow.

Build-versus-buy decisions can also change as AI capabilities become more standardized. Differentiation is often driven less by rebuilding common capabilities and more by how they are applied, such as unique data assets, specialized configurations, and novel applications that fit the business context. As a result, resource allocation choices tend to focus proprietary development on areas that create genuine competitive advantage, while relying on commodity services for broadly available functions.

Development practices and team composition often evolve as AI assistance becomes part of daily workflows, and this can change both productivity metrics and quality expectations. Teams sometimes see faster first drafts of code, tests, or documentation, but also encounter new work, such as validating generated output, addressing subtle defects, and enforcing consistent patterns across repositories.

In my own experience leading large engineering efforts, clarity about responsibility matters as much as the tools themselves. Integrating AI into development workflows raises practical questions about ownership and accountability, including who approves changes, who maintains generated components over time, and how QA adapts when code can be produced quickly yet still requires careful review. Product strategy and roadmaps often reflect similar trade-offs. They evaluate how deeply AI should be embedded into the product experience, while balancing near-term user value with investment requirements and the added technical complexity of operating AI features reliably at scale.

12.8.4 Near-Term Evolution: Agents, Twins, and Edge

Near-term Copilot evolution is likely to be incremental and focused on controlled domains with clear success criteria and reversible outcomes, such as developer tooling, customer service routing, and structured data analysis. Limited autonomous agents are emerging in these constrained environments. Broader deployment depends on demonstrating reliability, building trust, and establishing governance practices. Pilot results and organizational risk tolerance typically drive decisions on timelines and scale.

Digital twin integration could extend Copilot-style and agent-based systems by helping them reason about physical operations when accurate digital representations of buildings, manufacturing lines, or supply chains are available.

The value for use cases such as predictive maintenance depends on sensor coverage, model fidelity, integration maturity, and the availability of domain expertise to interpret the resulting insights.

These applications build on established digital twin concepts while adding natural language interfaces and analytical capabilities. A central challenge is data synchronization: keeping the digital representation aligned with the physical system it models. Synchronization latency, sensor failures, data quality issues, and schema mismatches can all degrade the reliability of AI-generated insights. Consequently, teams implementing these integrations usually invest heavily in the data pipeline and synchronization layer before the natural language interface delivers reliable value.

Modern edge computing facilitates an efficient hybrid model: on-device processing minimizes latency and enhances privacy, while cloud connectivity remains the anchor for model orchestration and intensive workloads. The optimal distribution of processing depends on specific use cases, regulatory requirements, and infrastructure capabilities. Edge deployments introduce operational costs and complexity, including secure update channels, synchronized versioning, and management of disparate node configurations.

These potential developments build on established engineering principles, including clear component interfaces, traceable reasoning supported by citations, thorough monitoring, auditable decision logs, and staged validation. Progress is often incremental rather than revolutionary, with each advance requiring careful validation before broader rollout. The benefits and the conditions for safe deployment tend to depend on data quality, observability, authorization controls, and governance maturity. Organizations that track these trajectories commonly incorporate pilot results, risk tolerance, and compliance constraints into their planning and prioritization.

12.9 Summary

Through integration across Microsoft's technology stack, orchestration capabilities, and an expanding partner ecosystem, Copilot has progressed from an experimental feature to production deployments across many organizations, often focusing on specific teams or workflows rather than uniform, enterprise-wide installations.

Copilot's value derives from platform integration within the Microsoft ecosystem and from how it is configured and governed. The system interoperates with Microsoft 365 applications through established APIs and data models, extending native capabilities when feature availability, token and context limits, and licensing permit. It can operate across Windows and Azure with varying depth, depending on licensing tier, tenant configuration, connector set, and tenant data residency settings.

With governance through Microsoft Entra and Microsoft Purview, organizations can deploy AI capabilities while maintaining security and compliance controls appropriate to their requirements, provided tenant settings, connectors, permission models, and operational policies are correctly configured and enforced. The ecosystem continues to expand as independent software vendors, systems integrators, and developers add specialized capabilities and connectors.

Organizations planning to deploy Copilot often weigh several factors beyond feature selection. A data foundation assessment is commonly treated as a starting point, because Copilot effectiveness tends to track with data quality, organization, and accessibility. Graduated rollouts are frequently used. Many programs begin with lower-risk use cases, such as document assistance, and then expand into more complex analytical tasks as reliability and governance mature.

Governance frameworks are often established early and clarified in operational terms. Typical elements include acceptable use policies, decision rights, review processes, and documented connector and permission configurations. Entra and Purview can be strong foundations, but their impact usually depends on clear policies and consistent enforcement. Change management also receives attention, since organizational adaptation, including process redesign and user training, often proves more challenging than the technical deployment itself.

Looking forward, Copilot may evolve from a discrete tool to a more pervasive intelligence layer across enterprise operations, though this transformation will vary by organization and industry. As AI assistance becomes more integrated into standard workflows, organizations may need to reassess their operational assumptions about decision-making processes, organizational structures, and value creation. This evolution depends on numerous factors, including technical advancement, regulatory frameworks, connector availability, tenant settings, and organizational readiness.

Technology adoption often succeeds through thoughtful integration rather than isolated implementation. Copilot's potential is shaped not only by its AI capabilities but also by how well those capabilities fit into existing workflows and systems through configuration, connectivity, and ongoing operations. This principle has guided my work over the years, from designing COM interface contracts at Microsoft to implementing enterprise architectures at global financial institutions.

Aspirations are usually tempered by the realities of practical implementation. Outcomes often vary with data readiness, change management capacity, and strategic alignment, as well as with how well human factors are addressed alongside technical architecture.

The Copilot ecosystem described in this chapter is undergoing a fundamental shift—from assistants that respond to prompts toward agents that autonomously pursue goals. Copilot Studio's agent capabilities, the Microsoft 365 Agents SDK, and Foundry Agent Service represent this transition in tooling. The governance, telemetry, and deployment patterns examined here apply equally—and with greater urgency—to agentic systems that operate with greater autonomy and broader reach. In an agentic context, governance must evolve beyond static permissions to incorporate dynamic safety guardrails that monitor an agent's execution path and tool invocation boundaries in real time. Telemetry also shifts its focus; rather than merely logging user queries, it must now capture multistep execution traces and, where available, reasoning summaries that help explain an agent's actions. Finally, deployment strategies must account for the nondeterministic nature of these systems, requiring continuous evaluation and canary testing to verify that autonomous behaviors remain aligned with enterprise policies even as the underlying models and data sources evolve.

This foundation of AI assistance connects to broader platform capabilities. While Copilot provides intelligence services, organizations also need platforms for building custom applications and workflows, including APIs, secure connectors, orchestration, and deployment and runtime controls. As part of rollout planning, they need to confirm the production status and scope for each deployment and document the configurations for connectors, permissions, and data residency.

The next chapter examines Microsoft's Power Platform, which gives citizen developers a practical path to create solutions that can benefit from Copilot's capabilities. Together, these platforms provide a framework for developing, deploying, and scaling AI-enabled business solutions.

CHAPTER 13

The Power Platform

Across industries and continents, organizations are seeking ways to turn their data into meaningful insights and automate routine work that slows them down. This search has fueled the rise of low-code and no-code platforms—tools that allow people to build digital solutions without becoming software engineers. Low-code platforms blend visual design, drag-and-drop components, and configurable logic, while still offering room for custom code when needed. No-code tools go a step further, relying entirely on templates and visual workflows. Microsoft Power Platform sits at the center of this movement, offering a collection of tools that make data analysis, application development, process automation, and website creation accessible to a far broader audience than traditional development ever allowed.

Each component of the Power Platform plays a distinct role in this ecosystem. Power BI helps people make sense of their data through interactive dashboards and reports. Development teams use Power Apps to build business applications that run across devices, from simple forms to sophisticated enterprise tools. Power Automate connects systems and services, reducing manual effort through automated workflows. Power Pages (formerly Power Portals) allows organizations to build secure, external-facing websites and portals. Many Power Platform solutions use Microsoft Dataverse as a common data foundation, particularly those built with Power Apps, Power Automate, and Power Pages, while Power BI also connects to a broad range of enterprise and external data sources.

The integration of AI has expanded the capabilities of these tools. ML models now support scenarios ranging from predictive analytics to document processing and natural language interaction. When configured thoughtfully, these capabilities can be woven into applications and workflows created by users with diverse technical backgrounds. The term "citizen developer" has emerged to describe business users who build solutions on these platforms, but real success typically comes from collaboration—domain experts shaping the logic, and IT professionals keeping those solutions secure, governed, and scalable.

K. C. Mukherjee, *The Microsoft AI Insider's Playbook*, https://doi.org/10.1007/979-8-8688-2730-3_13

This chapter explores how low-code development and AI intersect within the Power Platform. It aims to provide practical guidance on building intelligent business solutions that apply the platform's strengths while acknowledging its constraints. We begin with an overview of the platform's core components and their connection to the broader Microsoft ecosystem, including Microsoft 365, Azure, and Dynamics 365. From there, we trace the evolution of AI within the platform—from early predictive features to today's AI Builder and Copilot capabilities.

The chapter then turns to practical application. We examine how organizations across industries—from health care and retail to financial services and education—use AI Builder and Copilot to streamline processes, improve decision-making, and enhance customer experiences. These examples highlight both the opportunities and the challenges, reminding us that outcomes depend heavily on data quality, governance, and organizational readiness.

Design considerations for AI-driven solutions receive particular attention. Issues such as data preparation, model performance, ethical use, and the balance between automation and human oversight are explored in depth. The chapter concludes by looking ahead to emerging trends and how they may shape the future of low-code development.

For me, the Power Platform represents more than a set of tools—it reflects principles that have guided my work for decades. When I developed INTELLIFM, my goal was to empower subject matter experts to express their knowledge directly in system logic rather than relying on long chains of translation between business and engineering. I helped build component architectures that separated business logic from technical implementation, creating modular, composable systems built on Microsoft technologies. Power Platform brings these ideas to life at a global scale. It allows business experts to participate directly in creating solutions while IT provides the guardrails that keep those solutions secure and sustainable. Having witnessed the evolution from early expert systems to today's AI-enhanced platforms, I see Power Platform as a natural progression—one that unites domain expertise and technical capability in a way that resonates with organizations worldwide.

13.1 Understanding the Power Platform

The Microsoft Power Platform provides a suite of low-code tools for data analysis, application development, process automation, and website creation. The platform is commonly discussed in terms of four core products—Power BI, Power Apps, Power Automate, and Power Pages—supported by closely related platform elements such as Microsoft Dataverse, AI Builder, and Copilot Studio. Dataverse can serve as a common data foundation for many Power Platform solutions, particularly those built with Power Apps, Power Automate, and Power Pages, while Power BI also connects to a broad range of other enterprise and external data sources. This shared architecture reduces coding requirements while maintaining governance and security controls.

Note Service limits, pricing, and feature availability for Power Platform components change frequently. Specific figures, packaging details, and availability statements cited in this chapter are based on documentation available during the chapter's preparation and should be verified against Microsoft's current licensing and product documentation before implementation decisions are made to avoid costly surprises.

13.1.1 Core Components

The core components of the Power Platform form a cohesive toolkit for building data-driven applications, automating processes, analyzing data, and creating conversational experiences. This section outlines the purpose and roles of each component, both individually and collectively, within an enterprise context. The distinctions among the major Power Platform products and related platform elements become clearer when viewed side by side, as summarized in Table 13-1.

Table 13-1. *Comparison of Microsoft Power Platform products and related platform elements summarizing their primary functions, typical user groups, common application scenarios, and licensing approaches.*

Component	Primary Function	Key Users	Typical Use Cases	Licensing Model
Power BI	Data visualization and analytics	Analysts, business users, managers	Dashboards, reports, key performance indicators, self-service analytics	Per-user or capacity-based licensing
Power Apps	Low-code application development	Citizen developers, professional developers, solution architects	Data entry apps, mobile apps, internal tools, model-driven apps	Per-user and pay-as-you-go licensing; Dataverse, premium connectors, and related capacity may introduce additional costs
Power Automate	Workflow and process automation	Business users, automation specialists, developers	Approvals, notifications, system integration, RPA	Per-user, process-based, and pay-as-you-go licensing
Power Pages	Low-code external and internal websites	Business users, designers, developers	Customer/partner portals, secure data collection sites, public informational pages	Authenticated user and anonymous user capacity-based licensing
Dataverse	Enterprise data platform	Solution architects, developers, administrators	Centralized data storage, security, relational modeling, integration	Capacity-based (database, file, log) allocated through Power Platform or Dynamics licenses
Copilot Studio	Low-code agent and copilot development	Business users, solution architects, professional developers	Custom AI agents, chatbots, automated customer service, cross-platform orchestration	Consumption-based licensing centered on Copilot Credits, with pay-as-you-go options

Power BI

Power BI serves as a primary platform for data modeling, analytics, and the distribution of interactive insights. It supports connectivity through a wide range of built-in connectors, from file-based sources such as Excel and JSON to cloud services such as Amazon Redshift and Google Analytics. While basic reporting is accessible through a visual interface, more complex scenarios often require proficiency in DAX for calculations and Power Query M for data transformation.

Service operations are governed by capacity limits that vary by licensing tier. Semantic model size and refresh frequency differ substantially between shared capacity and Premium capacity. Verifying these constraints during architectural planning is necessary to avoid sizing errors and performance bottlenecks.

In 2023, Microsoft introduced Microsoft Fabric as a unified analytics platform, integrating data engineering, warehousing, real-time analytics, and Power BI. Within this ecosystem, Power BI functions as the analytics and visualization layer on top of OneLake—Fabric's unified logical data lake. Direct Lake mode allows Power BI to query data in OneLake without traditional imports or caching, simplifying the architecture and reducing latency.

Licensing has evolved alongside this architecture. Fabric capacities can support Power BI Premium workloads in addition to broader data platform capabilities. Teams evaluating Power BI should determine whether a Fabric-aligned architecture aligns with their data strategy, as that decision affects both cost modeling and the technical skills required for long-term environment management.

Power Apps

Power Apps supports two primary application approaches. Canvas apps offer fine-grained control over the user experience, which makes them well suited to custom layouts and mobile-first scenarios. Model-driven apps generate much of the interface from Dataverse tables, forms, views, and relationships, which makes them well suited to data-centric applications that revolve around standard create, read, update, and delete operations.

Canvas apps rely heavily on Power Fx, an Excel-like formula language, for logic and calculations. In model-driven apps, Power Fx is also used for commanding, custom pages, and low-code plugins, although the overall application model remains centered on Dataverse metadata and server-side behaviors. Although Power Apps is often described as low-code or no-code, effective development still requires a strong understanding of variables, collections, delegation limits, and performance optimization.

Canvas apps are subject to delegation limits when working with large datasets. Delegation means that filtering, sorting, or other operations are executed by the data source rather than locally in the client. When an operation is not delegable, Power Apps processes only a limited number of records locally—500 by default and up to 2,000 when configured, though these thresholds are subject to change, which can lead to incomplete results.

Model-driven apps depend on Dataverse and generally require Power Apps licensing that includes Dataverse entitlement. Additional costs can arise from Dataverse capacity, premium connectors, and enterprise-scale requirements. In larger enterprise applications, complex business logic is often better implemented in Dataverse plugins or external services such as Azure Functions rather than in the client, because this improves scalability and keeps critical processing on the server side.

Power Automate

Power Automate creates automated workflows, known as flows, that connect applications and services. Cloud flows support API-based integrations across services, whereas desktop flows (formerly known as Power Automate Desktop) handle RPA for applications that lack APIs. The platform includes an AI Builder integration for document processing, form recognition, and text analysis.

Flow complexity influences both licensing requirements and execution boundaries. Run allocations vary by license tier, and some scenarios can be supported through consumption-based pricing. Execution is constrained by tier-specific timeouts and service thresholds, and certain actions introduce additional caps, such as limits on HTTP requests and array operations. In practice, teams account for these constraints during design and add error handling and retry logic for business-critical processes.

Microsoft Power Automate documentation outlines service protection limits and execution thresholds, which are important considerations during the solution design phase. Human-in-the-loop orchestration is a critical design pattern, especially when AI-generated outputs have low confidence scores or affect high-stakes business processes.

Without explicit review gates, automated flows may propagate inaccurate classifications or predictions through downstream systems, a phenomenon known as silent failure. By integrating approval steps, exception queues, and configurable confidence thresholds, teams gain the visibility needed to intercept and correct errors before they degrade business outcomes.

Power Pages

Power Pages (formerly Power Portals) creates external-facing websites that connect to Dataverse. These sites address scenarios in which external users require controlled access to organizational data without Microsoft 365 licenses. The platform provides templates for common scenarios, including customer self-service portals, partner collaboration sites, and community forums.

Security configuration warrants close attention because these sites can expose internal data to external users. Controls such as row-level security, page permissions, and API access are typically configured explicitly rather than assumed. Licensing follows a capacity model, with charges tied to authenticated and anonymous user capacity and additional storage costs. For deployments involving sensitive data, a formal security review commonly forms part of the release process before moving the solution to production.

Copilot Studio

Copilot Studio is Microsoft's low-code platform for building custom AI agents and copilots. Evolved from Power Virtual Agents, it reflects a shift from scripted conversation flows toward agent-based, goal-oriented execution. Makers define agent instructions, triggers, knowledge sources, tools, and orchestration settings for deployment across Microsoft Teams, websites, and mobile applications.

At its core, Copilot Studio supports agents that go beyond basic retrieval. An agent can use knowledge from Dataverse or SharePoint, execute actions through tools and agent flows, and hand conversations off to human reviewers or live agents when judgment is required. The platform also provides analytics and telemetry to evaluate performance during development and in production, while generative orchestration can use conversation history and context to improve ongoing interactions.

By 2025, Copilot Studio had become Microsoft's primary low-code environment for autonomous agent development. These agents can operate proactively by responding to event triggers, monitoring conditions, and initiating multistep workflows without an explicit user prompt. This capability, which reached general availability in 2025, marked a move toward goal-directed execution within defined guardrails.

Governance remains a prerequisite for deployment. Teams must define the functional scope of each agent, establish audit trails and documented processes, and implement review checkpoints for high-stakes decisions. Licensing follows a consumption-based model centered on Copilot Credits, which requires close monitoring as usage scales. Organizations must also apply industry-specific controls and internal governance policies to support compliant use.

13.1.2 Microsoft 365 Integration

Power Platform components integrate with Microsoft 365 services through Graph API and native connectors. Power Apps can be embedded in SharePoint pages or Teams tabs. However, performance may vary depending on the app's complexity and network conditions. Power Automate includes templates for common Microsoft 365 scenarios, such as approval workflows and document processing, but these require appropriate permissions and may be subject to service throttling under high-usage conditions.

Through Microsoft Teams integration, apps and flows can be launched directly within channels and chats. However, guest users are subject to restrictions, and some features require specific Teams license levels. SharePoint lists serve as data sources for Power Apps and Power Automate, subject to list size limits and view thresholds documented in Microsoft's SharePoint service descriptions.

Azure Services Connection

Power Platform integrates with Azure services to provide extended capabilities. Azure Functions can be invoked from Power Apps and Power Automate to execute custom logic. However, this requires an Azure subscription and incurs additional charges. Azure AI Services (formerly Azure Cognitive Services) provides AI capabilities, including vision, language, and speech processing.

APIM can expose custom APIs to the Power Platform for integration with on-premises systems via hybrid connectivity. This approach requires configuration of data gateways, network security, and authentication protocols. Performance depends on network latency, gateway configuration, authentication design, and the selected Azure service tier.

Dynamics 365 Relationship

Organizations using Dynamics 365 benefit from native integration with Power Platform components. Model-driven Power Apps runs on the same platform as Dynamics 365 applications, supporting deeper customization. Power Automate includes Dynamics 365 triggers and actions for automating CRM and ERP processes.

This integration requires appropriate Dynamics 365 licenses and may involve additional costs for Power Platform usage beyond included allowances. Data synchronization requires careful planning to prevent conflicts, avoid duplication, and maintain consistency across environments.

Dataverse Foundation

Microsoft Dataverse (formerly Common Data Service) provides the unified data platform that underpins the Power Platform. It offers relational data storage with built-in business logic, security, and integration capabilities. Dataverse includes standard tables for common business entities (Account, Contact, and Product) and supports the creation of custom tables.

Capacity is tied to tenant licensing, with base allocations for database, file, and log storage that vary by plan, and additional capacity available for purchase. Performance is shaped by platform constraints such as API request limits, plugin execution timeouts, and workflow boundaries. Accordingly, solution designs reflect these constraints through patterns such as pagination for large datasets and asynchronous processing for more complex operations. The specific thresholds differ by license tier and are published in Microsoft Dataverse reference material.

Security operates at multiple levels, including business units, security roles, field-level security, and row-level permissions. Proper configuration requires an understanding of security model inheritance, role assignment, and the interaction between different security mechanisms.

Development Considerations

Power Platform development requires striking a balance between ease of use and governance requirements. While business users can quickly create solutions, production deployments require proper application life-cycle management (ALM), including version control, testing, and deployment pipelines. Microsoft provides tools, including the Power Platform command-line interface and Azure DevOps integration, though these require technical expertise beyond the typical skill set of a citizen developer.

Solution boundaries and dependencies shape long-term maintainability and upgrade paths. Managed solutions support structured packaging for deployment while limiting certain changes that could compromise solution integrity. Unmanaged solutions are more flexible during development, but they often introduce friction during upgrades and environment synchronization. To manage this, teams adopt governance practices around solution architecture, naming conventions, and deployment procedures to keep the application life cycle predictable.

13.2 Evolution of AI in the Power Platform

The integration of AI into Microsoft Power Platform has occurred through several phases, each adding specific capabilities while presenting new technical and organizational challenges. This evolution reflects broader trends in making ML accessible to users without specialized data science training. However, successful implementation still requires an understanding of AI limitations and appropriate use cases.

13.2.1 Timeline of AI Integration

Microsoft's initial AI integration focused on analytical capabilities within Power BI. Early features included time-series forecasting, clustering, and anomaly detection, which became available through built-in visualizations starting around 2017. Many of these capabilities required Premium capacity, and their constraints varied by release and licensing tier.

The platform can connect to Azure AI Services through premium connectors, bringing capabilities such as text analytics, computer vision, and form recognition into low-code solutions. This integration typically relies on a separate Azure subscription, with costs determined by the specific Azure AI Services that are used. Operationally, teams treat these calls as external dependencies by securing API credentials, accounting for rate limits, and designing for transient failures and service interruptions through appropriate error handling.

Figure 13-1 illustrates a conceptual timeline of how AI capabilities have been incorporated into the Power Platform.

2016
Power BI AI visuals introduced
First AI capabilities with automated insights and Quick Insights feature

2019
AI Builder introduced
Preview launched at Build 2019; general availability released in October 2019 with prebuilt models and custom training capabilities

2021
GPT integration begins
Early experiments with LLMs in Power Platform

2023
Copilot features launched
Natural language app creation and workflow generation

2024
Autonomous agents preview
Self-directed AI agents for complex business processes

2025
Autonomous agents reach general availability
Copilot Studio established as the central hub for custom agent development and cross-platform orchestration

***Figure 13-1.** Timeline showing the progressive integration of AI capabilities into the Microsoft Power Platform from 2016 to 2025. (Image by author)*

13.2.2 AI Builder Introduction

Microsoft announced AI Builder at Build 2019, with public preview beginning in June 2019 and general availability in October 2019. AI Builder integrates ML models directly into Power Apps and Power Automate, but access requires additional licensing beyond the base Power Platform subscriptions.

AI Builder uses a credit-based licensing model in which credits cover both training and prediction. Credit usage varies by model type, with document processing, image analysis, and text operations each drawing credits at different rates. Consequently, teams track consumption as part of routine operations to avoid unexpected interruptions when credits run low. The current consumption rates are published in Microsoft AI Builder pricing material.

Prebuilt models address common scenarios, including invoice and receipt extraction, business card capture, sentiment analysis, and key phrase extraction. Output quality varies with document layout, image quality, and language. The invoice model returns per-field confidence scores that can be used to route low-confidence results for review. Business card extraction can capture a broad range of contact fields, including name, job title, phone numbers, email, company, website, and address components. In AI Builder, object detection is typically implemented as a trained model that recognizes only the labels and visual conditions represented in the training images.

Custom models give organizations the ability to train on proprietary data. Minimum example requirements vary by model type. Some models can begin training with dozens of examples, but dependable production performance typically requires plenty more, along with iterative refinement to achieve acceptable accuracy. Model training may take several hours depending on model type, dataset size, and service load. Maintaining separate environments for development and production deployment protects against training disruptions affecting live systems.

Table 13-2 compares prebuilt and custom models across setup time, training requirements, accuracy, customization, maintenance, cost, and best-fit scenarios.

Table 13-2. *Comparison of prebuilt and custom AI Builder models across key implementation factors, including setup time, accuracy expectations, and resource requirements.*

Aspect	Prebuilt Models	Custom Models
Setup time	Ready to use within minutes; minimal configuration required	Requires data preparation, labeling, and iterative training; setup time varies by scenario
Training required	None; Microsoft provides and maintains the underlying model	Yes; representative training data and iterative refinement over time
Accuracy	Depends on input quality, document structure, and language; suitable for standardized scenarios	Depends on training data quality and quantity; can improve with iteration and domain-specific examples
Customization	Limited to available parameters and supported document types	Full control over labels, fields, and domain-specific patterns
Maintenance	Microsoft manages updates and model improvements	The organization is responsible for retraining, monitoring, and life-cycle management
Cost (AI credits)	Consumption varies by model type and operation	Consumption includes training and prediction operations; it varies by model complexity
Best for	Common, repeatable business scenarios with predictable formats	Unique or domain-specific requirements not covered by prebuilt models

Note AI Builder credit consumption varies by model type, operation, and whether the model is prebuilt or custom-trained. Current consumption rates are published in Microsoft's AI Builder documentation and are subject to change.

13.2.3 Copilot Integration

Microsoft began introducing Copilot capabilities across Power Platform in 2023, with availability varying by product, region, and licensing tier. Power Apps received Copilot features in March 2023, initially as a preview in North American regions. Power Automate and Power BI Copilot features followed by staggered releases through 2023 and 2024.

Copilot in Power Apps generates initial application structures based on natural language descriptions. When a user describes requirements, Copilot creates basic data tables, forms, and galleries. However, the resulting applications entail extensive tuning, as Copilot establishes a framework rather than a comprehensive, finished product. Modifying formulas, adjusting layouts, adding validation logic, and implementing security configurations appropriate to the requirements are all part of the finishing work.

Power Automate's Copilot assists with flow creation by interpreting natural language descriptions of desired automations. It suggests appropriate connectors and actions, but cannot handle complex branching logic or error handling without manual configuration. Generated flows require testing and often need adjustment for edge cases and exception handling.

Power BI Copilot facilitates the creation of report pages and DAX measures via natural language queries. Effectiveness depends on well-structured data models and clear naming conventions. Complex calculations still require manually writing DAX formulas, and generated visuals may need formatting adjustments.

13.2.4 Technical Considerations

AI features in Power Platform operate within technical constraints that affect implementation planning. Model execution is subject to timeouts that may affect high-volume processing scenarios. Batch processing capabilities vary by model type and may change as Microsoft updates the service. Both data privacy and residency requirements impact the availability of AI features. AI Builder processes data in specific regions, which may not align with organizational data residency mandates. Some models send data to Azure AI Services for processing, potentially crossing geographic boundaries.

Verifying that AI processing locations comply with regulatory and data residency requirements is a compliance obligation. For example, organizations subject to the GDPR must confirm that personal data remains within approved regions or that valid transfer mechanisms are in place. Similarly, under the CCPA, organizations must account for how AI-processed information is handled, retained, and disclosed. These constraints often shape architectural decisions regarding model selection and data pipeline design.

Training custom models requires an understanding of ML concepts, including training/validation splits, overfitting prevention, and the interpretation of performance metrics. While AI Builder abstracts away much of the complexity, achieving production-ready accuracy often requires iteration and expertise in data preparation and feature engineering.

13.2.5 Adoption Patterns

Organizations typically begin AI adoption with prebuilt models for document processing, as these provide immediate value with minimal configuration. However, effectiveness varies with the degree of document standardization. Structured forms, such as invoices, achieve higher success rates than variable formats, like contracts or correspondence.

The transition from prebuilt to custom models often reveals gaps in data quality and quantity. Many organizations find that their training data is insufficient or too inconsistent to train effective models. This realization often drives data cleanup initiatives and process standardization before successful AI implementation.

Copilot adoption patterns reveal initial enthusiasm, followed by adjustment periods as users learn prompt engineering techniques and become familiar with output limitations. Organizations report productivity gains primarily in prototype development and initial solution scaffolding, with less impact on implementing complex logic or optimizing performance.

13.3 Operating the Power Platform

Power Platform's accessibility to citizen developers introduces governance challenges that differ from traditional IT management. Organizations establish frameworks that foster innovation while preventing the uncontrolled proliferation of applications, security vulnerabilities, and technical debt. Effective governance combines technical controls, organizational policies, and ongoing monitoring so that solutions meet enterprise standards regardless of who builds them.

This governance challenge aligns with patterns I observed decades ago, when component-based development first enabled the rapid assembly of business solutions. At Wolters Kluwer, we learned that the INTELLIFM system's accessibility to domain experts required corresponding investment in governance frameworks—without which the efficiency gains were offset by maintenance complexity and inconsistent quality. Power Platform operates at a greater scale, but the fundamental tension between enablement and control remains unchanged.

13.3.1 Environment Strategy and Management

Power Platform environments provide isolated containers for applications, flows, and data. Organizations typically implement a three-tier structure, comprising development, testing, and production.

Development environments allow unrestricted experimentation but limit external connections to protect production systems and third-party services. Test environments mirror production configurations for validation while restricting access to end users. Production environments, by contrast, enforce strict change controls and require formal approval workflows for all modifications.

Without a clearly defined environment strategy, users may inadvertently create assets in the default environment. This leads to shadow IT: unmanaged solutions that bypass governance controls, expose sensitive data, and generate unplanned storage costs. Microsoft recommends restricting default environment permissions and directing all development activity to managed, purpose-built environments from the outset. This approach makes the life cycle of every solution auditable and governed by the relevant teams.

Environment creation policies control who can provision new environments and under what conditions. With default tenant settings, licensed users may be able to create environments, leading to uncontrolled growth and uneven governance. Many organizations limit this capability to designated administrators or route requests through an approval process using Microsoft Entra ID groups. Because each environment draws database and file storage from the tenant capacity pool, environment strategy is often linked to capacity planning to avoid resource exhaustion.

Solution deployment across environments typically follows ALM principles. Managed solutions package components for consistent promotion and, in target environments, limit direct modification so that releases remain traceable and repeatable. This model reinforces separation between development and production while supporting version control and practical rollback options when issues arise. In mature release processes, promotion criteria commonly include peer review, test evidence, and explicit business approval before a deployment moves into production.

13.3.2 Security and Data Protection

DLP policies govern data movement between connectors by grouping connectors into business, personal/consumer (nonbusiness), or blocked categories and restricting which groups can be used together in the same app or flow. Business connectors commonly include SharePoint, SQL Server, and Dataverse, whereas personal/consumer connectors often include social media or personal cloud storage services. These policies help prevent sensitive organizational data from being shared via unapproved channels—for example, by blocking flows that attempt to copy Dataverse records to the Gmail connector.

Connector governance extends beyond DLP to include custom connector approval workflows. Organizations can block specific connectors entirely, require approval for premium connectors, or restrict custom connector creation to designated developers. These restrictions apply at the environment level, allowing different policies for development versus production environments.

Microsoft Purview integration applies sensitivity labels and retention policies for Power Platform components. Apps and flows that contain sensitive data can be automatically classified, with access restricted based on users' clearance levels. Audit logs capture all administrative actions, app launches, and data access events, providing forensic capabilities for security investigations.

13.3.3 Center of Excellence Implementation

The Power Platform Center of Excellence (CoE) Starter Kit provides prebuilt solutions for governance and monitoring. The kit includes components for inventory tracking, compliance monitoring, and automated governance enforcement. Core components track all apps, flows, and makers across the tenant, identifying orphaned resources and unused licenses.

The governance components implement policies such as automatically notifying creators of unused apps, quarantining noncompliant solutions, and enforcing documentation requirements. The audit log component synchronizes Power Platform activity with centralized logging systems, supporting oversight and reporting. The kit requires a Power Apps or Power Automate Premium license for full functionality and a dedicated environment for deployment.

Organizations typically customize the CoE kit to align with their specific governance requirements. Common modifications include adding approval workflows for production deployments, integrating with IT service management systems, and implementing charge-back mechanisms for resource consumption. The kit's Power BI reports provide insights into adoption patterns, maker productivity, and compliance status.

13.3.4 Cost Management and Licensing

Power Platform licensing requires active management to contain operational costs. Power Apps and Power Automate combine user-based, process-based, and pay-as-you-go models, depending on the workload and deployment pattern. Microsoft's process-based tier, branded as the Process license, is designed for automating business processes without user interaction. In practice, selecting the wrong licensing model can make an otherwise useful solution cost-prohibitive at scale. Architects, therefore, evaluate licensing early, alongside expected usage patterns, connector requirements, Dataverse consumption, and AI-related costs.

High-volume automations are subject to Power Platform request limits, which govern the number of API calls a flow or application can make within a given period. Architects should design for batch processing rather than row-by-row operations. Processing individual records in a loop is a common architectural antipattern that can quickly exhaust request allocations, trigger throttling, and generate unexpected costs. Microsoft publishes current request limits in the Power Platform licensing documentation, and these should be reviewed during architecture and capacity planning.

Capacity-based resources such as AI Builder credits, Dataverse storage, and Power Pages often require deliberate allocation strategies. In many enterprises, show-back or charge-back approaches make consumption visible to business units and support clearer cost accountability. The Power Platform admin center provides usage analytics, while deeper cost analysis is frequently handled by exporting usage data to external BI tools.

Governance of premium features helps prevent unplanned use of higher-cost capabilities. Features such as AI Builder, premium connectors, and on-premises gateways are often limited to specific environments or controlled user groups. Microsoft Entra ID groups govern license assignments and access boundaries, restricting premium resource consumption to approved users.

13.3.5 Monitoring and Compliance

Continuous monitoring identifies governance violations before they become operational issues. The Power Platform admin center provides built-in analytics for resource usage, user activity, and error tracking. However, thorough monitoring typically requires integrating with broader IT monitoring platforms via Power Platform Management connectors or REST APIs.

Governance monitoring often relies on a small set of operational metrics. Common examples include the number of apps per maker as an indicator of sprawl, connector usage patterns that can surface shadow IT, error rates by solution as a signal of quality issues, and data growth trends that help anticipate capacity needs. In more mature setups, threshold-based alerts are used to flag exceptions, such as unusually high app creation by a single maker or error rates that exceed agreed service levels.

Compliance reporting provides evidence that governance policies and regulatory obligations are being met. Power Platform maintains audit logs for a configurable retention period, and integration with Azure Monitor or a third-party SIEM system can support longer retention. Default retention varies by license tier. Hence, retention settings are commonly reviewed in the Power Platform admin center as part of compliance oversight. Ongoing review cycles also tend to revisit DLP policies, identify unused resources for decommissioning, and confirm that production solutions remain documented and traceable.

13.3.6 Balancing Innovation with Control

Successful governance frameworks balance control with speed, avoiding bureaucratic friction that can push makers back toward shadow IT. In effective programs, environment requests are handled quickly, often within a business day, and production approval workflows are streamlined through automation where practical. Documentation expectations are typically aligned with solution complexity and business impact, with lighter requirements for simpler apps and greater rigor for high-impact systems.

Governance maturity typically evolves through phases. Initial adoption focuses on basic controls, such as DLP policies and environment restrictions. Intermediate maturity adds monitoring, documentation standards, and formal review processes. Advanced governance incorporates automated testing, continuous compliance monitoring, and predictive analytics for capacity planning.

Governance policies often evolve as adoption patterns and business needs change. Many organizations use quarterly reviews to assess policy effectiveness, surface emerging risks, and adjust controls in response to platform updates. Maker feedback commonly informs these updates so that governance supports, rather than inhibits, business value creation.

13.4 Trustworthy Power Platform

Deploying AI at an enterprise scale requires more than technical capability. It requires governance frameworks, safety mechanisms, and an unwavering focus on human benefit. Organizations face the challenge of balancing innovation with control, efficiency with ethics, and automation with accountability. Success depends on practical habits that foster trust, systematic risk management approaches, and continuous adaptation as technology and understanding evolve.

13.4.1 Building Trust Through Transparency

Trust typically develops through consistent, observable behaviors more than through promises alone. AI systems earn trust through specific practices that demonstrate reliability and accountability. These habits seem mundane. However, they determine whether organizations adopt AI as operational infrastructure or treat it as an interesting experiment.

Effective systems cite sources rather than claiming omniscience. When Copilot provides information, it includes references to specific documents or data sources. Users can verify claims independently. This citation discipline extends beyond simple attribution. The system indicates which documents informed its reasoning, what data supported its conclusions, and where uncertainty persists.

Marking content status prevents false authority. AI-generated text appears with clear indicators: "Draft," "AI-generated," or "Requires review." This labeling sets appropriate expectations. A drafted email shows as preliminary. An extracted data point indicates its source. A generated analysis notes its automated origin. Users know exactly what they are reviewing.

Providing provenance makes validation possible. Modern systems can supplement answers with citations to source documents, confidence indicators, and auditable logs—though the depth of explanation varies by model and workload. When Copilot generates a response, it may cite the documents it referenced. When AI Builder makes a prediction, it provides confidence scores. This transparency, while not exposing the true internal model reasoning, helps professionals to assess the reliability of outputs and trace information back to its sources.

Consistency in behavior builds confidence over time. Reliable systems respond predictably to similar inputs, provide informative error messages, and degrade gracefully under load rather than failing abruptly. In practice, these operational characteristics can matter as much as accuracy, particularly when systems encounter edge cases and ambiguous requests.

13.4.2 Ethical Frameworks and Explainability

Ethical AI involves more than compliance checklists. It requires systematic approaches to fairness, accountability, and human welfare. Organizations typically implement frameworks that address bias, promote explainability, and maintain human oversight where decisions affect lives and livelihoods.

Explainable Artificial Intelligence (XAI) has evolved from an academic concept to an operational requirement. Many regulated use cases require explainability, documentation, auditability, and human oversight. In fact, some organizations prohibit the use of opaque models for certain high-impact decisions. This does not mean exposing every weight in the neural network. It means providing meaningful explanations that connect inputs to outputs through interpretable reasoning, at a level appropriate to the risk and regulatory context.

Consider loan approval systems. Traditional models may simply output "approved" or "denied." XAI-compliant systems explain the factors contributing to the decision, including the impact of credit history, income verification, and debt ratios. They show how each factor influenced the decision and what changes would alter the outcome. Applicants understand not only the decision but also the reasoning behind it. Regulators can audit not just results but logic.

Bias detection and mitigation require continuous vigilance. Training data reflects historical patterns, including historical discrimination. Models trained on past hiring data may perpetuate gender or racial biases. Systems are expected to actively monitor for discriminatory patterns. This involves tracking outcomes across demographic groups, testing with synthetic data, and adjusting strategies when disparities emerge.

Microsoft's responsible AI framework provides a practical structure. It emphasizes six principles: fairness, reliability, privacy, inclusiveness, transparency, and accountability. Each principle translates into specific practices. Fairness requires bias testing. Reliability demands error monitoring. Privacy necessitates data governance. These are not abstract ideals but operational requirements with measurable compliance.

13.4.3 Decision Criteria for Enterprise Adoption

Organizations face complex choices about AI deployment. The following criteria guide thoughtful adoption:

Key Decision Criteria for Enterprise AI Adoption

- **Data Readiness**: Is organizational data clean, accessible, and properly governed? AI tends to amplify data quality issues, and weak data foundations often produce weak outcomes. Many organizations evaluate data readiness as a prerequisite for successful AI deployment.
- **Integration Complexity**: How deeply does AI need to integrate with existing systems? Simple overlays can be deployed quickly, but deep integration with core systems requires extensive planning, testing, and change management.
- **Risk Tolerance**: What happens when AI makes mistakes? Low-risk scenarios, such as document summarization, allow experimentation. High-risk decisions that impact safety, finances, or legal compliance necessitate stringent safeguards.
- **Regulatory Requirements**: Which regulations apply? Health care is subject to HIPAA. Finance navigates Securities and Exchange Commission (SEC) and Financial Industry Regulatory Authority (FINRA) requirements. European operations must comply with the GDPR. The regulatory landscape shapes deployment options.

- **Change Management Capacity**: Can the organization support adoption? Technical deployment often accounts for a smaller share of total effort than training, process redesign, and cultural change. Organizations benefit from honestly assessing their capacity for change.
- **Use Case Maturity**: Are you solving established problems or exploring new territory? Document processing and customer service have proven patterns. Novel applications require more experimentation and a higher tolerance for risk.

Successful deployments typically begin with high-volume, low-risk scenarios in which AI assists rather than makes decisions. Document classification, meeting transcription, and data extraction provide immediate value with manageable risk. Organizations build confidence through success before tackling critical decisions.

13.4.4 Continuous Evolution and Monitoring

AI systems exist in dynamic environments. Data distributions shift, user behaviors evolve, regulations change, and new vulnerabilities emerge. Static deployment can degrade performance and increase risk. Organizations need systematic approaches to monitoring and evolution.

Performance monitoring extends beyond simple accuracy metrics. Systems track response latency, resource consumption, and error patterns. They monitor for model drift, which is the gradual degradation as real-world data diverges from the training distribution. Financial models trained before the pandemic required a lot of adjustment as economic patterns shifted. Early detection prevents crises.

Feedback loops support continuous improvement over time. User corrections can be captured to refine models, while error analysis often surfaces systematic failure modes. A/B testing is commonly used to validate changes before broad rollout. Much as the Indianapolis Motor Speedway has advanced safety through proactive iteration rather than waiting for accidents, AI systems tend to mature fastest when improvements are made ahead of failures.

Security monitoring plays a central role in addressing emerging threats. Adversarial attacks attempt to mislead AI systems with carefully crafted inputs, data poisoning aims to corrupt training sets, and model inversion seeks to extract information from training data. In operational settings, these risks are handled through ongoing monitoring and layered controls, including input validation, anomaly detection, and periodic security assessments.

Governance processes often evolve as system capabilities mature. Early deployments may rely on human review for most decisions, with oversight later shifting toward sampling or exception-based review as confidence grows. Over time, governance can support a move from strict control to earned autonomy, while keeping oversight aligned with the risk profile of each use case.

13.4.5 Human-Centered Design Principles

A key measure of AI success extends beyond algorithmic performance to include human benefit. Systems augment human capability rather than simply automating tasks. This requires deliberate design choices that preserve human agency, develop human potential, and respect human values.

Augmentation over replacement guides architectural decisions. AI handles routine processing, freeing humans to focus on judgment and creativity. Lawyers focus on negotiation rather than document review, and doctors concentrate on patient care rather than paperwork. This approach aims for job elevation rather than elimination. The work becomes more meaningful, more impactful, and more satisfying.

Preserving human agency means keeping meaningful control in human hands. Users benefit from understanding what the system is doing, the basis for its recommendations, and the points where intervention is possible. Practical mechanisms for overriding, correcting, and providing feedback support this collaboration. Agency is not limited to emergency stops. In fact, it is reflected in the ongoing interaction between human judgment and machine capability.

Developing human potential requires investment in learning. As AI handles routine tasks, humans need new skills. This is not just technical training on AI tools. It is developing judgment about when to trust AI, how to validate its outputs, and where human insight adds value. Organizations succeeding with AI invest heavily in human development alongside technical deployment.

The path forward involves balancing multiple imperatives. Organizations pursue AI-driven efficiency gains while building trust through transparency and advance innovation while relying on governance to support safety. At the same time, the aim is often to augment human capability while preserving human agency and dignity. This balance, alongside technological progress, tends to shape successful intelligence transformation.

With governance frameworks and human-centered principles established, organizations can confidently navigate the journey from current capabilities to future possibilities. The path unfolds across distinct time horizons, each requiring different strategies and preparations.

13.5 AI Builder: Accessible ML

AI Builder is Microsoft Power Platform's integrated AI capability, designed to make ML accessible to business users without requiring formal training in data science. With AI Builder, organizations embed intelligence directly into apps and workflows using a low-code interface—accelerating the shift from procedural automation to intelligent automation. By abstracting the complexity of model development, infrastructure management, and algorithm selection, AI Builder allows teams to operationalize AI across departments with minimal friction. Its integration with Power Apps and Power Automate means intelligent features can be invoked within applications and workflows without disrupting existing business logic.

13.5.1 Prebuilt Models

AI Builder includes a suite of prebuilt models trained on Microsoft datasets to address common business scenarios with minimal configuration. These models are production-ready and can be quickly deployed to Power Apps and Power Automate workflows. Document processing models extract structured data from artifacts such as invoices, receipts, and tax forms, identifying key-value pairs, tables, and checkboxes. The platform provides standardized models and reference datasets that accelerate the development of extraction flows for common fields, such as invoice identifiers and vendor metadata. Straight-through processing rates are typically governed by confidence score thresholds, with low-confidence extractions routed to manual review queues. Achievable rates vary with invoice standardization, layout variability, and input quality.

Object detection allows retail teams to audit shelf inventory by identifying and counting items in images captured via mobile devices. These domain-specific models are optimized for retail shelf scenarios, allowing for the detection of densely packed products and brand logos. Retailers apply this capability to automate inventory checks, verify planogram compliance, and monitor shelf health in real time.

Sentiment analysis classifies text as positive, negative, or neutral, supporting customer service triage and social media monitoring. In Power Automate, this pattern is commonly used to route negative feedback to support queues and log sentiment scores for operational reporting.

Text classification automates document triage by assigning inbound communications to predefined categories. This pattern is well suited to routing support requests to appropriate departments based on content analysis. Language detection complements this by identifying the primary language of text inputs, allowing organizations to trigger localized workflows and direct inquiries to native-language support teams. The prebuilt language detection model supports more than 100 languages and integrates with Power Apps and Power Automate. Global organizations use this capability to direct inquiries to native-language support agents, improving response times and meeting service-level commitments.

Prompt Builder extended AI Builder with generative AI capabilities. It allows makers to add generative AI behavior directly in Power Apps and Power Automate via a low-code experience, without writing custom integration code or managing a separate Azure OpenAI subscription for this standard capability.

Makers define a prompt, a natural language instruction describing the desired generation or analysis, and AI Builder manages the underlying model call. The system returns generated output that the application or flow can process immediately; when needed, prompts can also be configured to return structured JSON output. Common architectural uses include document summarization, drafting context-aware responses, classifying free-form input, and extracting entities from unstructured content.

As with other AI Builder capabilities, prompts operate on a consumption-based model, with rates published in the current Microsoft documentation. In Power Apps and Power Automate, execution may consume AI Builder credits or Copilot Credits, depending on the environment's available capacity. Because output quality depends heavily on prompt design, teams should validate results carefully and introduce human review gates before using these outputs in high-stakes automated decisions. This evaluative step is an important part of the solution life cycle and helps support safety, accuracy, and governance.

13.5.2 Custom Models

For domain-specific needs, AI Builder supports the creation of custom models using proprietary data. Business users can train models through a guided interface that includes data labeling, annotation, and iterative refinement. Minimum training requirements vary by model type—document processing, object detection, and classification models each have different thresholds. Although some models can begin training with relatively few examples, dependable production performance typically requires more data. Current requirements are documented in Microsoft's AI Builder guidance.

Microsoft documentation illustrates how health care providers use custom models to extract patient intake data from structured forms, reducing manual data entry and improving onboarding efficiency. Model performance is evaluated using *precision, recall,* and *F1 scores*. Precision measures the proportion of correct predictions among all instances the model labeled as positive, while recall measures the proportion of actual positives the model correctly identifies. The F1 score is the harmonic mean of precision and recall, providing a balanced metric when there is a trade-off between false positives and false negatives.

These scores help organizations determine whether a model is sufficiently reliable for production use or requires further refinement. Thresholds for acceptable performance vary by use case—for example, document classification may tolerate lower recall when manual review is available. In contrast, sentiment analysis in customer service may demand higher precision to avoid misrouting critical feedback. Teams should establish a strategy for periodic retraining of the AI models because business conditions, form layouts, and data distributions change. This ongoing process helps prevent model drift and maintains the level of accuracy required for clinical and administrative workflows.

AI Builder supports continuous refinement, allowing users to add new examples and retrain models to maintain accuracy and relevance. ALM for custom AI Builder models requires deliberate planning. Unlike standard Power Platform components, AI Builder models are not automatically included in solutions and must be explicitly added before they can be promoted across development, test, and production environments. Model versions, training data, and performance baselines should be tracked alongside the solution to maintain consistency and support rollback when a retrained model underperforms in production. This is one of the more common implementation gaps in AI Builder deployments and is worth addressing early in the architecture phase.

13.5.3 Integration and Implementation

AI Builder supports both synchronous and asynchronous processing, giving organizations flexibility to tailor their integration strategies to meet operational requirements. Synchronous execution in Power Apps provides immediate feedback but may introduce latency for complex operations. Asynchronous execution patterns in Power Automate support long-running and background workflows, which commonly require status tracking and robust error handling. Teams often apply confidence score thresholds to determine whether to proceed automatically or route predictions for human review. The appropriate threshold varies by model, by field, and by business risk. For example, Microsoft's invoice processing sample routes the invoice total field for review when its confidence score falls below 0.65.

Implementing fallback logic, retry mechanisms, and alerts for threshold violations are essential practices for dependable production deployment. Optimization strategies include preprocessing documents to remove unnecessary pages, resizing images before object detection, and batching text operations to minimize overhead. These practices help organizations reduce consumption costs and improve model performance.

13.5.4 Licensing and Cost Management

AI Builder operates on a credit-based consumption model. Organizations purchase capacity that is consumed through model training and predictive operations. Consumption rates vary by model type; document processing, object detection, and text analysis each have distinct credit requirements. Credits are acquired through capacity add-ons or pay-as-you-go arrangements, and tenant-level pooling supports sharing across environments. Current consumption rates are published in Microsoft's AI Builder documentation and should be verified before committing to a deployment architecture.

In practice, credit consumption is often a primary barrier to broader adoption. Teams may underestimate credit requirements during the proof-of-concept phase, only to encounter serious budget constraints when scaling to production volumes. Establishing a FinOps strategy early, including consumption alerts, per-environment budgets, and regular usage reviews, helps avoid unexpected costs and supports a sustainable business case for ongoing investment.

13.5.5 Industry Impact

AI Builder supports a range of use cases across industries. In financial services, organizations apply it to invoice validation and fraud detection. In retail, it supports inventory management and customer sentiment analysis. In health care, it assists with patient intake and document classification. In government, it contributes to service delivery and multilingual communication. Outcomes vary based on data quality, implementation approach, and organizational readiness.

These implementations validate AI Builder's role as a strategic enabler of intelligent automation—one that aligns with enterprise governance, scales across environments, and supports responsible AI deployment within a low-code framework. By lowering the barrier to entry for ML, AI Builder empowers organizations to innovate rapidly while maintaining operational control and cost efficiency.

13.6 Copilot in the Power Platform

Microsoft introduced Copilot capabilities across Power Platform components in 2023, with features rolling out at different rates across products and regions. These generative AI features assist with initial application creation, flow design, and report generation. However, the outputs require refinement and validation before they can be used in production. These capabilities are powered by LLMs and vary in maturity across Power Platform components. While some features are generally available, others remain in preview and are subject to change. Table 13-3 summarizes the natural language capabilities, current limitations, and best use cases for Power Apps, Power Automate, Power BI, Power Pages, and Copilot Studio.

Table 13-3. *Copilot features across the Microsoft Power Platform showing natural language capabilities, current technical limitations, and recommended use cases for each component.*

Platform	Natural Language Capabilities	Current Limitations	Best Use Cases
Power Apps	Generate initial app screens and simple logic from natural language descriptions; add controls and data connections via chat	Complex logic, data relationships, and performance optimization still require manual design	Simple data entry apps, forms, and prototypes
Power Automate	Create draft workflows from plain-language prompts, including triggers and basic actions	Multistep branching, loops, expressions, and error handling require refinement	Approvals, notifications, and simple data synchronization
Power BI	Generate visuals and answer natural language questions when data is well modeled	Advanced DAX, complex calculations, and semantic modeling remain manual tasks	Quick insights, exploratory analysis
Power Pages	Generate basic page layouts, text, and simple forms from prompts	Custom styling, security configuration, and advanced logic require pro-dev skills	Informational pages, simple data collection forms
Copilot Studio	Build conversational agents and autonomous workflows from natural language; connect to data sources, APIs, and Power Automate flows; deploy across Teams, web, and mobile channels	Complex orchestration, multiagent coordination, and regulated decision-making require careful governance design; consumption costs should be monitored closely because usage is governed through Copilot Credits and related consumption controls	Custom AI agents, customer service automation, internal helpdesks, cross-platform task orchestration

13.6.1 Power Apps Copilot

In Power Apps, Copilot supports rapid prototyping by generating a starter canvas app from natural language prompts. When users describe requirements such as "build an app for tracking inventory," Copilot can propose one or more Microsoft Dataverse tables (including suggested columns and relationships) and then generate an initial app based on that data model. This initial generation reduces the blank-page problem, but makers typically perform additional work before production deployment—refining the data model, screen layouts and navigation, security roles, validation rules, integrations, and testing.

While Copilot generates foundational components, several critical elements still need to be added manually. Security configuration, role-based access, business logic, validation rules, complex formulas, table relationships, user interface refinement, and performance optimization—all require manual implementation.

Effective prompt engineering improves initial results. Specific requirements yield better structures than vague descriptions. For example, "Create an app to track inventory with fields for item name, quantity, and location" yields better results than "Make an inventory app." Including field names, data types, and relationships in prompts helps generate more complete data models. However, even well-crafted prompts often produce applications that require substantial modification. Organizations report that Copilot reduces initial setup time from hours to minutes, but does not meaningfully reduce total development time for production applications.

13.6.2 Power Automate Copilot

In Power Automate, Copilot streamlines the creation of automated workflows by interpreting natural language descriptions and generating initial flow structures. It is particularly effective for common business scenarios such as approvals, notifications, and data synchronization, offering a rapid starting point for automation design. For example, the statement "when an email arrives, save attachments to SharePoint" generates a flow with appropriate triggers and actions. The system identifies standard connectors and suggests basic action sequences.

Generated flows often work well for straightforward scenarios, but they rarely include the advanced logic needed for production use. Error handling, retry logic, conditional branching, variable management, data transformation, authentication setup, and performance tuning typically require manual configuration. Copilot performs best with established patterns such as approval workflows, notification flows, and basic data synchronization. Complex business logic and scenarios such as multistep approvals with delegation, parallel processing, and error recovery still require substantial human design. As a result, additional effort is commonly devoted to exception handling, testing of edge cases, and performance optimization.

13.6.3 Power BI Copilot

In Power BI, Copilot enhances report development by translating natural language queries into visualizations, DAX formulas, and narrative summaries. It helps users explore data patterns and build dashboards, especially when working with well-structured models and standard analytical requirements. Users can request visualizations, such as "show sales by region for last quarter," and Copilot attempts to create the appropriate charts. The feature also generates narrative summaries of data patterns and suggests report layouts.

Effectiveness depends heavily on the quality of the data model. Well-structured star schemas with clear naming conventions produce better results than complex or poorly organized models. Copilot-generated DAX measures often require refinement for performance and accuracy. Complex calculations involving time intelligence, running totals, or advanced filtering typically need manual creation.

Natural language queries are most effective for straightforward requests. Simple aggregations and filters generally succeed. Fundamental comparative analysis produces usable results. Standard chart types are generated correctly. However, complex analytical requirements often fail or produce incorrect results. Statistical analysis beyond basic aggregation requires manual implementation. Custom visualizations demand traditional development approaches.

13.6.4 Custom Agent Development

Copilot Studio is the primary low-code environment for architecting custom AI agents within the Power Platform. While embedded Copilot features in Power Apps, Power Automate, and Power BI assist with localized task completion, Copilot Studio provides the authoring, orchestration, and governance infrastructure for designing, validating, and deploying production-ready agents across diverse channels and enterprise systems.

Shift to Autonomous Agency

Copilot Studio supports the design of agents that coordinate across multiple systems, use conversation history and context, and operate autonomously under defined conditions.

Building an agent begins with defining its functional scope: the topics it handles, the actions it can execute, and the conditions that require human escalation. Makers configure knowledge sources, including SharePoint sites, Dataverse tables, and public websites, which the agent consults to produce grounded responses. Actions then connect the agent to external systems through Power Automate flows, connectors, or direct REST API calls, allowing it to create records, retrieve status information, and trigger downstream processes. By 2025, the platform supported autonomous agents and event-triggered execution, allowing agents to monitor environmental signals or event queues and initiate action sequences without an explicit user prompt.

An accounts payable agent, for example, might monitor an invoice queue, extract metadata using AI Builder, verify totals against purchase orders in Dataverse, and route exceptions to a human reviewer, all without manual intervention. The distinction between an automated workflow and an autonomous agent lies in goal-directed behavior: the agent evaluates context and selects an appropriate course of action rather than following a fixed, deterministic sequence.

Governance and Resiliency

Governance is a prerequisite for autonomous deployments. Organizations must define explicit boundaries of authority, maintain immutable audit trails, and require human approval for high-stakes actions such as financial modifications or external communications. In addition, testing must account for the nondeterministic nature of large language model reasoning, in which similar inputs may produce different response paths. In regulated industries, these agents undergo rigorous peer review and validation before promotion to production.

13.6.5 Technical Limitations and Requirements

Copilot and generative AI capabilities in the Power Platform involve licensing and availability considerations that vary by product and feature. Some Copilot experiences in Power Apps are available to makers, while other AI capabilities consume AI Builder credits or Copilot Credits and may require Premium licensing or capacity add-ons, depending on the organization's plan and tenant configuration. Feature availability also varies by geography, language, and release status. In some regions, full functionality requires cross-region data movement to align with available processing capacity.

Processing and service limits also affect the user experience. Response times vary based on workload complexity, retrieval scope, and regional capacity. Execution is bounded by platform constraints, including token context limits and Power Platform request quotas. To address these constraints, solutions often incorporate monitoring, retry logic where appropriate, and standardized handling for rate limit failures.

Several considerations typically arise before widespread adoption. Improvements in Copilot-assisted development often come from structured prompting practices and domain-specific examples rather than formal training in the traditional sense. Many organizations establish prompt templates, usage guidelines, and peer review practices to improve consistency and quality across teams. This investment in prompting infrastructure—while less visible than model training—has a direct impact on the reliability and maintainability of AI-assisted outputs. Review processes for AI-generated components help maintain quality and security. Governance policies for Copilot usage can reduce ungoverned sprawl, while documentation standards for AI-assisted development support transparency and accountability. In mature programs, Copilot usage aligns with internal AI governance frameworks and Microsoft's responsible AI guidance, emphasizing traceability of generated components and auditability of decision logic.

13.6.6 Practical Implementation Patterns

Successful Copilot implementations follow consistent patterns. Organizations typically begin with low-risk prototyping, where rapid iteration provides value without the concerns of production. Power users and professional developers experiment first, establishing patterns that citizen developers later adopt. Clear use case definitions determine where Copilot adds value versus traditional development.

Common implementation challenges include overreliance on initial generation without adequate validation, limited testing of edge cases and error conditions, insufficient security review of generated components, and poor documentation of

AI-assisted development. In response, many teams introduce review checkpoints, structured testing protocols, and documentation expectations as part of Copilot-assisted development practices.

Realistic expectations improve adoption success. Copilot accelerates initial development but does not eliminate the need for technical skills. Generated solutions require refinement before deployment to production. Hence, complex business logic still demands traditional development approaches, and professional developer involvement remains necessary for enterprise applications.

Copilot in the Power Platform represents a shift toward AI-assisted development. While it can accelerate prototyping and lower barriers to entry for initial solution development, successful enterprise adoption depends on disciplined governance, skilled refinement, and realistic expectations. Organizations that treat Copilot as a collaborative assistant—rather than a replacement for expertise—tend to achieve better outcomes.

13.7 Designing AI-Driven Solutions

Creating effective AI-enhanced applications in Power Platform requires a systematic design approach that addresses technical, operational, and ethical considerations. Success depends on a clear problem definition, the selection of appropriate technology, and sound implementation practices.

The design principles that follow echo lessons from my early work on expert systems. Whether building rule-based engines in the 1990s or configuring AI Builder models today, the same fundamentals apply: understand the problem before selecting the technology, invest in data quality before expecting model quality, and design for human oversight before automating decisions. The tools have evolved dramatically; the discipline required has not. Figure 13-2 illustrates the maturity model for AI implementation in Power Platform.

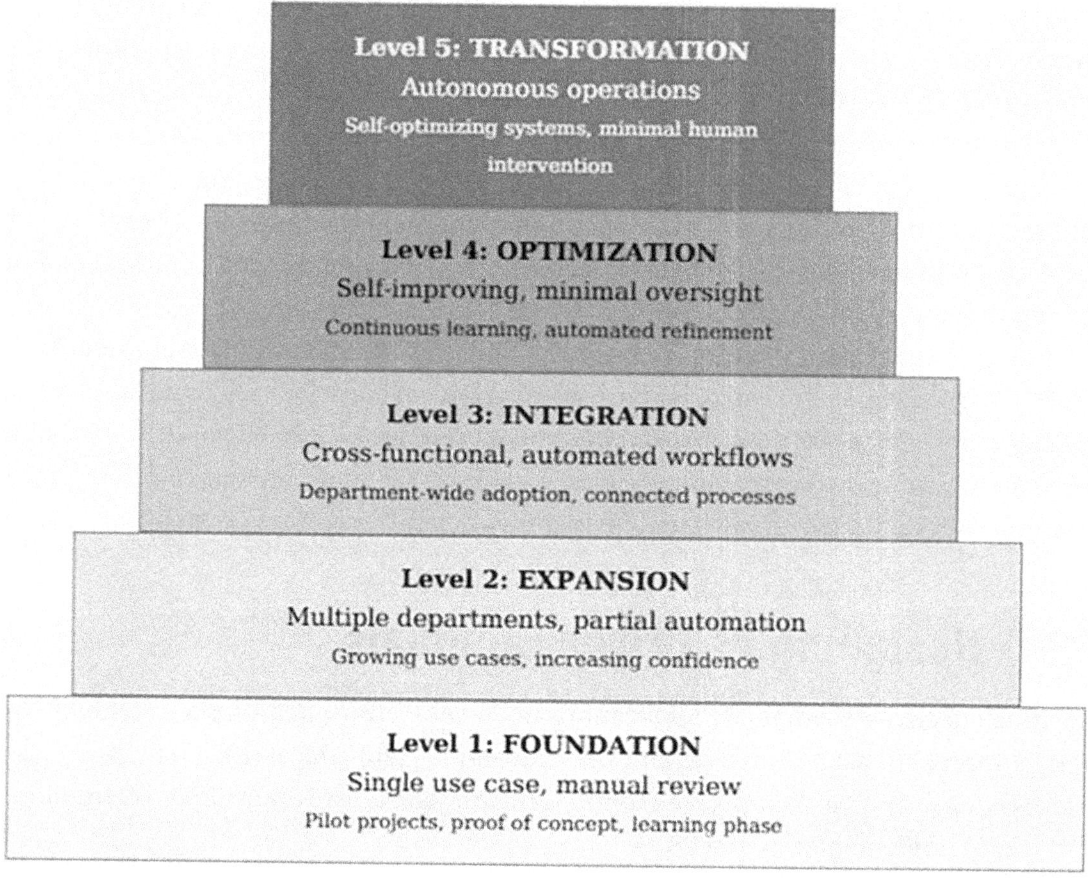

Figure 13-2. *Five-level maturity model for AI implementation in Microsoft Power Platform, showing progression from single use cases to autonomous operations. (Image by author)*

13.7.1 Solution Architecture Patterns

Architecture patterns guide how solutions are structured, assembled, and scaled across environments. The following subsections present practical patterns that balance clarity, reuse, and operational reliability.

Problem Definition and Scoping

AI implementation is most effective when it targets specific business problems with measurable outcomes. Many teams document baseline process metrics, expected improvements, and success criteria before development begins. For example, an invoice processing automation effort often captures the current processing time, error rate, and cost per transaction, along with target improvements for each measure.

Initial implementations benefit from MVP approaches. An MVP for document processing may handle only a single document type and route exceptions to human review. This approach validates technical feasibility and business value before expanding the scope. Delivery timelines vary based on data readiness, integration complexity, and governance requirements. Many teams implement an MVP in a small number of sprints and then invest additional sprints to harden the solution for production (security, monitoring, error handling, performance, and change management).

Technology Selection Criteria

Selecting between AI Builder prebuilt models, custom models, and Copilot assistance often depends on the scenario, data variability, risk tolerance, and governance requirements. Prebuilt models can fit standard use cases, but performance varies with input quality and layout diversity. Consequently, model evaluation is commonly used to validate results. Custom models are often chosen when domain-specific extraction or classification is needed, when prebuilt models do not cover the requirement, or when the workflow demands higher precision. Copilot can speed prototyping and initial app creation. However, production deployments typically involve additional refinement, including data modeling, security configuration, testing, monitoring, and integrations. Some scenarios also benefit from pro-code extensions.

Integration patterns affect solution architecture. Synchronous processing in Power Apps provides immediate feedback but can introduce noticeable latency for complex AI operations. Asynchronous processing in Power Automate supports long-running and batch workflows without blocking users. It requires status tracking, notifications, and error handling and helps prevent caller timeouts (for example, a child flow must respond within 120 seconds unless an asynchronous response pattern is used). Hybrid approaches commonly use synchronous processing for lightweight validation and asynchronous processing for longer-running analysis.

13.7.2 Data Requirements and Preparation

Sound data practice begins with precise requirements and disciplined preparation. The material below frames what "good data" looks like and how to ready it for trustworthy outcomes.

Data Quality Standards

Model performance depends heavily on the quality of the training data. Although the minimum thresholds for AI Builder may appear modest, achieving production-grade accuracy typically requires many more examples with consistent formatting.

Classification models require balanced datasets. Imbalanced datasets, in which one category contains far more examples than others, often produce biased predictions that favor overrepresented classes. To address this, teams must verify that the training set reflects the actual variety and frequency of data encountered in the production environment.

Effective data preparation involves multiple phases. Raw data collection must capture the variety found in production data, while annotation requires consistent labeling standards documented for multiple reviewers. A common architectural starting point allocates 70% to training, 15% to validation, and 15% to testing, although optimal partitioning depends on dataset size and model type.

Teams working with smaller datasets may use alternative splits or cross-validation techniques to make the most of limited labeled examples. Although data augmentation can expand small datasets, architects must remain cautious: synthetic data may fail to capture the nuanced complexity of real-world business artifacts.

Privacy and Compliance Considerations

Training data must comply with regulatory requirements. Personal information must be anonymized or used with consent for AI training. Health care data under HIPAA needs business associate agreements and audit trails. Financial data may require encryption at rest and in transit. European data under the GDPR requires explicit consent and the right to erasure.

Data residency shapes how AI Builder handles information. Training data and model outputs are typically stored in Microsoft Dataverse, which supports RBAC, audit logging, and governance features aligned with enterprise compliance standards. Training jobs run in designated Microsoft regions, which may not align with an organization's preferred locations. For sensitive data, AI processing and storage locations are often reviewed against regulatory and contractual requirements before data is uploaded.

13.7.3 Implementation Patterns

Implementation patterns translate design intent into repeatable build practices. Let us explore approaches that reduce friction, enhance maintainability, and facilitate rapid iteration.

Error Handling and Fallback Mechanisms

AI components require error handling strategies that extend beyond traditional application patterns. Common failure modes include credit exhaustion, service timeouts, low-confidence predictions, and malformed input data. In addition, AI Builder models are subject to documented processing limits and per-environment call quotas, which architects must account for during solution design.

Each failure mode requires a specific mitigation strategy. Fallback patterns provide continuity when AI services are unavailable. Items that fall below confidence thresholds are routed to human review queues, thus keeping high-stakes decisions subject to professional oversight. Cached predictions can serve requests during service outages, provided the inputs are repeatable and the business logic is deterministic.

For workloads involving unique artifacts, such as documents, images, or variable data, cached outputs are typically unsuitable. In these scenarios, teams should implement progressive degradation, which maintains core application functionality while alerting administrators to service disruption. Establishing these circuit breakers early in the architectural phase helps prevent silent failures in automated processes.

Human-in-the-Loop Design

Production AI solutions often incorporate human review at critical decision points. Teams commonly use confidence scores to route predictions: high-confidence outputs may be processed automatically, mid-confidence outputs may be sampled or reviewed based on risk, and low-confidence outputs are routed for manual review. Thresholds are typically configured per use case, often per extracted field, and validated against test data.

Review interfaces generally present predictions alongside supporting evidence. For document extraction, extracted fields are often highlighted with their confidence scores. For classification, probability distributions across categories can be displayed. For automation scenarios, decision logic and data sources are commonly surfaced. This level of transparency helps reviewers validate outputs efficiently and correct errors when needed.

13.7.4 Testing and Validation

Quality is established through thoughtful test design and objective validation. We will walk through practical methods for assessing correctness, resilience, and user experience—both before release and in production.

Accuracy Measurement

Model evaluation uses standard metrics interpreted in the business context. Precision measures the correctness of positive predictions, which is crucial for fraud detection because false positives can cause customer friction and dissatisfaction. Recall measures the completeness of positive identification, which is vital for document extraction, as missing data can lead to downstream errors. F1 scores balance precision and recall for overall performance assessment.

Business metrics supplement technical accuracy. Reductions in processing time, improvements in error rate, and cost savings provide tangible value metrics. User satisfaction scores and adoption rates indicate the solution's usability. Audit results verify compliance and adherence to governance.

Testing Strategies

AI component testing differs from traditional software testing. Unit tests verify individual model predictions against known inputs. Integration tests confirm proper data flow between AI services and applications. Performance tests measure response times under load. Regression tests detect model drift over time.

Edge case testing reveals model limitations. Test with poor-quality inputs (blurry images, handwritten text), unusual formats (rotated documents, nonstandard layouts), boundary conditions (maximum file sizes, character limits), and adversarial inputs (intentionally misleading data). Document failure modes and implement appropriate handling.

13.7.5 Governance and Ethics

Governance and ethics anchor responsible adoption of the Power Platform. The material below addresses oversight, accountability, and safeguards so that innovation proceeds with care and transparency.

Bias Detection and Mitigation

AI models can perpetuate or amplify biases present in training data. Regular auditing often examines whether predictions differ systematically across demographic groups, geographic regions, or business segments, and statistical tests can help surface variations that warrant investigation.

Mitigation approaches depend on the source of bias. Data rebalancing can adjust training set composition, algorithm changes can introduce fairness constraints, and postprocessing corrections can adjust outputs to meet equity targets. In mature programs, documentation captures bias testing procedures, identified issues, and applied mitigations.

Transparency and Explainability

Users benefit from visibility into AI decision-making processes. AI Builder surfaces confidence scores for predictions, while additional explainability features, such as contributing factors, can vary by model type and workload. Power Automate can capture execution paths and decision outcomes for audit purposes, and Power Apps can present confidence scores and source citations where available.

Model cards provide structured summaries of system characteristics, including intended use cases, performance metrics, limitations, and ethical considerations. However, they are not yet standardized across all Power Platform components. In mature practices, these materials are made accessible to stakeholders and updated when models are retrained or modified. Version control provides traceability over time and supports rollback when issues arise.

13.8 Challenges and Limitations

Successfully integrating AI within an organization is often filled with formidable, unexpected hurdles. While the low-code Power Platform democratizes AI, it does not entirely eliminate the inherent complexities of deploying intelligent systems in real-world scenarios. Power Platform's AI capabilities are constrained by technical, organizational, and operational factors that affect implementation success. Understanding these limitations helps organizations set realistic expectations and develop mitigation strategies. Table 13-4 summarizes key challenges in deploying AI solutions, their typical impacts, recommended mitigation strategies, and the success metrics used to track progress.

Table 13-4. *Microsoft Power Platform implementation challenges with quantified impacts, recommended mitigation strategies, and measurable success criteria.*

Challenge	Impact	Mitigation Strategy	Success Metric
Data quality	Reduces the reliability of AI models and automated workflows; increases manual correction effort	Implement data validation rules, establish data stewardship practices, and use cleanup tools	Data is complete, consistent, and suitable for automated processing; fewer exceptions triggered
Model drift	Gradual decline in model performance as business conditions or data patterns change	Monitor model outputs, schedule periodic retraining, and maintain feedback loops	Model performance remains stable over time with minimal unexpected variance
User adoption	Slow uptake of new applications; inconsistent usage across teams	Provide targeted training, identify champions, and offer ongoing support	Sustained usage of applications and positive feedback from end users
Governance gaps	Increased risk of noncompliance, inconsistent solution quality, and unmanaged proliferation of apps	Establish a CoE; define policies, and implement review processes	Solutions adhere to governance standards and follow approved life-cycle processes
Integration complexity	Delays in connecting to legacy or specialized systems; increased development effort	Use standard connectors, reusable templates, and documented integration patterns	Integrations function reliably and can be implemented without excessive custom development

13.8.1 Technical Limitations

Every platform has boundaries that shape what can be built and how it performs. This section highlights typical technical constraints and provides practical solutions for working within them.

Performance Constraints

AI Builder models operate within defined processing limits. File size, page limits for certain document scenarios, and image dimension constraints can shape solution design. At the implementation level, teams address these boundaries by using tactics such as splitting large documents, processing only relevant pages, and resizing or compressing high-resolution images.

Model quality also varies by document type, layout variability, and input quality. Rather than relying on generic accuracy ranges, teams often validate performance with representative test samples and use evaluation results to identify weak fields or layouts. For both prebuilt and custom models, confidence scores can help route uncertain extractions to human review, with thresholds set to match business risk. Over time, performance is typically monitored, and models and workflows are refined as new document variants appear.

Scale and Capacity Issues

Credit consumption limits can affect production scalability. AI Builder allocations vary by license tier and shape processing capacity for document processing, text classification, and related operations. In high-volume scenarios, additional capacity purchases or architectural changes are sometimes used to keep consumption within practical bounds. During solution planning, expected consumption is often compared with available allocation to reduce the risk of throughput constraints.

Administrators monitor usage through the Power Platform admin center, which provides real-time visibility into credit utilization, consumption trends, and environment-level allocation. When workloads exceed available capacity—whether due to high document volumes, bursty prediction patterns, or sustained production growth—organizations may need to purchase additional capacity or adjust their architecture. Common strategies include batching, asynchronous processing, and selectively offloading workloads to Azure AI Services or Azure OpenAI Service to maintain predictable performance at scale.

Dataverse storage limits impact custom model training. Training datasets consume storage capacity shared with operational data. Large image datasets for object detection can quickly exhaust allocated storage, necessitating capacity planning and data life-cycle management.

13.8.2 Data Quality Challenges

Weak data undermines even the best solution design. The discussion that follows highlights recurring quality issues and suggests methods for detecting, diagnosing, and correcting them.

Training Data Requirements

Insufficient or nonrepresentative training data is a common cause of underperformance in custom models. While minimum training thresholds vary by model type, performance often improves as more high-quality examples are added, but gains typically diminish over time. Classification models benefit from adequate representation across categories. Classes with very few examples often yield weaker results and require targeted data collection or rebalancing strategies.

Data preparation often consumes a large share of the effort in applied ML projects. Many organizations report that 60–80% of a data scientist's time is spent preparing data for modeling.[1] Teams collect representative samples, standardize formats, annotate consistently, validate labels, and split data appropriately. This work frequently reveals data quality issues that require remediation before model training.

Model Drift and Degradation

Model performance can degrade when production data diverges from training data. Document formats change, new categories emerge, and business terminology evolves. The rate of degradation varies by use case and data stability. Consequently, treating drift as an operational risk rather than a fixed annual pattern reflects the reality of production systems.

[1] Holger Hürtgen, Sebastian Kerkhoff, Jan Lubatschowski, and Manuel Möller, "Rethinking AI Talent Strategy as Automated Machine Learning Comes of Age," McKinsey & Company, August 14, 2020, `https://www.mckinsey.com/capabilities/quantumblack/our-insights/rethinking-ai-talent-strategy-as-automated-machine-learning-comes-of-age`.

Monitoring typically tracks signals such as data drift, changes in prediction confidence distributions, segment-specific error rates, processing time trends, and user-reported errors. Continuous monitoring can reveal emerging issues early. Retraining triggers are often defined in terms of business key performance indicators and tested against historical baselines. Because no universal threshold applies across all models, many teams plan to regularly evaluate representative production samples. Retraining may follow a domain-appropriate cadence or be initiated when monitoring shows sustained drift or a measurable decline in performance.

13.8.3 Organizational Challenges

Organizational dynamics often have a greater influence on outcomes than tools. Let us explore skills, roles, and collaboration patterns that help teams adopt the Power Platform effectively.

Skills and Knowledge Gaps

Citizen developers may have limited familiarity with key AI concepts such as confidence scores, precision–recall trade-offs, overfitting, and bias. Without this foundation, teams can set unrealistic expectations, apply models to unsuitable scenarios, and implement insufficient error handling.

Training requirements extend beyond tool usage. Developers benefit from a practical understanding of ML principles, hands-on experience with data preparation, the ability to interpret model evaluation metrics, and awareness of ethical considerations. Training duration varies by role and prior experience. Many organizations combine targeted learning paths with guided labs, coaching, and governance reviews to build capability over time.

Change Management Resistance

Employee concerns about automation can create barriers to adoption. Workers may worry about job displacement and may mistrust AI-supported decisions, particularly when AI is perceived as a threat rather than an augmentation of human work. Effective adoption programs address these concerns through transparent communication about how AI will be used, evidence of practical benefits, and active involvement of affected staff in solution design and rollout.

Cultural dynamics influence implementation outcomes. Organizations with cultures that support collaboration, learning, and experimentation tend to adopt and scale new digital capabilities more effectively than those that rely heavily on rigid hierarchy and control. Teams with stronger existing digital and automation capabilities may ramp up faster because they already have the processes, data discipline, and operating routines needed to integrate AI into daily work.

13.8.4 Integration Complexities

Integration ties new solutions to existing systems, where mismatches frequently arise. The discussion below identifies common friction points and outlines strategies to achieve stable, predictable exchanges.

Legacy System Compatibility

Power Platform AI capabilities work best when data is accessible through well-defined connectors and APIs. Legacy systems often require intermediate integration layers, including data extraction and transformation, format conversion, adapter or wrapper services, and error handling to address inconsistent schemas and operational quirks.

Real-time integration introduces additional design constraints. Synchronous calls can increase end-to-end transaction latency when AI operations are complex, and long-running work can exceed caller time limits in certain patterns. In a child-flow pattern, a response is required within 120 seconds unless an asynchronous response pattern is used. Batch processing adds operational considerations as well, including scheduling coordination, monitoring, and failure recovery mechanisms. Mature designs balance responsiveness with reliability while staying within platform limits and quotas.

Security and Compliance

AI processing introduces new security considerations. Models trained on sensitive data may leak information through predictions. Adversarial inputs can manipulate model outputs. API endpoints for AI services become potential attack vectors that require protection.

Compliance requirements can complicate AI deployment. GDPR's "right to explanation" can be difficult to satisfy for complex model architectures. HIPAA emphasizes audit trails for AI-driven health care decisions, while financial regulations often require model validation and ongoing monitoring. In regulated environments, controls commonly include access restrictions, audit logging, and disciplined model versioning.

13.8.5 Cost Management

Financial stewardship is part of sustainable platform use. This section explains cost drivers, common blind spots, and practical controls for keeping spending aligned with value.

Hidden Expenses

AI implementation costs extend beyond licensing. Organizations often incur additional ongoing expenses, including data preparation effort, monitoring and retraining, increased storage for training and evaluation datasets, and specialized operational support. These costs vary by organization size, data complexity, and solution scope. Hence, completing cost modeling before major initiatives prevents the budget overruns that erode organizational support for AI programs.

ROI calculations can overlook ongoing operational costs. Productivity gains may erode when models are not monitored, evaluated, and refreshed as data and business conditions change. As a result, many teams frame TCO over a multiyear horizon, such as three to five years, and compare realized value against ongoing runtime and maintenance costs.

Resource Allocation

AI Builder credit allocation creates governance challenges. Without charge-back mechanisms, individual departments may consume disproportionate resources. Establishing usage quotas, implementing approval workflows, and creating consumption dashboards allocate resources fairly.

Premium capacity requirements for advanced features can influence budget planning. Licensing decisions often involve trade-offs between per-user licensing for broad access and capacity-based licensing for intensive usage. Hybrid approaches that apply different license types to distinct user populations are often the most cost-effective.

13.9 Use Cases and Applications

Power Platform's AI capabilities often deliver value through small, practical improvements to daily work. A retail manager walking the floor dictates inventory adjustments on their phone, with the changes reflected in the system without returning to a terminal. An insurance adjuster at an accident site records observations verbally while a flow parses the narrative, extracts structured fields, and drafts claims documentation for review. A nurse completing rounds dictates patient notes, and the system automatically inserts medical terminology into the corresponding sections of the EHR.

These scenarios typically require days of development effort rather than months. Each combines a few components: STT services, language extraction models, system connectors, and basic logic rules. The builders are often the workers themselves, who understand process requirements firsthand. This section examines implementation patterns across industries, with realistic assessments of effort, outcomes, and limitations.

13.9.1 Health Care: Patient Intake Automation

Health care organizations increasingly use AI Builder to streamline patient intake workflows, particularly for processing insurance documents and standardized intake forms. Outcomes vary widely depending on the degree of form standardization, the quality of scanned documents, and the complexity of integration with EHR systems.

Implementation Approach

Deployments typically begin with highly structured documents such as insurance verification forms or demographic intake sheets. AI Builder's form processing capabilities can extract fields such as patient identifiers, insurance details, and demographic information when the underlying layout is consistent and the scanned images are of sufficient quality.[2] Handwritten content, variable layouts, and low-quality scans generally require additional human review, as Microsoft does not guarantee accuracy thresholds for specific field types.

[2] Microsoft, "Train and use a form processing model," Microsoft Learn, `https://learn.microsoft.com/en-us/ai-builder/form-processing-model-overview`.

Human validation remains essential for clinically sensitive information—including medication lists, allergies, and surgical history—because AI Builder is not a clinical decision support tool and is not regulated for autonomous extraction of medical data. Accordingly, health care organizations design intake workflows that include human review steps before information is committed to clinical systems.

Integration patterns differ materially across EHR platforms. Modern cloud-based EHRs that expose REST APIs or Fast Healthcare Interoperability Resources (FHIR) endpoints allow relatively direct ingestion of extracted data. In contrast, legacy EHRs may require Health Level Seven (HL7) v2 messaging, flat-file transfers, or intermediary databases, which introduce additional transformation layers and operational complexity.[3] These integration requirements often determine the overall project timeline more than the AI model training itself.

Typical Outcomes

Organizations generally report reductions in manual data entry effort, particularly for repetitive administrative fields. AI Builder can prepopulate structured data fields, after which staff review and correct extracted values. This review-and-approve model reduces—but does not eliminate—the time required for intake processing. The degree of efficiency gain depends on form consistency, document quality, and the proportion of handwritten or clinically sensitive fields requiring manual verification.

Implementation projects typically include form analysis, dataset preparation, model training, workflow design, EHR integration, validation, and staff onboarding. The duration varies widely depending on the number of document types, the complexity of the integration architecture, and organizational compliance requirements. Ongoing maintenance focuses on monitoring extraction quality, updating models when forms change, and addressing data quality issues that emerge during routine operations.

13.9.2 Retail: Inventory Forecasting

Retail organizations use Power BI's forecasting capabilities to support inventory planning and demand-shaping decisions. The effectiveness of these forecasts depends heavily on the quality, completeness, and stability of the underlying time-series data, as well as the degree of seasonality present in historical sales patterns.

---

[3] HL7 International, "Introduction to HL7 Standards," HL7.org, `https://www.hl7.org/implement/standards`.

Implementation Approach

Power BI's built-in forecasting uses an exponential smoothing model to project future values based on historical data.[4] The feature performs best when the dataset exhibits consistent periodic behavior, such as weekly or annual seasonality, and when missing data points or irregular reporting intervals have been addressed. Retailers often augment their sales history with contextual information—such as promotional calendars, weather data, and local events—by integrating external datasets via APIs or data flows.

Configuring the forecast requires balancing responsiveness and stability. More sensitive settings can capture recurring seasonal peaks, but they may also react to anomalies such as one-time promotions or supply disruptions. More conservative configurations produce smoother projections but may underrepresent emerging trends or shifts in consumer behavior. Retail teams typically iterate through multiple configurations as they refine data preparation practices, incorporate additional explanatory variables, and validate results against operational experience.

Typical Outcomes

Retailers generally report that Power BI's forecasting provides value by automating routine projection tasks and accelerating scenario exploration, rather than by delivering highly precise statistical forecasts. The tool can prepopulate baseline demand expectations, after which planners adjust for known business drivers such as upcoming promotions, assortment changes, or supply constraints. Forecast reliability tends to be highest for products with stable, repeatable demand patterns and lowest for trend-driven categories or those with a short life cycle, such as fashion.

The primary operational benefit is improved workflow efficiency. Power BI consolidates data sources, automates the generation of recurring forecasts, and provides interactive visualizations that help managers focus on exceptions rather than on manually assembling spreadsheets. Organizations that extend these workflows with Power Apps or Power Automate give field teams the ability to review and adjust forecasts directly, though effective use requires training in interpreting confidence intervals and understanding the limitations of statistical projections.[5]

---

[4] Microsoft, "Use the forecasting model in Power BI," Microsoft Learn, `https://learn.microsoft.com/en-us/power-bi/transform-model/desktop-analytics-pane#forecasting`.

[5] Microsoft, "Get started with Power Apps," Microsoft Learn, `https://learn.microsoft.com/en-us/power-apps/`.

13.9.3 Finance: Fraud Detection and Reporting

Financial institutions use AI Builder to support fraud detection and transaction monitoring workflows, but regulatory requirements and supervisory expectations limit the extent of automation that can be deployed in production environments. AI models typically augment existing rule-based systems rather than replace them, providing additional signals that help analysts prioritize alerts and investigate anomalous activity.

Implementation Approach

Organizations generally begin by training custom AI Builder classification models on historical transaction data labeled as either legitimate or suspicious.[6] Effective model development requires representative examples across fraud patterns, which can be challenging because fraudulent transactions constitute only a small fraction of the overall volume. This class imbalance affects model performance and often requires techniques such as threshold adjustment, targeted sampling, or additional contextual features. Even with these measures in place, institutions design workflows that incorporate human review so that risk-relevant decisions remain under human oversight.

Most deployments combine AI Builder with existing rule-based monitoring systems. Rules provide deterministic coverage for known fraud scenarios, while AI models help identify edge cases or subtle anomalies that static logic may miss. Integration with case management systems is typically implemented using Power Automate, routing flagged transactions to analysts for review. Institutions subject to regulatory oversight must document model behavior, validation procedures, and governance controls, which often influence the pace and scope of implementation.

Typical Outcomes

In production environments, AI Builder primarily supports alert prioritization rather than autonomous fraud adjudication. Institutions report that AI-generated signals help analysts focus on higher-risk transactions, reduce time spent on low-value alerts, and improve the consistency of investigative workflows. Because fraud patterns evolve rapidly, organizations maintain ongoing monitoring and periodic retraining to keep models aligned with emerging behaviors and updated regulatory expectations.

---

[6] Microsoft, "Train and use a classification model," Microsoft Learn, `https://learn.microsoft.com/en-us/ai-builder/text-classification-overview`.

Regulatory compliance frameworks—such as those governing anti-money laundering and fraud risk management—require that all flagged transactions undergo human review before any adverse action is taken.[7] As a result, AI Builder is used to enhance efficiency rather than eliminate manual oversight. Implementation timelines vary widely depending on data availability, governance requirements, and integration complexity, and institutions typically allocate additional time for validation, documentation, and postdeployment monitoring.

13.9.4 Education: Student Performance Dashboards

Educational institutions use Power BI and AI Builder to develop early-warning dashboards that help identify students who may require additional academic support. Adoption varies widely due to concerns about data quality, privacy regulations, and the institutional readiness required to act on predictive insights.

Implementation Approach

Power BI dashboards typically consolidate data from learning management systems, attendance records, and assessment platforms to provide a unified view of student engagement. AI Builder classification models can be trained to flag students who exhibit patterns associated with academic risk, using indicators such as assignment submission timing, participation in online discussions, and frequency of resource access. The effectiveness of these models depends on the completeness and consistency of the underlying data, which can vary across departments and instructional modalities.

Privacy regulations—most notably the Family Educational Rights and Privacy Act—govern how student information may be collected, processed, and shared.[8] Institutions must verify that predictive models do not rely on sensitive or potentially discriminatory variables and that dashboard access is restricted to authorized personnel. To balance insight with privacy, many institutions use aggregate or tiered risk indicators rather than exposing detailed model outputs, thereby reducing the likelihood of overinterpretation or inappropriate use.

[7] Federal Financial Institutions Examination Council (FFIEC), "BSA/AML Examination Manual," FFIEC.gov, `https://bsaaml.ffiec.gov`.

[8] US Department of Education, "Family Educational Rights and Privacy Act (FERPA)," ed.gov, `https://www2.ed.gov/policy/gen/guid/fpco/ferpa/`.

Typical Outcomes

Early-warning dashboards generally provide value by improving visibility into student engagement patterns and facilitating earlier intervention. Institutions with well-established advising or support programs report that dashboards help staff prioritize outreach and coordinate interventions more effectively. However, predictive insights alone do not guarantee improved outcomes. The impact depends heavily on the quality, timeliness, and consistency of the support structures that accompany them.

Implementation efforts often encounter both technical and cultural challenges. Integrating data from disparate systems requires coordination across IT, academic departments, and student services teams, and the process can be slowed by inconsistent data definitions or legacy platforms. Faculty adoption also varies: some instructors embrace data-informed teaching practices, while others express concerns about algorithmic assessment or the interpretability of predictive models. Successful programs typically invest in training, change management, and clear communication about the purpose and limitations of predictive analytics.

13.9.5 Government: Permit and Service Automation

Public agencies increasingly use the Power Platform to modernize permit processing, license renewals, and citizen service delivery. These initiatives typically combine mobile intake, automated validation, and integration with back-office systems, while ensuring compliance with public sector transparency, accessibility, and records management requirements.

Implementation Approach

Public sector agencies at the federal, state, and municipal levels can use Power Pages for resident- and constituent-facing interfaces, while Power Apps can support responsive applications for agency staff and, in some scenarios, external users. These platforms can support permit applications, service requests, and document submissions directly within agency workflows. Microsoft's government accelerator documentation includes a sample government portal for residents and businesses to apply for services, programs, and benefits, supporting this use case.[9] AI Builder models extract structured data from uploaded materials, such as identification documents, proof of residence, or property records, reducing manual data entry.

Power Automate orchestrates validation steps and routes submissions to appropriate reviewers based on agency business rules. While updates to cloud-based systems are typically managed through standard connectors, integrations with legacy permitting or case management systems often rely on the on-premises data gateway and, in some architectures, intermediary integration components. This architectural decoupling allows agencies to modernize the user experience without requiring an immediate replacement of established recordkeeping systems.

Document processing performance depends heavily on the consistency of form layouts and the quality of scanned or photographed images. Teams typically implement exception handling rules to flag missing information, unreadable fields, or ambiguous entries for manual review. This helps accelerate intake without compromising accuracy or compliance.

Integration patterns vary widely across jurisdictions. Cloud-native platforms that expose REST APIs support near-real-time updates, whereas older systems may rely on batch uploads, flat-file transfers, or intermediary databases. Public sector implementations must also account for statutory obligations such as records retention, auditability, and accessibility requirements. These include Section 508 of the Rehabilitation Act for federal agencies, Americans with Disabilities Act (ADA) Title II, Web Content Accessibility Guidelines (WCAG) 2.1 Level AA for state and local governments, and any applicable state accessibility rules. These obligations can introduce additional validation steps and documentation expectations into the final solution architecture.

Typical Outcomes

Agencies generally report that Power Platform–based automation reduces manual effort in routine permitting and service request workflows. Staff spend less time rekeying information and more time resolving exceptions or engaging directly with residents. Automated intake and routing also improve transparency by standardizing processes and providing clearer status tracking for applicants.

[9] Microsoft, "Dynamics 365 Government Accelerator," Microsoft Learn, `https://learn.microsoft.com/en-us/dynamics365/industry/accelerators/government-overview`.

The degree of improvement varies based on data quality, system architecture, and organizational readiness. Implementations typically include form analysis, model training, workflow design, integration with existing systems, and staff onboarding. Postdeployment activities focus on monitoring the quality of extractions, refining exception rules, and ensuring ongoing compliance with accessibility and public records requirements.[10]

13.10 Citizen versus Professional Developers

In many organizations, the Power Platform has opened the door for people who never saw themselves as "developers" to begin shaping the digital tools they use every day. This shift has created a development ecosystem in which business users and professional engineers work side by side, each bringing distinct strengths, expectations, and ways of thinking. Understanding how these groups operate—and how they collaborate—has become essential for building solutions that are both innovative and sustainable.

13.10.1 Citizen Developer: Capabilities and Constraints

Citizen developers often emerge from the front lines of the business. They are sales coordinators who are tired of juggling spreadsheets, analysts who want to automate repetitive tasks, or project managers who need a better way to track work. They rarely consider themselves programmers. Instead, they see a problem that slows their team and, sometimes by accident, discover they can solve it themselves.

Their tools are visual and familiar. A Canvas app begins with a blank screen and a drag-and-drop interface. A workflow starts with a template that mirrors a process they already understand. Power Fx formulas feel like the spreadsheets they have used for years. When they connect a button to a data source or watch an approval flow trigger automatically, there is often a moment of genuine empowerment: *I can build this.*

[10] US General Services Administration, "Section 508 Standards," Section508.gov, `https://www.section508.gov/manage/laws-and-policies/`.

Because they live inside the business process, citizen developers bring something professional developers cannot replicate—an intuitive understanding of how work actually gets done. They know which fields matter, which steps are routinely skipped, and which exceptions happen every week. When domain experts use low-code tools, the resulting solutions often feel natural to users.

But their strengths come with limits. As solutions grow more complex—more screens, more branching logic, more data sources—the initial clarity begins to blur. Variables and collections feel abstract. Authentication errors appear without warning. Performance issues surface when datasets grow. What began as a simple app for a small team can suddenly feel unwieldy.

Citizen-built solutions shine when the scope is clear and the audience is close. They digitize paper forms, automate reminders, and assemble dashboards that help teams stay aligned. These solutions often start quickly: a prototype built in a single afternoon, refined through hallway conversations or quick feedback from colleagues. Yet the same speed that fuels creativity can also create fragility. Documentation is sparse, naming conventions drift, and testing is informal. Over time, maintenance becomes more challenging, especially when the original creator moves into a new role.

13.10.2 Professional Developer Responsibilities

Professional developers enter the picture with a different mindset. They think in terms of architecture, life cycle, and scale. Some come from traditional software backgrounds and adopt low-code tools as part of a broader engineering toolkit. Others specialize in Power Platform development, mastering its extensibility and its constraints.

Where citizen developers rely on templates and visual tools, professional developers extend the platform through code. They build custom components, write plugins, design connectors, and integrate with enterprise systems. They understand delegation limits, security boundaries, and performance considerations that are invisible to most business users.

Their work is shaped by discipline. Requirements are documented before building begins. Code is reviewed. Automated tests validate behavior. Deployment pipelines help move changes safely from development to production. This rigor takes time, but it produces solutions that can support large user populations, withstand regulatory scrutiny, and operate reliably under heavy load.

Professional developers often inherit citizen-built solutions that have grown beyond their original intent. They refactor, stabilize, or rebuild them entirely. In doing so, they bridge the gap between grassroots innovation and enterprise-grade engineering.

13.10.3 Collaboration Models

Organizations that succeed with the Power Platform rarely segment citizen and professional developers into rigid categories. Instead, they foster collaboration patterns that allow each group to contribute where their expertise is most impactful.

- **Hub and Spoke Model**: In this model, professional developers build the foundational infrastructure—secure connectors, shared libraries, and approved templates—while citizen developers assemble departmental solutions on top of them. It resembles urban planning: IT provides the utilities and zoning, and business units build the structures that meet specific operational needs.
- **Mentorship Approach**: Some organizations take a more personal route. Professional developers hold office hours, review citizen-built apps, and offer guidance on tricky features. A citizen developer might arrive with a half-finished app and leave with both a solution and a deeper understanding of the platform. Over time, this mentorship builds confidence and raises the overall quality of solutions.
- **Graduated Support Tiers**: Other organizations define support levels based on complexity and risk. Simple, low-impact apps remain in the hands of citizen developers. Solutions that integrate with critical systems or serve larger audiences transition to professional oversight. Well-defined escalation paths safeguard the responsible evolution of solutions and prevent individuals from navigating complex challenges in isolation.

The boundary between citizen and professional development continues to narrow as agentic AI and autonomous software engineering tools mature. Tools such as GitHub Copilot, Claude, and similar coding agents allow makers with limited programming experience to generate and adapt code that previously necessitated professional intervention. While governance and QA responsibilities remain with professional teams, the practical gap in output capability is closing faster than traditional skills frameworks anticipated.

13.10.4 Skill Development and Training

Citizen developers typically begin with the fundamentals—how to build simple apps, create workflows, use prebuilt AI models, and follow governance guidelines. Their learning is often hands-on: workshops, hackathons, online tutorials, and community forums. With consistent practice, they grow from building small utilities to tackling more sophisticated tasks.

Professional developers pursue deeper specialization. Certifications help structure their learning, but real proficiency comes from understanding how low-code tools perform in enterprise environments. They study ALM, security, performance tuning, and integration patterns. Even experienced engineers need time to adapt to the Power Platform's unique blend of declarative and programmatic development.

13.10.5 Common Friction Points

When citizen and professional developers work together, friction is inevitable. Citizen-built apps may lack the polish expected in enterprise environments—interfaces feel inconsistent, error messages are vague, and edge cases are overlooked. Professional developers may overengineer simple needs or struggle to translate business language into technical requirements.

Ownership can also become unclear. A solution built by a citizen developer may quietly become mission-critical, leaving teams unsure who maintains it or who approves changes. Without clear governance, small misunderstandings can grow into operational risks.

Successful organizations address these challenges through shared standards, open communication, and well-defined responsibilities. Templates reduce inconsistency. Regular collaboration sessions build trust. Governance policies clarify who owns what. Over time, these practices transform friction into a productive partnership.

13.11 Future Trends

As of late 2025, the intersection of low-code development and AI continues to evolve, with emerging capabilities that may influence how organizations build and deploy business solutions. Current AI Builder and Copilot features already provide practical automation, and ongoing advances in generative AI, multimodal processing, and orchestration may broaden the capabilities of low-code platforms. At the same time, technical feasibility, regulatory considerations, and organizational readiness will shape how quickly these capabilities are adopted. Figure 13-3 presents a conceptual evolution model for the Power Platform, illustrating how AI capabilities might progress over time based on observable industry trends rather than on formal product commitments.

NEAR-TERM
(1-2 years)

- **Enhanced Copilot capabilities**
  More sophisticated natural language understanding
- **Better Microsoft 365 integration**
  Seamless data flow across applications
- **Improved AI Builder models**
  Higher accuracy, more prebuilt options
- **Advanced templates**
  Industry-specific solutions

MEDIUM-TERM
(3-5 years)

- **Autonomous agents**
  Self-directed process execution
- **Multimodal AI processing**
  Combined text, image, and voice understanding
- **Advanced predictive analytics**
  Proactive business insights
- **Edge deployment**
  Local AI processing capabilities

LONG-TERM
(5+ years)

- **Self-building applications**
  AI creates complete solutions from requirements
- **Predictive automation**
  Anticipatory process optimization
- **Full business process autonomy**
  End-to-end intelligent operations
- **Cognitive business systems**
  Human-like reasoning and decision-making

Figure 13-3. *Conceptual three-phase evolution model for the Microsoft Power Platform, depicting possible directions for AI capability development from near-term enhancements to longer-term autonomous systems. (Image by author)*

13.11.1 Generative AI Evolution in Low-Code Platforms

The rise of generative AI is reshaping low-code platforms in ways that feel both familiar and quietly transformative. Today, tools like Copilot can draft formulas, suggest workflows, and assemble the first version of an app. These capabilities are still in their early stages, but they hint at a future in which the boundary between "builder" and "assistant" becomes increasingly fluid. Progress is steady rather than explosive, with each step revealing new possibilities and new constraints.

Near-Term Possibilities

In the near term, generative AI is likely to become a more capable collaborator rather than a fully autonomous builder. Microsoft's public guidance points toward incremental improvements—better prompt understanding, smoother interactions, and more coherent suggestions. A user might describe a multistep approval process, and Copilot could assemble a draft workflow that captures the broad strokes. The result would still need refinement, but the starting point would be far more complete than today's single-step templates.

NLP will also become more nuanced. Instead of responding only to simple commands, AI assistants may begin to interpret more complex business requirements. A request such as "route approvals to different managers depending on the amount and department" could generate a more structured, multibranch workflow. Even so, human oversight will remain essential. Generated solutions still need to be validated, tested, and secured before they can be trusted in production.

These improvements will not eliminate the need for technical expertise, but they will make the early stages of development more accessible and reduce the friction of getting started.

Medium-Term Developments

Looking a bit further ahead, generative AI may become more contextually aware. Instead of treating each prompt as an isolated request, future systems could maintain continuity across a development session—remembering what the user built earlier, recognizing patterns, and suggesting refinements as the application evolves.

This kind of contextual intelligence could help users navigate complexity. A system might notice that a workflow is becoming unwieldy and propose a cleaner branching structure. It might suggest performance optimizations based on usage patterns or highlight security considerations that a nontechnical user might overlook.

Personalization may also deepen. Applications could adapt interfaces based on user roles, highlight frequently used features, or prefilter data based on past behavior. These ideas exist in early forms today, but generative AI could make them more fluid and intuitive.

Even with these advances, human judgment will remain central. AI may propose solutions, but people will decide which ones make sense.

13.11.2 Expanding AI Model Capabilities

Today's Power Platform AI features operate within well-defined boundaries. AI Builder handles specific document types. Copilot generates code for common patterns. Power BI analyzes structured datasets. Future evolution will likely expand these boundaries, but each step introduces new technical and operational challenges. Three areas show particular promise: multimodal processing, enhanced predictive analytics, and edge-based AI.

- **Multimodal Processing**: Most AI Builder models work with a single data type—text, images, or structured fields. Future versions may combine these inputs for richer scenarios. Imagine a quality control workflow that analyzes a product photo, reads inspection notes, and compares them against a specification database. This kind of multimodal reasoning is already visible in research prototypes, though not yet production-ready. Turning these prototypes into production-ready features is far more complex. Synchronizing different model types, managing latency, and maintaining accuracy across multiple inputs all introduce new engineering challenges. Costs rise, error rates compound, and infrastructure demands increase. The potential is real, but so are the hurdles.
- **Predictive Analytics Enhancement**: Predictive analytics may also grow more sophisticated. With richer datasets and improved algorithms, organizations could anticipate issues earlier and with greater nuance. Manufacturers might detect equipment anomalies sooner. Retailers might incorporate external signals—such as weather, events, and social trends—into demand forecasts. But these improvements depend on data quality and availability. Long

historical records, real-time feeds, and adequate processing capacity are prerequisites. Even then, prediction has limits. Complex systems contain uncertainty that no model can fully eliminate.

- **Edge Deployment Considerations**: Running AI models on edge devices offers appealing benefits: lower latency, reduced bandwidth usage, and improved privacy. A retail store might analyze customer interactions locally. A factory machine might make real-time quality decisions without relying on cloud connectivity. Yet edge deployment introduces its own constraints. Devices have limited processing power. Models need to be smaller and more efficient. Updates need coordination across distributed locations. Costs can rise quickly. Organizations will need to weigh these trade-offs carefully.

13.11.3 Autonomous Agents: Possibilities and Limitations

The idea of "agentic AI" has captured the industry's imagination—systems that can pursue goals, plan multistep actions, and adapt to changing conditions. It is an appealing vision, one that suggests software capable of operating with a degree of independence rather than waiting for explicit instructions. In practice, however, these capabilities remain early and experimental. The most realistic near-term agents will focus on structured, well-defined tasks with clear boundaries and predictable outcomes. They may monitor metrics and trigger predefined responses when thresholds are crossed, execute multistep workflows with straightforward decision branches, or gather information from multiple systems to assemble standardized reports. These scenarios represent meaningful extensions of today's automation rather than a leap into true autonomy.

A useful illustration is an inventory management agent that keeps an eye on stock levels across warehouses. It might identify items approaching reorder points, check supplier availability and pricing, draft purchase orders within approved limits, and route exceptions to human managers. This is sophisticated orchestration, but it operates within a tightly controlled environment. The agent is not "deciding" in any human sense. Essentially, it follows rules, applies logic, and escalates when conditions fall outside its scope.

For agents to become more capable, several technical prerequisites need to mature. Planning algorithms have to reliably decompose high-level goals into executable steps. Trusted autonomy requires systems that recover gracefully from individual failures instead of halting or causing cascading errors. Long-running tasks require a persistent context so that the agent can maintain continuity over hours or days. Learning from outcomes—improving performance based on what worked and what did not—demands careful feedback mechanisms to avoid reinforcing mistakes. These are active areas of research, not solved problems, and they illustrate why agentic behavior remains limited in production environments.

Even as the technology advances, governance is likely to shape how organizations adopt it. Accountability questions become central, including who is responsible when an agent makes a faulty decision, how audit trails are maintained for regulatory compliance, and which conditions warrant human intervention to override automated actions. Testing becomes more complex when systems behave nondeterministically, producing different outcomes under similar conditions. Explainability will be especially important in regulated sectors such as finance, health care, and government, where decisions need to be traceable, understandable, and defensible. Without clear visibility into how an agent reached a conclusion, organizations will be reluctant to entrust it with decisions that carry legal, safety, or compliance implications.

In short, autonomous agents hold promise, but their evolution will be gradual. The near future will bring more capable automation, not independent digital actors. The path forward depends as much on governance, accountability, and organizational readiness as on technical breakthroughs.

13.11.4 Organizational Implications

As AI capabilities expand, the skills organizations need will shift. Citizen developers will benefit from understanding concepts like confidence thresholds, prompt design, and data quality. Professional developers will spend less time on routine coding and more time on architecture, integration, and governance.

Business processes will evolve as well. Document-heavy workflows may be redesigned around automated extraction. Decision flows may incorporate AI-generated recommendations. Customer interactions may blend automated responses with human assistance based on their complexity.

These changes require thoughtful planning. Strengthening data foundations, investing in targeted skill development, and building adaptable governance frameworks will help organizations navigate this transition without overcommitting to unproven capabilities.

Generative AI in low-code platforms is advancing steadily, not explosively. The path forward will vary by industry, regulatory environment, and organizational readiness. The most successful adopters will experiment thoughtfully, invest in data quality, and build systems that can evolve alongside the technology.

13.12 Summary

Having worked on systems designed to capture and operationalize expert knowledge—from grammar engines to filing systems to enterprise architectures—I see Power Platform as the latest chapter in a long evolution. The aspiration that guided earlier work on INTELLIFM and other mission-critical systems—the idea that domain experts can shape their own tools—now operates at enterprise scale, supported by AI capabilities that were once unimaginable. Yet the core insight remains unchanged: technology succeeds when it amplifies human expertise rather than attempting to replace it.

Power Platform's integration of AI through AI Builder and Copilot catalyzes a fundamental expansion of accessibility, beyond the exclusive domain of traditional coding experts. Capabilities that once required specialized ML expertise are now exposed through visual interfaces and natural language prompts. Even so, effective use still depends on understanding data quality, model limitations, and the boundaries of appropriate use. AI can accelerate development, but it cannot compensate for unclear requirements, inconsistent data, or weak governance.

The practical impact of these capabilities varies widely across organizations. Prebuilt AI models deliver immediate value for common scenarios, such as document processing, while custom models offer teams the precision to address domain-specific needs. Copilot can generate initial application scaffolding and basic workflows, reducing the effort required to begin a project. However, the outputs still require refinement, validation, and alignment with organizational standards before they are ready for production use.

What stands out most in real deployments is the cumulative effect of incremental improvements. A team streamlines a manual process that once consumed hours. A service organization responds more consistently by using AI-suggested prompts.

A finance group reduces end-of-month friction by automating routine data entry. Individually, these changes may appear modest, but collectively, they reshape operational rhythms. Transformation emerges not from sweeping reorganizations but from steady evolution—process by process, team by team.

Organizations exploring Power Platform's AI capabilities benefit from a methodical approach. Beginning with well-defined problems allows teams to build confidence before tackling more complex scenarios. Assessing data quality and establishing governance frameworks early keep AI solutions reliable and compliant. Clear success criteria and human review processes maintain oversight while giving teams the opportunity to learn from each deployment.

Technical and organizational constraints can temper the potential of AI in low-code environments. Consumption-based licensing introduces cost considerations, model performance often requires ongoing monitoring and periodic refresh, and integrations with legacy systems frequently call for professional developer involvement. Taken together, these realities position Power Platform AI as one component of a broader digital strategy rather than a standalone solution.

Looking ahead, advances in multimodal processing, predictive analytics, and autonomous agents may expand the capabilities of low-code platforms. Yet these developments depend on technical feasibility, regulatory considerations, and organizational readiness. Monitoring progress with realistic expectations allows organizations to prepare for emerging capabilities without overcommitting to unproven technologies.

The convergence of low-code development and AI reflects a broader industry movement toward more accessible technology. While barriers to entry have decreased, successful implementation still requires thoughtful planning, targeted skill development, and ongoing management. Organizations that balance ambition with pragmatism—building from small wins, investing in data quality, and maintaining adaptable governance—tend to achieve more durable results than those pursuing rapid, disruptive change.

The Power Platform's evolution toward AI-driven automation and Copilot integration places it squarely within the emerging agentic landscape. As agents increasingly orchestrate Power Automate flows, invoke AI Builder models, and surface insights through Power BI, the governance and environment strategies examined in this chapter serve as guardrails to keep that autonomy trustworthy and auditable. Within this architecture, Power Platform serves as an execution layer, providing the secure connectors and prebuilt business logic that allow an agent to move from reasoning to action. As a result, DLP policies and environment routing are no longer merely administrative concerns. They define the security boundaries that govern what an agent can and cannot do with sensitive enterprise data. As these capabilities scale, organizations are moving beyond isolated task bots toward more orchestrated agent-based environments. By building on existing managed environments, they can expand autonomous operations without bypassing the compliance frameworks already established for their low-code ecosystems.

The next chapter synthesizes concepts across Microsoft's AI ecosystem, examining how Azure AI Services, Microsoft Foundry, Copilot, and Power Platform combine to support organizational intelligence initiatives. The focus shifts from individual capabilities to integrated architectural patterns and strategic considerations for enterprise-wide AI adoption.

CHAPTER 14

The Intelligence Revolution: Bringing It All Together

My work with AI began during my engineering studies. It deepened at Microsoft, where I developed automation features for Word and Excel, continued with the design of the AI-powered INTELLIFM at Wolters Kluwer, and extended to predictive valuation systems at Bloomberg. Since then, I have continued building AI systems for large enterprises, applying advanced technologies to real operational problems at scale. Each phase has reinforced a consistent principle: intelligence works best when it augments human capability, compresses cycle time, and fits naturally into existing workflows. That same principle runs through Microsoft's modern AI stack—Azure AI Services, Microsoft Foundry, Copilot, and Power Platform—capabilities that have evolved and converged into an integrated ecosystem for enterprise AI. They bring AI assistance into the workflows where enterprises actually do their work.

In February 2023, as generative AI gained widespread attention—with ChatGPT reaching 100 million users within two months of its November 2022 public release[1]—I spoke with *The Indian Express* about this moment in AI development.[2] The journalist, Anuj Bhatia, characterized it as an "iPhone moment" for AI, a comparison worth

[1] Krystal Hu, "ChatGPT Sets Record for Fastest-Growing User Base," *Reuters*, February 2, 2023, `https://www.reuters.com/technology/chatgpt-sets-record-fastest-growing-user-base-analyst-note-2023-02-01/`.

[2] Anuj Bhatia, "AI Pioneers Say ChatGPT, Bing and Bard Will Push Creativity, Take Over Mundane Jobs So That Humans Can Do Better," *The Indian Express*, February 19, 2023, `https://indianexpress.com/article/technology/artificial-intelligence/ai-pioneers-say-chatgpt-bing-and-bard-will-push-creativity-take-over-mundane-jobs-so-that-humans-can-do-better-8453549/`.

K. C. Mukherjee, *The Microsoft AI Insider's Playbook*, https://doi.org/10.1007/979-8-8688-2730-3_14

examining. Like the iPhone's transformation of mobile computing from specialized tool to everyday interface, current AI capabilities represent a shift from narrow technical applications to broader assistance with cognitive tasks. Both created platform effects in which value emerged not just from core technology but also from ecosystems of applications and integrations. The iPhone's impact came from reimagining portable computing rather than improving telephony. Similarly, ChatGPT and related systems matter less as language models than as conversational interfaces to computational assistance.

The relationship between humans and machines is continually evolving. As I told *The Indian Express*, Microsoft has been integrating AI into products like Word and Excel, as well as cloud computing environments such as Azure, for years. The integration of ChatGPT into Bing and the development of Copilot extend that trajectory rather than departing from it. These systems handle repetitive tasks, allowing people to focus on creativity and judgment. This shift reframes rather than replaces human work, making experience and insight more valuable. The article quoted another expert, Albert Meige, who suggested that "humans using AI in a smart way will definitely be going to replace humans who don't use it"—a perspective that resonates with patterns I have observed across enterprise deployments. The operative phrase is "in a smart way." Adopting AI tools without understanding their architectural constraints, governance requirements, and integration trade-offs rarely delivers the productivity gains the technology promises. The chapters in this book have attempted to equip readers with precisely that understanding.

This final chapter examines Microsoft's AI technologies and connects them to broader patterns in enterprise computing. The foundation rests on principles developed over decades: declarative logic that lets users specify outcomes rather than procedures, modularity that lets systems evolve without complete replacement, and semantic interoperability that allows components to share meaning and data. These concepts, while not new, remain essential for distinguishing experimental prototypes from production systems.

The chapter examines how these principles are implemented across four platform elements of Microsoft's AI stack: Azure AI Services, Microsoft Foundry, Copilot, and Power Platform. Azure AI Services provides the underlying cognitive capabilities—such as vision, speech, language, and document intelligence—through APIs and managed services. Microsoft Foundry serves as the unified development and operations platform that brings models, agents, tools, orchestration, evaluation, and deployment together for enterprise AI applications. Copilot serves as an interface for knowledge work, translating intent into action across applications. Power Platform extends these capabilities to a broader audience through low-code tools and AI Builder. Together, they demonstrate how AI capabilities transition from experimental features to operational tools.

The discussion encompasses governance and trust—essential yet often overlooked aspects of making AI systems reliable for regulated industries and sensitive decision-making. Through examples from customer service, field operations, and knowledge work, we examine how organizations deploy these capabilities while managing risk. The chapter concludes by considering emerging patterns: autonomous agents capable of executing multistep processes, context-aware systems that anticipate needs, and the gradual evolution of enterprise systems toward more adaptive architectures.

Organizations implementing AI face practical choices about architecture, governance, and human roles. Progress typically follows a measured approach: pilot programs in understood domains, careful measurement of outcomes, gradual expansion of scope, and continuous refinement based on experience. This systematic progression, rather than a dramatic transformation, characterizes how most organizations successfully integrate AI into their operations.

14.1 Foundational Principles

Four principles have shaped enterprise software design for decades: usability, automation, scalability, and declarative logic. While these concepts are not new, AI capabilities offer fresh approaches to their implementation. Each principle has evolved through distinct phases, providing lessons that now influence how organizations integrate intelligent systems.

14.1.1 The Evolution of Automation

Traditional automation followed predetermined scripts. Systems executed specific sequences: if condition A, then action B. Well-designed systems included error handling, but unexpected inputs often required manual intervention or process redesign. Change typically meant modifying code. INTELLIFM represented an early attempt to bridge the gap between rigid rules and contextual understanding. It parsed business intent from document content, demonstrating that machines could interpret meaning beyond simple pattern matching. Notably, the expert system allowed domain experts to specify the behavior of the applications without relying on traditional programming.

The shift toward adaptive systems introduced new possibilities. Instead of programming every scenario, developers train models on data. Systems identify patterns and make predictions within their training distribution. When inputs vary within expected ranges, intelligent systems can adjust their responses. This flexibility makes automation more resilient, though novel situations outside training parameters still pose challenges.

Current automation systems attempt to understand objectives rather than merely execute instructions. Azure AI Services illustrates this evolution. Speech recognition adapts to various accents through the diversity of training data. Language models interpret intent despite grammatical variations. Vision systems identify objects under different lighting conditions. Each service improves through retraining with new data, though this requires deliberate updates rather than automatic learning.

14.1.2 Scalability Redefined

Physical hardware was once constrained in scale. Adding capacity required purchasing servers, configuring networks, and managing increasing complexity. Cloud computing reduces infrastructure constraints, but effective scalability requires systems that handle complexity efficiently, not just increase volume.

ML affects scalability patterns differently from rule-based systems. Traditional systems often slow down as rules accumulate, as each condition adds processing overhead. ML models, once trained, process individual inputs at relatively consistent speeds regardless of training data volume. But this does not mean computational costs remain constant. Larger models require more processing power, and inference costs scale with usage. The key advantage lies in handling complex patterns without proportional increases in processing time per transaction.

Microsoft's implementation demonstrates practical approaches to scalability. Language models can serve multiple products through shared cloud infrastructure, while device and edge deployments may offload selected tasks to NPUs. In such hybrid designs, latency-sensitive or routine processing can occur closer to the user, and more compute-intensive inference can run in the cloud when appropriate. This distribution can improve responsiveness, but it also introduces coordination complexity, network dependencies, and additional governance considerations across device, edge, and cloud boundaries.

14.1.3 Usability Through Natural Interaction

Early usability improvements replaced command lines with graphical interfaces. Users clicked buttons instead of typing commands. Yet even sophisticated interfaces required training. Users learned system conventions—such as menu locations, function names, and sequence of operations.

NLP aims to reduce this learning curve. Copilot interprets requests like "schedule a meeting next week" without requiring users to specify the application or format. Power Platform accepts descriptions like "build an inventory tracker" and generates initial components. These interfaces lower barriers to entry, though users still need to understand system capabilities and limitations for effective use.

Context awareness extends interface improvements. Systems can surface relevant information based on current activities and suggest likely subsequent actions. However, these predictions are most effective for routine patterns. Unusual requests or complex workflows still require explicit guidance. Usability improvements make everyday tasks more efficient rather than eliminating complexity entirely.

14.1.4 Declarative Logic: From How to What

Imperative programming has dominated software development, requiring developers to specify exact steps, such as opening a file, reading a line, parsing data, and storing the result. Each instruction demanded precise syntax. Minor errors could break programs or produce incorrect results.

INTELLIFM introduced rule-driven automation for corporate filings and compliance management. Domain experts can configure rules determining when and how forms are prepared, submitted, and tracked. For example, the expert system can identify newly formed entities and generate the appropriate Certificate of Incorporation for printing. It can also dispatch electronic filings for annual reports based on state-specific deadlines, such as March 1 for Delaware or May 1 for Florida (filing requirements and dates vary by filing type and can change over time). These actions are governed by embedded filing rules, ensuring that forms are selected, populated, and routed in accordance with jurisdictional requirements and compliance calendars.

Modern AI systems extend the declarative capabilities introduced by INTELLIFM. Users state desired outcomes: "Summarize this meeting," "Find compliance issues," "Generate quarterly report." Platforms orchestrate necessary steps—transcription, analysis, formatting—behind the scenes. Copilot and Power Platform exemplify this approach, letting business users express their intent while systems handle the execution details.

This represents an architectural shift, accompanied by trade-offs. Declarative systems separate business logic from implementation, allowing changes to requirements without code rewrites. Components can be combined dynamically based on the expressed intent. However, complex or unusual requirements often still need imperative specification. The sweet spot lies in common business scenarios with well-understood patterns.

14.1.5 Bridging Intent and Execution

RAG illustrates how declarative principles connect user intent with system execution. Users ask questions in natural language, and the system retrieves relevant material and generates a contextual response grounded in that material. Many implementations also include supporting sources or excerpts to improve transparency, although the presence and quality of source attribution depend on design choices and governance policies. The underlying complexity, including semantic search, ranking, and synthesis, remains abstracted, and response quality still depends on data quality, access permissions, and query specificity.

Early NLP work explored similar patterns. Users described document types, and systems learned classification rules. While today's language models far exceed those rule-based systems in capability, the core principle remains: translate human intent into machine action without requiring users to understand the underlying mechanisms. Success rates have improved dramatically, though edge cases remain challenging.

Power Platform illustrates this bridge at an organizational scale. Citizen developers—business users who build solutions using low-code tools rather than writing code—describe applications conceptually. The platform generates initial data models, interfaces, and workflows. Professional developers refine details for production readiness. This approach democratizes basic development, though complex applications still require technical expertise.

14.1.6 Synthesis and Integration

These principles interact and reinforce each other. Scalability facilitates automation across enterprise workloads. Natural interfaces make declarative approaches accessible. Automation implements declarative intent efficiently. Each principle contributes to the overall capability of the system.

Azure AI Services provides a suite of pretrained models and APIs—accessible through various interfaces—that abstract the underlying AI infrastructure for developers. Microsoft Foundry serves as the development platform where those capabilities are assembled into applications and agents. Copilot adds the interaction layer—translating intent into actions across applications. Power Platform gives domain experts the tools to build solutions using these capabilities. Together, these four platform elements show how foundational principles, developed over decades, combine into practical implementations.

The evolution continues with both advances and limitations. Systems become more adaptive within defined parameters. Interfaces grow more intuitive for everyday tasks. Declarative approaches handle increasing complexity. Yet each improvement reveals new challenges. The intelligence revolution does not eliminate these principles' constraints, but instead explores their boundaries, finding practical applications while acknowledging their inherent limitations.

14.2 Architectural Synthesis

Modern intelligent systems require deliberate architectural layering that connects individual capabilities into functional solutions. This synthesis comprises three foundational layers that work together to support intelligence at an enterprise scale.

14.2.1 The Three-Layer Foundation

Microsoft's AI platform strategy rests on a three-layer foundation that connects infrastructure, organizational context, and intelligence services into a coherent whole.

Base Layer: Infrastructure

The foundational layer provides elastic cloud infrastructure, including IaaS and PaaS capabilities. Beyond compute and storage, this layer includes data lakes, advanced networking, and global distribution—all of which support high-scale AI workloads. Azure infrastructure supports data streaming, governance controls, and regional deployment strategies. However, infrastructure alone does not create business value; the higher layers provide the context and purpose that make intelligence useful.

Middle Layer: Organizational Context

The middle layer comprises enterprise applications and SaaS platforms, including ERP, CRM, and productivity suites. These systems provide essential organizational context through business logic, process definitions, and historical data. Without this layer, AI may produce technically impressive but operationally irrelevant outputs. With it, intelligence can align with specific business requirements, although the resulting integration complexity often requires substantial configuration by implementation teams.

Top Layer: Intelligence

The top layer consists of AI services, including pretrained models, cognitive APIs, and orchestration capabilities. Rather than operating independently, these services integrate with the lower layers to deliver agentic functionality. Intelligence is woven into existing workflows through deliberate API governance, performance tuning, and rigorous error handling. In mature architectures, grounding generated outputs in enterprise knowledge—through sources such as Dataverse, SharePoint, or Azure AI Search—and configuring permission-aware retrieval are important steps toward production-ready intelligence.

14.2.2 Microsoft's Implementation

The enterprise AI stack reflects this three-layer architecture. Azure AI Services provides the underlying cognitive services and APIs, including vision, speech, language, and document intelligence. Microsoft Foundry provides the unified platform layer for assembling models, agents, tools, orchestration, evaluation, and deployment into enterprise-ready AI applications. Copilot represents the family of AI assistants built on these services, surfacing capabilities through natural language interfaces embedded in productivity applications. Power Platform extends this ecosystem by giving implementation teams the tools to build custom solutions that draw on both foundational AI services and Copilot capabilities through low-code orchestration.

Copilot functions as a natural language interface that sits above an orchestration layer. That layer—implemented through Copilot Studio agent flows, Microsoft Foundry's orchestration runtime, or related infrastructure—translates user intent into coordinated actions across approved tools and data sources. In a configured environment with the right permissions and connectors, a request for quarterly customer feedback summaries can trigger the retrieval of relevant documents from SharePoint, invoke an analytics step such as sentiment classification, and produce a summary using a language model. This orchestration reduces visible complexity, but effective use still depends on governance, information access boundaries, and clear user intent, including what to include, what to exclude, and how to handle exceptions.

Power Platform gives domain experts—often acting as citizen developers—the tools to build applications incorporating AI capabilities. Citizen developers can create forms that extract data, validate against business rules, and route through workflows. The platform manages technical details—API calls, data transformations, basic error handling—though complex scenarios require professional developer intervention.

14.2.3 Core Design Patterns

Four patterns support reliable operation at scale, especially within regulated or sensitive business environments.

Composability allows specialized services to combine for complex tasks. Analyzing customer service calls typically involves STT, entity recognition, sentiment analysis, and summarization. Each component remains independently maintainable while preserving interface stability. Systems select service combinations based on task requirements, though optimal selection often requires manual configuration.

Extensibility allows organizations to add proprietary capabilities. Custom models trained on internal data work in conjunction with standard services. RAG techniques give generic models access to organization-specific knowledge. Fine-tuning adapts behavior to industry terminology. Organizations extend the foundation while preserving platform benefits, though managing custom extensions increases operational complexity.

Semantic interoperability allows services to share contextual understanding beyond simple data formats. When one service identifies "Contract Type: Master Services Agreement," downstream services can apply appropriate routing, compliance policies, and aggregation rules. This shared understanding, often built on standard data models, enhances system coordination. However, establishing semantic consistency across services requires ongoing maintenance.

Governance and transparency form the fourth essential pattern. Systems operating in regulated industries must prioritize auditability and accountability to build trust. In high-stakes domains such as finance, health care, and law, this means capturing inputs, sources, policy constraints, model versions, and approvals so that outcomes can be reviewed, challenged, and reproduced when necessary. The pattern requires recording the evidence trail behind an output, not merely presenting a final answer. Bloomberg Valuation Service (BVAL) exemplifies this approach.[3] Its success stems from transparent methodology, traceable valuation inputs, and defensible assumptions—qualities that promote independent review and withstand regulatory scrutiny. Governance and transparency help institutions apply meaningful oversight and maintain accountability.

14.2.4 Lessons from Precedent Systems

BVAL demonstrated these architectural principles in financial markets before the emergence of current AI platforms. It combined specialized models—such as yield curve construction, credit analysis, and volatility surfaces—into a unified valuation framework for pricing complex financial instruments. Each component maintained independence while contributing to integrated outputs. The system evolved from simple bonds to complex derivatives, using a consistent architecture.

BVAL succeeded through three key decisions that current AI architectures echo. First, clear component boundaries with explicit interfaces made parallel development and independent updates possible. Second, market data grounding aligns outputs with observable reality, neutralizing the abstractions inherent in purely theoretical models. Third, transparent reasoning—showing calculation paths, not just results—built trust with professional traders who needed to understand and defend valuations.

[3] "Evaluated Pricing Solutions (BVAL)," Bloomberg Professional Services, `https://professional.bloomberg.com/products/data/enterprise-catalog/pricing/evaluated-pricing/`.

These principles now operate across broader domains. While BVAL served thousands of financial professionals, current platforms serve millions across industries. The architectural patterns have proven to be transferable, although each domain presents unique challenges. Clear interfaces, grounded reasoning, and operational transparency remain important whether valuing securities or processing documents.

14.2.5 Integration in Practice

The architecture's value emerges when layers and patterns work together. Consider a procurement system processing vendor invoices. Cloud infrastructure provides document storage and computing for OCR processing. ERP systems supply vendor data, approval hierarchies, and accounting rules. AI services extract invoice data, validate against contracts, and identify anomalies.

Composability supports the handling of various invoice formats through configuration, rather than requiring reprogramming. Extensibility makes it possible to create custom models for organization-specific documents. Semantic interoperability keeps the extracted data flowing correctly into financial systems. Copilot lets users query invoice status in natural language. Power Platform gives accounts payable staff a way to build workflows for exceptions. The following examples draw on vendor case studies, partner reporting, and trade coverage; reported outcomes should be treated as instructive illustrations rather than universally generalizable findings.

Implementations in practice demonstrate how these architectural principles translate into operational improvements. In a documented deployment, the consulting firm Smartbridge automated invoice processing for a Texas-based natural gas company with more than 100 drilling sites. The company used Power Automate, AI Builder, and Azure to automate its invoice processing workflow. The solution used AI Builder's prebuilt text recognition model to extract metadata from vendor invoices received by email. The results were stored in an Azure SQL database. A Power Automate desktop flow then uploaded the extracted data into the company's document management tool, DocVue, for approval routing and payment processing. The automation ended reliance on a single individual for reconciliation, captured all available net-10-day vendor discounts through consistent processing, and generated daily reports to flag exception invoices alongside successful invoices.[4]

[4] Smartbridge, "Case Study: Invoice Processing Automation for an Oil & Gas Company," updated September 25, 2025, `https://smartbridge.com/invoice-processing-automation-case-study`.

A second example comes from Thermo Fisher Scientific—a global enterprise with more than 90,000 employees. The company's Smart Automation Global Business Services unit deployed UiPath Document Understanding to automate purchase-to-pay invoice processing through its Coupa spend management platform. The solution extracted data from PDF invoices and purchase orders, validated the results using the UiPath Action Center, and submitted the verified records for payment. According to UiPath, the deployment automated 53% of Thermo Fisher's approximately 824,000 annual invoices through straight-through processing and reduced invoice processing time by 70%. The company built regional models for key suppliers in both North America and Europe, with plans to expand the approach to additional workstreams and internal business unit invoicing.[5]

Across these cases, a consistent pattern emerges: automation delivers the greatest gains when documents are structured or semistructured; when integrations among extraction, validation, and payment systems are reliable; and when staff are trained to manage exceptions. The specifics vary—Microsoft Power Platform in one deployment and UiPath in another—but the architectural principles of composability, extensibility, and semantic interoperability apply regardless of vendor. Most organizations find that automation shifts staff responsibilities toward exception management, vendor communication, and oversight rather than eliminating roles entirely.

14.2.6 Evolution Toward Autonomous Systems

These architectural patterns are also evolving to support more autonomous operations—*agentic AI* systems that initiate actions based on conditions and goals rather than merely reacting to prompts. Chapter 13 examined the technical prerequisites and governance challenges in detail. The three-layer model offers a potential foundation for such systems, but architecture alone does not drive transformation. Organizational change emerges through workflow integration, user adoption, and process redesign. The following examples illustrate how architectural principles translate into operational outcomes, highlighting both successes and persistent challenges.

[5] UiPath, "Document Understanding Reduces Thermo Fisher Scientific's Invoice Process," `https://www.uipath.com/resources/automation-case-studies/document-understanding-reduces-thermo-fisher-scientific-invoice-process`.

14.3 Business Process Transformation

The integration of AI into business processes changes how organizations approach workflow design and execution. Linear workflows that proceed through fixed sequences are being supplemented or replaced by more adaptive systems. AI can route work based on current conditions. However, successful implementation requires careful design, testing, and ongoing adjustment.

14.3.1 Intelligent Orchestration

Traditional workflows follow predetermined paths. A customer request triggers step one, which leads to step two, and the process continues until completion. Deviations typically require manual intervention. AI-enabled orchestration introduces context-based conditional routing, and in many organizations this is emerging as an increasingly important operating pattern. But this flexibility comes with increased complexity.

Consider order processing. Standard workflows move through validation, inventory check, payment processing, and fulfillment. AI-enhanced systems can vary this sequence based on patterns. Orders from established customers may be exempt from specific validation steps. Transactions matching fraud indicators receive additional scrutiny. Inventory shortages can trigger checks with alternative suppliers. The workflow adapts within defined parameters, though edge cases still require human intervention.

This orchestration capability extends across connected systems. Azure Integration Services[6] can link ERP, CRM, and supply chain platforms. AI monitoring identifies potential bottlenecks and suggests rerouting options, though automatic redistribution typically requires human approval for critical processes. When a department experiences delays, the system may propose task redistribution to maintain throughput, with managers making final decisions based on broader contextual factors that the system may not capture.

14.3.2 Modern IVR and Customer Engagement

IVR systems illustrate both the promise and the limits of process transformation. Early generations, built around rigid menu trees ("Press 1 for sales, press 2 for support"), frequently created friction and constrained customer choice. Contemporary platforms

[6] "Azure Integration Services," Microsoft Azure, `https://azure.microsoft.com/en-us/products/category/integration`.

that use Azure AI and Nuance technologies support natural language interaction and more adaptive routing. Yet they continue to face challenges with multi-intent requests and with speech patterns that are underrepresented in training data—particularly in noisy environments or among speakers with uncommon dialects or pronunciation. These constraints reinforce the need for disciplined piloting, ongoing tuning, and a clearly defined escalation path to human agents.

Modern architectures also support preserving conversational context across channels. A customer may begin with voice, continue through chat, and conclude via email, with core context maintained throughout. This reduces repetition and shortens overall resolution time. When escalation occurs, agents receive the interaction history and an automated summary, though they often review details manually to capture nuances that current models may overlook. In regulated industries, cross-channel context persistence introduces governance and consent requirements that organizations must address explicitly—including data retention policies, customer consent for cross-channel tracking, and jurisdictional compliance obligations such as GDPR and CCPA.

Visual IVR extends the voice experience by adding a screen-based component. As customers speak, relevant information—such as account balances, transaction histories, or confirmation prompts—can appear on their devices. Well-designed implementations have produced meaningful reductions in call duration. Poorly designed ones, however, introduce friction, increase abandonment, or complicate authentication. Outcomes depend heavily on journey design, the sequencing of visual elements, and the balance between self-service and escalation.

Predictive engagement seeks to anticipate customer needs by analyzing behavioral patterns. A customer nearing a credit limit may be offered payment options; unusual account activity may trigger additional verification. These interventions require careful calibration: overly assertive outreach can feel intrusive, while overly passive systems miss opportunities to assist.

Published case studies from vendors such as Nuance (now part of Microsoft) and Genesys report improvements in containment, first-contact resolution, and average handle time following deployments of conversational and visual IVR. Reported gains typically reflect advances in intent recognition, journey design, and integration with downstream systems. Because vendor case studies are not independently verified and may be revised or removed over time, specific figures are best treated as directional rather than definitive benchmarks.

Across available implementations, a consistent pattern emerges. Organizations report measurable improvements in first-contact resolution for routine inquiries and reductions in handle time for standard requests. More complex issues may still require longer interactions as agents review AI-generated summaries or validate recommended actions. Ultimately, performance depends on selecting the right use cases, maintaining high-quality training data, and committing to continuous refinement. Real-time systems such as IVR introduce an additional architectural trade-off: high-accuracy models tend to incur latency that is perceptible in voice interactions, while lower-latency models may sacrifice intent recognition accuracy. Hybrid routing approaches address this by using faster, lighter models for initial intent classification and routing, reserving more accurate models for complex disambiguation or escalation decisions where additional processing time is acceptable.

14.3.3 Field Work and Mobile Intelligence

Field workers face unique challenges, including constant movement, hands-on tasks, and on-site decision-making. Traditional systems require documentation after returning to base, increasing the risk of detail loss. Mobile intelligence mitigates some of these issues while introducing new ones.

Power Platform supports voice-driven applications that fit many field environments. STT accuracy can vary widely with background noise, microphone quality, connectivity, and how closely terminology matches training and calibration conditions. NLP can extract structured data such as equipment identifiers, failure types, and required parts, but field workflows often still include a human confirmation step before downstream actions occur. For example, a technician might say, "The valve is leaking air on the left side," and the system can display a relevant schematic and propose a parts list for confirmation, creating a practical multimodal loop with human validation.

Adaptive interfaces adjust to situational context. Routine maintenance differs from emergency repairs. Systems present relevant procedures and safety warnings based on conditions. However, workers report that dynamic interfaces sometimes obscure necessary options, forcing them to revert to standard forms.

Real-world implementations illustrate both the promise and the constraints. Telstra—Australia's largest telecommunications provider—equipped its field technicians with role-specific mobile applications built on Microsoft Power Apps and embedded in Microsoft Teams. The solutions included TIDE, which helped teams resolve issues and identify opportunities; Sherloc, a damage investigation app that guided technicians through structured questions and geotagged photo capture; performance dashboards in Power BI; and product catalogs to support upselling on site. By embedding these tools in a single Teams interface, Telstra reduced the number of separate systems technicians had to navigate and brought field teams, office-based experts, and leadership into direct communication. Technicians could place video calls to the company's Brain Trust expert group for real-time guidance during active field situations, replacing the previous process of describing problems over the phone and waiting for instructions.[7]

Utility companies are exploring similar patterns with computer vision. Field crews routinely photograph equipment during inspections, and AI models can identify standard components and flag visible damage. In well-designed deployments, automated image classification reduces the volume of images requiring manual review and helps prioritize maintenance tasks. However, experienced technicians frequently need to override AI recommendations when local conditions, such as weathering patterns, unusual configurations, or environmental factors, fall outside the model's training distribution.

Resource coordination shows promise with limitations. AI systems track team locations and skills, recommending the most suitable responders for emergencies. But automatic dispatch rarely works without human verification. Factors such as team dynamics, local knowledge, and equipment conditions require human judgment. Organizations typically use AI suggestions as inputs for human dispatchers rather than relying on automatic routing.

Rail operators offer another perspective. Société Nationale des Chemins de fer Français (SNCF) has invested heavily in predictive maintenance for its rolling stock, deploying sensors across more than 1,000 trains to monitor doors, air conditioning and heating, compressors, batteries, brakes, and pantographs. The system can analyze over 8,000 variables per train, with 2,000 monitored in real time. It has reduced the number of routine preventive inspections substantially by replacing them with condition-based interventions. SNCF reports that remote diagnostics and predictive maintenance can reduce breakdowns by half to two-thirds for equipped fleets.[8]

---

[7] "Telstra Transforms Firstline Worker Experience, Improves Customer Support," Microsoft Australia News Centre, November 2019, https://news.microsoft.com/en-au/features/telstra-transforms-firstline-worker-experience-improves-customer-support/.

[8] "A Leader in Predictive Maintenance," SNCF Group, https://www.groupe-sncf.com/en/innovation/digitalization/predictive-maintenance.

Across these implementations, results vary by design quality, environmental conditions, and the maturity of supporting processes. The primary benefit often comes from faster information flow and reduced administrative burden rather than dramatic automation. Well-designed mobile tools reduce the number of systems field workers must navigate, improve communication between field and office teams, and capture structured data closer to the point of work.

14.3.4 Knowledge Work Augmentation

Knowledge workers—analysts, managers, lawyers, and consultants—spend considerable time on routine cognitive tasks. AI tools such as Copilot can automate portions of this work, though outputs require careful review and often substantial revision.

Document intelligence assists with contract review. AI can extract key provisions and compare them against templates, flagging deviations. However, accuracy varies considerably with document complexity, formatting, and the degree to which the contract language matches the model's training data. Standard commercial contracts with predictable clause structures yield better results than bespoke agreements with unusual terms or nested conditions. Legal teams typically report time savings during initial review, though they still must manually review critical sections. Microsoft's own Finance organization implemented an Azure AI–based contract review platform to triage and prioritize financial contracts. The Revenue team's Intelligent Transformation Finance group designed a solution that reads documents and assesses the likelihood that a contract requires an accounting assessment, replacing the manual preread that team leads had previously performed for each deal's document stack. According to Mathew Abraham, a technical program manager on Microsoft's Corporate Accounting team, the platform "significantly sped up and streamlined financial contract reviews," producing time savings and streamlining global coordination and prioritization.[9]

Compliance monitoring benefits from continuous scanning rather than periodic audits. AI systems can verify transactions against established rules, though they often struggle with nuanced regulations requiring human judgment. Organizations typically automate clear-cut rules while maintaining human review for interpretive requirements. False-positive rates remain a practical concern, necessitating human validation pipelines

[9] India Rodgers, "Scaling contract reviews at Microsoft with Microsoft Azure AI Services," Microsoft Inside Track, March 23, 2023, `https://www.microsoft.com/insidetrack/blog/scaling-contract-reviews-at-microsoft-with-microsoft-azure-ai-services`.

that can offset some of the efficiency gains. As organizations adopt tools like Microsoft 365 Copilot for compliance workflows, early reports suggest measurable efficiency gains in areas such as audit preparation and documentation review, though human oversight remains essential for complex regulatory interpretations.

Financial reporting shows measured improvements. AI can assist with transaction reconciliation, variance analysis, and narrative drafting. Microsoft's collaboration with Ernst & Young (EY) on AI-enabled finance operations illustrates an approach: the teams developed two internal tools, Finance Launch AI and Replay AI, that consolidated tens of thousands of historical financial documents into a knowledge library queryable in natural language. Over 100 Microsoft finance employees adopted Finance Launch AI, giving them the ability to query hundreds of documents and thousands of pages in seconds. The EY collaboration helped Microsoft successfully integrate AI-driven solutions in the finance department and achieve new levels of operational efficiency.[10]

Productivity gains vary widely across knowledge work domains. Analysts may spend less time gathering data, freeing time for deeper analysis; lawyers may increase contract throughput for standard agreements, with smaller gains for complex negotiations. These improvements are meaningful but fall short of the transformational claims sometimes made. Across published implementations, a consistent pattern emerges: AI accelerates routine tasks and improves consistency, but expert review remains indispensable.

14.3.5 Practitioner Perspective: Enterprise AI at FIS

My teams lived the FIS story from the inside. As an enterprise architect, I led engineering efforts to refine the SDLC and help position FIS not only as a financial technology provider but also as a technology-led software company. The work required translating the architectural principles described in this chapter—composability, extensibility, and governance—into production systems operating at the scale of a Fortune 500 financial services organization.

The engagement spanned multiple platforms within FIS's financial technology portfolio, including systems supporting payments, banking, and card-issuing operations. Structural discipline kept large-scale modernization traceable and governable across globally distributed teams. The infrastructure transformation included migrating

[10] "How AI Innovation Powers Microsoft's Finance Journey," EY Consulting Case Studies, March 5, 2025, `https://www.ey.com/en_us/insights/consulting/ey-consulting-case-studies/how-ai-innovation-powers-microsofts-finance-journey`.

on-premises workloads to Azure and AWS, deploying reusable domain services built on canonical APIs and event models, and unifying disparate data sources on a durable pub/sub messaging platform. A revamp of the SDLC addressed systemic delivery challenges and contributed to measurable improvements in operational efficiency and revenue outcomes at the scale of a major global financial technology organization.

My teams built sophisticated conversational AI systems, including IVR, chatbot, and virtual assistant technologies powered by NLP, and integrated them with the call distribution platform to improve customer self-service, reduce operating costs, and strengthen security protocols. My teams applied the INTELLIFM architecture and domain-driven design principles to develop internal applications, including the Merchant Authorization system. They built tools such as the Admin Console and Tagging Guide that empowered domain experts at FIS to update the AI systems in real time.

After Microsoft announced its acquisition of Nuance Communications in April 2021 (completed in March 2022), my teams helped forge a strategic partnership between FIS and Microsoft, with teams from both organizations collaborating on next-generation AI systems. That partnership has continued to bear fruit: in March 2025, FIS announced FIS Treasury and Risk Manager–Treasury GPT, a proprietary generative AI-driven product support tool built on Microsoft Azure OpenAI Service and embedded within the FIS Treasury and Risk Manager–Integrity Edition platform. FIS also announced plans to migrate Integrity to Microsoft Azure, and Treasury GPT received the Best Solution Innovation in AI award at the 2025 Treasury Management International Awards.[11]

14.3.6 Synthesis Across Domains

These implementations share consistent patterns. AI reduces friction at specific points—such as data extraction, format conversion, and initial routing—rather than eliminating entire processes. Humans remain essential for exceptions, relationship-driven work, and judgment calls. Success comes from identifying narrow, well-defined AI tasks while preserving human oversight for complex decisions.

[11] FIS, "FIS Launches Treasury GPT, a Pioneering AI-based Product Support Tool for the Treasury Industry," FIS Investor Relations, March 10, 2025, `https://www.investor.fisglobal.com/news-releases/news-release-details/fis-launches-treasury-gpt-pioneering-ai-based-product-support`.

The architectural foundations cultivate incremental improvement. Cloud infrastructure provides computing power. Enterprise applications supply business context. AI services deliver targeted capabilities. Together, they support process enhancement rather than wholesale transformation.

Professional services firms, whose business models depend on the same knowledge work processes discussed throughout this chapter, illustrate these patterns in their own operations. PricewaterhouseCoopers (PwC) is building AI into its global audit platform through tools such as Data PRO, which standardizes and validates client data for audit work, and Acquisition Hub, which gives clients a single location to share and track requested information. PwC has also deployed ChatNational, a generative AI (GenAI)–powered research platform. By automating routine data work, auditors can spend more time on the insights that matter most to clients. PwC expects end-to-end AI integration across the audit cycle sometime in 2026.[12]

Tax functions show similar patterns. Klynveld Peat Marwick Goerdeler (KPMG) deployed its Digital Gateway GenAI platform, which integrates generative AI capabilities across tax compliance, planning, and advisory workflows. The platform integrates document upload and AI-driven analysis, with automated data extraction and classification, and virtual assistants that handle tasks ranging from regulatory research to cross-jurisdictional translation. KPMG is simultaneously deploying AI agents to its Clara smart audit platform, aiming to augment the work of more than 95,000 auditors globally. In an illustration of the efficiency potential, KPMG Australia built a TaxBot on its Workbench multiagent platform, using a RAG model loaded with partner-written tax advice and Australian tax legislation. According to KPMG, the agent produces a first-draft 25-page advisory document in roughly a day's work that previously took the team about two weeks.[13]

---

[12] "PwC Expands AI Audit Suite with Data PRO Acquisition Hub," PwC US Newsroom, September 2025, `https://www.pwc.com/us/en/about-us/newsroom/press-releases/ai-audit-tools-data-pro-acquisition-hub.html`. See also Sean McCabe, "PwC expects end-to-end AI audit automation within 2026," Accounting Today, October 28, 2025, `https://www.accountingtoday.com/news/pwc-expects-end-to-end-ai-audit-automation-within-2026`.

[13] "KPMG advances AI integration in KPMG Clara smart audit platform," KPMG International, April 22, 2025, `https://kpmg.com/xx/en/media/press-releases/2025/04/kpmg-advances-ai-integration-in-kpmg-clara-smart-audit-platform.html`. For TaxBot details, see Simon Sharwood, "KPMG wrote 100-page prompt to build agentic TaxBot," *The Register*, August 20, 2025, `https://www.theregister.com/2025/08/20/kpmg_giant_prompt_tax_agent`.

Risk management organizations demonstrate parallel ambitions alongside cautionary examples. Deloitte Touche Tohmatsu Limited (Deloitte) has invested in AI capabilities for risk and compliance, including its Behavioral and Emotion Analytics Tool (BEAT) platform for monitoring interactions in financial services and a range of AI-driven threat detection and response services. However, a 2025 incident underscored the limits of these technologies. The Australian government discovered that a Deloitte report—commissioned by the Department of Employment and Workplace Relations (DEWR) to review the IT system used for automated welfare penalties—contained fabricated legal citations and nonexistent sources.[14] Following the discovery of multiple errors, including a faked quote attributed to a Federal Court judge, Deloitte admitted that it had used a GPT-4o-based toolchain hosted on DEWR's Azure tenancy. Although the initial contract was valued at AU$440,000, Deloitte agreed to refund more than AU$97,000.[15] The episode illustrates a central theme of this chapter: AI outputs require human validation, and skipping that step can have serious consequences.

These are illustrative snapshots drawn from vendor reporting, partner case studies, and trade sources; outcomes will vary by organization, implementation maturity, and context. Taken together, these examples suggest some patterns worth noting, albeit as directional observations rather than empirically validated conclusions. Across these examples, a consistent set of lessons emerges. AI accelerates routine cognitive tasks, such as data extraction, document classification, and initial analysis, and improves consistency for standardized work. Error reductions depend heavily on baseline quality and task type. Employee satisfaction often improves when AI handles tedious work, though frustration with AI limitations can offset these gains, especially when outputs require substantial correction. Processing-time improvements vary widely depending on how well defined the task is, the quality of training data, and the maturity of supporting workflows.

These capabilities can create value while also introducing new complexities. The benefits of automation are often weighed against implementation costs, along with new failure modes such as fabricated or unreliable outputs. Many deployments also retain human skills for oversight and exception handling. The following section examines governance frameworks associated with responsible deployment.

[14] Simon Sharwood, "Deloitte Refunds Australian Government over AI in Report," *The Register*, October 6, 2025, `https://www.theregister.com/2025/10/06/deloitte_ai_report_australia/`.

[15] Alexei Alexis, "Deloitte Refunds over $60K for Report with AI Errors, Australian Government Says," *CFO Dive*, October 21, 2025, `https://www.cfodive.com/news/deloitte-refunds-60k-report-ai-errors-australian-government-accounting/803321/`.

14.4 Strategic Implications and Future Trajectories

The intelligence revolution unfolds across distinct time horizons, each with its own challenges and opportunities. Organizations face decisions about immediate adoption while considering potential transformations ahead. The path from current capabilities to more autonomous systems involves progression through pilot programs, architectural evolution, and workforce adaptation. Throughout this journey, the relationship between humans and AI continues to evolve in complementary ways.

14.4.1 Near-Term: Foundations Through Staged Adoption

The immediate path forward often benefits from measured approaches rather than ambitious leaps. Many organizations begin with pilot programs in well-understood areas where success can be clearly measured and risks can be contained. Customer service, document processing, and routine analysis frequently serve as starting points. These areas involve high-volume, repetitive tasks for which AI assistance can deliver value without disrupting core operations.

Staged adoption patterns vary across organizations and industries. Initial pilots may involve anywhere from 20 to 200 users, depending on the organization's size and risk tolerance. Success metrics established up front typically include productivity improvements, error reduction, and user satisfaction. Reported gains vary widely depending on the use case selected and the quality of implementation. EY's 2025 Work Reimagined Survey indicates that organizations may be missing out on up to 40% of potential AI productivity gains because of talent-related gaps, highlighting the importance of workforce readiness alongside technical deployment.[16]

These quantitative results underscore the strategic need for workforce adaptation. The "iPhone moment" for AI, as described earlier, is not merely a technological shift but a competitive one, in which users of AI may gain advantages over those who do not. In response to this competitive evolution, organizations prioritize retraining. Investments

[16] EY, "EY Survey Reveals Companies Are Missing Out on Up to 40 Percent of AI Productivity Gains Due to Gaps in Talent Strategy," Ernst & Young, November 2025, https://www.ey.com/en_gl/newsroom/2025/11/ey-survey-reveals-companies-are-missing-out-on-up-to-40-percent-of-ai-productivity-gains-due-to-gaps-in-talent-strategy.

in programs that help employees—such as call center agents—shift from routine task execution to complex problem resolution and relationship management represent an early step toward transforming the workforce into "humans with AI assistance."

Starting with scenarios where AI assists rather than operates autonomously often reduces risk. Customer service exemplifies effective staging. Organizations may begin by using AI to classify and route initial inquiries. Success there can lead to automated responses for common questions. Next may come real-time agent assistance during calls. Eventually, AI could handle complete interactions for routine requests. Each stage builds on demonstrated success to gradually expand capability.

Document processing follows similar patterns of progression. Initial deployment may involve AI extracting data from invoices and integrating it into existing systems. Positive results can lead to automated validation against business rules. Over time, AI may handle workflows from ingestion through approval, with humans managing exceptions. This incremental approach helps maintain operational continuity during process transformation.

Timeline patterns show considerable variation. While some organizations succeed with 3-month pilots, 6-month expansions, and 12-month enterprise rollouts, others require extended periods for each phase. Industries with strict regulatory requirements often extend deployment timelines to 18–24 months. The appropriate pacing depends on technical complexity, organizational culture, and risk tolerance. The FIS engagement described in Section 14.3.5 illustrates this variability. A program of that complexity and regulatory scope—spanning payments, banking, and card-issuing systems—required sustained multiyear effort rather than a single discrete rollout, with each phase building governance structures and technical foundations that made subsequent phases viable.

Common success factors include executive support for resource allocation, clear communication about workforce impacts, well-structured training programs, and the maintenance of parallel manual processes during initial deployment. Organizations that address these areas report smoother implementations, though each deployment faces unique challenges.

14.4.2 Medium-Term: Architectural and Workforce Transformation

Medium-term transformation (three to five years) is likely to reshape both organizational architectures and workforce structures. Many enterprises are exploring modular, composable services as alternatives to monolithic applications. This architectural shift allows the dynamic assembly of capabilities, though implementation complexity and constraints imposed by legacy systems continue to influence adoption rates.

Modular architectures position AI services as interchangeable components. Organizations may use one vendor's language models for specific tasks while deploying specialized industry models for others. Components can be upgraded independently, reducing the risk of system-wide disruption. Updating a credit risk model, for example, need not affect customer service systems. This modularity can accelerate innovation, though it also increases integration complexity and demands stronger interface governance.

API-first design and microservices architectures are becoming more common, but adoption varies widely across industries. These approaches facilitate orchestration across AI-enabled services. However, legacy systems often require substantial modification to participate effectively. Organizations with inflexible architectures face greater challenges in adopting new AI capabilities, and the cost of accumulated technical debt becomes increasingly visible as AI adoption expands.

Workforce evolution occurs in parallel with technical change. Roles rarely disappear outright, but they shift as new capabilities alter how work is organized and executed. Data entry specialists may become data quality managers. Call center agents increasingly focus on resolving complex problems and managing relationships. Financial analysts devote more time to strategic analysis as AI handles routine reporting. These transitions require sustained training and support.

New roles reflect the emerging human–AI collaboration model. Organizations report creating positions such as AI trainers who customize models, prompt engineers who optimize interactions, and algorithm auditors who monitor fairness and compliance. These roles typically require a blend of domain expertise and AI proficiency, further blurring traditional boundaries between technical and business functions.

Workforce strategy involves balancing retraining and new hiring. While retraining preserves institutional knowledge, it demands a material commitment of resources. Conversely, hiring new talent introduces AI expertise but often lacks the specific business context required for implementation. Consequently, many organizations adopt hybrid models, pairing domain experts with technical specialists through cross-training initiatives.

Cultural adaptation often proves more challenging than technical implementation. The shift from task execution to AI supervision requires new competencies—judgment about AI reliability, error detection skills, and comfort with uncertainty. Organizations that invest in change management programs alongside technical deployment report smoother transitions, though outcomes vary widely.

14.4.3 Long-Term: Autonomous Enterprise and Ambient Intelligence

Looking further ahead, organizations may begin to resemble *adaptive systems* rather than static hierarchies. In this scenario, AI does not replace human judgment. Rather, it becomes the connective tissue that links processes, data, and decisions across the enterprise.

Operational autonomy emerges first in narrow domains. Supply chain platforms continuously ingest signals from weather forecasts, logistics networks, and market demand. Instead of waiting for human planners, these systems continuously rebalance inventory, optimize shipment routing in real time, and make precise, incremental adjustments to supplier coordination. Humans intervene only when the system encounters conflicting objectives or ethical constraints—such as prioritizing cost efficiency over resilience.

Finance functions evolve similarly. Reconciliation engines cross-check transactions across systems in real time, escalating only the exceptions that require interpretation. Forecasting models update continuously as new data arrives, shifting finance teams toward scenario design, risk framing, and strategic guidance.

Customer-facing systems become anticipatory. Service platforms detect anomalies—billing irregularities, subscription lapses, device failures—before customers notice them. Instead of waiting for a call, the system initiates a resolution workflow, drafts a message, and proposes next steps. Humans approve the outreach or adjust the tone, but the system handles the mechanics.

Ambient intelligence becomes the enterprise's background hum. Rather than issuing commands, employees work within environments that infer intent. A product manager reviewing a roadmap might see risk indicators surface automatically. A field supervisor preparing for a site visit might receive a synthesized briefing drawn from maintenance logs, weather data, and safety alerts. The system becomes less of a tool and more of a *contextual partner*—quietly shaping workflows without demanding attention.

This evolution does not eliminate human roles—it reshapes them. Employees spend less time navigating systems and more time interpreting outcomes, arbitrating trade-offs, and defining guardrails. New competencies emerge: understanding when to trust an autonomous process, when to override it, and how to design constraints that reflect organizational values.

Competitive dynamics shift as well. Organizations built with AI-native architectures may operate with fundamentally different cost structures and cycle times. Their processes adapt faster, their decision loops tighten, and their ability to experiment increases. Firms retrofitting legacy systems can still compete, but the gap between "AI-native" and "AI-enabled" becomes more visible—much like the gap between cloud-native companies and those that migrated later.

Platforms consolidate and deepen. Rather than stitching together dozens of tools, enterprises rely on a small number of integrated ecosystems. Microsoft's convergence of Azure AI, Copilot, and Power Platform illustrates this direction: a unified substrate where data, orchestration, and automation coexist. This consolidation brings greater coherence, while also increasing the need for platform expertise, governance, and architectural discipline.

The long-term enterprise is not fully autonomous—it is *selectively* autonomous. Humans remain responsible for objectives, ethics, and exceptions. AI handles the connective, repetitive, and anticipatory layers. The result is not a machine-run organization but a hybrid one: humans setting direction, AI shaping execution, and both adapting continuously to one another.

14.4.4 The Partnership Paradigm

Over time, a new pattern of work has begun to take shape—one defined not by competition between humans and machines, but by a growing partnership between them. Each side brings its own strengths. Machines excel at scanning large datasets, detecting patterns that humans cannot see, and executing tasks with consistent accuracy. Humans, by contrast, contribute creativity, ethical judgment, contextual understanding, and the ability to build trust. Organizations that learn to integrate these capabilities often achieve more than either could achieve alone.

You can already see this partnership in everyday scenarios. An AI system might surface subtle signs of customer dissatisfaction long before they appear in survey results, but a human decides how to respond, how to frame the outreach, and how to repair the relationship. AI can draft a proposal or summarize a negotiation, yet the delicate work of persuasion—reading the room, sensing hesitation, building rapport—remains firmly human. AI may optimize a logistics network to the minute, but when a storm disrupts deliveries or a supplier falters, people navigate the relationships and make the judgment calls.

These changes bring understandable concerns. History shows that automation has never produced uniform outcomes. Some sectors have expanded, others have contracted, and individuals have had to adapt at different speeds. AI may accelerate this cycle, requiring more frequent skill updates and career pivots. Organizations that invest in their workforce—through training, reskilling, and thoughtful role redesign—tend to experience smoother adoption and more durable benefits.

As noted in the *Indian Express* interview, the emerging divide is not between humans and machines, but between those who use AI effectively and those who do not. The competitive edge increasingly belongs to "humans with AI assistance"—people who know how to harness these tools to amplify their own capabilities. Encouraging this mindset means presenting AI not as a threat, but as an enhancer of human potential.

The road ahead does not follow a single, predetermined path. Instead, it unfolds through a series of possibilities. Near-term pilots help organizations build confidence and establish the foundations for architectural change. Those architectural shifts, in turn, may pave the way for greater autonomy in the future—while still preserving human roles in strategy, oversight, and exception handling. Organizations that move forward with measured steps, realistic expectations, and a commitment to their people often make more sustainable progress than those that pursue dramatic, all-at-once transformation.

14.5 Conclusion: The Intelligent Enterprise

The principles, architectures, and transformations explored throughout this chapter reflect a notable transition in enterprise computing. Organizations are increasingly deploying Azure AI Services for production workloads, integrating Copilot into daily workflows, and building applications on the Power Platform. For many users, these tools have become part of routine work rather than experimental features. The progression from early pilots to operational systems continues, though adoption rates and outcomes vary widely across industries.

Microsoft's ecosystem represents an approach to enterprise AI. Azure AI processes documents at scale across diverse organizations. Copilot assists knowledge workers with content creation, analysis, and decision support. Power Platform provides business users with tools to build applications with minimal coding. These capabilities are in use in production environments today, even as implementation challenges and inconsistent results remain common.

14.5.1 Considerations for Different Stakeholders

For technologists and architects, the evolution toward AI integration introduces new architectural choices. Some organizations pursue modular designs that allow AI services to be added incrementally. Semantic interoperability helps components share context. RAG can ground AI outputs in organizational data. Systems benefit from designs that accommodate model updates and shifting requirements, though this flexibility introduces additional complexity.

For business leaders, AI adoption extends beyond technology decisions. Organizations report better outcomes when training and change management efforts accompany technical deployment. Success metrics increasingly include employee satisfaction, decision quality, and process improvement—not just efficiency. Governance structures that incorporate diverse perspectives help address ethical, social, and organizational considerations alongside business objectives.

For IT professionals, supporting AI systems requires expanding traditional capabilities. Practical skills now include prompt engineering, model evaluation, and continuous monitoring. IT teams often serve as bridges between technical capabilities and business needs, promoting safe experimentation rather than restricting access.

For knowledge workers and citizen developers, AI tools offer opportunities to reduce routine tasks. Working effectively with AI—understanding its limitations, validating outputs, and recognizing where human judgment remains essential—has become a valuable skill. Tools such as Power Platform help organizations improve processes without formal development projects, but success depends on understanding the platform's capabilities and constraints.

14.5.2 The Path Forward

Alan Turing's observation in "Computing Machinery and Intelligence" (1950)—"We can only see a short distance ahead, but we can see plenty there that needs to be done"—remains relevant to AI adoption. The staged adoption patterns explored earlier in this chapter offer a proven path, but they are starting points rather than formulas. Each organization's trajectory depends on its data maturity, architectural readiness, regulatory context, and cultural appetite for change.

What distinguishes durable implementations from stalled pilots is less the technology chosen than the organizational scaffolding built around it. Data quality, governance, and change management are not one-time prerequisites to check off before deployment. Rather, they are ongoing disciplines that mature alongside the systems they support. Organizations that treat them as iterative rather than sequential tend to sustain momentum beyond initial wins.

14.5.3 Intelligence as the Quiet Force

A notable pattern positions intelligence as embedded infrastructure rather than a standalone feature. AI capabilities are increasingly integrated into existing workflows rather than requiring separate interfaces. A financial analyst may encounter draft reports with preliminary analysis. A lawyer may receive summarized precedents. A field technician may access repair procedures through augmented reality. The technology becomes less visible even as its benefits accumulate.

This integration shifts the focus of work from mechanical tasks to problem-solving. Time once spent on transcription, formatting, and searching becomes available for analysis and decision-making. Machines handle information retrieval while humans focus on interpretation and relationships. The nature of work evolves, though the pace and extent vary by role and industry.

The broader vision extends beyond individual productivity. Intelligence becomes an understated presence throughout organizational operations—available when needed, unobtrusive when not, informing rather than replacing human judgment. This represents a shift from AI as a distinct technology to intelligence as an embedded capability.

14.5.4 Organizational Choices and Outcomes

Organizations pursue AI adoption through varied strategies, and outcomes depend more on implementation quality than on timing alone. Those that invest in governance and human-centered design alongside technology often report more durable results than those that optimize for speed alone. Waiting for complete certainty may result in missed opportunities, whereas rushing ahead without a foundation introduces avoidable risks.

The distinguishing factor is rarely the sophistication of the AI itself. It is whether the organization treats intelligence as a capability woven into how people work or as a system imposed on top of existing processes. The former reshapes habits gradually; the latter generates resistance. Current deployments bear this out: reduced routine work, faster information retrieval, and improved pattern recognition emerge where AI fits naturally into existing workflows, not where it demands new ones.

Challenges persist around data preparation, system integration, change management, and governance. Organizations will follow different paths based on their culture, capabilities, and constraints. But across the implementations examined throughout this book—from conversational AI at FIS to contract review at Microsoft, from KPMG's TaxBot to Deloitte's cautionary episode in Australia—a common thread holds. The organizations that achieve lasting value are those that develop their people and their technology in tandem, treating each deployment as a step in a longer evolution rather than a destination.

The work of building intelligent enterprises continues. It is shaped not by any single platform or model but by the practical choices organizations make about where intelligence belongs, who it serves, and how it earns trust. Those choices, more than any architectural pattern or vendor roadmap, will determine what the intelligent enterprise becomes.

14.6 Summary

This concludes the journey through Microsoft's cloud and AI ecosystem that began in Chapter 1. From the declarative architecture of INTELLIFM to the agentic systems emerging on the Azure platform today, the principles that make software reliable, useful, and, above all, trustworthy have remained consistent through decades of change. The Glossary and Appendixes that follow provide reference material for further exploration of the concepts, technologies, and frameworks discussed throughout this book.

Appendixes

1. Appendix 1: Historical Computer Storage Formats

Chapter 1 includes an overview of punch cards and vacuum tubes—foundational technologies of the first age of computing, where punch cards served as storage and input media, and vacuum tubes functioned primarily as the logic and computation components that powered early electronic computers. Several other important, now obsolete (or largely obsolete) storage media followed, as outlined in this appendix.

1.1. Magnetic Storage

Magnetic drums, developed by Austrian inventor Gustav Tauschek, signaled the beginning of magnetic storage. These drums laid the foundation for magnetic disk storage, with dedicated read/write heads that improved data transfer rates and addressed the limitations caused by insufficient RAM in early computing systems.

Once a pioneering data storage technology, magnetic tape played a foundational role in the development of computing environments. Although initially designed for analog data storage, magnetic tapes quickly became integral to early mainframe systems. Magnetic tape offers vast storage capacity and cost-efficiency, making it an ideal solution for "cold" storage—data accessed infrequently, but preserved securely over time. Tape vaults, where valuable data is backed up and stored securely, protect against data loss from natural disasters or other damaging events.

Magnetic hard disk drives (HDDs), for example, meet different data storage needs than magnetic tapes do. Magnetic tapes excel in high-capacity, low-cost archival storage, while HDDs provide fast read/write speeds, making them suitable for active data storage. Together, magnetic tapes and HDDs form a comprehensive data management strategy, blending the speed and accessibility of disks with the cost-effectiveness of long-term tape storage.

K. C. Mukherjee, *The Microsoft AI Insider's Playbook*, https://doi.org/10.1007/979-8-8688-2730-3

While slower to access than other storage technologies, magnetic tape remains an economical solution for large-scale data management. The evolution of magnetic tape capacity reflects both technological progress and a fundamental shift in form factor. Early tape reels held approximately 2.3 megabytes in 1952. The introduction of tape cartridges in the 1980s—beginning with formats such as the IBM 3480—replaced open reels with enclosed, automated cartridges, improving handling, reliability, and capacity. By 2010, a single cartridge could hold approximately 4 terabytes of data. By 2023, 152.9 exabytes of compressed tape storage capacity had been shipped globally.[1]

1.2. Main Memory Technologies

The trajectory of main memory reflects substantial architectural advancements across successive eras. RAM development began with the Williams–Kilburn tube, created by Frederick C. Williams and Tom Kilburn in 1948. This cathode-ray tube enabled data to be read and written in any sequence, introducing the concept of volatile memory, where data persists only as long as its storage device is powered.

In the 1940s, magnetic-core memory emerged and dominated RAM from the mid-1950s to the mid-1970s, marking a leap in performance. The Massachusetts Institute of Technology pioneered this technology with the Whirlwind computer in 1953.

Andrew Bobeck at Bell Labs developed twistor magnetic memory in 1957. It reduced weight and power consumption, making it suitable for mass production. Bobeck also developed bubble memory, a compact storage technology that efficiently represented binary data, highlighting the potential for further miniaturization in memory storage.

The evolution of main memory, from the Williams–Kilburn tube to bubble memory, reflects the relentless innovation in memory technology that paved the way for high-capacity storage solutions.

[1] LTO Program Technology Provider Companies (Hewlett Packard Enterprise, IBM, and Quantum Corporation), "LTO Tape Capacity Shipments Achieve Significant Growth Amid Explosive Data Generation," Annual LTO Program Media Shipment Report, May 21, 2024, `https://www.lto.org/2024/05/lto-tape-capacity-shipments-achieve-significant-growth-amid-explosive-data-generation/`.

1.3. Optical Discs

The creation of optical discs in the 1960s also addressed the need for reliable, high-capacity storage. Inventor James T. Russell pioneered optical storage technology, which was later commercialized by Sony and Philips, resulting in the development of the compact disc, digital versatile disc, and Blu-ray.

In optical storage, laser beams are used to etch and read binary data. Initially, it only allowed read-only access, but it evolved in the 1990s with the introduction of rewritable formats. Although slower than magnetic storage, optical discs are durable and offer substantial storage capacity, making them ideal for storing multimedia content.

The distinction between "disk" (magnetic) and "disc" (optical) reflects the differing storage technologies used. Optical discs became the preferred solution for multimedia storage, and their development contributed to the data-sharing capabilities that supported AI research. They facilitated collaboration and innovation in AI by making it easier for institutions to share datasets.

Optical disc technology continues to influence modern storage solutions through its pioneering advances in standardized data formats and modular storage architecture—innovations that distinguished it from the fixed, sequential nature of earlier magnetic storage. Although the popularity of optical discs has waned with the rise of solid-state drives (SSDs) and cloud-based solutions, the foundational principles they introduced remain relevant.

SSDs, for instance, adopted the idea of organizing data into structured and standardized formats, while eliminating the mechanical components that limited the speed of optical drives. Instead, SSDs use fully electronic processes to achieve dramatically faster read/write performance. Similarly, cloud storage systems have inherited the distributed architecture and data management strategies that originated with optical media, scaling them to levels far beyond the limitations of physical storage.

This evolution underscores how foundational technologies like optical discs can pave the way for future innovations, even as newer systems render their original forms obsolete.

2. Appendix 2: Programming Languages Used with Mainframes

Programming languages are formal systems with syntactic and semantic rules that produce code directing a computer to perform a specific action. They translate human thought processes into algorithms that computers can execute, helping developers create software that performs specific tasks and powers applications that users interact with.

The programming languages used in mainframe environments are diverse, including COBOL, PL/I, C, C++, Java, Python, R, Assembler, SQL, Restructured Extended Executor, Job Control Language, and Command List. Each language has unique features and functionalities that developers use to deploy robust, scalable applications. Here, I provide an in-depth examination of key programming languages that have deeply shaped mainframe application development.

2.1. COBOL

Introduced in 1959, COBOL has long been a mainstay of mainframe computing. It is known for its human-readable syntax and powerful data processing capabilities. Its self-documenting nature—the meaning of its rules and variables is intended to be self-evident—makes COBOL highly understandable, and its detailed error messages aid efficient debugging.

Critics often point to COBOL's verbosity and reliance on outdated constructs, such as the "goto" statement, yet it remains essential to modern mainframe computing. According to IBM, COBOL remains deeply embedded in global financial infrastructure, supporting approximately 95% of automated teller machine transactions and 80% of in-person credit card transactions. It powers systems that generate more than $3 billion in daily commerce. The language serves as the foundation for more than 40% of all online banking systems worldwide.[2]

[2] IBM, "What Is COBOL?" IBM Think, November 17, 2025, `https://www.ibm.com/think/topics/cobol`.

While COBOL was initially procedural (that is, you programmed a series of steps for the computer to execute in a logical order), modern versions have incorporated object-oriented programming features such as classes, inheritance, and polymorphism, thereby increasing compatibility with current systems, including web applications.

Through APIs and service calls, COBOL can now integrate with AI models, giving applications access to NLP, predictive analytics, and ML. For example, COBOL-based financial systems can use AI to analyze transaction patterns and detect fraud in real time. Similarly, legacy COBOL applications in health care can integrate with AI to predict patient outcomes and optimize treatment plans. By interfacing with AI frameworks, COBOL programs remain relevant and practical.

2.2. C and C++

Developed at Bell Labs in the early 1970s, the C programming language evolved from its predecessor, the B language, which was initially used to create utilities for the Unix operating system. Although C was not native to mainframes, IBM and other vendors later introduced C compilers for mainframe environments, giving organizations the ability to write portable, systems-level code that could run across both mainframe and distributed platforms. Over time, C became a foundational language for systems development, underpinning the kernels—the core code that directs a computer's hardware to process and respond to inputs—of operating systems such as Windows and Linux. Its influence extends to languages such as C++, Objective-C, and C#, each tailored for specialized tasks but sharing the structure and efficiency of C.

The C family is prized for performance and control. C and C++ allow developers granular control over memory and direct access to hardware interfaces. This feature is advantageous when manipulating large datasets and executing parallel processing tasks. This makes C languages ideal for projects requiring optimization and resource management, which is why ML and other AI frameworks, such as TensorFlow and PyTorch, rely on C and C++ for their core components and performance-critical operations. The mature ecosystems of these languages include libraries and tools for numerical computation, which form the backbone of AI development.

Moreover, the interoperability between C/C++ and higher-level languages such as Python (which are better suited to developing software, websites, data management tools, and similar applications) allows a blend of high-performance back-end operations with user-friendly front-end interfaces. This combination provides developers with the performance benefits of C/C++ and the rapid development capabilities of Python, resulting in robust AI frameworks deployable across various platforms.

2.3. Java

Java emerged in the mid-1990s. It introduced platform agnosticism through bytecode compilation and the Java Runtime Environment. Java's flexibility allows applications to run on a wide range of devices, from mainframes to PCs and smartphones.

The Java ecosystem, enriched with frameworks and libraries like Deeplearning4j, H2O.ai, Apache Spark, and Waikato Environment for Knowledge Analysis, supports AI development on mainframes by providing ML, data processing, and analytics tools. These resources empower Java-based applications to excel in predictive analytics, NLP, fraud detection, and customer insights by drawing on mainframe processing power and reliability. Java improves business operations through historical data analysis, language processing for customer interactions, real-time fraud detection, and personalized marketing.

Java continues to expand its capabilities through regular updates. While these were irregularly spaced for its first two decades, Java has followed a six-month release cadence since September 2017, though the specific timing of individual releases may vary.

2.4. Python and R

Python and R are two open source programming languages that have become among the most widely used languages for AI today. Python's rich ecosystem, including libraries such as TensorFlow, PyTorch, and scikit-learn, facilitates rapid development and deployment of AI models. Mainframe applications, such as Anaconda and IBM Watson, use Python for data science and ML. R is widely used for its statistical computing and data visualization capabilities. RStudio, Caret, and Shiny are prevalent in mainframe environments for developing data science and AI applications.

3. Appendix 3: Key Moments in the History of Windows

The release of Windows 3.0 in May 1990 was a pivotal moment for both Microsoft and the broader computing world.[3] It introduced innovations and enhancements that materially bolstered functionality while democratizing its utility for a broader audience. This version played a key role in establishing Microsoft's dominance in the graphical operating system market and set a new benchmark for user expectations. As a software architect who contributed to its development, I also regard it as a personal milestone.

The Windows 3.0 GUI featured a vibrant and user-friendly design. This made it easier to navigate the operating system and was more visually appealing. Additionally, Windows 3.0 introduced the Program Manager, File Manager, and Print Manager, offering users a more organized and efficient way to manage applications, files, and printing tasks. These features made personal computing more accessible and manageable for the average user.

Windows 3.0 also marked a pivotal moment in terms of performance and capability. Its memory management techniques optimized system resource usage, resulting in smoother operation and more sophisticated applications. Furthermore, Windows 3.0 introduced cooperative multitasking, which allowed users to run multiple applications simultaneously. These innovations substantially boosted productivity and improved user experience, establishing a new benchmark for personal computing.

Windows 3.0 also supported 16-color Video Graphics Array graphics, opening new possibilities for both application developers and users. This led to richer visual content and more sophisticated graphical applications. The success of Windows 3.0 was further bolstered by its compatibility with a wide range of programs. From productivity tools and business applications to games and educational software, a diverse array of applications became available for Windows 3.0—most notably, the Microsoft Office suite—facilitating its adoption among both home and business users.

The launch of Windows 3.0 was met with critical acclaim and commercial success. It sold millions of copies and firmly established Windows as the leading graphical operating system. Its success demonstrated the market's readiness for a more powerful

[3] Microsoft, "History of Windows," Microsoft Learn, `https://learn.microsoft.com/en-us/archive/blogs/uktechnet/history-of-windows`.

and user-friendly computing experience, laying the groundwork for the future development of the Windows operating system.

As Microsoft continued to innovate Windows, the principles of user-centric design, performance improvements, and extensive application compatibility introduced in Windows 3.0 remained at the heart of its development philosophy. The legacy of Windows 3.0 is evident in subsequent Windows versions, each building upon its achievements to deliver increasingly sophisticated and powerful computing experiences to users worldwide.

3.1. Windows 95: The Game-Changing Operating System

Released in the summer of 1995, Windows 95 was both an evolutionary step in the Windows operating system lineage and a major influence on the broader computing landscape. Building on the successes and innovations of Windows 3.0, Windows 95 introduced new features and capabilities that improved the user experience and system functionality. This iteration marked the transition of Windows from an emerging operating system to a dominant force in the computing world, laying the groundwork for its enduring success.

Perhaps the most iconic feature introduced in Windows 95 was the Start menu, a centralized hub for accessing programs, files, and settings, and it has since become synonymous with the Windows experience. Complementing the Start menu, the Taskbar set new standards for how users interacted with open windows and applications, offering an efficient way to switch between tasks and monitor active processes.

Windows 95 also introduced Plug and Play technology, simplifying the installation and configuration of hardware devices. Users could expand their system's capabilities easily without the manual configuration hassles common in earlier computing environments.

Windows 95 represented a pivotal transition toward a 32-bit architecture, introducing advanced memory management and optimized system performance. While retaining some 16-bit components for backward compatibility, it supported more sophisticated applications and processes through its 32-bit features. Using this hybrid approach, Windows 95 bridged the gap between older 16-bit applications and the new 32-bit software ecosystem, facilitating a gradual transition in the computing world.

The ability to use long file names—up to 255 characters—was introduced, improving file management and navigation. Windows 95 also offered customizable desktop themes, allowing users to personalize the appearance of their interface.

Windows 95 included Internet Explorer as part of the Windows 95 Plus! Pack, marking Microsoft's initial steps toward acknowledging the growing importance of the internet. In addition, it introduced two notable improvements: enhanced multimedia capabilities for playing music and videos, and integrated dial-up networking, which simplified internet access. These features made personal computers more useful for home entertainment and online connectivity.

3.2. Evolution from Windows 98 to Windows 2000

Windows 98, released in 1998, expanded on Windows 95 by adding Windows Media Player and support for Universal Serial Bus (USB) and the Advanced Configuration and Power Interface (ACPI), reflecting the growing demand for digital media. This version contributed to the broader adoption of digital media playback, recording, and sharing.

Windows NT followed a parallel development track, focused on enterprise and professional users. Initially released as Windows NT 3.1 in 1993, it introduced a robust and secure operating system architecture. Notably, NT 4.0 merged the user-friendly Windows 95 interface with the robustness of NT.

Windows 2000, based on the NT codebase, targeted enterprise and professional users, providing plug-and-play compatibility, improved mobile support, and enhanced security. Windows Millennium Edition, also released in 2000, was aimed at home users and introduced System Restore—allowing users to roll back their system to a previous state—along with improved multimedia and home networking features.

3.3. Ambitious Releases: Windows XP to Windows 11

A series of ambitious releases followed. Windows XP (2001) combined the stability of NT with the accessibility of Windows 9x, winning widespread acclaim. Windows Vista (2007) introduced enhanced visual and security features, although it faced challenges due to its high system requirements.

Windows 7 (2009) addressed the issues in Vista, earning praise for performance and stability. Windows 8 (2012) introduced a touch-optimized Metro user interface, with user feedback leading to the development of Windows 8.1 (2013) and later Windows 10 (2015), which focused on integration and cloud connectivity.

Windows Server releases paralleled these developments, with Server 2012 and subsequent versions focusing on virtualization, cloud computing, and enhanced security.

In 2021, Microsoft introduced Windows 11, featuring a redesigned user interface and centralized taskbar settings. Each major release—from Windows XP to Windows 11—reflects the company's adaptability to technological change and evolving user expectations.

In recent years, Windows has become deeply integrated with cloud computing and AI technologies. Windows 11 now serves as a foundation for AI-powered computing, featuring Copilot+ PCs equipped with NPUs that perform over 40 trillion operations per second for tasks such as natural language translation.

The platform supports hybrid AI loops that distribute processing between local devices and Azure cloud services, using tools such as ONNX Runtime to dynamically allocate resources. This integration extends to Microsoft Copilot, which employs LLMs to deliver intelligent assistance across the Microsoft Cloud, while maintaining enterprise-grade data security and privacy. Together, these advancements have transformed Windows from a standalone operating system into a sophisticated platform that bridges on-device intelligence and cloud-based AI, paving the way for workflows and productivity improvements once unimaginable.

4. Appendix 4: Architecture of the Windows Operating System

This appendix supplements Section 1.6.1, which describes the architecture of the Microsoft Windows operating system and introduces Figure 1-4. The diagram illustrates the interaction between user-mode and kernel-mode components. A central vertical spine runs from Windows OS at the top to Hardware at the bottom, with user-mode subsystems branching to the left and kernel-mode subsystems branching to the right.

On the left side of the diagram, the user-mode subsystems include the Win32 subsystem, WSL, the Windows API subsystem, and the graphics subsystem. The Win32 subsystem is implemented through the Client/Server Runtime Subsystem (CSRSS). It remains the foundation for desktop applications built on frameworks such as WPF and WinForms. WSL allows native Linux applications to interface with the Windows kernel. The Windows API subsystem provides developers with wrappers around kernel system services, exposing them through a stable user-mode interface so that applications can request operating system functionality without directly invoking kernel routines. The graphics subsystem is positioned here to represent application-level rendering before data passes toward the hardware.

On the right side of the diagram, the kernel-mode subsystems include the NT Kernel, the Networking subsystem, the File System subsystem, and the Memory Management subsystem. These components handle low-level tasks such as process scheduling and memory allocation. Notably, the diagram shows the File System and Memory Management subsystems communicating directly with the HAL via vertical arrows, underscoring their critical role in managing physical resources.

A prominent red shaded block at the center of the architecture represents the integrated security model, which bridges the boundary between modes. Within this block, the Security Reference Monitor (SRM) operates in kernel mode to enforce access control decisions for every protected resource. Conversely, the Local Security Authority Subsystem Service (LSASS) operates in user mode to manage security policy and authentication. This design ensures that user-level policy management is backed by kernel-level enforcement.

At the base of the diagram, the HAL sits between the subsystems and the physical hardware. The HAL provides a uniform interface that shields the kernel from hardware-specific details, enabling Windows portability across various processor and chipset combinations.

Overall, the diagram illustrates the layered and modular architecture of the Windows operating system. The user-mode/kernel-mode boundary protects the system core, the HAL abstracts hardware complexity, and the integrated security block enforces a consistent protection model across the entire environment.

5. Appendix 5: Sophisticated Document Management Systems

Figure A5-1 outlines the INTELLIFM document capture and processing workflow in business environments across five interconnected stages: Capture, Sorting & Extraction, Process Integration, Application Integration, and Capture Throughout.

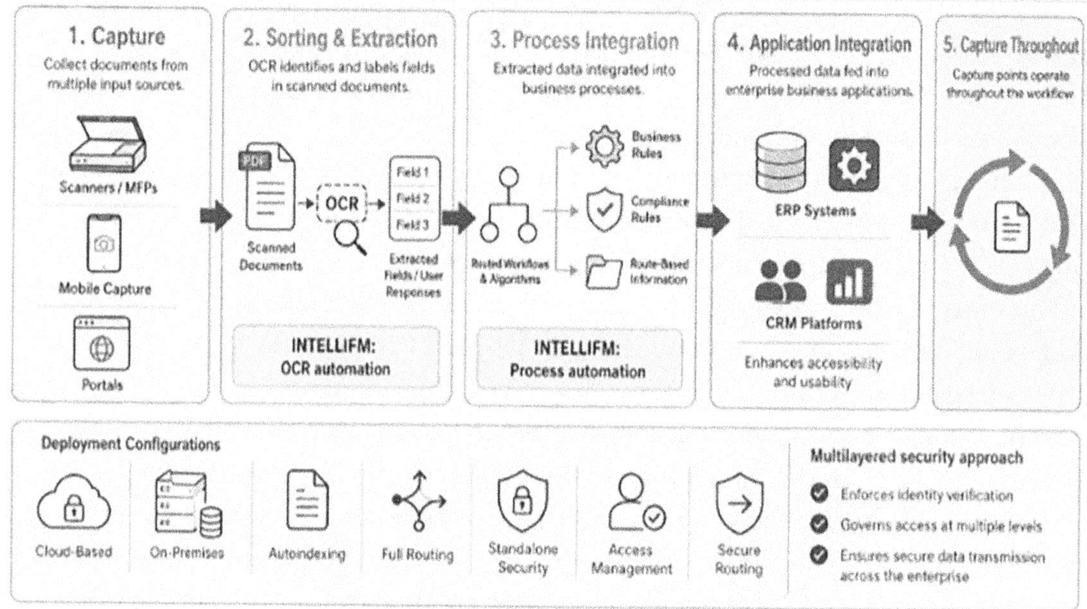

Figure A5-1. *The INTELLIFM document capture and processing workflow. Documents flow through five stages: Capture (via scanners/MFPs, mobile, and portals); Sorting & Extraction (INTELLIFM OCR automation identifies and labels data fields); Process Integration (INTELLIFM process automation applies business and compliance rules and routes workflows); Application Integration (integration with ERP and CRM platforms); and Capture Throughout (continuous operation across the workflow). The Deployment Configurations section illustrates support for cloud-based and on-premises environments, featuring autoindexing, full routing, and security controls. A multilayered security approach ensures identity verification, access management, and secure data transmission. (Image by author)*

In the initial Capture stage, documents are collected from multiple input sources, including scanners and multifunction printers (MFPs), mobile capture devices, and web portals. This flexibility allows organizations to ingest documents from wherever they originate, whether at a centralized scanning station, in the field, or through self-service portals.

In the Sorting & Extraction stage, INTELLIFM's OCR automation identifies and labels critical data fields within scanned documents. Where information cannot be extracted automatically, INTELLIFM prompts users via Q&A sessions to populate the remaining fields, ensuring complete and accurate data capture by minimizing traditional manual data entry and resolving exceptions in real time.

In the Process Integration stage, INTELLIFM's process automation routes the extracted data through rule-based workflows and decision-making algorithms. Business rules and compliance rules are applied automatically, initiating appropriate actions and enforcing regulatory and organizational standards across complex, diverse filing environments.

In the Application Integration stage, the processed data feeds enterprise applications, enhancing accessibility and usability across the organization. In a compliance filing context, these applications include ERP systems that manage regulatory deadlines and cost tracking, as well as CRM platforms that manage client matters and case tracking.

The final stage, Capture Throughout, indicates that document capture is an ongoing capability embedded at multiple points in the workflow—including mid-process documents such as supporting evidence or correspondence, as well as output documents generated at the end of the process—not solely at the initial intake stage.

Figure A5-1 highlights the Deployment Configurations band, which illustrates that INTELLIFM supports both cloud-based and on-premises data centers, with features including autoindexing, full routing, standalone security, access management, and secure routing. Together, these controls reflect a multilayered security approach that enforces identity verification, governs access at multiple levels, and ensures secure data transmission across the enterprise.

INTELLIFM's automation has its greatest impact in the Sorting & Extraction and Process Integration stages. In Sorting & Extraction, OCR technology processes scanned documents to identify and label fields, with any remaining gaps or exceptions populated from user responses gathered during Q&A sessions. This drastically reduces manual data entry and enforces consistency across multijurisdictional filing requirements. In Process Integration, INTELLIFM drives this data directly into business processes through rule-based workflows and decision-making algorithms that route information, initiate actions, and enforce compliance—converting what was once a labor-intensive, error-prone process into an efficient, governed, repeatable, and auditable workflow.

This automation reduces manual effort, accelerates response times, and delivers consistency and auditability across the workflows that process documents and manage data.

6. Appendix 6: INTELLIFM—AI Meets COM Architecture

This appendix supplements Section 5.2.2, which describes the COM-based architecture of INTELLIFM and introduces Figure 5-1. The original architecture of the expert system is organized into four modules: User Interface, Data Management, AI and Processing, and Document Management. Each module is implemented by one or more components. Figure 5-1 shows the primary component for each module.

The User Interface module handles user interactions to deliver an efficient experience. The *UIG component* dynamically generates user interfaces tailored to user needs during Q&A sessions for filings. It automatically enables relevant questions, disables irrelevant ones, and prepopulates fields with known information, improving efficiency and reducing input errors.

The Data Management module manages data retrieval and operations. The *SQL component* handles bidirectional interactions with the database for reference data queries and updates. It interfaces with two databases:

- The *Reference Data* database stores essential information.
- The *Reports and Reminders* database centralizes report storage and tracks tasks and deadlines.

This dual-database structure supports timely notifications and efficient workflow management, improving productivity, compliance, and accountability.

The AI and Processing module serves as the system's cognitive hub, employing the *EPS component* to manage complex logical operations. Using its in-memory knowledge base, EPS interprets business rules and applies them in real time to reliably and consistently automate workflows. Functioning as the system's formal memory, the knowledge base houses the structured facts and procedures required to validate every decision within an explainable, traceable framework. The EPS component communicates with the UIG to generate appropriate user interface controls, creating an adaptive system that handles complex filing processes with sophisticated rule interpretation.

The Document Management module oversees document storage and archiving. The *P&P component* serves two main functions:

- Managing the storage of completed filings in the saved-filings database
- Generating printed forms by combining filing data with form templates, ensuring that the output meets regulatory standards

As AI technology has advanced, enterprise systems built using the INTELLIFM blueprint have evolved beyond their Prolog-based origins. In some implementations, the dynamic logic was reimplemented using modern scripting and rule-based technologies. These hybrid architectures interface with ML systems to deliver holistic solutions, adding capabilities such as document classification, intelligent prefilling, and pattern detection. Throughout this evolution, the core principle has remained unchanged: ML models can propose, but rules decide. This principle continues to underpin responsible AI design, from enterprise guardrails to modern agentic systems where models reason but rules govern.

7. Appendix 7: Prompt Engineering in Practice

Prompt engineering can be understood as a control layer that shapes model behavior at runtime. The example in Listing A7-1 demonstrates how a developer might structure prompts when integrating an LLM into a customer service chatbot.

Listing A7-1. A Python example showing the message list format used in many modern chat-oriented LLM APIs, where a system or developer prompt defines the agent's role and behavioral guidelines and a user prompt represents a customer inquiry.

```
messages = [
    {"role": "system", "content": "You are a helpful customer service agent
    for an e-commerce company. Respond to customer inquiries politely and
    accurately. If you do not know the answer, kindly ask the customer to
    contact our Support team."},
    {"role": "user", "content": "What is the status of my order #12345?"}
]

response = generate_ai_response(messages)
```

In this pattern, the *system* (or *developer*) *prompt* provides the primary behavioral instruction for the model within a given request. It defines the agent's role, tone, and operational constraints. While LLMs may occasionally deviate from these instructions, a well-constructed system or developer prompt governs model behavior and reduces the likelihood of unpredictable outputs.

Prompt engineering works alongside several adjacent implementation mechanisms that address its inherent limitations. Although LLMs are stateless between calls, applications maintain conversational continuity through several mechanisms. These include passing the conversation history as part of the message list, maintaining session memory across interactions, retrieving relevant context via retrieval systems such as vector or hybrid search, and tracking tool state across multistep workflows.

The *user prompt* represents the task-specific input—in this case, a customer requesting the status of order *#12345*. The model does not inherently know the actual status of order #12345. Instead, it generates a response from the system-level instructions, the user's query, and any additional context or tool results the application provides.

The *generate_ai_response()* function encapsulates the orchestration logic. It packages the prompts, sends them to the model endpoint, and returns the generated output. In production systems, this function typically includes additional layers such as

- **Input validation** (for example, checking for malformed order numbers)
- **Guardrails** (for example, restricting the model from fabricating order details)
- **Postprocessing** (for example, formatting the response or routing unresolved queries to human agents)
- **Logging and telemetry** for monitoring model behavior over time

This example illustrates the declarative nature of prompt engineering: developers specify *what* the model needs to do, rather than *how* it should do it. Tool-calling capabilities extend this further; developers can instruct the model to invoke specific tools or functions for defined tasks, such as querying an order management system or escalating unresolved issues to a human agent. The orchestration layer invokes approved tools within those boundaries, while the model generates responses shaped by the defined role and constraints. When implemented carefully, this approach can improve consistency and control, making LLM-based systems more suitable for customer-facing applications.

8. Appendix 8: Overview of Software Development Roles

Software development involves a variety of roles, each bringing unique skills and perspectives to the process. These roles often overlap, and individuals may wear multiple hats, especially in smaller teams or startup environments. Some roles are directly involved in writing and designing software, while others contribute through strategy, coordination, and domain expertise. The interplay between these roles creates a symphony of expertise, driving innovation and the delivery of high-quality software solutions.

8.1. Roles in Software Product Delivery

The roles described below span product, design, engineering, operations, and domain expertise. Some are core technical roles directly involved in designing and building software, while others guide strategy, requirements, governance, delivery, and adoption. In practice, responsibilities often overlap, and one individual may perform multiple roles depending on the size and structure of the organization. Although some roles may appear similar, they differ in emphasis. Software architects focus on the internal structure of software systems, whereas solution architects align end-to-end technical solutions with broader business and integration needs. Platform engineers build internal platforms and tooling for development teams. DevOps engineers emphasize automation across delivery and operations, and site reliability engineers focus on reliability, availability, and operational resilience through software engineering practices.

(1) Product Managers

Primary Responsibilities:

- Define product vision, strategy, and roadmap.
- Conduct market research and competitive analysis.
- Bridge business stakeholders and development teams.
- Shape product requirements and guide prioritization.
- Measure product performance against business goals.

Key Skills Required:

- Strategic thinking and market awareness
- Communication and stakeholder management
- Analytical reasoning and data-driven decision-making
- Cross-functional collaboration
- Customer empathy and user advocacy

AI/Modern Tech Impact:

- Shape AI-powered product features and specifications.
- Collaborate with AI engineers, data scientists, and platform teams on model-driven capabilities.
- Evaluate emerging technologies for product opportunities.
- Navigate ethical considerations in AI product decisions.

(2) **Product Owners** (primarily in scrum-based environments)

Primary Responsibilities:

- Manage and refine the product backlog.
- Translate product strategy into sprint-ready work items.
- Clarify requirements and acceptance criteria for the development team.
- Participate in sprint planning, review, and related agile ceremonies.
- Accept or reject completed work based on defined acceptance criteria.

Key Skills Required:

- Backlog refinement and prioritization
- Communication and requirement clarification
- Analytical reasoning
- Cross-functional collaboration

AI/Modern Tech Impact:

- Manage AI-powered features in the product backlog.
- Oversee ML integrations and define acceptance criteria for model outputs.
- Define AI specifications in collaboration with data scientists and engineers.

(3) **Software Engineers**

Primary Responsibilities:

- Write, test, and maintain code.
- Translate specifications into functioning software.
- Debug and optimize applications.
- Collaborate across development teams.

Key Skills Required:

- Programming languages and algorithms
- Problem-solving and analytical thinking
- Communication and teamwork
- Continuous learning mindset

AI/Modern Tech Impact:

- Work with cloud-native technologies.
- Implement microservices architectures.
- Integrate AI/ML capabilities.

(4) **Software Architects**

Primary Responsibilities:

- Define the internal software system structure.
- Make technical direction decisions.
- Mentor development teams.
- Uphold architectural compliance.

Key Skills Required:

- Deep technical knowledge
- System design and integration skills
- Mentoring and leadership abilities
- Risk assessment capabilities

AI/Modern Tech Impact:

- Design systems that integrate AI/ML components.
- Establish architectural patterns for model serving and inference.
- Deliver scalability and maintainability of AI-enabled systems.

(5) **User Experience Designers**

Primary Responsibilities:

- Conduct user research and testing.
- Create user personas and journey maps.
- Design wireframes and prototypes.
- Uphold accessibility and inclusivity.

Key Skills Required:

- Empathy and user advocacy
- Research and analytical skills
- Communication and collaboration
- Creativity and problem-solving

AI/Modern Tech Impact:

- Use real-time data for personalized interfaces.
- Collaborate with data scientists on AI-powered features.
- Design transparent and ethical AI experiences.

(6) **User Interface Designers**

Primary Responsibilities:

- Create visual interface elements.
- Design color schemes and typography.
- Maintain visual consistency across platforms.
- Collaborate with developers on implementation.

Key Skills Required:

- Visual design and aesthetics
- Typography and color theory
- Responsive design skills
- Tool proficiency (Adobe, Figma)

AI/Modern Tech Impact:

- Use AI-powered design tools to accelerate prototyping.
- Adapt visual systems for AI-generated and dynamic content.
- Make interfaces consistent across multiplatform deployments.

(7) **Solution Architects**

Primary Responsibilities:

- Design structural foundations of complex systems.
- Bridge technical teams and business stakeholders.
- Select technologies and integration patterns.
- Deliver scalability and performance.

Key Skills Required:

- Strategic thinking and communication
- Technical expertise across multiple domains
- Risk management and analysis
- Leadership and collaboration

AI/Modern Tech Impact:

- Design enterprise architectures that incorporate AI and ML services.
- Define integration patterns for cloud-based AI platforms.
- Evaluate and select AI technologies aligned with business requirements.

(8) **Domain Experts and Subject Matter Experts**

Primary Responsibilities:

- Provide industry-specific knowledge.
- Define and validate requirements.
- Ensure regulatory compliance.
- Bridge business needs and technical implementation.

Key Skills Required:

- Deep domain knowledge
- Communication and translation skills
- Analytical thinking
- Ethical judgment and mentoring

AI/Modern Tech Impact:

- Stay current with rapidly changing AI technologies.
- Guide ethical AI decision-making in specific fields.
- Translate AI capabilities into domain-specific applications.

(9) **Business Analysts**

Primary Responsibilities:

- Gather and analyze business requirements.
- Manage stakeholder relationships.
- Evaluate solution viability.
- Support implementation and training.

Key Skills Required:

- Requirements analysis
- Stakeholder management
- Process modeling
- Data analysis and presentation

AI/Modern Tech Impact:

- Increasingly use data analytics tools and AI-driven insights for decision-making.
- Translate AI capabilities into business requirements.
- Evaluate the viability of AI-powered solutions.

(10) **Data Scientists**

Primary Responsibilities:

- Collect, clean, and analyze complex data.
- Build predictive models and algorithms.
- Create data visualizations and reports.
- Ensure ethical data use and compliance.

Key Skills Required:

- Statistics and ML
- Programming and data analysis
- Communication and storytelling
- Ethical judgment and collaboration

AI/Modern Tech Impact:

- Lead development of AI-powered features.
- Create personalization and recommendation engines.
- Address ethical AI considerations across the development life cycle.

(11) **ML Engineers**

Primary Responsibilities:

- Design, build, and deploy ML models and pipelines.
- Collaborate with data scientists to move models from experimentation to production.

- Optimize models for performance, scalability, and reliability.
- Maintain and monitor ML systems in production environments.

Key Skills Required:

- Programming and ML frameworks (Python, TensorFlow, PyTorch)
- Data engineering and feature engineering
- Cloud platforms and MLOps practices
- Problem-solving and cross-functional collaboration

AI/Modern Tech Impact:

- Build and manage MLOps pipelines for continuous model training and deployment.
- Implement model governance, versioning, and performance monitoring.
- Integrate large language models and foundation models into enterprise systems.

(12) **Data Engineers**

Primary Responsibilities:

- Design, build, and maintain data pipelines and infrastructure.
- Provide data quality, availability, and accessibility for downstream consumers.
- Integrate data from multiple sources into unified data platforms.
- Support ML and AI workloads with reliable, well-governed data.

Key Skills Required:

- Data pipeline and workflow orchestration tools
- SQL and programming languages such as Python and Scala

- Cloud data platforms and distributed computing
- Data modeling and governance practices

AI/Modern Tech Impact:

- Build and manage data platforms that support AI and ML workloads
- Implement real-time data streaming for AI-driven applications
- Safeguard data quality and lineage across both model training and inference

(13) **Security Engineers**

Primary Responsibilities:

- Design and implement security controls across systems and applications.
- Conduct threat modeling, vulnerability assessments, and penetration testing.
- Ensure compliance with security standards and regulatory requirements.
- Respond to security incidents and lead remediation efforts.

Key Skills Required:

- Security architecture and threat modeling
- Knowledge of regulatory frameworks such as GDPR, CCPA, and SOC 2
- Cloud security and IAM
- Problem-solving and cross-functional collaboration

AI/Modern Tech Impact:

- Secure AI/ML pipelines and model endpoints against adversarial attacks.
- Implement controls to prevent prompt injection and data poisoning.
- Ensure compliance with emerging AI governance and regulatory frameworks.

(14) **Platform Engineers**

Primary Responsibilities:

- Build and maintain internal developer platforms and tooling.
- Standardize development environments and deployment pipelines.
- Provide self-service infrastructure for development teams.
- Make platforms reliable, scalable, and secure.

Key Skills Required:

- Cloud infrastructure and Kubernetes
- Automation and infrastructure as code
- Developer experience and tooling
- Collaboration and communication across engineering teams

AI/Modern Tech Impact:

- Build platforms that support AI/ML workload deployment and scaling.
- Integrate AI-assisted developer tooling into internal platforms.
- Provide self-service access to AI infrastructure and model serving endpoints.

(15) **AI Engineers**

Primary Responsibilities:

- Design, build, and maintain AI-powered applications, workflows, and pipelines.
- Develop and refine prompts, retrieval strategies, and orchestration logic for LLM-based and other generative AI systems.
- Evaluate model outputs for accuracy, safety, and alignment with business requirements.
- Collaborate with product, data, and engineering teams to integrate AI capabilities into production systems.

Key Skills Required:

- Understanding of LLM behavior, limitations, and capabilities
- Programming and API integration skills
- Analytical reasoning and systematic experimentation
- Communication and cross-functional collaboration

AI/Modern Tech Impact:

- Design prompt frameworks and RAG pipelines.
- Implement guardrails, safety layers, and output validation for production AI systems.
- Stay current with rapidly evolving foundation models, tools, and AI engineering practices.

(16) **QA Analysts and Testers**

Primary Responsibilities:

- Develop test strategies and plans.
- Execute manual and automated testing.
- Document and track defects.
- Ensure quality standards compliance.

Key Skills Required:

- Attention to detail
- Analytical reasoning
- Communication and diplomacy
- Tool proficiency and adaptability

AI/Modern Tech Impact:

- Work with automated testing tools and AI-assisted test generation.
- Manage quality in CI/CD pipelines.
- Handle rapid release cycles in agile and DevOps environments.

(17) **DevOps Engineers**

Primary Responsibilities:

- Automate CI/CD pipelines.
- Manage IaC.
- Monitor applications and systems.
- Bridge development and operations teams.

Key Skills Required:

- Automation and scripting
- Cloud technologies
- Problem-solving and collaboration
- Security and compliance knowledge

AI/Modern Tech Impact:

- Implement containerization and serverless architectures.
- Manage multicloud environments.
- Integrate DevSecOps practices across the development life cycle.

(18) **Site Reliability Engineers**

Primary Responsibilities:

- Apply software engineering principles to infrastructure and operations.
- Monitor system reliability, availability, and performance.
- Manage incident response and postmortem analysis.
- Use automated testing at scale to prevent regressions across interdependent systems.

Key Skills Required:

- Systems engineering and distributed systems knowledge
- Programming and automation skills
- Incident management and problem-solving
- Communication and collaboration across development and operations teams

AI/Modern Tech Impact:

- Apply ML-based observability and anomaly detection tools.
- Manage reliability of AI/ML workloads in production.
- Implement AIOps practices to automate incident detection and response.

(19) **Database Administrators**

Primary Responsibilities:

- Design and maintain database systems.
- Implement data security and backup strategies.
- Optimize database performance.
- Plan for scalability and disaster recovery.

Key Skills Required:

- Database design and optimization
- Security and backup procedures
- Problem-solving and attention to detail
- Cloud and NoSQL technologies

AI/Modern Tech Impact:

- Increasingly work with cloud-based systems and NoSQL databases.
- Manage data pipelines supporting AI and ML workloads.
- Implement data quality and governance for model training and inference.

8.2. Additional Roles and Stakeholders

Supporting Roles

- **Project Managers**: Lead projects from inception to completion, managing timelines, budgets, resources, and stakeholder communication.
- **Network Engineers**: Design and maintain infrastructure for software reliability.
- **Sales and Marketing Professionals**: Analyze market trends and position products.
- **Finance Professionals**: Manage budgets, forecast costs, and allocate resources.
- **Stakeholders and End Users**: Provide feedback and participate in acceptance testing.

Role Specialization by Industry

- **Web Development**: Front-end and back-end developers with specialized positions.
- **Mobile Development**: Platform-specific expertise (iOS versus Android).

- **Enterprise Software**: Emphasis on integration specialists and business analysts.
- **Game Development**: Unique roles such as game designers and 3D artists.
- **Regulated Industries**: Stronger emphasis on compliance specialists and security experts.
- **Organization Scale**: Larger companies have more specialized roles, whereas startups require individuals who fill multiple roles.

8.3. Future Outlook

AI Integration:

- Many roles adapting to incorporate AI and ML capabilities where relevant
- Data scientists, ML engineers, and AI engineers playing increasingly prominent roles
- Growing focus on ethical AI, governance, and responsible innovation

DevOps Evolution:

- Continued blurring of development and operations boundaries
- Stronger emphasis on automation throughout the software life cycle
- Integration of security (DevSecOps)

Platform Evolution:

- Rise of low-code/no-code platforms creating new configuration-focused roles
- Continued emphasis on cloud-native development
- Growth in serverless and microservices architectures

Workforce Changes:

- Persistent trend toward remote work requiring new collaboration methods
- Cybersecurity becoming increasingly important across development and operations roles
- Continuous learning remaining important across nearly all positions

Ethical and Social Considerations:

- Growing importance of ethical considerations in software development
- Emphasis on responsible innovation and user privacy
- Need for roles focused on compliance and social impact

The roles involved in software product delivery form a complex ecosystem in which each role contributes distinct expertise through collaborative, multidisciplinary teamwork. Although these roles will continue to evolve with advances in platforms, cloud computing, AI, and software engineering practices, the central principle remains the same: successful systems are built through coordinated effort across product, design, engineering, operations, and domain knowledge. The pace of technological change makes adaptability and continuous learning increasingly important across the profession.

9. Appendix 9: Popular Design and Prototyping Tools

Blend for Visual Studio remains a useful tool within the Microsoft ecosystem for designing XAML-based user interfaces, especially when teams need visual support for animations, behaviors, and state-driven experiences. But the prototyping landscape is broader, encompassing many specialized tools for wireframing, interaction design, collaboration, and design-to-development handoff.

Among prototyping-first tools, UXPin emphasizes realistic, component-driven prototyping with logic, states, and code-backed components. Its Merge capability connects design work with production-ready React components, helping narrow the gap between design and development.

Sketch remains a Mac-native design and prototyping toolkit. Its prototyping features include links, hotspots, overlays, scroll areas, and preview support, making it well-suited for interactive user-flow exploration.

Mockplus supports rapid prototyping through drag-and-drop editing, interactive prototypes, and collaborative handoff workflows. Its cloud offering also supports broader team collaboration and design delivery.

Balsamiq remains especially useful in the early stages of design, where speed and low-fidelity thinking matter more than polished visuals. It is still centered on wireframing, but it now also supports interactive prototyping.

Figma is now an established platform for interactive prototyping, with support for flows, transitions, and presentation-based testing. It has also expanded into AI-assisted interactive demos through Figma Make.

Axure RP remains one of the strongest options for complex prototypes that require dynamic content, variables, conditional logic, and adaptive views. It is particularly useful when prototypes must simulate realistic workflows rather than only screen-to-screen navigation.

Origami Studio, created by Meta, is a free Mac-based tool for building interactive interfaces. Its Canvas and Patch Editor support detailed interaction design and component-based experimentation.

Proto.io is a browser-based prototyping platform with drag-and-drop editing, ready-made UI components, templates, and media support, including sound effects. It is designed to help teams create interactive web and mobile prototypes without code.

Marvel continues to offer wireframing, prototyping, and developer handoff features. Its handoff tooling supports CSS, Swift, Objective-C, and Android XML rather than the broader phrasing sometimes used in older summaries.

Some adjacent tools are worth mentioning separately because they extend beyond prototyping. Webflow is best described as a visual-first web development platform or website builder rather than a prototyping-first tool. It is valuable when teams want to move from visual design into production-oriented web experiences with a content management system and hosting support.

A few tools should now be framed more cautiously. Adobe XD remains available for existing customers, but Adobe says it is in maintenance mode and is no longer receiving ongoing feature development. "Framer X" is outdated terminology; the legacy desktop product formerly known as Framer X was deprecated and replaced by the current Framer product. InVision is now a historical reference rather than a current tool, as its design collaboration services shut down at the end of 2024.

The diversity of these tools reflects the varied needs of software development teams. The right choice often depends on project requirements, team expertise, and the fidelity needed at each stage of the design process. As the tooling landscape continues to evolve, AI-assisted workflows, component-driven design systems, and tighter design-to-development integration are becoming increasingly common. Staying current with available options remains an important part of delivering well-designed software.

10. Appendix 10: Popular AI Tools

Table A10-1 catalogs popular AI and automation tools across categories such as code generation, code review, testing, project management, documentation, and DevOps, with representative examples for each.

Table A10-1. *Representative AI-assisted and automation tools across nine categories of software development activities, reflecting the market landscape in early 2026.*

Category	Description	Examples
Code generation	AI tools that assist in writing and generating code based on requirements or specifications	• GitHub Copilot • Anthropic Claude Code • Google Gemini Code Assist • Amazon Q Developer • OpenAI Codex • Tabnine
Code review	Tools that analyze code for issues (including security vulnerabilities) and suggest improvements	• CodeClimate • CodeRabbit • PullRequest • Bito AI Code Review • DeepSource • GitHub Copilot • Qodo Merge • Snyk Code (DeepCode AI) • Amazon Q Developer

(*continued*)

Table A10-1. (*Continued*)

Category	Description	Examples
Testing	AI-powered solutions for test creation, execution, and maintenance	• Testim • ACCELQ Autopilot • Mabl • LambdaTest • Applitools • Test.ai • Tricentis Copilot
Project management	Tools that assist with planning, scheduling, and resource allocation in agile projects	• Forecast • Asana AI • Monday.ai • ClickUp Brain • Wrike Insights • Timely • Jira (sprint planning) • Azure DevOps • Project management chatbots
Documentation	AI systems that help create, maintain, and improve technical documentation	• GitBook AI • Writely • Notion AI • Docusaurus AI Assistant • Copy.ai
Communication	Tools facilitating team collaboration and information sharing	• Fireflies.ai • Slack AI • Microsoft Teams (with Copilot) • Zoom AI Companion • Otter.ai • Krisp AI • Loom

(*continued*)

Table A10-1. *(Continued)*

Category	Description	Examples
Data analysis and planning	Tools for analyzing data and providing insights for decision-making	• Tableau • Power BI • Jira Align • Aha! Roadmaps • Anaplan • Dataiku DSS
Development environments	AI-enhanced IDEs and coding workspaces	• VS Code (IDE) • GitHub Copilot Agent Mode (AI agent mode within VS Code) • Cursor • Warp • Windsurf (Cognition) • Amazon Q Developer
DevOps and CI/CD	Tools that assist with automating deployment pipelines and environment management, using AI assistance and rule-based automation	• GitHub Actions (agentic workflows) • CircleCI Insights dashboard • GitLab Auto DevOps • Jenkins (AI assistant plugins) • TeamCity AI Assistant • Harness AI DevOps Agent

The tools listed fall into two broad categories: standalone AI tools purpose-built for a specific function and AI features integrated into existing platforms. For example, GitHub Copilot is a standalone AI coding assistant, whereas Slack AI and Zoom AI Companion are AI capabilities integrated into existing collaboration platforms. Both categories are included here because practitioners encounter and evaluate them together in day-to-day development environments.

11. Appendix 11: Popular SaaS Products

This section examines influential SaaS products that exemplify the practical application of cloud computing and AI concepts discussed throughout this book. These platforms demonstrate how cloud infrastructure has fueled the delivery of sophisticated software capabilities through subscription-based models, transforming the way businesses operate and collaborate. Many of these solutions also showcase the integration of AI features—from automated workflows to intelligent analytics—illustrating the convergence of AI and cloud technologies in real-world applications.

By understanding these market-leading examples, readers can better appreciate how the theoretical principles explored in earlier chapters are applied in the tools and services that power modern digital business operations. The following overviews represent just a fraction of the many excellent SaaS offerings available in the market, each contributing uniquely to the diverse and innovative landscape of cloud-based solutions. Taken together, these examples span multiple phases of SaaS evolution and multiple forms of AI, from rule-based automation and predictive analytics to more recent generative and agentic features.

Under my leadership, Wolters Kluwer launched CTAdvantage.com, built on Microsoft technologies and incorporating AI for automated document management and compliance filing. It was an early enterprise SaaS platform that combined cloud delivery with AI-driven automation before such capabilities became common across the broader SaaS market.[4] At roughly the same time, Salesforce disrupted the market with its cloud-based CRM product in 1999. Its pay-per-user subscription model broke down traditional pricing barriers, bringing enterprise-grade CRM within reach of businesses of all sizes.

Salesforce's rapid growth to more than 150,000 customer companies worldwide reflected growing market confidence in cloud-based business software.[5] The company later extended its platform with Einstein, introducing predictive AI capabilities such as lead scoring, forecasting, and intelligent recommendations within sales and service workflows.[6]

---

[4] Krishna C. Mukherjee, "Automating Forms Publishing with the Intelligent Filing Manager," in *Proceedings of the IEEE International Conference on Systems, Man, and Cybernetics* (IEEE, 1999), I-308–I-313, `https://ieeexplore.ieee.org/document/814108`; Debra Levy, "Finding Forms," *Legal Assistant Today*, November/December 2001, `https://www.legalassistanttoday.com/feature_nd01-2/`.

[5] Salesforce, "World's #1 CRM," Salesforce.com, `https://www.salesforce.com/crm/worlds-number-one-crm/`.

[6] Salesforce, "Artificial Intelligence (AI) at Salesforce," Salesforce.com, `https://www.salesforce.com/artificial-intelligence/`; Jennifer W. Lee, "Get Started with Einstein Recommendation Builder," Salesforce Admins (blog), March 17, 2021, `https://admin.salesforce.com/blog/2021/get-started-with-einstein-recommendation-builder`.

Following Salesforce's lead, Google introduced its suite of productivity tools, Google Workspace (formerly G Suite), in 2006. Google Workspace—which includes Gmail, Google Drive, Google Docs, and Sheets—fosters seamless real-time collaboration and communication within teams. It quickly became a go-to choice for businesses of all sizes, growing from more than 6 million paying businesses in 2020 to over 11 million paying customers by 2025.[7]

Its integrations with other SaaS products, such as Salesforce and Slack, enhanced its value proposition. Google's "freemium" model, offering basic features at no cost and advanced features through subscription, fueled widespread adoption. The platform incorporates AI features, such as Gmail's Smart Compose and Smart Reply, which use ML to help users compose emails more efficiently.

Shopify emerged as a groundbreaking e-commerce platform in 2006, democratizing online retail for businesses of all sizes. Its user-friendly interface and robust features—such as customizable storefronts, payment processing, and inventory management—helped even those without extensive technical knowledge to succeed in the digital marketplace. By 2021, Shopify was powering over 1.7 million businesses in 175 countries.[8] Its tiered pricing model, from basic plans for small businesses to sophisticated solutions for large enterprises, broadened its appeal.

Also launched in 2006, HubSpot introduced a suite of software designed to boost inbound marketing and sales. Inbound marketing focuses on attracting customers through valuable content, search engine optimization (SEO), and social media rather than interrupting them with traditional advertising. By offering tools for CRM, marketing automation, and customer service, HubSpot helps companies attract, engage, and delight customers at every stage of their journey.

---

[7] Google Workspace, "How Google Meet Is Helping Our G Suite and Google Cloud Customers," Google Workspace Blog, `https://workspace.google.com/blog/productivity-collaboration/how-google-meet-supports-two-million-new-users-each-day` (6 million paying businesses and organizations, 2020); Google Workspace, "Google Workspace Study Reveals More Than 90% of Rising Leaders Want AI With Personalization," PRNewswire, December 4, 2025, `https://www.prnewswire.com/news-releases/google-workspace-study-reveals-more-than-90-of-rising-leaders-want-ai-with-personalization-302632689.html` (over 11 million paying customers, December 2025).

[8] Shopify Inc., "Shopify Black Friday 2021," US Securities and Exchange Commission, Form 6-K, November 2021, `https://www.sec.gov/Archives/edgar/data/0001594805/000159480521000042/shopifyblackfriday2021pres.htm`.

HubSpot's impact on digital marketing practices has been profound, with over 100,000 customers in more than 120 countries by 2021.[9] Its integration with platforms like Salesforce and Google Workspace has increased its utility across diverse business ecosystems. The platform integrates AI-driven predictive lead scoring and content optimization recommendations alongside automated chatbots that scale customer engagement.

In 2007, Dropbox was launched, offering secure cloud storage to facilitate file sharing and collaboration. As with Google Workspace, its "freemium" model contributed to rapid adoption. By 2020, Dropbox had over 600 million registered users, with 15 million paying customers. By 2023, it reported 18.12 million paying users.[10] In response to growing competition and the rise of AI-powered productivity tools, Dropbox has expanded beyond storage. It introduced Dropbox AI, which can summarize documents and answer questions directly from file previews. It also introduced Dropbox Dash, an AI-powered universal search product that brings together files, emails, and content from third-party platforms such as Google Drive, OneDrive, Notion, and Slack into a single searchable hub. These additions reflect Dropbox's strategic shift from a file storage provider to a broader AI-powered content management platform.[11]

Also introduced in 2007, Zendesk elevated customer service with its ticketing software. Zendesk helped businesses provide better customer support by centralizing inquiries from multiple channels. By 2020, Zendesk had served more than 160,000 customers across multiple industries worldwide.[12]

Slack reshaped workplace communication by organizing real-time conversations into channels dedicated to teams, topics, and projects. By fiscal year 2021, the company reported more than 156,000 paid customers, reflecting its emergence as a major

---

[9] HubSpot, "HubSpot Surpasses 100,000 Customers and $1 Billion in Annual Recurring Revenue," HubSpot Newsroom, February 16, 2021, `https://www.hubspot.com/company-news/hubspot-surpasses-100000-customers-and-1-billion-in-annual-recurring-revenue`.

[10] Dropbox, Inc., "Form 10-K for Dropbox Inc. Filed 02/16/2024," Dropbox Investor Relations, February 16, 2024, `https://investors.dropbox.com/static-files/eaffdb7c-727a-40c6-9308-1c1c062d2b30`.

[11] Dropbox, "Introducing Dropbox Dash, AI-Powered Universal Search, and Dropbox AI," Dropbox Blog, `https://blog.dropbox.com/topics/product/introducing-AI-powered-tools`; Dropbox, "Fall 2025 Release: Try the New Dropbox Dash, Your Context-Aware AI Teammate," Dropbox Blog, October 23, 2025, `https://blog.dropbox.com/topics/news/fall-2025-release-dropbox-dash-context-aware-ai-teammate`.

[12] Zendesk, "Zendesk Announces Third Quarter 2020 Results," Zendesk Newsroom, accessed April 15, 2026, `https://www.zendesk.com/newsroom/press-releases/zendesk-announces-third-quarter-2020-results/`.

enterprise collaboration platform.[13] More recently, Slack has extended the platform with Slack AI, adding AI-generated answers drawn from workspace messages and files, channel and thread summaries, recaps, and AI-assisted workflow creation.[14] Together with a broad ecosystem of more than 2,000 apps and a robust API, these capabilities have strengthened Slack's role as a central hub for communication, coordination, and workflow automation.[15]

Zoom, launched in 2013, became synonymous with video conferencing during the COVID-19 pandemic. Known for its high-quality video and audio, Zoom saw explosive growth, from 10 million daily meeting participants in December 2019 to 300 million by April 2020.[16] The pandemic spurred global adoption by businesses seeking to maintain connectivity with employees and clients, as well as by individuals seeking to stay connected with friends and family. The rapid growth exposed security vulnerabilities, which Zoom has worked to address. More recently, Zoom has extended the platform with Zoom AI Companion, introducing meeting summaries, task extraction, conversation highlights, and AI-assisted workflow automation. The most recent iteration, AI Companion 3.0, adds agentic retrieval capabilities that draw on meeting summaries, transcripts, and connected third-party applications to help users move from conversation to completed outcomes.[17]

Adobe Creative Cloud, introduced in 2013, brought Adobe's suite of creative tools into the cloud. Offering these tools on a subscription basis provided users with continuous access to the latest updates and features. While some long-time users initially resisted the subscription model, it ultimately proved successful, with an estimated 23 million

---

[13] Slack Technologies, Inc., "Slack Announces Strong Fourth Quarter and Fiscal Year 2021 Results," Slack Blog, March 4, 2021, `https://slack.com/blog/news/slack-announces-strong-fourth-quarter-and-fiscal-year-2021-results`.

[14] Slack, "Guide to AI Features in Slack," Slack Help Center, accessed April 15, 2026, `https://slack.com/help/articles/25076892548883-Guide-to-AI-features-in-Slack`.

[15] Business of Apps, "Slack Revenue and Usage Statistics," Business of Apps, accessed April 15, 2026, `https://www.businessofapps.com/data/slack-statistics/`.

[16] Eric S. Yuan, "A Year Later: Reflecting and Looking Ahead," Zoom Blog, March 2021, `https://www.zoom.com/en/blog/reflecting-looking-ahead/`; Zoom Video Communications, "90-Day Security Plan Progress Report: April 22," Zoom Blog, April 22, 2020, `https://blog.zoom.us/90-day-security-plan-progress-report-april-22/`.

[17] Zoom Communications, Inc., "Zoom Launches AI Companion 3.0 with Agentic Workflows, Transforming Conversations into Action," Zoom Newsroom, December 15, 2025, `https://news.zoom.com/zoom-launches-ai-companion-3-0/`.

subscribers by mid-2022.[18] The suite increasingly incorporates AI-powered features via Adobe Sensei. These include intelligent autotagging in Lightroom, content-aware fill in Photoshop, and automated video editing suggestions in Premiere Pro.

Microsoft, a dominant force in the SaaS landscape, has made substantial advancements in its cloud offerings. Launched in 2011, Microsoft 365 (formerly Office 365) has become a cornerstone of productivity for businesses worldwide. By early 2022, Microsoft 365 had reached approximately 345 million paid seats. By early 2026, Microsoft reported more than 450 million commercial paid seats.[19] A robust suite of AI-powered productivity tools—including Word, Excel, and Teams—fuels its widespread adoption. The shift toward remote work and online learning has further catalyzed the expansion of its user base.

The SaaS products discussed here have optimized business operations and collaboration, driving efficiency, productivity, and innovation. Their success stories continue to shape industries and accelerate progress across the global business landscape.

12. Appendix 12: API Architecture Overview

This appendix supplements Section 10.5.1 (specifically Section 10.5.1.5), which examines lessons from enterprise deployments of strategic cloud-AI architecture and introduces Figure 10-1. The diagram illustrates how components interact in a modern AI-enabled, cloud-based system, showing the high-level conceptual API architecture that connects human users, AI agents, gateway layers, orchestration components, and back-end services.

The figure is implemented using Microsoft Azure services—including APIM as the API gateway, Azure Logic Apps for workflow orchestration, and Azure Resource Groups for resource governance—though the architectural pattern it represents is broadly applicable across cloud platforms. It presents an updated architectural pattern that

[18] Photutorial, "Adobe Statistics: Creative Cloud Users, Employees, and More," `https://photutorial.com/adobe-statistics/`. Adobe does not publicly report Creative Cloud subscriber counts; this figure is an estimate based on available revenue data.

[19] Microsoft Corporation, "Microsoft FY22 Third Quarter Earnings Conference Call," Microsoft Investor Relations, April 2022; Microsoft Corporation, "Microsoft Fiscal Year 2026 Second Quarter Earnings Conference Call," Microsoft Investor Relations, January 28, 2026, `https://www.microsoft.com/en-us/investor/events/fy-2026/earnings-fy-2026-q2`.

incorporates AI agents and an AI gateway alongside the traditional API gateway and introduces MCP tools as the integration mechanism that connects the orchestration and logic layers to back-end systems.

12.1. Key Components

Human Users and External Client Applications: On the left side of the diagram, two types of consumers initiate interactions with the system. Human users connect through an authentication and authorization layer over HTTPS, entering the system through the gateway zone. External client applications appear as a distinct box at the top of the gateway zone, alongside a separate AI agents box. Both external client applications and AI agents connect downward into the gateway zone, where their traffic is handled by the combined AI gateway and API gateway component. Additionally, the left side of the diagram shows a developer (represented by a person icon) who interacts with the platform in two distinct ways: building applications against the gateway and consuming API documentation from the developer portal.

Example: In financial technology, human users such as bank customers and business analysts access services through secure HTTPS connections, while external client applications—such as budgeting tools or ERP systems—connect as programmatic consumers of the platform's exposed APIs.

AI Agents: Positioned in their own box at the top of the gateway zone, next to external client applications, AI agents represent autonomous software entities that interact with the system programmatically. They connect downward to the gateway zone, where the AI gateway handles AI-initiated traffic.

Example: An AI agent in a financial compliance system might autonomously monitor regulatory filings, query back-end line-of-business systems for relevant data, and trigger workflow actions—without human intervention at each step.

AI Gateway: The AI gateway appears as the upper label of the central gateway component, indicating its role in handling AI agent traffic. It handles authentication and authorization for AI-initiated requests and routes them into the workflow and orchestration layer. In Azure-based implementations, the AI gateway capabilities are typically delivered through Azure APIM extended with AI-specific policies, sharing the same platform as the API gateway shown below it in the figure.

Example: A retail platform might deploy an AI gateway to govern requests from recommendation and inventory optimization agents. This layer enforces authentication and rate limiting for each agent while routing traffic to specific back-end services—maintaining strict isolation from standard customer-facing API streams.

API Gateway: The API gateway appears as the lower label on the central gateway component, stacked beneath the AI gateway label, indicating that the two form a layered entry point. In Azure-based implementations, this layered entry point is delivered through Azure APIM, which provides the API gateway runtime, the developer portal, and a management plane as a unified platform service. The API gateway serves as the controlled entry point for standard external client application traffic and handles the following functions, depicted in the figure:

- Authentication and authorization of incoming requests
- HTTPS traffic management and routing
- In typical Azure APIM deployments, the API gateway also enforces policy controls such as rate limiting and access control, although these capabilities are not explicitly visualized in the diagram.

Example: Payment processors use the API gateway to authenticate merchant requests, enforce transaction limits, and route calls to the appropriate back-end services for processing payments.

Developer Portal: The developer portal is shown as a separate component within the gateway zone, connected to the API management layer through Publish Interfaces arrows. In Azure-based implementations, the developer portal is the externally facing, customizable website provided by Azure APIM through which API documentation, interface specifications, and developer resources are published and consumed by application developers building against the platform. The figure depicts the following developer portal interactions:

- Publish Interfaces arrows connecting both the gateway layer and the back-end web services layer to the developer portal.
- A Consume API Documentation flow representing developers accessing specifications, alongside a separate Build Applications flow showing developers interacting with the gateway as the system's entry point.

Example: A cloud banking platform publishes its APIs to the developer portal, allowing fintech partners to access documentation, test integrations in a sandbox environment, and build compliant applications against the platform's published APIs.

Workflow and Orchestration and Logic Apps: In the center of the diagram, the workflow and orchestration component and Logic Apps work together to coordinate complex multistep processes. They receive routed requests from the AI gateway and API gateway and connect to back-end systems via MCP tools. These components perform the following:

- Coordinate complex business processes across multiple back-end systems.
- Handle event-based and AI-triggered workflows.
- Orchestrate the sequencing of calls to line-of-business systems, SaaS services, and web services.

Example: In a loan processing platform, Logic Apps orchestrates the end-to-end application journey—from submission through credit checking, underwriting, document generation, and approval—coordinating across internal systems, third-party SaaS providers, and legacy web services.

MCP Tools: A notable addition in the updated architecture is the explicit presence of MCP (Model Context Protocol) tools. Three MCP tools nodes appear in the diagram, each positioned between the Logic Apps and workflow layer and one of the three back-end system categories: line-of-business systems, SaaS services, and web services. MCP tools serve as the standardized integration connectors that allow AI-aware orchestration layers to communicate with back-end systems in a structured, context-preserving manner. The figure also shows a direct HTTPS connection from the AI gateway and API gateway to the back-end web services layer, providing a secondary path for the gateways to call REST and SOAP web services directly. This bypasses the Logic Apps and MCP tools route for certain standard requests.

Example: An AI orchestration layer managing a multistep compliance workflow uses MCP tools to call a line-of-business compliance system, a third-party SaaS sanctions-screening provider, and a legacy SOAP-based reporting service—each through a dedicated MCP connector that translates and routes requests appropriately.

Back-End Systems: On the right side of the diagram, three categories of back-end systems are shown, each connected to the orchestration layer via its own MCP tools node:

- **Line-of-Business Systems:** Custom or internal applications such as core banking systems, ERP platforms, and proprietary enterprise applications
- **SaaS Services:** Third-party cloud-based services such as CRM platforms, compliance tools, and identity verification providers
- **Web Services:** REST and SOAP interfaces, as shown in the figure, representing the primary web service integration patterns[20]

Example: A digital bank integrates its internal core banking system (line-of-business), a third-party Know Your Customer verification provider (SaaS service), back-end payment services exposed via REST and a legacy interbank payment network via SOAP—all accessed through dedicated MCP tools connectors from the orchestration layer.

Resource Group: At the bottom of the diagram, a resource group boundary encompasses the internal components of the architecture—the AI gateway, API gateway, developer portal, workflow and orchestration, and Logic Apps. This boundary represents the logical grouping within which the platform's core components are deployed and managed, consistent with cloud governance and resource organization patterns such as those used in Azure Resource Groups. A legend at the bottom left of the figure defines the following abbreviations: API—Application Programming Interface; HTTPS—Hypertext Transfer Protocol Secure; REST—Representational State Transfer; SOAP—Simple Object Access Protocol; SaaS—Software as a Service.

12.2. Data Flow

The arrows in the diagram indicate the following flows:

- Human users, external client applications, and AI agents all route through the AI gateway, which serves as the primary entry point for all traffic entering the system.
- The AI gateway and API gateway route requests to workflow and orchestration and Logic Apps.

[20] Modern architectures may also expose services via GraphQL, gRPC, and event streams, depending on performance, flexibility, and real-time data requirements.

- Logic Apps connects to each back-end system category via dedicated MCP tools nodes.
- Publish Interfaces arrows flow from the API gateway and from back-end web services to the developer portal.
- A direct HTTPS connection runs from the AI gateway and API gateway toward the back-end web services layer, providing a secondary path to the MCP-based runtime flow.

12.3. Relevance of the Architecture

This architecture is particularly valuable because it does the following:

- **Integrates AI Agents as First-Class Consumers:** The explicit AI agent entry point and dedicated AI gateway reflect the shift toward agentic AI systems that interact with enterprise platforms autonomously, requiring their own authentication, routing, and governance controls.
- **Standardizes AI-to-Back-End Integration via MCP:** The MCP tools layer provides a structured, protocol-based mechanism for AI orchestration components to interact with heterogeneous back-end systems, reducing bespoke integration complexity.
- **Provides Security:** Both the API gateway and AI gateway establish controlled, authenticated entry points before requests reach sensitive back-end systems.
- **Fosters Innovation:** Companies can expose specific capabilities through published interfaces without exposing their entire system, letting third-party developers and AI agents build and operate on the platform.
- **Supports Compliance:** The API gateway enforces regulatory requirements by controlling and monitoring all data access, including AI-initiated requests.

- **Bridges Legacy and Modern Systems:** The MCP tools layer allows modern AI orchestration to communicate with legacy SOAP-based web services and proprietary line-of-business systems through well-defined connectors.
- **Enables Microservices and Agentic Workflows:** Products and AI agents can interact with independently deployed microservices via MCP tools, letting teams develop, scale, and govern functions independently.

Financial institutions deploy this architecture to manage secure access to banking services for both human users and AI agents. Health care organizations use similar patterns to share patient data across providers, insurers, and patient-facing applications in compliance with HIPAA. Retailers integrate inventory, logistics, and e-commerce systems with third-party sellers, delivery partners, and AI-driven demand forecasting agents. Transportation platforms coordinate real-time data flows among riders, drivers, mapping services, payment processors, and route optimization agents. The public sector adopts API and AI gateway patterns to streamline citizen access to government services while maintaining security and auditability. These examples illustrate how the API architecture shown in Figure 10-1 has evolved into a foundational pattern for secure, scalable, AI-aware integrations across industries.

Glossary

ACH	**Automated Clearing House:** A US-based network for processing electronic payments such as direct deposits and bill payments.
ACID	**Atomicity, Consistency, Isolation, Durability:** The four properties that define reliable transaction processing in relational databases. Atomicity means a transaction is completed entirely or not at all; consistency means it preserves database validity; isolation means concurrent transactions do not interfere with one another; and durability means committed changes survive system failure.
ACM	**Association for Computing Machinery:** A global professional organization founded in 1947 that advances computing as a science and profession through scholarly publications, conferences, educational initiatives, and the development of technical standards.
ADA	**Americans with Disabilities Act:** A US federal civil rights law enacted in 1990 that prohibits discrimination against individuals with disabilities. Title II applies to state and local government services, including digital services, which must be accessible to people with disabilities.
Agent	**Autonomous AI Agent:** A software system that can pursue goals by reasoning over inputs, invoking tools, retrieving data, and taking actions across one or more steps. Depending on the architecture, an agent may use memory, orchestration, and external services to maintain context and complete tasks beyond a single prompt. In Microsoft's AI ecosystem, agents can be developed using platforms such as Copilot Studio and Microsoft Foundry.
AI	**Artificial Intelligence:** A field of computer science concerned with building systems that perform tasks associated with human intelligence, such as perception, language processing, pattern recognition, prediction, and reasoning. Modern AI includes techniques such as ML, neural networks, and NLP.

(continued)

K. C. Mukherjee, *The Microsoft AI Insider's Playbook*, https://doi.org/10.1007/979-8-8688-2730-3

AIOps	**Artificial Intelligence Operations:** An operational framework and cultural practice that applies ML and analytics to IT operations data—including logs, metrics, and traces—to automate incident detection, root cause analysis, anomaly detection, and response. AIOps emphasizes proactive monitoring, intelligent alerting, and continuous learning from operational signals. It enables organizations to maintain reliability and performance at scale across complex, distributed systems by reducing manual effort and accelerating informed decision-making in IT operations.
AKS	**Azure Kubernetes Service:** A managed Azure service for deploying, scaling, and operating Kubernetes clusters. It reduces the operational complexity of managing the Kubernetes control plane and supporting infrastructure.
ALM	**Application Life-Cycle Management:** A framework for managing the full life cycle of a software application from initial requirements through development, testing, deployment, and ongoing maintenance. ALM encompasses processes, tools, and governance practices that coordinate work across development, QA, and operations teams. In Microsoft's ecosystem, ALM for Power Platform and AI Builder solutions includes managing environments, solutions, source control, and deployment pipelines across development, test, and production stages.
API	**Application Programming Interface:** A set of rules and protocols that defines how software components communicate and exchange data. APIs allow developers to integrate services, access external capabilities, and build modular applications without exposing underlying implementation details.
APIM	**Azure API Management:** A fully managed Azure service that allows organizations to publish, secure, monitor, and govern APIs at scale. It provides centralized capabilities for authentication, authorization, rate limiting, request and response transformation, versioning, and observability. APIM acts as a gateway layer between applications and back-end services, enforcing organizational policies and supporting consistent API behavior across distributed systems.
ARM	**Azure Resource Manager:** The deployment and management service for Microsoft Azure. ARM provides a consistent management layer for creating, updating, and deleting resources in an Azure subscription. ARM templates are JSON files that define infrastructure declaratively, specifying what resources should exist rather than scripting the steps to create them.

(*continued*)

AWS	**Amazon Web Services:** Amazon's cloud computing platform that provides a broad set of infrastructure services, including computing power, storage options, networking, and databases. It allows organizations to scale and grow without managing physical infrastructure, paying only for the resources they use.
Azure	**Microsoft Azure:** Microsoft's cloud computing platform that provides a wide range of services and solutions for building, deploying, and managing applications and services through Microsoft-managed data centers. The platform offers IaaS, PaaS, and SaaS capabilities.
BASIC	**Beginner's All-purpose Symbolic Instruction Code:** A high-level programming language developed in 1964 at Dartmouth College to make computing accessible to nonspecialists. BASIC's simple syntax and interactive design made it one of the most widely used languages during the personal computer era. Microsoft's implementation of BASIC for the Altair 8800 in 1975 was the company's first product.
BEAT	**Behavioral and Emotion Analytics Tool:** A proprietary AI-powered voice analytics platform developed by Deloitte. Unlike traditional call monitoring systems, BEAT analyzes vocal patterns, speech characteristics, and behavioral indicators to assess compliance, detect potential misconduct, and evaluate customer service quality in financial services environments.
BERT	**Bidirectional Encoder Representations from Transformers:** An NLP model introduced by Google researchers in 2018. BERT reads text in both directions simultaneously, allowing it to understand context more effectively than earlier models that processed text only left-to-right. The model achieved state-of-the-art results on multiple language tasks and strongly influenced the development of modern NLP models.
BI	**Business Intelligence:** The strategies, technologies, and practices used to collect, integrate, analyze, and present business data to support informed decision-making.
BVAL	**Bloomberg Valuation Service:** Bloomberg's award-winning pricing service that provides independent, evaluated prices for fixed-income securities and other financial instruments using proprietary models and extensive market data. BVAL combines multiple data sources—including dealer quotes, transactions, and benchmark curves—to generate objective price estimates for bonds and securities that may not trade frequently, serving as a trusted reference for portfolio valuation, risk management, and regulatory compliance.

(continued)

CCPA	**California Consumer Privacy Act:** A California privacy law that regulates how businesses collect, use, and share the personal information of California residents and grants consumers important rights regarding that data.
CDN	**Content Delivery Network:** A geographically distributed network of servers that caches and delivers web content, static resources, and media files from locations closer to end users. CDNs reduce latency, improve load times, and increase availability by distributing traffic across multiple edge servers rather than routing all requests to a single origin server.
CI/CD	**Continuous Integration/Continuous Delivery:** A method to frequently deliver apps and app updates to customers by introducing automation into the stages of app development.
CLM	**Contract Life-Cycle Management:** The process of managing contracts from initiation through execution, compliance monitoring, and renewal or termination. CLM systems automate workflows such as drafting, approval routing, obligation tracking, and expiration alerts, reducing manual effort and improving visibility across an organization's contractual commitments.
CLOUD	**Clarifying Lawful Overseas Use of Data:** A 2018 US statute that authorizes law enforcement to compel US-based providers to produce electronic data stored abroad through lawful process and permits qualifying foreign governments to request data from US providers under bilateral executive agreements.
CLR	**Common Language Runtime:** The execution engine for Microsoft's .NET Framework, introduced in 2002. The CLR provides services such as memory management, type safety, exception handling, and just-in-time compilation. It allows programs written in different .NET languages to interoperate by compiling them to a common intermediate language that the runtime executes.
CLU	**Conversational Language Understanding:** A capability in Azure Language that supports building custom NLU models to predict user intent and extract entities from conversational text (utterances), commonly used in chatbots and virtual assistants. Models are trained on labeled example utterances, evaluated, and then deployed for runtime predictions via an API.
COBOL	**Common Business-Oriented Language:** A compiled English-like computer programming language designed for business use.

(continued)

CoE	**Center of Excellence:** An organizational construct that centralizes expertise, governance, and best practices for a specific domain or technology. A CoE provides strategic direction, operational support, and standardized frameworks to accelerate adoption, maintain quality, and promote continuous improvement across teams.
COM	**Component Object Model:** A Microsoft object model and binary standard that defines how software components interact, including components written in different languages. COM provides a framework for creating reusable objects and is the foundation for technologies such as OLE and ActiveX.
Copilot	**Microsoft Copilot:** Microsoft's brand for AI assistants and related AI experiences across products such as Microsoft 365, GitHub, Windows, Security, and Azure. Different Copilot offerings vary in capabilities, grounding sources, and underlying architecture, but generally combine language models with relevant data, tools, and workflow integration.
CoT	**Chain-of-Thought:** A prompt engineering technique that instructs AI models to generate step-by-step reasoning before reaching conclusions, improving accuracy on complex analytical tasks by encouraging structured decomposition of problems. The intermediate steps produced are generated text that resembles reasoning rather than a direct window into the model's internal processing. CoT also increases latency and token consumption due to the additional text generated during the reasoning phase.
COVID-19	**Coronavirus Disease 2019:** An infectious disease caused by the SARS-CoV-2 virus, declared a global pandemic by the World Health Organization in March 2020.
CPU	**Central Processing Unit:** The principal processing component of a digital computer system, comprising the control unit, arithmetic-logic unit, and registers. The CPU interprets and executes instructions from software, coordinating with the RAM and other hardware components to perform computational tasks.
CRM	**Customer Relationship Management:** A strategy and set of technologies for managing customer interactions and data across the customer life cycle. CRM systems support sales, marketing, and customer service activities.
CSRSS	**Client/Server Runtime Subsystem:** The user-mode process that implements essential elements of the Windows (Win32) subsystem. CSRSS manages tasks such as console window handling and process and thread bookkeeping, and it remains a core part of the user-mode environment on which Win32 desktop applications depend.

(continued)

CSS	**Cascading Style Sheets:** A style sheet language used to describe the presentation of a document written in markup language like HTML.
CT	**Corporation Trust Company:** A wholly owned subsidiary of Wolters Kluwer that provides business incorporation, registered agent services, and corporate compliance solutions across US jurisdictions. Founded in 1892 and operating widely as CT Corporation, it serves as the official registered agent for businesses operating in multiple jurisdictions, receiving legal documents and regulatory correspondence on behalf of client companies. Its services range from business formation and foreign qualification filings to ongoing compliance management, serving clients from small businesses to Fortune 500 corporations. CT Corporation's web-based platform, CTAdvantage.com, is a pioneering example of knowledge-based AI, using a deterministic expert system to automate complex, jurisdiction-specific compliance workflows.
CUDA	**Compute Unified Device Architecture:** A parallel computing platform and programming model developed by NVIDIA for general-purpose processing on GPUs. CUDA provides APIs that allow developers to write code that executes across thousands of parallel GPU cores, making it widely used for training and running modern ML models.
DAD	**Disciplined Agile Delivery:** A process decision framework designed to simplify decisions around incremental and iterative solution delivery.
Dataverse	**Microsoft Dataverse:** A cloud-based data platform for storing and managing business data used by Power Platform and Dynamics 365 applications. Dataverse provides structured tables, security controls, auditing, and integration capabilities and often serves as a data layer for business applications, automation, and AI-assisted workflows.
DAX	**Data Analysis Expressions:** A formula language used to define calculations and queries in tabular data models for Power BI, Power Pivot (Excel), Azure Analysis Services, and SQL Server Analysis Services.
DEC	**Digital Equipment Corporation:** American computer company (1957–1998) that pioneered minicomputers, notably the PDP and VAX series. DEC systems were widely used in academic and research computing. The company was acquired by Compaq in 1998.

(continued)

DEC-1090	**DECsystem-1090:** A large, multiuser mainframe computer made by DEC, part of the PDP-10 line. At IIT Kanpur, the system ran from 1979 to 1989 and served as the institute's primary computing resource—a period alumni refer to as the DEC-10 years.
Deloitte	**Deloitte Touche Tohmatsu Limited:** One of the Big Four global professional services organizations, headquartered in London. Deloitte provides audit, consulting, tax, and risk advisory services, with major practice areas in AI-driven analytics, enterprise modernization, and digital risk management.
DENDRAL	A pioneering expert system developed at Stanford University in the 1960s that inferred the molecular structure of organic compounds from mass spectrometry data. DENDRAL demonstrated that computers could replicate expert-level reasoning in a specialized scientific domain by encoding chemists' knowledge as rules, establishing foundational techniques for knowledge-based systems.
DevOps	**Development and Operations:** A collaborative discipline that integrates software development (Dev) and IT operations (Ops) to accelerate the delivery of reliable, scalable applications. DevOps emphasizes automation, continuous integration and delivery, IaC, and real-time monitoring. It reduces the time between code changes and deployment, promotes cross-functional collaboration, and improves system resilience.
DevSecOps	**Development, Security, and Operations:** An extension of DevOps that integrates security practices throughout the SDLC rather than treating them as a separate phase. DevSecOps incorporates automated testing, vulnerability scanning, and compliance checks into CI/CD pipelines so that teams can identify and address risks early while sustaining rapid delivery.
DEWR	**Department of Employment and Workplace Relations:** A cabinet-level department within the Australian government responsible for national employment policy, workplace relations regulation, and workforce development programs. DEWR administers legislation governing industrial relations, employment conditions, and job services across Australia.
DLP	**Data Loss Prevention:** A set of policies and technologies designed to prevent sensitive data from being shared, transferred, or exposed outside authorized boundaries. In Power Platform, DLP policies control how connectors can be used together.

(continued)

DORA	**DevOps Research and Assessment:** A research program that studies and measures software delivery performance using four key metrics: deployment frequency, lead time for changes, mean time to recover, and change failure rate.
DOS	**Disk Operating System:** A command-line operating system used on early IBM-compatible PCs, commonly used as informal shorthand for MS-DOS. See MS-DOS.
DSPM	**Data Security Posture Management:** A security discipline and category of tooling that helps organizations discover, classify, and protect sensitive data across cloud environments. Microsoft's DSPM for AI extends this capability to AI-generated content and interactions, providing visibility into how sensitive data is accessed and used within Copilot and agent workflows.
EBITDA	**Earnings Before Interest, Taxes, Depreciation, and Amortization:** A financial metric used to evaluate a company's operating performance by excluding nonoperating expenses and noncash charges.
EC2	**Elastic Compute Cloud:** A web service that provides resizable compute capacity in the cloud, offered by Amazon Web Services. EC2 allows users to rent virtual servers to run their applications and workloads.
EHR	**Electronic Health Record:** A digital system that stores and manages patient health information, including medical history, medications, test results, and treatment plans. In health care AI implementations, EHRs serve as the primary data source for clinical decision support, automated intake, and AI-assisted workflows, subject to HIPAA compliance requirements.
ELIZA	An early NLP program created by Joseph Weizenbaum at MIT in 1966. ELIZA simulated conversation by using pattern matching and substitution rules to transform user inputs into responses, most famously in a script that mimicked a Rogerian psychotherapist. The program revealed how readily people attribute understanding to machines, even when the underlying mechanism is simple.
ENIAC	**Electronic Numerical Integrator and Computer:** The first general-purpose electronic digital computer, completed in 1945 at the University of Pennsylvania. ENIAC was designed to calculate artillery firing tables for the US Army and demonstrated that electronic computation could dramatically outperform mechanical methods, marking a pivotal moment in computing history.

(continued)

ENISA	**European Union Agency for Cybersecurity:** An agency of the European Union established to improve network and information security across member states. ENISA provides guidance on cybersecurity policy, supports incident response, and publishes research on emerging threats, including the security implications of AI.
EPS	**Encapsulated Prolog Services:** A Prolog-based inference component within the INTELLIFM architecture that performs real-time reasoning and communicates results to other system components to support dynamic decision-making.
ERP	**Enterprise Resource Planning:** An integrated software system for centralizing core business processes across multiple departments, including finance, HR, manufacturing, supply chain, services, and procurement. It streamlines operations, supports data sharing, and improves decision-making through an integrated database.
EU	**European Union:** A political and economic union of member states in Europe that establishes common regulations, trade policies, and legal frameworks. In enterprise AI and cloud computing, EU regulations such as the GDPR and the EU AI Act impose important requirements relating to data protection, transparency, risk management, and the responsible deployment of AI systems for organizations operating in, or serving customers in, the EU.
EY	**Ernst & Young:** A global professional services firm headquartered in London and one of the Big Four. EY provides assurance, tax, consulting, and advisory services and is known for its work in finance transformation, risk management, and AI-driven enterprise modernization.
F1	**F1 Score:** An ML evaluation metric representing the harmonic mean of precision and recall. An F1 score of 1.0 indicates perfect precision and recall, while a score of 0 indicates complete failure. The F1 score is particularly useful when evaluating models on imbalanced datasets where accuracy alone would be misleading.
FaaS	**Function as a Service:** A serverless computing model that extends PaaS by abstracting away server and container management. Developers write individual functions that execute in response to events, while the cloud platform automatically handles provisioning, scaling, and runtime management. The pay-per-invocation pricing model makes FaaS particularly well suited to intermittent and event-driven workloads.

(continued)

FAQ	**Frequently Asked Questions:** A compiled list of common questions and their answers on a particular topic, used to provide self-service support and reduce repetitive inquiries. FAQ resources help users find quick guidance for routine issues without requiring direct assistance.
FDA	**Food and Drug Administration:** A US government agency responsible for regulating food, drugs, and medical devices.
FERPA	**Family Educational Rights and Privacy Act:** A US federal law that governs access to and disclosure of student education records. FERPA grants parents and eligible students the right to inspect records and restricts the release of PII without consent. It applies to institutions that receive US Department of Education funding and is relevant to AI applications in education that involve student data.
FFIEC	**Federal Financial Institutions Examination Council:** A US interagency body that prescribes uniform principles, standards, and reporting requirements for the federal examination of financial institutions. FFIEC member agencies include the Federal Reserve, the Federal Deposit Insurance Corporation, the Office of the Comptroller of the Currency, the National Credit Union Administration, and the Consumer Financial Protection Bureau. The council publishes examination manuals and guidance on topics including financial crime compliance, cybersecurity, and IT risk management.
FHIR	**Fast Healthcare Interoperability Resources:** An international standard for exchanging health care information electronically among EHR systems, clinical applications, and other health information systems, using modern web technologies such as RESTful APIs and data formats such as JSON and XML.
FinOps	**Cloud Financial Operations:** An operational framework and cultural practice that integrates finance, engineering, and business teams to bring financial accountability to the variable spend model of cloud computing. FinOps emphasizes cross-functional collaboration, real-time cost visibility, and the optimization of cloud resources. It enables organizations to balance speed, cost, and quality so that cloud investments deliver maximum business value through data-driven decision-making.
FINRA	**Financial Industry Regulatory Authority:** A US self-regulatory organization that oversees broker-dealers and enforces rules governing trading practices, sales activities, and communications with investors. When broker-dealers use AI systems to generate customer-facing communications, those communications remain subject to FINRA rules, including Rule 2210.

(continued)

FIS	**Fidelity National Information Services, Inc.:** A global financial technology company that provides banking, payments, treasury, and capital markets platforms to financial institutions and enterprises.
FPGA	**Field-Programmable Gate Array:** A reconfigurable integrated circuit that can be programmed after manufacturing to perform specific computational tasks at hardware speeds. FPGAs are used in AI infrastructure to accelerate inference and real-time data processing workloads.
GCP	**Google Cloud Platform:** A suite of cloud computing services offered by Google.
GDP	**Gross Domestic Product:** The total monetary value of all finished goods and services produced within a country's borders in a specific time period. GDP is the primary indicator of national economic output and is used to compare economic performance across countries and time periods.
GDPR	**General Data Protection Regulation:** A European Union regulation setting rules for data protection and privacy for individuals.
GenAI	**Generative Artificial Intelligence:** A class of AI systems that create new content such as text, images, code, audio, and video by learning patterns from large training datasets.
GPT	**Generative Pretrained Transformer:** A family of LLMs developed by OpenAI that generate content by predicting the next token from prior context. GPT models are based on the transformer architecture and are widely used for tasks such as text generation, summarization, translation, and question answering.
GPU	**Graphics Processing Unit:** A specialized integrated circuit designed to accelerate the rendering of images, video, and other highly parallel computations. Originally developed for graphics processing, GPUs are now widely used in scientific computing and ML because they can process large volumes of data in parallel. GPUs may be integrated into a system or provided as separate dedicated components.
GUI	**Graphical User Interface:** A visual interface through which users interact with software using graphical elements such as windows, icons, buttons, and menus rather than text-based commands. GUIs are standard in operating systems, applications, and mobile devices and were pioneered at Xerox PARC before being commercialized by Apple and Microsoft.

(*continued*)

HAL	**Hardware Abstraction Layer:** A low-level Windows component between the kernel and the physical hardware that provides a uniform interface, shielding the kernel from hardware-specific details and enabling portability across processor and chipset combinations.
HCL	**Hindustan Computers Limited:** An Indian multinational IT services and consulting company, headquartered in Noida, India. Founded in 1976, HCL provides technology services including software development, infrastructure management, and business process outsourcing to clients across industries worldwide.
HDD	**Hard Disk Drive:** A data storage device that uses spinning magnetic platters and a read/write head to store and retrieve data. HDDs offer high capacity at a lower cost per gigabyte than SSDs, but are slower and more susceptible to physical damage.
HIPAA	**Health Insurance Portability and Accountability Act:** A US law that governs the privacy and security of health care information.
HL7	**Health Level Seven:** A family of international standards for exchanging electronic health information across clinical systems. HL7 defines messaging formats and interoperability protocols used by EHR systems, laboratory platforms, and billing applications.
HR	**Human Resources:** The organizational function responsible for managing employee-related processes, including recruitment, onboarding, training, compensation, benefits administration, and workforce planning. In AI implementations, HR processes are common targets for automation through chatbots, workflow assistants, and document processing systems.
HTML	**Hypertext Markup Language:** The standard markup language for creating web pages and web applications.
HTTP	**Hypertext Transfer Protocol:** A communication protocol that defines how requests and responses are exchanged between clients and servers on the web. HTTP uses standard methods such as GET, POST, PUT, and DELETE and operates as a stateless protocol in which each request is independent. HTTPS adds Transport Layer Security to encrypt HTTP traffic.
IaaS	**Infrastructure as a Service:** A cloud computing service that provides virtualized computing resources over the internet.

(continued)

IaC	**Infrastructure as Code:** The practice of defining and provisioning infrastructure (such as networks, virtual machines, containers, and permissions) using machine-readable configuration files rather than manual setup. IaC supports version control, repeatable deployments, reviewable changes, and consistent environments across development, testing, and production.
IAM	**Identity and Access Management:** A framework of policies, processes, and technologies that governs how digital identities are established, authenticated, and authorized to access resources. IAM enforces the principle of least privilege, manages user and service credentials, and serves as the primary security boundary in cloud environments.
IBM	**International Business Machines:** A multinational technology company known for hardware, software, and consulting services.
IDC	**International Data Corporation:** A global provider of market intelligence, advisory services, and events for the IT, telecommunications, and consumer technology markets.
IDE	**Integrated Development Environment:** A software application that provides an integrated set of facilities to programmers for software development.
IEC	**International Electrotechnical Commission:** A global standards organization that prepares and publishes international standards for electrical, electronic, and related technologies.
IEEE	**Institute of Electrical and Electronics Engineers:** The world's largest technical professional organization dedicated to advancing technology through standards development, conferences, peer-reviewed publications, and educational programs across engineering, computing, and related fields.
IID	**Independent and Identically Distributed:** A statistical assumption that each data point in a dataset is drawn from the same probability distribution and that all data points are statistically independent of one another. The IID assumption underlies many ML algorithms and statistical models; violations of this assumption can reduce model reliability and generalization.
IITs	**Indian Institutes of Technology:** A group of public technical and research universities in India recognized for excellence in engineering, science, and technology education. IIT alumni have made notable contributions to global technology and business, including in AI and enterprise software.

(continued)

INTELLIFM	**Intelligent Filing Manager:** An expert system and software architecture created to automate high-volume filing, workflow-driven operations, and document-centered business processes. Its modular, component-based design supported multiple knowledge bases and incorporated declarative techniques for generating user interfaces and separating interface definition from procedural logic, helping demonstrate how AI-driven automation could be delivered in enterprise environments and early SaaS models.
Interlisp	A dialect of Lisp developed at Bolt, Beranek, and Newman (BBN) beginning in 1966 and later advanced at Xerox PARC. Interlisp was notable for its integrated programming environment, including a debugger, spelling correction, and the DWIM ("Do What I Mean") facility, which attempted to automatically correct common user errors.
IoT	**Internet of Things:** A network of physical devices embedded with sensors and software that collect and exchange data over the internet. IoT spans consumer devices, industrial equipment, and infrastructure systems, supporting real-time monitoring, automation, and data-driven operations across industries.
IP	**Internet Protocol:** A network-layer protocol that routes data packets across interconnected networks by assigning unique addresses to devices and determining the best path for delivery.
IPO	**Initial Public Offering:** The first sale of a company's stock to the public, typically through a listing on a stock exchange.
ISO	**International Organization for Standardization:** An independent, nongovernmental body that develops and publishes voluntary international standards across industries. In the context of cloud and AI services, ISO 27001 (information security management) and ISO 27701 (privacy information management) are the certifications most frequently referenced in enterprise compliance programs.
IT	**Information Technology:** The hardware, software, networks, and related infrastructure used to create, process, store, and exchange digital information in organizational and business settings.
IVR	**Interactive Voice Response:** A telephony technology that allows humans to interact with a computer-operated phone system through voice and telephone keypad input.
JSON	**JavaScript Object Notation:** A lightweight data interchange format that is easy for humans to read and write and easy for machines to parse and generate.

(continued)

JTC	**Joint Technical Committee:** A standards development body formed by the ISO and IEC. JTC 1, established in 1987, is responsible for developing international standards in information technology, including standards relevant to AI, cybersecurity, and software engineering.
JVM	**Java Virtual Machine:** A runtime environment that executes Java bytecode and provides a consistent platform for programs written in Java to run on any device or operating system with a compatible JVM implementation. This "write once, run anywhere" capability made Java a widely adopted language for cross-platform and enterprise development.
KPMG	**Klynveld Peat Marwick Goerdeler:** A global network of professional services firms offering audit, tax, and advisory services. Headquartered in Amstelveen, the Netherlands, KPMG is a Big Four firm known for its work in risk management, tax automation, and AI-driven compliance solutions.
KWI	**Kliger-Weiss Infosystems Inc.:** A cloud-based retail technology company founded in 1985, providing point-of-sale, merchandising, e-commerce, and inventory management solutions primarily to specialty retailers. KWI's platform integrates retail operations across physical and digital channels.
LeSS	**Large-Scale Scrum:** A framework for scaling scrum to multiple teams working on a single product.
Lisp	**List Processing:** A programming language created by John McCarthy in 1958, designed for symbolic computation and AI research. Its distinctive features—tree-based data structures, automatic memory management, dynamic typing, and the treatment of code as data—made it particularly well-suited to AI applications such as NLP and expert systems.
LLM	**Large Language Model:** An AI model trained on vast amounts of text data to understand and generate human language.
LSASS	**Local Security Authority Subsystem Service:** A user-mode Windows process that enforces system security policy and handles authentication, verifying logons, managing password changes, and issuing access tokens in concert with the kernel-mode Security Reference Monitor.

(continued)

LTN	**Law Technology News:** A publication that provides insights and updates on the intersection of law and technology, focusing on how technological advancements impact legal practice and regulation.
Maclisp	A dialect of Lisp developed at MIT's Project MAC (from which it derives its name) in the late 1960s. Maclisp ran on PDP-10 systems under operating systems including ITS, TOPS-10, and TOPS-20 and was widely used for AI research through the early 1980s. Notable applications written in Maclisp include the Macsyma computer algebra system and Terry Winograd's SHRDLU natural language program.
MAUI	**.NET Multiplatform App User Interface:** A Microsoft framework for building cross-platform applications using a single codebase. MAUI extends earlier frameworks such as Xamarin.Forms, allowing developers to create native applications for Windows, macOS, iOS, and Android using C# and XAML. It continues the declarative approach of describing interfaces and binding them to application state.
MCP	**Model Context Protocol:** An open protocol for connecting AI applications to external tools, data sources, and services through a standardized interface. It reduces the need for custom point-to-point integrations by defining a common way for applications to discover and use external capabilities. Microsoft Foundry supports MCP integration.
METR	**Model Evaluation and Threat Research:** A nonprofit research institute based in Berkeley, California, that evaluates the capabilities and risks of advanced AI models. METR develops standardized evaluation frameworks and conducts independent assessments to help identify potentially dangerous capabilities in frontier AI systems before deployment.
MFA	**Multifactor Authentication:** A security mechanism that requires users to provide two or more verification factors to access a resource. MFA typically combines something the user knows (a password), something the user has (a security token or mobile device), and something the user is (a biometric). MFA reduces the risk of account compromise and is widely recommended as a baseline security control for enterprise deployments, including those involving Azure AI Services and Microsoft 365.
MFP	**Multifunction Printer:** A consolidated office hardware device that integrates the capabilities of multiple standalone machines into a single centralized unit. Modern MFPs serve as "document hubs" within a network, bridging the gap between physical and digital workflows.

(*continued*)

MIT	**Massachusetts Institute of Technology:** A leading research university founded in 1861, known for pioneering work in engineering, computer science, and the physical sciences, as well as its influential contributions to innovation, entrepreneurship, and technology policy.
MITRE ATT&CK	**MITRE Adversarial Tactics, Techniques, and Common Knowledge:** A globally accessible knowledge base of adversary tactics and techniques based on real-world observations, maintained by the MITRE Corporation. ATT&CK provides a structured framework that security teams use to classify and analyze cyber threats, assess defensive coverage, and prioritize detection and response capabilities. Microsoft security products such as Microsoft Sentinel use ATT&CK mappings to support threat investigation and incident response.
ML	**Machine Learning:** A branch of AI in which systems learn patterns from data to make predictions, classifications, or decisions without being explicitly programmed for each case. Deep learning is a subfield of ML that uses multilayer neural networks.
MLOps	**Machine Learning Operations:** A discipline that applies DevOps practices to the machine learning life cycle to support reproducibility, deployment, monitoring, and governance of ML systems.
MS-DOS	**Microsoft Disk Operating System:** A command-line-based operating system developed by Microsoft, widely used on IBM-compatible PCs in the 1980s and early 1990s. It served as the foundation for early versions of Windows and played a central role in establishing Microsoft's dominance in the PC software market.
MVP	**Minimum Viable Product:** A development approach in which a product is built with just enough features to test core functionality and gather user feedback before investing in full-scale development. For AI projects, an MVP is particularly valuable for surfacing data quality issues, model accuracy limitations, and bias before broader rollout.
MVVM	**Model–View–ViewModel:** A software architectural pattern that facilitates the separation of the development of the graphical user interface from the development of the business logic or back-end logic. It is used in platforms like Windows Presentation Foundation.

(continued)

MYCIN	An expert system developed at Stanford University in the 1970s that diagnosed bacterial infections and recommended antibiotics. MYCIN used approximately 600 rules derived from medical expertise and introduced certainty factors to handle the uncertainty inherent in medical diagnosis. Although never deployed clinically, MYCIN demonstrated that AI could match specialist-level performance in well-defined domains.
NASA	**National Aeronautics and Space Administration:** The US government agency responsible for the nation's civilian space program, aeronautics, and aerospace research.
NASSCOM	**National Association of Software and Services Companies:** The trade association of India's technology and business process management industry. Founded in 1988 and headquartered in New Delhi, NASSCOM represents over 3,000 member companies and advocates for policy, talent development, and industry standards across India's technology sector.
NIST	**National Institute of Standards and Technology:** A nonregulatory agency of the US Department of Commerce that develops and promotes measurement standards, cybersecurity frameworks, and technology guidelines to enhance innovation and industrial competitiveness. Established in 1901, NIST plays a central role in shaping technical standards across sectors.
NLP	**Natural Language Processing:** A field of AI concerned with the understanding, interpreting, and generation of human language by computers. NLP combines computational linguistics with ML and deep learning to support tasks such as translation, sentiment analysis, speech recognition, and conversational systems.
NLU	**Natural Language Understanding:** A branch of AI focused on interpreting human language by identifying meaning, intent, and entities in text or speech. It is commonly used in chatbots, virtual assistants, search, and document processing to convert user input into structured information that software can act on. Unlike NLP, which encompasses a broader range of language processing tasks, NLU focuses specifically on comprehension and meaning extraction.

(*continued*)

NPU	**Neural Processing Unit:** A specialized hardware accelerator designed for efficient execution of AI workloads, particularly neural network inference. NPUs offload tasks such as vision models, speech recognition, and transformer-based AI from the CPUs and GPUs, providing higher performance per watt. Modern NPUs are central to "AI PC" architectures, bringing on-device AI features with low latency and improved energy efficiency.
NRF	**National Retail Federation:** The world's largest retail trade association, representing department stores, specialty retailers, discount stores, and internet retailers. NRF conducts industry research, publishes retail benchmarks, and advocates for retail industry interests on policy matters.
NT	**New Technology:** A designation used by Microsoft for its Windows NT family of operating systems, introduced with Windows NT 3.1 in 1993. The NT architecture introduced features such as preemptive multitasking, hardware abstraction, and stronger security models that distinguished it from the earlier MS-DOS-based Windows line. NT technology later became the basis of mainstream Windows releases.
OAuth	**Open Authorization:** A standard authorization framework that allows an application to obtain limited access to protected resources on behalf of a user without requiring the user's password.
OCR	**Optical Character Recognition:** Technology that converts different types of documents, such as scanned paper documents or portable document format files, into editable and searchable data.
OLE	**Object Linking and Embedding:** A Microsoft technology that allows content created in one application to be embedded or linked in another. An embedded object is stored within the host document, while a linked object remains connected to its source and updates automatically. OLE was foundational to document interoperability in Microsoft Office.
ONNX	**Open Neural Network Exchange:** An open source format for representing ML models to establish interoperability across different AI frameworks and runtimes. ONNX allows models trained in one framework to be exported and deployed in another, reducing vendor lock-in and simplifying production deployment across diverse hardware and software environments.

(continued)

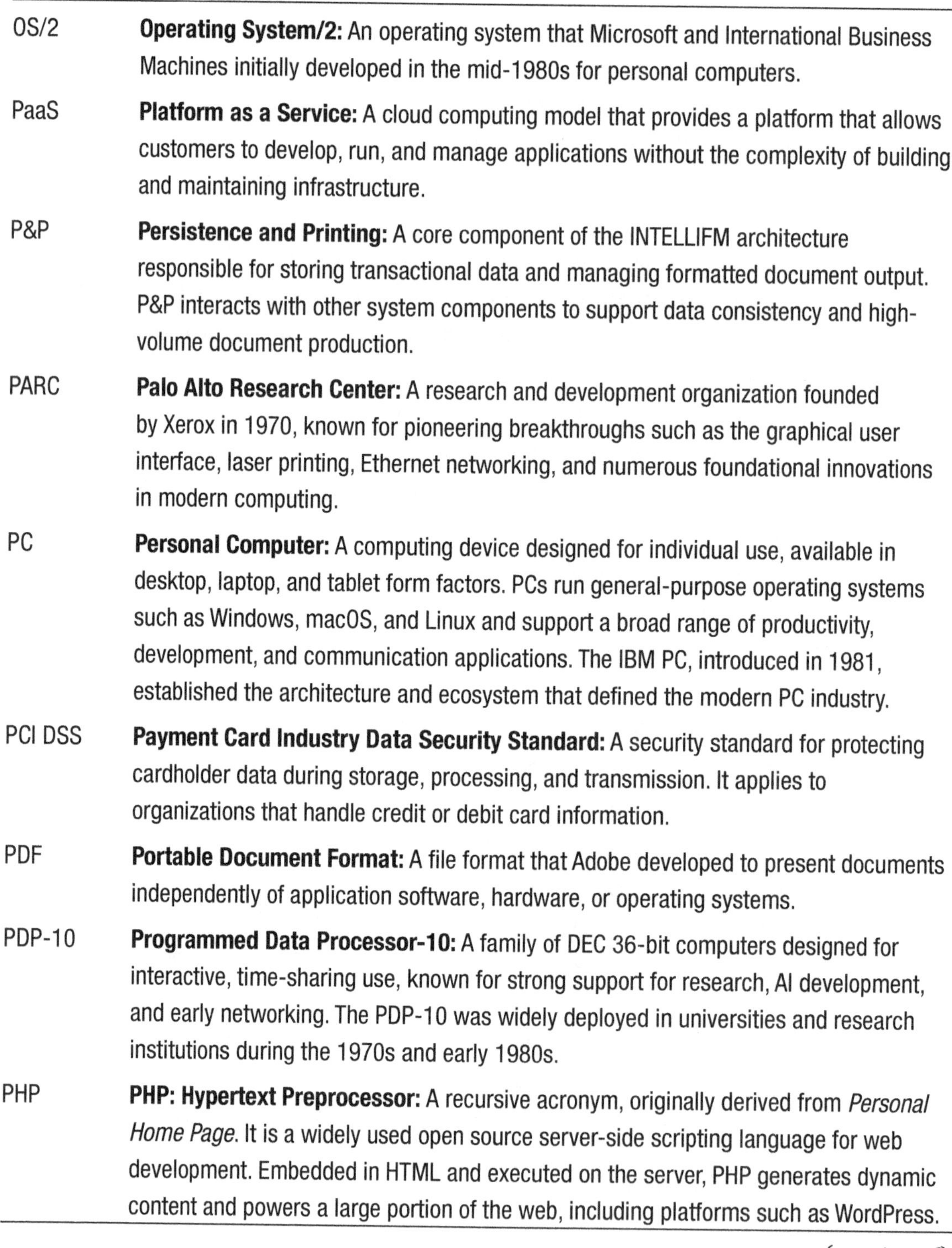

OS/2	**Operating System/2:** An operating system that Microsoft and International Business Machines initially developed in the mid-1980s for personal computers.
PaaS	**Platform as a Service:** A cloud computing model that provides a platform that allows customers to develop, run, and manage applications without the complexity of building and maintaining infrastructure.
P&P	**Persistence and Printing:** A core component of the INTELLIFM architecture responsible for storing transactional data and managing formatted document output. P&P interacts with other system components to support data consistency and high-volume document production.
PARC	**Palo Alto Research Center:** A research and development organization founded by Xerox in 1970, known for pioneering breakthroughs such as the graphical user interface, laser printing, Ethernet networking, and numerous foundational innovations in modern computing.
PC	**Personal Computer:** A computing device designed for individual use, available in desktop, laptop, and tablet form factors. PCs run general-purpose operating systems such as Windows, macOS, and Linux and support a broad range of productivity, development, and communication applications. The IBM PC, introduced in 1981, established the architecture and ecosystem that defined the modern PC industry.
PCI DSS	**Payment Card Industry Data Security Standard:** A security standard for protecting cardholder data during storage, processing, and transmission. It applies to organizations that handle credit or debit card information.
PDF	**Portable Document Format:** A file format that Adobe developed to present documents independently of application software, hardware, or operating systems.
PDP-10	**Programmed Data Processor-10:** A family of DEC 36-bit computers designed for interactive, time-sharing use, known for strong support for research, AI development, and early networking. The PDP-10 was widely deployed in universities and research institutions during the 1970s and early 1980s.
PHP	**PHP: Hypertext Preprocessor:** A recursive acronym, originally derived from *Personal Home Page*. It is a widely used open source server-side scripting language for web development. Embedded in HTML and executed on the server, PHP generates dynamic content and powers a large portion of the web, including platforms such as WordPress.

(continued)

PII	**Personally Identifiable Information:** Data that can be used to identify, contact, or locate a specific individual, either directly or indirectly. PII includes both standalone identifiers and combinations of data that, when linked, reveal personal identity.
PIN	**Personal Identification Number:** A numeric code used to authenticate a user's identity in banking, payment systems, and device access controls. PINs typically range from four to eight digits and are used in conjunction with a physical card or device to verify that the person presenting the credential is the authorized account holder.
PL/I	**Programming Language One:** A procedural, imperative computer programming language designed for scientific, engineering, business, and system programming tasks.
Prolog	**Programming in Logic:** A declarative programming language developed in the early 1970s, primarily associated with AI and computational linguistics. Prolog expresses computation in terms of relations defined by facts and rules, allowing programmers to describe what they want rather than how to compute it. The language excels at symbolic reasoning, pattern matching, and knowledge representation.
PwC	**PricewaterhouseCoopers:** A global professional services network headquartered in London and one of the Big Four accounting firms. PwC provides audit, tax, consulting, and advisory services to enterprises worldwide, with a strong focus on digital transformation and AI-assisted assurance.
QA	**Quality Assurance:** A systematic process of verifying that software meets defined requirements and standards before release. QA encompasses testing, code review, and process evaluation to identify defects and confirm reliability, performance, and usability.
Q&A	**Question-and-Answer:** A structured interaction used to elicit information from an AI system. In conversational AI, Q&A exchanges rely on intent recognition, retrieval mechanisms, and model-generated reasoning to produce relevant responses. They are central to evaluating system accuracy, uncovering edge cases, and identifying gaps in training data or knowledge integration.
QSR	**Quick-Service Restaurant:** A category of restaurants that offer fast food with minimal table service, standardized menus, and rapid order fulfillment. QSR operators have been early adopters of AI-driven technologies including dynamic menu pricing, demand forecasting, personalized digital ordering, and predictive inventory management.

(*continued*)

RAG	**Retrieval-Augmented Generation:** A technique that improves AI-generated responses by retrieving relevant content from knowledge bases or document stores and incorporating it into the model's context at inference time. RAG grounds outputs in organizational or domain-specific data rather than relying solely on training data, helping reduce hallucinations and improve factual accuracy. Microsoft Copilot Studio and Microsoft Foundry support RAG-based grounding of responses.
RAM	**Random Access Memory:** A type of volatile memory that temporarily stores data for quick access by the processor. Unlike persistent storage such as SSDs or HDDs, RAM loses its contents when the system is powered off. RAM capacity directly affects a system's ability to run multiple applications simultaneously and is a key factor in AI workload performance.
RBAC	**Role-Based Access Control:** A security model that restricts system access based on a user's assigned role, granting permissions according to job responsibilities rather than individual identity. In Azure and enterprise AI systems, RBAC enforces the principle of least privilege across resources, including data, AI models, and deployed applications.
REST	**Representational State Transfer:** A software architectural style for designing stateless web services. RESTful APIs use standard HTTP methods such as GET, POST, PUT, and DELETE to perform operations on resources identified by URLs and are widely used for web and enterprise application integration.
ROI	**Return on Investment:** A financial metric that measures the gain or loss generated by an investment relative to its cost. ROI is commonly expressed as a percentage and helps organizations evaluate the efficiency of expenditures, compare alternatives, and justify continued investment in projects or technologies.
RPA	**Robotic Process Automation:** A technology that uses software robots or "bots" to automate repetitive, rule-based tasks and processes in business operations by mimicking human interactions with digital systems and software.
SaaS	**Software as a Service:** A cloud-based model in which software applications are delivered over the internet. Users can access and use the software through a web browser without needing to install or maintain it on their local devices. SaaS typically provides centralized updates, scalability, and lower upfront costs than traditional software licensing.

(*continued*)

SAFe	**Scaled Agile Framework:** A set of organization and workflow patterns intended to guide enterprises in scaling lean and agile practices, providing a structured approach for implementing agile methodologies at enterprise scale by combining elements of agile, lean, systems thinking, and DevOps to help large organizations deliver value continuously and more efficiently.
SAP	**Systems, Applications, and Products in Data Processing** (originally Systemanalyse Programmentwicklung in German)**:** A German multinational enterprise software company and the platform it produces. SAP systems support core business functions such as finance, logistics, human resources, and supply chain management and are widely deployed in large enterprises across industries.
S/4HANA	**Suite 4 for High-Performance Analytic Appliance:** SAP's fourth-generation ERP platform, built on the SAP HANA in-memory database. S/4HANA combines real-time analytics, simplified data models, and cloud deployment with a framework to consolidate legacy SAP systems and integrate AI-driven capabilities into core business processes.
SDK	**Software Development Kit:** A collection of tools, libraries, sample code, and documentation provided by a platform vendor to help developers build applications for a specific platform, operating system, or device. Azure AI and Microsoft 365 offer SDKs that simplify service integration and reduce low-level implementation work.
SDLC	**Software Development Life Cycle:** A process that defines the various stages of software development for delivering a high-quality product, typically including planning, requirements analysis, design, implementation, testing, deployment, and maintenance phases.
SEC	**Securities and Exchange Commission:** A US federal agency that regulates securities markets and enforces laws against market manipulation, insider trading, and financial fraud. Its oversight extends to investment advisers, broker-dealers, public companies, and other market participants, including the use of automated and AI-driven systems in regulated activities.
SEO	**Search Engine Optimization:** The practice of improving a website's visibility and ranking in search engine results through content quality, technical structure, keyword relevance, and link authority. SEO techniques help organizations attract organic traffic by aligning web content with search engine algorithms that index and rank pages.

(*continued*)

SERFF	**System for Electronic Rate and Form Filing:** An electronic system used by US insurance companies and state regulators to streamline the submission, review, and approval of insurance policy rates and forms. SERFF facilitates regulatory compliance and accelerates the product filing process across multiple jurisdictions.
SIEM	**Security Information and Event Management:** A category of security software that aggregates, correlates, and analyzes log and event data from across an organization's IT infrastructure. SIEM systems centralize visibility into security activity for real-time threat detection, incident response, and compliance reporting.
SLA	**Service-Level Agreement:** A formal contract between a service provider and a customer that defines the services to be delivered, performance standards, responsibilities, and remedies or penalties for noncompliance, establishing shared expectations for service quality and accountability.
SMS	**Short Message Service:** A text messaging standard that facilitates the exchange of short text messages between mobile devices over cellular networks. SMS messages are typically limited to 160 characters and do not require an internet connection, making them a widely available channel for notifications, authentication codes, and customer communications.
SNCF	**Société Nationale des Chemins de fer Français:** France's national state-owned railway company, responsible for operating the country's passenger and freight rail services, managing rail infrastructure, and overseeing maintenance of rolling stock. SNCF is one of Europe's largest transportation organizations and an adopter of AI-driven field-service and maintenance technologies.
SOAP	**Simple Object Access Protocol:** A protocol for exchanging structured information in web services using XML. SOAP supports formal message definitions, security features, and contract-based enterprise integrations.
SOC	**System and Organization Controls:** A suite of audit reports developed by the American Institute of Certified Public Accountants that evaluate a service organization's controls over security, availability, processing integrity, confidentiality, and privacy. SOC 2 Type 2 reports, which assess control effectiveness over a defined period, are the variant most commonly required in enterprise cloud and AI service evaluations.

(continued)

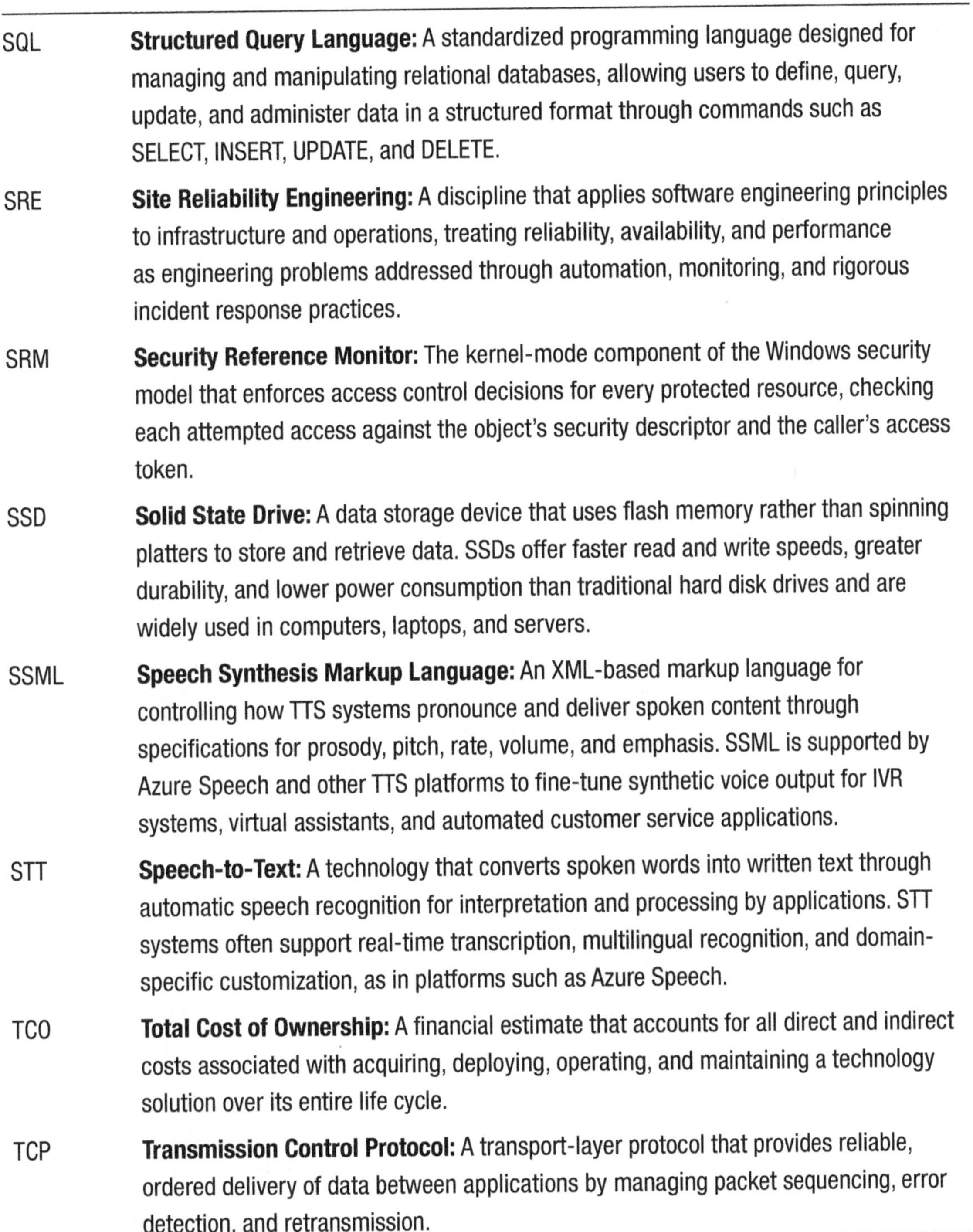

SQL	**Structured Query Language:** A standardized programming language designed for managing and manipulating relational databases, allowing users to define, query, update, and administer data in a structured format through commands such as SELECT, INSERT, UPDATE, and DELETE.
SRE	**Site Reliability Engineering:** A discipline that applies software engineering principles to infrastructure and operations, treating reliability, availability, and performance as engineering problems addressed through automation, monitoring, and rigorous incident response practices.
SRM	**Security Reference Monitor:** The kernel-mode component of the Windows security model that enforces access control decisions for every protected resource, checking each attempted access against the object's security descriptor and the caller's access token.
SSD	**Solid State Drive:** A data storage device that uses flash memory rather than spinning platters to store and retrieve data. SSDs offer faster read and write speeds, greater durability, and lower power consumption than traditional hard disk drives and are widely used in computers, laptops, and servers.
SSML	**Speech Synthesis Markup Language:** An XML-based markup language for controlling how TTS systems pronounce and deliver spoken content through specifications for prosody, pitch, rate, volume, and emphasis. SSML is supported by Azure Speech and other TTS platforms to fine-tune synthetic voice output for IVR systems, virtual assistants, and automated customer service applications.
STT	**Speech-to-Text:** A technology that converts spoken words into written text through automatic speech recognition for interpretation and processing by applications. STT systems often support real-time transcription, multilingual recognition, and domain-specific customization, as in platforms such as Azure Speech.
TCO	**Total Cost of Ownership:** A financial estimate that accounts for all direct and indirect costs associated with acquiring, deploying, operating, and maintaining a technology solution over its entire life cycle.
TCP	**Transmission Control Protocol:** A transport-layer protocol that provides reliable, ordered delivery of data between applications by managing packet sequencing, error detection, and retransmission.

(continued)

TCS	**Tata Consultancy Services:** A global IT services, consulting, and business solutions company headquartered in Mumbai, India. TCS is a subsidiary of the Tata Group and one of the world's largest IT services firms by market capitalization. It offers services in software development, digital transformation, cloud computing, AI, and enterprise solutions across diverse industries.
TDD	**Test-Driven Development:** A software development practice in which tests are written before the corresponding code so that every feature begins with a defined verification criterion and that the codebase remains reliable as it evolves.
TLS	**Transport Layer Security:** A cryptographic protocol designed to communicate securely over a computer network. TLS provides data privacy, integrity, and authentication between client-server applications such as web browsers, APIs, and email services.
Token	**Token (AI):** The basic unit of information processed by an AI model. In text-based models, a token typically represents a word, part of a word, or a punctuation character, depending on the tokenization method used. In multimodal models, tokens may also represent discrete patches of an image or segments of audio. Model capacity, context window size, and API pricing are typically expressed in tokens. As a general approximation, 100 tokens correspond to approximately 75 words in English, though this varies by language and content type.
TOPS-10	Digital Equipment Corporation's time-sharing operating system for PDP-10 systems, designed to support many users working interactively at terminals.
TPS	**Toyota Production System:** A lean manufacturing methodology developed by Toyota Motor Corporation that emphasizes waste reduction, continuous improvement (*kaizen*), and just-in-time production. TPS integrates principles such as *jidoka* (automation with human oversight) and *heijunka* (production leveling) to optimize efficiency and quality. Widely adopted across industries, TPS serves as the foundation for modern lean operations and agile supply chain management.
TSMC	**Taiwan Semiconductor Manufacturing Company:** The world's largest dedicated independent semiconductor foundry, headquartered in Hsinchu, Taiwan. Founded in 1987, TSMC manufactures chips designed by other companies, producing advanced processors for major technology firms. Its fabrication facilities represent critical infrastructure in the global semiconductor supply chain.

(*continued*)

TTS	**Text-to-Speech**: A technology that converts written text into synthetic speech through neural voice synthesis for voice responses and audio output in applications. TTS systems often include multilingual voice generation, custom voice creation, and prosody control, as in platforms such as Azure Speech.
UAT	**User Acceptance Testing:** A phase of software development in which the intended audience tests the product to verify it meets their requirements.
UCC	**Uniform Commercial Code:** A set of laws governing commercial transactions in the United States—including sales of goods, leases, negotiable instruments, bank deposits, fund transfers, letters of credit, bulk sales, warehouse receipts, bills of lading, investment securities, and secured transactions—aimed at standardizing business law across different states.
UIG	**User Interface Generation:** An automated process or technology that creates user interface elements, layouts, and designs based on predefined rules, data models, or AI, reducing manual design effort and improving consistency across applications. It is a core component of the INTELLIFM expert system.
UNESCO	**United Nations Educational, Scientific, and Cultural Organization:** A specialized agency of the United Nations established in 1945 to promote international collaboration in education, science, culture, and communication. UNESCO aims to foster peace, sustainable development, and intercultural dialog through knowledge sharing and capacity building.
USB	**Universal Serial Bus:** A standard interface for connecting peripherals to a computer or host system, supporting data transfer and power delivery across a wide range of devices.
VAX	**Virtual Address eXtension:** A line of 32-bit minicomputers developed by Digital Equipment Corporation, known for introducing virtual memory and serving scientific, engineering, and business computing in the 1980s and early 1990s.
VBA	**Visual Basic for Applications:** A programming language embedded in Microsoft Office applications for automating tasks, creating custom functions, and extending application functionality through macros. VBA evolved from WordBASIC and became the shared automation language across Excel, Word, Access, and other Office applications, allowing users without formal programming training to build custom workflows.

(continued)

VGA	**Video Graphics Array:** A legacy computer display standard and physical connector (15-pin D-sub) primarily for transmitting analog video signals. Introduced by IBM, it supports specific display resolutions and color depths. While largely superseded by modern digital interfaces, VGA remains prevalent in older hardware and projectors and is used to maintain backward compatibility.
VM	**Virtual Machine:** A software-based emulation of a physical computer that runs an operating system and applications as if it were independent hardware. VMs allow multiple isolated environments to share a single physical host, reducing hardware costs and improving operational flexibility. Cloud platforms such as Microsoft Azure offer VMs as on-demand compute resources that can be provisioned, scaled, and released as needed.
VS Code	**Visual Studio Code:** A free, open source, and highly customizable source code editor that Microsoft developed. It supports a wide range of programming languages; offers features such as syntax highlighting, code completion, debugging, and version control integration; and can be extended with numerous plugins to enhance functionality across various development tasks.
WCAG	**Web Content Accessibility Guidelines:** International standards from the World Wide Web Consortium for making web content accessible to people with disabilities. WCAG defines three conformance levels: A, AA, and AAA, with AA commonly required in public sector and enterprise contexts.
WordBASIC	Microsoft's macro programming language for Word, introduced in the early Windows era. It allowed users to automate document tasks through scripting and remained Word's primary macro language through Word 95. With Word 97, Microsoft introduced VBA and a new object model, bringing Word into the broader Office programmability model and replacing WordBASIC as its main macro language.
WPF	**Windows Presentation Foundation:** A Microsoft framework for building Windows desktop application user interfaces. WPF uses XAML for declarative interface definition, supports data binding, and provides rich graphics and layout capabilities within the .NET ecosystem.
WSL	**Windows Subsystem for Linux:** A compatibility layer in Windows that allows users to run native Linux distributions and command-line tools directly on Windows without a virtual machine or dual-boot configuration. WSL is widely used by developers who need access to both Linux and Windows tooling in a single environment.

(*continued*)

WYSIWYG **What You See Is What You Get:** A user interface approach in which on-screen content closely matches the final printed or published output. WYSIWYG editors are used in word processors, web design tools, and graphic editors, allowing users to format and edit content visually without writing code or markup. Microsoft advanced WYSIWYG fidelity in the early 1990s through TrueType font technology and improved print layout consistency in Office applications.

XAI **Explainable Artificial Intelligence:** An approach to developing AI systems that are transparent and interpretable, allowing humans to understand, trust, and effectively manage AI by providing clear explanations of the reasoning behind AI-generated outputs, predictions, or recommendations.

XAML **Extensible Application Markup Language:** A declarative, XML-based markup language used to define user interfaces in Microsoft .NET UI frameworks. XAML is used in frameworks such as WPF, UWP, and .NET MAUI to separate interface definition from code and support data binding and layout definition.

XCON **eXpert CONfigurer:** An expert system developed at Carnegie Mellon University and deployed by Digital Equipment Corporation beginning in 1980 to configure VAX computer systems. XCON used thousands of rules to determine valid component combinations, reducing configuration errors and saving DEC millions of dollars annually. It became one of the first commercially successful expert systems.

XML **Extensible Markup Language:** A markup language used to encode documents and structured data in a format that is both human-readable and machine-readable. It allows developers to create custom tags and organize data for exchange across different systems. XML is widely used in web services, configuration files, and document processing.

XP **Extreme Programming:** An agile software development methodology that emphasizes technical practices such as pair programming, TDD, and continuous integration to sustain code quality and support frequent releases.

XPS **XML Paper Specification:** A document format developed by Microsoft that preserves document fidelity across devices and platforms. XPS files use XML-based markup to describe page layout, fonts, and graphics so that documents print and display consistently across software and hardware. Windows Presentation Foundation includes native support for XPS printing.

Index

A

K. C. Mukherjee, *The Microsoft AI Insider's Playbook*, https://doi.org/10.1007/979-8-8688-2730-3

B

C

J

K

L

M

U

V

W, X, Y

Z

GPSR Compliance
The European Union's (EU) General Product Safety Regulation (GPSR) is a set of rules that requires consumer products to be safe and our obligations to ensure this.

If you have any concerns about our products, you can contact us on

ProductSafety@springernature.com

In case Publisher is established outside the EU, the EU authorized representative is:

Springer Nature Customer Service Center GmbH
Europaplatz 3
69115 Heidelberg, Germany

www.ingramcontent.com/pod-product-compliance
Lightning Source LLC
Chambersburg PA
CBHW081433100826
49614CB00018B/473
* 9 7 9 8 8 6 8 8 2 7 2 9 7 *